The Buddhist Self

T0376485

The Buddhist Self

On *Tathāgatagarbha* and *Ātman*

C. V. JONES

University of Hawai'i Press
Honolulu

© 2021 University of Hawai'i Press
All rights reserved
Paperback edition 2024

Printed in the United States of America

Library of Congress Cataloging-in-Publication Data

Names: Jones, Christopher V. (Christopher Victor), author.
Title: The Buddhist self : on tathāgatagarbha and ātman / C.V. Jones.
Description: Honolulu : University of Hawai'i Press, 2021. | Includes bibliographical references and index.
Identifiers: LCCN 2020043230 | ISBN 9780824883423 (cloth) | ISBN 9780824886493 (pdf) | ISBN 9780824886509 (epub) | ISBN 9780824886516 (kindle edition)
Subjects: LCSH: Tathāgatagarbha (Buddhism) | Ātman. | Mahayana Buddhism—Doctrines. | Buddhism—India.
Classification: LCC BQ4450 .J66 2021 | DDC 294.30954—dc23
LC record available at https://lccn.loc.gov/2020043230

ISBN 9780824899264 (paperback)

Cover Art: The head of a Buddha statue partially revealed from its mold, exhibited in the technology section of the Patan Museum, Nepal. Posterized image based on a photograph by Anica Mann.

University of Hawai'i Press books are printed on acid-free paper and meet the guidelines for permanence and durability of the Council on Library Resources.

To my parents,
Sue and Derek,
for everything

Contents

ACKNOWLEDGMENTS xi

ABBREVIATIONS xiii

CONVENTIONS xvii

1 Introduction 1

1.1 Self and Not-Self in Early Buddhism 1
1.2 *Tathāgatagarbha* Literature in Overview 11
1.3 Essences, Natures, Wombs, and Chambers 14
1.4 Buddhist *Ātmavāda:* Preliminary Thoughts 21

Part I Buddha-Nature, the Self

2 The *Mahāparinirvāṇamahāsūtra* and the Buddhist Self 29

2.1 The Text 29
2.2 The Buddha as Self 33
2.3 Buddha-nature and the Self 40
2.4 Contentions and Clarifications 47
2.5 The True Self and False Notions of It 55
2.6 Self and Absence of Self 59
2.7 Buddha-nature in Dharmakṣema's MPNMSD+ 62
2.8 Conclusions 67

3 The *Aṅgulimālīyasūtra* and the Essential Self 70

3.1 The Text 70
3.2 An "Essence" of One's Own 74
3.3 What Buddha-nature Is Not: More False Notions of the Self 77
3.4 Perceiving Buddha-nature 79
3.5 Essence, Action, and the Self 83
3.6 A "Single Essence" 87
3.7 Buddhism contra Other Systems 91
3.8 Conclusions 95

4 The *Mahābherīhārakasūtra* and Liberation of the Self 97

4.1 The Text 97
4.2 Continuity of the Self 100
4.3 The Sovereign Self 104
4.4 Buddha-nature and Buddhist Practice 107
4.5 Self, Not-Self, and Emptiness 109
4.6 Conclusions 114

Part II Buddha-nature, Not Self

5 The *Śrīmālādevīsiṃhanādasūtra* and the Perfection of Self 119

5.1 The Text 119
5.2 Reimagining *Tathāgatagarbha* 122
5.3 The *Dharmakāya* and Its Qualities 129
5.4 On "Singularity" 132
5.5 Conclusions 136

6 Other *Tathāgatagarbha* Sources 139

6.1 The *Anūnatvāpūrṇatvanirdeśaparivarta* 139
6.2 The *Tathāgatagarbhasūtra* 143
6.3 The *Mahāyānasūtrālaṃkāra* 148

7 The *Ratnagotravibhāga* and the Self That Is No Self 154

7.1 The Text 154
7.2 Buddha-nature and the "Basic" RGV 158
7.3 "Perfection of Self" in the RGVV 167
7.4 *Tathāgatagarbha* as, Once Again, the Self 175
7.5 Conclusions 178

8 The *Laṅkāvatārasūtra* and Rejecting the Buddhist Self 181

8.1 The Text 181
8.2 *Tathāgatagarbha* and Absence of Self 183
8.3 The "*Ālayavijñāna-Tathāgatagarbha*" 188
8.4 Selfhood in the *Sagāthaka* 191
8.5 Conclusions 194
8.6 Postscript: After the LAS 195

Part III Buddha-nature Reconsidered

9 Recurring Themes and Motifs 203

9.1 The Single Vehicle 203
9.2 "Cryptic" Utterances 210

9.3 The Intrinsically Pure Mind 214
9.4 "Sarvalokapriyadarśana" 217
9.5 Emptiness and Nonemptiness 218
9.6 Non-Buddhists and Their Teachings 223

10 Evolution of the Buddhist Self 229

10.1 The Course of Buddha-nature Teaching 229
10.2 Origins of the Buddha-nature Idea 237
10.3 Liberation and the Self 245
10.4 Buddhist Selfhood and the Mahāyāna 253
10.5 Closing Thoughts 261

REFERENCES 265

INDEX 287

Acknowledgments

The foundation of the current volume is research completed in late 2014 at the University of Oxford, and the subject of kind recognition by the Khyentse Foundation in 2017. By early 2015, it was apparent to me that my work on the *tathāgatagarbha* literature, and its relationship to the language of selfhood, was far from finished. These months saw the publication of Michael Radich's *The Mahāparinirvāṇa-mahāsūtra and the Emergence of Tathāgatagarbha Doctrine,* a book that invited those who work in the history of *tathāgatagarbha* in India to revisit our understanding of the early life of this tradition, so thoroughly examined by Takasaki Jikidō, Michael Zimmermann, and others.

Radich's contention that the *Mahāparinirvāṇamahāsūtra* may be our earliest surviving Indian text concerned with an account of the *tathāgatagarbha* complemented many things that I had discovered over the course of my own research. Observing a congruence between our findings, I set about reconstructing what I propose was the development of the *tathāgatagarbha* literature in India, using its interest in the language of selfhood, and the matter of how far the expression *tathāgatagarbha* intends something like an account of the self, as an instructive methodological guide. If this volume and its constituent studies achieve nothing else, I think it valuable that scholars and students of Buddhism—in its Indian, Tibetan, and East Asian modes and otherwise—are confronted by some of the more unconventional expressions of Buddhism that emerged in its homeland, together with the hypothesis that something as influential and productive as teaching about Buddha-nature could have begun life as an attempt by Buddhist authors to innovate beyond what was commonly acceptable in their scriptural heritage.

I am grateful to the University of Hawai'i Press for producing this volume, especially for scrupulous work on the manuscript by Ivo Fravashi, and to my anonymous reviewers for their methodical attention to its content. I thank the Glorisun Global Buddhist Network and the Indian Institute at Oxford University for support with its production, and the British Academy for the opportunity to pursue the further research required for the completion of this project. For inspiration and assistance with the cover art I am indebted to Anica Mann and Thomas Schrom, as well as the team behind the technology exhibition at the Patan Museum. Additional thanks to the exhibition curator, James Giambrone, and the artists responsible: Jeevan Shakya and Rajendra Shakya (wax image makers), Nanda Maya Shakya and Raju Shakya (mold makers), and Jeevan Shakya, Rajendra Shakya and Suman Shakya (casters).

For patient and diligent assistance with Japanese sources I would like to thank Ken Ishikawa and—from an earlier stage in the life of this research—Kazuko Yokoi. I am grateful for conversations and correspondences with a number of colleagues from across the breadth of Buddhist studies, whose advice and support helped my research along its way, including Diwakar Acharya, Naomi Appleton, Norihisa Baba, Cathy Cantwell, Lance Cousins, Richard Gombrich, Luis Gómez, Jowita Kramer, Robert Mayer, Ulrich Pagel, Akira Saitō, Sarah Shaw, Jonathan Silk, Péter-Dániel Szántó, Vincent Tournier, Dorji Wangchuk, and Jan Westerhoff. I am especially grateful to have received the generous help and encouragement of several scholars whose research and expertise on the *tathāgatagarbha* literature has been invaluable to this publication and my work toward it: Hiromi Habata, Kazuo Kanō, Michael Radich, Masahiro Shimoda, and Michael Zimmermann.

Afforded this opportunity, I would like to thank particular educators who have inspired my attitudes to research and teaching. I thank Julius Lipner for some of my first, vibrant exposures to the world of Indian religion, and Anna Williams for having been an early and formative influence on my scholarly career. I am very thankful for having had skilled, patient, and extraordinarily generous instructors in Sanskrit and Indian intellectual history: Jim Benson, Chris Minkowski, and Alexis Sanderson. Finally, a profound debt is that which I owe to my two mentors—Ulrike Roesler and Stefano Zacchetti—who assisted my voyage through the curious corner of the Indian Buddhist world that I have ventured to explore. Over the many years of work leading up to this volume they have been inspirational teachers, generous colleagues, and kind friends. This book would not have been possible without them.

My years of research in Oxford have been enriched by the camaraderie of the staff and fellows of St. Peter's College. I am also thankful for the love, patience, and many insights of my partner, Paula, and for the encouragement of a great many friends who have shown (or politely feigned) enthusiasm for a book that they will probably never read.

This volume is dedicated to my parents, Derek and Sue, who have supported me and my endeavors in more ways than I can express here.

Abbreviations

AAN	*Anūnatvāpūrṇatvanirdeśaparivarta* in Chinese translation: T.668—*Foshuo buzeng bujian jing* 佛說不增不減經
AMS	*Aṅgulimālīyasūtra*
AMS^{C}	*Aṅgulimālīyasūtra* in Chinese translation: T.120—*Yangjuemoluo jing* 央掘魔羅經
AMS^{T}	*Aṅgulimālīyasūtra* in Tibetan translation: e.g., D.213, Q.879—*Sor mo'i phreng ba la phen pa zhes bya ba theg pa chen po'i mdo*
AN	*Aṅguttaranikāya* of the Pāli *Suttapiṭaka:* Pali Text Society edition
BĀU	*Bṛhadāraṇyaka-upaniṣad:* Sanskrit edition of Olivelle 1998
BGVNS	*Bodhisattvagocaropāyaviṣayavikurvāṇanirdeśasūtra*
BGVNS^{B}	*Bodhisattvagocaropāyaviṣayavikurvāṇanirdeśasūtra* in Chinese translation, by Bodhiruci: T.272—*Dasazhe niqianzisuo shuo jing* 大薩遮尼乾子所說經
Ch.	Chinese
D	Derge edition of the Tibetan Buddhist canon
DN	*Dīghanikāya* of the Pāli *Suttapiṭaka:* Pali Text Society edition
DzG	*De bzhin gshegs pa'i snying po gsal zhing mdzes par byed pa'i rgyan*, by Bu ston Rin chen grub; translation by Ruegg 1973
IBK	*Indogaku bukkyōgaku kenkyū* 印度学仏教学研究
JIABS	*Journal of the International Association of Buddhist Studies*
LAS	*Laṅkāvatārasūtra*
LAS^{C1}	*Laṅkāvatārasūtra* in Chinese translation: T.670—*Lengqie abaduoluo bao jing* 楞伽阿跋多羅寶經
LAS^{C2}	*Laṅkāvatārasūtra* in Chinese translation: T.671—*Ru lengqie jing* 入楞伽經
LAS^{C3}	*Laṅkāvatārasūtra* in Chinese translation: T.672—*Dasheng ru lengqie jing* 大乘入楞伽經
LAS^{T}	*Laṅkāvatārasūtra* in Tibetan translation: e.g., D.107; Q.775—*Lang kar gshegs pa theg pa chen po'i mdo*
MBhS	**Mahābherīhārakasūtra*

MBhS^{C}	**Mahābherīhārakasūtra* in Chinese translation: T.270—*Da fagu jing* 大法鼓經
MBhS^{T}	**Mahābherīhārakasūtra* in Tibetan translation: e.g., D.222; Q.888—*Rnga bo che chen po'i le'u zhes bya ba theg pa chen po'i mdo*
MDh	*Mānava-dharmaśāstra:* Sanskrit edition of Olivelle 2005
MN	*Majjhimanikāya* of the Pāli *Suttapiṭaka:* Pali Text Society edition
MPNMS	*Mahāparinirvāṇamahāsūtra*
MPNMS^{D}	*Mahāparinirvāṇamahāsūtra* in Chinese translation, by Dharmakṣema: T.374—*Da banniepan jing* 大般涅槃經
MPNMS^{D}+	*Mahāparinirvāṇamahāsūtra* material exclusive to MPNMS^{D} (T.374[12] 428b17–603c30; see 2.1, 2.7)
MPNMS^{F}	*Mahāparinirvāṇamahāsūtra* in Chinese translation, by Faxian: T.376—*Da bannihuan jing* 大般泥洹經
MPNMS^{T}	*Mahāparinirvāṇamahāsūtra* in Tibetan translation: e.g., D.120; Q.788—*Yongs su mya ngan las 'das pa chen po'i theg pa chen po'i mdo:* all references are to the edition of Habata 2013
MPNMS-dhk	Earlier material in the composition of the *Mahāparinirvāṇamahāsūtra* that is for the most part focused on teaching about the *dharmakāya,* with no apparent knowledge of *tathāgatagarbha;* see 2.1n14
MPNMS-tg	Later material in the composition of the *Mahāparinirvāṇamahāsūtra* that includes, and has as its focus, teaching about the *tathāgatagarbha;* see 2.1n16
MSA(Bh)	*Mahāyānasūtrālaṃkāra(-bhāṣya)*
MSA(Bh)^{C}	*Mahāyānasūtrālaṃkāra(-bhāṣya)* in Chinese translation: T.1604—*Dasheng zhuangyan jing lun* 大乘莊嚴經論
MSA(Bh)^{T}	*Mahāyānasūtrālaṃkāra(-bhāṣya)* in Tibetan translation: e.g., D.4026; Q.5527—*Theg pa chen po mdo sde'i rgyan gyi bshad pa*
Q	Peking edition of the Tibetan Buddhist canon
RC	*Ri chos nges don rgya mtsho zhes bya ba mthar thug thun mong ma yin pa'i man ngag,* by Dol po pa Shes rab rgyal mtshan; translation by Hopkins 2006.
RGV	*Ratnagotravibhāga* (i.e., verse strata of the RGVV)
RGVV	*Ratnagotravibhāgavyākhyā*
RGV(V)^{C}	*Ratnagotravibhāga(-vyākhyā)* in Chinese translation: T.1611—*Jujing yisheng baoxing lun* 究竟一乘寶性論
RGV(V)^{S}	*Ratnagotravibhāga(-vyākhyā):* Sanskrit edition of Johnston (1950) 1991.
RGV(V)^{T}	*Ratnagotravibhāga(-vyākhyā)* in Tibetan translation: e.g., D.4025, Q.5526—*Theg pa chen po rgyu bla ma'i bstan bcos rnam par bshad pa:* all references are to the edition of Z. Nakamura 1967

ŚDS	*Śrīmālādevīsiṃhanādasūtra*
ŚDS^{C1}	*Śrīmālādevīsiṃhanādasūtra* in (first) Chinese translation, by Guṇabhadra: T.353—*Shengman shizihou yisheng dafangbian fangguang jing* 勝鬘師子吼一乘大方便方廣經
ŚDS^{C2}	*Śrīmālādevīsiṃhanādasūtra* in (second) Chinese translation, by Bodhiruci: T.310[11]672c14–678c4—*Shengman furen hui* 勝鬘夫人會 (text 48 in the *Dabaoji jing* 大寶積經)
ŚDS^{T}	*Śrīmālādevīsiṃhanādasūtra* in Tibetan translation: e.g., D.92; Q.760[48]—*Lha mo dpal phreng gi seng ge'i sgra zhes bya ba theg pa chen po'i mdo;* all references are to the edition of Tsukinowa 1940
Skt.	Sanskrit
SN	*Saṃyuttanikāya* of the Pāli *Suttapiṭaka:* Pali Text Society edition
SP	*Saddharmapuṇḍarīka(-sūtra)*: Sanskrit edition of Kern and Nanjio (1908–1912) 1970
T	*Taishō (shinshū daizōkyō)* 大正新脩大藏經 edition of the Chinese Buddhist canon
TGS	*Tathāgatagarbhasūtra*
TGS^{1}	*Tathāgatagarbhasūtra* (recension represented by TGS^{C1})
TGS^{2}	*Tathāgatagarbhasūtra* (recension represented by TGS^{C2}, TGS^{B}, and TGS^{T})
TGS^{B}	*Tathāgatagarbhasūtra,* in Tibetan translation from Bathang, published in Zimmermann 2002
TGS^{C1}	*Tathāgatagarbhasūtra* in (first) Chinese translation, by Buddhabhadra: T.666—*Dafangdeng rulaizang jing* 大方等如來藏經
TGS^{C2}	*Tathāgatagarbhasūtra* in (second) Chinese translation, by Amoghavajra: T.667—*Dafangguang rulaizang jing* 大方廣如來藏經
TGS^{T}	*Tathāgatagarbhasūtra* in Tibetan translation: e.g., D.258; Q.924—*De bzhin gshegs pa'i snying po zhes bya ba theg pa chen po'i mdo*
Tib.	Tibetan

Conventions

Where in the main text I present terminology from Chinese and/or Tibetan translations of an Indian work, it is my convention to present first the Chinese, then what is present in corresponding Tibetan material, and after one or both a reconstruction of underlying Sanskrit terminology. In many instances I employ an asterisk (*) to denote that it is not transparent what Indic terminology lies behind some or other translation, and hence that what follows it is hypothetical (e.g., *foxing* 佛性; *sangs rgyas kyi khams*: **buddhadhātu*).

Where footnotes include reconstructions of passages from damaged Sanskrit manuscripts (reproduced, for example, from Habata 2019), the following symbols apply:

[ ] surround damaged character(s)
( ) surround restored characters where there is a gap in the manuscript
< > surround an addition to the text where no gap is present in the manuscript
{ } surround superfluous characters, not considered in translation

CHAPTER 1

Introduction

What is called "the self" means the tathāgatagarbha.
The nature of the Buddha exists in every sentient being,
but because it is obscured by all manner of afflictions,
sentient beings cannot see, within themselves, its presence.

—*Mahāparinirvāṇa-mahāsūtra*

1.1 Self and Not-Self in Early Buddhism

This study traces the history of an association between two ideas in Indian religious history: what is often termed "Buddha-nature"—commonly articulated by the expression *tathāgatagarbha*—and the self (Sanskrit *ātman*), referring to the permanent and indestructible essence, or an unchanging central element, of any human or other sentient being.[1] Our primary sources will be a number of Indian Buddhist works that promote teachings that are in tension with commonly accepted norms and conventions of Buddhist doctrine. All of these sources belong to the Mahāyāna tradition of Buddhism, with origins in India no later than the early fifth century CE, and some of them claim that the Buddha taught the existence of something that could be deemed *ātman,* or the self.[2] At least ostensibly, this records a revision of the Buddha's hitherto unquestioned commitment to teaching *anātman*: that nothing is fit to be considered the self, and that

Epigraph: Translated from the Tibetan version of the *Mahāparinirvāṇamahāsūtra* (i.e., MPNMS^{T}—Habata 2013: §376.2–5): *bdag ces bya ba ni de bzhin gshegs pa'i snying po'i don to // sangs rgyas kyi khams ni sems can thams cad la yod mod kyi / de yang nyon mongs pa'i rnam pa rnams kyis bsgribs te / bdag nyid la yod bzhin du sems can rnams kyis mthong bar mi nus so /*

1. Throughout this volume the English term "self" will be used as a translation of *ātman,* which generally designates a permanent, unchanging, and intrinsically valuable aspect of one's person. I use different language to speak of "the conventional self": the "person" or "individual" whom Buddhism understands to suffer repeated death and rebirth through transmigration.

2. By "the Buddha" I intend the literary Śākyamuni, who in Buddhist tradition is understood to have been the sole speaker of mainstream (otherwise "Śrāvakayāna"; see note 4 below) Buddhist discourses (*sūtras*), and for followers of the Mahāyāna was responsible also for a wide variety of teachings about the correct practices of a bodhisattva.

thinking of personal identity in terms of the continuity of some enduring essence is detrimental to the pursuit of an end to the experience of transmigration (*saṃsāra*), or recurring death and rebirth.

Buddhist teachings about self and not-self are part of a struggle to articulate what it is that endures across the life (and over the successive lives) of a sentient being, when Buddhism generally teaches that all things are impermanent (*anitya*), and that nothing should be considered a stable, unchanging core of one's own identity. Space permits that this opening chapter can provide only an overview of Buddhist teaching about "not-self," which has been a rich vein for commentators within the Buddhist tradition, for scholars who have traced the development of Buddhist intellectual history in India and abroad, and for philosophers who find in Buddhism sophisticated discussion of problems regarding personal identity.[3] What should be established at the outset is that Indian Buddhist literature was invested in a discourse about personhood that distinguished Buddhist teaching from rival traditions of Indian religious thought and practice, concerned as these were with some or other account of what qualified to be called "the self."

Non-Buddhist Indian literature—much of which would eventually become associated with what is now called Hinduism—reflects many centuries of concern with the discernment, knowledge, and liberation of what was in Sanskrit known as *ātman:* a permanent, unchanging kernel to one's existence. By contrast, Indian Buddhist texts communicate that preoccupation with ideas about the self is a fundamental cause of the endless cycle of rebirth that characterizes the human condition. In short, if an account of *ātman* refers to a "central something" (Collins 1982: 80) in the constitution of a sentient being—that which is essential to them, and the unchanging core of their identity in this life and the next—Buddhist literature commits instead to teaching that things are not the self (*anātman*), and that investigation of our experience exhibits only an absence of the self (*nairātmya*). Realizing as such is an important step toward attaining soteriological goal(s) that were held to have been expounded by the Buddha: an end to transmigration (i.e., *nirvāṇa*)—otherwise status as an arhat, as sought by the "mainstream" Buddhist tradition (what came to be known as the Śrāvakayāna or "vehicle of 'hearers'/disciples [*śrāvaka*s]")[4]—and later the goal of supreme, complete awakening (*anuttarā samyaksaṃbodhi*) that was the aim of a bodhisattva, or otherwise a follower of the "great vehicle," or Mahāyāna.

---

3. Modern philosophical analyses of *anātman* teaching have often focused on the matter of whether or not Buddhism promotes a reductionist account of personal identity, and include publications by Albahari (2002; 2006); Duerlinger (1993); Ganeri (2007); and Siderits (e.g., 2007: 32–68; 2015). Some scholars have acknowledged a similarity between *anātman* teaching and the work of Derek Parfit (e.g., 1984; see also Kapstein 1986; 2018).

4. Regarding use of the term "Śrāvakayāna," and related nomenclature, see Ruegg 2004: 7–12, 28–31.

On the surface, Buddhist opposition to the category *ātman* constitutes a rejection of wider Indian concern with the self, its whereabouts, and the process of freeing it from bondage to rebirth: interests common to Brahmanism, Jainism, and other Indian traditions besides.[5] All of these traditions (or even families of traditions, given their internal diversities), shared with Buddhism a concern with the same underlying problem: the seemingly unending cycle of transmigration—from one life to another, suffering continual death, rebirth, and redeath—that is dictated in some manner or other by human action (*karma*). By far the greater share of Indian religious systems, to the exclusion of Buddhism, have understood the experience of transmigration to have at its center an enduring agent, or at any rate a "central something," that is continuously present, retains its identity as it passes from one life to the next, and witnesses repeated sickness, aging, and death ad infinitum. For all of their differences, we might understand Buddhism's opponents to have shared a common *ātmavāda* orientation: they engaged in "discourse about the self," which accepted, in one fashion or another, that liberation from perpetual rebirth is a process of finding, knowing, and releasing what is essential to one's identity from the vicious cycle within which it is trapped.

Indian notions of *ātman,* or that which undergoes transmigration, built upon ideas that were culturally specific to the late Vedic period of Indian history (c. 1000–500 BCE). Behind at least some of these notions lies the intellectual heritage of the Brahmanas (*brāhmaṇa*s or *brahmans*), who were awarded by birth access to ritual formulae and a position of privilege at the top of the prescribed Brahmanical social order. The expression *ātman* as it appears in early Vedic literature—for example, the hymns of the *Ṛgveda*—has connotations of animation, that which endures through a person's life, and otherwise that which is essential, substantial, or "most dear" to a person (Renou 1952). It is also that which the Brahmanical priest served and in some sense "saved" by conducting ritual sacrifice: securing for the ritual performer (or his patron) rebirth among the gods or his ancestors. Through the correct performance of sacrifice, the ritualist makes for himself ("his self") or for some donor a life in the next world, and so

5. Jain tradition considers one's "life" (*jīva,* but called also *ātman*) to be the embodied, suffering subject bound to the process of transmigration: see, for example, Jacobi 1908; Dundas 2002: 42–44, 102–105; Bronkhorst 2007: 28–34. Other teachings about the self include those proper to Brahmanical schools of philosophy such as Sāṃkhya and Vaiśeṣika, which reached maturity around perhaps the fourth century of the Common Era (Bronkhorst 2006: 287–290). For Sāṃkhya the highest and primary reality is *puruṣa,* related to musings on *puruṣa/ātman* in some Upaniṣads, which in the *Sāṃkhyakārikā* is plural (*bahutva*), possesses power (*adhiṣṭhāna*) over its environment, is the enjoyer (*bhoktṛ*) of experiences, and that which might achieve isolation (*kaivalya*) from rebirth: see, for example, Larson 1969: 167–176; Burley 2007: 147–150. The Vaiśeṣika system imagines the *ātman* to be one of nine fundamental substances (*dravya*), and one of a number of basic entities that are part of the constitution of a sentient being: see, for example, Kumāra 2013: 73–84.

through correct ritual action (*karma*) perpetuates the fortunes of that which endures beyond the physical body.[6]

By the late Vedic period, as visible in the early Upaniṣads, Brahmanism had come to reflect on this process, and recognized that rebirth into the presence of gods or ancestors led only to another inevitable death, and so subsequent rebirth back into the world of human beings.[7] This problem—that an agent feels the consequences of his actions over innumerable lives yet to come—was the major concern of many renunciants (*śramaṇa*s) active in the Northeast Indian region of Magadha, which evidence suggests was a hinterland of Brahmanical authority. Exponents of *śrāmaṇya* traditions—whom Indian authors would know as Jains, Ājīvikas, or otherwise—promoted renunciation from the established social order, along with any ties to familial or ritual obligations, in pursuit of an end to transmigration and the repeated suffering that it entails.[8] From the milieu of competing traditions of *śrāmaṇya* practice, the teachings of Siddhārtha Gautama—otherwise Śākyamuni, or the Buddha—emerged as the most historically successful response to the grim and apparently pervasive belief in seemingly endless rebirth. Though Buddhism accepts the basic premises of the late-Vedic concern—the fact of transmigration, and the role of *karma* in its perpetuation (in Buddhist teaching understood in terms of the "intention" proper to any activity, *cetanā*)—Buddhism is significant for having reimagined the model of transmigration assumed by Brahmanical and other renunciant traditions alike.

In what Buddhist tradition remembers as only the second teaching of the Buddha (in the Pāli canon the *Anattalakkhaṇasutta*, discussed further below), the Buddha challenged the premise that an end to transmigration entails discernment and liberation of some immutable, enduring kernel of personhood. Traditionally this is held to be the beginning of Buddhism's rejection of discourse about the self, and the groundwork for its commitment to instead teaching that things are "not-self" (*anātman*). Not only does Buddhism present the pursuit of such an entity as futile, but views about the self (*ātmadṛṣṭi*), or "grasping" to a notion of the self (*ātmagrāha*), are taught to be actively detrimental to the pursuit of release from rebirth. In accord with this, Buddhist authors developed a terminology that accounts for transmigration without recourse to the notion of an enduring, unchanging subject. This we might call the Buddhist *nairātmyavāda*, or "discourse about absence of self," which was perpetuated by Buddhist authors who took application of *anātman* teaching to be central to the pursuit

6. Regarding *ātman* in Vedic literature prior to the Upaniṣads, see Elizarenkova 2005; also Kazama 1962; Collins 1982: 27–84. Regarding the Vedic ritual world, see Killingley 2018a.

7. See Killingley 2018a: 58–66. Fine introductions to this literature remain Brereton 1990; Olivelle 1998: 3–37; and, more recently, chapters throughout Cohen 2018.

8. Regarding the thesis that the *śrāmaṇya* tradition originated apart from the world of Brahmanical authority, see, for example, Bronkhorst 2007; 2011. The most thorough discussion of the elusive Ājīvika tradition remains Basham 1951.

of *nirvāṇa*.[9] To take but a single well-known example, the closing verses of Vasubandhu's *Abhidharmakośabhāṣya* (fourth or fifth century CE)—at the end of a sustained rebuttal of various erroneous ideas about selfhood—states that "the only route to the city of *nirvāṇa* is absence of self (*nirātmatā*)," which, though having been disclosed by the Buddha, cannot be seen by those who possess only "weak vision."[10] Whereas other religious teachers and adepts were attached to some or other opinion or view about the self, the Buddha rejected preoccupation with any such thing, and was remembered as having promoted an alternative discourse about transmigration, and liberation from it, without any need for the idea of an enduring, unchanging self.

Crucially, sources for early Buddhist thought—for example, texts preserved in the Pāli *Suttapiṭaka*—suggest that Buddhism did not imagine teachings about absence of self to be diametrically opposed to the position that a self does indeed exist.[11] What I am calling Buddhist *nairātmyavāda* did not, at least early in its history, reject the existence of the self so much as oppose the wider Indian religio-philosophical preoccupation *with* the self—its presence, whereabouts, and nature—completely. This is in evidence where the Buddha is recorded as having been confronted with questions to which, we are told, he opted not to respond. For example, the *Atthattasutta* (SN.IV.400)[12] records the inquisitive renunciant Vacchagotta asking the Buddha whether or not there exists a self, to which the Buddha gives no answer.[13] The Buddha goes on to explain that to promote a self would be to subscribe to the "eternalist" position (*sassatavāda;* Skt. *śāśvatavāda*) that something endures across rebirths, while to deny this would promote the

9. In this volume I opt to call this the *nairātmyavāda* instead of the *anātmavāda* (against other publications, including my own: Jones 2016a), as I find that it is only the former expression that is clearly attested in any of the Indian sources relevant to this study: namely, in the *Laṅkāvatārasūtra* (Nanjio 1923: 355.10, 360.3; see also 8.4).

10. Pradhan 1967: 478.17–24: *nirvāṇapuraikavartiṇiṃ ... nirātmatām ... na mandacakṣur vivṛtām apīkṣate.* A philosophical study of this material is Duerlinger 2005, who elsewhere extends a similar approach (2012) to not-self teaching in Candrakīrti's (seventh century) *Madhyamakāvatārabhāṣya*. Regarding that which a bodhisattva wishes to "see" through their practice, see also 10.2.

11. This should not be mistaken for the now unpopular position that early Buddhism—in spite of its commitment to *nairātmyavāda* discourse—accepted an enduring self apart from anything that is discernible in our experience, regarding which see, for example, Grimm 1958; K. Bhattacharya 1973; Pérez-Remón 1980.

12. All references to Pāli sources, unless stated otherwise, are to volume and page numbers in the Pali Text Society (PTS) editions of texts.

13. Elsewhere, for example in the *Vacchagottasutta* (SN.IV.395), this same renunciant is interested in whether or not the world is eternal, whether or not it has an end, whether or not one's life (*jīva*) is identical to the body, and whether or not the Tathāgata survives after his death. The Buddha responds by rebuking other religious groups (*aññatitthiyas*) and their differing views about selfhood; see Anālayo 2011: 389–393. The last of Vacchagotta's queries—regarding the Buddha's status after his apparent *parinirvāṇa*—we will observe to have been an important interest of authors in the Buddha-nature tradition (see 2.2).

"annihilationist" position (*ucchedavāda*) that death brings an end to existence.[14] The Buddha of this and other related discourses prefers silence; to give answers that either affirm or deny views about the self would not be conducive, or "skillful" (*kuśala*), to directing an audience toward liberation.[15] As Stephen Collins (1982: 132) writes, questions posed by the Buddha's interlocutors are "linguistically ill-formed," and premised on the idea that talk of transmigration rests on whether or not what could be called the self does or does not exist. The Buddha's more nuanced position was that erroneous thinking in terms of the self or its negation must be set aside in pursuit of effective change to one's predicament in the turbulent floodwaters of ongoing death and rebirth.

Hence early Buddhist sources dispense with not only the search for the self but also an entire framework for understanding transmigration and prospective liberation from it. The foremost causes of transmigration are revealed to be ignorance (*avidyā*) and craving (*tṛṣṇā*): ignorance of the way in which things are—impermanent (*anitya*), unsatisfactory (*duḥkha*), and in all instances "not the self"—and a craving, crude or subtle, for things that are erroneously imagined to be otherwise. Buddhism holds that our experience of transmigration consists of the arising of transient events or phenomena (*dharma*s), each causally conditioned by others, all of which are necessarily impermanent; there is neither requirement nor room in such a model for an enduring agent or unchanging kernel of identity. The belief that somewhere amid these impersonal elements there must be something that is permanent—something that is "one's self," or anything that "belongs to the self" (*ātmanīya*)—is a subtle and foundational form of attachment, a root cause of further erroneous attitudes, and hence of continuing transmigration. The great irony of pursuing the self or knowledge of it is that supposing the possibility of such a thing, harboring any views or theories that this or that is *ātman*, is precisely the kind of mental activity that maintains transmigration and the persistent suffering that it entails.

The early Buddhist model outlined above preserves what Stephen Collins called "a kind of pragmatic agnosticism, in which the self is not so much denied as declared inconceivable" (1982: 10). What was taught in early discourses attributed to the Buddha could instead be characterized as a "soteriological strategy" (ibid., 78) that intends the rejection of wrong-minded views that obstruct alleviation from suffering, and otherwise the

14. Forms of annihilationism—which also denies the role of *karma* as that which perpetuates rebirth—came to be associated with the Cārvākas. Exponents of this tradition held that no self exists apart from the physical elements that comprise the body, and that bodily death must mean the end of one's existence; see R. Bhattacharya 2011; P. P. Gokhale 2015.

15. A rich and entertaining discussion of not-self teaching is Ṭhānissaro 2011, in which the author puts great emphasis on the Buddha's clarification that his teachings promote what is skillful (*kuśala*) rather than what may be philosophically satisfying, and that otherwise all that is "categorical" in the Buddha's dharma are the four noble truths concerning suffering, its emergence, its cessation, and the path that leads to it (ibid., 8–9, 57–60).

unhelpful conceits that pervaded the wider Indian religious landscape. Among the most pernicious of views are any that take an aspect of experience, or some imagined entity beyond experience, to be permanent, unchanging, or—by virtue of its being fleetingly pleasant (*sukha*)—that which one should hold dear, as if it were "one's self" or "one's own." The production of such views are themselves instances of *karma,* which promote craving and attachment, and so serve only to perpetuate transmigration. Hence the central "strategy" endorsed by generations of Buddhist authors, and attributed to the Buddha himself, teaches that there is nothing in one's experience that meets the criteria for being called the self, and that amid phenomena one can observe only the absence of such a thing, and so nothing worthy of attachment or clinging.[16]

Staying with Collins, whose *Selfless Persons* (1982) remains a classic analysis of early Buddhist teachings about not-self, we might briefly review some early Buddhist arguments that contend that there is nothing within our experience (nor inferred beyond it) that befits the label *ātman,* and as a consequence that discourse about the self is not proper to soteriologically efficacious thought or activity (95–110). We cannot attempt a comprehensive survey of Buddhist *nairātmyavāda,* but could attend to some themes and language that reoccur throughout Buddhist teachings on this matter. A good starting point is the *Anattalakkhaṇasutta* (SN.III.66–68), in which the Buddha discusses the content of human existence in terms of five composite "heaps" (*skandha*s)—of physical form (*rūpa*), sensation (*vedanā*), conceptualization (*saṃjñā*), "constructing activities" (*saṃskāra*), and consciousness (*vijñāna*)—that categorize different constituent aspects or moments of our experience. The Buddha first makes clear that because no agent has the ability to will that any of these heaps be different—"that my body be this, or not this"—there is no self that exhibits any power (*vaśa*) over them. We infer that a self is that which should allow for control or freedom over its circumstances; if no power can be exerted over elements of our experience, there is no good reason to consider the "self" to be present among them.

By contrast, Brahmanical tradition promoted an association between *ātman* and the animating power, or *brahman,* that underpins both the world and the sacrifices that can affect it.[17] In this model, what endures across lives is the hidden epicenter of the agent who can make a better lot for himself in a next life through the performance of Vedic ritual or, as developed in the Upaniṣads, through the pursuit of empowering, eventually liberating, self-knowledge.[18] An early and influential example of *ātmavāda*

16. One might consider the conclusion to the *Mahāpuṇṇamasutta* (MN.III.15), in which the result of the Buddha's teaching about *anātman* is that his audience "do away with" (*nibbindati;* Skt. *nirvindati*) the content of their five "heaps," realizing none of them to be the self.

17. Gonda 1950: 40–41; Suthren Hirst 2018: 107–108.

18. We return to sources for non-Buddhist *ātmavāda* in later chapters; for example, 9.6, 10.3.

discourse—proper to the late Vedic period also—is the *Bṛhadāraṇyaka-upaniṣad* (BĀU), which refers to the "inner controller" (*antaryāmin*) that has dominion over the elements of the body, as well as knowledge of all things considered valuable to the Brahmanical worldview.[19] Though the acquisition of liberating knowledge or insight (*prajñā*) is also an integral part of Buddhist soteriology, this is not located "in the self" as some locus of absolute truth or power; insight is acquired through contact with Buddhist teaching (dharma), and otherwise cultivated throughout a career of disciplined self-transformation over this and successive lives.

The BĀU also holds that this "inner controller" is undying (*amṛta*), distinguishable from the physical body in which it resides.[20] But again Buddhism poses a challenge: the Buddha of the *Anattalakkhaṇasutta* implores his audience to observe that all moments within their experience—again categorized in terms of five composite "heaps"—are impermanent (*anicca;* Skt. *anitya*), subject to change (*vipariṇāma*), and so are "unsatisfactory" (*dukkha;* Skt. *duḥkha*). The Buddha's audience agrees that none of the constituents of these heaps should be treasured as one's self, and that the correct attitude toward any phenomenon is to deny that "it is mine, this is I, this is myself" (*etaṃ mama, eso 'ham asmi, eso me attā*).[21] No element of lived experience must be mistaken for the self, and thoughts or desires for such a thing must be set aside.

This last point invites a further argument: if nothing worthy of being called the self can be found amid lived experience, it is erroneous to postulate such a thing outside of what can be known or felt. For comparison we might again consider the BĀU, in which the self is enigmatically both "within" bodily functions and sensory experience (breath, speech, sight, etc.), but although "he sees, he cannot be seen" (*adṛṣṭo draṣṭā*).[22] By contrast, Buddhist texts such as the *Mahānidānasutta* (DN.II.55–71) reject the idea that the self can be found either within sentient experience (which by

19. BĀU 3.7.1: Sanskrit edition of Olivelle 1998: 84–89.

20. BĀU 3.7.3–23: Olivelle 1998: 86–89.

21. This same refrain is found elsewhere in the Pāli canon, for example, in the *Alagaddūpamasutta* (MN.I.130–142). According to Norman (1981), it is in this text that we encounter a refutation of the self that is expounded by the Upaniṣads: a self that is the same as the world, and which after death will be "permanent, lasting, enduring, not characterized by any change" (*nicco dhuvo sassato avipariṇāmadhammo*), predicates that we encounter throughout our *tathāgatagarbha* sources also. Its metaphysically grand claims notwithstanding, I do not believe that the *Alagaddūpamasutta* provides definitive proof that early Buddhist authors (or indeed the Buddha) knew particular Upaniṣads themselves, so much as responded to a broader discourse that was concerned with transmigration and the notion that some "self" must suffer through it. Making the case that Pāli *sutta* materials exhibit knowledge of the *Bṛhadāraṇyaka-* and *Chāndogya-upaniṣads* in particular, see Gombrich 1996: 31–64; also Wynne 2011: 105–114. The position that early Buddhist literature shows no conclusive evidence of knowing ideas from these Upaniṣads was articulated by Horsche (1968); see also Ruegg 2008: 88n123; Cohen 2018: 73–80.

22. BĀU 3.7.14–23: Olivelle 1998: 88–89.

nature changes from moment to moment) or apart from it, as an absence of mental activity would not lead anyone to claim that they (or "their self") still exists.[23] In short, close attention to the content of our experience shows there to be nothing about us that endures, which rules unhindered, or is some self-reflexive locus of timeless knowledge or wisdom: nothing—to return to what Louis Renou observed in the Vedic *ātman*—that one should treasure as "dear" to oneself, and so worthy of pursuit, discovery or attachment.[24]

In place of discourse about the self, Buddhist authors supply an account of lived experience, as well as transmigration between successive lives, in terms of impersonal conditioned events, none of which is fit to be considered the self or what belongs to it. Again we might take the *Mahānidānasutta* as instructive. This is a locus classicus for the Buddhist account of what more accurately describes the process of transmigration: those realities that can (unlike the self) be observed amid the flow of transient phenomena, and that constitute the seemingly endless process of dependent origination (*pratītyasamutpāda*) as one event gives rise to another. Repeated birth, aging, and death ultimately come about due to ignorance about the transience of all things and, indeed, erroneous thinking about selfhood.[25] This pattern of events—outside of which is a state that is "unconditioned" (*asaṃskṛta*), otherwise the achievement of *nirvāṇa*—explains the experience of transmigration without recourse to any account of some elusive, enduring entity that is bound within a process of death and rebirth. Given the absence of anything worthy of the title *ātman* in this process, Buddhist teaching has no recourse to the notion of any static, unchanging entity within the correctly apprehended process of birth, death, and rebirth.

Whereas other religious systems propounded some or other account of the self (by the name *ātman* or other near synonyms; see 2.6), discourses attributed to the Buddha employ arguments against this mode of thinking, together with a different model of what it means to transmigrate and how one might draw this process to an end. Buddhist authors developed a sophisticated vocabulary to describe the impersonal and transient phenomena of which our experience consists, and attempted to balance this with the Buddha's caution regarding the trappings of metaphysical speculation—regarding the self or otherwise—and its deleterious effects on the pursuit

23. See Collins 1982: 98–100.

24. This concern with the self that is "dear" is part of the famous debate between Yājñavalkya and his wife, Maitreyī, in the BĀU (4.5: Olivelle 1998: 126–131); see Black 2007: 162–167. A possible reference to this episode is intended by the Pāli *Mallikāsutta* (SN.I.75), regarding which see Gombrich 1996: 62–64.

25. The Pāli *Gaddulabaddhasutta* (SN.III.149) compares someone who takes some or another constituent of their experience to hide the self with a dog that is tied to a post, circling endlessly through transmigration.

of liberation.[26] Avoiding speculative thinking about the self (or other moot issues, such as how to conceptualize the experience of *nirvāṇa* after the death of the physical body), Buddhist authors promoted attention to the immediate experience of conditioned reality, and taught strategies of detachment from any fallacious belief that some element of our person or experience can be taken to be the self.[27]

To summarize, we might understand the conventional Indian Buddhist position, reflected in the wealth of dialogues attributed to the Buddha (and much commentarial literature besides) to be a rejection of discourse about the self, and hence of an *ātmavādin* mode of teaching common to other Indian religious traditions. What the vast majority of early Buddhist sources promoted—be they attributed to the Buddha or to commentators who unpacked his teachings—can be termed a discourse about absence of self, or *nairātmyavāda*. This is best understood not as a flat denial of the existence of the self, so much as the position that there is *no place* for ideas about the self in a perspective that is conducive to liberation; that preoccupation with thoughts about a self—or what endures across lives and, potentially, into a state of liberation—is actively detrimental to the pursuit of an end to suffering.[28]

---

26. This sentiment is expressed in the well-known parable of the arrow, found in the *Cūḷamālunkyasutta* (MN.I.426–432). Wynne (2011: 167) eloquently characterizes early Buddhist teachings about *anātman* as having avoided the promotion of "a direct statement of philosophical truth," but contends that abhidharmic formulations in later centuries reflect "reductionist realist" interpretations of *anātman* that proved persistent in Buddhist thought—and into Western reception of it—to the present day; see note 3 above. See also Schmithausen 2014: 633–635. Regarding possible ties between the early Mahāyāna and the development of *abhidharma* specifically, see Bronkhorst 2018. It is otherwise worth remembering that abhidharmic thinking—of the Sarvāstivāda, Theravāda, or otherwise—may not have been fully formed during the period in which the Mahāyānist texts addressed by this study were produced; see 10.2.

27. Bronkhorst (2011: 8) expresses this very succinctly: "The aim of the teaching of the Buddha is evidently not to discover the real self. In his teaching, the insight that the self does not play a part in the activities of body and mind does not help to attain liberation. On the contrary, the preoccupation with the true nature of the self has to be given up. Only then is one ready to follow the path shown by the Buddha. Seen from this practical point of view, the question as to the existence of the self is of minor importance. The main thing is that knowledge of the self plays no useful role on the Buddha's path to liberation."

28. A commitment to *nairātmyavāda* discourse is still exhibited in the *pudgalavāda* tradition, to which various Indian Buddhist schools subscribed, which affirmed that some "person" (*pudgala*) survives through transmigration as the "bearer" of the existential burden that is the five *skandhas*. Exponents of the *pudgalavāda* did not understand this person to be *ātman* in the sense of an abiding "essence" of a sentient being that is worthy of discovery, and did not conflate their slippery notion of an enduring *pudgala* with notions of *ātman* that are rejected throughout the Buddha's discourses. The most thorough discussion of the *pudgalavāda* remains Priestley 1999; see also Chau 1984; Cousins 1994; Eltschinger and Ratié 2013: 64–87; and a useful overview in Harvey 1995: 34–38. Regarding Buddha-nature vis-à-vis *pudgalavāda,* see Eltschinger and Ratié 2013: 62n49. There is curious evidence, in the *Tarkajvālā* of Bhāviveka (c. 490–570), that members of one Buddhist school, the Haimavatas (not among most surviving lists of those who accepted the *pudgalavāda*), argued that

1.2 *Tathāgatagarbha* Literature in Overview

Commitment to *nairātmyavāda* discourse extends beyond our sources for early Buddhism and develops in literature of the Mahāyāna tradition. Literature proper to the Mahāyāna may have begun to emerge in India around the final century before the Common Era, and presents the Buddha as having promoted not merely the pursuit of *nirvāṇa* but also the superlative status of a completely awakened Buddha, an aspirant to which is called a bodhisattva.[29] Our surviving Indian Mahāyānist texts—Indian sources as well as materials preserved in Chinese and/or Tibetan translation—in diverse ways reflect upon the challenging prospect of progressing along the long and arduous path toward complete awakening, commonly understood to take an immeasurable number of lifetimes.[30] Relatively early examples of Mahāyānist literature, such as texts proper to the "perfection of insight" (*prajñāpāramitā*) tradition, continued to stress the importance of *anātman* teaching, and understood this to be an articulation of the fundamental "emptiness" (*śūnyatā*) of all phenomena. Mahāyānist sources concerned with emptiness explain absence of self to go beyond the context of personhood (called sometimes *pudgalanairātmya*) and relate it to all phenomena (*dharmanairātmya*), such that nothing—up to the content of the Buddha's own teachings, and indeed the experience of liberation itself—should be understood to possess an independent nature (*svabhāva*) apart from the impermanent, conditioned character of all entities, and so should not be conceptually hypostasized, let alone serve as objects of attachment.[31]

The wealth of Mahāyānist literature available to us either promotes or takes for granted a commitment to Buddhist *nairātmyavāda,* whether this was articulated in terms of the emptiness of phenomena or, more simply, the futility of believing in—let alone searching for—the self. And yet in one corner of the Indian Mahāyāna we find a set of texts that dabbled with other modes of expression, and in so doing challenged the fundamental postulate of Buddhist teaching with which we have so far been concerned. A small corpus of Mahāyānist texts consider the Buddha's dharma to include affirmation of what is called the *tathāgatagarbha.* This expression makes some or other statement—depending on the literary work in question—about the essential or underlying nature of a sentient being, and in all instances holds something about them to be permanent, enduring, and indestructible. As evident in the quotation that began this chapter, some

---

the *pudgala* is apart from the *skandhas*, permanent and also the experiencer of *nirvāṇa*: ideas distinct from the more "conventional" *pudgalavāda* to which the Sāṃmitīya and Vātsīputrīya schools of Buddhism subscribed (Priestley 1999: 37–42), but closer to what is promoted by some sources of the *tathāgatagarbha* tradition.

29. Regarding the origins of the Mahāyāna tradition(s), see, most recently, the range of perspectives represented in Harrison 2018b.

30. Expressed eloquently throughout Silk 2002; see also Harrison 1995a.

31. An erudite introduction to these ideas is Williams 2009: 51–55.

Mahāyānist sources go so far as to declare that the expression *tathāgatagarbha* refers to some entity "within" the constitution of a sentient being, and moreover that the Buddha revealed its existence as his authoritative account of what could indeed be called the self.

The most thorough discussion of *tathāgatagarbha* thought in all of its aspects, and across all Indian texts concerned with it, remains Jikidō Takasaki's monumental *Nyoraizō shisō no keisei* (The Formation of *Tathāgatagarbha* Thought, 1974). Takasaki's study concerns all texts that we might consider proper to an Indian *tathāgatagarbha* "corpus," but privileges those that did not understand this to refer to the Buddha's account of the self. Takasaki's proposed chronology of this literature imagined the expression *tathāgatagarbha* to have its origins in the language and imagery of the *Tathāgatagarbhasūtra*. The *Tathāgatagarbhasūtra* became the focus of an influential study by Michael Zimmermann (2002), which cemented in the minds of other authors (in particular those publishing in Western languages) the importance of this text in the early development of the *tathāgatagarbha* tradition.[32] Other important studies of *tathāgatagarbha* texts—about which more will be said in later chapters—include David Seyfort Ruegg's investigation of the *Ratnagotravibhāgavyākhyā* (1969), Alex and Hideko Wayman's translation and analysis of the *Śrīmālādevīsiṃhanādasūtra* (1974), and Jonathan Silk's edition, translation, and study of the *Anūnatvāpūrṇatvanirdeśaparivarta* (2015b). Other learned discussions—for example, by Sallie King (1991) and Brian Edward Brown (1991)—have considered the philosophical content of one or more sources of the *tathāgatagarbha* tradition, though with limited scope regarding the historical development of its relation to discourse about the self. A more recent and very insightful account of Indian *tathāgatagarbha* literature features in Kazuo Kanō's study of the transmission and interpretation of the *Ratnagotravibhāgavyākhyā* (2016: 1–14), while a valuable overview of all works in this corpus is that by Michael Radich (2015b).[33]

That some sources of the *tathāgatagarbha* tradition flirted with the language of selfhood is well-known, though some of the texts most relevant to this issue have received little attention next to others that were better remembered by the Indo-Tibetan commentarial tradition. The most "infamous" Indian text to have propounded an account of the self is that which is quoted at the beginning of this chapter: the Mahāyānist *Mahāparinirvāṇamahāsūtra,* which had a significant impact on East Asian Buddhist thought after its translation into Chinese in the early fifth century (see 2.1).[34]

---

32. A recent discussion of the *tathāgatagarbha* literature, which follows Takasaki's model and otherwise the reception of this literature in Tibetan tradition, is Brunnhölzl 2014: 3–52.

33. See also Kanō 2016: 385–392, which traces the development of the *tathāgatagarbha* tradition up to its reception by the Tibetan master rNgog Blo ldan shes rab (1059–1109), responsible for the Tibetan translation of the RGVV. Other discussions of the *tathāgatagarbha* corpus as a whole include H. Nakamura (1980) 1987: 229–233 and Williams 2009: 103–128.

34. Here one might begin with the life and work of the "Nirvāṇa School" master Daosheng 道生 (c. 355–434); see Liebenthal 1955; 1956. The current study will, for the most part, limit itself to what we can discern about *tathāgatagarbha* teaching in South Asia.

The most significant studies of the *Mahāparinirvāṇamahāsūtra* (MPNMS) include that by Masahiro Shimoda (1997),[35] a wealth of publications by Hiromi Habata, and the first thorough analysis of the MPNMS in English, by Michael Radich (2015a).[36] However, the MPNMS is not alone in having promoted what could be called a form of Buddhist *ātmavāda,* and two other Indian texts—virtually untouched by surviving instances of Indian Buddhist commentary—present the *tathāgatagarbha* as a Buddhist account of the self. These are the *Aṅgulimālīyasūtra* (AMS) and **Mahābherīhārakasūtra* (MBhS), which belong to what Takasaki classified as the "*Mahāparinirvāṇa*-group" of *sūtra*s (henceforth MPNMS-group).[37] All three texts share a number of unusual thematic and doctrinal elements, and take the expression *tathāgatagarbha* to refer to some entity that sentient beings "possess," or that otherwise resides "within" their constitution, and which is otherwise called the self. Apart from these texts are better-known sources for teaching about the *tathāgatagarbha,* including the *Tathāgatagarbhasūtra* (TGS), *Śrīmālādevīsiṃhanādasūtra* (ŚDS), and *Laṅkāvatārasūtra* (LAS), as well as the compendious, commentarial *Ratnagotravibhāgavyākhyā* (RGVV).

Grouping all of these works together, I will refer frequently to a "*tathāgatagarbha* corpus" of texts: those Indian Buddhist works that held this expression to be highly significant, and which committed to explaining for an audience to what *tathāgatagarbha* must refer. But we require also a distinction between the forms and explanations of *tathāgatagarbha*—which differ from text to text—and their common commitment to a central idea that is communicated by this expression in all instances. With some debt to the title of Michael Zimmermann's study of the *Tathāgatagarbhasūtra* (2002), I will refer to what is common to texts of this corpus as the "Buddha-nature idea": *that something proper to all sentient beings across their successive births and deaths is, at all times, that which is proper also to a Buddha.*[38] The subtle difference between this and discrete literary discussions of *tathāgatagarbha* doctrine in different Mahāyānist texts—including differing articulations as to what the very term *tathāgatagarbha* itself refers—must be kept in mind as we proceed.

Attempts to make sense of the challenging *ātmavādin* orientation of some *tathāgatagarbha* sources include those by Kenryū Tsukinowa (1938)

---

35. An English overview of this and Shimoda's wider work on the MPNMS is Shimoda 2015; see also Sasaki 1999.

36. Radich's argument owes a debt also to compelling and erudite studies by Stephen Hodge (2006; 2010/2012), about which more is said in the next chapter (especially 2.1 and 2.8).

37. A recent overview of both the AMS and MBhS is T. Suzuki 2014. Previous studies of these texts will be discussed in chapters 3 and 4.

38. See also Zimmermann 2014a: 515–516. This phrasing understands that other Mahāyānist sources could reflect teachings that are proximate to the Buddha-nature idea apart from the expression *tathāgatagarbha:* for example, in the *Tathāgatotpattisaṃbhavanirdeśa* (*sūtra*)—which teaches the pervading presence of the Buddha's knowledge (*buddhajñāna*)—or a number of other texts cited by the compendious *Ratnagotravibhāgavyākhyā;* see 7.1–2.

and by Ruegg (1989a: 17–55).[39] For all of their erudition, these discussions approach some texts of the *tathāgatagarbha* literature—in particular the MPNMS—without the benefit of more recent reassessments of their composition and textual history. For example, we will see in the next chapter (2.1 and 2.7) that a lengthy portion of the MPNMS, which survives in just one of its available recensions, very probably had origins apart from core material of the MPNMS that we know to have been composed in South Asia. Moreover, likely earlier material in the composition of the MPNMS began by introducing a discussion about the self without explicitly stating that this refers to some content of a sentient being (2.2), in other words, some abiding "Buddha-nature." Finally—as we shall discuss below—scholarly understanding of this literature has been challenged by Michael Radich's contention that the MPNMS may in fact be our earliest source for teaching about *tathāgatagarbha* in general.[40] If we accept Radich's arguments, an immediate repercussion is that our earliest source for the expression *tathāgatagarbha* presented Buddha-nature as nothing short of an account of *ātman*. A central claim of this study, with the benefit of renewed attention to Indian sources that teach about Buddha-nature, is that we should indeed understand the *tathāgatagarbha* tradition to have begun its life as a Buddhist account of something that deserved to be called *ātman,* and that the early history of *tathāgatagarbha* teaching in India entailed an attempt by Buddhist authors to present, and then explain, a Mahāyānist account of what was an enduring concern for Indian religious teachers and adepts in general: the pursuit and liberation of that which could be called the self.

1.3 Essences, Natures, Wombs, and Chambers

Before venturing into the corpus of Mahāyānist works that teach some or other articulation of the Buddha-nature idea, we must address head-on the meaning—or better, meanings—of two Indic expressions central to our sources. The first is of course *tathāgatagarbha,* variously understood to refer to "the matrix of the Tathāgata (i.e., Buddha)" (Takasaki 1966: 22), the germinal "Essence" or "Embryo-Essence" of the Tathāgata (Ruegg 1989a: 4, 19), or the state of "containing a Tathāgata" (Zimmermann 2002: 45). I consider all of these interpretations—by no means an exhaustive account of how *tathāgatagarbha* has been unpacked—to have their merits, and to

39. Tsukinowa (1938) addressed the self or "great self" as an articulation of absence of self ("無我の(大)我"); see also 6.3, 7.3. Ruegg's valuable considerations on this theme will be addressed in later chapters (especially chapter 10). A thoughtful study of this topic is the work by Khosla (2015), though with comparatively less attention to explicitly *ātmavādin* articulations of Buddha-nature (those in the "MPNMS-group" of *sūtra*s, discussed below), to which this study is particularly attentive. Publications focusing specifically on the *ātmavādin* language of the MPNMS include Liu 1982: Fujii 1983; 1993; and Habata 1990; as well as Takasaki 1974: 144–148; see also 2.1.

40. Radich 2015a: 35–58.

attest to the many nuances and plausible renderings of a highly productive and enigmatic Indian term.[41]

Texts that will concern us appear to have employed the expression *tathāgatagarbha* in different ways, to reflect subtle but critical distinctions between ways of teaching that all sentient beings possess some kind of enduring Buddha-nature. In some instances, the expression *tathāgatagarbha* can be read as a dependent determinative compound (*tatpuruṣa*), and hence designates "the chamber" or "womb," or instead "embryo" (*garbha*) of/for a Buddha that a sentient being "has," as stated by the MPNMS (*tathāgatagarbho 'stīti*).[42] But elsewhere *tathāgatagarbha* seems to have been used as an exocentric compound (*bahuvrīhi*): sentient beings are those who "contain" a Buddha, or who are in possession of the chamber/womb of/for a Buddha. The exocentric reading appears to be in play where our sources take the expression *tathāgatagarbha* to apply to sentient beings themselves, for example in the RGVV (*sarvasattvās tathāgatagarbhā iti*).[43] This phrasing could intend that sentient beings "are [themselves] the chamber for a Buddha," but the exocentric interpretation can also accord with instances where *tathāgatagarbha* unambiguously refers to something discrete that sentient beings somehow "possess": sentient beings are those who have a "chamber" or "womb" for a Buddha within themselves.

In later chapters we will return to the matter of how best to understand the expression *tathāgatagarbha* and to what it refers across different texts of this tradition. At the outset I venture to suggest that we should not feel unduly burdened by the issue of what manner of compound is being used in one instance or another. Some texts (including the MPNMS) clearly refer to the *tathāgatagarbha* as something that sentient beings *themselves have*, somehow "within" yet apart from other elements of their constitution. However, elsewhere (e.g., in the ŚDS; see 5.2–3) it may be that *tathāgatagarbha* more loosely refers to some *aspect* of a sentient being—specifically, we shall

---

41. More recently, Brunnhölzl (2014: 53–54) has focused on *garbha* in the sense of a "core" or "heart": in part informed by the curious Tibetan translation of this expression with *snying po* ("heart," "essence"). Meanwhile, Saitō (2020), with a debt to Hara (1994), has argued that the RGVV understands *tathāgatagarbha* to mean that sentient beings are "children of a *tathāgata*." My sense is that throughout Indian *tathāgatagarbha* literature—and in particular in *sūtra* materials—we more frequently encounter *garbha* in the sense of a "chamber" or "womb," closer to the standard Chinese rendering of this expression (*zang* 藏), and justified in various sections throughout this volume (e.g., 2.3, 5.2, 7.2). This is not to dismiss, however, the multivalent nature of (*tathāgata*)*garbha* as it is used across these and other sources, inviting here and there the sense of something "embryonic." See also Kanō 2020 and Zimmermann 2020.

42. See Habata 2015b: 185; also 2019: 141–142 (featuring Habata's edition of Sanskrit fragment no. 18.4: [*t*](*a*)*thāgatagarbho* <'>*stīti*); see also Radich 2015a: 26n23. Regarding this as still a *bahuvrīhi* compound—with a sense something like "there exists that which is *tathāgatagarbha*, i.e., a *stūpa* [in every sentient being]"; see Kanō 2017. In each instance, the presence of the *dhātu*, or otherwise *stūpa*, can designate the presence of the Buddha himself: see notes 50 and 52–53, below; also Bronkhorst 2011: 196–197.

43. Johnston (1950) 1991: 25.18, 26.7. See also Zimmermann 2002: 39–46, regarding *tathāgatagarbha* in the context of the TGS.

later see, of their mind—such that it is not so much something that they "have" about themselves but instead refers to their underlying or proper nature, or "what they fundamentally are." On such occasions *tathāgatagarbha* refers to that which is proper to a sentient being and which is, in every instance, the generative space or "womb" from which a new Buddha can, in time, emerge. However it is used, in every instance *tathāgatagarbha* makes some claim about what is enduringly real in or about all sentient beings, which is their possession already of some nature that constitutes the presence of a fully developed (though as yet "undisclosed") Buddha.[44]

Where texts of the *tathāgatagarbha* corpus refer to it as something that a sentient being "has," the expression *tathāgatagarbha* was used interchangeably with the second key term that must concern us: the *buddhadhātu,* or some "essence" or "nature" of a Buddha.[45] The relationship between the expression *buddhadhātu* (sometimes *tathāgatadhātu*) and *tathāgatagarbha* (sometimes *buddhagarbha*)—whether these terms are reflected in surviving Sanskrit, or inferred from passages available only in translations of Indian texts—will be a key concern of the chapters that follow. In the MPNMS-group of texts the expression *tathāgatagarbha* functions as an epithet for the presence of some *buddhadhātu* that is "within" a sentient being. Explanation of the *tathāgatagarbha* in terms of the *buddhadhātu* is preserved in the Sanskrit RGVV (see 7.2), though the absence of the word *buddhadhātu* in any surviving Indian fragments of the MPNMS-group means that we can only reconstruct its presence in those works from Chinese and Tibetan translations of them.[46] Frequent correspondence between Tibetan terms that almost certainly translated *buddhadhātu* (e.g., *sangs rgyas kyi khams/dbyings*) and Chinese terms that very likely reflect the same (e.g., *foxing* 佛性), along with other supporting evidence besides,[47] puts it beyond reasonable doubt that

44. Regarding Buddha-nature teaching in terms of "disclosure" of what is already present, see Zimmermann 2014a.

45. The connotations of the Sanskrit *dhātu* exceed this: it can refer to a constituent part of some composition (e.g., the physical "elements" of the body; see 2.4), and frequently that which is most fundamental in some structure (e.g., a mineral present within rock, or the linguistic root of some or other utterance; see 4.4), or sometimes a "cause" for something as yet unproduced (see 7.4). In the context of the relic cult, the *buddhadhātu* is the enduring essence of the Buddha localized somewhere in the world. In our Buddha-nature literature, *dhātu* can denote something very close in sense to *ātman:* that which is most precious, and "essential," to any sentient being. See also, for example, Habata 2015b: 177–178; 2019: 33–38; Radich 2015a: 23–34, 159–168; Jones 2020.

46. Especially throughout part 1 of this volume, in which we are concerned with passages from texts of the MPNMS-group, I attach an asterisk to the expression **buddhadhātu* where appropriate. We have yet to discover a Sanskrit fragment of the MPNMS that preserves the expression *buddhadhātu,* so this reflects a probable but still hypothetical reconstruction of the term that was very likely present in Indic material underlying our Chinese and Tibetan translations. See Radich 2015a: 24n16, 25n19; also Habata 2015b.

47. Imagery found in the MPNMS, AMS, and MBhS all play on multiple senses of the Sanskrit *dhātu,* in the senses of, for example, the "essence(s)" of language, minerals, the physical body, or otherwise: see, for example, 3.5, 4.4; also Jones 2020: 60–64.

texts of the MPNMS-group all used *tathāgatagarbha* to refer to the presence of the *buddhadhātu*.

Associations between the *tathāgatagarbha* and the "nature" (*dhātu*) of a Buddha in the MPNMS-group specifically—again, the MPNMS, AMS, and MBhS (see above, 1.2)—were explored already by Takasaki.[48] Takasaki understood these texts, and the account of the *buddhadhātu* that they promoted, to reflect a derivation or tangent from the main trajectory of the *tathāgatagarbha* literature in India, which he otherwise considered to begin with the TGS and culminate in the RGVV.[49] But an alternative explanation, proposed by Michael Radich (2015a: 101–173), understands that the origins of the expression *tathāgatagarbha* are entwined with the claim that sentient beings possess the nature or essence of a Buddha, and that the expression *buddhadhātu* became less significant as teachings about Buddha-nature, under the name *tathāgatagarbha,* continued to develop. Hence, at its origins—and better reflected by the MPNMS-group of texts—Buddha-nature thinking was associated with the revelation that in sentient beings there abides the *dhātu* of the Buddha, where *dhātu* refers to the enduring and superlatively valuable "essence" of an awakened being.

Both Shimoda and Radich explored the hypothesis that this "internalized" *buddhadhātu* drew upon a pervasive Indian Buddhist interest: the supposedly indestructible relics of the Buddha (also [*buddha*]*dhātu*) that were believed to be housed in relic-mounds (*stūpa*s), and were potent foci for Buddhist worship and "merit making."[50] From early in Buddhist history—indeed, presumably, no later than the Buddha's death—the veneration of the *stūpa* was of great importance for both the monastic community (sangha) and for the laity who supported it.[51] The defining feature of any *stūpa* was that which it was commonly believed to contain: a trace of the Buddha's physical person that constituted his continuing presence in the world. Inscriptional evidence suggests that as far back as the turn of the Common Era, relics of the Buddha were considered to have been infused with the qualities

48. Takasaki 1974: 127, 182; also Shimoda 1997: 35–39; Radich 2015a: 32–34; 2015b: 264–269.

49. Takasaki 1971; 1974: 768–769; also Radich 2015a: 24n17; Silk 2015b: 1n2. Takasaki (1971: 3) refers to the TGS, AAN, and ŚDS as "the three basic scriptures of the *tathāgatagarbha* theory." A critique of the assumptions on which Takasaki's chronology relies is Radich 2015a: 93–94.

50. Regarding *dhātu* in the sense of "relic," see, for example, Schopen 1988: 530; also Edgerton 1953: 282–284. An excellent introduction to the veneration of Buddhist relics, or of the *stūpa,* is Trainor 2004; see also Schopen 1998; Skilling 2005; Bronkhorst 2011: 193–206. Regarding the subtle distinction between these two objects of reverence—that is, *stūpa* and relic—see Radich 2007: 455–457.

51. I put little stock in the now mostly discredited position, championed by Akira Hirakawa (e.g., 1990: 270–274), that veneration of the *stūpa* was a concern of lay Buddhists to the exclusion of monastics, and moreover that the (supposedly lay) cult of the *stūpa* was formative in the emergence of Mahāyāna Buddhism. See also, for example, Schopen 1991; Harrison 1995a: 57–63.

of a living Buddha—his morality, concentration, insight, and otherwise—such that reverence for the relic was functionally equivalent to worship of the Buddha himself.[52] These physical relics were not necessarily imagined as pieces of bone or teeth: in at least some instances they were conceptualized as tiny, radiant, beadlike objects, akin to jewels.[53] Hence we need not imagine the expression *buddhadhātu* to designate anything recognizably anatomical so much as the precious but concealed content of the *stūpa:* a trace of the Buddha that remains endowed with his qualities, functionally equivalent to the Buddha himself, and enduring in the world even when there is no clearer sign of his living presence.

Few surviving Indian Buddhist texts are devoted exclusively to the importance of *stūpa*s and their contents, but a far greater number, sometimes only in passing, attest to the importance and value of relics in Indian Buddhist culture.[54] Among such sources are various forms of the *Mahāparinirvāṇasūtra,* recounting the Buddha's final days, in which the pivotal event after the Buddha's death and cremation is the distribution of his relics between communities of his followers, who enshrined them in *stūpa*s.[55] Elsewhere, in texts representative of the Mahāyāna tradition, we find references to the established function of the relic as a source of merit making. In the *Aṣṭasāhasrikāprajñāpāramitā* the value of circulating the text is said to be more than that which is generated by the construction of a tremendous number of *stūpa*s; the value of relics—which is implicitly acknowledged—is due to their having entered the world because of the Buddha's attainment of the perfection of insight.[56] There is also the *Saddharmapuṇḍarīka,* which venerates the site at which the text itself is taught, expounded, written, studied, or recited as one on which a *stūpa* could be built without any need for a physical relic, because the text itself constitutes the bodily presence of the Buddha.[57] Though both

52. For a discussion of relevant inscriptional evidence—primarily reliquary inscriptions in Kharoṣṭhī script, dated to decades either side of the turn of the Common Era—see Radich 2007: 523–570. An example of the Buddha's qualities having been attributed to relics is the so-called Senavarman inscription (early first century CE), regarding which see Schopen 1987: 203–209; also von Hinüber 2003: 23–27. Concerning the unreliable claim that relics of this period were held to possess the very "life" (*prāṇa*) of the Buddha, exhibited by text inscribed on the relic casket from Shinkot in Bajaur (c. second century BCE), see H. Falk 2005 (a response, in part, to Schopen 1987: 203–204); see also Schopen 1988 (particularly 209–211); Strong 2004: xvi; Radich 2007: 512–516. Regarding the efficacy of beholding a relic (perhaps "seeing a *buddhadhātu*"), see N. Falk 1977; regarding relic worship as it developed in China, see Kieschnick 2003: 29–36.

53. Strong 2004: 10–12, 46–47.

54. Regarding texts that are directly concerned with relics, see Bentor 1988; also Shimoda 2002.

55. For a survey of different Buddhist literary accounts of these events, see Strong 2004: 116–123, and regarding the legendary redistribution of relics in the third century BCE by the emperor Aśoka, see ibid., 124–149.

56. Vaidya 1960: 28.29–29.27.

57. Kern and Nanjio (1908–1912) 1970 (henceforth SP; see also note 80): 231.7–232.10; Kern 1884: 220–221.

of these works promote themselves or their teachings over the efficacy of the Buddha's relics, each does so by acknowledging the importance of the relic cult in the imagination of its intended Indian audience.

So then to the *tathāgatagarbha* literature—surely later than both of the Mahāyānist *sūtras* named above—and in particular to the MPNMS, which Radich has suggested is our earliest Indian source for this expression and the challenging kinds of Buddhist teaching to which it refers (see 2.1). Radich's argument develops Shimoda's earlier observation that the MPNMS exhibits two stages in its composition, the first of which makes no mention of the Buddha-nature idea, nor of the expressions *tathāgatagarbha* or *buddhadhātu,* but is instead concerned (as the title of the text suggests) with the matter of the Buddha's apparent death and departure from transmigration (*parinirvāṇa*). As a radical retelling of the Buddha's ostensibly final teachings, the MPNMS first reveals that the Buddha exists permanently beyond his physical body. It is only later, and in what Shimoda takes to be a second stage in the composition of the text, that we find a reimagining of what endures after the Buddha's death—his relics or enduring essence (*dhātu*)—that in this work are said to be present in the constitution of all sentient beings (see 2.3).[58]

Our extant versions of the MPNMS preserve the sense that what persists in sentient beings was called not simply *buddhadhātu* but also *tathāgatagarbha.* Radich persuasively shows that surviving versions of the MPNMS (including available Sanskrit fragments) reflect a preponderance of the expression *tathāgatagarbha* over *buddhadhātu.*[59] If *buddhadhātu* denotes the Buddha's abiding relic, and if *tathāgatagarbha* is an epithet of this, then the expression *tathāgatagarbha* most naturally refers to the chamber (*garbha*) for a Buddha (*tathāgata*): the space at the center of a *stūpa,* where lies hidden that which is essential to a Buddha and most precious to the world after his (apparent) departure from it. Radich demonstrates that the notion of the *stūpa* as the "chamber for a relic" (*dhātugarbha*) is attested across a wide range of Buddhist literature, and so argues (beyond Shimoda's earlier discussion of these categories) that the expression *tathāgatagarbha* developed as a complement to the idea of an internalized *buddhadhātu:* the presence of a Buddha's qualities—a mode of his being, or his "embodiment"—not in any *stūpa* but rather in sentient beings themselves.[60] A narrative retelling of the Buddha's death provides a compelling "scenario of origin" for the expression *tathāgatagarbha*; insofar as each sentient being possesses the

58. Shimoda 1997: 283–292; also Takasaki 1971: 7–8.

59. Radich 2015a: 23–32.

60. For example, in the *Aṣṭasāhasrikā-prajñāpāramitā* (Vaidya 1960: 31.10–11), which instructs followers of the Buddha to build *stūpas* that are each "a chamber for the relic of the Buddha" (*tathāgatadhātugarbha*). See Radich 2015a: 160–164, especially 161n434 and 162n436; also Ruegg 1969: 504–505, 514–516 (following Liebenthal 1956: 93–95); 1977: 288; 2004: 27n32, also 8.6n50.

"tomb" of the Buddha, Radich contends, this can intend also the "womb" (*garbha* also) from which a Buddha might, someday, emerge.[61]

Hence *tathāgatagarbha* denotes the locus from which a new Buddha could appear, and in a manner quite distinct from the normal sequence of birth, maturation, and death associated with bondage to the process of transmigration. Radich interprets this as a complement to a "docetic" account of the Buddha that is evident across the rest of the MPNMS and in many other Mahāyānist sources besides.[62] As articulated very directly in the *Lokānuvartanasūtra*—composed no later than the second century of the Common Era—this is the view that the Buddha exists before, after, and truly *beyond* the appearance of his worldly life and teaching.[63] In a similar vein, the *Saddharmapuṇḍarīka* states that the Buddha achieved awakening countless myriad eons ago, such that what audiences saw of his birth, life, and death could only have been displays that are instruments of his teaching.[64] Whereas the MPNMS focuses on denying the finality of the Buddha's (apparent) departure from the world, other Buddhist sources produced in the early centuries of the Common Era venerate the miraculous purity of the Buddha/bodhisattva's final birth, and in each instance deny that such a superlatively reverend being could participate normally in worldly processes.[65] Hence, Radich argues, the innovation of the *tathāgatagarbha* played an important "kataphatic" function next to the "negative docetic" denial that the Buddha in his final life was conceived and born: from the perspective of a Buddha, completely awakened beings are not "produced" at all so much as "revealed" from a bodhisattva, and apart from any "display" that a Buddha may make of his apparently final birth, awakening, and subsequent departure from the world.[66]

To summarize, Radich's account of the MPNMS and its place in the early life of the Buddha-nature idea invites a reassessment of a central concern in both this text and throughout other *tathāgatagarbha* works that came after it. Early teaching about *tathāgatagarbha* explains from where a Buddha can emerge—from some enigmatic, imperceptible "true nature" of sentient beings—and in order to make sense of the idea that Buddhas are entities that exist apart from the ordinary processes of transmigration, even when they appear to be have been born, achieved awakening, imparted the dharma, and died. The interest of this study is that the MPNMS,

61. Radich 2015a: 159–168 (also 101–104, with a debt to Schmithausen 1987: 1–7).

62. See Radich 2015a: appendix 5, regarding "kataphatic gnostic docetism."

63. Regarding Lokakṣema's 支婁迦讖 (late second century) translation (T.807: *Neizang baibao jing* 內藏百寶經), see Harrison 1982; 1993: 159–161.

64. SP 315.11–317.4; Kern 1884: 298–299. See also Radich 2012a: 239–244; also Bielefeldt 2009: 74–78.

65. Radich (2015a: 118–129) attends also to the *Upāyakauśalyasūtra, Lalitavistara,* and *Mahāvastu* as sources for accounts of the Buddha's miraculous or even "apparitional" birth; see also Sasson 2008.

66. See Radich 2015a: 105–158.

together with other texts that are seemingly early in the life of the Buddha-nature tradition, declares not only that the *tathāgatagarbha,* otherwise the presence of the *buddhadhātu,* is an enduring characteristic of all sentient beings, but that this can also be called the self, or *ātman.*

1.4 Buddhist *Ātmavāda:* Preliminary Thoughts

The aim of this study is to address systematically the relationship between Indian teachings about Buddha-nature and discourse about the self, or *ātman,* as represented by all Indian texts that are concerned with the expression *tathāgatagarbha.* My central claim is that association between Buddha-nature teaching and the promotion of a kind of Buddhist *ātmavāda* is a feature of what we should take to be early works in the *tathāgatagarbha* corpus (those addressed in part 1 of this volume), and that texts which seek to distance their audience from the idea of a Buddhist teaching of the self (those of part 2) can be considered inheritors of the expression *tathāgatagarbha* that wished to salvage Buddha-nature thinking from association with discourse about selfhood. This is not to presume that by understanding Buddha-nature teaching as "a Buddhist account of the self" we can unpack every aspect of its value or function for Indian Buddhist authors, let alone their audiences. More modestly, I hold that we benefit from using the acknowledged proximity between the expression *tathāgatagarbha* (and various epithets) and discourse about the self as a lens through which to examine the development of Buddha-nature thinking in India, and so observe hitherto underappreciated aspects of to what the expression *tathāgatagarbha* was understood to refer. Most importantly, I believe that through such a lens we observe a more compelling picture of the relative chronology of works in this tradition, and we should adopt the perspective that Buddha-nature thinking began and developed as—at least in part—a Buddhist account of the self.

Here, I acknowledge, looms a kind of circularity: by prioritizing Buddha-nature texts that discuss *tathāgatagarbha* in terms of selfhood, I attempt to defend the position that these reflect earlier articulations of the Buddha-nature idea. However, I take as my starting point Michael Radich's proposal—which does not attend to Buddha-nature understood as an account of the self—that from within this corpus of texts it is indeed the MPNMS that is our likely earliest source concerning the expression *tathāgatagarbha* and to what it can refer. I hence take Radich's analysis of the MPNMS as a prompt to reconsider the trajectory of Buddha-nature thinking in Indian literature in general. Takasaki's picture of the literature associated with the *tathāgatagarbha,* and of the development of its central Buddha-nature idea, has proved influential.[67] But if the MPNMS is at the source of this tradition (or as close as any surviving work of literature allows us to approach such a

67. Most influentially by Michael Zimmermann (1999; 2002), by whom see also, more recently, 2014b; 2020; also, for example, H. Nakamura (1980) 1987: 229–230; Williams 2009: 104.

thing), we must contend with the fact that the earliest work in this corpus considers the expression *tathāgatagarbha* to refer to nothing less than a Buddhist account of the self. If we take the MPNMS to be our earliest work in this tradition, then the immediate repercussion is that the *Aṅgulimālīyasūtra* (AMS) and **Mahābherīhārakasūtra* (MBhS)—other works belonging to Takasaki's "MPNMS-group"—may also be earlier than texts that do not so clearly understand *tathāgatagarbha* to refer to a teaching about the self. Even if this is not the case, it is undeniable that both these texts reflect a form of Buddha-nature thinking conspicuously close to what is exhibited by the MPNMS, and so articulate teachings that are conceptually closer to the proposed origins of this tradition. Part 1 of this volume will attend to the content of these three *sūtra*s: their explanations of the *tathāgatagarbha,* otherwise the "essence" or "nature" of a Buddha in all sentient beings, and the degree to which it is appropriate for a Buddhist audience to understand this as one's "self."

In part 2 we turn to texts that challenge an *ātmavādin* mode of Buddha-nature thinking. Works including the *Śrīmālādevīsiṃhanādasūtra* (ŚDS), *Ratnagotravibhāga(-vyākhyā)* (RGV[V]), and *Laṅkāvatārasūtra* (LAS) are at pains to qualify the relationship between the *tathāgatagarbha* and discourse about the self, to an extent that would have seemed unnecessary had these two things not already been associated with one another in earlier Buddhist thought and, presumably, literature. These texts continue to promote the *tathāgatagarbha* as something that is permanent (*nitya*), lasting (*dhruva*), tranquil (*śiva*), and enduring (*śāśvata*), though they are also concerned to explain that the *tathāgatagarbha* is not anything like an account of the self except—in some instances—when such a notion is of expedient benefit for particular audiences prone to *ātmavādin* thinking (see 8.2). We will consider also some other works of the *tathāgatagarbha* corpus—such as the *Tathāgatagarbhasūtra* (TGS) itself, which many scholars have previously taken to be the fountainhead of this tradition (see 1.2, above)—that ignore association between Buddha-nature teaching and the notion of selfhood entirely, but which also show no persuasive evidence of having predated the MPNMS and other what we might call "*ātmavāda*" *tathāgatagarbha* sources.

As we are concerned with the development of Buddha-nature thinking in India, I will not with any thoroughness consider texts that likely originated outside of the Indian subcontinent. I will not attend to works that are of very likely Chinese origin, for example, the *Dasheng qixin lun* 大乘起信論 (T.1666), traditionally but tenuously attributed to the Indian poet Aśvaghoṣa (second century CE), or the *Foxing lun* 佛性論 (T.1610), attributed to Vasubandhu but more likely produced by its supposed translator, Paramārtha 真諦 (499–569 CE), under the influence of the RGVV.[68] An exception to this rule will be made for material found in our second

68. See S. King 1991: 21–26; also (regarding Paramārtha as author of the *Dasheng qixin lun*) Grosnick 1989; Tarocco 2008. Regarding Paramārtha's oeuvre as a whole, see Radich

Chinese translation of the MPNMS—that by Dharmakṣema 曇無讖 (385–433 CE)—which, though perhaps not of Indian origin, deserves attention due to its impact upon both Chinese and Tibetan reception of the "core," certainly Indian, MPNMS (see 2.7). Finally, the wealth of commentarial and exegetical literature regarding the RGVV—in Tibet especially—is beyond the scope of this study, and is not so relevant bearing in mind the several centuries between the composition of the RGVV (prior to the fifth century) and renewed interest in its teachings in Indian works produced much later, during and after the eleventh century.[69]

Though we will limit our attention to forms of what were known to be Indian works, we remain very dependent upon translations of relevant texts into Chinese (between, primarily, the fifth and sixth centuries), and/or Tibetan (between, for the most part, the eighth and ninth centuries).[70] All too frequently we must read important statements regarding Buddha-nature thinking through the words and phrasing of translators who may or may not have captured the details or nuances of originally Indian materials.[71] Very often our Chinese and Tibetan translations reflect differing recensions of Indian works, and in some instances we find good evidence of doctrinal developments between one version of a text and another. I will often use footnotes to attend to differences between versions of a literary work, but will discuss at length only those variations that have a bearing on how we should understand the Buddha-nature thinking of any given work across its different surviving versions.[72] On occasion we must attempt to prize apart the stages in the composition of a text, especially where there is evidence to suggest that some author(s) developed its account of Buddha-nature thinking over time. Although I do not in any instance seek for an Indian original or "urtext" of one source or another, I will make occasional judgments regarding whether or not material surviving in one version of

2012b. For a thorough discussion of Buddha-nature and selfhood in the *Foxing lun,* see S. King 1989.

69. Regarding later reception of the RGVV in India, see Kanō 2016: part 1.

70. For Chinese texts I rely on the Taishō (*shinshū daizōkyō*) 大正新脩大藏經 edition of the canon (henceforth T) made widely available through CBETA online, and with recourse to it I refer to variants preserved in the Song (宋), Yuan (元), Ming (明), and "Palace" (宮) editions and Shōgozō manuscript collection (聖語藏). For Tibetan texts I include references to the widely used Derge (D) and Peking (Q) editions of the *bka' 'gyur* (for "*sūtra*" texts) and *bstan 'gyur* (for others), unless an edition that makes use of these and more is otherwise available (e.g., Habata 2013, a critical edition of the MPNMS). In instances where I translate long passages of Tibetan material, I have consulted a wider range of witnesses: the London, Narthang, and Stog Palace editions, and—where content of these survive—the fragmentary Gondhla and Tabo editions also. Space permits that I refer to these editions only where their content has affected my reading of a passage (e.g., omitting purely orthographic variations). Critical editions of texts other than the MPNMS, which might emulate the exemplary work of Habata (2013), remain desiderata.

71. See Nattier 2003: 70–72.

72. This while acknowledging that material preserved only in a longer recension of a text need not necessitate that it is later; see Ruegg 2004: 20–24.

a text is likely to reflect content that could be older or more "basic" to the history of that work.[73]

In part 3 we will at first suspend the central issue of Buddha-nature and selfhood to address some related themes, motifs, and terminology that reoccur throughout the *tathāgatagarbha* literature. Consideration of how these other themes are treated across our sources—for example, the paradigm of a "single vehicle" (*ekayāna*) of Buddhist teaching, the idea that the Buddha employed "cryptic" utterances (*sandhāvacana*) in the interest of educating certain audiences, and the meaning and value of teachings about emptiness (*śūnyatā*)—will buttress the relative chronology of Buddha-nature works that informs the structure of parts 1 and 2. In the final chapter we return to our guiding concern, and hypothesize regarding what may have motivated Indian authors to articulate teachings about the *tathāgatagarbha,* otherwise the existence of Buddha-nature, as an account of the self. Investigating this matter, I contend, helps us to situate the *tathāgatagarbha* literature—especially the earlier, "*ātmavāda*" phase of its development—in a particular matrix of Mahāyānist innovations that was proper to the early centuries of the Common Era, at a time when wider Indian discourse about the self had developed beyond what was known to the earliest Buddhist authors, who had dismissed it tout court.

I acknowledge at the outset that proposing a relative chronology of Mahāyānist works is a challenging endeavor, and often our only hard evidence regarding absolute dating is the *terminus ante quem* provided by records of when texts were translated into Chinese.[74] Criteria for establishing a relative chronology of thematically related texts, such as those that all concern the *tathāgatagarbha,* include whether or not one source mentions another by name. However, unless there is clear evidence that the title mentioned intended a work that we *also* know by that name, such inferences about relative dating may be unreliable.[75] Otherwise we might look for instances where one text draws upon material found in another but without mentioning its name.[76] But here the direction of influence may not be easy to discern, and both texts may have instead drawn from a lost third source

73. Excellent discussions of related issues include Silk 2015a; 2016; also Nattier 2003: 49–51.

74. For further consideration of this kind of enterprise, see Harrison 2018a: 12–16. For a discussion very apposite to literature discussed in the present volume, see Takasaki (1982) 2014. I revisit the issue of the absolute dating of our Buddha-nature texts in the final chapter: see 10.2.

75. See Harrison 1995a: 55. Radich (2015a: 35–57) demonstrates that what have been taken to be references to the *Tathāgatagarbhasūtra* in the MPNMS may well be self-referential (i.e., describing the MPNMS itself). However, mention of the *Saddharmapuṇḍarīka* (SP) in the MPNMS (see Radich 2015a: 52; see also 2.1n13) refers to a theme of that other text specifically, and so can be taken as reliable evidence that authors of the MPNMS knew of the SP, and in some form that we would find recognizable today.

76. Such evidence leads me to believe the ŚDS to have known ideas of the MPNMS (see 5.2–3), even if it is not decisively clear that the authors of the ŚDS knew the MPNMS itself.

that predates both.[77] Of some value are instances where a text introduces terminology better known from another corner of Buddhist intellectual history, such that we judge ourselves to be reading either a recontextualization of ideas or language from one doctrinal context to another, or sometimes a marriage of what were taken to be complementary elements from discrete literary or intellectual climates.[78] But we must be open also to the prospect that ideas or terminology could have fallen out of favor; concepts or phrasing found in one source could have been knowingly rejected or jettisoned by another. Such may well have been the case if indeed (1) the MPNMS is our oldest source within the *tathāgatagarbha* corpus, but (2) sources later than it hesitated to refer to the *tathāgatagarbha* as the presence of the Buddha's relic or "essence" (*dhātu*) within any sentient being. In short, an investigation such as ours requires careful judgment deciding whether or not sources did indeed know or build upon ideas present in others, especially where it may be the case that a later source attempted to reimagine important but contentious ideas that were promoted by another.

With all of these caveats in mind, we will use the issue of how Buddha-nature relates to discourse about the self as a means by which to order texts concerned with the interpretation of the expression *tathāgatagarbha*. This, in turn, invites further suggestions about the doctrinal heritage of our sources, which help us to situate the *tathāgatagarbha* literature in the broader religious landscape of India in the early centuries of the Common Era. Takasaki understood there to be two primary influences upon the *tathāgatagarbha* tradition: the *prajñāpāramitā* literature (which seems to have been considered authoritative for the vast majority of Mahāyānist authors in general), and the *Saddharmapuṇḍarīka(sūtra)* (henceforth SP)—commonly called the *Lotus Sūtra*—that became one of the most influential texts for East Asian Buddhism, though was by comparison less influential in the Indian subcontinent itself.[79] It will become apparent as we proceed that while texts of the *tathāgatagarbha* corpus certainly knew and accepted the authority of *prajñāpāramitā* literature, the stronger ties are those that bind Buddha-nature thinking to the SP.[80] Hence while we might abandon Zimmermann's

---

77. For example, the MBhS echoes a wealth of material found in the SP (see 4.1). Though we cannot prove conclusively that the former borrows from the latter, the material in question coheres better with the content of the SP, which reads very much like the earlier source for ideas "borrowed" by the MBhS.

78. Here our best example is the LAS, which takes the term *tathāgatagarbha* to in fact refer to the substratum consciousness (*ālayavijñāna*) that is proper to the Yogācāra-Vijñānavāda tradition (see 8.3).

79. See Takasaki 1974: 369–445. Regarding the SP in its Indian context, see Silk 2001; Nattier 2007: 181–183.

80. All references to the SP are to the Sanskrit *editio princeps* of Kern and Nanjio (1908–1912) 1970, having discerned that other versions of the text (e.g., Kumārajīva's 鳩摩羅什 [359–409 CE] influential *Miaofa lianhua jing* 妙法蓮華經 [T.262]), as well as other surviving Sanskrit manuscripts not consulted by Kern and Nanjio (e.g., those discussed in various publications by Seishi Karashima [e.g., 2003–2006]) present nothing to challenge claims

earlier contention—after Takasaki—that the TGS represents our earliest available source for the expression *tathāgatagarbha,* his recognition that the SP was of paramount importance for authors of that text, and for exponents of the Buddha-nature idea in general, remains instructive.[81]

In the textual studies that follow we will see the ideas of the SP loom large, and its conception of the Mahāyāna as the single vehicle (*ekayāna*) a consistent complement to the idea that all sentient beings share a common nature with the Buddha(s).[82] We will see that the likely earliest authors in the *tathāgatagarbha* tradition articulated their teachings in a climate of Mahāyānist innovation shaped by the principle that there can exist only one kind of liberation from rebirth—the complete awakening proper to a Buddha—and hence that all expressions of Buddhist dharma must work to lead every sentient being toward this single goal. By understanding early *tathāgatagarbha* works as properly "ekayānist" in type, and that they all affirmed that the Buddha's involvement in the world went beyond what some Buddhist audiences supposed, we can make better sense of the conditions under which Buddhists began to propose that the Buddha revealed an account of the self. This, we will see, was an attempt by some Buddhist authors to promote a definitive and unifying account of Buddhist liberation, which could eclipse not only wider Buddhist teaching but all Indian discourse about liberation in general.

---

that I make about the SP, its content, and its likely influence on the *tathāgatagarbha* tradition. I also frequently include reference to Kern's 1884 English translation of the (Sanskrit) SP.

81. Zimmermann 1999; 2002: 56–57, 60, 77, 81.

82. Good introductions to this theme, and its importance in the SP, include Bielefeldt 2009; Lopez and Stone 2019.

PART I

Buddha-Nature, the Self

CHAPTER 2

The *Mahāparinirvāṇamahāsūtra* and the Buddhist Self

2.1 The Text

Undoubtedly the text of the *tathāgatagarbha* tradition that is most associated with teaching about selfhood is the *Mahāparinirvāṇamahāsūtra* (MPNMS): a Mahāyānist retelling of the final days and teachings of Buddha Śākyamuni at Kuśinagara.[1] We possess four complete translations of the text, representative of three recensions of the Indian MPNMS. The first is the Chinese translation attributed to Faxian 法顯 (d. 418–423) and Buddhabhadra 佛陀跋陀羅 (358–429), perhaps also Baoyun 寶雲 (d. 449), produced c. 416–418 CE (T.376: *Dabannihuan jing* 大般泥洹經; henceforth MPNMS^{F}), which—as the shortest and earliest translation of the MPNMS—is the text used for most passages translated in this chapter.[2] The second and by far longest version is the Chinese translation of Dharmakṣema 曇無讖 (385–433), produced sometime between c. 421 and 432 CE (T.374: *Dabanniepan jing* 大般涅槃經; henceforth MPNMS^{D}).[3] The translation of this version into English is an ongoing venture by Mark Blum (e.g., 2013). The final translation of significance regarding the Indian MPNMS is that into Tibetan, produced in the early ninth century by Jinamitra, Jñānagarbha, and Devacandra (e.g., D.120; Q.788: *Yongs su mya ngan las 'das pa chen po'i theg pa chen po'i mdo;* henceforth MPNMS^{T}), for which a critical edition is that of Hiromi Habata (2013).[4]

1. The final days of the Buddha are otherwise recounted in the Pāli *Mahāparinibbānasutta* (DN.II.72). Regarding the Sarvāstivādin form of this narrative, see Waldschmidt 1950–1951; regarding its form preserved in the Chinese *āgama*s, see Silk 2006.

2. Hodge (2010/2012: 8–9) expresses doubt regarding Faxian's involvement in the translation of MPNMS^{F}, but as this does not appear to have any direct bearing on its interpretation, I follow, for example, Radich (2015a: 20–21n9), Habata (e.g., 2015b), and Shimoda (e.g., 2015) and the traditional association of this translation with Faxian.

3. Regarding the dating of Dharmakṣema's translation work, which revolves around when one believes him to have arrived at Guzang—sometime between 412 and 421 CE—see Chen 2004; also Hodge 2010/2012: 9–27.

4. Stephen Hodge has prepared an English translation of this version, making reference to both MPNMS^{F} and MPNMS^{D} also, which is as yet unpublished.

We possess forty (known) Central Asian fragments of the Sanskrit MPNMS, drawn from twenty-eight leaves and likely from three manuscripts, from the vicinity of Khādalik in the present-day Xinjiang province of China. A final fragment is preserved at Kōyasan, in Japan.[5] Most of these fragments contain material not directly relevant to discussion of Buddha-nature, though several provide valuable insights into the language used to promote this idea in an Indian climate. A further portion of the MPNMS is preserved in the Sanskrit *Ratnagotravibhāgavyākhyā* (RGVV), and will be considered below (2.2; also 7.3).

There exists also a second version of the MPNMS in Tibetan (e.g., D.119, Q.787), though this is a translation from the Chinese MPNMS^{D}, replete with lines confused by a crude rendering of the Chinese phrasing used in Dharmakṣema's original.[6] A likely motivation for the preservation of MPNMS^{D} in the Tibetan *bka' 'gyur*—in which it was more common practice that the canon retained only one version of a text under any title—is that MPNMS^{D} is around four times the length of either of our other two complete versions of the MPNMS. Most of the content exclusive to MPNMS^{D} (and its Tibetan derivative) is contained in additional chapters that follow the material that it shares with MPNMS^{F} and MPNMS^{T}, which Chinese sources hold was obtained by Dharmakṣema in either Khotan or Dunhuang.[7] As none of this material is shared by our other versions of the MPNMS, nor reflected in any surviving Sanskrit fragments of the text, it remains plausible that this content was composed in Central Asia or China, and may even owe its existence to Dharmakṣema himself.[8]

Material common to MPNMS^{F}, MPNMS^{D}, and MPNMS^{T}—and hence reliably of Indian origin—will be referred to simply as the MPNMS, and will be the primary focus of this chapter. Material in MPNMS^{D} that follows and exceeds the core content of the MPNMS, and which is of more questionable origin, will be called MPNMS^{D}+, and remains slightly suspect if we are concerned only with material that had Indian provenance.[9] Nevertheless, as both Chinese and Tibetan tradition understand that the additional content we will call MPNMS^{D}+ was ultimately of Indian origin, and was believed to include authoritative utterances by the Buddha, we will later consider the manner in which this material developed ideas of the (core) MPNMS (see 2.7).

---

5. Regarding these see Habata 2007; 2009; 2015a; and 2019. See also Radich 2015a: 21n11.

6. We can exclude another form of MPNMS^{D}, the Chinese "Southern Version" (T.375), produced some time c. 430–440, which is in essence a revision of T.374.

7. See Shimoda 2015: 158 (citing the *Gaoseng zhuan* 高僧傳, T.2059, and *Chu sanzang jiji* 出三藏記集, T.2145).

8. Hodge 2010/2012: 25–29. There is, however, convincing evidence that this material is familiar with Indian literature unknown to any other Chinese materials that we know from Dharmakṣema's time; see Radich 2011: 49–50, 160–163; Granoff 2012: 203–210.

9. The material I am calling MPNMS^{D}+ is T.374(12)428b17–603c30.

A significant feature of the MPNMS is that it is framed by an account of the departure of the Buddha from the world, but in which his actual death is conspicuously omitted: when the Buddha reclines onto his right side, presumably to "enter *parinirvāṇa*" and leave the world for good (as is the case in other texts recording his death), the narrative simply ends.[10] This underscores the central theme of the MPNMS apart from its teaching about Buddha-nature: that in spite of appearances, and of prior literary accounts of the Buddha's death, the Buddha should be considered to be permanent (*nitya*), and so remains influential in the world even though his physical body can no longer be perceived.[11] The MPNMS teaches that the Buddha exceeds what was seen of his birth, life, and death, and in fact became awakened in the far distant past.[12] This perspective is shared by one of the few identifiable Indian works mentioned by name in the MPNMS (and preserved in a Sanskrit fragment of it): the *Saddharmapuṇḍarīka* (SP).[13]

According to Masahiro Shimoda (1997: 163–171), it is earlier material in the composition of the MPNMS that is concerned with establishing the permanence of the Buddha.[14] This is what Michael Radich has called MPNMS-dhk: that portion of the text concerned with the Buddha in his *dharmakāya*—called also his "adamantine body" (*vajrakāya*)—that is his transcendent, indestructible mode of being apart from what is seen of him in the world.[15] As discussed in the previous chapter (1.3), I agree with both

10. MPNMS^{F} 899c22–23; MPNMS^{D} 428b11–12; MPNMS^{T} §587. The Buddha is said to have displayed, for the sake of his audience, a body that exhibits sickness (現身有疾); the Buddha himself did not suffer.

11. Regarding permanence (*nitya*[*tā*]) in the MPNMS—and relevant, I believe, to the MPNMS-group as a whole—see Habata 2014: 150–152; 2015b: 183–184 (following Hara 1959).

12. See, at length, MPNMS^{F} 870b10–872a4; MPNMS^{D} 388a11–390a5; MPNMS^{T} §187–214.

13. See MPNMS^{F} 893c6; MPNMS^{D} 420a23–24; MPNMS^{T} §495.17. Also Habata 2009: 580; 2019: 161–162, in which Habata reconstructs a Sanskrit fragment (no. 21.3) to read *saddharmapauṇḍar*[*ī*]*k*(*a*)[*m*](*ahāsūtra-*). The MPNMS cites the SP in connection with the idea that many sentient beings who did not think themselves capable of attaining awakening indeed have the potential for it. At its most extreme, the SP declares that any sentient being who has heard the *sūtra* being taught will—in some future life—arrive at the status of a Buddha; see SP 53.3–4 (v.2.100; also Kern 1884: 53, in which this is presented as verse 2.99).

14. The material of "MPNMS-dhk" is as follows: MPNMS^{F} 853a3–868a17; MPNMS^{D} 365a2–385b5; MPNMS^{T} §1–168. See Radich 2015a: 21–22; Shimoda 2015: 161.

15. See Radich 2012a. An important connotation of this *vajrakāya* is the sense of power or "unimpededness" associated with the term *vajra;* see Salvini 2016: 233–242. In the MPNMS, the *dharmakāya* is a body that is not sustained by food (Radich 2015a: 129–132)—an idea articulated also, for example, in the *Vimalakīrtinirdeśasūtra* (Taishō University 2006: 34 [20a3]: *dharmakāyās tathāgatā nāmiṣakāyāḥ*), in which context it is just as clear that this body could not sustain injury or illness, and is apart from all things that are conditioned (*asaṃskṛta*). Though we have little clarity about to what precisely the expression *dharmakāya* refers (bearing in mind that in many literary contexts *dharmakāya* refers to the Buddha's "embodiment in dharma," or his presence via his teachings, and is nothing to hypostatize beyond this; see Harrison 1992a), the consistent contrast that the MPNMS makes is between

Shimoda and Radich that this material likely predates the rest of the MPNMS, which goes on to introduce the different but clearly related idea that all sentient beings possess, permanently and so across all rebirths, the nature of a Buddha (*buddhadhātu*), referred to otherwise, and frequently, as possession of the *tathāgatagarbha*. Material concerned with *tathāgatagarbha,* which clearly builds upon ideas found in MPNMS-dhk, Radich calls MPNMS-tg.[16] A distinction between these two strata of the MPNMS will prove integral to how we understand the development of Buddha-nature presented as an account of a permanent, unchanging self.[17]

Shimoda's analysis of the MPNMS proposed much about the social history underlying the composition of the text, much of which is beyond the scope of this volume.[18] However, his observation that it is only later material of the MPNMS that concerns the *buddhadhātu,* and that this was intended to constitute an internalization of the Buddha's relic, is key to understanding the development of the Buddha-nature idea. Studies of the MPNMS have also been produced by Stephen Hodge (2006; 2010/2012), who has focused on a prophecy complex found in this text and shared by other works of the so-called MPNMS-group, and has highlighted complexities in the textual history of our three recensions of the MPNMS. Invaluable editions of both MPNMS^{T} and many fragments of the Sanskrit MPNMS have been produced by Hiromi Habata (e.g., 2007; 2009; 2015a; 2019), who has also published widely on a number of themes found throughout the text (e.g., 1989; 1990; 2014; 2015b; 2018). A significant and provocative discussion of the MPNMS is that of Michael Radich (2015a), who builds upon work by Shimoda to argue that we have good reason to believe that the MPNMS (or specifically MPNMS-tg) is our oldest literary source for a discussion of *tathāgatagarbha,* and that in its content we find clues regarding the origins of this expression, and the Buddha-nature idea for which it stands (for more details, see also 1.3).

Radich broadly accepts the stratification of the MPNMS proposed by Shimoda, into what we can continue to call MPNMS-dhk and MPNMS-tg.[19]

---

the *dharmakāya* as the Buddha's enduring existence beyond the world and his displayed appearance in it, which is characterized by birth, suffering, and death. A thorough discussion of the Buddha's embodiments—including different senses of the expression *dharmakāya*—is Radich 2007 (especially 813–824, 895–1029); see also Makransky 1997.

16. The material of "MPNMS-tg" is as follows: MPNMS^{F} 868a24–899c23; MPNMS^{D} 385b12–428b12; MPNMS^{T} §169–588. See Radich 2015a: 21–22; Shimoda 2015: 161.

17. Another study of this topic in the MPNMS is Habata 1990. Liu (1982), Ruegg (1989a: 17–55), and Fujii (1983; 1993) all consider Dharmakṣema's text (i.e., T.374, or otherwise T.375; see note 6 above) without distinguishing MPNMS^{D}+ from MPNMS^{D}, or in other words, material that we know to have some basis in an Indian text. See also 2.7.

18. See Shimoda 1997; 2014; also Sasaki 1999. Insights into Shimoda's Japanese publications are available in English in Shimoda 2015.

19. Shimoda's stratification (see, e.g., 2015: 161–163) proposes a further complication: that material in what Radich calls MPNMS-dhk—called in MPNMS^{F} the chapter on "Longevity" (長壽品: 863b21–866a14; corresponding to MPNMS^{D} 379b23–382c25; MPNMS^{T}

MPNMS-dhk represents a text very much of the "*Mahāparinirvāṇa*" genre, concerned with the significance of the Buddha's (bodily) demise and the fate of the dharma and sangha after it, to which MPNMS-tg adds, by its account of *tathāgatagarbha,* a reimagining of the distribution of the Buddha's enduring postmortem relics (*dhātus*). Assessing MPNMS-dhk as a discrete text is in one sense problematic: every version of this material survives together with MPNMS-tg, and hence may have undergone further development after the composition of the later stratum of the text. However, the content of MPNMS-dhk does reflect an internally coherent text, which made statements about the nature of a Buddha that predate and inform the discussion of Buddha-nature (vis-à-vis sentient beings) that came after it. While MPNMS-dhk does not affirm the existence of the *tathāgatagarbha,* its description of the Buddha—in which he is himself said to somehow "be" *ātman*—must be our starting point.

2.2 The Buddha as Self

Where MPNMS-dhk approves the language of selfhood it is not in relation to the status or nature of sentient beings but rather describes how the Buddha (or the state of awakening that he has achieved) should be understood in contrast to them. The *ātman* taught in MPNMS-dhk presents a special usage of this term: not once mentioning the constitution of sentient beings, and yet—importantly—explicitly contrasting this *ātman* to the ideas of non-Buddhist traditions that certainly *did* teach that the language of selfhood is appropriate when discussing transmigration.[20] There is no doubt that the *ātman* taught in MPNMS-dhk was formative for the authors of MPNMS-tg: both strata of the MPNMS introduce the correct usage of this term through a discussion of four conceptual distortions (*viparyāsa*s) that plague sentient beings, one of which is the muddling of what should be thought to be the self and what should not. Hence by attending to MPNMS-dhk we address the literary prehistory of Buddha-nature teaching in an *ātmavādin* form—our likely earliest source for the idea that the Buddha revealed some account of what deserves to be called the self.

More conventional Buddhist teaching holds that sentient beings have distorted perspectives in which they consider there to be something permanent (*nitya*) in what is properly impermanent; the self (*ātman*) in what is not the self; pure (*śubha/śuci*) in what is impure; and pleasant or blissful

---

§113–143)—was inserted into the body of MPNMS-dhk after the composition of MPNMS-tg. I am here in a similar situation to Radich (2015a: 207–210), in that my interest in the content of the MPNMS regarding *tathāgatagarbha* and discourse about the self does not benefit from further scrutinizing Shimoda's proposed "Stratum 2b." Further light may be shed on the composition of the MPNMS in as yet unpublished work by Hodge (see Radich 2015a: 210).

20. See Eltschinger 2014: 36n3. This distinction between two senses of *ātman*—here with reference to the Buddha, and only later (in MPNMS-tg) with reference to Buddha-nature—is observed already in Habata 1990.

(*sukha*) in what is unsatisfactory or constitutes suffering (*duḥkha*).[21] However, both strata of the MPNMS affirm that the notions of permanence, selfhood, purity, and bliss still have some correct application.[22] In MPNMS-tg—as we shall see later (2.3)—these "inverted" distortions refer to teachings about Buddha-nature.[23] In MPNMS-dhk the picture is not so clear. Monks who are in the presence of the Buddha describe to him a simile, stating that just as a dizzied person can perceive that things around him are spinning when in fact they are not, so must sentient beings come to see impermanence, absence of self, impurity, and suffering in all things. The Buddha explains that the monks have not fully grasped the simile's meaning. "In the manner that a person says that the sun, moon, mountains and earth are spinning when they are not; but only those who are dizzy say that these things are spinning, likewise do sentient beings foolishly, distortedly impute self, permanence, bliss, and purity. But after this [is corrected, one knows that], the Buddha is the meaning of 'self,' the *dharmakāya* of 'permanence,' *nirvāṇa* of 'bliss,' and what are designated as *dharma*s is the meaning of 'purity.'"[24] Our other translations, MPNMS[D] and MPNMS[T], clarify that sentient beings are guilty of imputing, for example, absence of self with respect to that which is, after all, the self. Here the Buddha explains that although sentient beings see "distortedly," this does not mean that a corrected perspective is one that *never* conceptualizes permanence, selfhood, etcetera, so much as one that takes there to be, for example, permanence or

21. For example, see the *Vipallāsasutta* (AN.II.52); also the *Abhidharmakośabhāṣya* (Pradhan 1967: 283.8–284.22), or Śāntideva's (eighth century) *Śikṣāsamuccaya* (Bendall [1897–1902] 1970: 198.11–13).

22. That there is a correct application of the positive attributes *nitya, ātman,* and so on is stated also in the *Mahāmeghasūtra* (e.g., *Da fangdeng wuxiang jing* 大方等無想經, T.387[12]1082b29–c1: 眾生真實不知如來常住不變, 如來為然智慧法燈, 悉令得見常樂我淨). The *Mahāmeghasūtra* is another work in the "MPNMS-group" of texts (see Radich 2015a: 97–99; 2015b: 266–267; also Takasaki 1974: 275–301), sharing the same prophetic account of the decline of the dharma found in the other three (see also 9.4, 10.2) but showing only passing and uninformative concern with Buddha-nature (T.387[12]1100a26–27: 一切眾生悉有佛性; also 1102b21). T. Suzuki (2001) has argued that the *Mahāmeghasūtra* may have been composed around the same time as the MPNMS, and that the two texts likely influenced one another during their production. A summary of the Chinese *Mahāmeghasūtra* (T.387) is Forte 2005: 333–349.

23. See Takasaki (1974: 172) and Shimoda (1997: 202–205; English 16–17). It should be noted that explicit reference to the inversion of the distortions as "qualities" (*guṇa*) is found only in the RGVV, in which these constitute the four *guṇapāramitā*s proper to the *dharmakāya*. See, however, note 41 below.

24. MPNMS[F] 862a11–14: 如人言日、月、山、地轉此非為轉, 但眩惑謂之[a]為轉, 如是眾生[b]愚癡顛倒計我、計常、計樂、計淨。然後[c]佛者是我義, 法身是常義, 泥洹是樂義[d], 假名諸法是淨義。

[a] T 之 = Song/Yuan/Ming/Palace 呼

[b] T 眾生 = Song/Yuan/Ming/Palace 眾生心常, Shōgozō 眾生常

[c] Shōgozō 後 = T 彼

[d] Shōgozō omits 義

Compare MPNMS[D] 377b16–c14; MPNMS[T] §101.4–12.

impermanence where these are the *correct* attributes of some or other phenomenon.[25]

The identifications that conclude this passage—indicating that selfhood refers to the Buddha specifically—should be read with caution. In their place MPNMS[D] supplies a longer list of equations,[26] which could support Hodge's hypothesis that these reflect some form of interlineal gloss that became inserted into our main text, with the intention of mapping these four positive designators—self, permanence, bliss, and purity—onto four different Buddhist categories.[27] This is persuasive, as these precise identifications are not explored anywhere else in the MPNMS, and may reflect some kind of interpolation. Although it is correct, as Shimoda writes, that MPNMS-dhk identifies the Buddha "as" *ātman,* the status of this equation relative to the rest of this material requires, at least initially in our analysis, some caution.[28]

The position of MPNMS-dhk is that it is erroneous to take what is in fact the self to be otherwise. The matter of quite what should be taken to be the self remains unclear even after another simile, in which the Buddha compares his monks to a group of merchants who construct a bathing pool for nocturnal swimming. One of them drops a precious beryl stone (*vaiḍūrya*) into the water, and the merchants take turns diving to retrieve it. Most of them emerge with pebbles or stones, thinking themselves to have found the jewel, but its enduring radiance from the bottom of the water informs them that they are mistaken.[29] For the explanation of this simile, we can in this one instance refer to a Sanskrit quotation of the MPNMS preserved in the Sanskrit RGVV:

> Likewise, monks, you who are ignorant mentally cultivate, repeatedly and increasingly and with full acceptance, the reality of *dharma*s: that everything is impermanent, unsatisfactory, without self, and impure,[30] all that you have dealt with is worthless; therefore, monks, do not be like those who were fixated on the pebbles and gravel in the pond, but be skilled in your methods![31]

25. An important Sanskrit fragment (no. 8a1–2) preserves corresponding material, and has been reconstructed by Habata (2019: 105–106) to reflect *(cat)*[*uv*]*(i)*[*p*]*(a)ryā*[*s*]*(ā)*, along with the expressions "*(ni)*[*t*]*yam anityam iti,*" "*ātmā*[*n*]*(am)*," and "*sukh*[*āt*]*(m)*[*ā*]."

26. MPNMS[D] (377c9–12) appears to state, elliptically, that *anātman = saṃsāra; ātman =* the Tathāgata; *anitya = śrāvaka*s and *pratyekabuddha*s; *nitya = tathāgatadharmakāya; duḥkha = tīrthika*s, *sukha = nirvāṇa; aśubha = saṃskṛta;* and *śubha* = the *saddharma*.

27. Hodge 2010/2012: 42

28. Shimoda 2015: 163–164.

29. See MPNMS[F] 862b8–14; MPNMS[D] 377c29–378a7; MPNMS[T] §104.1–15; also Johnston (1950) 1991: 74.22–75.12.

30. MPNMS[F] (862b15) alone refers to emptiness (*kong* 空) in place of not-self/absence of self (e.g., *wuwo* 無我).

31. This refers to "skill-in-means/methods" (*upāyakauśalya*), not in the sense of a Buddha's use of different teachings (a prominent theme in the SP; see, e.g., Pye 2003; Lopez and

> Monks, whatever you mentally cultivate, repeatedly and increasingly and with full acceptance, to be in all instances impermanent, unsatisfactory, without self, and impure, amid these there is that which exhibits permanence, bliss, purity and selfhood; hence [states the RGVV], to be understood in detail, according to this [*Mahāparinirvāṇa*]*sūtra,* is the explanation of obstruction by [conceptual] distortions, which concerns being fixed on the reality of the supreme *dharma*s.[32]

The framing of this passage by the RGVV understands its message to be remedial: that teaching about the four distortions can lead to error if one does not consider also the unique qualities of that which is "supreme" (see 7.4). The form that this passage takes in all versions of the MPNMS (together with its use by the RGVV in all versions of it) is essentially the same, with only subtle divergence over what is being described in the simile. In the Sanskrit RGVV this is "the reality of the supreme *dharma*(s)" (*paramadharmatattva*), and in MPNMS^{F} we find "the real *dharma*(s)" (*zhenshifa* 真實法: possibly Skt. **paramadharma*); in MPNMS^{T} and the Tibetan RGVV we find "the reality of *dharma*(s)" (*chos kyi de kho na nyid dam pa;* perhaps again **paramadharmatattva*), while in MPNMS^{D} and the Chinese RGVV this is simply "reality" (*zhenshi* 真實: **tattva*).[33]

These expressions do not clarify what precisely we should consider to be permanent, self, blissful, and pure, other than that which is certainly supreme, or supermundane, in contrast to that which is not. If we follow Hodge and suspend the slightly suspect (i.e., perhaps later) claim that "the Buddha is *ātman,*" etcetera, we do not have any further indication that these four attributes pertain to the Buddha specifically. But if the message of the MPNMS is that it is correct to mentally cultivate not-self, but not in regard to *all* phenomena, what precisely is it that is left that could rightly be called the self, and by virtue of what? This material makes no mention of sentient beings, nor Buddha-nature (called *tathāgatagarbha* or otherwise),

---

Stone 2019: 53–73) but rather a bodhisattva's ability to stay on track toward the goal of complete awakening, especially during their practice of meditation; see de Breet 1992; Nattier 2003: 155.

32. Johnston (1950) 1991: 75.6–12: *evam eva bhikṣavo yuṣmābhiḥ sarvam anityaṃ sarvaṃ duḥkhaṃ sarvam anātmakaṃ sarvam aśubham iti sarvagrahaṇena bhāvitabhāvitaṃ bahulīkṛtabahulīkṛtaṃ dharmatattvam ajānadbhis tat sarvaṃ ghaṭitaṃ nirarthakam / tasmād bhikṣavo vāpīśarkarakaṭhalyavyavasthitā iva mā bhūta*[a] *upāyakuśalā yūyaṃ bhavata / yad yad bhikṣavo yuṣmābhiḥ sarvam anityaṃ sarvaṃ duḥkhaṃ sarvam anātmakaṃ sarvam aśubham iti sarvagrahaṇena bhāvitabhāvitaṃ bahulīkṛtabahulīkṛtaṃ tatra tatra eva nityasukhaśubhātmakāni santi iti vistareṇa paramadharmatattvavyavasthānam ārabhya viparyāsābhibhūtanirdeśo*[b] *yathāsūtram anugantavyaḥ.*

[a] Emended after Schmithausen 1971: 159: *mā bhūtā* to *mā bhūta.*

[b] Emended by Schmithausen (ibid.): *viparyāsabhūtanirdeśo* to *viparyāsābhibhūtanirdeśo.* Compare MPNMS^{F} 862b14–19; MPNMS^{D} 378a7–11; MPNMS^{T} §104.16–23.

33. MPNMS^{F} 862b20; MPNMS^{D} 378a11–12; MPNMS^{T} §104.24. Regarding versions of the RGVV, to which I refer above (specifically: RGVV^{T} D.4025, 113b3; Q.5526, 118a3 (Z. Nakamura 1967: 145–147); RGVV^{C} 839c29), see 7.1.

and so we must conclude that these positive designators describe some enduring state of existence that is apart from transmigration and conditioned existence: the state that is enjoyed by a Buddha.[34]

Though we will see these four distortions revisited in MPNMS-tg (2.3), in MPNMS-dhk there is only one of the set that receives further elaboration. The monks who are in the Buddha's company inquire how a positive account of selfhood can be reconciled with teaching about *anātman*. "As the Lord has taught that all phenomena are without self, so should we practice; when we practice like that the [erroneous] notion of a self is destroyed, and when the notion of a self is destroyed, then do we enter *nirvāṇa*. What does this [talk of the self] mean? We entreat the Lord to take pity, and explain further!"[35] The Buddha responds with a parable, embedded in which is an important recognition that his account of selfhood could be compared with discourse about the self found in non-Buddhist traditions, even if a self is not (yet) something that the Buddha describes as proper to sentient beings. The parable recounts a king who had in his service a naïve physician, whose judgement the king held to be authoritative.[36] This physician prescribed to the king's subjects, without discrimination, the same milk-based medicine for all kinds of ailments, with predictably mixed results. The physician is eventually replaced in his duties by a more skilled doctor, who had pretended for a great time to be a willing but inexperienced apprentice. He promptly has the king outlaw any use of this milk-based medicine, going so far as to have the king threaten execution for any who imbibe it. The king himself then succumbs to an illness, the cure for which is this same milk-based medicine, which the skilled physician duly prescribes. The king questions his new physician's instruction, and is given the following response: "Take for example a sheet of wood that has a trail of bite-marks left by a woodworm, which appear to be writing. Those who are not skilled in writing consider these to be real letters; those who are

34. See Shimoda 2015: 163–164.

35. MPNMS[F] 862b21–24: 如世尊説一切諸法皆悉無我; 當如是修[a], 如是修時我想即滅, 我想滅已正向泥洹[b]。此有何義? 唯願世尊哀愍[c]更説。

[a] Song/Yuan/Ming/Palace omit 如是修

[b] T 泥洹 = Song/Yuan/Ming/Palace/Shōgozō 涅槃

[c] Song/Yuan/Ming/Palace 愍 = T 故

Compare MPNMS[D] 376b3–9; MPNMS[T] §88.

36. This parable, and others from the MPNMS-group, is mentioned in two influential Tibetan commentaries from the fourteenth century, representative of different opinions regarding the "provisional" or "definitive" status of Buddha-nature teachings (see T. Wangchuk 2017: 43–55; 69–81): the *Ri chos nges don rgya mtsho zhes bya ba mthar thug thun mong ma yin pa'i man ngag* (henceforth RC) by Dol po pa Shes rab rgyal mtshan (1292–1361), regarding which see Hopkins 2006: 128–129, and the *De bzhin gshegs pa'i snying po gsal zhing mdzes par byed pa'i rgyan* (henceforth DzG, after "*mDzes rgyan*") by Bu ston Rin chen grub (1290–1364), regarding which see Ruegg 1973: 82. I include references to translations of these commentaries as examples of different and competing interpretations of Buddha-nature outside of India, about which much more can be (and has been) written; see, for example, publications named at 9.5n63.

thoroughly discerning know that these are not letters. Your previous [and naïve] physician was like this: though concocting the milk-remedy, he did not discern the occasion for its prescription."[37] The Buddha explains that he is like the skilled physician, while the naïve physician can be compared to teachers of other religious systems (*waidao* 外道; *mu stegs pa: *tīrthikas*). Quite shockingly, the Buddha then reveals that the doctrine of *anātman* was taught for the purpose of subjugating teachers of rival doctrines. Though this sentiment is present in all three versions, its clearest articulation is preserved in MPNMS^{T}:

> In order to subjugate persons of other systems, I said that there was no *ātman, sattva, jīva,* or *pudgala.* The teaching of other systems—that there is an existing self—is like the letters carved out by the insect: hence do I teach, with respect to all sentient beings, absence of self.[38]

We encounter similar lists for erroneous notions of selfhood—"self" (*ātman*), "[enduring] sentient being" (*sattva*), "[enduring] life" (*jīva*), "person" (*pudgala*), etcetera—throughout our *tathāgatagarbha* sources; these appear earlier and wider in Buddhist literature, and must reflect well-known designators for notions of selfhood that, according to Buddhist teaching, should be rejected.[39]

This example with the woodworm is important for several reasons. First, even though MPNMS-dhk does not clearly acknowledge the self as a category applicable to sentient beings, the text still recognizes that discourse about the self was understood to have been a defining characteristic of non-Buddhist systems. To evoke the language of selfhood—even here, where the subject appears to be the selfhood of the (liberated) Buddha rather than (transmigrating) sentient beings—the authors of MPNMS-dhk knew themselves to be courting language and ideas associated with non-Buddhist teachings. Secondly, we might have expected the Buddha to

---

37. MPNMS^{F} 862c15–17: 譬如板木有虫食跡似生[a]名字。不善書者謂是真字; 其善別者知非書字本[b]。先醫如是：雖合乳藥，不知分別時節所應。

[a] Yuan/Ming 生 = T王

[b] Song/Yuan/Ming/Palace 別者知非書字本 = T 書者乃知非真, Shōgozō 別者乃知非書字本

Compare MPNMS^{D} 378b27–c2; MPNMS^{T} §106.69–74.

38. MPNMS^{T} §107.7–12: *mu stegs pa rnams tshar gcad pa'i phyir bdag med do // sems can med do // srog med do // gang zag med do zhes gsung ngo // mu stegs pa rnams kyis bdag bstan pa ni srin bus brkos pa'i yi ge dang 'dra ste / de'i phyir nga sems can thams cad la bdag med do zhes bstan pa ston par mdzad do //* Compare MPNMS^{F} 863a7–9; MPNMS^{D} 378c21–23.

39. A very early list of ten such erroneous notions occurs in the *Mahāniddesa,* commenting on the *Aṭṭhakavagga* of the *Suttanipāta* (4.6.5: Andersen and Smith 1913: 159; La Vallée Poussin and Thomas 1916: 127). The *Kāśyapaparivarta* exhibits a list of fifteen such erroneous notions (Vorobyova-Desyatovskaya 2002: 50 [§142]), while Skilling (1997: 300–301, 331) finds in the *Bimbisārapratyudgamanamahāsūtra* a list of as many as seventeen. See also Habata 1990: 177–178; see also 2.5n101.

have clarified that his teaching *anātman* was for the purpose of educating sentient beings in terms of what is true, but instead it is presented as having been taught to deter sentient beings from wrong-minded views of the self that they may encounter in the world. As such, MPNMS-dhk implies that teaching about not-self is in the end expedient, and employed by the Buddha not because of its verity but rather for the sake of eventually revealing a *correct* doctrine of the self that must be distinguished from the *ātmavādin* teachings of rival religio-philosophical systems.[40]

Some further implications follow. In the example of the woodworm, these creatures—though ignorant of what they do—nonetheless produce what at least *appear* to be convincingly constructed letters. Similarly, though the naïve physician does not know when to prescribe the milk-medicine, we infer that occasionally this was indeed the correct treatment for a given patient. The implication is that the language of selfhood as used by non-Buddhist teachers must, by virtue of resembling what is taught now by the Buddha, have at least the semblance of truth: a resemblance to the Buddha's own teaching about the true self. In spite of this (or, indeed, because of it), this portion of MPNMS-dhk concludes by stressing that the Buddhist self is nothing like ideas that the Buddha had otherwise, earlier, opposed:

> All sentient beings accepted the teaching of the Tathāgata, then taught one another, in every case teaching absence of self. In this manner, because the Tathāgata knew the time and means for rescuing sentient beings, he taught that all phenomena are without self. Because [the real self] is not like the self that is accepted by persons in the world, [the Buddha] taught that all phenomena are by nature without self. When again he teaches about the self, it is like the good doctor understanding the workings of the milk-medicine.
>
> Know that the self is real; the self is permanent, not subject to change, not subject to destruction. The self has good qualities,[41] the self has sovereignty. Like the doctor skilled in [use of] the milk-medicine, the Tathāgata likewise teaches the true dharma for the sake of sentient beings. All four communities [monastics and laypersons, male and female], should train in accordance with this.[42]

40. We see this line of thinking again in the *_Mahābherīhārakasūtra_ (see 4.6).

41. Here MPNMS^F *de* 德; corresponding to MPNMS^T *yon tan nyid:* perhaps Skt. *_guṇatā_.

42. MPNMS^F 863a9–15: 一切眾生承如來教[a], 展轉相教, 皆説無我。此是如來知時方便濟眾生故, 説一切法其性無我。非如世間所受吾我, 故説一切諸法[b]無我。時復説我, 如彼善[c]醫明乳藥法。當知我者是實: 我者常住、非變易法、非磨滅法。我者是德、我者自在。如善乳藥醫, 如來亦然為諸眾生説真實法。一切四眾當如是學。

[a] Song/Yuan/Ming/Palace/Shōgozō 教 = T 言
[b] Song/Yuan/Ming/Palace/Shōgozō 諸法 = T 法其性
[c] Song/Yuan/Ming/Palace/Shōgozō 善 = T 良
Compare MPNMS^T §107.20–27; MPNMS^D 378c24–379a5.

In slightly more detail, MPNMS^{T} includes some examples of erroneous, worldly notions of the self—comparable to the size of a thumb, or of a millet grain—and so reminiscent of imagery encountered in the Upaniṣads (a feature to which we will return later: 9.6).[43] But across all versions of MPNMS-dhk there is still no mention of the self with reference to sentient beings themselves; the self that is permanent, indestructible and so forth is contrasted with worldly notions of the self, but we have no sense of how it relates to transmigration or the character of those who experience it. Therefore we cannot conclude that MPNMS-dhk introduces the idea of a self apropos of sentient beings—articulated in terms of Buddha-nature or otherwise (indeed, with no mention yet of *tathāgatagarbha*)—though it does include a contrast between the Buddha's liberated "self" and wrong-minded discourse about selfhood proper to other religio-philosophical systems.

Although MPNMS-dhk approves the language of selfhood to say something about the status of the Buddha, it does not with any certainty introduce a true *ātmavāda:* that is, an account of the self as something proper to sentient beings. Nevertheless, that the expression *ātman* has some referent was singled out from the four "inverted" distortions for further elaboration. Promoting an account of the Buddha's "selfhood," as the authors of MPNMS-dhk likely realized, raises difficult questions: if liberation can be described in terms of *ātman*—with which non-Buddhist systems were so concerned—from where can this status come, or where can it be discovered? Could something befitting the term *ātman* be "created," that is, be caused to exist, at the point of awakening? If not, then locating the self at the attainment of liberation invites an account of *ātman* in regard to transmigration also—the position, we shall see, developed in MPNMS-tg.

2.3 Buddha-nature and the Self

As discussed in the previous chapter (1.3), there is good reason to believe that the expression *tathāgatagarbha* begins with MPNMS-tg, and the internalization of the relic of the Buddha in the constitution of every sentient being. Indeed, in one very important passage MPNMS-tg makes a bold declaration about how the bodhisattva should imagine himself: already of the same nature as a Buddha, so that for sentient beings he should become the true *stūpa,* or site of a true relic (*sheli* 舍利: *śarīra*) and so an object of reverence.[44] Our clearest account of this thought is preserved in MPNMS^{T}:[45]

---

43. MPNMS^{T} §107.17–19: *bdag mthe bong tsam dang / khre rgod kyi 'bru tsam.* MPNMS^{D} (378c28–29) adds that the self might be thought of as like a tiny particle (*weichen* 微塵).

44. MPNMS^{F} 885a5–7: 若禮舍利塔 / 應當敬禮我 / 我與諸眾生 / 為最真實塔 / 亦是真舍利 / 是故應敬禮。

45. Addressed also by Habata 2015b: 180–181; and Kanō 2017: 20–23, 48–50; also Takasaki 1974: 148–152; Shimoda 1997: 278–283.

> Having gone to the Buddha for refuge, may I attain the same body as him; then having become a Buddha, may I do the activities of a Tathāgata.[46] Having become equal to a Tathāgata, I need not bow reverentially to the Buddhas: may I become like a great refuge for all sentient beings! Without abandoning the *dharmakāya,* may I give reverence to the relic of the Buddha (*buddhadhātu*) and to the *stūpa*. May I be like a *stūpa* for all those sentient beings who are not willing to revere [the Buddhas]; may my body become a site of worship for all sentient beings![47]

While the bodhisattva is not yet, in a literal sense, a Buddha, his status "like a *stūpa*" in possession of the relic/nature of a Buddha would make him a fitting object of devotion. Corresponding material in MPNMS^{D} clarifies that this status can be extended to all sentient beings. Physical relics are established by the Buddha "because of a desire to develop sentient beings towards salvation; but if sentient beings are led to the idea that they possess a reliquary in their own body, and so make offerings to it, in this fashion can sentient beings make my *dharmakāya* a site of refuge."[48] It seems likely that Buddha-"nature" (*dhātu*) throughout the MPNMS refers to this internalized "relic" (*dhātu* also), and so quite reasonably—after Shimoda and Radich—that the *tathāgatagarbha* is the "relic chamber" hidden within the constitution of any sentient being. This hidden nature is cause for the bodhisattva, akin to a *stūpa,* to be an object of reverence for any devotee of the Buddha. In the person of a bodhisattva already are the (thirty-two) major and (eighty) minor physical characteristics that adorn the body of a fully realized Buddha;[49] though he may not express these characteristics outwardly, what is essential to a Buddha resides within him.

---

46. Here MPNMS^{T} reads *de bzhin gshegs pa'i rlabs,* regarding which see Habata 2015b: 181n14. Habata hypothesizes that this may include a translation of **udāra,* so translates "the power of the Tathāgata." Kanō (2017: 20) opts for something like the "conduct/behaviour" of the Tathāgata ("如来蔵としてのふるまい"); I have no better suggestion of what the Tibetan may mean, or may have rendered from an Indian original.

47. MPNMS^{T} §391.10–18: *bdag sangs rgyas la skyabs su song nas sku gcig par gyur cig / de nas sangs rgyas nyid du gyur nas de bzhin gshegs pa'i rlabs byed par gyur cig / de bzhin gshegs pa dang mnyam par gyur nas sangs rgyas rnams la thal mo btud par mi bya'o // bdag sems can thams cad kyi skyabs chen po lta bur gyur cig / bdag gis chos kyi sku yang mi gtang bar sangs rgyas kyi khams dang mchod rten la phyag bya'o // phyag byed mi 'dod pa'i sems can thams cad kyi mchod rten lta bur bdag gyur cig / bdag gi lus sems can thams cad kyis phyag bya ba'i gnas su gyur cig /*

48. MPNMS^{D} 410a7–9: 為欲化度諸眾; 亦令眾生於我身中[a]起塔廟想, 禮拜供養, 如是眾生以我法身為歸依處。

[a] T 中 = Yuan/Ming 即

Here is some similarity to the Buddha's instruction to Ānanda at the end of the Pāli *Mahāparinibbānasutta* (see Takasaki 1971: 7–8): that his disciples remain "islands unto themselves, refuges unto themselves, having no other refuge" (DN.II.100: *attadīpo viharati attasaraṇo anaññasaraṇo*). We will later see that the MPNMS and other Buddha-nature works prioritize the Buddha (who might be "within" oneself, or one's *true* self) as the only true refuge (see 5.4).

49. See MPNMS^{F} 885b7–21; MPNMS^{D} 410b6–14; MPNMS^{T} §394.13–25, and accompanying discussion by Radich (2015a 139–140); also (differing from MPNMS^{F} and MPNMS^{T})

What is yet more striking is that where MPNMS-tg discusses *tathāgatagarbha,* otherwise *buddhadhātu,* this is usually also presented as the Buddha's teaching about the self, and often in connection to the body of a sentient being. Even when this is not explicitly called the self, MPNMS-tg acknowledges that the existence of Buddha-nature sits in tension with teachings about *anātman.* For example, the MPNMS is consistent with other *tathāgatagarbha* works in its denial that Buddha-nature can be seen by persons other than a Buddha (see 3.4): it cannot be known directly by the arhat, or "solitary buddha" (*pratyekabuddha*).[50] However, an important caveat is that the bodhisattva at the tenth stage (*bhūmi*) of accomplishment—in other words, close to the achievement of complete awakening—is able to perceive their Buddha-nature, albeit in an indistinct manner, once the Buddha has taught about its existence. The MPNMS uses the example of a doctor who treats a patient suffering from some eye disease; after surgically clearing the retina, gradually the patient regains their vision: "Likewise, good son, the venerable bodhisattva who purifies the stages of practice, attaining the tenth stage, looking in their body for the real nature of the Tathāgata, is nonetheless misled by the wheel of the absence of self; how much less, then, would the *śrāvaka* and *pratyekabuddha* be able to know this! You should know, good son, that in this way the nature of the Tathāgata is difficult to see."[51] MPNMS^{D} states that these bodhisattvas transmigrate "continually confused by absence of self."[52] Whatever the case, it is quite clear that wrong-minded understanding of *anātman,* seeing what is not the self where there is in fact Buddha-nature, continues to hinder even advanced bodhisattvas. The implication is that teaching about *tathāgatagarbha* indeed sits in some kind of difficult tension with the Buddha's well-established teachings about *anātman,* even when *tathāgatagarbha* is not explicitly unpacked in terms of the self.

Both MPNMS^{D} and MPNMS^{T} specify that a bodhisattva of the tenth stage is able to discern the **buddhadhātu* "in part" (Ch. *shaojian* 少見; Tib. *de'u*): that advanced beings who are not yet Buddhas can indeed perceive, albeit imperfectly, their Buddha-nature. This idea is absent from directly corresponding lines of MPNMS^{F}, but is encountered briefly in another of its short similes: the tenth-stage bodhisattva, compared now to someone

mention of the same marks at MPNMS^{D} 419a9–10. Regarding these physical marks, associated with a "superior being" (*mahāpuruṣa*), see, for example, Radich 2007: 295–331; Zysk 2016: 162–172, 195–222; McGovern 2016.

50. Regarding the *pratyekabuddha,* see Kloppenborg 1974; Norman 1983; also Ray 1994: 212–250.

51. MPNMS^{F} 887a9–12: 如是善男子, 菩薩摩訶薩淨治道地成就十住, 於自身中觀察如來真實之性, 猶為無我輪之所惑; 況復聲聞及辟支佛而能知之! 當知善男子, 如來之性, 難見如是。Compare MPNMS^{T} §405.10–20. This terminology is unusual: the "wheel of the absence of self" (無我輪) is found also in MPNMS^{T} (*bdag med pa'i 'khor lo*); the meaning is clearer in MPNMS^{D} (see next note).

52. MPNMS^{D} 411c23–412a1 (including 常為無我之所惑亂).

trying to discern birds in the sky, "scrutinizes his own body for the nature of the Tathāgata, but still produces deluded notions, until eventually [seeing it] in part."[53] This simile introduces further comparisons between the tenth-stage bodhisattva and someone with imperfect vision. In each instance the tenth-stage bodhisattva looks for the *tathāgatagarbha* "in his own body" (MPNMS^F 自身中觀; MPNMS^T *rang gi lus la*)—where it is somehow, enigmatically, located—but even he cannot yet see it clearly.[54] The point that the Buddha is making is quite clear: the presence of the *tathāgatagarbha,* within one's own constitution, is difficult to see. This prompts the Buddha's interlocutor, the bodhisattva Kāśyapa, to ask whether or not Buddha-nature is something that can be seen by the physical eye (*rouyan* 肉眼: *māṃsacakṣus*).[55] The Buddha's response is unambiguous: "Like the heaven of neither ideation nor of non-ideation (**naivasaṃjñānāsaṃjñāyatana:* i.e. something beyond the experience of regular sentient beings), this [Buddha-nature] is only within the domain of the Buddhas; how could all of the *śrāvaka*s and *pratyekabuddha*s perceive it? Only one who follows the teachings of the Tathāgata, faithfully committing oneself to them, after that sees their equality [to the Buddha]."[56] Though their precise wordings are different, all three versions of the MPNMS state that it is only through faith (*xinshou* 信受 / *xinshun* 信順; *yid ches: *pratyaya*) that inferior beings can have any access to their Buddha-nature, guided by the MPNMS itself.[57]

So far these statements are little different from *tathāgatagarbha* taught in other Mahāyānist texts that we will address later: Buddha-nature is difficult to ascertain, visible only to a Buddha, but is nonetheless a permanently abiding truth about all sentient beings. But a central feature of Buddha-nature teaching throughout the MPNMS in particular is that this unseen treasure can be called the true self. In a clear evocation of what we

---

53. MPNMS^F 887a14–15: 於自身中[a]觀如來性，猶生惑想，久乃髣髴。

[a] T 於自身中 = Song/Yuan/Ming/Palace 自於身上 (see also next note).

54. For these comparisons in full, beginning with that which concerns the diseased eye, see MPNMS^F 887a6–887b17; MPNMS^D 411c20–412b8; MPNMS^T §405–414. Curiously, the apparatus of the Taishō (and, in this instance, supported also by consultation of the *Zhonghua Dazangjing* 中華大藏經: Beijing, 1984–1988) records variant readings throughout this passage (see previous note for one example). Apart from the opening example (of the cataract, in which case all editions reflect 自身中觀察), these variants record that the bodhisattva looks for his Buddha-nature "above/upon his body" (身上). This is not reflected in our other versions of the MPNMS but accords with a Sanskrit fragment of another passage, discussed below (2.3n72), and certainly requires further scrutiny outside of this study.

55. Notably this is not the better-known Kāśyapa, an arhat, who is conspicuously absent from the Buddha's deathbed both in the MPNMS and in other accounts of the *parinirvāṇa* narrative. This is perhaps significant: it is not an arhat who struggles with Buddha-nature teaching but rather a bodhisattva, which suggests that the MPNMS knew or expected objection from Mahāyānist, rather than simply Śrāvakayānist, audiences.

56. MPNMS^F 887b18–21: 譬如非想非非想天， 唯佛境界； 一切聲聞及辟支佛， 云何能見? 但彼隨順如來契經， 信心方便， 然後等觀。 Compare MPNMS^D 412b9–14; MPNMS^T §415.

57. MPNMS^D 412b11: *Da niepan jing* 大涅槃經; MPNMS^T §415.11: *yongs su mya ngan las 'das pa chen po'i mdo chen po.*

read in MPNMS-dhk (2.2), MPNMS-tg returns to the matter of what are correct notions of permanence, selfhood, bliss, and purity, and explains that selfhood refers to what is otherwise called the *tathāgatagarbha,* or **buddhadhātu:* "The notion that what is not self is the self is a distortion; the notion that what is the self is not self is a distortion. Saying that every worldly being possesses a self is a distortion. The Buddha teaches that the nature of the Tathāgata (如來性) is the real self (真實我), but if with respect to this tenet one mentally cultivates [the thought] that it is not the self, this is called the third distortion [of four]."[58] Language that was in MPNMS-dhk used to describe the reality or status of the Buddha in MPNMS-tg refers now to Buddha-nature (in MPNMS^{T} *de bzhin gshegs pa'i snying po: tathāgatagarbha*), and while we are yet to read explicitly that this pertains to something about sentient beings (indeed, we are told that it is still distorted to think that sentient beings possess a self), the explanation that follows this confirms that Buddha-nature is that which somehow endures across their successive lives. Just as the story of the skilled physician in MPNMS-dhk followed the declaration that the Buddha was in some sense *ātman,* this second "inversion" of distorted views proper to MPNMS-tg introduces a great many more similes, concerned throughout with the manner in which Buddha-nature refers to the self of sentient beings. These similes are initiated by a further, very reasonable question put to the Buddha by his perplexed interlocutor, Kāśyapa:

> Lord, [if] the Tathāgata has [a teaching about] the self, does this or does this not exist within the twenty-five existences?
>
> The Buddha said to Kāśyapa: The real self is the nature of the Tathāgata (如來性). Know that all sentient beings have this, but as those sentient beings are enshrouded by immeasurable afflictions, it is not manifested.[59]

Our other two versions of the MPNMS inquire also whether or not there is a self amid "twenty-five existences," which the MPNMS mentions several more times later on (see below, 2.4), and likely refer to possible forms of existence (or "births": Skt. **bhava?*) as sentient beings undergo transmigration.[60] Crucially, the Buddha does not give Kāśyapa a straight answer to his

58. MPNMS^{F} 883b3–5: 非我我想顛倒，我非我想顛倒。言一切世間有我，是為顛倒。佛說如來性是真實我，而於此義作非我修，是名第三顛倒。Compare MPNMS^{D} 407a20–26; MPNMS^{T} §373. See also Shimoda 1991: 9–15.

59. MPNMS^{F} 883b14–b17: 世尊，如來有我，二十五有，為有為無? 佛告迦葉：真實我者，是如來性。當知一切眾生悉有，但彼眾生無量煩惱覆蔽不現。Compare also MPNMS^{D} 407b7–10; MPNMS^{T} §375.4–376.5.

60. E.g., MPNMS^{T} §375.4–5: *srid pa nyi shu rtsa lnga la bdag mchis zhes bgyi 'am / ma mchis zhes bgyi.* See also 4.5. The MPNMS also states that these twenty-five existences are described in the *Śūraṅgamasamādhisūtra* (MPNMS^{F} 872a7; MPNMS^{D} 390a7–8; MPNMS^{T} §215.1–6), though I do not find such a thing in any surviving form of that text (e.g., T.642; D.132;

question but states only that the nature of the Buddha is indeed also the self (*wo* 我; *bdag: ātman*) of a sentient being.[61]

The Buddha's more thorough response bears a resemblance to one of the nine similes for explaining Buddha-nature encountered in the *Tathāgatagarbhasūtra* (TGS; see 6.2).[62] The Buddha explains how an impoverished man might be ignorant about a treasure buried beneath his house. A kindly visitor, who knows about the treasure, promises to show it to the man if he agrees to do work for him. Having agreed, the poor man has his fortune—hidden beneath his feet all along—revealed to him.[63] "All sentient beings are also like this: each of them has the nature of the Tathāgata (如來之性), [but] concealed by and sunken into immeasurable afflictions, they are unable to know it for themselves; the Tathāgata, skilfully teaching and developing [them], makes known that in their own body is the nature of the Tathāgata, so that they delight and have faith in it."[64] We should note that the Buddha has not confronted Kāśyapa's question regarding whether or not this Buddha-nature is something amid (twenty-five) types of existence. Nor does this simile focus on the *tathāgatagarbha* as the self of sentient beings, though it is clear that it is somehow "within" them, and cannot be known other than through revelation by a Buddha.

A second simile, or perhaps short parable, is more illuminating, and attends to the Buddha teaching successively—and with echoes of what we saw in MPNMS-dhk (2.2)—first *anātman* and then, contentiously, a doctrine of *ātman*. The parable concerns a woman who has a sick infant.[65] A doctor prescribes to the child a kind of medicinal butter, which must be fully digested in order for it to take effect.[66] In the meantime the child

---

Q.800); see also Shimoda 1997: 275–278. H. Nakamura (1980: 1045c) refers to a tradition that these intend types of birth in different realms of existence: fourteen in the realm of sense desire (*kāmadhātu*), seven in the realm of form (*rūpadhātu*), and four in the formless realm (*arūpyadhātu*). See also Blum 2013: 372.

61. Corresponding material in MPNMS^T provides the quotation at the start of this volume, which appears to reflect the terms *ātman* (*bdag*), *tathāgatagarbha* (*de bzhin gshegs pa'i snying po*), and *buddhadhātu* (*sangs rgyas kyi khams*) in succession.

62. See Zimmermann 2002: 120–125. This also resembles an image in the *Chāndogya-upaniṣad* (v.8.3.1: see Olivelle 1998: 276–277). As Radich argues (2015a: 56–57), we have no good reason to suppose that the simile of the MPNMS borrows from the TGS; see also 6.2.

63. MPNMS^F 883b17–b24. Both MPNMS^D (407b12–b20) and MPNMS^T (§376.6–26) instead preserve a version of the story in which a poor woman, not knowing about the treasure beneath her house, agrees to work for a visitor only if he will make known to her son the location of the hidden treasure. Both versions are mentioned in Dol po pa's RC; see Hopkins 2006: 53–54.

64. MPNMS^F 883b24–b26: 一切眾生亦復如是：各各皆有如來之性，無量煩惱覆蔽隱沒，不能自知。如來方便誘進開化，令知自身有如來性，歡喜信受。Compare MPNMS^D 407b24–28; MPNMS^T §376.29–38.

65. This parable is cited in Dol po pa's RC (Hopkins 2006: 131) and Bu ston's DzG (Ruegg 1973: 82–83).

66. The MPNMS is replete with other examples of medicinal imagery, a theme explored in detail by Habata (1989; also 2019: 27–38). A further notable example, used also by Bu ston

should not feed from its mother's breast, so the mother smears onto her breast a pungent ointment made of nimba leaf and tells the child that it is poisonous. When the time is right the mother removes the nimba and invites her child back, but he is now understandably reluctant. The mother finally explains that all of this was so that the medicinal butter had opportunity to work.[67]

> Likewise, good sons, for the sake of leading and maturing sentient beings, the Tathāgata first taught to them the mental cultivation of absence of self in regard to all phenomena. When they mentally cultivate absence of self, they eliminate any [erroneous] view of the self; having eliminated any view of the self, they enter into *nirvāṇa*.
>
> In order to remove [notions of] the worldly self, I taught the strategic, cryptic teaching that negates the self;[68] after that, I teach to them the nature of the Tathāgata, which is the supermundane, supreme self.[69]

The Buddha teaches *anātman* in order to eliminate erroneous notions of selfhood; only once this has been achieved can he reveal Buddha-nature, which can indeed be called the self. Like the child of the parable, members of the sangha may be reluctant to accept a Buddhist account of the self, but the MPNMS is clear that the doctrine of *anātman* is succeeded by a correct teaching about what can be called *ātman*.

An expression corresponding to this "supermundane, supreme self" (離世真實之我: **lokottaraparamātman?*) is absent from both MPNMS^{D} and MPNMS^{T}, in which what is named is simply the *tathāgatagarbha*. However, MPNMS^{T} does also here state that what the Buddha reveals to monks is his "great self" (*che ba nyid*), which with the aid of a Sanskrit fragment (no. 18.3) we can verify is the revelation of the Buddha's "*māhātmya*."[70] Rather than an account of the self, this could intend something like the Buddha's

in his DzG (Ruegg 1973: 70), compares the Buddha's earlier teachings to basic medicines, drawn directly from plants, that are taught by a doctor to his son; only after mastering these can the son learn about advanced medicines. Here teaching about *anātman* is listed as just one "early" teaching of the Buddha, surpassed by revelations about *tathāgatagarbha;* see MPNMS^{F} 893c22–894a1; MPNMS^{D} 420c2–15; MPNMS^{T} §498.

67. MPNMS^{F} 883b27–c2; MPNMS^{D} 407b29–c10; MPNMS^{T} §377.

68. Both MPNMS^{D} and MPNMS^{T} here omit reference to any "cryptic utterance" (likely Skt. **sandhāvacana*); see 9.2.

69. MPNMS^{F} 883c3–6: 如是善男子，如來誘進化眾生故，初為眾生說一切法修無我行。修無我時，滅除我見。滅我見已，入於泥洹。除世俗我故，說非我方便密教；然後為說[a]如來之性，是名離世真實之我。

[a] T 說 = Sheng 說經

Compare MPNMS^{D} 407c10–c19; MPNMS^{T} §378.14–20.

70. Reconstructed in Habata (2019: 140–141: (*māhāt*)[*m*]*y*(*a*)*saṃdarśa*[*n*](*āya*)). Habata translates the *māhātmya* that the Buddha reveals as "die überweltliche Erhabenheit," his "supermundane majesty." See also Habata 2009: 570–572n150.

"majesty" or "great character."[71] Whether or not this is what is meant by the declaration that "all sentient beings possess the *tathāgatagarbha*"—that is, that what they possess is the majestic person, already, of the Buddha—is an incomplete answer regarding the intentions of the MPNMS, as it more frequently refers to the *tathāgatagarbha* as, more plainly, "the self" (*bdag: ātman*).

What is beyond doubt is that Buddha-nature is introduced to us as an account of some precious constituent in the body of sentient beings, harboring already the qualities of a fully realized Buddha.[72] Even where it is not called the self, the revelation of this nature sits in an acknowledged and problematic tension with prior teachings about absence of self with respect to all phenomena. Defending the idea of a Buddha-nature—and its place alongside the earlier teaching that there is nothing that endures, or is worthy of attachment, in the constitution of any sentient being—is a major occupation of the remaining content of MPNMS-tg, and appears to have been no mean feat.

2.4 Contentions and Clarifications

Having heard these last two parables, Kāśyapa presents to the Buddha a number of objections regarding Buddha-nature and its status as the true self. These are particularly pertinent, not only as they suggest genuine problems that opponents of an *ātmavādin* form of Buddha-nature teaching may have had, but also because these tell us what the authors of the MPNMS held the term *ātman* to have commonly signified. Below are summarized Kāśyapa's objections as presented in each available version of the MPNMS. Discernible categories of objection are listed numerically, taking MPNMS^{F} as a base. Objections in our other two versions that interrupt the trajectory of this basic list are numbered to reflect this (e.g., 4.i); what are

71. See Harvey 1995: 55–57; also 6.3.

72. A further Sanskrit fragment (no. 18.4; see Habata 2019: 141–142; also Habata 2009: 572; 2015b: 185) does, however, raise some difficult questions. Here Habata reconstructs (and interprets) the phrase *asmākam u[p]ari [t]athāgatagarbho* <'>*stīti:* most naturally "the *tathāgatagarbha* exists above (*upari*) us" (see also Kanō 2017: 42–47; 2020: 25–26). Corresponding Tibetan (MPNMS^{T} §378.18) reads simply *bdag cag la* … : "regarding/in us"; our Chinese translations do not significantly differ from the Tibetan (regarding which, see the reference in note 69 above). In this context the Sanskrit *upari* could have been intended in the sense of "in relation to" (Apte 1957: 458a), though this is somewhat irregular. Curiously, editions of MPNMS^{F} also preserve the suggestion that the *tathāgatagarbha* is some entity that resides "above" or "upon" the body (身上; see 2.3nn53–54). While acknowledging the difficulties that these materials present, I nonetheless stick to the dominant reading throughout our versions for the MPNMS, and understand its author(s) to have intended that concerning all sentient beings, there exists the *tathāgatagarbha* somehow "in" or "about" their constitution. There is no doubt that traces of the idea that Buddha-nature resides "above" or "upon" a sentient being require further study.

further nuances within some forms of an objection are expressed alphabetically (e.g., 3a and 3b).

MPNMS^{F} 883c7–18

1. The existence of a self (我) means that a child should not acquire knowledge as it ages.
2. As there is birth and death, there can be no self (我).
3. Due to Buddha-nature (如來性), there should be no difference between sentient beings, yet they are born as *brāhmaṇa, kṣatriya, vaiśya, śūdra,* or *caṇḍāla* (i.e., "classes" [*varṇa*s] of person according to Brahmanical, normative social strata); all sentient beings should be of the same character.
4. For the same reason (如來性), people should not commit improper deeds, such as killing, stealing, and so forth (and yet they do).
5. For the same reason (如來性), no one should suffer deafness, blindness, nor muteness.

6a. Is this Buddha-nature (如來性) united with the body, somewhere within the variously colored blue, yellow, red, or white (substances) therein …

6b. … or does it pervade all of them?

MPNMS^{T} §379.4—§380.15

1. If there is a self (*bdag*), a newborn child should not need to acquire knowledge.
2. It is not reasonable that a self (*bdag*), having been born, should die.

3a. Despite Buddha-nature (*de bzhin gshegs pa'i khams*), and due to *karma,* there exist various rebirths, as *brāhmaṇa, kṣatriya, vaiśya, śūdra, caṇḍāla,* or as an animal …

3b. … rather, if there is a self (*bdag*), there should be no such differentiation.

4. Because there is a "nature" (*khams: dhātu*), no one should take up the path of ten improper deeds: of killing, stealing, sexual impropriety, and so forth.

4.i. (Moreover) when drinking alcohol, no one should become drunk.

5. If there is a nature of sentient beings (*sems can gyi khams: sattvadhātu*), there should be no blindness, deadness, or muteness.

6a. Does a self, which is the nature of sentient beings (*bdag sems can gyi khams*), reside amid phlegm, embryonic matter (*nur nur po*), or blue or yellow [bodily humors]?

6b. Does the self (*bdag*) reside in just one of these, or pervade all of them, like a fluid?

6c. Can the self (*bdag*), if the body is injured in battle, lose part of itself, or be crippled?

MPNMS^{D} 407c20–408a9

1. A newborn child has no knowledge at birth, so there is no self (我).
2a. If there is a self (我), then having been born, there should be no death.
2b. If there is Buddha-nature (佛性), then sentient beings should exist permanently, and not suffer decline (as they transmigrate).
3a. There being no such decline, there should be no distinctions in terms of *brāhmaṇa, kṣatriya, vaiśya, śūdra, caṇḍāla,* or animals; but there is, due to *karma.*
3b. If there is a self (我), there should be neither superiority nor inferiority among sentient beings; hence the nature of a Buddha (佛性) is not characterized as permanent (常法).
4. If Buddha-nature (佛性) were permanent, there should not be any killing, theft, licentiousness, deception, insult, lying, prattle, craving, anger, or wrong views.
4.i. If one's own nature is permanent (我性常), then why do some people become violent having drunk alcohol?
5. For the same reason (我性常), there should be no blindness, deafness, muteness, or lameness.
5.i. For the same reason (我性常), we would not need to avoid fire, flood, poison, swords, wicked persons, or animals.
5.ii. For the same reason (我性常), no one should ever lose memory of anything.
6a. For the same reason (我性常), does this nature reside in mucus, or in that (in the body) which is blue, yellow, red, or white?[73]
6b. Does one's nature that is permanent (still 我性常) pervade all of the above, like the oil of a sesame seed, without gaps?
6c. If the body is destroyed, would the self (我) be destroyed also?

The shortest and simplest list of objections is found in MPNMS^{F}; the list in MPNMS^{T} seems to have developed some form of this, and MPNMS^{D} has done similarly while retaining some interesting agreements with MPNMS^{F} (for example, the list of colored humors in objection 6).[74] The Indic expressions **tathāgata-/buddhadhātu* and *ātman* seem to dominate this passage, while MPNMS^{D} suggests also "one's own essence/nature" (**ātmadhātu; *svadhātu;* see 3.2) and MPNMS^{T} "the essence/nature of sentient beings (*sattvadhātu*). All three versions reflect an apparent and notable absence of

73. Following MPNMS^{T}, I believe MPNMS^{D} reflects a list beginning with mucus (*tituo* 涕唾), and then four differently colored humors (see, alternatively, Blum 2013: 229).

74. This list of colors—blue, yellow, red, white—reflects a sequence that may be very ancient in Indian thought, in which what is blue (or otherwise "dark") is most inferior, and white the most superior; see Goudriaan 1978: 175–190; Wynne 2007: 30–31. See also 9.6.

the expression *tathāgatagarbha,* which could suggest the relative antiquity of this passage in the composition of MPNMS-tg.[75]

The inclusion of these objections communicates that the authors of the MPNMS acknowledged concerns that Buddhist audiences would have had regarding a Buddhist account of the self.[76] Though Indian Buddhist texts from all periods condemn attachment to notions of selfhood (*ātmagrāha*), they do not so often include so much discussion of the self that should be rejected. Following the numerical list of objections provided above, we can infer that *ātman* as opposed by Kāśyapa refers to something (1) immutable (in terms also of knowledge that is proper to it), (2) permanent, and (3) undifferentiated (yet numerically distinct) across sentient beings.[77] Meanwhile some *(*buddha*)*dhātu*—if our authors here intended any distinction between this and *ātman*—must also (4) possess various virtues, (5) lack impairment, and (6) be situated—in one place, or pervasively—in the body. Both MPNMS^{T} and MPNMS^{D} add that (4.i) existence of the self should mean that one cannot become inebriated, and both versions also query how (6c) injury to the physical body could allow the self, presumably beyond harm, to be damaged. MPNMS^{D} adds that the existence of some **dhātu* should ensure (5.i) invulnerability from harm and (5.ii) reliability of memory.

It was Kāśyapa's earlier question—regarding the self amid twenty-five types of existence—that prompted the previous two parables, concerning the buried treasure and the sick infant (2.3). This list of objections introduces more parables that may have been intended to address some (if not all) of the issues that Kāśyapa—a surrogate for a skeptical Buddhist audience—has raised, but it is questionable how far any of these satisfactorily address one or more of his concerns. The first parable initially seems to concern objection 6, regarding the relationship of the self to the physical body, but then in its explanation appears to address objections 3 through 5 also, and so is framed as a response to the problem of how there are differentiations between rebirths if all sentient beings have the same, essentially awakened (Buddha-)nature.[78] The Buddha tells the story of a wrestler who fights for the amusement of a king. The wrestler wears a precious jewel on his forehead, which—during the course of a bout—is pushed firmly

75. This supports Hodge's hypothesis (2010/2012: 42–43, 53–54, 82–84) regarding the preeminence of the expression *ātman* in the MPNMS before the introduction of the expressions *buddhadhātu* and *tathāgatagarbha;* see 2.8.

76. Some of these arguments appear also in a curious passage of the *Sāṃmitīyanikāyaśāstra,* a *pudgalavādin* text that comes as close as any in that tradition to affirming the existence of not only an enduring "person" (*pudgala*) but a substantial self (*ātman*); see Priestley 1999: 84–85.

77. The MPNMS does not appear to suggest the self to be a numerically single substance, but only a qualitatively identical, common nature; see also 3.6.

78. This material is discussed in Dol po pa's RC (Hopkins 2006: 130–131) and Bu ston's DzG (Ruegg 1973: 72–73), which notes distinctions between MPNMS^{T} and the Tibetan translation of MPNMS^{D}.

and imperceptibly into his brow. A doctor inspects the wound and finds that the jewel has sunk deep into the wrestler's flesh. The wrestler believes the jewel to have been lost elsewhere, until the doctor brings it out from his body and shows it to him.

> All sentient beings are likewise: each of them possesses the nature of the Tathāgata (如來之性), [but] by keeping bad company, generating desire, anger, and delusion, they fall into the three bad destinies, and receive various bodies that belong to twenty-five types of existence.
>
> The precious jewel that is the nature of the Tathāgata is sunk into the abscess of afflictions—of desire, anger, and delusion—so that it is not known to be there.
>
> Cultivating the notion of absence of self in regard to the worldly self, [sentient beings] do not comprehend the strategic, cryptic teaching[79] of the good doctor who is the Tathāgata; generating the notion of absence of self, one is not able to know the true self: hence the Tathāgata again uses his [skill in] methods to bring about the end of the torment of immeasurable afflictions, disclosing and revealing the nature of the Tathāgata (如來之性).[80]

Hence differentiation between sentient beings (objection 3) is explained by the fault of keeping poor company (**akalyāṇamitra*s: i.e., not exemplars of Buddhist dharma) and the influence of afflictions: desire, anger, delusion, and so forth. Both MPNMS^D and MPNMS^T are more detailed, and list not only types of rebirth (as hell-beings, animals, through the four *varṇa*s and otherwise) but also types of disability and deformity throughout twenty-five forms of existence: hence this version of the parable's explanation preserves something of a response to objection 5, regarding disability. Note that the origin of these afflictions (which underlies objection 4, regarding improper activities) is still not considered. A more detailed explanation of this parable is exclusive to MPNMS^T.

> To those who wonder "Where is the self? Where does it reside? Is it like the content of a pot or, if not, does it pervade [the body], like a liquid? Does it remain, like the ornament on the brow of the wrestler?" the

---

79. Notably MPNMS^T reflects simply the Buddha's "cryptic utterance" (*dgongs pa'i tshig: *sandhāvacana*). My suspicion is that MPNMS^F and MPNMS^D may have occasionally supplied the adverbial *fangbian* 方便—"strategically"—without this having corresponded directly to anything in an underlying Indic text. See 9.2 (also note 69 above).

80. MPNMS^F 883c29–884a7: 一切眾生亦復如是: 各各皆有如來之性，習惡知識，起婬、怒、癡，墮三惡道，乃至周遍二十五有種種受身。如來之性摩尼寶珠，沒在煩惱、婬、怒、癡瘡，不知所在。於世俗我修無我想[a]，不解如來良醫方便密教; 作無我想而不能知真實之我。於是如來復為方便令滅無量煩惱熾然，開示顯現如來之性。

[a] T 想 = Ming 修

Compare also MPNMS^D 408a26–b1; MPNMS^T §382.1–13.

Tathāgata has said to them, like the doctor, that the self does not reside in any place, but is radiant like the precious jewel, even while it is obscured by various afflictions. After this has been taught, sentient beings then have faith, and will eradicate their afflictions completely. Then, just like the jewel, they see the *tathāgatagarbha*.[81]

This appears to address objection 6, regarding the location of the self in the body: initially it was thought to be nowhere, but the Buddha reveals now that the self does, somehow, exist, but can be seen only after one produces the faith, and appropriate activities, to reveal it. By realizing the end of a bodhisattva's practice, the *tathāgatagarbha*—indeed, a new Buddha—is revealed.

The next two parables—at least as they appear in MPNMS^D and MPNMS^T—have more to say about how far we can speak of the *tathāgatagarbha* as somehow "within" a sentient being. The first concerns again, and in greater depth, objection 3, regarding differentiation between types of sentient being. A rare, sweet medicine is said to grow in the Himālayas (hidden, according to MPNMS^D and MPNMS^T, in thick flora), and can only be drawn out by a great emperor (*cakravartin*). In his absence, people suffering from illnesses attempt to extract the medicine using pipes, but find that they each attain a different constituent flavor of the elixir, and not its desirable essence.[82] Likewise, the Buddha-nature that belongs to sentient beings is of superior taste but remains inaccessible to them; hence sentient beings experience various rebirths, of differing quality, as they transmigrate.

That nature of the Tathāgata (如來性) cannot be killed or harmed: what dies can be called short of life, [but] the nature of the Tathāgata is called true longevity (真壽), not ending or being destroyed up until the attainment of buddhahood.

The nature of the Tathāgata cannot be harmed or killed; only the body that is subject to nourishment can be harmed or killed. Like those sick people [of the parable], doing many wicked actions, [sentient beings]

81. MPNMS^T §382.25–34: *bdag ga la yod / gang na gnas / ci rdza ma'i nang na rdza ma 'dug pa lta bu zhig gam / 'on te rlan lta bur khyab par 'dug gam / gyad rmongs pa'i smin mtshams kyi rgyan lta bur 'dug gam snyams pa la sman pa bzhin du de bzhin gshegs pas de dag la 'di skad du / bdag ni thams cad du gnas pa ma yin la / rin po che rdo rje ltar 'od gsal zhing nyon mongs pa'i rnam pas bsgribs pa yin no zhes bka' stsal te / de skad ces bka' stsal pa la sems can rnams yid ches par 'gyur la nyon mongs pa zad par bya dgos pa tsam du zad do // de nas rdo rje bzhin du de bzhin gshegs pa'i snying po mthong bar 'gyur ro //* Compare MPNMS^D 408b5–b10.

82. MPNMS^T calls this the "elixir of bees" (*bung ba'i bcud*); ordinary beings cannot draw out any form of it, but the *cakravartin* employs pipes to separate its different flavors. The essence of the elixir (*bcud kyi khams*) then rises into the air and remains there (§383.1–16). MPNMS^T, used by Bu ston in his DzG (Ruegg 1973: 72–73), distinguishes between forms of crude existence (the flavors) and the underlying essence of all of them (in gaseous form). In MPNMS^D (408b13–22), the *cakravartin* alone can draw out the elixir, which then changes in flavor in accordance with the manner in which it is preserved.

> receive various results such as birth as a *kṣatriya, brāhmaṇa* and so forth, throughout the twenty-five existences, because they do not attain the true nature of the Tathāgata.[83]

Hence MPNMS[F] seems to address objection 2, regarding permanence. However, the equivalent explanations, in MPNMS[D] and MPNMS[T], could be read also as responses to objection 6c (absent from MPNMS[F]), regarding the relationship between a finite body and an immortal, essential nature. According to MPNMS[T] "the cause of becoming a Buddha" (*sangs rgyas su 'gyur ba'i rgyur*) is said to be of one flavor (*ro gcig:* Skt. *ekarasa*); apart from this there are "many flavors" that are birth as a man, woman, or otherwise, which are the results of the differing *karma* of sentient beings.[84] MPNMS[T] also equates the **tathāgatadhātu* with "the nature of persons" (*skyes bu'i rang bzhin*) that survives their apparent demise, and explains the relationship between the *tathāgatagarbha* and bodily death: "If there was the destruction of a living creature (*srog chags*), then life (*'tsho ba po: jīvaka*) would cease; but it is not possible for life to cease. Here, that which is called 'life' is the *tathāgatagarbha:* that nature (*khams: dhātu*) cannot be destroyed, killed, or perish, but as long as one does not attain buddhahood, one cannot see its great purity. This being so, there is no person that kills a living creature."[85] The end of this passage in both MPNMS[D] and MPNMS[T] is particularly striking, and in response Kāśyapa objects that this would mean there could be no bad *karma* when someone kills another sentient being. In MPNMS[T] the Buddha responds that the build-up of "external" (*phyi rol gyi bsags pa'i*) bodily elements (*khams: dhātus*) is like the thicket in the parable that hides the mysterious elixir.[86] In corresponding material of MPNMS[D] the **buddhadhātu* is said to reside among the five "heaps" of experience (*yin* 陰: *skandhas*), and we learn that the destruction of these constitutes killing a living being (see 1.1).[87] Hence there can still be karmic repercussions for the killing of another sentient being, but this does not equate to destroying

83. MPNMS[F] 884a16–20: 彼如來性[a]無可殺害; 其諸死者名為壽短[b]。如來之性名為真壽，不斷不壞乃至成佛。如來之性無害無殺，唯長養身有害有殺: 如諸病人，作眾邪業，種種報應刹利、梵志乃至生死二十五有，不得真實如來性故。

[a] T 彼如來性 = Song/Yuan/Ming/Palace/Shōgozō 若得如來真實性者

[b] T 短 = Song/Yuan/Ming/Palace/Shōgozō 斷

Compare also MPNMS[T] §383.16-§384.26 (reflecting both *tathāgatagarbha* and *tathāgatadhātu*); MPNMS[D] 408b22–c14 (featuring only 佛性).

84. MPNMS[T] §383.18–21.

85. MPNMS[T] §384.3–8: *gal te srog chags bsad par gyur na ni 'tsho ba po gtan med par byas par 'gyur la / 'tsho ba po gtan med par 'gyur ba ni mi srid do // de la 'tsho ba po zhes bya ba ni de bzhin gshegs pa'i snying po yin la / khams de ni gzhig pa 'am / gsad pa 'am / gtan med par bya mi nus la sangs rgyas nyid ma thab kyi bar du shin tu rnam par dag par mthong bar yang mi nus so // de bas na srog chags gsod pa'i mi med do //*

86. MPNMS[T] §386.14–21.

87. MPNMS[D] 408c7–8: 眾生佛性住五陰中; 若壞五陰名曰殺生。

what is essential to them: their *(buddha)dhātu*.[88] This is a significant claim, and more so still if the position of the Indic text underlying MPNMS^{T} was that the *(buddha)dhātu* is somehow buried "within" yet apart from the very physical "elements" (*dhātu*s) that make up the body. Moreover, if MPNMS^{D} reliably translates a text that contrasted the **buddhadhātu* with the *skandha*s, this would constitute a rare and uncharacteristic mention of these five "heaps"—a staple of wider Buddhist teaching regarding sentient beings and the content of worldly experience—in our *tathāgatagarbha* corpus. At any rate, both MPNMS^{D} and MPNMS^{T} exhibit the sense that Buddha-nature is apart from whatever else comprises the experience, and so existence, of a sentient being.

At this juncture our two longer versions of the MPNMS return to erroneous notions of selfhood that should be rejected. MPNMS^{T} rejects a self that is held to be the size of some fruit shell, of a rice grain, of a thumb, and so forth.[89] MPNMS^{D} mentions the self that is imagined to be the size of a millet or rice grain, a bean, or a thumb.[90] The **buddhadhātu* is said to be like none of these notions, which are again reminiscent of imagery regarding the self found in the Upaniṣads (see 2.2). Similar comparisons appear also in the *Aṅgulimālīyasūtra* (AMS), and will be dealt with in greater detail later in this study (see 3.3, 9.6). In the meantime, it is enough for us to acknowledge that versions of the MPNMS reflect and repeat an awareness that the Buddha's teaching about the self could be confused for Brahmanical musings about (nominally) the same thing.

The next parable in this sequence is shorter than those discussed above, but elegant in its simplicity. It seems to confront objection 2, regarding the deathlessness of the self. A man digs into stone, smashing it to dust, while looking for a diamond. Whereas the surrounding rock crumbles, the diamond alone remains undamaged: "Likewise is the nature of the Tathāgata (如來之性): it cannot be harmed by the sharp swords of the Māras.[91] Only the body that must be nourished is affected; that which is damaged or destroyed is not the nature of the Tathāgata. Therefore you should know that the nature of the Tathāgata cannot be harmed, and cannot be killed."[92] Again, both MPNMS^{T} and MPNMS^{D} provide the most

---

88. Habata (1990: 186) finds similarity between this and claims made in both the *Kaṭha-upaniṣad* (v.2.18–19: Olivelle 1998: 384–385) and—more famously—the *Bhagavadgītā* (v.2.17–20: Sargeant 2009: 102–105); see also 3.3, 9.6. This passage is cited by Dol po pa's RC (Hopkins 2006: 358–359).

89. MPNMS^{T} §384.22–25: *'jig rten pa rnams kyi bdag ni sdum bu sha ma ka'i 'bras bu tsam dang / 'bras kyi 'bru tsam dang / mthe bo tsam zhes bya ba la sogs par rtogs pa ste / mi bden pa'i rtog pa yin no //*

90. MPNMS^{D} 408c11–12: 猶如稗子，或如米、豆、乃至母[a]指。

[a] T 母 = Song/Yuan/Ming/Palace 拇

91. A class of deity associated with obstructing the path of the bodhisattva, and who otherwise represent ongoing death through transmigration.

92. MPNMS^{F} 884a23–25: 如來之性，亦復如是：天魔利劍所不能傷。唯長養身受，其傷壞非如來性。是故當知如來之性無害無殺。

explanation. Here MPNMS^{T} refers to "the self of living beings" (*skye ba po'i bdag*), and contrasts this again to the "collection of bodily elements" (*bsags pa'i khams*) that correspond to the stone in the parable. MPNMS^{T} continues as follows: "The *tathāgatagarbha* is that which lives (*'tsho ba pa*), and is like the precious diamond. This being so, by taking the lives of people there is destruction of life; because of this, by destroying the collection of elements, a living creature is killed."[93] In place of this "collection of elements," MPNMS^{D} again refers instead to the five heaps (*wuyin* 五陰), the destruction of which constitutes the death of a living being.[94] These details, again missing from MPNMS^{F}, may reflect later contributions to the text in order to make sense of how the permanent, indestructible *tathāgatagarbha* relates to mortal sentient beings, which in wider Buddhist literature are more conventionally discussed in terms of the congruence of physical elements or—more frequently still—the interdependence of ephemeral mental and physical states or events (see 1.1).

At any rate, these parables do not present a very systematic reply to the objections to which they seem, at first, to be a response. But what we learn about the Buddha's account of the self is significant: Buddha-nature is apart from the actions that cause sentient beings to transmigrate, and is unharmed by the perils that a sentient being may suffer from one life to the next. While the self can be contrasted to the afflictions that obscure its presence, it is also separate from either elements of the physical body (according to MPNMS^{T}) or the constituent heaps of normal, worldly experience (MPNMS^{D}). Moreover, that which can be called the self is not any erroneous, worldly notion of selfhood found in non-Buddhist discourse, despite the fact that the Buddha was required to teach about absence of self in order to dismiss forms of *ātmavādin* teaching already prevalent in the world. This relationship between Buddhist and non-Buddhist teachings about the self is a particularly tricky issue, with which the MPNMS deals in its final exposition of Buddha-nature and to what it does, and moreover does not, refer.

2.5 The True Self and False Notions of It

So ends the first string of parables concerning Buddha-nature as a doctrine of the self. After this the MPNMS explains at some length the relationship between the *tathāgatagarbha* and the path of the bodhisattva, including the claim that one's Buddha-nature is perceptible—in some limited manner—to those bodhisattvas who occupy the tenth *bhūmi* (see 2.3). At the end of this material the MPNMS employs a final parable that

93. MPNMS^{T} §385.9–11: *de bzhin gshegs pa'i snying po 'tsho ba pa ni rdo rje rin po che dang 'dra ste / de bas na mi rnams kyi srog bcad pas 'tsho ba 'jig par 'gyur te / de'i phyir bsags pa'i khams bshig pas srog chags bsad par 'gyur ro //*

94. See MPNMS^{D} 408c19–22.

confronts a pressing concern: the relationship between the Buddhist account of the self and the nominally similar doctrines of rival, non-Buddhist systems. As the closing discussion of Buddha-nature qua selfhood in the MPNMS, this can be considered the final word that the text has to offer regarding *tathāgatagarbha,* and it provides an important insight into the perceived place of early Buddha-nature teaching in wider Indian religious discourse.[95]

Kāśyapa asks the Buddha about ideas of the self already found in the world.[96] The Buddha's response is a parable about two friends: a prince and a pauper.[97] The prince is in possession of a marvelous sword, which he shows to his friend before departing for his homeland.[98] The pauper is then overheard talking about the sword in his sleep, and is summoned before a king, who desires it. The pauper explains that he has seen the sword but can offer no assistance finding it. The king dismisses him, realizing that the sword comes from another kingdom, but a succession of later rulers forget this and ponder where the legendary sword can be found. "In just this way, a venerable bodhisattva appeared in the world and explained the true character of the self. Ignorant persons, hearing that all sentient beings have the nature of a Buddha (佛性: **buddhadhātu*), did not understand the truth, and so explain, with deluded imagination, that the self is like an inch-long lamp in the heart, or various [notions such as] *sattva, ātman, pudgala,* or *jīva.*"[99] MPNMS^{T} provides a longer list of erroneous views about the self: comparable to a thumb-sized man, the shell of a fruit, or a grain of rice burning in the heart (see also 3.3); MPNMS^{D} provides these same analogies but omits mention of the list *sattva, ātman,* etcetera.[100] Contributors to the MPNMS clearly wished to discredit not only conceptions of what we might call the "intuited" self (*sattva, ātman, pudgala,* etc.) but also of a "speculated" self: some kernel of identity hidden within the

95. For more detail on this passage, see Jones 2016a: 129–137; also Schmithausen 2009: 135n369.

96. MPNMS^{F} 887b24–25: 世尊，世間眾生皆言有我: 比義云何? Compare the subtly different MPNMS^{D} 412b15–16 and MPNMS^{T} §416.1–3, which state that worldly persons (MPNMS^{T} *'jig rten pa rnams*; but MPNMS^{D}非聖凡夫: **anāryapṛthagjanas*) consider the nature of sentient beings (眾生性; *sems can gyi khams: sattvadhātu*) to constitute a self (我) or enduring "person" (*gang zag:* **pudgala*).

97. MPNMS^{F} 887b25–c9; MPNMS^{D} 412b15–c13; MPNMS^{T} §416.

98. In MPNMS^{F} the prince does not possess a sword but rather a rhinoceros (*si* 兕), a translation likely based on some confusion regarding the Sanskrit *khaḍga,* or some other Indic equivalent, meaning either "sword" or, indeed, "rhinoceros." Both MPNMS^{D} and MPNMS^{T} concern a sword, and the narrative of MPNMS^{F} makes better sense if we assume that this story was originally about a precious sidearm. The explanatory material following each version of the parable is much the same: I assume the Indic text underlying MPNMS^{F} to have originally understood the object of the king's desires to be a sword.

99. MPNMS^{F} 887c9–12: 如是菩薩摩訶薩出於世時，為眾說真實之我。其無知者，聞一切眾生皆有佛性，不知其真便妄想說: 我如寸燈在於心中[a]，種種眾生、我、人、壽命。

[a] Shōgozō omits 我如寸燈在於心中

100. MPNMS^{D} 412c14–20; MPNMS^{T} §417.1–16.

body, akin to what is taught in the Brahmanical Upaniṣads.[101] What is particularly intriguing is that the Buddha's teaching about Buddha-nature is said to have been heard before, when some bodhisattva (Śākyamuni himself?) revealed the correct account of the self to an earlier audience. The inability of sentient beings to comprehend this teaching led to the perpetuation of ideas that fall short of the *true* self, despite having their origin in the bodhisattva's account of precisely that.

The Buddha's explanation of the parable then provides one of the boldest statements made in the MPNMS: that at least some ideas about the self exist in the world not simply through miscomprehension of what was taught by a Buddha or bodhisattva, but by design:

> If a worldly person expounds a self that is in accordance with the dharma, know that person to be beyond what is worldly; know that in all cases this is some emanation by a bodhisattva (*pusa bianhua* 菩薩變化: **bodhisattvanirmita*) manifested in conformity with conventional discourse ...[102]
>
> ... the Buddha again said to Kāśyapa: all speech, incantations and treatises; that which is taught by the Tathāgata is the root of all of these.[103]

MPNMS^{T} differs only to say that whatever in the world "is in all ways highest dharma" is emanated (*sprul pa:* Skt. *nirmita*) by bodhisattvas,[104] and goes on to list that all treatises (*bstan bcos: śāstra*), spells or "sciences" (*rig sngags: vidyā*), and incantations (*gsang sngang: mantra*) are taught by the Buddha.[105] MPNMS^{D} clarifies that these "worldly" persons are common people (*fanfu* 凡夫: **pṛthagjanas*)—in other words, certainly no one who obviously speaks for Buddhist dharma—and adds that "all discourses, incantations, and speech" belong to the Buddha and not, as an audience might otherwise

---

101. This distinction between "intuited" (*sahaja*) selfhood, assumed by sentient beings or philosophers, and "speculative" (*vikalpita; parikalpita*) notions of selfhood, proposed by one or other philosophical system or school, is proper to Buddhist commentarial literature of later centuries, regarding which see Eltschinger 2014: 271–275 (especially note 91).

102. My translation disregards a chapter division that appears, and breaks the flow of this passage, only in MPNMS^{F} (887c18: 文字品第十四). Such divisions occur only in this version of the MPNMS, and may have been supplied by its Chinese translators. See Blum 2013: 357n131; Shimoda 2015: 160–161.

103. MPNMS^{F} 887c16–20: 若世間說我隨順法者，當知是則為離世俗，當知皆是菩薩變化，現同俗說 ... [text omitted; see previous note] ... 佛復告迦葉：一切言說、呪術、記論，如來所說為一切本。

104. Ruegg (2008: 31) explains what is *nirmita* (or a *nirmāṇa*) to be "a second-order ectype of its original, first-order, archetype, be the latter a Buddha or high Bodhisattva, who may emanate or project it as a soteriological device with the purpose of assisting a trainee." See also Lamotte 1962: 324–325; also 10.4n66.

105. MPNMS^{T} §418.1–6. These three terms might be intended to reflect the three branches of Vedic literature beginning with *mantra* ("liturgies") and *arthavāda* ("explanations"), though the third, *vidhi* ("injunctions"), maps only imperfectly onto what seems to reflect Sanskrit *vidyā* ("sciences," "knowledges").

expect, "to non-Buddhist teachers."[106] The claim that "worldly" beings who speak persuasively about the self are somehow produced by a bodhisattva is slightly at odds with the main thrust of the parable and of its initial explanation, in which wrong-minded notions of the self are presented as misunderstandings of what was once explained correctly by a bodhisattva. The intriguing conclusion to this material is a reduction of ostensibly non-Buddhist teaching about the self, where it bears any similarity to what is taught by the Buddha, to activities by some bodhisattvas.

That broader religious discourse—"speech, incantations, and treatises"—find their origin in the Buddha or his teachings is a subtly different idea, which may still relate to "covert" activities of bodhisattva(s). This line also serves as an introduction to the next topic of the MPNMS: concern with the esoteric meanings of all different syllables (*akṣaras*), which are said to have been produced by the Buddha.[107] This is no longer a discussion of Buddha-nature per se, but reflects still the position that the influence of the Buddha reaches further than audiences may have thought, to the extent that the Buddha is somehow responsible for the efficacy of all magical or ritual language that one might encounter in the broader Indian religious landscape.

In the next chapter we will encounter another instance of the claim that non-Buddhist religious discourse—in particular that which pertains to the self—finds its origin in the activities of Buddhas or bodhisattvas (see 3.7), and in the final chapter we will revisit the idea that the Buddha's influence accounts for ideas and practices not obviously under his purview (10.4). In the meantime we can conclude that teaching about *tathāgatagarbha* in the MPNMS culminates in just such a claim: that the proximity of any ostensibly non-Buddhist account of the self to what is now taught by the Buddha can be explained with recourse to one of two ideas. The first is that foreign *ātmavādin* discourse—with echoes of what is taught in the Upaniṣads—arrives at a teaching about the self by misremembering what was taught by some bodhisattva. The second, more ambitiously, contends that some teachings about the self derive any persuasiveness that they may have from having been produced by bodhisattvas, such that non-Buddhist accounts of the self are (re)imagined as stratagems promoted for the purposes of introducing sentient beings to the Buddha's own, definitive account of the self, or otherwise the presence of Buddha-nature in all sentient beings.

---

106. MPNMS^{D} 412c26–413a1: 皆是佛說非外道說. This version refers to these **pṛthagjanas* as being *bodhisattvanimitta* (菩薩相貌). This is likely a mistranslation of precisely *-nirmita:* a muddling found otherwise at, for example, T.227[12]564b15, where 相貌 clearly corresponds to a form of *nirmita* preserved in the Sanskrit *Aṣṭasāhasrikā-prajñāpāramitā* (Vaidya 1960: 163; see also Karashima 2011: 308n54). Hence I understand the Indian source for MPNMS^{D} to have been concerned also with some "emanation(s)." See also Habata 1990: 182–183.

107. MPNMS^{F} 887c20–889a14; MPNMS^{D} 413a2–414b19; MPNMS^{T} §419–436.

2.6 Self and Absence of Self

For all that we have seen of Buddha-nature articulated in terms of the self, it is also demonstrably clear that the authors of the MPNMS accepted Buddhist teaching about not-self apropos of the many and various wrong-minded notions of the self that circulate in the world. Although a central claim of the MPNMS is that the revelation of Buddha-nature constitutes a teaching about the self, it is worth highlighting that the text does not mean to jettison Buddhist challenges to erroneous notions of such a thing, nor prior Buddhist teaching about *anātman*. For example, prior to the simile of the dizzied man featured in material of MPNMS-dhk (see 2.2), the Buddha's audience of monks presents an interpretation of their *nairātmyavāda* position, of which the Buddha approves:

> In the manner that reeds, grass, and the castor tree have no substance to them, so also is this body.[108] The [notions of] *ātman, puruṣa, jīva* and so forth have no substance to them.
>
> The Buddha said to the monks: Like this should you cultivate the notion of absence of self![109]

Here MPNMS^{T} supplies a long list of erroneous, "intuited" notions of the self (see 2.5, above), likely reflecting the Sanskrit expressions *ātman* (*bdag*), *sattva* (*sems can*), *jīva* (*srog*), *pudgala* (*gang zag*), *manuja* (*shed las*), *mānava* (*shed bu*), and *kartṛ* (*byed pa po*).[110] Both MPNMS^{T} and MPNMS^{D} share a few more lines on the same theme: "Just as planting ten million husks of chaff is pointless, likewise does this body have no self. Just as the blackboard tree (*saptaparṇa*) lacks any fragrance, likewise this body has no self; like this do we [monks] continuously cultivate the notion that there is no self."[111] Here MPNMS^{D} adds that the physical body is without self, or any "master" (*zhu* 主), and that it is abandoning a sense of self in regard to all phenomena that leads to liberation. It is then very clear that the authors of MPNMS-dhk still adhered firmly to teaching about not-self.

After the passage translated above, MPNMS^{T} adds that absence of self is akin to the absence of any visible trail left by a bird in the sky.[112]

108. The castor bean (also in MPNMS^{T}: *e raṇḍa*) is odorless and tasteless: without, in a sense, any "essence."

109. MPNMS^{F} 862a2–a5: 猶如蘆草及伊蘭樹無有堅實，此身如是。我、人、壽命等無有堅固。佛告比丘：汝等如是修無我想耶。Compare MPNMS^{D} 377a25–28; MPNMS^{T} §98.

110. MPNMS^{D} supplies a similar list (337a27: 我、人、眾生、壽命、養育、知、見、作), from which it is harder to reconstruct specific Indic terms. See Zacchetti 2005: 327nn5–8.

111. MPNMS^{T} §99.1–5: *dper gsol na phub ma skon pa bye ma snyed bor ba ni cir yang mi gces pa de bzhin du / lus 'di la yang bdag ma mchis so // dper gsol na / kha sral gyi me tog la dri bda' ba ma mchis pa de bzhin du lus 'di la yang bdag ma mchis te / de ltar bdag cag gis bdag ma mchis pa'i 'du shes bsgoms te / mang du bgyis lags so /* Compare MPNMS^{D} 377b1–5.

112. MPNMS^{T} §99.12–15; compare MPNMS^{D} 377b5–6. This image is surely very old, and can be found also in the *Dhammapada*, where it describes the status of an arhat (v.7.92–93; von Hinüber and Norman 1994: 26).

This foreshadows material found in all forms of MPNMS-tg, which in MPNMS^{F}—and concerning now Buddha-nature—runs as follows: "In the manner that lack of divine vision means that one cannot see the trail left by a bird in the sky, by not yet being rid of afflictions one cannot see for oneself the nature of the Tathāgata (如來之性) in one's own body. Hence do I teach for them absence of self. For the purpose of [clearing] afflictions, I explain my cryptic teaching,[113] regarding which sentient beings who lack divine vision impute the [false, worldly] self."[114] In corresponding material, MPNMS^{D} clarifies that sentient beings without divine vision impute the self while not knowing the *true* self, otherwise their Buddha-nature (**tathāgatadhātu*), while MPNMS^{T} states instead that sentient beings cannot see the existence of their "supreme essence" (*snying po'i mchog*). The salient point in all of the above is that the MPNMS does not deny the value of Buddhist teaching about absence of self in regard to any number of erroneous notions of such a thing. But while the constitution of sentient beings is otherwise so much ephemera, such that there exists no "worldly" self, MPNMS-tg clarifies that all sentient beings nevertheless have "within" their person the *tathāgatagarbha,* which might otherwise be correctly called their (true) self.

The *ātmavāda* articulation of Buddha-nature in the MPNMS comes with an important caveat. At one juncture, and amid articulation of its *tathāgatagarbha* doctrine, MPNMS-tg evokes by name the *prajñāpāramitā* tradition, and with it refers to selfhood and absence of self as "nondual" (*advaya*). The idea that self and not-self are two sides of the same conceptual coin is one that will raise its head elsewhere in other *tathāgatagarbha* sources (e.g., 7.3–4), but is something of a departure from the otherwise very pronounced *ātmavādin* orientation of the MPNMS. Due to its relative clarity—especially in regard to what appear to be references to other Buddhist texts—we consider this material as it is preserved in MPNMS^{T}:

> Foolish persons cling to the view that the Buddha's teaching about absence of self means that all phenomena are without self; the wise know that the existence of the self and absence of self are non-dual: such is the nature of those who are wise. In the "discourse that gathers together all

113. Our other versions suggest that absence of self constitutes a cryptic utterance (MPNMS^{D} 無我密教; MPNMS^{T} *dgongs pa'i tshig gis bdag med*), behind which lies the Buddha's account of the *tathāgatagarbha;* see 9.2.

114. MPNMS^{F} 890a7–a10: 如鳥飛空不見其跡無有天眼，煩惱未斷不自見身如來之性。是故我為彼說[a]無我。為煩惱故說微密教，其諸眾生無有天眼而計吾我。

[a] Yuan/Ming/Palace/Shōgozō 為彼說 = T 說有法

Compare MPNMS^{D} 415c14–17; MPNMS^{T} §451. Elsewhere the MPNMS ascribes the vision proper to a Buddha (*foyan* 佛眼) to followers of the Mahāyāna, perhaps by virtue of accepting (though not yet seeing) their Buddha-nature: see MPNMS^{F} 876b20–25; MPNMS^{D} 397b22–27; MPNMS^{T} §307. The example of the bird's trail appears also in the AMS; see 3.4.

> merits" (*Sarvapuṇyasamuccayasūtra*)[115] I have taught the *tathāgatagarbha*, which is praised by limitless Buddhas, and so it should be understood that the existence and absence of the self are non-dual. Good son, from the [above named] discourse, and from the **Prajñāpāramitā-mahāsūtra*,[116] and this [current] illumination of the entry into non-duality, reflect on my teaching concerning the non-duality of the existence and absence of self.[117]

The first *sūtra* listed here may refer to a text by a similar name (*Sarvapuṇya-samuccayasamādhisūtra*) preserved in two Chinese translations, one Tibetan version, and in a number of Gāndhārī fragments.[118] Among these we do find the very similar claim that self and absence of self are "the same" (though not strictly that they are "nondual").[119] Meanwhile some instances of *prajñāpāramitā* literature do indeed promote the idea that self and not-self are "nondual,"[120] and even—in at least superficial agreement with MPNMS-dhk—that the Buddha can be called "the self."[121] This is one of a

115. Blum (2013: 244; 357n124) suggests that this is likely the MPNMS referring to its own content; however, see the discussion below my translation, and also Radich 2015a: 42–45.

116. MPNMS^F 般若波羅蜜大經; MPNMS^D 摩訶般若波羅蜜經; MPNMS^T *shes rab kyi pha rol tu phyin pa'i mdo chen po*.

117. MPNMS^T §400.9–20: *byis pa rnams ni sangs rgyas kyis bdag med par gsungs pa la chos thams cad bdag med par 'dzin to // shes rab can rnams kyis ni bdag yod pa dang / bdag med pa gnyis su med par shes te / de ni shes rab can rnams kyi rang bzhin yin no // de bzhin gshegs pa'i snying po dpag tu med pa sangs rgyas kyis bsngags pa ni bsod nams thams cad bsdus pa'i mdo las ngas bstan te / bdag yod pa dang bdag med pa gnyis su med par gzung bar bya'o // rigs kyi bu bsod nams thams cad bsdus pa'i mdo dang / shes rab kyi pha rol tu phyin pa'i mdo chen po las / gnyis su med pa la 'jug pa'i snang ba de nyid las bdag yod pa dang / bdag med pa gnyis su med par ngas bstan pa de rjes su dran par gyis shig //* Compare MPNMS^F 886b17–25; MPNMS^D 411a2–411a8.

118. Regarding these translations (e.g., T.381–382), see also Radich 2015a: 43nn78–79. The Gāndhārī text is edited and discussed in Harrison et al. 2016.

119. For example, T.382(12)999a26–27: 我與無我二俱平等. See Habata 1992: 161.

120. Most reminiscent of this passage is the *Suvikrāntavikrāmiparipṛcchā-prajñāpāramitā* (Hikata 1958: 20.17–23): *saṃdhāya nirdiṣṭaṃ: yo hy advayam ātmānaṃ prajānāti, sa buddhaṃ dharmaṃ prajānāti … ātmabhāvaṃ sa bhāvayati sarvadharmāṇaṃ, yenādvayaparijñayā sarvadharmāḥ parijñātāḥ, ātmasvabhāvaniyatā hi sarvadharmāḥ … advayadharmaparijñayā buddhadharmaparijñā, ātmaparijñayā sarvatraidhātukaparijñā* ([I have] taught obliquely that he who knows that the self is non-dual knows both the Buddha and dharma … he cultivates a self (or perhaps "character": *ātmabhāva*) that consists of all *dharmas*; because the knowledge that is non-dual understands all *dharmas*, all *dharmas* are by nature established in the/one's self (*ātmasvabhāvaniyata*) … after knowing the non-duality of *dharmas* there is knowledge of the *dharmas* of the Buddha; after knowing the/one's self there is knowledge of all that is within the three-fold world.) This text employs the rhetoric of paradox as well as the Buddha's use of oblique or cryptic (*saṃdhāya*) utterance—with meaning or intent not clear to his audience—though in a manner that can be distinguished, I believe, from what we find in the *tathāgatagarbha* literature (see 9.2). See also Conze 1978: 56–58; Zacchetti 2015: 197.

121. *Saptaśatikā-prajñāpāramitā* (Masuda 1930: 221.7–9): *yasyaitad adhivacanam ātmeti tasyaitad adhivacanaṃ buddha iti* (That which is denoted by "self" is that which is denoted by "Buddha"). The passage goes on to state that this is so because the Buddha, like the self, is

couple of instances in which the MPNMS shifts its tone to promote the nondual nature of different teachings.[122] Yet even in these passages the MPNMS privileges an account of the *presence* of something: in the passage translated above it is not the *tathāgatagarbha* that is under scrutiny but rather the "foolish" interpretation of *nairātmyavāda* discourse that understood there to be nothing worthy of being called the self. The point, I believe, is that Buddha-nature was not *explicitly* taught in the other texts that the MPNMS names, but is rather the enigmatic, kataphatic complement, revealed only now, to Buddhist teachings about not-self with respect to all worldly phenomena.

All versions of the MPNMS—employing subtly different phrasing—also express that the presence of Buddha-nature in all sentient beings amounts to a "middle way" between extreme positions: according to MPNMS^{D} this is a middle way between eternalism and annihilationism (see 1.3); in MPNMS^{T} it is explained to be the Mahāyānist account of how, in spite of teachings about the conditioned nature of phenomena, there can be no destruction of the self.[123] I suggest that these passages reflect a desire on the part of authors to contextualize Buddha-nature teaching in the wider Mahāyāna tradition, and square what they teach with some interpretation of *prajñāpāramitā* literature, with which affirmations about Buddha-nature sit somewhat uncomfortably. Otherwise, as we have seen at length (2.3–5), the MPNMS declares that *tathāgatagarbha* is something of a corrective to existing understanding about absence of self; we shall see later that it was a significant concern of later works in the *tathāgatagarbha* corpus that they address tension between Buddha-nature teaching and the decidedly apophatic character of the *prajñāpāramitā* tradition (see 9.5).

2.7 Buddha-nature in Dharmakṣema's MPNMS^{D}+

As discussed above (2.1), we have reason to doubt that material following the end of the common core of the MPNMS—present only in Dharmakṣema's translation, which I am calling MPNMS^{D}+—was composed in India.[124] We lack any Sanskrit fragments of this material, or any reference to its content in a source that is of Indian origin. As Chinese tradition holds that this material was recovered by Dharmakṣema in Central Asia, it is possible that it was composed there, or even that Dharmakṣema was himself its author.[125]

something that cannot be discerned or apprehended (ibid., 222.6–223.2). See Conze 1978: 98–60; Zacchetti 2015: 197–198.

122. See also (in MPNMS-dhk) MPNMS^{F} 866a21–b19; MPNMS^{D} 383a2–b4; MPNMS^{T} §146.

123. MPNMS^{D} 405b6–10; MPNMS^{T} §356.15–16. Compare also MPNMS^{F} 882a9–12.

124. See, however, 2.1n8.

125. The position of Hodge (2010/2012: 27–29). We need not go this far, but I agree that there is no good reason to hold that MPNMS^{D}+ was produced by the same Indian milieu responsible for the rest of the MPNMS (ibid., 25–27); see also 2.1n8.

Suspending the issue of where MPNMS^{D}+ originated, and with close attention to the manner in which this material elaborates its account of Buddha-nature, it looks all but certain that the author(s) of MPNMS^{D}+ did not belong to the same intellectual milieu as those responsible for the rest of the MPNMS.

Material of MPNMS^{D}+ is known for having been thought to redeem some persons, called *icchantika*s (*yichanti* 一闡提), who in the core MPNMS seemed to be denied the potential for buddhahood, in spite of the seemingly "universalist" message of the text as a whole.[126] MPNMS^{D}+ states in clear terms that the *icchantika* is not beyond the attainment of awakening, because they do indeed possess the nature of a Buddha.[127] In a thematically similar vein, MPNMS^{D}+ is known also for an account of the redemption of the patricidal king Ajātaśatru.[128] A further interesting feature is that MPNMS^{D}+ makes frequent reference to the doctrine of the single vehicle (*yisheng* 一乘: Skt. *ekayāna*)—integral to the *Saddharmapuṇḍarīka* (SP)—which though no doubt known to the MPNMS (the core text mentions the SP by name; see 2.1) is not mentioned in any of its undeniably Indian content.[129]

The content of MPNMS^{D}+ is vast and varied. Much of its material concerning Buddha-nature is repetitive, and does not provide much clarity regarding it beyond what we find in the "core" material of the MPNMS. Significantly, even if MPNMS^{D}+ was originally composed in some Indic language, it does not appear that the Chinese in which it survives reflects usage of the term *tathāgatagarbha* in the sense understood by the core MPNMS: *tathāgatagarbha* (如來藏), referring to the presence of Buddha-nature (佛性) that is somehow "within" sentient beings. Like MPNMS^{D} (i.e., the content of Dharmakṣema's translation, or T.374, that precedes

126. Admonishment of *icchantika*s runs, at greatest length, through MPNMS^{F} 891c8–894a1; MPNMS^{D} 417b25–420c15; MPNMS^{T} §468–498. The tone of this material is that the *icchantika*s cannot reap the benefits of the MPNMS as a powerful *sūtra* that reveals the *tathāgatagarbha,* cleanses afflictions, and inspires the intention to achieve awakening (*bodhicitta*). Interpretation of this material in China—across MPNMS and MPNMS^{D}+—is played out in the biography of Daosheng, regarding which see Liebenthal 1955: 303–308.

For more regarding the *icchantika,* see Karashima 2007. It is clear that this expression underwent development before its use in the RGVV (see 7.3), and in the MPNMS is used to designate individuals who rejected the Mahāyāna as presented by it.

127. MPNMS^{D}+, 519b19–21: 若一闡提信有佛性, 當知是人不至三惡, 是亦不名一闡提也。以不自信有佛性故, 即墮三惡, 墮三惡故, 名一闡提 (If an *icchantika* were to have faith in the existence of Buddha-nature, know that he will not descend into the three bad [destinies], and also is then not called an *icchantika*. By not believing in the existence of the Buddha-nature one falls into the three bad [destinies]; falling into these, he is called *icchantika*).

128. See Radich 2011: 33–41.

129. For example, MPNMS^{D}+ 524c14–15: 一乘者名為佛性: 以是義故, 我說一切眾生悉有佛性 (The single vehicle is called Buddha-nature: hence do I teach that all sentient beings possess Buddha-nature). One occurrence of what may refer to the *ekayāna*—not found in either other version of the core MPNMS, or in any surviving Sanskrit fragments—is MPNMS^{D} 383a25.

MPNMS^{D}+), much is made of the "secret store of the *tathāgata*" (e.g., 如來密藏), but this now seems to refer to all that is taught across the MPNMS rather than just Buddha-nature, which MPNMS^{D}+ always refers to as *foxing* 佛性.[130] Yet there is no question that the articulation of Buddha-nature thinking in MPNMS^{D+} at once inherits and develops what was taught in the core MPNMS. For example, when MPNMS^{D}+ describes the Buddha miraculously radiating a number of colored lights, we are told that "in each light was proclaimed the secret store of the Tathāgata: saying that all sentient beings possess Buddha-nature."[131] Elsewhere MPNMS^{D}+ unpacks the content of this "secret store": that all sentient beings possess Buddha-nature; that there is no discrimination between the Buddha, dharma, and sangha; that the characteristics of these three jewels are precisely permanence, bliss, selfhood, and purity, and that Buddhas do not finally enter *nirvāṇa* as if it were some other plane of existence, but are rather permanent and unchanging.[132]

On several occasions MPNMS^{D}+ alludes to discussion of Buddha-nature found in the core MPNMS: it refers briefly to the examples of the treasure buried beneath a house and of the wrestler with the lost jewel (see 2.4).[133] But elsewhere its account of Buddha-nature is distinctive: MPNMS^{D}+ states that Buddha-nature is "like space," and can otherwise be identified with kindness or compassion.[134] These identifications are unlike anything found in the core MPNMS, and do not receive much clarification in MPNMS^{D}+ itself. Moreover, while it appears that the author(s) of MPNMS^{D}+ accepted

---

130. Dharmakṣema's preference for this expression is well demonstrated by Habata (2015b: 191); in the curious doctrinal abecedary that appears late in the MPNMS (see 2.5n107; also 8.2n11), we are told that the syllable *ga* stands for "*tathāgatagarbha*" (MPNMS^{T} §426.6–7); in MPNMS^{D} (413c3) *ga* is taken to refer to the existence of *foxing* 佛性, where an Indian text would have surely referred to (*tathāgata*)*garbha*.

131. MPNMS^{D}+ 430a2–3: 是光明中宣說如來祕密之藏: 言諸眾生皆有佛性。

132. MPNMS^{D}+ 487a15–18: 何等不聞, 而能得聞? 所謂甚深微密之藏[a]: 一切眾生悉有佛性, 佛、法、眾僧無有差別, 三寶性相常、樂、我、淨, 一切諸佛無有畢竟入涅槃者常住無變。

[a] T 藏 = Yuan/Ming/Palace 義

The text then elaborates that the *nirvāṇa* of the Buddha is neither "being" nor "absence," "created" nor "uncreated," "contaminated" nor "uncontaminated," and so on. Such interest in oppositions between "*x* and not-*x*" is not a primary theme in the earlier, definitely Indian MPNMS (which nevertheless features some discussion of "nonduality"; see 2.6), but is a hallmark of MPNMS^{D}+; see also 7.3.

133. MPNMS^{D}+ 523c15–23; 572b8–9; then 572b6–7. A curious detail is that this allusion to the example of the buried treasure refers only to a person who is informed that his/her house has gold buried beneath it; that is, it agrees with the content of MPNMS^{F}, and not the parable found in MPNMS^{D}, which concerned—more convolutedly—a woman and her son (see 2.3n63).

134. MPNMS^{D+} 456a18 (淨佛性猶如虛空); 456b21–22 (慈者即是眾生佛性). Other teachings unique to MPNMS^{D}+ (though they are not identified as such) are discussed by Liu (1982: 68–69; translating MPNMS^{D}+ 574b15–20), including a passage in which Buddha-nature is said to possess various concentrations (*samādhi*s), but lack action, afflictions, the *skandha*s, and the twelve stages of dependent origination. The comparison of Buddha-nature to space is referenced in Dol po pa's RC; see Hopkins 2006: 83.

the idea that all sentient beings have what is called "Buddha-nature," they developed a different account of how far this should be articulated as a teaching about the self.[135]

At the expense of further discussion of Buddha-nature, MPNMS^{D}+ attends more to the four positive counterparts to the distorted views: that something is permanent, the self, blissful, and pure. These, however, are taken to refer to the status of a fully awakened being: in other words, close to the use of these positive terms reflected in material of MPNMS-dhk (see 2.2). Crucially, MPNMS^{D}+ exhibits some reluctance to extend the language of selfhood to Buddha-nature, or what is proper to all sentient beings: when the text lists six aspects of Buddha-nature, these are "permanence, purity, reality, goodness, visibility, and reality/truth" (omitting "self"); only a couple of lines later is the Buddha *himself* described in terms of permanence, bliss, selfhood, and purity.[136] We see this also when the Buddha is questioned by the "six masters" of non-Buddhist systems, who are better known from forms of the *Samaññaphalasutta* (e.g., DN.I.47).[137] The Buddha states that notions of (worldly) selfhood are untenable, but explains that the Buddha himself is *ātman* due to (in short) his "limitlessness" (*wubian* 無邊), and so his non-Buddhist interlocutors accept his teaching.[138] Elsewhere we encounter a lengthy list of arguments, attributed to these same non-Buddhist teachers, for the existence of the self, followed only lines later by a series of responses from the Buddha regarding absence of self in all phenomena, which makes no mention of Buddha-nature.[139] In short, MPNMS^{D}+ exhibits a greater focus on the Buddha as somehow worthy of being called the self, and some caution about promoting the idea that this language is appropriate with respect to anything proper to lowly sentient beings.

In one instance MPNMS^{D}+ falls in line with what we find in the core MPNMS: the Buddha contests to an audience of Brahmanas that he does not, contrary to their accusations, teach a kind of annihilationist view (*duanjian* 斷見):

> I do not teach that all sentient beings are without a self! I constantly teach that all sentient beings possess Buddha-nature; is Buddha-nature not the self? Hence, I have not taught an annihilationist view.

---

135. MPNMS^{D}+ adds other interesting details, and states that one can come to "see" one's Buddha-nature by copying and reciting the *sūtra;* MPNMS^{D}+ 487b19–20: 聽是經者, 聞有佛性, 未能得見。書寫、讀誦、為他[a]廣説、思惟其義, 則得見之。

[a] T 他 = Yuan/Ming/Palace 人

136. MPNMS^{D}+ 513a3–4: 佛性有六 … 一常、二淨、三實、四善、五當見、六真; 513a6–7: 如來即是覺相善相, 常樂我淨。This material is referenced in the RC; see Hopkins 2006: 64.

137. Regarding other versions of this narrative, see Vogel 1970; MacQueen 1988.

138. MPNMS^{D}+ 544c11–21. See also Ruegg 1989a: 21–23.

139. MPNMS^{D}+ 444c22–445a20, and responses at 446b16–447a9.

> All sentient beings do not see Buddha-nature, hence [I teach] impermanence, absence of self, unpleasantness, and impurity; because of this is it said that I teach an annihilationist view.[140]

The Buddha uses an account of the self to defend the dharma from its critics, and in the process converts rival religious authorities to it. But with the important exception of the passage just cited, MPNMS^{D}+ does not usually associate selfhood with Buddha-nature at all so much as with the figure or achievement of the Buddha himself. Far more typical is the following, which follows just lines after the passage translated above: "Good son, this Buddha-nature is in truth not the self; for the benefit of sentient beings is it called the self.… Buddha-nature is absence of self, [but] the Tathāgata teaches the self [for the sake of some audiences]: because of his permanence, the Tathāgata is the self, but he teaches absence of self, because he has achieved sovereignty."[141] This reads as if the authors of MPNMS^{D}+ were uncomfortable with the idea that sentient beings possess something that could rightly be called the self, even if the Buddha is prepared to teach this in order to educate certain audiences. More central to MPNMS^{D}+, we discover, is the Buddha's own "selfhood" by virtue of his power or "sovereignty" (*zizai* 自在: perhaps related to Skt. *aiśvarya;* see also 4.3). Elsewhere MPNMS^{D}+ tells us that the Buddha's "great *nirvāṇa*" (*daniepan* 大涅槃) is the realization of a "great self" (*dawo* 大我: Skt. **mahātman*), which is characterized by "great sovereignty" (*dazizai* 大自在) that consists of eight kinds of power. Someone possessing the great self is able to (1) manifest many bodies and (2) travel the grand "trichiliocosm" of worlds (*sanqian daqian shijie* 三千大千世界: evoking Skt. *trisāhasramahāsāhasralokadhātu*) freely while (3) possessing neither lightness nor heaviness; (4) by one-pointedness of mind endow his consciousness to multiple bodies; (5) by each sense organ perceive ("synesthetically") any type of sense datum; (6) apprehend all *dharma*s (but without having the erroneous notion of there being any *dharma*s to apprehend!); (7) expound all teachings (though in reality, we are also told, none properly exist), and (8) pervade all places, like space.[142]

---

140. MPNMS^{D}+ 525a21–25: 我亦不説一切眾生悉無有我; 我常宣説一切眾生悉有佛性。佛性者豈非我耶? 以是義故, 我不説斷見[a]。一切眾生不見佛性, 故無常、無我、無樂、無淨。如是則名説斷見也。

[a] Song/Yuan/Ming/Palace omit 見

141. MPNMS^{D}+ 525a28–b6: 善男子, 是佛性者, 實非我也, 為眾生故, 説名為我 … 佛性無我, 如來説我: 以其常故, 如來是我, 而説無我, 得自在故。Regarding the use of this material in Bu ston's DzG, see Ruegg 1973: 113–114, 123–124; also 1989a: 22–23.

142. MPNMS^{D}+ 502c13–503a22. See also H. Nakamura (1980: 1103b), who associates these with a set of eight powers from Yoga and (later) Vedānta tradition. MPNMS^{D}+ may have intended something like the set of eight powers (*siddhi*s), beginning with the ability to assume a minute size, found in Patañjali's *Yogasūtra* (3.45; see Feuerstein 1979: 118) and subsequently unpacked in the *Yogabhāṣya* of Vyāsa (fourth century?); see, for example, R. S. Bhattacharya 1975. An influential (but very different) list of the Buddha's powers is found in the *Daśabhūmikasūtra;* see, for example, Vaidya 1967: 45.7–15.

Some final extracts from MPNMS^{D}+ highlight differences between the doctrine of this material and the antecedent content of MPNMS-tg, but also echo the positions of some other *tathāgatagarbha* works, to which we turn in later chapters, that must postdate the Indian MPNMS. MPNMS^{D}+ makes an important distinction between declaring that the Buddha himself can be discussed in terms of selfhood, and what—by virtue of their Buddha-nature—can be said about sentient beings: "The Tathāgata, being permanent, is called the self. The *dharmakāya* of the Tathāgata is without limit, obstruction, origin, or destruction, and is endowed with the eight types of sovereignty, so is called the self. Sentient beings do not in reality have such a self or what is of the self; only because they will certainly attain emptiness in the ultimate sense (畢竟第一義空: evoking, if not translating, Skt. *paramārthaśūnyatā*) is there said to be 'Buddha-nature.' "[143] Comprehension of emptiness (*śūnyatā*) is not a theme that dominates the reliably Indian content of the MPNMS (see, however, 9.5). Otherwise the claim that selfhood is a property of the Buddha—but *not* of sentient beings—is an important feature of MPNMS^{D}+. We also read that "all sentient beings do not *yet* have all the qualities of a Buddha [including] permanence, bliss, selfhood, and purity."[144] This neatly encompasses the position of MPNMS^{D}+: that talk of the self is appropriate with regard to the Buddha, but that this language is *not* appropriate in an account of Buddha-nature, in description of that which is proper to the nature of sentient beings.

In summary, MPNMS^{D}+ teaches Buddha-nature in a manner that is conspicuously distinct from the core material of MPNMS-tg, to the extent that the author(s) of MPNMS^{D}+, whoever they were, express some discomfort with the *ātmavādin* orientation of what came before them. They do not share the aim of the MPNMS to explain and defend how possession of Buddha-nature equates to the Buddha's revelation of the true self, and instead step away from presenting this as anything like a revision of *nairātmyavāda* discourse that characterized the Buddha's earlier teachings. Undoubtedly MPNMS^{D}+ requires further study on its own terms, apart from any conflation with the core MPNMS. In the meantime it is enough to remember that MPNMS^{D}+ may not be of Indian origin, or at least that it likely did not originate in the same intellectual milieu as that which produced the *ātmavādin* account of Buddha-nature articulated in MPNMS-tg.

2.8 Conclusions

This chapter has taken as authoritative Radich's argument that the MPNMS likely represents our earliest available account of the *tathāgatagarbha*, which

143. MPNMS^{D}+ 556c11–14: 如來常住則名為我。如來法身無邊、無礙、不生、不滅、得八自在, 是名為我。眾生真實無如是我及以我所; 但以必定當得畢竟第一義空, 故名佛性。See also Liu 1982: 71.

144. MPNMS^{D}+ 572b21–22: 一切眾生現在未有一切佛法: 常、樂、我、淨。

may have its origins in an internalization of the Buddha's lasting essence (*buddhadhātu*)—otherwise held to reside in a *stūpa*—in the constitution of every sentient being. We have supposed also that the notion of the internalized Buddha-nature developed from a particular account of the Buddha found in MPNMS-dhk, in which the Buddha is said to exist permanently and beyond the world of conditioned entities or events, and so to somehow constitute what could be called *ātman*. To complement this, MPNMS-tg teaches the internalization of some "essence" of the Buddha, which denotes a permanence and indestructability apart from the physical body; each sentient being is imagined as the locus for a new and properly transcendent Buddha: in other words, Buddhas as they are venerated already in MPNMS-dhk. The claim that each sentient being has the chamber (*garbha*) for such an essence, as Radich has contended (see 1.3), could be understood also as an account of the "womb" (*garbha* also) from which a prospective future Buddha might eventually emerge.

Before we leave the MPNMS, attention must be given to a hypothesis of Stephen Hodge, who has written eruditely regarding the relationship between the term *ātman* and the categories *tathāgatagarbha* and *buddhadhātu* in MPNMS-tg. Based on the distribution of what seems to represent the expression *ātman* across our various translations, Hodge has contended that the expressions *tathāgatagarbha* and *buddhadhātu* may have begun their life in the MPNMS as glosses—perhaps interlinear additions to early Indian manuscripts—that were later absorbed into the main text to clarify or even transform what was meant when the MPNMS taught that sentient beings "have *ātman*." His hypothesis is that passages of MPNMS-tg originally promoted—very simply—a doctrine of the self, which only later was revised in terms of what we are calling Buddha-nature: first the presence of the (*buddha*)*dhatu*, and then *tathāgatagarbha*.[145] This hypothesis is attractive bearing in mind (1) the irregular distribution of what seem to be the terms *tathāgatagarbha, buddhadhātu,* and *ātman* across available forms of the text, but also (2) the fact that MPNMS-dhk introduces the idea that the Buddha himself can be described in terms of the self, before material of MPNMS-tg teaches about the presence, in all sentient beings, of Buddha-nature.

However, it could be argued that some essential element (indeed, some "*dhātu*") is missing from this hypothesis. My proposal, after Hodge, is that MPNMS-tg may well have originally featured a greater reliance on the language of selfhood—what we find, for example, in the objections voiced by the bodhisattva Kāśyapa (see 2.4)—but that such an apparent departure from established Buddhist teaching had to emerge in tandem with another idea. Seeing as the framework of the MPNMS is indeed the Buddha's (apparent) death, and other accounts of this event usually entail a discussion of what happens to his relics, MPNMS-tg could reinvent the distribution of the Buddha's postmortem remains into an account of that which is enduring

145. Hodge 2010/2012: 42–43, 52–54.

and indestructible in any sentient being, and which in each instance can foreshadow the realization of a new Buddha.[146] This was the *buddhadhātu;* no longer resident at the *stūpa* but enigmatically present in the constitution of every sentient being (i.e., the *tathāgatagarbha;* see also 1.3). The Buddha-nature idea—imagined as a new account of the location of the Buddha's abiding nature—bridges the conceptual gap between the experience of liberation as the achievement of the self, otherwise an enduring state of freedom and power, and the claim that in every sentient being there is something precious and permanent, some "*dhātu,*" that might otherwise deserve to be called the self that is enigmatically present throughout transmigration.

We have then a preliminary answer to why MPNMS-tg couched its form of Buddha-nature teaching in terms of the self of sentient beings: that the status of a Buddha could be described in terms of *ātman* gave license, at the birth of the *tathāgatagarbha* tradition, to the affirmation that something that could be called *ātman*—enduring, indestructible, and uncreated—must exist in the constitution of sentient beings in general (see 10.3). Such a self is "about" any sentient being but also nowhere to be found by them; the self and its grandeur are manifested in the person of a Buddha, which any diligent bodhisattva strives to become. This reflects a new perspective on Buddhist soteriology: liberation becomes an achievement possible for anyone, the cause of which is extant already, albeit imperceptibly, in the constitution of all sentient beings. While authors of the MPNMS still valued the *nairātmyavāda* discourse of earlier and wider Buddhist tradition, they had also at their disposal an account of that which persists across rebirth and can eventually, with effort, enjoy liberation from it (see 10.4).

Among other benefits, Buddha-nature teaching provided Buddhist authors with an affirmative response to *ātmavāda*-oriented interlocutors—exhibited most clearly in the parable of the lost sword—and their perhaps persuasive sermons about what it is that survives through transmigration and is the basis, in all beings, for release from it. And yet an innovation such as this clearly came at a cost: MPNMS-tg shows awareness that its ideas invited, and surely received, substantial criticism. We will see that Buddha-nature articulated as a teaching about the self was rejected by later Indian authors, who developed the expression *tathāgatagarbha* apart from any claim that this in any way corrects or succeeds teachings about absence of self. Nevertheless, as we shall explore in the next two chapters, the MPNMS was not the only Mahāyāna text to develop and defend the idea that Buddha-nature constitutes a definitive account of what is enduring and valuable in the constitution of any sentient being.

146. See Strong 2004: 98–123.

CHAPTER 3

The *Aṅgulimālīyasūtra* and the Essential Self

3.1 The Text

After the MPNMS, what may be next in the relative chronology of *tathāgatagarbha* works—at least those concerned with an *ātmavādin* form of it—is the Mahāyāna *Aṅgulimālīyasūtra* (AMS), which has received little attention in modern scholarship. We possess two versions of the AMS, and (to date) no Sanskrit fragments of it. The Chinese version of the text (T.120: *Yangjuemoluo jing*央掘魔羅經; henceforth AMS^{C}) was translated by Guṇabhadra 求那跋陀羅 (394–468 CE).[1] The Tibetan translation (e.g., D.213, Q.879: *Sor mo'i phreng ba la phen pa zhes bya ba theg pa chen po'i mdo;* henceforth AMS^{T}) was produced in the late eighth or early ninth century, and is attributed in its colophon to Dharmatāśīla, Śākyaprabha, and the enigmatically named Tong Ācārya.[2]

After work by Takasaki (1974: 191–233), the greatest attention shown to the AMS has been by Kazuo Kanō (2000) and Takayasu Suzuki (1999a; 1999b; 2000a; 2000b; 2014), with contributions also by Ichijō Ogawa (1999; 2001) and Lambert Schmithausen (2003).[3] An absence of greater scholarly attention to the AMS may be due to the lack of interest Buddhist commentators seem to have shown the text in the intervening centuries. References to the AMS do appear in some later Indian works, though for the most part

1. An English translation of AMS^{C}—together with translations of some other *tathāgatagarbha* works—is that by Rulu (如露), published online (http://www.sutrasmantras.info; also in print, 2016). While there is no doubt great merit to making Chinese Buddhist materials accessible to a wider audience, these translations lack strong philological grounding and are, in some places, misleading.

2. Kanō (2000: 75–76n4) notes how the colophon of the Tabo edition records that the Tibetan translation relied upon both a Sanskrit manuscript and, where this Sanskrit was lacking, a Chinese translation. The Tabo edition is the only one to call this Tong Ācārya an Indian *paṇḍita* (*rgya gar gyi mkhan po*), whereas others instead refer to him as a "Chinese translator" (*rgya'i lo tshā ba*). See also Radich 2015a: 62n127.

3. An overview of AMS^{T}, informed by Tibetan reception of Buddha-nature teaching, is Brunnhölzl 2014: 20–22.

these show interest not in its account of the *tathāgatagarbha* so much as its prescription of vegetarianism.[4] Perhaps most significant is the *Laṅkāvatārasūtra* (LAS), which lists the AMS after the MPNMS in its knowledge of *sūtra*s that teach abstention from meat, which makes it likely that its authors knew the AMS vis-à-vis Buddha-nature also.[5] The longest Indian quotation of the AMS is found in the Tibetan translation of Bodhibhadra's tenth-century *Jñānasārasamuccaya-nibandhana*, which we will consider below (3.7).

The AMS belongs to the MPNMS-group of *sūtra*s, and shares with the MPNMS—among other features—a prophecy about the disappearance of the Buddha's dharma eighty years after the reemergence of the text in which the prophecy features (see 2.1, 10.2).[6] The AMS appears to be more heavily indebted to the MPNMS than to the remaining *tathāgatagarbha*-oriented text in this group, the **Mahābherīhārakasūtra* (MBhS). Suzuki has contended that some language used in the AMS (pertaining to "a teacher of what is beneficial": **hitopadeṣṭṛ*; see 3.1) appears less developed here than in the MBhS, and so argues for a relatively early date for the AMS.[7] There is little else to help determine the relative ages of these two works, although both advance different aspects of Buddha-nature thought visible already in the MPNMS. What is certainly the case is that the AMS develops more themes from the MPNMS than the comparatively short MBhS, and so is perhaps more accurately imagined as the direct successor to their mutual predecessor.

Like the MPNMS, the AMS also records that it was sometimes known as a *mahāsūtra*, or specifically "the very extensive *mahāsūtra* of he who wields the sword" (**Mahāvaipulya-Śastradhara-mahāsūtra?*),[8] a fitting title given the narrative's preoccupation with violence.[9] Some of this violence has to do with the serial killer Aṅgulimāla, the eponymous "protagonist" of the AMS,

4. See 3.5. Regarding vegetarianism in the MPNMS, see, for example, MPNMS^F 868c23–25: 善男子, 我從今日制諸弟子不聽食肉; 設得餘食, 常當應作食子肉想 (Good son, from this day I restrict my disciples, and do not permit them to eat meat; when one obtains an offering of meat, always should one think of it as if it were the flesh of one's own son). Compare MPNMS^D 386a11–14; MPNMS^T §173. See also Kanō 2000: 58–59; Schmithausen 2002: 315–323; 2003: 21–46; and Schmithausen forthcoming.

5. Nanjio 1923: 258.4–5: *hastikakṣye mahāmeghe nirvāṇāṅgulimālīke laṅkāvatārasūtre ca mayā māṃsaṃ vivarjitam*. See also 8.1n5. Regarding other Indian texts that mention the AMS, see Kanō 2000: 58.

6. In its own prophecy the AMS states how remarkably difficult it will be, during the decline of the dharma, for anyone to teach about the permanence of the Buddha's existence or the existence of the *tathāgatagarbha* (AMS^C 537c17–538c7; AMS^T D.213, 189a2–191a6; Q.879, 196b4–198b7).

7. T. Suzuki 2000b: 157–158; see also 3.1.

8. AMS^T D.213, 126a4; Q.879, 133b6: *shin tu rgyas pa chen po'i mdo sde chen po mtshon cha thogs pa;* also AMS^C 512b: 執劍大方廣經. See Habata 1994.

9. Regarding justification of violence in defense of the dharma, see AMS^C 521b27–c24; AMS^T D.213, 142b7–143a3; Q.879, 150a1–5. The MPNMS also endorses the protection of monks by armed devotees (e.g., MPNMS^F 867a12–27; MPNMS^D 384a19–b11; MPNMS^T §153–154); see Habata 2018: 242–244; also Kanō 2016: 4–5n11.

known otherwise from (for example) the Pāli *Aṅgulimālasutta* (MN.II.97–106).[10] Like the MPNMS, the AMS reimagines what was likely an already well-established Buddhist narrative framework to deliver an account of the bodhisattva path, as well as a defense of its own formulation of the Buddha-nature idea. Much of this is delivered by the Buddha himself, though a great deal of the teaching is done also by Aṅgulimāla, who receives questions from esteemed arhats, bodhisattvas, and deities (in a manner reminiscent of the celebrated *Vimalakīrtinirdeśasūtra*). The AMS is hence not only another reimagining of a preexisting Buddhist story but moreover—in a form common also to the *Śrīmālādevīsiṃhanādasūtra* (ŚDS)—involves the exposition of Buddhist dharma by a figure who is not ostensibly a likely spokesperson for it.

Though it is a less prominent theme than in the MPNMS, the AMS also discusses the Buddha's *dharmakāya,* again, in contrast to the Buddha's physical form, and in a manner reminiscent of what we encountered in the previous chapter: "The Tathāgata is without bones or sinew; how can he have bodily remains or relics? Lacking any relics, the *dharmakāya* that is supreme in methods is the inconceivable Buddha: inconceivable is the Tathāgata. In order that those who lack faith are led to faith, the Buddha strategically deposits [in the world] his relics; for the sake of making a *stūpa,* he deposits his relics."[11] The establishment of icons, we are told, was a means of venerating deities that was already practiced by other cults already in the world; the Buddha displays the existence of physical relics to appeal to persons who would have observed these practices.[12] But beyond these is his *dharmakāya,* and although the AMS grants us little insight into how this should be understood (the Buddha is, after all, "inconceivable"), there is little doubt that *dharmakāya* again stands for the Buddha's mode of existence apart from whatever appearances he manifests in the world. With echoes of the MPNMS, the AMS understands the Buddha's enduring *dharmakāya* to be something apart from his physical remains, although what is "essential" (*dhātu*) to him is present in the constitution of every sentient being.[13] In one instance, in which the AMS denies that the Buddha, beyond appearances, relies on

---

10. For a comprehensive list of Aṅgulimāla's appearances in wider Buddhist literature, see Kanō 2000: 74–75n2; also Anālayo 2008.

11. AMS^{T} D.213, 158b2–3; Q.879, 166a1–2: *de bzhin gshegs pa la rus ba'ang med / rgyus pa yang med na / sku gdung dang ring bsrel lta ga la yod de / ring bsrel med pa thabs kyi mchog chos kyi sku ni sangs rgyas bsam gyis mi khyab pa ste / de bzhin gshegs pa ni bsam gyis mi khyab pa'o // ma dad pa rnams dad pa bskyed pa'i phyir ring bsrel bzhag pa'i thabs mdzad de / sangs rgyas kyi mchod rten bya ba'i phyir ring bsrel bzhag go //* Compare AMS^{C} 526c17–21, in which relics are something that the Buddha "displays" for the world (*shixian* 示現). Regarding the survival of one of these verses in Sanskrit, see note 13 below.

12. AMS^{C} 526c22–24; AMS^{T} D.213, 158b3–4; Q.879, 166a2–5.

13. A very similar critique of relics occurs in the *Mahāmeghasūtra* (T.387[12]1096c4–1097a27; especially 1097a20–24); see Forte 2005: 336–340), a fourth text of the so-called MPNMS-group that is concerned primarily with the permanence of the Buddha rather than the Buddha-nature idea; see also Takasaki 1974: 276–301. One verse translated above—regarding

food, we read that the Buddha is replete with the virtues of the "great self" (*dawo* 大我; *bdag nyid chen po*: **mahātman* or perhaps **māhātmya*), similar to content of MPNMS-dhk, though we are offered no more explanation of what this means.[14]

This difference between truth and appearance is a prominent theme throughout the AMS. A central revelation of the text is that murderous acts committed by Aṅgulimāla—for which he was perhaps well known by Buddhist audiences—were merely illusory.[15] Although it may seem apposite that Aṅgulimāla be chosen as a mouthpiece for the guarantee that all sentient beings have at all times the propensity for complete awakening (regardless of their past actions), the authors of the AMS were cautious of the possibly antinomian dimension of their message (see 3.5). Indeed, a focus of the AMS are the difficulties and demands of the bodhisattva path, and a confirmation that possession of Buddha-nature is no free ticket to liberation.[16]

Though this describes no easy task, the AMS understands the path of the bodhisattva to be defined by the cleansing and discovery of the *tathāgatagarbha,* which is again the site of what can be called the nature or essence of a Buddha. "One who is on the path of the bodhisattva declares that 'all sentient beings have the *tathāgatagarbha.* Having first gradually removed afflictions, I attain the nature of a Buddha (**buddhadhātu*) [that is] unshakably pleasant and extremely blissful.' "[17] In this passage and elsewhere our versions of the AMS seem to reflect use of the terms *tathāgatagarbha* and *buddhadhātu* interchangeably, just as we find in the MPNMS (see 1.3). It is worth demonstrating early in this chapter that the phrasing preserved in AMS^T often differs from what we find in AMS^C: corresponding to the above, AMS^T presents the following: "One who is on the path of the bodhisattva should declare: 'All sentient beings have the *tathāgatagarbha;* having become unshakeable (*mi g.yo ba*) with regard to my own *dhātu,* I shall in the manner intended by the Sugata [i.e., Buddha] eliminate the ten million afflictions [that obscure it].' "[18] The passage above includes a reference to "one's own *dhātu*" (*nga'i dbyings:* Skt. **maddhātu*); we will see much more of the expression *dhātu*—in what appear to have been a number of constructions—throughout this chapter. While it is beyond reasonable doubt that the expression *buddhadhātu* is represented by both AMS^C and AMS^T, what

---

the Buddha's lack of bones or sinew—appears to be common to both texts (T.387[12]1097a21–22), and is preserved in the Sanskrit *Suvarṇaprabhāsasūtra;* see 10.4n69.

14. See AMS^C 523b20–21; AMS^T D.213, 147b3–4; Q.879, 154b5.

15. See AMS^C 528b11–19; AMS^T D.213, 161a4–b7; Q.879, 168b1–169a6; also Kanō 2016: 5n11.

16. See Grosnick 1990: 65; Schmithausen 2003: 22.

17. AMS^C 539c6–c8: 菩薩道者謂:「一切眾生皆有如來藏。我次第斷諸煩惱得佛性,不動快樂甚可愛樂」。

18. AMS^T D.213, 194a1; Q.879, 201a7–8: *byang chub sems dpa'i lam zhes bya ba ni sems can thams cad la de bzhin gshegs pa'i snying po yod de / nga'i dbyings su ngas mi g.yo ba thob pa ltar / bde bar gshegs pas dgongs pa'i tshul gyis nyon mongs pa bye ba gcad* [Q. *bcad*] *par bya'o //*

is most characteristic of the AMS is its use of other ways of describing some "essence" that is proper to sentient beings, and which describes that which is permanent and unchanging within each and every one of them.

3.2 An "Essence" of One's Own

A frequently occurring expression in the AMS appears to be **ātmadhātu,* which might be translated as "one's own *dhātu*" or "what is essential in/to/of one's self." This is represented wherever AMS^{T} provides either *bdag gyi khams* or *bdag gyi dbyings,* and where corresponding material of AMS^{C} provides *woxing* 我性 or *wojie* 我界 (though the latter, employing *jie* 界, does not best reflect *dhātu* in the sense of "essence" or "nature"; see also 6.1). In other instances we find slightly different renderings of "one's own essence/nature" (*zixing* 自性; *rang gi dbyings: *svadhātu* or perhaps **maddhātu*). The AMS uses these expressions as further epithets for *buddhadhātu,* or otherwise *tathāgatagarbha,* as we saw also in the MPNMS.[19] There is little doubt that all of these expressions intend still some Buddha-nature present in all sentient beings, albeit with some caution about going so far as to call this the self.[20] But while the AMS (for the most part) steers clear of declaring that this, the *tathāgatagarbha,* should be called the self, it remains the case that the abiding, precious essence of a sentient being functions like just that, and was acknowledged to sit in problematic tension with teachings about absence of self.

Again like the MPNMS, the AMS also describes Buddha-nature in terms of a "cryptic" or even "secret" teaching" (*mijiao* 密教; *ldem po ngag,* also *dgongs pa'i tshig:* e.g., **sandhāvacana* or **saṃdhābhāṣya*) that is explained to disciples of the Buddha who were more accustomed to teachings about *anātman.* In the MPNMS the expression *sandhāvacana*—the Buddha's use of cryptic utterances—refers to the revelations that the Buddha exists permanently, as well as the existence of the *tathāgatagarbha* or self, all in contrast to what he had taught already to his disciples (see 9.2). But in the AMS what seems to have been the same language is used to explain that previous declarations by the Buddha were oblique references to Buddha-nature all along. The sense is that the *tathāgatagarbha* doctrine is not an entirely new teaching so much as something that has been latent or even "hidden" within the Buddha's earlier pronouncements. A pertinent example of this motif comes in Aṅgulimāla's discussion with the arhat Pūrṇa, who among the Buddha's disciples is renowned for being a skilled expositor of the dharma. Pūrṇa recites to Aṅgulimāla the following verse:

---

19. Versions of the MPNMS also reflect the expression **ātmadhātu;* see 2.4; also Habata 1990: 180. However, it is not clear that in the MPNMS **ātmadhātu* is so endorsed as an epithet for the *tathāgatagarbha* as it is in the AMS.

20. Bu ston's DzG quotes the AMS as having taught that the *tathāgatagarbha* is the self (*de bzhin gshegs pa'i snying po de bdag yin no;* see Ruegg 1973: 80), but I am unable to find this explicit identification in either surviving version of the AMS.

> That which all the Buddhas and *śrāvaka*s did not discern,
> Such a teaching did the truly awakened one explain to living beings.[21]

Quite reasonably, Pūrṇa unpacks this to refer to the inability of Buddhas in past, present, or future—together with any *śrāvaka*s or *pratyekabuddha*s—to discern any kind of self in the constitution of sentient beings. Pūrṇa understands that the Buddha could not find any "intuited" notion of the self (see 2.5), using a list of designations similar to those we find in versions of the MPNMS (AMS^{C} 我、人、壽、命), including also the less common expression **sattvadhātu* (*zhongshengjie* 眾生界; AMS^{T} *sems can gyi khams*): "the essence of sentient beings," to which we must return later (3.3). In response, Aṅgulimāla explains that the Buddha's verse reflects a "cryptic teaching" (*yinfu zhishuo* 隱覆之說; *ldem po ngag*; **sandhāvacana/saṃdhābhāṣya*) that concerns precisely what *is* discerned by Buddhas: that is, they find the *tathāgatagarbha*. Without having understood the truer or "secret" meaning of the initial verse, Pūrṇa is said to have "declared the [Buddha's] teaching to be absence of self," such that he "falls into the lamp of delusion, like a moth that casts itself into a flame."[22] The alternative interpretation provided by Aṅgulimāla is certainly creative, and interprets previous articulations of the dharma to be cryptic allusions to Buddha-nature:

> "That which the Buddha-Tathāgatas did not discern" refers to the fact that exalted Buddhas of the past, searching very diligently in all sentient beings, could not discern the absence of the *tathāgatagarbha*.
>
> All exalted Buddhas of the present … do not discern the absence of the **ātmadhātu*.
>
> All exalted Buddhas of the future … will not discern the absence of the **svadhātu*.
>
> The *śrāvaka*s and *pratyekabuddha*s of the three times … also do not discern the absence of the *tathāgatagarbha*.[23]

This passage must be referring to a single idea by three names: *tathāgatagarbha*, which can be called also **ātmadhātu* and **svadhātu*.[24] The AMS

---

21. AMS^{T} D.213, 150b6; Q.879, 157b8–158a1: *sangs rgyas kun dang nyan thos kyis // gang de kun du ma brnyes pa // chos de mngon par sangs rgyas nas // srog chags rnams la bstan par bya //* Compare AMS^{C} 525a18–19: 諸佛及聲聞 / 聖所不得法 / 正覺善通達 / 廣為眾生說。This discussion with Pūrṇa is repeated, at some length, in Dol po pa's RC (Hopkins 2006: 143–146).

22. AMS^{C} 525a27–29: 謂法無我，墮愚癡燈如蛾投火。Compare AMS^{T} D.213, 151a5–151a6; Q.879, 158a8: *gang po de bzhin gshegs pa'i ldem po ngag mi shes pas bdag med pa la chos su sems pa* [Q. + *de*] *ni gti mug gi chos kyi mar me'i nang du phye ma leb ltar lhung ngo //.*

23. AMS^{C} 525a29–b6: 諸佛如來所不得者，謂過去一切諸佛世尊，於一切眾生所極方便求，無如來藏不可得。現在一切諸佛世尊，於一切眾生所極方便求，無我性不可得。未來一切諸佛世尊，於一切眾生所極方便求，無自性不可得。三世一切聲聞緣覺，於一切眾生所極方便求，無如來藏亦不可得。Compare AMS^{T} D.213, 151a6–b1; Q.879, 158a8–b3.

24. AMS^{T} reflects instead of **svadhātu* the expression *sattvadhātu* (*sems can gyi khams*), though this is also listed in an account of (erroneously) "intuited" notions of selfhood (with

then provides a lengthy account of what kind of "essence" resides in sentient beings. For example, Buddhas do not discern a *tathāgatagarbha* "that is produced" (AMS^C 如來之藏生), but do discern what is unproduced, which is Buddha-nature (不生是佛性: see note 25 for full details).[25] This passage equates the *tathāgatagarbha* with the **buddhadhātu,* but also often refers to this throughout as simply "the **dhātu* that has *x* quality," where *x* is permanence, changelessness, etcetera. Hence we can take expressions such as **ātmadhātu* to mean simply some "essence"—called unproduced, permanent, changeless, without sickness, and so forth—that sentient beings all possess. In each instance this **dhātu* is also said to be adorned with all of the major and minor marks of a superior being (*mahāpuruṣa*): its qualities are the desirable characteristics of some "self," but also the presence of the physical attributes of a fully realized Buddha.[26]

Taking all of this into account, my suggestion is that we understand **ātmadhātu* to mean "the essence of/within the (conventional) self/person," which—being an uncreated, indestructible *dhātu*—is some entity that explains the capacity of sentient beings to become Buddhas. It is nothing less than the **buddhadhātu,* though **ātmadhātu* casts this as "what is proper to sentient beings" in contrast to what is not: adventitious afflictions that obscure their true nature. Preference for the expression **ātmadhātu* may reflect a strategic move on the part of the AMS in order to avoid explicitly stating that the Buddha teaches the existence of the self, even though the substance of its Buddha-nature teaching is still that there exists an enduring, indestructible essence in the constitution of all sentient beings, and one that is associated with the goal of the Buddhist path (i.e., attainment of a Buddha's qualities). As we have seen above, the AMS still presents this *dhātu,* otherwise the *tathāgatagarbha,* to be a remedy to wrong-minded understanding of *anātman* from earlier Buddhist teaching, represented in the text by the arhat Pūrṇa. Elsewhere the AMS will indeed suggest that the Buddha has taught nothing less than a doctrine of the self (see 3.7), but we should otherwise note a different tone to the AMS that distinguishes it somewhat from the MPNMS: that Buddha-nature be considered what is

---

ātman, jīva, etc.) just lines above this passage (see note 29 below). My suspicion is that the reading **svadhātu* in AMS^C may be older, and that some corruption (e.g., a mistaken reading of *sattva-* in place of *sva-*) may have led to the reading preserved in AMS^T.

25. In full, AMS^C (526a27–b22) calls the *dhātu* unproduced (不生), true (真實), permanent (常), lasting (恒), unchanging (不變易), quiescent (寂靜), indestructible (不壞), unbreakable (不破), without sickness (無病), not aging or dying (不老死), and without contamination (無垢). In the second and third of these the term 如來之藏 is replaced by 自性.

AMS^T (D.213, 157a3–157b6; Q.879, 164b2–165a6) calls the *dhātu* unproduced (*ma skyes pa*), unoriginated (*ma byung ba*), permanent (*rtag pa*), unchanging (*ther zug*), everlasting (*g.yung drung ma yin pa*), without disease (*nad med*), without age or death (*rga shi med pa*), without fear (*mi 'jigs pa*), indestructible (*mi shigs pa*), and without contamination (*dri ma med pa*). This material features in Dol po pa's RC (Hopkins 2006: 100–101).

26. See also 2.3n49.

permanent and unchanging in any sentient being but not, more contentiously, that it be called explicitly the Buddha's account of the self.

3.3 What Buddha-nature Is Not: More False Notions of the Self

As was the case in the MPNMS, the AMS recognizes that the existence of the *tathāgatagarbha*, called *ātman* or otherwise, is not something that will be easily accepted by its audience. In defense of this teaching, the authors of the AMS articulate at some length what Buddha-nature is not. This is done with reference to lists of false notions of selfhood—*ātman, jīva, pudgala,* etcetera—for which the *tathāgatagarbha* must not be confused, but also by clarifying what the existence of the *tathāgatagarbha,* or otherwise *(buddha)dhātu,* means for the conduct of a bodhisattva. This suggests that the authors of the AMS confronted similar criticisms to those that informed apologetic content of the MPNMS (see 2.4), but that they went to further lengths to justify teaching the existence of something that looks very much like an account of the self.

We should first return to Pūrṇa's apparently limited understanding of the verse quoted in the previous section, concerning what Buddhas apparently "cannot discern." Pūrṇa's interpretation is surely not something that the authors of the AMS want to reject outright; in the same way that the authors of the MPNMS still accepted teaching about not-self with regard to erroneous, worldly accounts of the self, those of the AMS certainly would not want the *tathāgatagarbha* to be confused for any falsely intuited notions of the self. Pūrṇa's complete articulation of "that which the Buddhas did not discern," before his correction by Aṅgulimāla, runs as follows:

> All the Buddhas of the past, though searching diligently amid all phenomena, did not discern any *sattvadhātu, ātman, *pudgala,* or **jīva.*[27]
>
> All the Buddhas of the present and of the future, together with the *śrāvaka*s and *pratyekabuddha*s of all three times, though searching diligently amid all phenomena, did not discern the *ātman;* and in accordance with that taught for sentient beings abstention from [notions of] *sattvadhātu, ātman, *pudgala* and **jīva,* expounding the teaching that is absence of self, and the teaching of emptiness: in this way is the dharma taught.[28]

So runs AMS^{C}.[29] The structure of Pūrṇa's teaching is reminiscent of the *prajñāpāramitā* literature, which teaches that among *dharma*s there can be

27. Regarding similar lists in other Buddhist literature, see 2.2n39.

28. AMS^{C} 525a20–25: 謂過去一切諸佛, 於一切法中極方便求, 不得眾生界及我、人、壽命。現在未來一切諸佛及三世一切聲聞、緣覺, 於一切法中極方便求亦悉不得我, 亦如是為眾生說離眾生界、我、人、壽命; 說無我法、說空法, 如是說法。

29. Corresponding material in AMS^{T} (D.213, 150b7–151a4; Q.879, 158a1–158a6) is a little confusing. To begin with, AMS^{T} does not list *ātman* among things that Buddhas of the present and future do *not* discern; if this is intended to mean that they do know Buddha-nature as *ātman,* then why not exclude this also from what is not discerned by Buddhas in the

discerned none of these various notions of personhood, each of them being—in the language of that literature—empty (*śūnya*).[30] Indeed, Pūrṇa frames this as an account of not only *anātman* but also emptiness (*śūnyatā*): it is an account of what Buddhas "do not discern" (Ch. *bude* 不得; Skt. *an-upa-√labh*), which audiences would have likely recognized as an evocation of older Buddhist teachings that are of an avowedly *nairātmyavādin* orientation.

As in the case of the MPNMS, the authors of the AMS opposed various notions of what we have called the "intuited" self—*ātman, pudgala, jīva,* etcetera—which were associated, since very early in Buddhist tradition, with erroneous "commonsense" views about worldly personhood and identity (see 2.5). It is these that Pūrṇa rejects, and which Aṅgulimāla surely also takes to be misguided concepts. Yet Aṅgulimāla's response to Pūrṇa shows us that Buddha-nature can invite other comparisons, between the *tathāgatagarbha* and notions of "speculated" selfhood reminiscent of what is taught in the Brahmanical Upaniṣads:

> The meaning [of the Buddha's verse] is that the exalted Buddhas of the past searched diligently amid all phenomena for various kinds of a worldly self: [said to be] like a thumb; like a grain of millet, hemp or barley; or like a mustard seed; either blue, yellow, red, or white in colour; square or round, long or short.
>
> Some say it resides in the heart; some above or below the navel; some say in the head or eye, or across various parts of the body; some say it is spread throughout the body like a bodily fluid. In such a way are there countless kinds of deluded ideas [about the self].
>
> Thus are worldly conceptualizations of the self, which is also said to be permanent, pleasant, and tranquil. All of the Buddhas together with the *śrāvaka*s and *pratyekabuddha*s did not discern a self such as this. One who is perfectly awakened gives such a teaching [about not-self] for the sake of all sentient beings: this is the correct meaning of that verse of the Tathāgata.[31]

---

past (unless, somehow, earlier Buddhas did *not* know the *tathāgatagarbha*)? Moreover, all of this occurs in the account of the arhat Pūrṇa, who would surely have simply stated that all Buddhas, in all times, taught about absence of self. My suspicion is that this material in AMS[T] exhibits some corruption at some stage in its transmission (see also note 24 above).

30. See, for example, *Pañcaviṃśatisāhasrikā-prajñāpāramitā*, e.g., Dutt 1934: 39.3–5: *tad yathāpi nāma śāriputra ātmeti cocyate na cātmā upalabhyate na sattvo na jīvo na poṣo na puruṣo na pudgalo na manujo 'pi upalabhyante anupalambhaśūnyatām upādāya.* See also Zacchetti 2005: 207, 327–329. Regarding this kind of formulation in the Pāli tradition, see Harvey 1995: 24–28.

31. AMS[C] 525b7–14: 謂過去一切諸佛世尊, 於一切法極方便求世間之我, 如拇指、粳[a]米、麻、麥、芥子; 青、黄、赤、白; 方圓、長短: 如是等比種種相貌。或言在心、或臍上下、或言頭、目、及諸身分; 或言遍身猶如津液[b], 如是無量種種妄想。如世俗修我, 亦言常住、安樂、蘇息。如是比我, 一切諸佛及聲聞緣覺, 悉皆不得。正覺彼法為眾生說: 此是如來偈之正義。

[a] T 粳= Ming 秔

[b] T 液 = Song/Yuan/Ming 膩

In its own slightly different list of "speculative" notions of selfhood, AMS^{T} provides the following: a self the size of a thumb; the size of a millet or rice grain, or of a mustard seed; red, blue, yellow, or white; short, long, very long ("and so on"); resident in the heart; near the navel; in the head, eye, or ear; or like the heat at the heart of an oil lamp. The worldly self is said to have been called permanent (*rtag pa: nitya*), lasting (*brtan pa: dhruva*), and enduring (*ther zug: śāśvata*).[32]

Designators for the "intuited" self—such as those opposed by Pūrṇa—appear throughout Buddhist literature, and are repeatedly said to refer to nothing within the constitution of a sentient being. Here, however, the AMS takes specific aim at notions of "speculated" selfhood—within one's constitution but in some manner "hidden"—in the vein of the Upaniṣads. For example, the thumb-sized man is mentioned in both the *Śvetāśvatara-*[33] and *Kaṭha-upaniṣad*s, the latter of which focuses repeatedly on the self that resides in the heart,[34] while comparison to barley, millet, and mustard seeds is found in the *Bṛhadāraṇyaka-*[35] and *Chāndogya-upaniṣads*.[36] Locating the self in the head or eye appears also in the *Bṛhadāraṇyaka-*[37] and *Chāndogya-upaniṣad*s,[38] while comparison to a lamplight—found just in AMS^{T}—brings to mind an analogy made by the *Śvetāśvatara-upaniṣad*,[39] which also provides a comparison of the self to a bodily fluid.[40]

We will return to these erroneous notions of selfhood, and their parallels in wider Indian literature, in the concluding chapters of this study (see 9.6, 10.3). For now, we acknowledge that the AMS affirms that what an awakened observer does *not* discern in human experience is both (1) an *absence* of the *tathāgatagarbha* (otherwise "one's own *dhātu*"), but also (2) the *presence* of any notion of a "speculated" self that is hidden somewhere within the body, as explored within Brahmanical tradition. This second conclusion is significant, as the account of the (*buddha*)*dhātu* found elsewhere in the AMS is still very reminiscent of some account of the self even when it is not called, by name, *ātman*.

3.4 Perceiving Buddha-nature

Like the MPNMS, the AMS relies on similes and parables to explain what the *tathāgatagarbha* is and how to understand its role in the liberation of

32. See AMS^{T} D.213, 151b1–b4; Q.879, 158b3–b7.

33. See Olivelle 1998: 422–423 (v.3.13), 428–429 (v.5.14).

34. Ibid., 376–377 (v.1.14), 386–387 (v.3.1), 392–393 (v.4.6–7), 394–395 (v.4.12–13), 402–403 (v.6.17).

35. Ibid., 134–135 (v.5.6).

36. Ibid., 208–209 (v.3.14.2–3).

37. Ibid., 66–67 (v.2.3.5), 118–119 (v.4.4.2).

38. Ibid., 224–225 (v.4.15.1), 280–281 (v.8.7.3).

39. Ibid., 418–419 (v.2.15).

40. Ibid., 416–417 (v. 1.15–16).

sentient beings. We must keep in mind that such examples are not necessarily intended to elucidate every detail of how Buddha-nature should be understood; they were likely employed to clarify specific concerns of actual or potential audiences, which in some instances go beyond those that are suggested in the MPNMS.[41] Our challenge then is to ascertain the significant import of each simile as intended by our authors, and to avoid investing undue importance in other aspects or implications of their language or imagery.

We saw in the previous chapter that the position of the MPNMS was that advanced bodhisattvas could indeed perceive the existence of the *tathāgatagarbha,* although only in an imperfect or incomplete manner (2.3). The AMS explores this same idea with recourse to two similes. In the first, the Buddha's son Rāhula is described inspecting a pool of water inhabited by tiny creatures. At first Rāhula cannot make out if what he sees are living things or not, but gradually he comes to discern tiny insects. This simile echoes content of the MPNMS, which among many other short comparisons likened the tenth-stage bodhisattva to a monk who faces the same problem as Rāhula.[42] We should not overlook the fact that to peer into water in classical India would mean that the agent was confronted also with the relatively novel sight of their own physical self or person, flecked with the presence of small objects or creatures. Keeping all of this in mind, the explanation of the simile in AMS^{C} runs as follows:

> Likewise is the tenth-stage bodhisattva: scrutinizing his own body for his own nature (**svadhātu*), he generates various different views concerning innumerable types of nature. In this way is the *tathāgatagarbha* difficult to attain.
>
> A teacher of what is beneficial, during a time when the wicked world is said to be all aflame, will with disregard for his own life teach about the *tathāgatagarbha* to sentient beings: hence do I teach that venerable bodhisattvas, heroes among men, are themselves Tathāgatas.[43]

41. Zimmermann (2002: 34–35), in relation to the *Tathāgatagarbhasūtra,* urges caution regarding the difference between "allegory" and "simile": "In contrast to what we normally call 'allegory,' a simile does not allow parallels to be drawn between a whole range of congruent factors featuring in the *upamāna* [i.e., the literary comparison] on the one hand and the *upameya* [that which is to be understood by it] on the other.... Let us keep in mind that it was not the intention of the author(s) to construct allegories with perfect proportional relations in regard to all single elements."

42. See MPNMS^{F} 887b6–9; MPNMS^{D} 412a12–a25; MPNMS^{T} §412. Behind both of these passages there is an older tradition, represented in the *Ambalaṭṭhikarāhulovādasutta* (MN.I.414), which concerns Rāhula's education by analogies involving water. A further comparison might be drawn with a passage of the *Chāndogya-upaniṣad* (v.8.8; Olivelle 1998: 280–281), in which enquiring deities are instructed to look for the self by observing their reflections in water.

43. AMS^{C} 525b26–c2: 十地菩薩亦復如是: 於自身中觀察自性, 起如是如是無量諸性種種異見: 如來之藏如是難入。安慰説者, 亦復甚難謂於惡世極熾然時, 不惜身命而為眾生説如來藏: 是故我説諸菩薩摩訶薩, 人中之雄, 即是如來。

AMS^{T} differs slightly: the tenth-stage bodhisattva searches for and does eventually see his **ātmadhātu* in his own body, and sees this to be "a limitless *dhātu*" (*mtha' yas pa'i dbyings*).[44] This could still have translated "limitless (notions of) *dhātu*" (Skt. **anantadhātu*), closer to what we find in AMS^{C}, translated above. In which case, are we to believe that wrong-minded notions of the self can originate in the imperfect faculties of bodhisattvas, generating ideas that fall short of Buddha-nature as known to a Buddha? It would be out of character for a Mahāyānist *sūtra* to be quite so critical of a tenth-stage bodhisattva—close to buddhahood, and so the pinnacle of all that can be accomplished by any sentient being—and this passage may have only intended to draw attention to the difficulties that even advanced bodhisattvas face when making intelligible that which they themselves cannot see in full. Either way, the AMS appears to accept that a tenth-stage bodhisattva has some limited access to the *tathāgatagarbha,* but, like the MPNMS, emphasizes that only a Buddha can fully perceive its presence and character.

The simile regarding Rāhula is followed by a further example concerning the arhat Aniruddha, who in accounts of the Buddha's disciples is associated with being foremost among those with supernatural "divine vision" (*divyacakṣus*).[45] Again with echoes of the MPNMS (see 2.3), the AMS remarks that Aniruddha can see the trails left by birds in the sky, but that companions of his cannot, and so must rely on his testimony.[46] Similarly, "the *śrāvaka*s and *pratyekabuddha*s, being fools with regular vision, trust in discourses by the Buddha that explain the existence of the *tathāgatagarbha.* How could they be able to see [for themselves] the nature (**dhātu*) that is within the range of what is knowable to a Buddha? The *śrāvaka*s and *pratyekabuddha*s rely on faith in another; how can a person of the world who is blind from birth know anything by themselves, without receiving it from another?"[47] The AMS goes on to laud those who have faith in the *tathāgatagarbha,* and offers an explanation as to why so many in the sangha do not accept teachings about it. Their incredulity, Aṅgulimāla explains, is due to their not having heard about this in past lives; those who do accept it must have in a previous existence heard about the *tathāgatagarbha,* directly from a Buddha.[48] There are also individuals who have long studied the "cryptic teaching about absence of self," but "through the three times

44. AMS^{T} D.213, 152a1–4; Q.879, 159a5–a7.

45. See Lamotte 1944: 527.

46. We again find this same example, albeit with less detail, in the MPNMS, in the context of bodhisattvas of the tenth stage being able to discern, in part, their Buddha-nature (see 2.6); MPNMS^{F} 887a12–16; MPNMS^{D} 412a1–4; MPNMS^{T} §406.

47. AMS^{C} 525c4–7: 肉眼愚夫聲聞緣覺信佛[a]經説有如來藏。云何能見佛境界性？ 聲聞緣覺尚由他信：云何生盲凡夫，而能自知不從他受？

[a] T 佛＝Shōgozō 解

Compare (for this, and the preceding simile concerning Rāhula) AMS^{T} D.213, 152a4–152a7; Q.879, 159a7–159b3.

48. A motif found in early Mahāyānist literature also, including the *Aṣṭasāhasrikā-prajñāpāramitā*, regarding which see Drewes 2019: 18–28.

they do not understand these cryptic teachings; hearing about the *tathāgatagarbha,* but not believing in it."[49]

From this we draw two conclusions: first, that the AMS praises those who do accept its doctrine by affirming that these persons have, in past lives, been taught by a Buddha already. But for those who cannot accept it, a major stumbling block is their age-long observance of teachings about *anātman* without access to the Buddha's hidden meaning or intent. Again, although the AMS mostly avoids referring to the *tathāgatagarbha* as the self, Buddha-nature is presented as the counterintuitive content of teachings about absence of self, which somehow alludes to the truth that something superlatively precious does, imperceptibly, exist. Fortunate for all, we are told that the Buddha time and again appears in the world to "explain to gods and humans that the *tathāgatagarbha* is like the trail of a bird in the sky," revealing their Buddha-nature (佛性); the Buddha does this "to turn gods and men from attachment to the view of absence of self."[50]

A final word is needed about the striking conclusion to the simile about Rāhula—translated above—regarding the bodhisattvas as "heroes among men … themselves Tathāgatas." Corresponding material in AMS^{T} echoes this sentiment: "To the venerable bodhisattvas, [who are] tigers,[51] I teach *tathāgatagarbha,* but not to others. Those sentient beings are themselves Tathāgatas."[52] Both versions of this passage make bold assertions about those who tread the path of the bodhisattva: that they are, by virtue of their Buddha-nature, already Buddhas. Such a sentiment we have observed already in the MPNMS, where possession of the Buddha's essence (*dhātu*) seems to mean that the bodhisattva does indeed, in at least some sense, constitute the presence of a Buddha in the world (see 2.3). In a similar fashion, the AMS seems to narrow the distinction between those who commit to becoming Buddhas—who accept their Buddha-nature, and work to cleanse it—and Buddhas themselves. But this still does not grant the

49. AMS^{C} 525c25–28: 久習無我隱覆之教 … 去來現在不解密教, 聞如來藏, 不生信樂。AMS^{T} (D.213, 153a6–7; Q.879, 160a3–4) refers to the *tathāgatagarbha* as the Buddha's *dgongs pa'i tshig*: **saṃdhāvacana*; see 9.2.

50. AMS^{C} 536c4–9 (including, regarding absence of self: 我於無量阿僧祇劫恒河沙生, 轉無量眾生諸天及人執無我見。) Compare AMS^{T} D.213, 186a1–4; Q.879 193b3–6.

51. AMS^{T} describes these bodhisattva as "tigers" (*stag*), an image used several times in this version. AMS^{C} (translated above) calls them "heroes among men" (人中之雄), something like which occurs also in MPNMS^{F} (853b16: 人中雄). Corresponding material is preserved in MPNMS Sanskrit fragments no. 1.5 (Habata 2007: 8; and similar in no. 20.2; see Habata 2019: 152), and gives us *narakuṃjarāḥ* ("preeminent"—or "elephants"—among men), though in place of this expression MPNMS^{T} (§4.19) provides simply *mi mchog* ("best of men"). The title "tiger among men" (*puruṣavyāghra*) occurs frequently throughout the Brahmanical epics: see, for just one example, Hara 1994: 42. See also the next note.

52. AMS^{T} D.213, 152a4; Q.879, 159a7: *byang chub sems dpa'* [Q. + *sha*] *stag de dag la nga de bzhin gshegs pa'i snying po ston gyi / gzhan la mi ston to // sems can de dag ni bdag nyid de bzhin gshegs pa yin no /* The variation in Q.—"to bodhisattvas alone" (*sha stag*)—I find only in this edition, and it helps us little with the repeated use of simply (*byang chub sems dpa'*) *stag* across other editions of AMS^{T} (see previous note).

bodhisattva license to assume the achievement of buddhahood, which—we are elsewhere told—still requires dedication to the task of clearing away the afflictions that obscure the character of a Buddha.

3.5 Essence, Action, and the Self

Perhaps guilty of this themselves, the authors of the AMS were certainly aware that teaching about *tathāgatagarbha* could overstate the proximity of sentient beings to their goal: the achievement of buddhahood. In spite of the claim that the bodhisattva is in a sense "(already) a Tathāgata," the AMS also clarifies that *tathāgatagarbha* teaching does not undermine the importance of diligence along the path of the bodhisattva.

It has been said that texts that espouse forms of *tathāgatagarbha* doctrine are not overly concerned with how one goes about pursuing the bodhisattva path.[53] The AMS itself acknowledges that teaching about Buddha-nature could promote laxity or even a spirit of antinomianism: if one has the *tathāgatagarbha* already, and attainment of awakening is ultimately just a matter of (a very long) time, then lapses of conduct in this life are a trivial matter. However, the AMS gives particular emphasis to the bodhisattva's observance of celibacy (*brahmacārya*) and the need for continual self-sacrifice in service to the dharma. It confronts the accusation that teaching about *tathāgatagarbha* may be used to legitimize wickedness, and in the process clarifies further how what is proper to sentient beings—their "own nature" (**ātmadhātu*)—differs from the conventional person who acts and feels consequences in the world. In the following passage the Buddha explains the nuances of *tathāgatagarbha* teaching to the bodhisattva Mañjuśrī, his and Aṅgulimāla's most persistent interlocutor throughout the text.

> Furthermore, Mañjuśrī, someone who knows there to be butter in milk will diligently churn it, but because it has no butter will not churn water; likewise, Mañjuśrī, because sentient beings know [themselves] to have the *tathāgatagarbha,* they keep observation of the precepts and practice celibacy. And furthermore, Mañjuśrī, someone who knows there to be gold in a mountain will dig to find gold, but because it has no gold will not dig into a tree; likewise, Mañjuśrī, because sentient beings know [themselves] to have the *tathāgatagarbha,* they keep observation of the precepts and practice celibacy, declaring: "I shall certainly attain awakening!"

53. Zimmermann 2014a: 519–520. Elsewhere Zimmermann (2002: 76–77), I think correctly, hypothesizes that Buddha-nature literature has less interest in ethics because its foremost concern is to establish a universality to the "family of the Buddhas": the ubiquity of the cause of awakening in all sentient beings. But this does not mean, as the AMS demonstrates, that authors within this tradition were uninterested in matters of how the bodhisattva—the Buddha's "true sons"—should act in the world. Regarding the theme of the paternal Buddha (or even the "paternal *sūtra*") in the context of the *Tathāgatagarbhasūtra,* see Cole 2005: 197–235; also Saitō 2020.

> Further still, Mañjuśrī, if there were no *tathāgatagarbha,* then practicing celibacy would be futile, just as one who churns water for an entire aeon will never obtain butter.[54]

Corresponding material in AMS[T] is concerned with what it calls the *dhātu* (*dbyings*) rather than *tathāgatagarbha;* fitting because the examples used include "the element of gold" (*ser gyi dbyings:* Skt. *suvarṇadhātu*) that is present in some rock but never in wood. Buddha-nature is understood to be the necessary condition for awakening: the presence of the *tathāgatagarbha* is that which grounds the possibility of attaining the status of a Buddha, because it is nothing less than the permanent, indestructible character of a Buddha already.

Yet Mañjuśrī's concern about *tathāgatagarbha* goes further, and he inquires about how Buddha-nature relates to the discipline and dedication that is required of a bodhisattva along his tremendously lengthy career:[55]

> If in all sentient beings there exists the *tathāgatagarbha,* then all sentient beings should become Buddhas. All sentient beings will then kill, steal, engage in sexual misconduct, lie, drink alcohol, and so on, engaging in unwholesome courses of action.
>
> Why so? If all sentient beings possess Buddha-nature (佛性: **buddhadhātu*), they should all at one time attain liberation. If there exists Buddha-nature, then [some beings, reassured by this] will commit many heinous deeds, including those of the *icchantika.*
>
> If there is a self, then one's own nature (*wojie* 我界: **ātmadhātu*) should liberate all existents [which is not the case]; therefore, in what is worldly there is neither self nor some "essence" (*jie* 界: *dhātu*): the teaching of the Buddha is absence of self with respect to all phenomena.[56]

At an extreme, Mañjuśrī thinks it possible that sentient beings who are assured of the *tathāgatagarbha* will pursue the course of the *icchantika,* who in

---

54. AMS[C] 540a18–25: 復次文殊師利, 如知乳有酥[a]故方便鑽求, 而不鑽水以無酥[a]故。如是文殊師利, 眾生知有如來藏故, 精勤持戒淨修梵行。復次文殊師利, 如知山有金故鑿山求金, 而不鑿樹以無金故。如是文殊師利, 眾生知有如來藏故, 精勤持戒淨修梵行言「我必當得成佛道 」。復次文殊師利, 若無如來藏者, 空修梵行, 如窮劫鑽水終不得酥[a]。

[a] T 酥 = Shōgozō 蘇

Compare AMS[T] D.213, 195a4–195b1; Q.879, 202b2–6. This material features in Dol po pa's RC (Hopkins 2006: 154–155).

55. Similar concerns are voiced in MPNMS[D]+ 405b11–18; see also Liu 1982: 71–72.

56. AMS[C] 539a15–20: 若一切眾生悉有如來藏者, 一切眾生皆當作佛。一切眾生皆當殺、盜、邪婬[a]、妄語、飲酒等, 不善業迹。何以故? 一切眾生悉有佛性, 當一時得度。若有佛性者, 當作逆罪, 及一闡提。若有我者, 我界當度一切有。是故世間無有我、無有界: 一切法無我, 是諸佛教。

[a] T 婬 = Song/Yuan/Ming 淫

Compare AMS[T] D.213, 192a7–192b3; Q.879, 199b7–200a2.

the AMS is otherwise associated with the nadir of improper behavior.[57] Teaching about Buddha-nature, Mañjuśrī fears, will legitimize a lapse from the practices of the bodhisattva: a thought that may well have troubled real-world audiences of this and other *tathāgatagarbha* works besides.

Notably, AMS^C also appears to hold that the existence of the **ātmadhātu* should lead to the liberation of "all existents" (我界當度一切有), and perhaps even that this should happen "[all] at one time" (當一時得度): the liberation of one entity in possession of Buddha-nature should liberate all, implying that the *dhātu* of sentient beings might be numerically singular. Here the use of *wojie* 我界 (literally "the realm [*dhātu*] of the/one's self") in place of the more common *woxing* 我性 (more clearly "one's essence/nature [*dhātu*]") may be pertinent, and we shall return to this detail below (3.6). But suggestion of any "singularity" to Buddha-nature is absent from the corresponding material of AMS^T, which concludes as follows: "If in all sentient beings there exists an **ātmadhātu* (*bdag gyi dbyings*) then they themselves (*bdag nyid*) will be liberated; [but] as there is no **ātmadhātu* involved in the fruition of actions, then in no worldly being, nor in oneself (*bdag*), is there any essence (*dbyings: dhātu*): hence did the Buddha teach absence of self (*bdag med*) with respect to everything."[58] Here AMS^T reflects a contrast between sentient beings as agents (*bdag nyid*) and the **ātmadhātu* (*bdag gi dbyings*) that exists, in some manner, "within" them: their Buddha-nature that exists apart from actions done in the world. Mañjuśrī holds such an agent to be determined by their past actions and, in future, to be heir to the fruits of their present deeds. Because no enduring "essence" is required in this process, then talk of any such thing is misplaced.

The Buddha responds by restating the existence of the *tathāgatagarbha* in all sentient beings, and compares it—veiled by innumerable afflictions—to a lamp residing in a jar.[59] He then introduces the example of an ascetic boy training at the time of the previous Buddha (Kāśyapa),[60] who promises the boy that in seven years he will become a universal emperor (*cakravartin*) who will rule over the world. The ascetic boy is overjoyed, and with the certainty of the Buddha's prediction instructs his mother to bring vast quantities of food so that he might increase his strength. This overindulgence results in what AMS^C calls the boy's "untimely death" (非時而死); he is said in AMS^T to have "killed himself" (*bdag nyid shi ba*).[61] The Buddha

57. See also 2.7n126.

58. AMS^T D.213, 192b2–192b3; Q.879, 200a1–200a2: *gal te sems can thams cad la bdag gi dbyings yod na / bdag nyid sgrol par 'gyur te / las kyi rnam par smin pa la bdag gi dbyings med pas na / de'i phyir 'jig rten dang bdag la dbyings med de / thams cad la bdag med pa de ni sangs rgyas kyi bstan pa'o //*

59. An image found also in the MBhS; see 4.2.

60. Not to be confused with the Buddha's disciple (Mahā)Kāśyapa, nor the bodhisattva of the same name who is the Buddha's interlocutor in the MPNMS.

61. AMS^C 539a23–a29; AMS^T D.213, 192b3–192b6; Q.879, 200a2–200a6. The final remark—that the boy merely killed himself—is missing from corresponding material in a Gondhla edition fragment of AMS^T (Gondhla 25.04, 47a7–9).

asks Mañjuśrī to explain the boy's ill fortune: whether the Buddha (Kāśyapa) had lied, was not all knowing, or whether the karmic fruit of becoming an emperor had somehow not ripened? Mañjuśrī's response is that the boy must have died due to past evil actions, and the Buddha corrects him, "Do not say this! He simply died an untimely death, not as a repercussion of previous unwholesome actions. Mañjuśrī, does the Buddha predict without knowing about previous unwholesome actions? Without previous unwholesome actions, at that time [the boy] transgressed, and so simply lost his life."[62] It is far more common for Indian Buddhist literature to emphasize the role that past actions play in the current or future prospects of sentient beings. However, the Buddha stresses the role of diligence here and now, and goes on to articulate that the enemy of liberation—given the presence of the *tathāgatagarbha* in all sentient beings—is negligence (*pramāda*):

> Likewise, Mañjuśrī, if a man or woman should think "I have in my body the *tathāgatagarbha:* I shall [certainly] attain liberation, so will do evil," and if in that way they do evil, will they because of Buddha-nature (佛性) be liberated, or will they not?[63] It is like the ascetic boy, just described, who though in truth had the nature of a ruler did not achieve this status. Why so? Because of excessive negligence. In just such a way Buddha-nature will not liberate those sentient beings, due to their excessive negligence.
>
> Do all sentient beings lack Buddha-nature? Truly there exists Buddha-nature, like the reward of becoming a universal emperor [in the case above]. Does the Buddha tell falsehoods? Sentient beings tell falsehoods and do negligent acts. By hearing the dharma but being negligent, or by their own unwholesome actions, they do not attain buddhahood.[64]

We should keep in mind that the claim that all sentient beings are indeed capable of attaining awakening does not at all guarantee that any one of

---

62. AMS^{C} 539b3–b5: 勿作是說！ 彼非時死耳, 非本惡業報也。文殊師利, 彼佛不知先惡業報而記之耶？ 無先惡業，今自作過以致失命耳。Compare AMS^{T} D.213, 192b6–193a2; Q.879, 200a6–200b1.

63. AMS^{T} (D.213, 193a2–3; Q.879, 200b1–b2) suggests **ātmadhātu* instead of **buddhadhātu.*

64. AMS^{C} 539b5–13: 如是文殊師利, 若男子女人作是念言:「我身中有如來之藏;自當得度, 我當作惡」, 若如是作惡者, 為佛性得度耶,不得度耶？ 如上所說彼調伏子, 實有王性,而不得度: 所以者何？ 以多放逸故。佛性不度, 亦復如是, 以彼眾生多放逸故。一切眾生為無佛性耶？ 實有佛性, 如轉輪[a]王報。為佛妄語耶? 眾生妄語作諸放逸。以聞法放逸故, 自過惡故, 不得成佛。

[a] T 輪 = Shōgozō 輪聖

Compare AMS^{T} D.213, 193a2–5; Q.879, 200b1–5. AMS^{T} states that beings "are not liberated by [virtue of] the *dharmadhātu*" (*chos kyi dbyings*); the expression *dharmadhātu*—the nature/realm of phenomena, or otherwise perhaps simply "reality" (see 6.1)—is virtually absent from AMS^{T} (see also 3.6n76), and this passage otherwise takes its subject to be the *buddhadhātu* (*sangs rgyas kyi dbyings*).

them necessarily *will,* let alone with any ease or speed. The actions of sentient beings certainly matter, though what lies apart from or "beneath" these is their ever-present Buddha-nature. The *tathāgatagarbha* refers to something that all sentient beings possess, and yet it is separate from the timeless process of action and retribution that conditions their transmigration. Hence sentient beings can each blame their own negligence (*fangyi* 放逸; *bag med pa: pramāda*) for their not having made greater progress toward the goal of awakening. In short, the existence of Buddha-nature—the cause for awakening in all sentient beings—does not promise an easy or short journey toward the status of a Buddha.

As is the case in the MPNMS, understanding sentient beings in terms of the standard categories available to Buddhist authors—the mechanics of *karma,* the "heaps" (*skandhas*) of experience, dependent origination and so forth—does not provide much insight into Buddha-nature teaching. The status of the *tathāgatagarbha* remains indiscernible amid one's constitution, unknowable to anyone apart from Buddhas and (imperfectly) advanced bodhisattvas. Its role in progress toward awakening is at once fundamental and, in practical terms, in a sense inconsequential: the presence of Buddha-nature is that upon which liberation depends, and yet it is distinct from the worldly agent who works to remove the afflictions that obscure it.[65]

3.6 A "Single Essence"

The previous section introduced the curious suggestion that the AMS (or at any rate AMS^{C}) understands that possession of the (*buddha*)*dhātu* by one sentient being should mean that if one person achieves the status of a Buddha, then all sentient beings—by virtue of their all having the same Buddha-nature—should be liberated "all at once" (*yishi* 一時). In that passage, AMS^{C} seems to understand **ātmadhātu* to have meant "the realm" to which a sentient being belongs (*wojie* 我界): a development in Buddha-nature thinking found otherwise in the *Anūnatvāpūrṇatvanirdeśaparivarta* (AAN; see 6.1).[66] A corresponding statement is missing from AMS^{T}, but this feature of AMS^{C} coheres with a curious idea that is suggested elsewhere in both versions of the text: that the "essence" or "nature" proper to a sentient being is not something discretely present in each sentient being—identical in kind but immeasurable in number—but rather a (*buddha*)*dhātu* that is

65. The very next portion of the AMS undermines the idea that the cleansing of afflictions is entirely one's own responsibility. The Buddha explains to Mañjuśrī that due to simply hearing this *sūtra* innumerable misdeeds of the audience are removed, and that even hearing Śākyamuni's name means that the hearer becomes a bodhisattva capable of clearing his afflictions and achieving "the body of the Buddha." See AMS^{C} 539b21–c1; AMS^{T} D.213, 193b1–6; Q.879, 200b7–201a5.

66. Regarding the possibility of one of these texts exhibiting knowledge of the other, see Kanō 2000: 68.

somehow singular, and hence that the achievement of liberation in one instance should, in theory, mean its realization by all sentient beings.

Elsewhere both versions of the AMS touch upon the notion of a "single essence" (*yixing* 一性; *dbyings gcig: *ekadhātu*), which on first impression seems to raise some interesting metaphysical repercussions of Buddha-nature teaching. We first encounter this when the AMS lauds the practice of celibacy (*brahmacārya*).[67] The Buddha explains to Mañjuśrī that due to the ubiquity of the *tathāgatagarbha* in all sentient beings, they should think of each other as siblings.[68] Aṅgulimāla inquires how the Buddha's own parents could have conceived him if this was the case. In the familiar mold of the MPNMS and other texts that discuss the Buddha's life as a series of instructive (docetic) manifestations, the Buddha explains how his birth and even the existence of his parents were all just magical displays for the benefit of sentient beings. He otherwise reminds Aṅgulimāla that all sentient beings who transmigrate must have, at some point or other, been each other's mother, father, sibling, and so on;[69] each is like a performer who has played various roles, hence one should practice celibacy.[70] Some lines later, the Buddha informs Mañjuśrī that attachment to sexual desire does not befit men or women, as both possess the *tathāgatagarbha:* "because of the single essence (*yixing* 一性), a Buddha practices celibacy.[71] AMS^{T} differs only slightly, and declares that the *dhātu* of sentient beings (*sattvadhātu*) is a single *dhātu* (*dbyings gcig: *ekadhātu*), and that by taking up the practice of celibacy one begins their steady trajectory toward the status of a Buddha.[72]

Though the Buddha may display "worldly" events in his own life—his birth, marriage, and fathering a child—sentient beings genuinely engage in all manner of "impure" worldly activities, and yet they are supposed to have within themselves that which is proper to a Buddha, and so should be "beyond" any such activities.[73] The AMS expresses discomfort with sexual activity, either because—depending on our interpretation of this "single

67. See Dhirasekera 1982: 21–54; McGovern 2019: 99–122.

68. AMS^{C} 540a27–b1; AMS^{T} D.213, 195b2–3; Q.879, 202b8–203a1. In AMS^{T} sentient beings are called "brothers in dharma" (*chos kyi spun*: **dharmabhrātṛ*) and all women are called sisters (*sring mo*).

69. For an early example of this trope, see the Pāli *Mātusutta* (SN.II.189); also Lamotte 1944: 500.

70. AMS^{C} 540b2–17; AMS^{T} D.213, 195b3–196a3; Q.879, 203a1–203b1. The image of a "performer" (*jier* 伎兒; *bro mkhan:* Skt. *naṭa*) features also in the LAS (see 8.3), but is better known as an image used in the *Sāṃkhyakārikā* (42, 59; see Mainkar 1964: 113–114, 149–150) that describes mercurial "nature" (*prakṛti*) in opposition to the primary, immutable substance (*puruṣa*) that works through it, and is the classical Sāṃkhya response to inquiry about the self. In the AMS and LAS the comparison is drawn between a performer and Buddha-nature, whereas in the Sāṃkhya analogy the performer is compared to *prakṛti*: that which is not *puruṣa*, so not what a sentient being "truly is."

71. AMS^{C} 540b20–22 (including: 以一性故，是故如來淨修梵行).

72. AMS^{T} D.213, 196a5–6; Q.879, 203b3–4.

73. See AMS^{C} 540b23–c1; AMS^{T} D.213, 196a6–b2; Q.879, 203b4–8.

essence"—(1) sentient beings each possess a *dhātu* of "like-kind" that is, essentially, a Buddha, making this activity inappropriate, or, more problematically still, (2) sentient beings possess seemingly localized instances of the *same* Buddha-nature: "a single essence" in a numerical sense, which (we infer) would also make these kinds of activities perverse. We see no clear statement that in the MPNMS the *tathāgatagarbha* refers to a numerically singular entity expressed across many sentient beings, and yet here or there the AMS preserves material that could suggest just this. Where the AMS turns its attention to abstention from killing, AMS[C] tells us the following:

> Mañjuśrī addressed the Buddha, saying: "Lord, because the essence of all sentient beings is a single essence (*yijie* 一界: *ekadhātu*), is this why Buddhas abstain from taking life?"
>
> The Buddha replied: "It is so. Taking life in the world is just like taking one's own life, because it is killing one's own essence (*zijie* 自界: **svadhātu*)."[74]

Here AMS[C] again translates *dhātu* with *jie* 界 over *xing* 性, though in the Indic text it could be hard to distinguish whether the intention was *dhātu* in the sense of "realm" (better rendered by Chinese *jie* 界) or, as my translation reflects, "essence" (by *xing* 性). Some lines later, when Mañjuśrī inquires whether or not it is because of the *tathāgatagarbha* that Buddhas do not eat meat, the Buddha tells him that this is indeed the case: because all beings have been each others' relatives in previous lives, in the manner that a performer takes on many guises or personae (i.e., echoing arguments in favor of celibacy, discussed above). Moreover, the Buddha says, "one's own flesh and that of another are then a single flesh (*yirou* 一肉; *sha gcig*: **ekamāṃsa*): therefore the Buddhas do not eat meat."[75] The Buddha develops this teaching further, and with recourse again to the notion of a "single essence": "Moreover, Mañjuśrī, the essence of all sentient beings (*yiqie zhongsheng jie* 一切眾生界: **sarvasattvadhātu*) and the **ātmadhātu* (*wojie* 我界) are a single essence (*yijie* 一界). The flesh that is eaten is a single flesh; hence all the Buddhas do not eat meat."[76] This could support the

74. AMS[C]: 540c2–4: 文殊師利白佛言: 世尊, 以一切眾生界是一界故, 諸佛離殺生耶? 佛言: 如是。世間殺生如人自殺, 殺[a]自界故。

[a] Shōgozō omits殺

Compare AMS[T] D.213, 196b2–3; Q.879, 203b7–203b8. See also Schmithausen 2003: 24–25.

75. AMS[C] 540c22–26: 文殊師利白佛言: 世尊, 因如來藏故諸佛不食肉耶?
佛言: 如是一切眾生, 無始生死生生輪轉, 無非父、母、兄弟、姊妹, 猶如伎[a]兒, 變易無常。自肉他肉則是一肉: 是故諸佛悉不食肉。

[a] T 伎 = Yuan/Ming 技

Compare AMS[T] D.213, 197a3–a5; Q.879, 204b1–204b3.

76. AMS[C] 540c26–27: 復次文殊師利, 一切眾生界我界即是一界。所食[a]之肉即是一肉, 是故諸佛悉不食肉。

earlier notion—implied by Mañjuśrī in AMS[C]—that the existence of the *(buddha)dhātu* in all sentient beings suggests a numerically identical "essence" that pervades all of them. Though the Buddha does not accept that liberation is something that could be attained by sentient beings "all at once," the AMS could intend that to eat another sentient being is still a kind of autophagia.[77] And yet this position would be doctrinally very problematic. The prescription not to eat meat entails an equation between the "single flesh" of sentient beings and their "single essence," though if the *(buddha)dhātu* is that which is indestructible, even supermundane, in the constitution of a sentient being, and is apart from the workings of *karma* (3.5), it should be apart from and undisturbed by (impure) worldly activities and their results, including what is done by, and also to, the flesh of the physical body.

More likely, then, is that these "singularities"—a "single essence" and "single flesh"—were intended to reflect an ideological rather than metaphysical position (see also 5.4). Crucially, the key interest of the AMS appears not to be the intricacies of a metaphysical account of sentient beings and their common "essence" so much as prescriptions about certain kinds of activities that are conducive or not conducive to a bodhisattva's career. In the midst of the material outlined above, Mañjuśrī asks how the Buddha can prescribe abstention from killing but also the subjugation of "wicked persons, who are [also] in possession of the *(*sva-)dhātu* (*zijie* 自界)."[78] The distinction, we read, is one of purity: someone can follow prescriptions to eat only once a day, but in so doing kills innumerable microscopic beings that live in his body and so do not receive sustenance; though such a person undoubtedly kills, this is not "the impurity of taking life" (非殺生不淨).[79] Considerations of violence and taking life are secondary to what is correct or "pure" activity, which is buttressed by the revelation that all beings possess, somewhere about themselves, the nature of a Buddha.

This "single essence" in the AMS certainly requires further scholarly attention, but in the meantime I suggest that its authors did not intend the idea that all sentient beings are literally "of one flesh" but rather that they possess an enduring essence or nature (*dhātu*) that is single in the sense of

---

[a] T食 = Song/Yuan/Ming/Shōgozō 宅

Compare AMS[T] D.213, 197a5–a6; Q.879, 204b3–204b4. AMS[T] takes the *dhātu* of all sentient beings (**sarvasattvadhātu*) that is "one *dhātu*" to be also the *dharmadhātu* (*chos kyi dbyings*), an expression that is with one exception otherwise absent from AMS[T], and unattested in AMS[C] (see above 3.5n64).

77. I tentatively suggest that this evokes ancient issues concerning the Buddha's physical relics: specifically, the matter of whether they were diffused across several sites, or remained essentially "one" despite location at (allegedly, thousands of) different sites; see Strong 2007.

78. AMS[C] 540c5–6: 有自界諸惡像類者。 In AMS[T] (D.213, 196b3–4; Q.879, 204a1–2), these are "wicked non-Buddhists [*pāṣaṇḍas*], who possess their own *dhātu* (*bdag nyid kyi dbyings 'chang ba skyon chags pa ya mtshan can rnams*)."

79. AMS[C] 540c7–10; AMS[T]: D.213, 196b4–5; Q.879, 204a3: *srog gcod pa dag par mi 'gyur ro.*

"like-kind." The foremost concern of the AMS is to provide some explanation of why certain activities can be considered impure, which may have been compelling for audiences interested in the conduct proper to a bodhisattva.[80] Otherwise, the AMS proscribes violence (in its endorsement of vegetarianism) as much as it legitimizes it (in defense of Buddhist dharma): violence is justified if "pure" in type, primarily if it is required as part of the bodhisattva's commitment to the long-term benefit of all sentient beings.[81]

There is more besides to support the view that a foremost concern of the AMS is the purity of the bodhisattva's practice, and what this does (and does not) entail. Amid its promotion of vegetarianism, the AMS states that the bodhisattva need not take a strictly "vegan" attitude and so abstain from contact with all animal products under all circumstances. This view is found also in the MPNMS, in which this is said to distinguish the Buddha's dharma from the activities of *nirgrantha*s (non-Buddhist mendicants, and likely Jains specifically).[82] Both the MPNMS and AMS are concerned with the austereness of the bodhisattvas' practice, and with the Buddha-nature idea as some complement to it, but are insistent—as we saw in the MPNMS—that the Buddha's teachings should not be confused with those found in other systems (see 2.2, 2.6). A final portion of the AMS displays an awareness that similarities between Buddhism and elements of non-Buddhist systems are all too apparent, but that in any such confusion—including in regard to teachings about the self—it is the Buddha's dharma alone that has real authority.

3.7 Buddhism contra Other Systems

The last portion of the AMS that we will consider breaks a trend visible throughout the rest of the text: it states explicitly that the Buddha did indeed teach the existence of a self.[83] Whereas the AMS otherwise reflects some caution with respect to this terminology, we here encounter the recognition not only that the existence of some **ātmadhātu* corrects erroneous thinking about *anātman* (see 3.3) but that this *dhātu* amounts to the Buddha's teaching about the self. This same material is significant for its preoccupation with the ideas and practice of non-Buddhist systems in general, and along the way echoes the claim of the MPNMS that non-Buddhist ideas and practices come about not by the insight or ingenuity of other teachers but due to the influence of the Buddha himself (2.5).

80. The impurity of eating meat is discussed also in the LAS, regarding which see 8.1n5.

81. See 3.1n9.

82. For example, MPNMS^{F} 869a7–8; also, for example, AMS^{C} 540c28–541a11. See also Schmithausen 2005: 190–191.

83. This content is discussed further in Jones 2016a: 139–144; see also Kanō 2000: 66.

The relevant passage begins with Mañjuśrī stating that only the Buddha's teachings about liberation—and the renunciation that leads to it—are authoritative, in spite of the fact that others in the world lay claim to knowledge about such topics, and teach things such as absence of self and abstention from eating meat.[84] This prompts from the Buddha an explanation regarding the origins of other teachings about liberation outside of his own (*waidao* 外道; *ya mtshan can:* Skt. *pāṣaṇḍa*s: teachers of non-Buddhist ideas and practices). The Buddha recounts a story that takes place after the passing of a previous Buddha,[85] and some unfortunate circumstances that befall the final practitioner of the dharma left in the world at that time: a forest-dwelling monk named Buddhamati. Buddhamati receives a robe from a pious layman, but is subsequently kidnapped by thieves who strip him and tie him to a tree. A passing Brahmana sees Buddhamati's predicament and wrongly thinks that he is seeing a practice that is proper to Buddhist dharma; he emulates the monk and becomes what the AMS calls the first "renunciant without possessions" (裸形沙門; *dge sbyong gcer bu pa: *nirgranthaśramaṇa*). Buddhamati frees himself, covers his body with tree bark and ochre, and fashions a flywhisk from bound grass. Another Brahmana sees him, emulates this, and becomes the first "renunciant Brahmana" (出家婆羅門; but AMS^{T} *mur 'dug kun du rgyu ba: *pravrājyatīrthya*, "renunciant non-Buddhist"). Later that day Buddhamati bathes himself, treats his wounds with moss, and dons the discarded rags of a cowherd; again he is seen, and the observer becomes the first of "Brahmanas who practice hardships" (苦行婆羅門; but AMS^{T} *ya mtshan can dka' thub byed pa: *duṣkarapāṣaṇḍa*, "non-Buddhists who practice hardships"). In a further attempt to treat his wounds, Buddhamati covers himself in ashes, and an onlooker becomes the first "ash-smeared Brahmana" (灰塗婆羅門; but AMS^{T} *phyugs bdag pa: *pāśupata*, see 9.6). Finally, Buddhamati builds himself a fire, but as his wounds become more painful, he hurls himself from a cliff in desperation. A Brahmana who sees him becomes the first of "those who hurl [themselves] from cliffs, worshipping fire" (投巖事火; absent from AMS^{T}).[86]

---

84. AMS^{C} 541a20–24 (including 世間亦說我不食肉，彼等無我亦無不食肉；唯世尊法中有我決定不食肉。) Corresponding material in AMS^{T} (D.213, 198a3–4; Q.876, 205a8–b1) focuses only on the Buddha's teaching about vegetarianism, though does at the end of the ensuing myth acknowledge that the Buddha taught about the self (discussed below).

85. This Buddha has the curious name *Kosantabhadra: AMS^{T} D.213, 198a5; Q.879, 205b2: *ko san ta bzang po*; AMS^{C} 541a29: 拘孫陀跋陀羅.

86. See AMS^{C} 541a27–c3; also AMS^{T} D.213, 198b2–199a5; Q.879, 205b8–206b3. AMS^{T} in the final instance refers to "those who pursue suffering to the stage of being immovable/the unmoving ground" (*mi g.yo ba'i sar mya ngan du 'gro ba*)—still, in likelihood, reference to suicide. The final practice named in AMS^{C}—suicide over a precipice (*bhṛgupāta*)—is mentioned in a list of ascetical practices that the MPNMS explains are not proper to the Buddha's teaching; see MPNMS^{F} 882b19–c4; MPNMS^{D} 406a16–b6; MPNMS^{T} §364–365. On this practice described in Brahmanical literature, see Thakur 1963: 80–81.

For a Mahāyānist *sūtra* this is an uncommon degree of attention to non-Buddhist practices, all of which arise after misunderstandings about what is entailed in Buddhist dharma. But crucially the AMS uses the myth to make a subtly different point, much more in accordance with the explanation of the parable of the lost sword found in MPNMS-tg (2.5):

> In such a way, Mañjuśrī, all superior conducts and various kinds of deportments that are produced in the world are all emanated by the Tathāgata (**tathāgatanirmita*). When the dharma has disappeared, then such things appear. In this way the true dharma disappears.
>
> Likewise, Mañjuśrī, in regard to the true self, worldly beings [have] this-or-that distorted view and various false notions: namely, that liberation is like this-or-that, and that the self is like this-or-that. Those who pertain to what is supermundane also do not understand the cryptic teaching of the Tathāgata; they claim that the teaching of the Buddha is absence of self [and] reason in accord with it, just like in the origins of non-Buddhist systems [described above].[87] Those worldly beings accord with what is foolish, and those concerned with what is supermundane have lost understanding of the cryptic utterances [of the Buddha].[88]

This passage accepts that the Buddha indeed taught a doctrine of—explicitly—the self, and that this is once again the enigmatic content behind the Buddha's use of cryptic utterances (*yinfu zhijiao* 隱覆之教; *ldem po ngag*: **saṃdhābhāṣya*) that many within the sangha are not able (or ready) to grasp. There is no mention of the *tathāgatagarbha* or (*buddha*)*dhātu*, and yet the intended contrast must surely be between the Buddha's account of the self and notions of selfhood found in other systems. Moreover, and as we saw in the MPNMS, there is also a sense that non-Buddhist systems are somehow "creations" by the Buddha: not simply derivative of the dharma (as seems to be taught in the myth itself) but manifested by the Buddha for some strategic purpose. A similar idea is present elsewhere in the AMS, though mentioned only fleetingly. Aṅgulimāla reveals to the arhat Mahāmaudgalyāna that all "precepts and deportments" in the world—be they "worldly or supermundane"—were in fact taught by the Buddha.[89]

---

87. AMS^{T} elaborates that the error of holding the Buddha to have taught only that all things are not-self belongs to non-Buddhists (*mur 'dug*: Skt. *tīrthyas*); see D.213, 199b2; Q.879, 206b7.

88. AMS^{C} 541c7–c15: 如是文殊師利，世間一切所作之上尸羅、威儀，種種所作，一切悉是如來化現。法滅盡時，如是事生。若如是者，　正法則滅。如是文殊師利，於真實我，世間如是如是邪見諸異妄想：　謂解脱如是，　謂我如是。出世間者，亦不知如來隱覆之教：　謂言無我是佛所説，彼隨説思量，如外道因起[a]。彼諸世間隨順愚癡；出世間者，亦復迷失隱覆説智。

[a] Song/Yuan/Ming omit 起

Compare AMS^{T} D.213, 199a7–199b3; Q.879, 206b5–8.

89. AMS^{C} 529b27–28 (乃至世間有 / 隨順戒威儀 / 世間出世間 / 當知皆佛説). Compare AMS^{T} D.213, 164a2–3 Q.876, 171a7–8, which lists all "rites (*chos*), codes of conduct (*'thun pa'i*

Still this does not sit well with the content of the Buddhamati myth itself, in which erroneous teachings and practices occur not by the Buddha's design but due to human ignorance. The view that these things are somehow created by the Buddha appears only in the explanation of the myth, suggesting perhaps that the Buddhamati narrative was appropriated by the authors of the AMS, and is used to make a slightly different point: that non-Buddhist teachings and practices, including those that resemble the Buddha's own (about the self, vegetarianism, and so forth), originate in not only the activities (wrongly understood) but also the *purposes* of the Buddha.

Hence, both the MPNMS (in its parable about the lost sword; 2.5) and the AMS indebt non-Buddhist ideas and practices to the Buddha. This interpretation of the Buddhamati myth is referenced also by the tenth-century Mādhyamika author Bodhibhadra, who in his *Jñānasārasamuccaya-nibandhana* provides one of the few references to the AMS to survive in another originally Indian source.[90] Bodhibhadra cites the misfortunes of Buddhamati, and recognizes this story to belong to the AMS. He explains that apart from the different schools of Śrāvakayāna and Mahāyāna thought there are outsiders (*phyi rol pa: *bāhyaka*) who—quoting now the AMS—practice "worldly modes of conduct, behaviors and rites" that are all emanated by a Buddha (*sangs rgyas kyi sprul pa: *buddhanirmita*). The AMS states as much, Bodhibhadra concludes, "so that persons [of these traditions] might become objects of compassion."[91] In other words, Bodhibhadra understood the account of things produced by the Buddha in the AMS to promote compassion for persons following non-Buddhist ideas and practices who unknowingly participate in the Buddha's ongoing work to lead all sentient beings out of transmigration.

Returning to the myth as it appears in the AMS, a further line of its explanation requires special attention. The text concludes its discussion of the myth as follows: "Therefore the Tathāgata taught the middle path of the single vehicle (*ekayāna*), which is apart from the two extremes. He taught the self to be real, the Buddha to be real, the dharma to be real, the sangha to be real: hence is taught the middle way that is known as the Mahāyāna."[92] Here AMS^{C} refers to the notion of the single vehicle, which occurs several more times in the AMS and is better known as the pivotal

---

tshul khrims), injunctions (*cho ga*) and virtues (*yon tan*)" in the world as the Buddha's teachings.

90. For detail about this and other later citations of the AMS, see Kanō 2000: 77.

91. D.3852, 41a5–a7; Q.5252, 47b1–b5 (... *de dag snying rje'i yul du gyur pa'i phyir* ...).

92. AMS^{C} 541c15–17: 是故如來說一乘中道離於二邊： 我真實、佛真實、法真實、僧真實：是故說中道名摩訶衍。Compare AMS^{T} D.213, 199a7–199b4; Q.879, 206b5–207a1. AMS^{T} states that the Buddha teaches "the reality of the dharma, Tathāgata and sangha"; it omits mention of the self together with the three jewels. However, this material in AMS^{T} still states that the Buddha teaches the reality of the self (*bdag gi de kho na*). I am grateful to Kazuo Kanō for assistance with this difficult passage.

doctrine of the *Saddharmapuṇḍarīka* (SP).[93] We have acknowledged already that the MPNMS knew the SP by name (see 2.1), and we will see in the next chapter an even stronger influence of the SP upon the MBhS. In the final part of this study, we will return to the importance of teaching about the single vehicle in the early development of Buddha-nature thought (see 9.1), and consider further why the MPNMS and AMS in particular exhibit what is, for Mahāyāna *sūtra* literature, an uncommon interest in addressing the presence and status in the world of non-Buddhist systems and their ideas (9.6).

3.8 Conclusions

In spite of what may be expected of a text that uses the murderer Aṅgulimāla to teach an exposition about Buddha-nature, the AMS stops short of arguing that sentient beings are destined for awakening in spite of their past misdeeds.[94] Whereas its authors could have presented Aṅgulimāla as an ideal case in point—a being burdened by a history of violence and bloodshed, now seemingly devoted to the path of the bodhisattva—his past crimes are explained to be little more than illusions created by a being who is revealed, at the end of the *sūtra,* to be nothing other than an emanation by a Buddha.[95] Its authors' primary interests are otherwise to what we might prima facie assume, and its message one of assiduousness if the bodhisattva is to ever discover his "own nature" that has the qualities, already, of a Buddha.

The AMS inherits and develops ideas that we have seen already in the MPNMS, and continues to use the expressions *tathāgatagarbha* and *buddhadhātu* interchangeably. It refers frequently to simply "the *dhātu*": that which has the character of the Buddha but which is also essential or proper to "oneself" (**ātmadhātu* or **svadhātu*). This is, to all intents and purposes, an account of a self by another name: *dhātu* here stands for that which is permanent and indestructible in the constitution of a sentient being, for which the bodhisattva may search inside himself, and which—after much hardship—allows him to attain the status of a Buddha. The AMS contrasts Buddha-nature with erroneous notions of selfhood that must be rejected, but like the MPNMS also teaches about the *tathāgatagarbha* in relation to the bodies of sentient beings, though apart from all worldly activities in which they engage. Moreover—and again with echoes of the MPNMS—the AMS considers Buddha-nature to have been a cryptic teaching

93. See also AMS^{C} 532b8–12, in which the AMS teaches that the vehicles of the *śrāvaka* and *pratyekabuddha* are mere expediencies (compare AMS^{T} D.213, 169a6–7; Q.879.48, 176a8–b1).

94. The AMS takes steps to excuse Aṅgulimāla's crimes from the start: his killings are an act of obedience to a commandment issued by his teacher (e.g., AMS^{C} 512c9–19), and are elsewhere explained away as instructive illusions (see 3.1n9).

95. See AMS^{C} 543a7–b9; AMS^{T} D.213, 203b3–204b5; Q.879, 211a5–212a8. Regarding this Buddha's name, which suggests further ties between the AMS and SP; see 9.4.

by the Buddha: about a nature that is of a single kind (**ekadhātu*) with his own, which in each instance is the precious trace of a fully liberated being.

In summary, the foremost concern of the AMS is the sanctity of the internalized essence of the Buddha, no longer in the physical *stūpa* but somehow present "within" the body of a bodhisattva. In one instance the AMS tells us that teaching anyone who opposes the dharma is "to make an offer to one's own *dhātu* (**svadhātu*)";[96] whereas coming to harm as one tries to subjugate enemies of the dharma can be called "knowing the *tathāgatagarbha*."[97] Though the AMS exhibits caution in regard to calling this one's "self," it still generally agrees with the *ātmavādin* orientation of the MPNMS: Buddha-nature endures, somehow, about a sentient being's constitution, when all other notions of the self are negated, but because it is supermundane must be distinguished from notions of selfhood taught in non-Buddhist religious discourse. In part 3 of this volume we shall discuss further why both the MPNMS and AMS, as perhaps our two oldest sources for teachings about Buddha-nature, opted to articulate *tathāgatagarbha* in the openly contentious fashion that they do. But next we turn to the final text of the MPNMS-group, and of our *ātmavādin* sources for Buddha-nature teaching, which shows comparatively little caution in teaching that Buddhist dharma does indeed exhibit, at its culmination, an account of the self.

96. AMS^C 540c18–20: "則爲供養自界." Corresponding material in AMS^T (D.213, 197a2; Q.879, 204a7–8) concludes that this is done "to honor one's self" (*bdag la mchod pa*), or perhaps "to honor the Buddha" (who is speaking in this passage); see also 10.3.

97. AMS^C 540c20–21: 如自求畢竟樂, 棄捨、欲樂、衣、食、命、樂。如自ヵ害身, 而調伏彼: 是名善知如來之藏。Compare AMS^T D.213, 197a2–3; Q.879, 204a8–b1, where those who need to be subjugated are "wicked non-Buddhists (*skyon chags pa ya mtshan can* [Skt. *pāṣaṇḍas*])."

CHAPTER 4

The *Mahābherīhārakasūtra* and Liberation of the Self

4.1 The Text

The third *sūtra* of the MPNMS-group, and final *tathāgatagarbha* text that espouses an unquestionably *ātmavādin* form of Buddha-nature teaching, is the **Mahābherīhārakasūtra* (MBhS), or "the discourse of one who bears the great drum."[1] We have available two translations of the MBhS. The earlier is that into Chinese, again produced in the fifth century by Guṇabhadra (T.270: *Da fagu jing* 大法鼓經; henceforth MBhS^{C}). The second is a Tibetan translation produced in the ninth century by Vidyākaraprabha and the Tibetan dPal gyi lhun po (e.g., D.222; Q.888: *Rnga bo che chen po'i le'u zhes bya ba theg pa chen po'i mdo;* henceforth MBhS^{T}).[2] MBhS^{T} contains some material not present in MBhS^{C}, and otherwise our two versions differ in details when explaining that the culmination of the Buddha's teaching is his revelation of the *tathāgatagarbha* or, very frequently, the self.[3]

Little has been written about the MBhS: a number of articles by Takayasu Suzuki (e.g., 1997; 2000a; 2000b; 2002; 2014; 2015) and, as ever, an investigation by Takasaki (1974: 234–253). The longest treatment of the MBhS in any Western language is likely that by the present author (Jones 2016b) and concerns themes common to the MBhS and to the

1. Like the AMS, the title of the MBhS evokes an environment of violence or conflict: the Buddha compares this discourse to the beating of King Prasenajit's war drum, which when beaten reassures his troops but scatters enemies; similarly, those who oppose the Mahāyāna scatter when they hear it. The content of the *sūtra* is also referred to as the Buddha's "secret" (*mimi* 祕密; *gsang ba:* Skt. **guhya*); see MBhS^{C} 291a17–a21; MBhS^{T} D.222, 87b2–5; Q.888, 91b5–92a2: see also 9.2.

2. The translation and colophon to the Tibetan version of the text records the title *Mahābherīhārakaparivarta;* the Chinese translation, and the content of both versions, reflect instead *Mahābherīsūtra*.

3. Notably, material exclusive to MBhS^{T} states that the text can be considered a "*mahāsūtra*" (MBhS^{T} D.222, 113a4; Q.888, 118a7: *mdo chen po 'di*), much like both the MPNMS and AMS; see Habata 1994.

Anūnatvāpūrṇatvanirdeśaparivarta (AAN).[4] Both of these texts discuss the *tathāgatagarbha* in order to argue that there can be neither decrease nor increase in the totality of sentient beings or Buddhas, a similarity that gives the superficial impression of some debt between one *sūtra* and the other. However, if there was indeed such a debt (which is far from clear), then it is still the case that the MBhS reflects a response to this issue that is based on the form of the Buddha-nature idea found in the MPNMS, which is quite unlike how *tathāgatagarbha* is explained by the AAN (see 6.1).[5]

As mentioned in the previous chapter (3.1), both the AMS and MBhS refer to "the teacher of what is beneficial" (*anweishuozhe* 安慰説者; *phan pa[r] ston pa:* Skt. **hitopadeṣṭṛ*), attention to which has led Suzuki to argue that the MBhS is the later of these two works. In the MBhS the expression **hitopadeṣṭṛ* appears frequently and designates someone who preserves and recites the MBhS specifically, suffering rebuke from audiences that do not accept it.[6] Suzuki infers that by the time of the composition of the MBhS **hitopadeṣṭṛ* had been accepted as a technical expression—a variation on the idea of the preacher of the dharma (*dharmabhāṇaka*)—that was cemented after the AMS, in which it was used more broadly for a promulgator of teachings about *tathāgatagarbha.* There is little other evidence to conclude that the AMS is necessarily the earlier text of these two, other than the fact that the AMS seems to inherit more ideas and motifs from the MPNMS than does the MBhS.

There is virtually no mention of the MBhS in any other Indian source that is available to us.[7] One reason for this may have been that its account of the *tathāgatagarbha* as a teaching about the self appears to be more provocative than what is found in either the MPNMS or AMS. Otherwise the MBhS also lacks any teaching about vegetarianism, for which these other two texts were better remembered. Concerning Buddha-nature, the MBhS takes a hard line regarding the relative status of earlier Buddhist texts with which its content appears to jar, and declares that teachings about emptiness (*śūnyatā*) must be understood as "intentional" (*ābhiprāyika*) or of provisional meaning (*neyārtha*), so require further explanation.[8] Hence the MBhS preserves for us a challenging conclusion to the Buddha-nature idea developed across the MPNMS-group of texts: a model of sentient beings that has some aspect of them transmigrate endlessly until they are released from the afflictions that bind them to perpetual rebirth, and that makes

4. An English translation of MBhS^{C} is that of Rulu (2016): see 3.1n1. A short description of the MBhS, based on its Tibetan translation, is Brunnhölzl 2014: 23–24.

5. For an alternative perspective, see T. Suzuki 2002, and—in passing—Silk 2015b: 50.

6. See T. Suzuki 2000b; also 2.1.

7. The MBhS is mentioned, together with the AMS, in Bodhibhadra's tenth-century *Jñānasārasamuccaya-nibandhana;* see D.3852, 29a3; Q.5252, 32a7–8.

8. See T. Suzuki 2000a; there are also reflections on this material in Dol po pa's RC (Hopkins 2006: 126–128). Regarding "intentional" and "provisional" teachings, see Ruegg 2004: 37–38.

precious little recourse to more established Buddhist teachings such as the dependent or conditioned nature of phenomena, or otherwise their fundamental "emptiness."

Another striking feature of the MBhS is its reproduction of content better known from the *Saddharmapuṇḍarīka* (SP). Influence of the SP is apparent across the MPNMS-group (see 9.1), though never as clear as in the case of the MBhS, which reproduces from the SP the now well-known parables of the lost son and of the magically conjured city.[9] The MBhS also makes repeated reference to the idea of the single vehicle (*ekayāna*) and MBhS^{C} explicitly addresses how this teaching relates to the *tathāgatagarbha:* "If all sentient beings have the *tathāgatagarbha*—that is a single essence, a single vehicle—then why does the Tathāgata say that there are three vehicles: of the *śrāvaka*s (i.e., Śrāvakayāna), *pratyekabuddhas* and the Buddhas (i.e., Mahāyāna)?"[10] Otherwise the MBhS exhibits strong Buddhological ties to both the SP and the MPNMS. While the AMS may have developed the account of *tathāgatagarbha* found in the MPNMS, it does not devote as much attention to the other core theme of its predecessor: the permanence of the Buddha apart from his apparent *parinirvāṇa.* Whereas the AMS uses the language of secrecy and revelation with regard to *tathāgatagarbha,* the MBhS believes that what is taught cryptically by the Buddha's pronouncements (*yinfushuo* 隱覆説; *dgongs pa'i tshig:* Skt. **sandhāvacana*)—much like in MPNMS-dhk—is the permanence of the Buddha apart from the death of his physical body: "The cryptic teaching is that while it is said that the Tathāgata has completely passed over into *nirvāṇa,* in reality the Tathāgata is permanent and not subject to destruction: *parinirvāṇa* is not characterized by annihilation."[11] We shall see that the central affirmation of the MBhS is that buddhahood constitutes a kind of enduring, pleasant existence. This, its authors contend, is in opposition to what they believe was understood by *sūtra*s that taught emptiness (*śūnyatā*). What is paramount to the MBhS is that the Buddha be understood as not only a permanently existing being but also one who enjoys true freedom from transmigration, and superlative influence over the world that he appeared to leave behind. As much as the Buddha himself can be considered a kind of permanent, awakened

---

9. T. Suzuki 2015; also T. Suzuki 2002: see also 4.5. Early in the MBhS a large portion of the Buddha's audience, who are not yet capable of accepting teachings about *tathāgatagarbha,* leave before he begins teaching, reminiscent of an episode early in the SP (38.12–39.6; also Kern 1884: 38–39).

10. MBhS^{C} 297b20–22: 若一切眾生有如來藏，一性、一乘者，如來何故説有三乘聲聞乘、緣覺乘、佛乘? Compare also MBhS^{T}: D.222, 106a7–106b1; Q.888, 111a1. MBhS^{T} asks only "Why has the Buddha taught the existence of three vehicles?," though agreement with the *ekayāna* position is evident throughout the rest of the text. Elsewhere MBhS^{T} understands itself to be "a *mahāsūtra* in which is taught the single vehicle" (MBhS^{T} D.222, 113a4; Q.888, 118a7: *mdo chen po 'di*).

11. MBhS^{C} 291a29–b1: 隱覆説者，謂言如來畢竟涅槃，而實如來常住不滅；般涅槃者非毀壞法。MBhS^{T} (D.222, 88a3–4; Q.888, 92a6–7) clearly lists four separate qualities (*rtag pa, brtan pa, zhi ba, ther zug pa;* Skt. *nitya, dhruva, śiva, śāśvata;* see also 5.2).

subject, so too must the Buddha-nature of sentient beings be considered their true self, their *ātman,* which might someday know this same liberated state.

4.2 Continuity of the Self

The MBhS presents the core of its *tathāgatagarbha* teaching through a series of concise similes, which are stylistically more reminiscent of what we find in the *Tathāgatagarbhasūtra* (TGS) than the lengthier similes or parables that dominate the MPNMS and AMS.[12] Four similes of the MBhS are introduced as explanations of what the Indian text likely called *tathāgatagarbha* (*fozang* 佛藏; but MBhS^{T} *snying po*: simply Skt. **garbha*). Both versions also refer to the subject of these similes as "the *dhātu* of sentient beings" (*zhongshengjie* 眾生界; *sems can gyi khams: sattvadhātu*). The same expression is used at the end of these similes; the Buddha concludes, "Just as I have the nature of all sentient beings (*sattvadhātu*), know that all sentient beings are like that: the nature of all sentient beings is limitless and radiant."[13] Although MBhS^{C} translates this *sattvadhātu* as the "realm" (*jie* 界) of sentient beings (a slippery feature of AMS^{C} also; see 3.6), the similes themselves seem to concern more simply the "essence" of a Buddha hidden in all sentient beings, in accordance with what is taught in the MPNMS.[14]

The last three of these four similes are illuminating but do not present *tathāgatagarbha* teaching in terms of selfhood, and can be discussed with some brevity. The second of the set compares the *tathāgatagarbha* to a moon concealed by cloud, an example found also in the AMS;[15] like the clouds, afflictions cover the nature of a Tathāgata (如來性) so that it remains impure.[16] The third example emphasizes the need for diligence if one is to make manifest the awakened qualities of a Buddha. A person digging for water continues to work until the hard earth gives way to mud and, in time, water. Similarly, one must dig out "the earth of afflictions" to find their Buddha-nature (如來性; but MBhS^{T} *de bzhin gshegs pa'i snying po: tathāgatagarbha*).[17] The fourth simile compares the *tathāgatagarbha* to a lamp in a jar, again echoing an image found also in the AMS.[18] As long as the lamp remains concealed, it is of no benefit to anyone; the *tathāgatagarbha* (MBhS^{C} exhibits

12. These are quoted in both Dol po pa's RC (Hopkins 2006: 150–151) and Bu ston's DzG (Ruegg 1973: 78–81).

13. MBhS^{C} 297b18–20: 如我有眾生界，當知一切眾生，皆亦如是。彼眾生界無邊明淨[a]。

[a] T 明淨= Song/Yuan/Ming/Palace 淨明

Compare MBhS^{T} D.222, 111a5; Q.888, 114a4.

14. This is in contrast to slippery wordplay concerning *dhātu* exhibited by the AAN; see 6.1.

15. AMS^{C} 526b29–c23.

16. MBhS^{C} 297b7–9; MBhS^{T} D.222, 110b5–6; Q.888, 115b4–115b6.

17. MBhS^{C} 297b9–12; MBhS^{T} D.222, 110b6–111a2; Q.888, 115b6–8. This is also reminiscent of an example used in the tenth chapter of the SP (233–234; Kern 1884: 221–222).

18. MBhS^{C} 297b12–17; MBhS^{T} D.222, 111a2–4; Q.888, 115b8–116a4.

both 如來藏 and 如來性), once its sheath of afflictions has been destroyed, presents to the world the qualities and activities of a Buddha, which are for the benefit of all sentient beings. The focus is on the unrealized potential of all sentient beings; once their afflictions are cleared away, what remains is a Buddha who can continue to lead all sentient beings toward the same goal.

However, it is the sequentially first of these four similes that warrants special attention. It is only in this first example that the *tathāgatagarbha* is explicitly referred to as the self.[19] A patient suffers poor vision due to the influence of some eye disease—removable, like a cataract—and suffers as long as no doctor is found to treat him. When a doctor is found, the patient's sight can be improved. Our two translations of this passage differ, of which MBhS[T] is the most coherent:

> Likewise, this essence (*khams: dhātu*) is concealed by a sheath of ten million afflictions. So long as one delights in *śrāvaka*s and *pratyekabuddha*s, the self is not the self, and there are [notions of] "I" and "mine." When one delights in the exalted Buddhas, the self becomes the [true] self, and after that a person is able to be treated.
>
> Afflictions should be thought of as being like the cloudy vision due to the yellow and blue cataracts of that person's diseased eye; the *tathāgatagarbha* is like the eye that continues to exist [either side of its affliction].[20]

Corresponding material in MBhS[C] is problematic; it groups Buddhas, *śrāvaka*s, and *pratyekabuddha*s together as persons who can lead someone to the true self.[21] This suggests an unusual generosity to *śrāvaka*s and *pratyekabuddha*s, which is not in keeping with the rest of the text (nor the opinion of Indian Mahāyānist literature in general, in which the *śrāvaka* and *pratyekabuddha* are more often objects of ridicule). MBhS[C] also omits the sense that encountering a Buddha makes someone "treatable" (*bsgrub tu rung ba;* Skt. **sādhya*). But both versions agree that there is what is erroneously taken to be either "I" or "mine" (*ātman, ātmanīya*), and apart from this is what MBhS[C] calls the "true self" (*zhenwo* 真我). Here we find no clear sense

19. A simile involving eye surgery is found also in the MPNMS, though in that context it explains how sentient beings other than tenth-stage bodhisattvas are incapable of perceiving the *tathāgatagarbha;* see 2.3.

20. MBhS[T] D.222, 110b3–5; Q.888, 115b2–4: *de bzhin du nyon mongs pa bye ba'i spubs kyis khebs pa'i khams 'di ji srid du nyan thos dang / rang sangs rgyas rnams la dga' bar byed pa de srid du bdag ni bdag ma yin par 'gyur zhing bdag gi bdag tu 'gyur ro // gang gi tshe sangs rgyas bcom ldan 'das rnams la dga' bar gyur pa de'i tshe bdag tu 'gyur zhing de'i 'og tu bsgrub tu rung ba'i mir 'gyur ro // mi de'i mig nad ling tog ser po dang sngon po'i rab rib gang yin pa ltar nyon mongs pa rnams blta bar bya'o // de bzhin gshegs pa'i snying po ni mig bzhin du nges par yod do //*

21. MBhS[C] 297b4–7: 如是無量煩惱藏翳障如來性。乃至未遇諸佛、聲聞、緣覺， 計我非我，我所為我。若遇諸佛、聲聞、緣覺， 乃知真我。如治病愈其目開明。翳者[a]， 謂諸煩惱；眼者謂如來性。

[a] T 翳者 = Palace 不翳

that this Buddha-nature is something "within" sentient beings—as expressed by both the MPNMS and AMS—but certainly what is otherwise called *tathāgatagarbha* constitutes one's self that is somehow hidden where it has always been, and is of great value.

The end of this simile communicates that the *tathāgatagarbha,* or the self, is that which survives between a state of affliction and into its true mode of being apart from obscuration or obstruction. But the MBhS also provides something irregular for the MPNMS-group: a systematic argument for the necessity of the self, if indeed sentient beings can all, in theory, achieve the status of a Buddha.

This is introduced by what at first seems to be a laudation of the Buddha but which invites important implications about the status of sentient beings in general: "The Tathāgata is a god among gods. If *parinirvāṇa* is complete annihilation, the world would be [gradually] destroyed; if it is not annihilation, then it is lasting and tranquil. Since it is lasting and tranquil, then certainly there exists a self, just as smoke means there is fire."[22] MBhS^{T} confirms that the Indian text described *parinirvāṇa* as both lasting (*brtan pa: dhruva*) and tranquil (*zhi ba: śiva*); because it exhibits these qualities, we are told, there must exist a self.[23] The logic is quite clear: if *nirvāṇa* refers to a state of being (and so is not "annihilation"; see 4.3, below), then something of the sentient being must endure after liberation and enjoy its benefits. While the AMS contends that Buddha-nature must exist in order for liberation to be possible (see 3.5), the MBhS reflects at greater length on the absurdity of there being no self if liberation is indeed the permanent, pleasant mode of existence enjoyed by a Buddha. Its further argument is somewhat terse, and our clearer account is that preserved in MBhS^{C}:

> If there was [first] no self, and [then] there existed a self, then the world would increase in content [which is untenable].
>
> In reality there is a self, which negates the [principle of] absence of self, and also cannot be destroyed.
>
> If in reality there were no self, the self would not be established [as it just has been, above].[24]

Bracketed between two reductio-style arguments we find the position of the MBhS: that there does indeed exist a self, which can be neither created nor destroyed, and which stands in opposition to the teaching that all things should be considered "not-self." We will see below that the MBhS takes the bold step of relegating teachings about absence of self to only

22. MBhS^{C} 296c23–26: 如來是天中之天。若般涅槃悉磨滅者， 世間應滅。若不滅者， 則常住安樂。常住安樂，則必有我， 如煙有火。

23. MBhS^{T} D.222, 109a7–b1; Q.888, 114a4–6. Zimmermann (2002: 81) detects a similar line of thinking in two similes of the TGS (numbers 6 and 8; see 6.2).

24. MBhS^{C} 296c26–c27: 若復無我而有我者， 世間應滿。實有我非無我亦不壞。若實無我，我則不成。 Compare MBhS^{T} D.222, 109b1–2; Q.888, 114a5–6.

provisional status, deployed by the Buddha in anticipation of his later revelation about the self that is the enjoyer of liberation (see 4.3). Otherwise this passage highlights a central premise at the heart of our *ātmavāda tathāgatagarbha* sources: if the liberation of a Buddha constitutes realization of what can be called the self (taught already by MPNMS-dhk; see 2.2), this cannot refer to something that comes into existence or is created (so must be *asaṃskṛta;* see also 10.2), and must have always been apart from the world of cause and effect.

Each "self" must then pertain to an entity that exists, without beginning, and waits for the achievement of liberation. This is how the MBhS proceeds: first defining what is meant by "a being" (*you* 有; MBhS[T] *mchis pa* but also *yod pa:* Skt. **bhava?*), and clarifying—in terminology familiar from the MPNMS (see 2.3–4)—that this refers to entities that are subject to twenty-five forms of existence.[25] These transmigrating entities can be contrasted with "non-beings" that are not in possession of a mind (*wusi zhiwu* 無思之物; *sems pa med pa*) and which make up the rest of conditioned existence. These two categories, we are told, are of fundamentally different natures:

> "Non-being" means an entity without a mind.
>
> If a non-being were [to become] a sentient being, then that [sentient being] must come [into being] from elsewhere [which is untenable]. If entities with minds are destroyed, then sentient beings would decrease [in the world, which is untenable]. If non-beings were [to become] sentient beings, they would fill up [the world, by increase, which is untenable].
>
> Because sentient beings do not come into existence, nor are they destroyed, [their number] neither decreases not increases.[26]

MBhS[T] concludes that "these two (i.e., beings and non-beings) do not arise and are not destroyed." What are called non-beings are certainly still existing entities, but they are qualitatively different from sentient beings, who cannot cease to exist and so have something about themselves that endures: their self, or otherwise the nature of a Buddha.

As I have argued elsewhere, this discussion of neither decrease nor increase in the totality of existing beings is markedly different from what we find in the superficially similar AAN.[27] Such differences are important, as they are indicative of two distinct understandings of Buddha-nature teaching. The account of the MBhS is quite radical: *tathāgatagarbha* is a designator for an entity possessed by sentient beings, otherwise some essence (*dhātu*) that has the qualities of the Buddha, and can otherwise be called the self.

---

25. MBhS[C] 296c28–29; MBhS[T] D.222, 109b2; Q.888, 114a6–7.

26. MBhS[C] 296c29–297a3: 非有者，無思之物。若非有是眾生者， 應從他來。設有思之物壞者， 眾生當滅。若[a]非有是眾生者， 則應充滿。以眾生不生不壞故， 不減不滿。

[a] T若 = Yuan/Ming 不壞

Compare MBhS[T] D.222, 109b2–4; Q.888, 114a7–b1.

27. Jones 2016b: 75–79.

Selves appear to be discrete (and innumerable) entities, each of which can work to end their bondage to the process of transmigration. Unlike in the metaphysically sophisticated AAN—in which Buddha-nature is identified with a single underlying basis for the existence of sentient beings and Buddhas alike (see 6.1)—the MBhS teaches the indestructibility of something proper to each individual sentient being: something that can be called the self. All of which, as we saw above, is because Buddhas are understood to enjoy a state of being that is permanent, pleasant, and—as "god among gods"—characterized by tremendous power.

4.3 The Sovereign Self

The idea that the Buddha embodies superlative freedom or power is integral to the Buddhology of the MBhS, and so also to its account of *tathāgatagarbha*.[28] On occasion this is explained by what seems to have been the expression **aiśvarya,* or "sovereignty" (present where MBhS^{C} *zizai* 自在 corresponds to MBhS^{T} *dbang phyug*),[29] and elsewhere some or other form of the Indic **vaśa/vaśitā*, or "power." To explore this theme, it is worth following the trajectory of the MBhS as it explains the extent of the Buddha's power, and how this relates to the status of sentient beings who are all, for the time being, bound to transmigration.

Earlier Buddhist sources concerned with teaching about *anātman* argued that there is nothing that deserves to be considered the self because sentient beings lack power over the conditions of their existence. Indeed, the Buddha's first argument in the *Anattalakkhaṇasutta*—held to be his earliest teaching on this matter (see 1.1)—is that one cannot will one's physical form, sensations, or otherwise to be other than they are or will be, with the consequence that none of the five "heaps" of experience (*skandha*s) can be home to something worthy of calling the self. Other early discourses, such as the *Cūḷasaccakasutta* (MN.I.231–232), state that this can be explained in terms of a lack of power (*vaśa*) over the constituents of one's existence, a sure sign that there is nothing present that warrants consideration as the self. Other *tathāgatagarbha* sources—both the *Śrīmālādevīsiṃhanādasūtra* (ŚDS) and AAN—use the expression *aiśvarya* in reference to the power of Buddhas and bodhisattvas.[30] But what is unique to the MBhS is a preoccupation with this power in contrast to the impotence of sentient beings as

28. See also, on this same topic, T. Suzuki 1997.

29. A relevant Sanskrit parallel to this usage is found in the RGVV (Johnston [1950] 1991: 32.11–12): *sarvatra paramadharmaiśvaryavibhūtvasaṃdarśanād ākāśadhātuparyavasānaḥ*. A passage quoting the AAN preserves another occurrence, which refers to the Buddha's "sovereign power over all *dharmas*" (ibid., 41.4–5: *sarvadharmaiśvaryabalatāmadhigatas*). See also Lamotte 1944: 392.

30. For example, in the ŚDS, where our Tibetan version exhibits *dbang 'phyug* (e.g., Tsukinowa 1940: 10.2, 104.16; see 5.1); or in the AAN (Silk 2015b: 108 [§15i]). See also note 29 above.

they suffer through transmigration: "As long as sentient beings transmigrate through birth and death, the self is not sovereign: hence, for [those beings] I teach absence of self. But the *mahāparinirvāṇa* that is attained by Buddhas is lasting and tranquil. For this reason, I wipe out both annihilationism and eternalism."[31] In corresponding material MBhS^T makes no mention of sovereignty but instead states that transmigration goes hand in hand with preoccupation with the (worldly) self (*bdag 'jug pa*).[32] But both versions state that *anātman* is taught in order to undermine views of annihilation (*ucchedavāda*) and eternalism (*śāśvatavāda*), the conceptual Scylla and Charybdis avoided by earlier Buddhist teaching. The authors of the MBhS attempt to sail a precarious course between these two positions, and arguably do not manage to avoid promoting what would have likely been received as a form of eternalism: the view that transmigration, and liberation from it, entails the enduring existence of some entity. Elsewhere, the MBhS defends its teaching that there must indeed be something about sentient beings that endures into liberation:

> Kāśyapa said to the Buddha: Lord, if [sentient beings] attain liberation and sovereignty, one should know that sentient beings certainly ought to have permanence. For example, when one sees smoke one knows that there is necessarily fire. If there exists a self, there must be liberation. If it is taught that there is a self, this explains that liberation has some form; this is not the worldly view of a self, nor either annihilationism or eternalism.[33]

The MBhS invests a great deal in the idea of liberation "having a form" (*youse* 有色; *gzugs dang bcas pa: *rūpavat*), which we will explore further below (4.6). For now it is sufficient to conclude that for the authors of the MBhS, liberation is anything but an end to existence; it is the continuation of what is proper to a sentient being, avoiding—at least by their own testimony—the conceptual pitfalls of annihilationism and eternalism.

In what fashion, then, does a Buddha exist? The MBhS shows very clearly that it commits to the same form of docetic Buddhology encountered in MPNMS-dhk (see 2.2): that the Buddha's activities were displayed

---

31. MBhS^C 296b22–b24: 乃至眾生輪迴生死, 我不[a]自在。是故我為說無我義。然諸佛所得大般涅槃常住安樂。以是義故, 壞彼斷常。

[a] T我不 = Song/Yuan/Ming/Palace 不得

32. See MBhS^T: D.222, 108b1–2; Q.888, 113a5–6. The unusual expression *bdag 'jug pa* appears in the Tibetan translation of the *Ugraparipṛcchā*(*sūtra*) (e.g., D.63, 266b6; Q.760[19]308a8), in which it seems to mean interest in what is proper to one's self, and in the earlier of two Chinese translations of that text (T.322[12]18b4–5) corresponds to *hu* 護, a "desire" or "hankering" for the self.

33. MBhS^C 296c8–11: 迦葉白佛言: 世尊, 得解脱自在者, 當知眾生必應有常。譬如見煙, 必知有火。若有我者, 必有解脱。若説有我, 則為已説解脱有色。非世俗身見, 亦非説斷常。Compare MBhS^T D.222, 108b7–109a1; Q.888, 113b3–5.

"in conformity with the world" (*lokānuvartana*), whereas his true nature abides beyond whatever has been seen of him.

> Kāśyapa said to the Buddha: Lord, why is it that while the Tathāgata does not attain *nirvāṇa,* he displays his *nirvāṇa;* while not being born, he displays his birth?
>
> The Buddha replied to Kāśyapa: For [the purpose of] destroying the notion of permanence on the part of sentient beings, the Tathāgata displays *nirvāṇa* without attaining it, and shows birth while having not being born. Why is this? Sentient beings say that "even the Buddha had a demise, and does not attain sovereignty;"[34] how much worse off are we, who have [erroneous notions of] "I" and of "mine"?[35]

So power or "sovereignty" is that which the Buddha *appeared* to lack, hence the perceived inevitability of his own death. However, it is precisely his transcendent power that allows the Buddha to make a show—in conformity with the needs of his audience—of his birth, life, and bodily demise. A couple of similes explain this further, one of which remains focused on the benefits of the Buddha making a display of his mortality:

> It is like a man pursued by a robber—with blade raised and wanting to do harm—who thinks: "I am powerless to avoid this death!" To avoid such things as the various sufferings of birth, old age, sickness, and death, sentient beings think: "I resolve to become Indra or Brahmā!" In order to eradicate such thoughts, the Tathāgata displayed [his own] death.[36]

The perception of the MBhS is that sentient beings, frightened by the ubiquity of suffering, might wish to become deities with whom they associate freedom from death.[37] The Indic term *aiśvarya* shares a root with *īśvara,* an epithet for gods (*deva*s) such as those named above; to be *īśvara*—in the manner of illustrious figures such as Indra or Brahmā—is to possess *aiśvarya.* Of course, this is not how the status of these deities was commonly

34. In place of 自在 (**aiśvarya*), MBhS^{T} has the unusual expression *bdag gi dbang,* "the power of the self," or "my/one's own power" (Skt. **ātmavaśa*?).

35. MBhS^{C} 296c12–16: 迦葉復白佛言：世尊，云何如來不般涅槃示般涅槃，不生示生？佛告迦葉：為壞眾生計常想故，如來不般涅槃示般涅槃，不生示生。所以者何？眾生謂：「佛尚有終沒[a]不得自在，何況我等有我我所」？

[a] T 沒 = Song/Yuan/Ming/Palace 歿

Compare MBhS^{T} D.222, 109a1–3; Q.888, 113b5–8.

36. MBhS^{C} 296c20–c23: 譬如有人為賊所逐，擧刀欲害，作是思惟：「我今無力當得免[a]此死難」。以不如是生老病死種種眾苦成就眾生思想：「願作帝釋梵王」。如來為壞彼思想故示現有死。

[a] T 免 = Palace 勉

Compare MBhS^{T}: D.222, 109a5–7; Q.888, 114a1–4.

37. Comparison of the *skandha*s to murderers, communicating the lack of influence that one has over them, is found already in the Pāli *Suttapiṭaka*; for example, the *Yamakasutta* (SN.III.114–142).

understood by Indian Buddhism: the gods whom ignorant persons considered to be "sovereign," beyond the grasp of birth and death, are no more outside of the cycle of transmigration than any other sentient being. To rectify the misplaced aspirations of sentient beings, the Buddha displayed that even he is subject to death, despite in actuality being both permanent and having true, sovereign power over the conditions of his existence.

In a further simile, the MBhS suggests that this power of a Buddha is not something that sentient beings eventually produce but is that which can be "discovered" if only they were to attend to, and properly comprehend, their circumstances. "For example, it is as if a king were captured by a neighboring kingdom, and bound up in chains, and should then think: 'Am I still a king; am I still a lord? I am neither!' What is the cause of his trouble? It is due to negligence. Likewise, as long as sentient beings wander through transmigration, the self lacks sovereignty; because it lacks sovereignty, [the Buddha] teaches the doctrine of absence of self."[38] In corresponding material MBhS^{T} concludes that sentient beings transmigrate "saying 'I,' or 'having a view of the self' "; hence the Buddha taught about absence of self.[39] Again the subject of the simile is a figure who supposedly exhibits sovereignty, but here the king *should* enjoy power were it not for the predicament in which he currently finds himself. Sentient beings do not enjoy the status of a Buddha, but this is not proper to their true nature; liberation, in short, can be imagined as the process of freeing the sovereign individual (or what is essential to them) from a state of frustrating, but unessential, imprisonment. Moreover, we can infer that the MBhS takes teaching about not-self to be a kind of expediency, taught by the Buddha to highlight the lack of power sentient beings exhibit while in transmigration, but not applicable to the true self that is their enduring Buddha-nature.

4.4 Buddha-nature and Buddhist Practice

In the simile just discussed, the king's imprisonment is attributed to his negligence (*pramāda*). We have seen the AMS also identify negligence as the reason why sentient beings do not enjoy the status of a Buddha, akin to an ascetic who is distracted from his practice (see 3.5). Whereas the MPNMS reads like a justification for belief in the existence of Buddha-nature (or otherwise acceptance of this as the Buddha's newly revealed teaching about the self), both the AMS and MBhS stress that this does not mean that liberation is assured, and should still be pursued with the assiduous diligence expected of a bodhisattva.

38. MBhS^{C} 296c16–20: 譬如有王為隣國所執繫縛枷鎖作是思惟:「我今復是王是主耶? 我今非王非主」何縁乃致如是諸難? 由放逸故。如是眾生乃至生死輪迴, 我不自在。不自在故, 説無我義。

39. MBhS^{T} D.222, 109a3–5; Q.888, 113b8–114a1: *nga ni bdag go zhes bdag tu lta ste / bdag med par lta ba'i don yin no.*

Discussion of this matter in MBhS^{C} begins when the Buddha's interlocutor, the arhat Kāśyapa, asks how the self first becomes associated with the afflictions that obscure it.[40] The Buddha responds with the example of a goldsmith who observes impurities in some gold, and who desires "the element of gold" from it (*jinxing* 金性; *gser gyi dbyings: *suvarṇadhātu*). Though the simile is presented as an exposition of "the self," our translations suggest that the Indic MBhS must have evoked the (*buddha*)*dhātu*—an "essence" or "element"—specifically. We read that even if the goldsmith searches his whole life, he will not find the source of the gold's impurities; he must simply work to remove them.[41]

> Likewise, regarding the self, there arise adventitious afflictions. If someone who wishes to see the self thinks: "Now I should look for the self, and the root of defilement," would that person find their origins or not?
>
> Kāśyapa said to the Buddha: No, Lord!
>
> The Buddha said to Kāśyapa: If with diligence one removes the dirt of afflictions, then one will obtain the self. Hearing *sūtra*s such as this, believing and rejoicing deeply [in them], being neither sluggish nor hurried, being very skilled in one's methods, attending to the three modes of action [i.e., of body, speech, and mind]: by these causes and conditions one obtains the self.[42]

Here the self—like the "essence" (*dhātu*) of the gold—is an achievement: it is that which is realized at the attainment of liberation, obtained by the bodhisattva's perseverance in his practice. The MBhS teaches that afflictions adventitious to the self should not be pondered further, and that sentient beings must only work diligently toward their eradication.

This thought is developed in a further simile. Kāśyapa asks why sentient beings cannot perceive the self.[43] The Buddha responds with the example

40. MBhS^{C} 297a3–a5: 世尊，若有我者，云何生彼煩惱諸垢？佛告迦葉：善哉善哉，應以是問。Notably MBhS^{T} (D.222, 109b4–5; Q.888, 114b1) instead asks, "How does one know that the self exists?," to which the Buddha responds that this "must not be asked." The question about the origin of afflictions appears slightly later in MBhS^{T} (see note 43 below), at a point that makes considerably less sense (given the Buddha's response): I therefore follow the trajectory of MBhS^{C}.

41. The import of the simile is reminiscent of the better-known parable of the man shot with an arrow, found in the *Cūḷamāluṅkyasutta* (MN.I.426). In both instances, the Buddha discourages speculation on metaphysical issues—such as the nature of the self—that distract from the practical pursuit of liberation.

42. MBhS^{C} 297a10–a16: 如是我者，生客煩惱。欲見我者，作是思惟：「今當推尋我及垢本」，彼人云何為得本不？迦葉白佛言：不也世尊。佛告迦葉：若勤方便除煩惱垢，爾乃得我。謂聞如是比[a]經，深心信樂，不緩不急，善巧方便，專精三業，以是因緣爾乃得我。

[a] T 比=Ming 此

Compare MBhS^{T} D.222, 109b7–110a2; Q.888, 114b4–7.

43. MBhS^{C} 297a17: 迦葉復白佛言：世尊，若有我者，何故不見？MBhS^{T} here has Kāśyapa ask about the origin of afflictions; see note 40 above.

of a teacher of language who instructs impetuous students to learn by rote the "linguistic roots" (*zijujie* 字句界; *skad kyi dbyings:* *[*akṣara*]*dhātu?*) of their language: an image that again likely reflects use of the Indic *dhātu* specifically.[44] The teacher's students are interested only in the meanings of these linguistic roots, which he reveals only after the hard graft of learning the roots has been accomplished.

> Likewise, I now say for the benefit of sentient beings who are covered by afflictions: "Good sons! The *tathāgatagarbha* is like this, or like that." Those who desire to see it, do they then see it?
>
> Kāśyapa replied: No, Lord.
>
> The Buddha said to Kāśyapa: Just as one does not understand the meaning of linguistic roots, and should rely upon a teacher, likewise, Kāśyapa, know that the Tathāgata is one who speaks truly, by true speech teaching that there are sentient beings. You will understand later, like one who has accomplished their studies.[45]

What is most perplexing in the final lines of this passage, and represented in both translations, is the claim that sentient beings (*sattva*s) themselves exist.[46] This introduces arguments for the continuity, and indeed necessity, of the self—discussed above (4.2)—which concern the identity between sentient beings and, in time, liberated Buddhas. The guarantor for this is indeed some manner of "existent" or otherwise an enduring "nature": that which is otherwise known by the expression *tathāgatagarbha,* and which constitutes the Buddha's account of the self.

4.5 Self, Not-Self, and Emptiness

Whereas both the MPNMS and AMS evince that the ideas they expound were not well received, the MBhS adopts what seems to be a more combative stance against more established Buddhist thinking. It reminds its audience that there are many who reject *sūtra*s that explain the *tathāgatagarbha,* and who instead focus on texts that expound teachings about the emptiness of all phenomena. More striking still, the MBhS states that *sūtra*s which espouse emptiness do so with some special intention (*youyushuo* 有餘説, literally "needing further explanation"; but MBhS^{T} *dgongs pa can: ābhiprāyika*),

---

44. See Scharfe 1977: 83–85.

45. MBhS^{C} 297a22–27: 如是我今為煩惱藏所覆眾生說言: 「善男子, 如來藏如是如是」, 彼便欲見當得見不? 迦葉白言: 不也世尊。佛告迦葉: 如彼不知界成句義, 當緣師信, 如是迦葉, 當知如來是誠實語者, 以誠實語說有眾生。汝後當知, 如彼學成。 Compare MBhS^{T} D.222, 110a2–7; Q.888, 114b8–115a6. This is reminiscent also of an example found in the MPNMS (MPNMS^{F} 872a28–b7; MPNMS^{D} 390c15–c24; MPNMS^{T} §221–222), although there it is grammar (Skt. **vyākaraṇa*) that follows a child's education in written characters.

46. MBhS^{T} (D.222, 110a6–7; Q.888, 115a5–6): *sems can yod pa nyid do zhes gsung na yang rig par byos shig.*

and that the MBhS itself reflects the Buddha's "supreme teaching" (*wushangshuo* 無上説; *bla na med pa'i mdo: *anuttarasūtra*) that concerns the permanence of the Buddha and of Buddha-nature.[47]

In some instances the MBhS celebrates the diversity of the Buddha's teaching; he is compared to King Prasenajit, who at an annual feast offers his guests meals that accord with their specific appetites[48]: "The exalted Buddhas do likewise: in accord with the various inclinations of sentient beings, they expound for them various teachings."[49] The MBhS accepts that the Buddha uses different teachings for different audiences, but some teachings are still more definitive than others. Apart from declaring that the three vehicles are in fact only one (see 4.1), the MBhS follows the SP by employing the examples of the lost son and of the magically conjured city, in which followers of the vehicles of the *śrāvakas* and *pratyekabuddhas* are reassured that they are all "true sons of the Buddha," and—though they may not know it—already following teachings of the Mahāyāna.[50] This sentiment is explored further in material exclusive to MBhS^T (and plausibly later than content that is shared by both versions), in which the Buddha explains that his use of his skill-in-methods (*thabs mkhas pa:* Skt. *upāyakauśalya*) to teach different audiences does not constitute any contradiction (*'gal ba: virodha*), but does require from an audience the ability to distinguish between teachings that are provisional (*drang ba'i don: neyārtha*) and those that are definitive (*nges pa'i don: nītārtha*).[51]

There is no doubt that the reduction of certain teachings to "strategies" was a contentious move by the SP; the same can be said about the MPNMS and AMS where they reveal that teaching about absence of self did not intend that the Buddha could not teach the *true* self that refers to Buddha-nature (see also 9.2). But it is the MBhS that presents in the boldest terms what is implied by other Buddha-nature works: that teaching about not-self was some manner of expediency, and is succeeded by revelation of the *tathāgatagarbha*.

> The Buddha said to Kāśyapa: In order to refute worldly [notions of] self, I taught the doctrine of absence of self. If I did not teach in this fashion,

47. MBhS^C 296b8–10. Compare MBhS^T D.222, 107b6–108a1; Q.888, 112b2–3. This last expression is conspicuously close to the epithet "*uttaratantra*" found in both the MPNMS and RGVV; see 7.2; see also Radich 2015a: 48–49. This passage could intend an inversion of a statement by the *Akṣayamatinirdeśasūtra*, which prioritizes texts that teach emptiness over any that do not; see T. Suzuki 1997: 43–44; Jones 2016b: 67n56; also Ruegg 2004: 37.

48. MBhS^C 296b10–12. Compare MBhS^T D.222, 108a1–4; Q.888, 112b3.

49. MBhS^C 296b12–14: 諸佛世尊亦復如是：隨順眾生種種欲樂而為演説種種經法。Compare MBhS^T D.222, 108a4–5; Q.888, 112b8.

50. Regarding the magically conjured city, see SP 187–189; Kern 1884: 181–183; then MBhS^C 296a7–b7; MBhS^T D.222, 106b1–107b6; Q.888, 111a2–112b1. Regarding the lost son, see SP 101–110; Kern 1884: 99–108; then MBhS^C 297b22–c21; MBhS^T D.111a6–112a3; Q.888, 116a6–117a4.

51. MBhS^T D.222, 115a3–4; Q.888, 120b3–5.

> how could anyone accept the dharma of the great teacher [who is the Buddha]?
>
> When the Buddha teaches absence of self, sentient beings are amazed, and upon hearing what has not before been heard, they come to the Buddha and are then, by a hundred thousand methods, led into the Buddha's teaching. Having entered into the Buddha's teaching, their faith increases, they become more diligent, they become learned in regard to teachings about emptiness; only then do I teach for them the lasting and tranquil liberation that has a form.[52]

In MPNMS-dhk we encountered the idea that the Buddha taught *anātman* for the purpose of vanquishing teachers who espoused wrong-minded notions of the self (see 2.2); here, similarly, *anātman* is said to have been taught to win audiences away from worldly ideas about the self. Faith in the Buddha leads to acceptance of teachings concerned with emptiness, and only then—finally—does the Buddha teach liberation "with a form," which is lasting (*dhruva*) and tranquil (*śiva*), and attainment of what can be called *ātman*, realized in the status of a Buddha.

This "liberation with form" (*gzugs dang bcas pa: *rūpavat*), which we also encountered earlier (see 4.3), is revealed only after sentient beings have been led into the dharma not by an account of the self but rather by teachings about absence of self with respect to all phenomena. Again the MBhS shows a debt to the MPNMS, which also presents a distinction between liberation "with form" (*se* 色; *gzugs*), proper to the Buddhas, and another that is "without form" (*wuse* 無色; *gzugs med*), which is how liberation was explained to *śrāvaka*s.[53] The Buddha's liberation is characterized by "separation from bondage to fetters," what the MBhS understands as the freedom or "sovereignty" of the Buddha, due to which he is said to have realized the self.[54]

The MBhS provides another account of the trajectory of the Buddha's teaching, which repeats, with subtle differences, what we have seen above:

> Furthermore, there are sometimes worldly persons teaching such a liberation [i.e., with form]. In order to refute them, I taught that liberation is non-existence. If I did not teach in this manner, how could anyone accept the dharma of the great teacher?

---

52. MBhS^{C} 296b26–c2: 佛告迦葉：為破世間我故說無我義。若不如是說者，云何令彼受大師法？佛說無我，彼諸眾生生奇特想，聞所未聞，來詣佛所然後以百千因緣令入佛法。入佛法已，信心增長，勤修精進，善學空法，然後為說常住安樂有色解脫。Compare MBhS^{T} D.222, 108b2–5; Q.888, 113a6–b1.

53. MPNMS^{F} 872c27–873a4; MPNMS^{D} 391c28–392a11; MPNMS^{T} §229.

54. MPNMS^{F} 873a4–8 (一切縛和合悉離); MPNMS^{D} 392a12–17; MPNMS^{T} §230 (featuring *'ching ba thams cad dang bral ba*: "freedom from all bondage").

> By a hundred thousand methods I explained that liberation is annihilation, without a self. After that, I observed those sentient beings who took absolute annihilation to be liberation; lacking insight, they head toward annihilation. [So] after that, I expound by means of a hundred thousand methods the teaching that liberation is existence.[55]

We can express this succession of teachings concisely:

1. There exist worldly teachings about liberation that is "with form."
2. The Buddha opposes these, teaching a kind of liberation proximate (at least to some minds) to annihilation, while eschewing any account of the self.[56]
3. To correct any misunderstanding, the Buddha now teaches a kind of liberation that is existence, and talks again about the self and its realization.[57]

So the MBhS understands the development of the Buddha's teaching as dialectical, in which erroneous accounts of liberation already in the world are challenged by teaching about not-self, which in turn must be balanced by the Buddha's eventual revelation of the true self that is realized at awakening. Material exclusive to MBhS^{T} explains this to be an example of the Buddha's skill-in-methods: absence of self is taught to undermine worldly conceptions of a self somewhere about the body (*'jig tshogs la lta ba:* Skt. *satkāyadṛṣṭi*), whereas the culmination of the dharma is indeed the existence and reality of the self (*bdag yod pa nyid;* also *bdag gi de kho na nyid*), revealed only to those who are prepared to receive it.[58]

However, the MBhS does not stop here and undermines the learnedness of any audience that privileges discourses concerned with emptiness. Above we saw that teachings about emptiness were expounded "intentionally" (*ābhiprāyika*); elsewhere, MBhS^{C} laments that there are unruly monks who either comply with (*sui* 隨) or even augment (*zengyi* 增異) the content of emptiness-oriented texts.[59] Blame is leveled at Buddhist audiences—likely detractors of *tathāgatagarbha* teaching—who misunderstand the

---

55. MBhS^{C} 296c2–7: 復次或有世俗説有是解脱。為壞彼故，説言解脱悉無所有。若不如是説，云何令彼受大師法？是故百千因縁為説解脱滅盡無我。然後我復見彼眾生見畢竟滅以為解脱，彼無慧人趣向滅盡。然後我復百千因縁説解脱是有。Compare MBhS^{T}: D.222, 108b5–7; Q.888, 113b1–3.

56. MBhS^{C} 解脱滅盡無我; MBhS^{T} *thar pa chud gzon pa nyid kyi bdag med pa*: "liberation that is without the self, which is a kind of annihilation (Skt. **vināśa*)." See note 55 above for references.

57. MBhS^{C} 解脱是有, MBhS^{T} *thar pa yod pa nyid*. See note 55 for references.

58. MBhS^{T} D.222, 115b1–3; Q.888, 121a3–5.

59. MBhS^{C} 296b15–16; MBhS^{T} D.222, 108a5–6; Q.888, 113a1–2. In MBhS^{T} we are instead told that these monks either (wrongly) interpret (*'dren pa*) or reject (*spong ba*) the content of *sūtras*.

Buddha's teachings about emptiness, and who have not grasped that emptiness was taught in preparation for the Buddha's account of the self:

> Those [who espouse emptiness teachings] say that "all discourses of the Buddha, in all cases explain absence of self," while not knowing the meaning of emptiness or of absence of self; those ignorant persons head toward annihilation.[60]
>
> Yet still the teachings of emptiness and absence of self are also pronouncements by the Buddha. How is this? The store of immeasurable defilements and afflictions conceals the *nirvāṇa* that is always empty [of them]; in this way, what is meant by "*nirvāṇa*" is the meaning of all [teachings]; such longevity and tranquility [enjoyed by the Buddha] is what is meant by the *mahānirvāṇa* that is attained by the Buddha.[61]

The passage above translates content of MBhS^{C}, with which MBhS^{T} essentially agrees.[62] We can take this passage to mean that *(mahā) nirvāṇa* taught by the MBhS—a condition that is both permanent and pleasant—is what is ultimately intended where other accounts of *nirvāṇa* have been delivered in other *sūtra*s. These, as we have read, sometimes adopted a tone that the MBhS takes to have been annihilationist in character, but the liberation to which these teachings must finally refer is one that is "with form," and the attainment of the superlative power and freedom of a Buddha.

In light of all that we have seen above, it is not surprising that the MBhS also expresses caution regarding how liberally its ideas should be shared. Its authors recognized that a Buddhist account of the self should not be taught to just anyone, and categorizes beings into three types: those who cannot be helped and who "shall fall into hell [in their next rebirth]," those who believe in the *sūtra,* and those who by the four modes of persuasion (*saṃgrahavastu*) can be led to it, and hence—gradually—toward liberation.[63] The last of these are compared to individuals who suffer some illness but who should not be treated with medicine immediately; one should wait until the proper time, "once the illness is fully manifested," in order to

60. The MBhS may intend, for example, "those persons will be destroyed [by virtue of their ignorance]," or otherwise that they lean toward annihilationist views about liberation.

61. MBhS^{C} 296b16–b20: 彼如是言：一切佛經皆說無我，而彼不知空無我義；彼無慧人趣向滅盡。然空無我說亦是佛語。所以者何？無量塵垢諸煩惱藏常空涅槃。如是涅槃句[a]是一切句。彼常住安樂是佛所得大般涅槃句[b]。

[a] Song/Yuan/Ming/Palace 槃句 = T 槃

[b] Palace omits 句

62. MBhS^{T} D.222, 108a7–b1; Q.888, 113a3–4, especially: *mya ngan las 'das pa nyid kyi tshig gi gzhi rnams ni / de dag thams cad kyi gzhi yin te / sangs rgyas bcom ldan 'das / de dag ni zhi ba ther zug pa'i mya ngan las 'das pa thob pa yin no //* (the meaning [*gnas*: Skt. **padārtha*?] of the expression *nirvāṇa* is the meaning of all [of the Buddha's teachings]; the exalted Buddhas attain the enduring *nirvāṇa* that is tranquil).

63. See MBhS^{C} 297c27–28; also MBhS^{T} D.222, 112a6–7; Q.888, 117b1.

cure them.[64] The MBhS also compares unready audiences to a man who is scared by the cries of birds; taking them to be thieves, he flees from his path into the territory of a hungry tiger. Similarly, monastics and lay followers, "hearing about both the existence and absence of self, fear hearing about the existence of the self; they enter the annihilationist view of great emptiness (*dakong* 大空: **mahāśūnyatā*), and mentally cultivate absence of self. In this manner, they do not produce faith in the very profound *sūtra*(s?) that concern *tathāgatagarbha* and the permanence of the Buddhas."[65] In other words, some (or most) of the Buddhist community will remain attached to the *nairātmyavāda* mode of practice found in the Buddha's earlier teachings, or to teachings about emptiness that were prevalent in texts proper to the Mahāyāna. These monks struggle to accept the status of a Buddha articulated in terms of the self, as well as the idea of attaining such a thing by discovery of the *tathāgatagarbha*. Teachings about emptiness remain a curious sort of comfort for those not ready to accept that the culmination of the Buddha's teaching is the definitive account of what was, all along, the self.

Like those of the MPNMS and AMS, the authors of the MBhS had a pessimistic sense of how their ideas were likely to be received by new audiences. This complements the prophetic warning in the MBhS—very similar to that found across the MPNMS-group—that it will resurface during the final eighty years that the dharma has left in the world (see also 9.4, 10.2).[66] There is little doubt that Buddha-nature understood in terms of the self, as well as the explicit devaluing of teachings about emptiness, would have made the content of the MBhS, to adapt its own metaphor, a difficult pill for some audiences to swallow. All of this provides ample reason why we are left with scant evidence of the MBhS having been read by later Indian commentators: it may have been so irregular in both its choice of language and attitude to wider Buddhist teachings that the influence of the MBhS may have been minimal indeed.

4.6 Conclusions

Of our three *ātmavāda tathāgatagarbha* texts—all works of the so-called MPNMS-group—the MBhS is the most difficult to situate in relation to the wider *tathāgatagarbha* corpus. Our two extant translations boast challenges both philological and conceptual, but there is little doubt that the MBhS articulates the boldest, most contentious defense of Buddhist *ātmavāda* available to us. Not only does the MBhS teach a Buddhist account of the self, it does so while explicitly relegating teachings about absence of self,

64. MBhS^{C} 298a3–6; MBhS^{T} D.222, 112a7–8; Q.888, 117b3–4.

65. MBhS^{C} 298a10–12: 於有我無我聲，畏有我聲，入於大空斷見，修習無我。於如是如來藏、諸佛常住甚深經典，不生信樂。 Compare MBhS^{T} D.222, 115b4–5; Q.888, 121a7–8. This material features in Dol po pa's RC (Hopkins 2006: 127–128).

66. MBhS^{C} 298c19–299a29; MBhS^{T} D.222, 118a6–121a8; Q.888, 124a4–27b2.

and of emptiness, to an "intentional" or "provisional" status. We are told that such a thing as the self—otherwise still the essence (*dhātu*) of a Buddha, proper to him and to all sentient beings (*sattvadhātu*)—must exist in order for a Buddha to enjoy the enduring, tranquil state of liberation that any number of other Mahāyānist sources attribute to him.

An interesting detail, in contrast to both the MPNMS and AMS, is the near absence from the MBhS of the expression *dharmakāya*. The MBhS makes hardly any mention of the *dharmakāya*, and may have—in its Indian forms—contained only a single occurrence of this expression.[67] Instead of making a distinction between the Buddha's physical body and his immutable *dharmakāya* (otherwise, in MBhS^{T}, the Buddha's "unbreakable body": *mi phyed pa'i sku: *abhedyakāya*), the MBhS prefers to speak simply about the enduring existence of the Buddha, who enjoys the lasting, tranquil state of a liberation that exhibits some "form." Another text that talks more straightforwardly about the Buddha—without so much focus on his different "bodies," *dharmakāya* or otherwise—is the SP, with which the MBhS was certainly familiar. Ties between the SP and the wider *tathāgatagarbha* corpus will continue to be of interest as this study progresses (see 5.4, 9.1), but in the MBhS we find its influence all too clearly, as evinced by the reproduction of entire parables from the SP (of the lost son and of the magically conjured city) that celebrate the Mahāyāna as the single vehicle (*ekayāna*) in which all Buddhist teachings are included.

In summation, the MBhS contends unapologetically that the attainment of liberation requires something that could be called the self. Though this self is knowable only to fully awakened beings, the MBhS attempts to justify that such a thing must exist in order for liberation to be anything that a sentient being might eventually come to enjoy. Otherwise the self is a byword for freedom: it is that which can be apart from transmigration, from conditioned existence, and is the liberation that the Buddha experiences beyond his (apparent) death. This coheres with much of what was taught by the MPNMS, and in a sense the MBhS joins the dots between the self that is proper to liberation in MPNMS-dhk (the status enjoyed by a Buddha) and the self that prefigures this status taught in MPNMS-tg (the self proper to sentient beings, or *tathāgatagarbha*). Because the Buddha's liberation permits that he be described as the self, there must exist that upon which this achievement depends; because all sentient beings have the potential to achieve his status, as taught already in the SP, all must possess a precious trace of this self, of Buddha-nature, already.

We have now addressed the three texts of the so-called MPNMS-group—the MPNMS, AMS, and MBhS—that teach the existence of the *tathāgatagarbha* in terms of a permanent, unchanging, indestructible, and

---

67. See MBhS^{C} 299b13–17; MBhS^{T} D.222, 124a4–6; Q.888, 130b7–131a1; for further discussion, see Jones 2016b: 67–68; also T. Suzuki 2002.

superlatively valuable "essence" of every sentient being: otherwise, as was more common in wider Indian thought, what can be called *ātman*. We must now turn to those texts that most scholars, after Takasaki, have held to be the backbone of the Indian *tathāgatagarbha* tradition, and first of all a *sūtra* that shows signs of having known Buddha-nature teaching as it was articulated in the three works to which we have so far attended. An objective of part 2 of this volume is to demonstrate that remaining works of the *tathāgatagarbha* corpus did not set the stage for an *ātmavādin* form of this teaching but instead responded to earlier, more contentious articulations of the Buddha-nature idea exemplified by the MPNMS, AMS, and—perhaps most ardently—the MBhS.

PART II

Buddha-nature, Not Self

CHAPTER 5

The *Śrīmālādevīsiṃhanādasūtra* and the Perfection of Self

5.1 The Text

We turn now to the *Śrīmālādevīsiṃhanāda(nirdeśa)sūtra* (ŚDS), or the discourse that explains "the 'lion's roar' delivered by Queen Śrīmālā."[1] Undoubtedly the ŚDS is a text better known to modern scholarship than both the AMS and MBhS, in no small part due to its importance for the author(s) of the much-studied *Ratnagotravibhāgavyākhyā* (RGVV) and to its influence on the *Laṅkāvatārasūtra* (LAS).[2] This chapter and those that follow it contend that the ŚDS reflects an important turning point in the development of Buddha-nature thinking in India, away not only from discourse about the self but also from anything that was imagined to be some "essence" or precious "element" in the constitution of a sentient being. For authors of the ŚDS, and other works that can be demonstrated to be later than it, the expression *tathāgatagarbha* refers instead to that which underpins the existence of both a sentient being and of a liberated Buddha, otherwise referring to the mind that is intrinsically pure (e.g., *prakṛtipariśuddhacitta;* see also 9.3).

Several Sanskrit fragments of the ŚDS are preserved in the Schøyen collection of manuscripts, though the content of these fragments does not

1. Matsuda (2000: 74) reconstructs a Sanskrit fragment of the colophon to read *śrīmālādevīsiṃha[nāda]nirde[śa](sūtraṃ)*, which accords with the title of the text as translated by Guṇabhadra (i.e., in ŚDS^{C1}; see main text, above), including the qualification that the text is "a great extensive discourse concerned with the methods proper to the single vehicle" (ibid., 74: *[e](kayāna)ṃ [ma](h)[opā](ya)vaitulye;* ŚDS^{C1} 217a4; also 223b15: 一乘大方便方廣經). Regarding the motif of the "lion's roar," see Anālayo 2009: 5–10.

2. The ŚDS is also mentioned by name in Śāntideva's (eighth century) *Śikṣāsamuccaya* (Bendall [1897–1902] 1970: 42.12). From likely the same century, Kamalaśīla's *Madhyamakāloka* quotes the ŚDS and its account of "death that is an inconceivable transformation" (Skt. **acintyā pāriṇāmikī cyuti*), in order to explain continuing transmigration of the arhat, and hence offer justification for teaching about the single vehicle (D.3887, 240a4–b1; P.5287, 269b2–8: see Kanō 2016: 9; also 5.4 below).

shed much light on how the text understands Buddha-nature.[3] We also possess valuable quotations of the ŚDS preserved in the Sanskrit RGVV, and indeed concerning its understanding of *tathāgatagarbha*. However, for much of its content we are still very much dependent upon translations of the ŚDS into other Asian languages, the earliest of which is the Chinese translation by Guṇabhadra from 436 CE (T.353: *Shengman shizihou yisheng dafangbian fangguang jing* 勝鬘師子吼一乘大方便方廣經; henceforth ŚDS^{C1}). After this is another Chinese version preserved in the *Mahāratnakūṭa* collection of *sūtra*s (*Dabaoji jing* 大寶積經—T.310[11]672c14–678c4: *Shengman furen hui* 勝鬘夫人會; henceforth ŚDS^{C2}), translated by Bodhiruci 菩提流志 (d.727) around 710 CE.[4] A third version is preserved in the Tibetan *bka' 'gyur* (e.g., D.92; Q.760[48]: *Lha mo dpal phreng gi seng ge'i sgra zhes bya ba theg pa chen po'i mdo;* henceforth ŚDS^{T}), which was produced in the early ninth century by Jinamitra, Surendrabodhi, and Ye shes sde, and which in content closely resembles ŚDS^{C2}. An edition of ŚDS^{T}—based on the Derge, Peking, and Narthang editions, and which is referenced throughout this chapter—is that by Kenryū Tsukinowa (1940), who presented this together with a Japanese translation and reproductions of both Chinese versions. An English translation of ŚDS^{C1} is that by Diana Paul (2004), while ŚDS^{C2} has been translated (along with other materials from the *Mahāratnakūṭa* collection) by Garma Chang (1991: 363–386).[5] There is also the English translation, based primarily on ŚDS^{T} (or "the *Ratnakūṭa* recension") by Alex Wayman and Hideko Wayman (1974), who advanced the influential hypothesis (though by no means universally accepted) that the ŚDS was a product of the Mahāsāṃghika Buddhist tradition.[6] As ever, the ŚDS and its place in the *tathāgatagarbha* tradition was addressed also by Takasaki (1974: 97–126).[7] Discussions of the doctrine of the ŚDS include those by Diana Paul (1979) and Richard King (1995b), while a recent treatment of themes explored in this chapter is by Jarosław Zapart (2017).

Like some other Mahāyānist *sūtra*s (including the AMS), the ŚDS frames much of its content as having been delivered by someone other than the Buddha himself. In this instance it is Queen Śrīmālā of Kosala, daughter of King Prasenajit, who is praised by the Buddha not only for her devotion to him and to the Mahāyāna but also for her eloquence in regard to explaining

---

3. Matsuda 2000; see also note 1 above.

4. Lost to us is a Chinese translation by Dharmakṣema, which may have shed light on the relationship between the MPNMS and ŚDS as perceived by that author; see Wayman and Wayman 1974: 9.

5. A further English translation of ŚDS^{C1} is that of Rulu (2016): see 3.1n1.

6. See Paul 1976a; Wayman 1976; and Paul 1976b regarding the conclusions of the Waymans' study. Wayman 1978 presents a comprehensive list of reasons to suppose a Mahāsāṃghika influence upon the ŚDS. More recently Vincent Tournier (2017: 196n253, 285n119) has persuasively challenged the Waymans' identification of doctrinal ties between the ŚDS and the *Mahāvastu,* a central text of the Mahāsāṃghika tradition. See also 10.2n7.

7. Regarding earlier Japanese scholarship concerning the ŚDS, see Radich 2015b: 263.

the path of the bodhisattva.[8] Śrīmālā teaches in the company of a magical apparition of the Buddha, created by him, who empowers her to speak eloquently about the path of the bodhisattva, *tathāgatagarbha,* and the Mahāyāna understood as the single vehicle (*ekayāna*), as expressed most famously in the *Saddharmapuṇḍarīka* (SP). Though influence of the SP is not as pronounced as we saw in the MBhS (see previous chapter), the ŚDS still understands the vehicles of the *śrāvaka* and *pratyekabuddha* to be stages along what is ultimately the path to complete awakening (see 5.4). Together with the texts of the MPNMS-group, we can consider the ŚDS to be a true "ekayānist" work that accepts the soteriological paradigm promoted by the SP (see, for further discussion, 9.1).

In the course of her teaching Queen Śrīmālā outlines differences between those who follow the Mahāyāna and the various "saints" of earlier Buddhist tradition: the arhat and other followers of the Śrāvakayāna who are close to achieving that status. She articulates three vows proper to the bodhisattva: that (s)he should (1) work for the liberation of all sentient beings, (2) explain the dharma without wearying, and (3) "abandon body, life and wealth while upholding the *saddharma*" (i.e., "true dharma").[9] This certainly evokes the difficulty of the bodhisattva path imagined by both the MPNMS and AMS, but in other regards the ŚDS departs from the ideas and language of the MPNMS-group in some significant ways. We encounter no mention of the prophecy complex common to the MPNMS-group of texts, nor any focus on Buddha-nature or the Buddha's enduring existence as the explanation of the Buddha's strategically cryptic methods of teaching (see 9.2).[10] The ŚDS also shows no interest in celebrating the

---

8. Wayman and Wayman take this to be related to the origins of the ŚDS, they claim, in the Andhra region after the fall of the Śātavāhana empire (c. 220 CE), in which the female royalty of the otherwise Brahmanically oriented Īkṣvāku dynasty supported Buddhism. See Wayman and Wayman 1974: 1–2; Nilakanta Sastri 1958: 96. The influence of the Waymans' hypothesis is clear in work by Barber (2008: 152–156), whose attention to *tathāgatagarbha* sources develops the association between this literature and the region of Andhra. See also 10.2n7.

9. ŚDS^{C1} 218a9: 捨身命財, 護持正法. See also, for example, ŚDS^{C1} 219a1–10; also ŚDS^{T} 54.16–58.16, in which we read that one must abandon body, life, and wealth in order to achieve the permanent, indestructible body of the Buddha (*sangs rgyas kyi sku: buddhakāya*). The body of the Buddha is the subject of verses at the beginning of the ŚDS (e.g., ŚDS^{C1} 217a16–b9; SDS^{T} 6–12), said to be inexhaustible, and the site of permanently abiding *dharmas*. This language, which is closer in tone to what we find in the MPNMS-group, is somewhat left behind as the ŚDS launches into its exposition of the *tathāgatagarbha-dharmakāya,* discussed below.

10. At its climax the ŚDS is said to have explained the underlying truth of emptiness and about the intrinsically pure mind (e.g., ŚDS^{C1} 223b4–6, including 空義隱覆真實; ŚDS^{T} 168.2–9, including *stong pa nyid kyi don gyi dgongs pa*). In ŚDS^{T} we find occasional reference to the "intent" behind the Buddha's teaching (ŚDS^{T} 68.5–16 *dgongs pa can: ābhiprāyika*). No doubt the ŚDS does claim to offer a definitive account of how one should understand these and other topics—especially the reduction of the three vehicles of Buddhist teaching to just one—though unlike the MPNMS-group the ŚDS does not dwell on the fact that some

Buddha's longevity beyond his apparent death, an idea especially important to both the MPNMS(-dhk) and MBhS. Instead it concerns the Buddha's *dharmakāya,* which is not so explicitly contrasted with his physical person so much as used to denote a collection (*kāya*) of supermundane qualities that one achieves upon liberation.[11] Among these—to which we will turn later—is "the perfection of self" (*ātmapāramitā*), a legacy of *ātmavādin* discourse inherited, in all likelihood, from the MPNMS itself.

5.2 Reimagining *Tathāgatagarbha*

We should begin with how the ŚDS understands the expression *tathāgatagarbha,* which does not clearly refer to anything "within" the constitution of any sentient being. In fact the ŚDS omits any form of the declaration that "all sentient beings possess the *tathāgatagarbha*"—either "within their bodies" or otherwise—which is our first sign that its authors assumed their audience to have an acquaintance with this expression already, if only insofar as teaching about *tathāgatagarbha* is assumed to say something "about" sentient beings in general terms. Moreover, no available form of the ŚDS shows any evidence of using the expression *(buddha)dhātu:* its account of Buddha-nature teaching is concerned strictly with the *tathāgatagarbha* and, at the end of its exposition, an identification between this and the intrinsically pure mind (*zixing qingjingxin* 自性清淨心; *sems rang bzhin gyis yongs su dag pa: *prakṛtipariśuddhacitta*) that persists apart from, or "beneath," afflictions: "There are two teachings that are difficult to understand: the mind that is intrinsically pure is difficult to understand, and that this mind is defiled by afflictions."[12] While this fails to make a clear equation between these two categories, the fact that conjunction with afflictions (*kleśa*s) is a feature of the *tathāgatagarbha* (and what distinguishes it from the *dharmakāya;* see 5.3) leaves us in little doubt that the *tathāgatagarbha* is being identified with the intrinsically pure mind. By comparison, texts proper to the MPNMS-group exhibit little interest in the mind, its nature, or composition; the only mention of a "pure mind" in any of these occurs in the AMS, in which this is presented as a doctrine taught in the Śrāvakayāna that is superseded by teaching about Buddha-nature (see 9.3). In the ŚDS the identification is the other way around: what is called *tathāgatagarbha* refers to the mind, or properly to its basic nature apart from the afflictions that sully it.

---

of the Buddha's earlier pronouncements, taken at face value, jar with teachings about Buddha-nature.

11. See Harrison (1992a: 55–57) regarding this interpretation of *dharmakāya*—a "collection of the Buddha's qualities"—found also in Sarvāstivādin sources such as the *Abhidharmakośabhāṣya.*

12. ŚDS[C1] 222c4–5: 有二法難可了知：謂自性清淨心難可了知；彼心為煩惱所染亦難了[a]知。
[a] T 了 = 可了 Song/Yuan/Ming/Palace
Compare ŚDS[C2] 678a4–5; ŚDS[T] 152.13–16.

Unlike in the MPNMS-group, this *tathāgatagarbha* cannot be set in opposition to other components of experience (e.g., the "heaps" of experience, or other bodily elements; see 2.3). It does not refer to the static "essence" (*dhātu*) of a Buddha, nor seems to intend the idea of a "chamber" (*garbha*) within which such a sacred element could be imagined to reside. If, as Michael Radich has argued, the expression *tathāgatagarbha* began life in a creative internalization of the Buddha's essential "relic" resident in every sentient being, then the ŚDS shows no signs of understanding it as such: no interest in the (relative) value of *stūpa*s, nor of the relics that they were understood to house. The *tathāgatagarbha* is certainly still some aspect of sentient beings, but the ŚDS avoids any language that suggests it to be something "hidden" or "within" them. In other words, in the ŚDS the expression *tathāgatagarbha* certainly refers to the causal ground for a fully awakened being—that is to say, they possess the generative locus or "womb" (*garbha*) for such a thing—but now without clearly evoking the sacred chamber (*garbha* also) that was thought to preserve the essence of a Buddha after his bodily demise.[13]

At the conclusion of its discussion about the *tathāgatagarbha* and to what it must refer, the ŚDS relates *tathāgatagarbha* to various signifiers for reality as it is known to a fully awakened being: "Lord, the *tathāgatagarbha* is the *garbha* of the *dharmadhātu* (Skt. **saddharmadhātugarbha*); it is the *garbha* of the *dharmakāya* (**dharmakāyagarbha*); it is the *garbha* of the supremely supermundane (**lokottaradharmagarbha*); it is the *garbha* of what is intrinsically pure (**prakṛtipariśuddhadharmagarbha*). This naturally pure *tathāgatagarbha*, which is defiled by adventitious afflictions, is the inconceivable domain of the Tathāgatas."[14] Though this translates material from ŚDS[C1], the Sanskrit expressions supplied above are reconstructed with the aid of a corresponding and seemingly identical list from ŚDS[T]; all but the last of these expressions are represented in the Sanskrit RGVV.[15] Clearly a great deal rides on how we understand the linguistic unit "-*garbha*," which in the ŚDS has eclipsed any interest in the expression *dhātu* and reference

13. My phrasing—in terms of a "generative locus"—is reminiscent of that used by Matsumoto (e.g., in Hubbard and Swanson 1997) in his discernment of a "*dhātuvāda*" orientation in the ŚDS: that is, some account of "a singular, real locus (*dhātu*) that gives rise to a plurality of phenomena" (ibid., 171). What I stress is that the expression *tathāgatagarbha* refers foremost to the generative locus for specifically a Buddha, whose qualities are already dormant in every sentient being. I moreover do not subscribe to Matsumoto's view that the *tathāgatagarbha* of the ŚDS or any other works in this tradition is by any means "un-Buddhist" (see 5.5, 10.5). A similar, but more favorable, reading of the ŚDS is that of Zapart (2017), who presents the *tathāgatagarbha* as something like a "basis" to phenomenal existence.

14. ŚDS[C1] 222b22–24: 世尊，如來藏者，是法界藏、法身藏、出世間上上藏、自性清淨藏。此自性[a]清淨如來藏而客塵煩惱上煩惱所染，不思議如來境界。

[a] Song/Yuan/Ming/Palace/Shōgozō 自性 = T 性

Compare ŚDS[C2] 677c21–25; ŚDS[T] 150.4–11.

15. Johnston (1950) 1991: 76.16–77.1. A longer list, closer to what we see in the ŚDS, is preserved in the Chinese RGVV (T.1611[31]839a22–25).

to what is "most essential" about a sentient being. These compounds are all creative (re)interpretations of the expression *tathāgatagarbha,* presented in such a fashion that they suggest an audience's familiarity with this expression, if not also with how it should be understood. Following the Tibetan translation of *garbha* in the sense of some "embryo" (*snying po*), we could understand these equations to mean that the *tathāgatagarbha* is something like the "seed" of each of these categories.[16] However, this is a little odd in—for example—the expression *dharmadhātugarbha:* the "*garbha* of the essence/nature/realm of phenomena (i.e., "reality" properly known)" is not something that we could imagine to "grow" or "develop" but rather is the true or fundamental state of things that is known to a Buddha.

Buddhist literature beyond the *tathāgatagarbha* tradition frequently employed the language of gestation and birth to explain the achievement of awakening: the *Aṣṭasāhasrikā-prajñāpāramitā,* for example, remarks that awakening is "born" through the perfection of insight (*prajñāpāramitānirjāta*),[17] which is "mother and begetter" (*mātā janayitrī*) of all Buddhas.[18] The *Vimalakīrtinirdeśasūtra* explains that the *dharmakāya* is similarly "born" by the perfections—the perfection of giving (*dānanirjāta*), discipline (*śīlanirjāta*), and so forth—and records that the perfection of insight is "the mother of bodhisattvas."[19] However where the expression *tathāgatagarbha* is taken to be the *garbha* for *what is already supermundane,* apropos of any sentient being, it is hard to imagine that this should be taken to be anything itself in need of growth or development. A better reading, I propose, is to continue to understand *garbha* in the sense of some "chamber," or more broadly some imperceptible "locus": the *tathāgatagarbha*—an enduringly present aspect of any sentient being—is the space at which these supermundane qualities, and the penetrating understanding of phenomena proper to a Buddha, can be realized or (by great effort) "found." The *tathāgatagarbha* is then also something like the "womb" for the emergence of a Buddha, but also of his transcendent mode of being (*dharmakāya*), supermundane qualities, awareness of reality, etcetera. Though the ŚDS shows no trace of the idea that the *tathāgatagarbha* holds the Buddha's "essence," or permits any identification between bodhisattva and Buddha (see 2.3), the ŚDS retains the sense that this expression refers to that aspect of a sentient being from which a liberated Buddha can emerge, because realization of the *dharmadhātu, dharmakāya,* etcetera are located "in it" and can be born "from it." To sum up, we might understand *tathāgatagarbha* as it appears in the ŚDS to designate the enduring locus at which awakening, and what is properly supermundane, can be found, which can be identified also with the underlying, fundamentally pure nature of the mind.

16. See Ruegg 1969: 501–502; also Hara 1994, and more recently (focusing on *tathāgatagarbha* as understood by the RGVV) Saitō 2020.

17. Vaidya 1960: 29.12–13, 36.1–2

18. Ibid.,125.26–27, 134.26–27. See also Radich 2015a: 150–151.

19. Taishō University 2006: 18–19 (2, §12), 79 (7, §6).

Insofar as *tathāgatagarbha* refers to something "about" sentient beings, the message of the ŚDS is that reality properly understood—together with the true mode of the Buddha's existence (*dharmakāya*)—is not apart from the character of a sentient being as he or she undergoes transmigration. This retains the sense of the Buddha-nature idea outlined at the start of this study (1.2) and found throughout the MPNMS and other texts that teach the existence of the *tathāgatagarbha*. The ŚDS remains committed to this idea, and the very flexible expression *tathāgatagarbha* with which it became associated, without taking it to require some valuable element that is in any way "within" and so somehow "hidden" about a sentient being.

Whereas the texts of the MPNMS-group employ colorful similes to explain something that is beyond the faculties of a sentient being, the ŚDS—a comparatively short text—attempts to unpack the *tathāgatagarbha* in a single, extended description, which is noticeably more technical than what we have encountered in earlier chapters of this study:

> Lord, <u>birth and death</u> depend upon the *tathāgatagarbha;* because of the *tathāgatagarbha,* it is taught that no beginning to these can be known.[20] Lord, because of the existence of the *tathāgatagarbha,* there is taught <u>birth and death</u>; this is called the correct teaching.
>
> Lord, <u>birth and death</u> are the end of the sense faculties and the successive arising of new sense faculties: this is called birth and death. Lord, the two phenomena, birth and death, are the *tathāgatagarbha;* it is because of worldly speech that there is said to be birth and death: death being the destruction of the faculties, and birth the arising of new faculties; [but] it is not the case that the *tathāgatagarbha* has either birth or death. The *tathāgatagarbha* is apart from the characteristics of what is conditioned; the *tathāgatagarbha* is permanent and unchanging: hence the *tathāgatagarbha* is a basis (*yi* 依: *niśraya*), a support (*chi* 持: *ādhāra*), and a foundation (*jianli* 建立: *pratiṣṭhitā*).
>
> Lord, [the *tathāgatagarbha*] is not separate nor apart from, not other nor different to the inconceivable qualities of a Buddha. Lord, the *tathāgatagarbha* is a basis, support, and foundation that is apart from, different to, outside of conditioned phenomena.[21]

---

20. In ŚDS[C1] this is *benji* 本際, regarding which see Sharf 2002: 229–238. This may reflect the Sanskrit *pūrvakoṭi* (ŚDS[T] *sngon gyi mtha'*), a start to the process of transmigration, which can never be found. A similar idea is found in both the AAN (T.668[16]467b27) and RGVV (e.g., Johnston [1950] 1991: 72.15–16).

21. ŚDS[C1] 222b5–14: 世尊，生死者，依如來藏。以如來藏故，說本際不可知。 世尊，有如來藏故說生死，是名善說。世尊，生死，生死者，諸受根沒，次第{不}受根起：是名生死。世尊，死生者[a]，此二法是如來藏；世間言說故，有死有生：死者，謂根壞；生者新諸根起，非如來藏有生有死。如來藏者[b]，離有為相。如來藏常住不變：是故如來藏是依、是持、是建立。世尊，不離、不斷、不脫、不異不思議佛法。世尊，斷、脫、異、外有為法，依、持、建立者：是如來藏。

[a] T 死生 = Song/Yuan/Ming/Palace 生死

[b] Song/Yuan/Ming/Palace omit 者

Though our Chinese translations do not reflect this, corresponding material in ŚDS^{T} preserves a (perhaps insignificant) distinction between "birth and death" (*'chi 'pho ba dang skye ba*) and *saṃsāra* (Tib. *'khor ba;* instances where ŚDS^{T} reflects this have been underlined in the translation of ŚDS^{C1} above). The sense of all three versions is nevertheless the same: the cycle of transmigration, that of perpetual birth, death, and rebirth, "depends upon" the *tathāgatagarbha*. The *tathāgatagarbha* is "the basis, support, foundation" for recurring transmigration but is also somehow apart from phenomena that are conditioned (*saṃskṛta*) and make up our experience of it. We are fortunate that the middle portion of the above passage (after "it is because of worldly speech …") is preserved in the Sanskrit RGVV, which mostly accords with what we find in ŚDS^{T}: "Lord, it is worldly convention to say that something has died or is born. 'Death,' Lord, is the cessation of the sense organs; 'birth,' Lord, is the occurrence of new sense organs. However, Lord, the *tathāgatagarbha* is not born, does not decay, does not die, does not pass away, nor arise again. Why is this? Lord, the *tathāgatagarbha* is apart from the domain of things characterized as conditioned: it is permanent, lasting, tranquil, and enduring."[22] Here the *tathāgatagarbha* is called permanent (*nitya*), lasting (*dhruva*), enduring (*śāśvata*), and (absent from ŚDS^{T}) tranquil (*śiva*). The Sanskrit RGVV goes on to agree that the *tathāgatagarbha* is called the basis (*niśraya*), support (*ādhāra*) and foundation (*pratiṣṭhitā*) that underlies all conditioned phenomena, or the stuff of repeated death and rebirth, and is somehow apart from, and unaffected by, the content of our transmigration.[23]

So the *tathāgatagarbha* is something that endures across successive births, but is best imagined as some basis or foundation on which all of our experience (though this is not explained) depends. It is always in possession of the properties of a Buddha, and indeed somehow wants for the realization of awakening; the ŚDS continues: "Lord, if there were no *tathāgatagarbha,* one could not feel revulsion for suffering, nor aspiration for *nirvāṇa*.[24] Why so? Because seven kinds of *dharma*s—the six modes of consciousness as well as knowledge of mental phenomena—do not abide

---

Compare ŚDS^{C2} 677c7–16; ŚDS^{T} 144.9–148.1. The exclusion of {不} from my translation brings ŚDS^{C1} into agreement with both ŚDS^{C2} and ŚDS^{T}. This character is excluded in a quotation of this passage (of ŚDS^{C1}) found in Zongmi's 宗密 *Yuanjue jing da shu chao* (圓覺經大疏鈔: 823/823 CE), preserved in the *Dainippon zokuzōkyō* 大日本續藏經, text no. 245(9)578a9–10 (accessed via CBETA, December 2018). I thank Stefano Zacchetti for bringing this to my attention.

22. RGVV^{S} 1.65; Johnston (1950) 1991: 45.20–46.4: *lokavyavahāra eṣa bhagavan mṛta iti vā jāta iti vā / mṛta iti bhagavann indriyoparodha eṣaḥ / jāta iti bhagavan navānām indriyāṇāṃ prādurbhāva eṣa / na punar bhagavaṃs tathāgatagarbho jāyate vā jīryati vā mriyate vā cyavate votpadyate vā / tat kasmād dhetoḥ / saṃkṛtalakṣaṇaviṣayavyativṛtto bhagavaṃs tathāgatagarbho nitya dhruvaḥ śivaḥ śāśvata iti /*

23. Johnston (1950) 1991: 72.15–73.8; also ŚDS^{T} 146.14–148.1.

24. Subtly different from the claim in the AMS (see 3.5) that the *tathāgatagarbha* is required in order for there to be such a thing as liberation.

for even an instant, and are not pained by various kinds of suffering; they are without revulsion for suffering and the aspiration for *nirvāṇa*. Lord, the *tathāgatagarbha* has no prior limit; it is characterized by a lack of origin or end; it is pained by all kinds of of suffering; it has revulsion for suffering, and aspiration for *nirvāṇa*."[25]

Here the *tathāgatagarbha* is the enduring basis of the desire for liberation. In many other Mahāyānist works this might be explained in terms of *bodhicitta,* the thought or intention (*citta*) for awakening that motivates a bodhisattva through successive rebirths toward the hard-won goal of complete awakening. Though featuring in both the MPNMS and AMS, mention of the *bodhicitta* is absent from the MBhS and also, now, the ŚDS.[26] In the ŚDS, *tathāgatagarbha* is the basis for the experience of transmigration and for the desire of its cessation, and remains, throughout, the locus for the awakened qualities of a Buddha (i.e., *dharmakāya*). Its authors perhaps acknowledged that the Buddha-nature idea can serve one of the primary functions of the *bodhicitta,* and has the advantage of referring to something that endures across lives, and so throughout the career of the bodhisattva, apart from any implied need for this to be sustained by exposure to the Mahāyāna.[27] We see also that the ŚDS contrasts *tathāgatagarbha* with the content of six modes of consciousness (operating through the six senses, including thought), as well as what is known by the mind, which are by nature transient.[28] There is no sign that *tathāgatagarbha* designates any constituent of their person that a bodhisattva might attempt to "discover"; it is instead something like an explanatory principle, relating to (1) how there is continuity for a sentient being across successive deaths, rebirths and—after due diligence—the attainment of awakening, and (2) how this same foundation, operating "beneath" the normal functions of the mind, is some basis for the desire to achieve said goal.

Importantly, apart from understanding it to be both (a) permanent and (b) unchanging, the account of *tathāgatagarbha* in the ŚDS does not bear much resemblance to the "embodied" (*buddha*)*dhātu,* or otherwise the *ātmavādin* account of *tathāgatagarbha* that is espoused and defended throughout the MPNMS, AMS, and MBhS. There is much less, in short, that resembles a notion of *ātman,* or some self that somehow "undergoes"

25. ŚDS^{C1} 222b14–19: 世尊, 若無如來藏者, 不得厭苦、樂求涅槃。何以故? 於此六識及心法智, 此七法刹那不住, 不種眾苦、不得厭苦樂求涅槃。世尊, 如來藏者, 無前際不起、不滅法、種諸苦; 得厭苦樂求涅槃。Compare ŚDS^{C2} 677c16–20; ŚDS^{T} 148.1–15. See also Eltschinger and Ratié 2013: 62n49.

26. A comprehensive study of *bodhicitta* is D. Wangchuk 2007; regarding this and its relation to *tathāgatagarbha* teaching, see ibid., 157.

27. Ibid., 291–356.

28. ŚDS^{C2} (677c17–18) refers to "six [modes of] consciousness and what is known by them" as a set of seven *dharmas*; ŚDS^{T} (148.4–6) calls the seventh simply "consciousness" (*rnam par shes pa*: *vijñāna*). See also 8.3n28; also Wayman and Wayman 1974: 105n97; also Takasaki 1974: 350–366.

transmigration (amid "twenty-five forms of existence," as stated by both the MPNMS and MBhS; see 2.3–4; 4.2). In short, the ŚDS gives its audience little cause to consider *tathāgatagarbha* to be reminiscent of *ātmavādin* teachings found in wider Indian thought, or anything like a worldly notion of a self: it is not "within" oneself, nor is it "bound" within a process of ongoing rebirth.

It is then telling that the ŚDS nonetheless clarifies that its doctrine is nothing like a such a thing: "Lord, the *tathāgatagarbha* is no *ātman,* no *sattva,* no *jīva,* no *pudgala.* The *tathāgatagarbha* is not within the domain of sentient beings who are fallen into the view of a worldly self, who have distorted [views], who are bewildered by emptiness."[29] We are by now familiar with lists of erroneous notions of selfhood, as well as the claim that the *tathāgatagarbha* cannot be known by the vast majority of sentient beings (see, e.g., 2.5, 3.3). But the presence of such a list in the ŚDS—given that it does not teach anything that strongly resembles an account of the self as this is known in wider Indian literature—is conspicuous, and leads us to hypothesize that the ŚDS reflects an audience's expectations about to what the expression *tathāgatagarbha* must refer. If an audience knew the expression *tathāgatagarbha* already, they may have known also that it carried associations with ideas that were of an *ātmavādin* orientation, about which the ŚDS expresses caution. Whereas the MPNMS presents and defends *tathāgatagarbha* as the Buddha's account of the (true) self, the ŚDS simply rejects the idea that this teaching resembles anything like selfhood, and uses the expression *tathāgatagarbha* to articulate a different account of what is consistent across the lives of sentient beings.

In summary, to the authors of the ŚDS *tathāgatagarbha* refers to the correct account of what sentient beings properly *are:* that underlying aspect of their existence that is permanent, unchanging, and the locus at which can be realized the nature/realm of phenomena (*dharmadhātu*), or the true body of the Buddha (*dharmakāya*). This refers also to some stratum of the mind, which must be understood to exist apart from all of the afflictions that obstruct its true nature. In a fashion that was particularly productive for the LAS (see 8.3), the ŚDS sets *tathāgatagarbha* in opposition to the regular operations of consciousness; hence it is no "part" of a sentient being, let alone their "self," so much as a proper understanding of the naturally pure basis to their cognitive activities and, moreover, the experience of transmigration.

In spite of this distancing from the *ātmavādin* orientation of earlier Buddha-nature works, the ŚDS still betrays clear debts to the innovations of the MPNMS. Aside from a caution about worldly notions of the self, or that which endures "within" any sentient being, the ŚDS continues to hold

29. ŚDS^{C1} 222b19–21: 世尊, 如來藏者, 非我, 非眾生, 非命, 非人。如來藏者墮身見眾生、顛倒眾生、空亂意眾生, 非其境界。Compare ŚDS^{C2} 677c20–21; ŚDS^{T} 149.15–150.4.

that the language of selfhood could still be used apropos of the Buddha's true mode of being apart from his physical person, the *dharmakāya*.

5.3 The *Dharmakāya* and Its Qualities

We have seen that in the ŚDS the term *tathāgatagarbha* refers to something like the underlying nature of a sentient being, conceptualized in mentalistic terms, without this referring to anything "hidden" about their constitution. But the ŚDS maintains the idea that each sentient being is the locus for the actualization, in the world, of a Buddha, and employs the expression *tathāgatagarbha* to refer to the basis for the emergence of a Buddha in the world that runs "beneath" successive births into the experience of liberation. The perspective of the ŚDS is that at the other end of this process—the eradication of afflictions, and so the actualization of a Buddha—the *tathāgatagarbha* is better known as the *dharmakāya:* the mode of the Buddha's existence that is characterized by supermundane properties.

There is likely no single interpretation of the term *dharmakāya* that will do justice to its different usages across Mahāyānist, let alone wider, Buddhist literature.[30] However, we can reliably understand that this refers in any instance to a "truer" mode of the Buddha's existence than any impermanent, physical body of his that was seen and heard in the world. The ŚDS ties its own account of the *dharmakāya* to the position that there exists only a single vehicle (*ekayāna*) of Buddhist teaching, and so only one form of liberation: that which is proper to a Buddha. "Attainment of supreme, complete awakening is attainment of the realm (*dhātu*) of *nirvāṇa;* the realm of *nirvāṇa* is precisely the *dharmakāya* of the Tathāgata; the supreme *dhamakāya* is the supreme, single vehicle. Between the Tathāgata and *dharmakāya* there is no difference: the Tathāgata is the *dharmakāya*. Attaining the profound *dharmakāya,* one attains the supreme, single vehicle: that which is supreme is without limit or cessation."[31] At face value these equations seem to communicate little, but for some audience it may well have been worth establishing that inhabiting the realm of *nirvāṇa,* otherwise "being liberated," constitutes attainment of what can be called the *dharmakāya*. Equating this with both the Tathāgata (presumably, by implication, the awakened person Śākyamuni), and indeed with the single vehicle that is his teaching, establishes that buddhahood and knowledge of the vehicle that leads to it refer also to the liberated reality that lies behind any physical Buddha: the *dharmakāya*.

It is at this juncture that the ŚDS reintroduces its understanding of Buddha-nature, and declares that "the *dharmakāya,* not separated from the

30. See also 2.1n15.

31. ŚDS^{C1} 220c22–26: 阿耨多羅三藐三菩提者，即是涅槃界。涅槃界者，即是如來法身。得究竟法身者，則究竟一乘。無異如來無異法身：如來即法身。得究竟法身者，則究竟一乘。究竟者，即是無邊不斷。 Compare ŚDS^{C2} 676b8–12; ŚDS^{T} 108.9–16.

sheath of afflictions, is called *tathāgatagarbha*."[32] Hence these two expressions—*tathāgatagarbha* and *dharmakāya*—refer to the same thing, but so long as there exist afflictions (which obscure, as we read above, the pure status of the mind), we should speak about the *tathāgatagarbha,* the basis for transmigration that underlies ongoing birth and death. The *dharmakāya,* meanwhile, refers to a mode of the Buddha's being (a "body," *kāya*) that is precisely a collection (*kāya* also) of supermundane qualities (*dharmas*) that distinguish it from anything proper to mundane existence.

The qualities that the ŚDS holds are proper to the *dharmakāya* are familiar. Having repeated the classic Buddhist formula of four distortions (*viparyāsas*)—that is, that sentient beings impute selfhood in regard to what is not the self, permanence in regard to what is impermanent, and so forth (see 2.2)—the ŚDS states that there are still *correct* thoughts about self, permanence, bliss, and purity, with clear echoes of the MPNMS: "The *dharmakāya* of the Tathāgata is the perfection of permanence, the perfection of bliss, the perfection of self, and perfection of purity; those who see the *dharmakāya* of the Buddha as such have the correct view."[33] Based on the quotation of this passage in the Sanskrit RGVV, we know that our translations of the ŚDS reflect expressions including *ātmapāramitā,* "the perfection of self."[34] The RGVV refers to this set of four as the "perfected qualities" (*guṇapāramitās*) of the *dharmakāya,* though this expression is absent from the ŚDS and so should be avoided while we attend strictly to this text on its own terms. Indeed, the RGVV has much more to say about these qualities (see 7.3–4), but their occurrence in the ŚDS—which offers no further elaboration—must have had some relevance for its own, certainly earlier audience. We must take care to contextualize these predicates of the *dharmakāya* and not misrepresent the position of the ŚDS through the lens of either the RGVV or, indeed, the MPNMS.

These four predicates are all proper to the *dharmakāya*—"perfections," we presume, in the sense of the "highest" form of some or other quality.[35] The *ātmapāramitā* is perhaps then a superlative or supermundane form of *ātman* or selfhood (which the RGVV on one occasion explains to mean *paramātmapāramitā,* or "the perfection of a self that is supreme/other"; see 7.3). The *tathāgatagarbha,* we have seen, is the *dharmakāya* rid of afflictions; the ŚDS understands the *tathāgatagarbha* to possess already the properties of the Buddha (and so is also "not-empty" of them; see 9.4). Otherwise the ŚDS teaches that the *tathāgatagarbha* refers to nothing like a worldly notion of selfhood, so this is surely not meant to be contradicted by attribution of *ātmapāramitā* to the *dharmakāya* (which is, lest we forget, the Buddha's existence

32. ŚDS^{C1} 221c10–11: 世尊，如是如來法身，不離煩惱藏，名如來藏。Compare ŚDS^{C2} 677a18–19; ŚDS^{T} 130.6–8.

33. ŚDS^{C1} 222a23–25: 如來法身是常波羅蜜、樂波羅蜜、我波羅蜜、淨波羅蜜。於佛法身, 作是見者, 是名正見。Compare ŚDS^{C2} 677b26–28; ŚDS^{T} 142.1–4.

34. Johnston (1950) 1991: 31.3–4.

35. See Hikata 1958: x–xii; Dayal 1970: 165–166.

apart from all that is worldly). It is likely an important detail that these perfections predicate the *dharmakāya* and not, explicitly, the *tathāgatagarbha,* or the state of the *dharmakāya* while it remains afflicted, and an aspect of sentient beings as they continue to transmigrate.[36]

Moreover, the "perfected" self of the *dharmakāya*—unlike the "self that is the Buddha" in MPNMS-dhk (see 2.2)—is not called merely *ātman* but rather *ātmapāramitā.* We have no evidence of this term, nor of the other "perfections" among which it is numbered, in demonstrably earlier Buddhist sources, and these were perhaps inventions by the authors of the ŚDS to distinguish what could be said about the *dharmakāya* from any (erroneous) notions of selfhood, permanence, etcetera in regard to worldly phenomena. The ŚDS provides no further detail regarding what *ātmapāramitā* might mean; for this we have only the interpretation of these categories offered by the RGVV, to which we turn later (7.3). But it is likely very significant that the authors of the ŚDS approved of the idea, found otherwise in the MPNMS (specifically MPNMS-dhk), that inverted perspectives of the four distortions correctly describe the Buddha in his transcendent mode of being.[37] What the authors of the ŚDS did *not* want was for these qualities to be confused for worldly notions of, for example, selfhood, and hence the *dharmakāya* must exhibit specifically the "perfection" of selfhood that is somehow above, beyond, or at any rate "different to" *ātman* as any worldly person could possibly understand such a thing.[38]

The account of *ātmapāramitā* in the ŚDS must represent some response to language exhibited by the MPNMS. The true mode of the Buddha's existence can be expressed in terms of the "perfection" of self, etcetera, but not—as expressed more simply, in MPNMS-dhk—as simply "the self" (see 2.2). The picture that is emerging is one in which the ŚDS finds that innovative terminology found in the MPNMS was in need of not only refinement but also some creative reinvention. The expression *tathāgatagarbha* still describes a fundamental identity between transmigrating and liberated beings, but does not resemble at all an account of the self; it is nothing "within" sentient

36. This disagrees with S. King 1991: 12; 1997: 177; also Matsumoto 1997: 170. See also Zapart 2017: 151–152.

37. Though Takasaki held that the ŚDS belongs to the main trajectory of the *tathāgatagarbha* literary tradition (1974: 111–126), he nevertheless acknowledges that the account of these four "inversions" appears more developed in the ŚDS than in the MPNMS (ibid., 167); see also Shimoda 1991. The current chapter agrees with Radich's contention (2015a: 85–97) that the ŚDS exhibits no good evidence that it predates the MPNMS.

38. The absence of any detail regarding what "perfection" means in this context is frustrating, but perhaps the authors of the ŚDS intended little besides a distinction between "worldly" qualities and what is proper to the Mahāyāna and its teachings about that which is supermundane. In complement to established Mahāyānist interest in the "perfection" of virtues—giving (*dānapāramitā*), discipline (*śīlapāramitā*), etcetera—the ŚDS may simply be employing *pāramitā* as a hallmark of Mahāyānist teaching, to communicate that, for example, *ātman* proper to the *dharmakāya* is a superlative quality (*pāramitā*), realized at the terminus of the path of superlative virtues (*pāramitā*s also) that is known to bodhisattvas.

beings, but something that underlies or underpins successive births. The Buddha himself, meanwhile, should not be imagined in terms of some enduring self, but could be thought to exhibit some "perfected" form of selfhood beyond any worldly account of anything by a similar name. All of this, the ŚDS reminds us, is of course above the comprehension of arhats and *pratyekabuddhas*, persons who are new to the path of the bodhisattva, and other sentient beings besides.

At this juncture we might take stock of the distinction between the Buddha-nature idea as expressed in the MPNMS-group and as we find it taught by the ŚDS. The MPNMS-group articulates *tathāgatagarbha* in a manner that understands sentient beings to be in possession of some self ("*ātmavāda*"), whereas the ŚDS conceptualizes sentient beings in terms of the composition and workings of the mind ("*vijñānavāda*").[39] The MPNMS-group consistently presents the *tathāgatagarbha* (otherwise some *dhātu* or "essence") as something like a transmigrating *subject,* or the kernel of one's personhood that undergoes transmigration and eventually achieves the status of an awakened subject acting in the world, a Buddha. But in the ŚDS the expression *tathāgatagarbha* says nothing about the corporeal constitution of a sentient being so much as that which underlies their successive transmigrations and, eventually, their liberation: something like an awakened *substrate,* which possesses the qualities of what is a markedly impersonal conceptualization of the Buddha's true form, his *dharmakāya.* This is a "body" of supermundane qualities rather than any personal entity that enjoys a pleasant, enduring state apart from (yet still operating in) the world, the latter of which would better describe the Buddha of the MPNMS-group of *sūtras* and their own articulations of what it means to discover one's enduring Buddha-nature or, indeed, the self.

5.4 On "Singularity"

We have seen in previous chapters that the MPNMS-group of *sūtras* revisits and reimagines some important aspects of earlier Buddhist teaching, most notably the Buddha's complete rejection of discourse about the self but also—in the same vein as the SP—dismissing the vehicles of the *śrāvaka* and *pratyekabuddha* by teaching that all sentient beings possess already the nature of a Buddha. Though the ŚDS disagrees with the MPNMS about how to understand the expression *tathāgatagarbha,* it shares both a commitment to the single vehicle paradigm (*ekayāna*) promoted by the SP, and—like other texts concerned with Buddha-nature—continues to provide novel interpretations of some other central Buddhist teachings.[40]

39. I here intend *vijñānavāda*, "discourse/teaching about consciousness," in a broad sense that is not reducible to the Yogācāra-Vijñānavāda tradition of philosophy; see also 8.1n6.

40. There is a possibility that the ŚDS is quoting the SP where it declares that "who has the correct view [about the *dharmakāya*] are the Buddha's true sons, born from his mouth,

For example, the MPNMS(-tg) reinterprets the "four truths"—of suffering, its arising, its possible cessation, and the path that leads to this—that were supposedly the content of the Buddha's very first discourse.[41] In the MPNMS, the truth of "suffering" (*duḥkha*) refers to ignorance regarding the permanence of the Buddha,[42] and the truth of its cessation (*nirodha*) to the *tathāgatagarbha* that lies dormant beneath myriad afflictions.[43] The ŚDS also reconfigures the four truths in order to affirm that only one of them is "ultimately true" (*diyi yidi* 第一義諦; *don dam pa'i bden pa: *paramārthasatya*): the truth of the cessation of suffering.[44] Insofar as both texts understand "what is ultimate" to refer to Buddha-nature (however this is conceptualized), they are in agreement that an end to the experience of suffering constitutes the removal of afflictions from that which exhibits already, were it only to be cleansed, the superlative qualities of a Buddha.

This reduction of Buddhist categories to single principles is a recurring theme in the ŚDS, but also—here and there—in both the MPNMS and AMS.[45] In the midst of its account of the *tathāgatagarbha*, just before the pivotal suggestion that a bodhisattva make himself "like a *stūpa*" (see 2.3), the MPNMS established that there are not, ultimately speaking, three distinct refuges (i.e., the Buddha, dharma, and sangha) but that "the Buddha is himself the three refuges."[46] This same idea is found in the AMS,

born from true dharma, emanations of the dharma, attaining a portion of the dharma" (e.g., ŚDS^{C1} 222a24–26, echoing SP 61.2–3 [Kern 1884: 61]). However, this refrain is found in a number of other texts, including the *Pañcaviṃśatisahāsrikā-prajñāpāramitā* (Dutt 1934: 122.20–123.2) and *Mahāvastu* (Senart 1897: 54.17–55.4). This has likely origins in language proper to the Brahmanical tradition, as suggested by the *Assalāyanasutta* (MN.II.147) and what seems to be an allusion to *Ṛgveda* verse 10.90, the well-known *Puruṣasūkta* (van Nooten and Holland 1994: 531–532).

A further detail is that according to our Chinese translations the Buddha predicts that Queen Śrīmālā, in a future life, will become a Buddha by the name Samantaprabhāsa (ŚDS^{C1} 217b15–16; ŚDS^{C2} 673a29: 普光), a name from a series of future Buddhas predicted in the SP (206; 207.9, 208.10, 209.4; Kern 1884: 198–200). In ŚDS^{T} we find instead Samantabhadra (*kun tu bzang po*); a bodhisattva by this name has an entire (likely late) chapter of the SP devoted to him (SP 472–483; Kern 1884: 431–440).

41. See, for example, the Pāli *Dhammacakkappavattanasutta* (SN.V.420–424).

42. See MPNMS^{F} 882c4–16; MPNSM^{D} 406b6–12; MPNMS^{T} §367. Here MPNMS^{T} celebrates *de bzhin gshegs pa'i che ba nyid,* perhaps Skt. **tathāgatamāhātyma,* "the majesty of the Tathāgata." See also 2.3; also 6.3.

43. MPNMS^{F} 883a4–12; MPNMS^{D} 406c11–19; MPNSM^{T} §369.6–13.

44. ŚDS^{C1} 221c25–222a3; ŚDS^{C2} 677a29–b9; ŚDS^{T} 132.15–136.6. See also R. King 1995b: 7.

45. Indeed, a Sanskrit fragment of the ŚDS preserves the claim that the text reveals the definitive meaning (*nītārtha*) based on "singularity" (*ekatvapratisaraṇa*); Matsuda 2000: 72–73.

46. Expressed most clearly in MPNMS^{T} §391.3–6: *gcig pu la skyabs su song shig / ye shes 'di la ni skyabs gsum med de / chos dang dge 'du ba yang med do // sangs rgyas nyid chos kyang yin / dge 'dun yang yin te / de bzhin gshegs pa nyid gzhi gsum pa yin no //* (Take refuge in but one thing: in this knowledge [taught here] there are not three refuges, as there is neither dharma nor the assembly of the sangha. Rather, the Buddha is the dharma, and also the sangha; the Tathāgata is himself the three refuges). Compare MPNMS^{F} 884c21–24; MPNMS^{D} 409c27–410a1. See also Habata 2015b: 180–183; Radich 2015a: 139–140.

which explains the single vehicle to mean also a "single refuge" (**ekaśarana*), which we are again told refers to the Buddha; because both the dharma and sangha depend on a Buddha for their (re)appearance in the world, these two can be called "strategic" refuges (*fangbianyi* 方便依; *thabs kyi skyabs: *aupāyikaśaraṇa*)—so taught by the Buddha for some expedient purpose—whereas a Buddha alone is the "ultimate refuge" (*diyi yiyi* 第一義依; *don dam thabs: *paramārthaśaraṇa*).[47] In a very similar fashion, the ŚDS relates the teaching of the single vehicle to the authority of only a single refuge:

> The dharma is the path of the single vehicle; the sangha is the assembly of the three vehicles. These two refuges are not the supreme refuge; they are called partial refuges. Why is this? Teaching the dharma that is the path of the single vehicle, one attains the supreme *dharmakāya;* there is no teaching higher than the practice of dharma proper to the single vehicle.
>
> ...
>
> The ultimate meaning of the two refuges is the supreme refuge: the Tathāgata. Why is this? Because the Tathāgata is not different from the two refuges. The Tathāgata is precisely the three refuges. Why is this? Because he teaches the path of the single vehicle.[48]

Both the AMS and ŚDS envisage teachings about a single vehicle and single refuge to complement one another, though the latter is an innovation beyond what we find in the SP.[49] Both the AMS and ŚDS emphasize that the refuges of the dharma and sangha are only either "strategic" (AMS: *fangbian* 方便; *thabs*) or "partial" (ŚDS: *shaofen* 少分; *yan lag gi*); in either instance, they are not the ultimate refuge that is the Buddha himself. The Buddha as the one true refuge is the fountainhead of the other two; the single vehicle (i.e., the Mahāyāna) is the mechanism by which new Buddhas are produced.

Hence the ŚDS reflects a kind of "streamlining" of Buddhist doctrine: that there is but one truth (the cleansing of one's Buddha-nature) and one refuge (a Buddha, after one's Buddha-nature has been fully revealed). Very likely this kind of thinking is indebted to the SP, which earlier than both the ŚDS and AMS had reduced the three vehicles of discrete kinds of liberation (those proper to the *śrāvaka, pratyekabuddha,* and bodhisattva)

---

47. AMS^{C} 530a8–20; compare AMS^{T} D.213, 165a4–b1; Q.879, 172b1–5.

48. ŚDS^{C1} 221a4–15: 法者即是說一乘道；　僧者是三乘眾。此二歸依非究竟歸依，名少分歸依。何以故？說一乘道法，得究竟法身；於上更無說一乘法事[a] … 此二歸依第一義是究竟歸依如來。何以故？無異如來，無異二歸依。如來即三歸依。何以故？說一乘道。

[a] Yuan/Ming/Palace 事 = T 身

Compare ŚDS^{C2} 676b19–29. Compare ŚDS^{T} 112.5–116.4.

49. The idea that the Buddha is the "supreme refuge" (*śaraṇaṃ param*) survives into the RGV (v.1.20; Johnston [1950] 1991: 18.12–13); I am grateful to Dorji Wangchuk for bringing this to my attention.

to the single vehicle that is the Mahāyāna.[50] According to the ŚDS, "The vehicles of the *śrāvaka* and *pratyeka[buddha]* are included in the Mahāyāna. The Mahāyāna is the vehicle of the Buddha(s); hence the three vehicles are a single vehicle."[51] But whereas the SP introduces the single vehicle as something that the Buddha makes clear only for some audiences (see 9.2), the ŚDS—just as in its treatment of Buddha-nature thought—attempts a formalization of this idea, and an account of how persons previously believed to be liberated (i.e., arhats and *pratyekabuddhas*) still, in some subtle fashion, remain bound to transmigration (see 9.2).[52] With the benefit of Sanskrit terminology preserved in the RGVV, we can determine that the ŚDS teaches that arhats, *pratyekabuddhas*, and bodhisattvas "who possess great power" (*vaśitāprāpta*) are all still reborn via "mind-made bodies" (*manomayakāya*). This survives what is called "the death consisting of an inconceivable transformation" (*acintyā pāriṇāmikī cyuti*), which has left behind transmigration as it is normally understood.[53] The ŚDS tells us that while all of these revered beings have eliminated four kinds of fundamental "bases" or "entrenchments" (*vāsabhūmis*) that hinder all sentient beings, they have not yet eliminated all afflictions due to the "basis of ignorance" (*avidyāvāsabhūmi*) that is the fundamental cause of all other kinds of mental affliction.[54] Eradicating this underlying cause results in the attainment of awakening, which—in accordance with the central revelation of the SP—is the only definitive kind of liberation that there is.

Crucially, and unlike the SP, the ŚDS does not present the single vehicle as something controversial or unheard of. It stresses the superiority of the Mahāyāna, and refers to the arhat and *pratyekabuddha* only in order to undermine their achievements; for example, their inability to comprehend the *tathāgatagarbha*, and their continuing bondage, in some subtle manner, to transmigration. Just as it does not need to explain that *tathāgatagarbha*

50. For example, SP 48.13–14 (v.2.69); Kern 1884: 48 (presented there as v.2.68). See also 9.1.

51. ŚDS^{C1} 220c19–21: 聲聞，緣覺乘皆入大乘，大乘者即是佛乘，是故三乘即是一乘。Compare ŚDS^{T} 108.2–7.

52. ŚDS^{C1} 219c2–7: 有餘生法不盡 … 言得涅槃者是佛方便 ([arhats and *pratyekabuddhas*] have not exhausted further birth … saying that they have attained *nirvāṇa* is a stratagem of the Buddha[s]). Compare ŚDS^{C2} 675a27–b4; ŚDS^{T} 74.6–76.1.

53. See, for example, ŚDS^{C1} 219c20–23 (compare ŚDS^{C2} 675c2–3; ŚDS^{T} 80.3–9). For more on *manomayakāya*, see Radich 2007: 224–284, together with Pāli *sutta* material that he cites (e.g., AN.V.17.166), concerned with celestial forms that can be attained by highly accomplished *śrāvakas*; also Radich 2010. Lee (2014: 65–79) discusses *manomayakāya* in light of the Sarvāstivādin *Mahāvibhāṣā* (T.1545[27]363a20–21); also Kubota (1999) attends to the same term as it appears in Vasubandhu's (also Sarvāstivādin) *Abhidharmakośabhāṣya* (e.g., 3.40: Pradhan 1967: 153.10–12; La Vallée Poussin 1923: 122, 209n2).

54. These Sanskrit expressions are known through quotations in the Sanskrit RGVV; see Johnston (1950) 1991: 33.4–34.7. The other four "bases"—sometimes translated "entrenchments"—being those in (1) views of monism, (2) desire for sense pleasure, (3) desire for physical form, and (4) desire for existence; regarding these, see ŚDS^{C1} 220a3–a5; ŚDS^{C2} 675b19–22; ŚDS^{T} 84–86.

refers to something about the status of sentient beings, the ŚDS takes for granted that its audience has encountered before—and is not shocked by—the idea that the Buddha taught vehicles that are inferior to the Mahāyāna (the "Hīnayāna") as only strategies or expediencies. For all of its technicality, the intent of the ŚDS is quite clear: to explain, after the SP, how there can exist only a single vehicle, and how individuals who were commonly believed to have achieved a kind of liberation—arhats and *pratyekabuddhas*—must have more work to do, in some subtle mode of existence, before they fully escape transmigration.

In summary, the ŚDS presents a systematic treatment of how the Buddha-nature idea and the doctrine of the single vehicle can complement one another. In contrast to what we see in the MPNMS-group, these two tenets are presented in such a fashion that they do not seem to be new or contentious, though they were in need of careful exposition—perhaps what was seen to be lacking in works such as the SP, or in others that had experimented already with Buddha-nature articulated as an account of the self.

5.5 Conclusions

Authors of the MPNMS, AMS, and MBhS shared not only common ideas about the *tathāgatagarbha,* or otherwise *buddhadhātu,* but also a preoccupation with defending what are "cryptic" utterances of the Buddha that require further explanation, and a shared prophetic narrative about the prospects of the dharma after the Buddha's (apparent) disappearance (see chapter 9). The ŚDS, by contrast, reflects a different understanding of Buddha-nature, and one apart from any sense that teaching it will endanger its advocates. Its pivotal claim is that the expression *tathāgatagarbha* must refer to the intrinsically pure nature of the mind, and after this—once this mind has been cleansed of all that afflicts it—exhibits the superlative, transcendent qualities of the *dharmakāya.* In accordance with its "ekayānist" orientation, the ŚDS still understands *nirvāṇa* to refer to the only definitive kind of liberation that exists, or otherwise the achievement of full buddhahood. In the meantime, *tathāgatagarbha* is the basis of our desire for this liberation, which endures across successive lives; it is something like a substratum that functions unaffected beneath the events of successive moments of consciousness, across one life and those that succeed it. Whereas in the MPNMS-group afflictions obscure the nature of the Buddha, which is understood as some static element (*dhātu*), in the ŚDS they are impurities that sully sentient beings understood in mentalistic terms, an understanding of Buddha-nature that proved especially productive for authors of the RGV(V) (7.1) and of the LAS (see 8.3).

As the *tathāgatagarbha* is no enduring, constituent element, it makes little sense for such a thing to be articulated in terms of selfhood. The insistence in the ŚDS that *tathāgatagarbha* refers to nothing like such a thing, in spite of the fact that the *sūtra* promotes nothing like a permanent, unchanging kernel to experience, implies that its authors knew of the *ātmavādin* flavor of Buddha-nature teachings expressed in another corner of the Mahāyāna literary tradition. It is also quite clear that the ŚDS develops other themes found otherwise in the MPNMS, AMS, and, predating all of these sources, some form of the SP.[55] That the ŚDS reconfigures the four truths, prioritizes the Buddha as a single refuge, and accepts the single vehicle paradigm suggest influence by these other Mahāyānist works. But nothing is more telling than the manner in which the ŚDS explains the *dharmakāya* and its four "perfections," in a manner that evokes Buddhological statements that were made by the MPNMS specifically (see 2.2, 2.3).

Hence the ŚDS represents an important turning point in the *tathāgatagarbha* tradition: a reinvention of the *ātmavādin* form of Buddha-nature teaching into something new and, evidence suggests, more palatable for a wider Buddhist audience (see also chapters 7 and 8). The ŚDS recycles terms and categories from the MPNMS (or, at any rate, some milieu that accepted its teachings), but rejects the central claim that *tathāgatagarbha* refers to some "thing" that resides in every sentient being, or otherwise what could be called their self. Its authors preserve the central Buddha-nature idea—a commonality between transmigrating and liberated beings—but explain this to refer to some mentalistic foundation common to both kinds of existence. Buddha-nature is hence nothing "within" a sentient being: it is the enduring basis for the existence of a sentient being that is already, were it not for the presence of afflictions, the "womb" (*garbha*) wherein one can find, and from which can emerge, the qualities of a Buddha.

Before leaving the ŚDS, and with the benefit of having observed distinctions between its teachings and the *ātmavādin* mode of the Buddha-nature idea that came before it, we should at least acknowledge some of the criticism that this text has received from modern scholarship. Some

55. The ŚDS and AMS share an unusual simile: a comparison of the *saddharma* to four great burdens (*mahābhāras*) that are felt by the physical earth (its oceans, mountains, and vegetation, and the mass of sentient beings; see Kanō 2000: 69); these are also mentioned briefly in the *Mahāyānasūtralaṃkāra* (15.2); Lévi 1907: 97–98). In the AMS these are compared to four kinds of condemnation that the bodhisattva will face when trying to teach about the Buddha's permanence, and the *tathāgatagarbha,* in the final eighty years of the dharma (e.g., AMS^{C} 537c20–538a21; see also 3.1n6). In the ŚDS these burdens are compared to a need to impart either (1) good moral conduct or (2–4) the vehicles of the *śrāvaka, pratyekabuddha,* or bodhisattva to different sentient beings (e.g., ŚDS^{C1} 218b7–b15). While the AMS reflects an environment in which Buddha-nature teaching was contentious, the ŚDS folds this simile into a picture of the ("ekayānist") Mahāyāna providing different teachings for different audiences. It is also possible that the ŚDS intends allusion to the AMS in the name of its key speaker. Śrīmālā is a queen and daughter of King Prasenajit, whose name (absent from any assuredly earlier Buddhist sources, so perhaps an invention of the text's authors) is "pleasant/auspicious garland" (*śrī-mālā*), and whose teaching about *tathāgatagarbha* is perhaps preferable to that which was associated with the terrible "garland of fingers" (*aṅguli-māla*).

readers of the ŚDS—for example, Shirō Matsumoto, on behalf of the "Critical Buddhist" (Hihan Bukkyō) movement—have suggested that by virtue of presenting the *tathāgatagarbha* as something like a permanent, unchanging stratum upon which transmigration is based, the ŚDS relinquishes any right to be considered an authentically "Buddhist" text.[56] According to Matsumoto, the ŚDS espouses a "*dhātuvāda*" orientation: an account of transmigration which posits that impermanent, conditioned phenomena are generated by a permanent, unconditioned substratum (*dhātu* in the sense of a "cause" or "basis" from which phenomena are generated), in opposition to wider Indian Buddhist denial of any conceptual need for a such a thing (see 1.1).

Even if one is persuaded by Matsumoto's reading of the ŚDS, and of its lack of credibility as a truly "Buddhist" text (which entails a questionably essentialist model of Indian Buddhism, and a disapproval of Indian Buddhist innovation; see 10.4), it is in our interest to recognize that the ŚDS makes an undoubtedly different kind of claim to that found in our *ātmavāda tathāgatagarbha* sources. All three texts that espouse *ātmavādin* modes of Buddha-nature teaching suggest that audiences will struggle with what is being revealed in the text; the ŚDS, by contrast, does not *itself* claim that its doctrine sits at odds with established Buddhist tradition.[57] On the contrary, the ŚDS understands *tathāgatagarbha* to refer to a teaching established elsewhere in the dharma—namely the intrinsic purity or luminosity of the mind (see also 9.3)—and so may be our earliest source for a second phase of teaching about Buddha-nature in India.

---

56. See articles reproduced in Hubbard and Swanson 1997. Recent responses to the Hihan Bukkyō critique are Yamabe 2017 and Shimoda 2020.

57. Matsumoto (2014: 283–292) has since argued that the MPNMS also exhibits "*dhātuvāda*" teaching in a manner comparable to the ŚDS, by virtue of (a) presenting the Buddha/*buddhadhātu* as *ātman,* and (b) this *ātman* referring to some ground of existence (i.e., the "*dhātu*" as a "generative monism" in any instance of some "*dhātuvāda*"). However, any Upaniṣadic undertones to the MPNMS do not extend to its account of the self being anything that can be identified with an empowering force of creation (e.g., *brahman*), specifically, so much as with the Buddha. While Matsumoto's *dhātuvāda* model is superficially closer to the picture painted by the ŚDS (in which the expression *dhātu* is itself never used, which is an irony of Matsumoto's focus on the ŚDS as a "*dhātuvāda*" text), the MPNMS-group of texts understand *dhātu* as the presence of a discrete instance of Buddha-nature in the constitution of any individual sentient being, with no sense of it being the cause or basis for the content of transmigration.

CHAPTER 6

Other *Tathāgatagarbha* Sources

At this juncture we benefit from turning our attention to three exceptional works that sit on the periphery of the main interest of this study. Both the *Anūnatvāpūrṇatvanirdeśaparivarta* and *Tathāgatagarbhasūtra* are Indian Buddhist *sūtra*s that teach about the expression *tathāgatagarbha*. These two, together with the ŚDS, constitute a triad of *tathāgatagarbha* works that were prioritized by Jikidō Takasaki (see 1.2). However, both of them are conspicuous for making no reference—approving or otherwise—to the *tathāgatagarbha* and its relationship to discourse about the self. They are nevertheless both significant works in this textual tradition, and their relative positions in the development of Buddha-nature thought warrant attention before we turn to the *Ratnagotravibhāgavyākhyā* (RGVV; see the next chapter), which they both influenced. A third text, the *Mahāyānasūtrālaṃkāra*—together with Indian commentarial materials associated with it—is exceptional for the more obvious reason that it does not provide a full-throated account of *tathāgatagarbha* at all. However, it does reflect an awareness of this expression and *sūtra*s concerned with it, likely predates the completion of the RGVV, and attends also to the claim that the Buddha can be considered to have achieved something worthy of articulation in terms of the self, or *ātman*.

6.1 The *Anūnatvāpūrṇatvanirdeśaparivarta*

The *Anūnatvāpūrṇatvanirdeśaparivarta* (AAN) survives only in one Chinese translation, produced by Bodhiruci 菩提流支 (d.527; distinct from the translator named in 5.1) in 520 CE (T.668: *Foshuo buzeng bujian jing* 佛說不增不減經; see Silk 2015b: 3–14). Some of its content is otherwise available in quotations by the RGVV, which takes the AAN, together with the ŚDS, as its central authorities on the *tathāgatagarbha*. An edition and thorough study of the AAN is that by Jonathan Silk (2015b), who contends—contra Takasaki—that the AAN is likely influenced by the ideas and language of the ŚDS, and not the inverse.[1] As the AAN does not consider *tathāgatagarbha*

1. Silk 2015b: 9–12; especially note 36.

in terms of selfhood—and Silk's study does much to unpack the language and doctrine of the text besides—we need not consider it in tremendous depth here.[2] But we should observe that the AAN reflects something like a maturation of ideas present already in the ŚDS, and in particular the identification of the *tathāgatagarbha* with a particular conception of the *dharmakāya*. Like the ŚDS, the AAN does not present the *tathāgatagarbha* as something that resides "within" sentient beings, or as a component element of their being. Hence the AAN constitutes a further development of *tathāgatagarbha* teaching after this expression had been extricated from its *ātmavādin* roots, in reference now to a common basis to the existence of sentient beings and of liberated Buddhas, which is here called the single nature (*yijie* 一界: *ekadhātu*) of reality itself.

The AAN is framed as a discussion between the Buddha and the arhat Śāriputra. Its ideas are presented more systematically than in other works of the *tathāgatagarbha* tradition, and it has the flavor of other short Buddhist discourses—such as the *Brahmajālasutta* (DN.I.1–46)—that categorize and confront a plethora of wrong-minded views.[3] In particular, and as befits its title, the AAN establishes how there can be neither decrease (*anūnatva*) nor increase (*apūrṇatva*) in the "realm" of sentient beings (*sattvadhātu*), which refers to the totality of transmigrating entities. The problem, considered in other Buddhist compositions besides, is whether or not an awakened being's achievement of *nirvāṇa* constitutes a decline in the number of sentient beings, and a swelling of the "realm of *nirvāṇa*" (*nirvāṇadhātu*) as an alternative plane of existence.[4] Something like this issue is broached also in the MBhS (see 4.5), but there the slightly different angle is the continuity of a sentient being, or what is proper to them (*dhātu*), rather than the extent of what may be distinct realms of existence (*dhātu* also) proper to sentient beings or to Buddhas. Similarities between these two *sūtra*s are superficial, and their approaches to the matter of decrease or increase reveal differences rather than similarities between their respective forms of Buddha-nature teaching.[5]

The answer to the problem of decrease or increase provided by the AAN is that there is in fact only a single "nature/realm of phenomena" (*yi fajie* 一法界: *ekadharmadhātu*), which accounts for the existence of both sentient beings and Buddhas, and which experiences no fluctuation in its extent.[6] From the perspective of a Buddha, this single reality can be called

2. For a guide to prior scholarship concerning the AAN, see ibid., 1n4.

3. Ibid., 15–16.

4. Ibid., 22–29.

5. See Jones 2016b.

6. Silk 2015b: 29, 64 (§4i); see also Grosnick 1977. The expression *dharmadhātu* can refer to the causal basis for all phenomena (i.e., *dhātu* in the sense of *hetu*, an aspect of *tathāgatagarbha* as understood by the RGVV: see 7.4; also Johnston [1950] 1991: 72.5–73.8), and is otherwise a synonym for reality properly understood; see, for example, *Madhyāntavibhāgakārikābhāṣya* 1.14–15 (Nagao 1964: 23.14–24.2). It is also the subject of the

either *tathāgatagarbha* or *dharmakāya,* and depending on its degree of "purity" (*śuddhi*) refers to the existence of a sentient being, a bodhisattva, or—when entirely cleansed of afflictions—a Buddha.[7] The AAN teaches that all three categories of being depend upon the same *dharmadhātu,* on the same underlying nature of all phenomena, and so, as Silk writes, the AAN treads close to a form of monism.[8] We read otherwise that this *dharmakāya,* when it is afflicted (and so better called *tathāgatagarbha*) is nothing other than the "essence/nature" (*dhātu*), as well as the "realm" (*dhātu* also) of all sentient beings who undergo transmigration: "When this *dharmakāya,* Śāriputra, covered by the sheath of ten thousand afflictions, is being swept along by the stream of transmigration, moving though the course of birth and death that is beginningless transmigration, this is referred to as 'the realm of sentient beings' (*sattvadhātu*)."[9] This translates a Sanskrit portion of the AAN preserved in the RGVV.[10] The "realm" of sentient beings—which can also be understood as "that which is their essence"—is also the presence of the *dharmakāya;* when it is sullied (and so called *tathāgatagarbha*) there occurs transmigration, but when it is cleansed there is liberation. Between these two poles exists the bodhisattva, who works to purge the *tathāgatagarbha* from that which obscures or pollutes it.

With echoes of what we have seen in the ŚDS (5.1), the AAN also relates *tathāgatagarbha* to the intrinsic purity of the mind (**prakṛtipariśuddhacitta*).[11] However, the *tathāgatagarbha-dharmakāya* is also said to be inseparable from "the *dharmadhātu* of insight and pure reality."[12] While the AAN does refer

---

Dharmadhātustava, traditionally attributed to Nāgārjuna but more likely composed in the latter half of the first millennium, though prior to the eighth century (Zhen 2015: xxxii; also Ruegg 1971). Here *dharmadhātu* is said to abide in all sentient beings (v.1: *sarvasattveṣv avasthita*), though one surviving Chinese form of the text instead understands this to refer to the *dharmakāya* (*fashen* 法身; see Zhen 2015: 8n2). Otherwise the *Dharmadhātustava* echoes the similes of the lamp in a pot that is found in the MBhS (ibid., 9 [v.5–7]; see 4.1), compares the *dharmadhātu* to an embryo (ibid., 13 [v.27]), and stresses that its teaching implies no notion of *ātman* (ibid., 13 [v.24–25], 15 [v.35]). In short, *dharmadhātu* expounded in this short and curious text resembles a form of Buddha-nature teaching, though likely postdates the sources considered in this volume. For other examples of Buddha-nature articulated in terms of *dharmadhātu,* see 8.6.

7. Silk 2015b: 36, 103–111 (§14i–15i).

8. Ibid., 33–34; also 113 (§16): 皆真實如不異不差 (All [three modes of the *tathāgatagarbha,* or *dharmadhātu,* i.e., distinguished by levels of purity] are true reality [*(*bhūta*)*tathatā*?], not distinct and not separate).

9. Johnston (1950) 1991: 40.16–18: *ayam eva śāriputra dharmakāyo 'paryantakleśakośakoṭigūḍhaḥ saṃsārasrotasā uhyamāno 'navarāgrasaṃsāragaticyutyupapattiṣu saṃcaran sattvadhātur ity ucyate.* See also AAN 467b6–8; Silk 2015b: 103 (§14i).

10. Our Chinese translation of the AAN concludes that the *dharmakāya* refers simply to "sentient beings" (i.e., 眾生)—not specifically the *sattvadhātu*—although a quotation of the AAN in the **Mahāyānadharmadhātunirviśeṣa* (e.g., T.1626[31]893a9–11; see Silk 2015b: 9–10; also 103–104 regarding the passage in question) exhibits *sattvadhātu* (i.e., 眾生界), in agreement with the quotation of the AAN in the RGVV.

11. Ibid., 40–41, 118–119 (§17ii), 121 (18ii); see, for example, AAN 467b29: 自性清淨心.

12. Ibid., 116–117 (§17i); including AAN 467b27: 智慧清淨真如法界.

to the intrinsically pure mind (more than once), and seems to understand this as an authoritative account of what the *tathāgatagarbha* must be, the central concern of the AAN—to which the *tathāgatagarbha-dharmakāya,* or the intrinsically pure mind, must in the end refer—is instead the singular nature of reality: "Śāriputra, regarding this unborn, unperishing, constant, tranquil, unchanging refuge, [otherwise the *tathāgatagarbha,* or the intrinsically pure mind, or] the pure *dharmadhātu,* I call this 'sentient beings.' "[13] This seems to be the doctrinal crux of the AAN: that sentient beings can be understood in terms of reality, or the nature/realm of phenomena (*dharmadhātu*), such that their true nature is nothing other than the same reality from which emerge Buddhas. Though otherwise an account of what has been called *tathāgatagarbha*—or indeed the "inconceivable" teaching of a mind that is not truly afflicted—the AAN presents an account of reality properly understood, which is timeless, tranquil, and suffers no fundamental change as sentient beings either transmigrate or, in time, liberate themselves from this process.

We are by now far removed from anything like Buddha-nature understood as some entity hidden "within" the body of a sentient being, and the AAN shows no awareness of *tathāgatagarbha* teaching having any association with discourse about the self, nor as any contentious "secret" that Buddhist audiences will find difficult to accept. If the AAN is something like an inheritor of ideas present already in the ŚDS—in particular the identity of the *tathāgatagarbha* and *dharmakāya,* which refer also to the intrinsically pure nature of the mind—then the authors of the AAN may have taken for granted that the expression *tathāgatagarbha,* and its articulation in mentalistic terms, had been clarified already. While the ŚDS responds to ideas and terminology present in the MPNMS (foremost the inversion of the four distortions; see 5.3), the AAN explores in greater depth to what the expression *tathāgatagarbha* should properly refer: the underlying basis to both transmigration and liberation, which must otherwise be that which accounts for all sentient existence. We will see a similar line of thought, even more clearly influenced by the ŚDS, in the *Laṅkāvatārasūtra* (LAS; see 8.3). At this stage, it is enough to conclude that whereas the MPNMS-group understood Buddha-nature to refer to an abiding reality "within" sentient beings, which might be confused for a worldly teaching about the self, the AAN joins the ŚDS in presenting *tathāgatagarbha* as a continuity that runs "beneath" modes of existence, more akin to a metaphysical (or "metapsychological") continuum that underpins successive births and, eventually, liberation.[14]

13. Ibid., 123 (§19ii); AAN 467c10–12: 舍利弗, 我依此不生、不滅、常恒、清涼、不變歸依、不可思議、清淨法界, 說名眾生。

14. Regarding this idea in the AAN, see ibid., 122 (§19i), or otherwise AAN 467c4–6.

6.2 The *Tathāgatagarbhasūtra*

It is common in other scholarly discussions of Buddha-nature teaching that some treatment of the *Tathāgatagarbhasūtra* (TGS) features as the starting point, and its mention relatively late in this volume requires further justification. The TGS does not at any stage discuss *tathāgatagarbha* in terms of the self, nor does it hold that the Buddha, his liberated status, or the *dharmakāya* that is the true mode of his being should be described in anything like such terms. The authors of the TGS make no contribution in regard to this contentious issue, which could be taken as evidence that the TGS predates any suggestion that Buddha-nature teaching resembles something like a Buddhist account of the self. Indeed, previous accounts of the development of the *tathāgatagarbha* literature, after Takasaki, have understood the TGS to be our earliest Indian source for this term and to what it refers, and that it is in this text that we find the foundations for different interpretations of Buddha-nature, exhibited by the MPNMS and ŚDS.[15]

However, we have several good reasons to question this hypothesis. As discussed at the outset of this study (see 1.2), a major contribution of Michael Radich's analysis of the MPNMS is the argument that it is instead our best contender for earliest available *tathāgatagarbha* text. We have seen that the MPNMS defends not only its presentation of a Buddhist account of the self, but also that this is understood as the existence of the *tathāgatagarbha,* and that this terminology is intertwined throughout its content (see 2.3–5). Together with the AMS and MBhS, the MPNMS reflects opposition from Buddhist audiences who were not willing to accept its ideas, which is evidence of difficulties in the early life of teaching about *tathāgatagarbha* in general. Otherwise—as we have considered already—the MPNMS provides a coherent account of the emergence of the expression *tathāgatagarbha:* the enduring existence of the Buddha apart from his apparent death (in MPNMS-dhk) invites the idea that something about sentient beings, who could become Buddhas, should be of the same, transcendent nature as the Buddha already (MPNMS-tg; see 1.2, 2.8). The TGS does not offer any doctrinal explanation for the emergence of Buddha-nature thinking, and is in essence a collection of similes that describe different perspectives on how Buddha-nature can be conceptualized. Indeed, the TGS exhibits no discernible debts to other *sūtra*s of the *tathāgatagarbha* corpus, which in turn show no clearly discernible influence by it. Though the similes of the TGS were known to contributors to the RGVV (see below;

15. This is evident throughout Takasaki 1974 (see, e.g., 46–48, 768–769), while the subtitle of Zimmermann's exemplary 2002 study of the TGS declares this to be "the earliest exposition of the Buddha-nature teaching in India." Regarding this claim, see 1.4n67; also Zimmermann 2020.

also 7.2), the relative position of the TGS in the development of Buddha-nature teaching is otherwise hard to establish.[16]

The TGS has survived in a number of versions, all of which have been discussed thoroughly and with great erudition by Michael Zimmermann (2002). Despite the question mark over one of Zimmermann's central claims—that the TGS is likely our earliest source of the *tathāgatagarbha* tradition—his study of the imagery and likely development of the text remains invaluable. Zimmermann finds that of the four forms of the TGS available to us, the oldest Chinese translation—that ascribed to Buddhabhadra 佛陀跋陀羅 in the early fifth century (T.666: *Dafangdeng rulaizang jing* 大方等如來藏經; henceforth TGS^{C1})—represents an independent recension of the text ("TGS^{1}"), apart from that which underlies the other three (henceforth TGS^{2}).[17] Representative of recension TGS^{2} are (1) the Chinese translation ascribed to Amoghavajra 不空金剛 (705–774 CE) from the middle of the eighth century (T.667: *Dafangguang rulaizang jing* 大方廣如來藏經; henceforth TGS^{C2}); (2) the canonical Tibetan translation from circa 800 CE (e.g., D.258; Q.924: *De bzhin gshegs pa'i snying po'i mdo;* henceforth TGS^{T}); and (3) the Tibetan paracanonical translation from Bathang (TGS^{B}).[18] Available also are versions of the nine similes of the TGS in all surviving forms of the verse *Ratnagotravibhāga* (RGV), which Zimmermann finds to be in greater agreement with recension TGS^{2}.[19]

The TGS presents the nine similes that are its main content in both prose and verse forms. In brief, the similes refer to (1) a Buddha who is hidden in a lotus calyx, (2) honey guarded by bees, (3) a corn kernel within a husk, (4) a gold nugget buried in excrement, (5) treasure buried beneath a house,[20] (6) a sprout emerging from a seed, (7) an abandoned Buddha image wrapped in rags, (8) the embryo of a *cakravartin* in the womb of a poor woman, and (9) a golden icon within a clay mold. In every instance some precious "content" is concealed by some expendable shell or exterior, which in each simile stands for Buddha-nature and the afflictions that obscure it, respectively. Zimmermann has argued that the earliest contents of the TGS are likely the prose forms of eight of its nine similes, those numbered

16. Regarding possible influence of the TGS on the *Mahāyānasūtrālaṃkāra,* see Zimmermann 2002: 77–79.

17. English translations of TGS^{C1} are those of Grosnick (1995), and of Rulu (2016: see 3.1n1).

18. Zimmermann 2002: 16–20. All references to TGS^{T} and TGS^{B} are to Zimmermann's editions in that volume. The four versions of the TGS to which Zimmermann refers, as well as his English translation of TGS^{T}, are also reproduced synoptically via the University of Oslo Faculty of Humanity's *Bibliotheca Polyglotta: Thesaurus Literaturae Buddicae,* available at https://www2.hf.uio.no/polyglotta/.

19. Zimmermann 2002: 23–24.

20. Highly reminiscent of the simile of the buried treasure found in the MPNMS (see 2.3); Radich (2015a: 56–57) demonstrates that there is no strong evidence that the MPNMS inherits this from the TGS, though it need not have been transmitted from the MPNMS to the TGS either.

2 through 9.[21] These were then framed by a narrative in which the Buddha reveals to his assembly a host of shining Buddha who are hidden inside putrid lotus calyxes. This provided the basis for a final simile (numbered 1) that essentially repeats this image in the same style as the earlier eight, and became the sequentially first of them in the TGS as it is known to us today. Zimmermann observed that in the prose content of the TGS it is only this sequentially first but likely *latest* simile that employs the term *tathāgatagarbha* itself; apart from in the title of the text, and in the (likely later) verse form of each simile, it is otherwise absent. This means that the expression that gives the TGS its title was perhaps a late addition to its content, which is otherwise a heterogeneous collection of musings on the central Buddha-nature idea.

While there is demonstrably greater agreement among witnesses to TGS² than among any of them and TGS¹, there remains tremendous variety across all of our versions of the text, especially in regard to how the nine similes refer to what is "precious" in the constitution of sentient beings, or in other words, their Buddha-nature. At no stage is this referred to as one's "self," though across our four versions of the TGS we encounter a wide array of expressions used to describe Buddha-nature, some of which definitely warrant our attention. In order to locate the similes under discussion (most easily accessed via Zimmermann's 2002 editions of each version), in the footnotes that accompany this section I refer to versions and similes of the TGS in the following format: translation (or recension, if common to all forms of TGS²): simile number (1–9) and prose (p) or verse (v) form.[22]

In every form of the first simile (the Buddha hidden in a lotus calyx), the term *tathāgatagarbha* is used to refer to sentient beings themselves, which Zimmermann has understood to be an exocentric (*bahuvrīhi*) compound, such that sentient beings are all "containers for a Tathāgata."[23] In the introductory framework for this simile, TGS^{C1} alone understands *tathāgatagarbha* to refer to "that which sentient beings possess," so understands a determinative (*tatpuruṣa*) compound.[24] This translation (our one witness to recension TGS¹) frequently takes *tathāgatagarbha* (that is, 如來藏) to refer directly to the content of a sentient being—that is, it does not seem to understand it to be an exocentric compound, and so is in agreement with the sense of *tathāgatagarbha* taught in works of the MPNMS-group (i.e., that sentient beings somehow "have" it). TGS¹, in other words, may reflect a form of the Indian TGS that was in greater accord with the use of this expression found in our *ātmavādin* sources for Buddha-nature teaching.[25]

---

21. Zimmermann 2002: 27–34.

22. See also ibid., 50–51, as well as note 18 above.

23. Zimmermann 2002: 39–50; 2020.

24. TGS^{C1} 457c2–3: 一切眾生，雖在諸趣煩惱身中，有如來藏，常無染污。

25. Zimmermann 2002: 22. TGS^{C2} also sometimes reflects a *tatpuruṣa* reading, such that it is possible that this betrays a habit of Chinese translators when encountering the expression

Otherwise the TGS declares that what is present in sentient beings is one or another specific quality or aspect of a Buddha, most frequently his knowledge (e.g., *rulaizhi* 如來智; *de bzhin gshegs pa'i ye shes*).[26] This does not look like the substantialized "essence" or "nature" of a Buddha implied by the corporeal *dhātu* of the MPNMS-group. But otherwise we very frequently encounter the "body" (*shen* 身; *lus/sku*) of a Buddha that is hidden beneath afflictions.[27] Sometimes we find the ambiguous Chinese expression *ti* 體, which may have the sense of "the nature of a Buddha" (plausibly a translation of *svabhāva,* evident in a simile reproduced in the Sanskrit RGV), but which could also have had in mind something of a Buddha's physical body.[28] This may have even intended the Buddha's body understood as something like the "relic," that which resides at the *stūpa,* and was "internalized" in the articulation of Buddha-nature found in the MPNMS (see 1.3, 2.3).

Very frequently, and with echoes of what we find in the MPNMS-group, our Chinese forms of the TGS refer to the precious content of a sentient being as something that is "within the body."[29] In prose material dealing with the eighth simile, we find some evidence for the Indic expression *dhātu* (TGS^{C2} *rulaijie* 如來界; TGS^{B} *de bzhin gshegs pa'i khams*: Skt. **tathāgatadhātu*), though in corresponding material TGS^{T} exhibits instead "the lineage of a Buddha" (*de bzhin gshegs pa'i rigs:* **tathāgatagotra*), which could well underlie all three of these translations.[30] Moreover, TGS^{C1}—again, our single witness to recension TGS^{1}—quite frequently refers to "the nature of a Buddha" (*foxing* 佛性 / *rulaixing* 如來性: **buddhadhātu*), though this Chinese rendering may again translate instead, for example, **buddhagotra,* or **buddhatva.*[31] We find also many other more abstract expressions—primarily across TGS^{T}—that refer to that which sentient beings are meant to "possess": "buddhahood" (*buddhatva*),[32] "self-existence"

tathāgatagarbha (i.e., understanding it to refer directly to "something that sentient beings *have,*" in the manner of the MPNMS-group). It is noteworthy that TGS^{C1} is a work by Buddhabhadra, who was involved—to at least some degree—in the translation of MPNMS^{F}; see 2.1.

26. For example, TGS^{C1}: 3p; TGS^{C2}: 3v; TGS^{2}: 5p; TGS^{2}: 7p; TGS^{2}: 9v.

27. TGS^{2}: 1v; TGS^{C2}: 3v; TGS^{2}: 5v; TGS^{2}: 6v; TGS^{C1}: 7v; TGS^{2}: 7v; TGS^{C1}: 9p.

28. TGS^{C2}: 3p; TGS^{C2}: 6v; TGS^{C2}: 7v; TGS^{C2}: 8p. See also Johnston (1950) 1991: 26.12 (compare also RGVV^{C} 828b11: 體及因果業). Further examination of *ti* 體, related Chinese expressions, and their relation to the relic-cult of Indian Buddhism can be found throughout Silk 2006.

29. TGS^{C1}: 1v; TGS^{C1}: 5p; TGS^{C1}: 5v; TGS^{C2}: 5v; TGS^{C1}: 6v; TGS^{C1}: 7p; TGS^{C1}: 8p; TGS^{C2}: 8p; TGS^{C2}: 8v; TGS^{C1}: 9p.

30. TGS^{T}: 8p.

31. TGS^{C1}: 1p; TGS^{C1}: 4v; TGS^{C1}: 7v; TGS^{C1}: 8p; TGS^{C1}: 9v; regarding, for example, 如來性 as a translation of *tathāgatagarbha,* see Radich 2015a: 23–34; also note 25 above.

32. TGS^{T}: 2p.

(*svayaṃbhūtva*),[33] "the ground of awakening" (*buddhabhūmi*),[34] an "original state" (*prakṛti*),[35] or a "real nature" (e.g., *dharmatā*).[36]

Though scholarship has long treated the TGS as a locus classicus for the Buddha-nature idea, our surviving versions of it are not of one voice on the matter of how the notion of an abiding Buddha-nature should be articulated. In likelihood this is because the similes of the TGS are evocative, and perhaps did not intend the kind of explanatory account of *tathāgatagarbha,* and to what this expression refers, found in other works of this tradition.[37] The matter of how to read the compound *tathāgatagarbha* across versions of the TGS is hard to determine, but where this expression may refer (exocentrically) to something that sentient beings "possess" (i.e., they are defined by *tathāgatagarbha*), this can still accord with the doctrine of the ŚDS or AAN, in which Buddha-nature is not an "element" of a sentient being's constitution but a designator for that aspect which is most vital to them (i.e., the site of the qualities of a Buddha). It is only in some versions of the similes (and mainly in TGS^{1}, reflected by TGS^{C1}) that the expression *tathāgatagarbha* clearly refers to some content "within" sentient beings, as taught by the MPNMS-group of texts. However, on occasion different versions of the TGS share with our *ātmavādin* sources the sense that what is present, in the body of a sentient being, is the Buddha's physical body.[38] Another interesting detail—to which we will return in the next chapter (see 7.2)—is that the nine similes of the TGS reproduced in the RGV frequently teach the existence of the nature of the Buddha (e.g., *tathāgatadhātu*) existing "within" sentient beings, which suggests that some form(s) of the TGS, or at any rate the similes preserved in it, focused on Buddha-nature as the presence of some indestructible "essence," in closer agreement still with what we find in the MPNMS-group.

Our many and varied forms of the TGS and its similes are difficult to situate in the development of Buddha-nature thought in India. It may not reflect a very early form of Buddha-nature thinking, exemplified better by the MPNMS-group and their *ātmavādin* mode of this idea. But there is room to hypothesize that Buddha-nature as taught by the TGS is more ancient than what we read in the ŚDS and AAN. In distinction to these two texts, versions of the TGS include the sense that Buddha-nature is something corporeal: the body of the Buddha, resident in the bodies of sentient beings. Moreover, we find no clear reference to Buddha-nature identified with the intrinsically pure nature of the mind, a feature central to both the ŚDS and AAN (see 9.3). Although the TGS offers us little in terms of understanding the relationship between the expression *tathāgatagarbha* and

33. TGS^{T}: 3p.
34. TGS^{T}: 3v.
35. TGS^{T}: 4v. See also Zimmermann 2002: 53.
36. TGS^{T}: 3v; TGS^{2}: 8v.
37. Zimmermann 2002: 15; also 1999: 153–155.
38. Zimmermann's (2002) section 10.10; see ibid., 151, 338–339.

discourse about the self, it is plausible that its similes have origins closer to the MPNMS-group than to the ŚDS and AAN, which reflect a reconfiguration of the Buddha-nature idea into an account of some mentalistic foundation to both transmigration and liberation from it.[39] While we have insufficient grounds to situate the TGS at the dawn of the *tathāgatagarbha* tradition, it is possible that its poetic musings on Buddha-nature took inspiration from the *ātmavādin* form of this idea, and in some instances retained the image of a Buddha's "body," or the "essence" of his person, resident in the constitution of all sentient beings.

These matters aside—and even after having rejected the notion that the TGS is our earliest source for the expression *tathāgatagarbha*—another aspect of Zimmermann's analysis of the TGS remains very significant. The importance of the *Saddharmapuṇḍarīka* (SP) for the authors of other works in the *tathāgatagarbha* tradition is, by now, clear enough (see 2.1, 3.7, 4.1, 5.4; also 9.1, 10.4). Zimmermann suggests that authors of the TGS composed a text that was meant to evoke the SP, or at least portions of it, in both style and structure.[40] This being the case, it is all the more likely that the TGS—a collection of evocative similes, framed otherwise by an account of the Buddha's miraculous revelation of Buddha-nature—is a relatively early source for teaching about it, and its similes could predate the reinvention of the expression *tathāgatagarbha* into an epithet for the intrinsically pure state of the mind, as seems to have been the preoccupation of the ŚDS, the AAN, and, finally, the RGVV (see especially 9.3).

6.3 The *Mahāyānasūtrālaṃkāra*

The next text that we should consider is somewhat anomalous. Though the *Mahāyānasūtralaṃkāra* (MSA) and the commentarial literature that depends upon it show awareness of the expression *tathāgatagarbha*, and moreover an association between this and Buddhist teaching about the self, it would be inaccurate to consider these to be part of the *tathāgatagarbha* corpus proper. An important treatise of the Yogācāra-Vijñānavāda tradition, the MSA accepts at least one key teaching that is in opposition to the Buddha-nature idea: the existence of discrete lineages (*gotra*s) to which sentient beings belong, which determine—and in some instances also limit—their capacity for attaining liberation.[41] For the MSA, beings who do not belong to the "*buddhagotra*" or who are not of "undetermined lineage" (*aniyatagotra*) are necessarily incapable of attaining the status of a Buddha, while those who are "without lineage" (*agotra*) are condemned to endless transmigration,

39. Indeed, simile number 5—that of the buried treasure—may have drawn upon the very similar simile found in the MPNMS (see 2.3), though it is conspicuous that no other similes found across the MPNMS, AMS, or MBhS find equivalents in any form of the TGS.

40. Zimmermann 1999: 156–168; 2002: 77.

41. These lineages are outlined in chapter three of the MSA: Lévi 1907: 10–13; also Obermiller (1931) 1991: 97–104; Takasaki 1974: 721–724; Griffiths 1990: 48–51.

and cannot achieve even the comparatively lowly status of an arhat or *pratyekabuddha*.[42] Hence the Yogācāra-Vijñānavāda literature does not subscribe to the single vehicle paradigm on which early Buddha-nature teaching seems to depend, and instead accepts the older, more conventional three-vehicle model of liberation (*triyāna*), under which *śrāvaka*s and *pratyekabuddha*s end transmigration differently from the bodhisattva.[43]

The MSA is traditionally attributed to the bodhisattva Maitreya (or Maitreyanātha) and is after that understood to have been written by Asaṅga (fourth century), who is sometimes taken to have been Maitreya's earthly amanuensis.[44] We have available a Sanskrit text of the MSA, which is preserved embedded within a prose commentary—the *Mahāyānasūtrālaṃkārabhāṣya* (MSABh)—that is ascribed to Vasubandhu. A Chinese translation of the MSABh (T.1604: *Dasheng zhuangyan jing lun* 大乘莊嚴經論; henceforth MSABh^{C}) was made between 630 and 633 CE by Prabhākaramitra 波羅迦頗蜜多羅 (564–633), and a Tibetan translation (e.g., D.4026; Q.5527: *Theg pa chen po mdo sde'i rgyan gyi bshad pa;* henceforth MSABh^{T}) in the late eighth century by Śākyasiṃha and dPal brtsegs.[45] The study of the Sanskrit MSABh begins with the edition of Sylvain Lévi (1907), while an investigation of Buddha-nature teaching as represented in the MSABh is that by Paul Griffiths (1990).

There is little doubt that the author of the MSABh had some knowledge of *tathāgatagarbha* tradition. At one point the text refers to the ŚDS, which suggests that the author of the MSABh knew some version of it and, if so, presumably its account of *tathāgatagarbha* also.[46] Though the term *tathāgatagarbha* does not feature in the MSA itself, it does occur once in the MSABh, and there in association with a verse of the MSA that must be some allusion to Buddha-nature teaching. The verse in question (MSA 9.37) explains the lack of differentiation (*nirviśiṣṭa*) in reality (*tathatā*) when this is properly understood: "Although being without differentiation

42. For example, MSA 1.14, 3.11 (Lévi 1907: 6, 11).

43. Asaṅga's (fourth century) *Mahāyānasaṃgraha* (10.32; see Lamotte 1938a: 95–96; 1938b: 325–328) defends the three-vehicle (*triyāna*) model of liberation, and with recourse to the *Mahāyānasūtrālaṃkāra* (11.53–54; Lévi 1907: 69–69) teaches that the notion of a single vehicle was expounded for the purpose of either maintaining or attracting certain audiences.

44. Griffiths 1990: 43–44. Other works attributed to Asaṅga certainly knew the MSA: it is named in the *Viniścayasaṅgrahaṇī* and cited (though not by name) in the *Mahāyānasaṃgraha;* see Griffiths 1990: 44n8. See also discussion of Maitreya and works attributed to him in Ruegg 1969: 39–55.

45. The verses of the MSA in isolation are also preserved under the title *Theg pa chen po mdo sde'i rgyan;* for example, D.4020; Q.5521.

46. MSABh 11.59; Lévi 1907: 70: *śrīmālāsūtre: śrāvako bhūtvā pratyekabuddho bhavati punaś ca buddha iti* ([The Buddha said] in the *Śrīmālāsūtra:* having become a *śrāvaka,* one becomes a *pratyekabuddha,* and after that a Buddha). Though this line encapsulates the "ekayānist" orientation of the ŚDS I can find no directly corresponding phrase in any surviving version of that text.

anywhere, when reality reaches purity it achieves the state of a Tathāgata; hence all corporeal beings are the womb (*garbha*) for that [i.e., a Tathāgata]."[47] All three versions of the MSA seem to understand that sentient beings are characterized by this *garbha* for a Buddha; that is, *tathāgatagarbha* is employed as an exocentric compound.[48] The same is evident in the accompanying commentary of MSABh, all versions of which use *tathāgatagarbha* to qualify sentient beings (e.g., *sarve satvās tathāgatagarbhā*): they "contain" a Buddha.[49] This may again understand *tathāgatagarbha* in a manner reminiscent of the ŚDS and AAN, the latter of which—as we saw above (6.1)—also makes an equation between *tathāgatagarbha* and reality (**tathatā*) itself. If intending an exocentric compound, the MSA and MSABh may have held that sentient beings are characterized by "*tathāgatagarbha,*" but not necessarily as some "constituent" of their body, as taught in the MPNMS-group.

Other content of the MSA exhibits knowledge not simply about *tathāgatagarbha* teaching but also about Buddhist discourse regarding the self, or specifically some "higher" self that is achieved at liberation. Verses in the same chapter (9.20–21) describe the goal of awakening in terms of "the uncontaminated realm" (*anāsrava dhātu*), which here seems to refer to reality at its fundamental level (i.e., *dhātu* in the sense of *dharmadhātu,* "the nature/realm of phenomena").[50] Again with echoes of the AAN, MSA 9.22 then describes reality as neither impure nor pure, yet identifiable with buddhahood (*buddhatā*).[51] Most compelling, however, is the next verse, MSA 9.23: "In the purity that is emptiness, having attained the path through absence of self, [and] because they have attained the pure self (*śuddhātman*), Buddhas have arrived at their own great self (*ātmamahātman*)."[52] The expression corresponding to *ātmamahātman* in MSA^{T} is *bdag nyid chen po'i bdag,* "they themselves attain *mahātman*."[53] MSA^{C} states simply that what Buddhas

47. MSA 9.37 (Lévi 1907: 40): *sarveṣām aviśiṣṭāpi tathatā śuddhim āgatā / tathāgatatvaṃ tasmāc ca tadgarbhāḥ sarvedehinaḥ //* Gadjin Nagao (2007: 224) suggested this verse to be a later addition to the text, a detail brought to my attention by an anonymous reviewer. This is one instance in which the expression *garbha* may intend "embryo" (i.e., "corporeal beings are destined [for being Tathāgatas]"), as visible also in the RGVV (see 7.4).

48. MSA^{T} D.4026, 156b7; Q.5527, 167b4–5: *de yi snying po can;* MSA^{C} 604c10: 故說諸眾生 / 名爲如來藏。

49. See Lévi 1907: 40 (after MSA 9.37).

50. Lévi 1907: 36. Compare MSA^{C} 603b23–29; MSA^{T} D.4026, 155a3–5; Q.5527, 165b3–4. This language is carried through the ensuing verses, for example, MSA 9.26; Lévi 1907: 38: *buddhānām amale dhātau naikatā bahutā na ca / ākāśavad adehatvāt pūrvadehānusārataḥ //* (In the uncontaminated realm of Buddhas they are neither one nor many; [not many] due to having no body, like space, [and not one] due to correspondence with a prior [bodhisattva] body).

51. Lévi 1907: 36–37.

52. MSA 9.23; Lévi 1907: 37: *śūnyatāyāṃ viśuddhāyāṃ nairātmyān mārgalābhataḥ / buddhāḥ śuddhātmalābhitvāt gatā ātmamahātmatām //*

53. MSA^{T} D.4026, 155a6; Q.5527, 165b7–8. See also Tsukinowa 1938.

achieve can be called the "great self" (*dawo* 大我).[54] If nothing else is clear, the MSA holds that at the pinnacle of Buddhist practice—and after complete comprehension of absence of self in regard to all phenomena—the status proper to a Buddha can be called *mahātman*.[55]

We should not rush to conclusions. The similar expression *māhātmya* is preserved in a Sanskrit fragment of the MPNMS (see 2.3), and either may have featured in the AMS (see 3.1), hence it is possible that the MSA knew of the claim that the Buddha possesses a kind of "great" selfhood that is superior to all erroneous, worldly notions of a self. But there is also the chance that these verses mean something closer to *mahātman/māhātmya* in the common and ancient Indian sense of being "high-minded" or "majestic"; that is, that through proper comprehension of teaching about not-self the Buddha becomes a superior type of being, or has "great character," but does not necessarily obtain something that should be called *ātman* in any contentious metaphysical sense. This is supported by commentary provided by the MSABh:

> In the above, regarding the uncontaminated realm, there is taught the supreme self (*paramātman*) of Buddhas. For what reason? Because they have a character that is at the pinnacle that is absence of self (*agranairātmyātmakatvāt*). The pinnacle that is absence of self is reality purified, which is the self of Buddhas in the sense of their real nature (*svabhāva*); that [reality] having been purified, Buddhas attain the pure self, the pinnacle that is absence of self.[56] Hence, due to the attainment of the pure self, Buddhas are said to have attained their own great self (*ātmamāhātmyaṃ*); with this intention, regarding the uncontaminated realm, there is established the supreme self of Buddhas.[57]

By knowing absence of self the bodhisattva can achieve the "supreme self" (*paramātman*) that is proper to a Buddha; language that could have been drawn from any of our *tathāgatagarbha* sources. The claim that a Buddhist account of the self refers to a full comprehension of teaching about ab-

54. MSA^{C} 603c9–10.

55. Two later commentaries, surviving only in Tibetan, offer no further clarity on this passage. These (for the sake of completeness) are the (*Mahāyāna-*)*Sūtrālaṃkāravṛttibhāṣya*, traditionally ascribed to the sixth-century commentator Sthiramati (regarding whom, see Kramer 2016), and—from perhaps the same period—the *Mahāyānasūtrālaṃkāraṭīkā*, attributed to *Asvabhāva/Niḥsvabhāva (Griffiths 1990: 46–48).

56. The subject in *tasyāṃ viśuddhāyāṃ* is found in MSA 9.38 (Lévi 1907: 40: *tathatā śuddhiṃ āgatā*).

57. Lévi 1907: 38: *tatra cānāsrave dhātau buddhānāṃ paramātmā nirdiśyate / kiṃ kāraṇaṃ / agranairātmyātmakatvāt / agraṃ nairātmyaṃ viśuddhā tathatā sā ca buddhānām ātmā svabhāvārthena tasyāṃ viśuddhāyām agraṃ nairātmyam ātmānaṃ buddhā labhante śuddhaṃ / ataḥ śuddhātmalābhitvāt buddhā ātmamāhātmyaṃ prāptā ity anena abhisaṃdhinā buddhānām anāsrave dhātau paramātmā vyavasthāpyate* / Compare also MSA^{C} 603c11–17; MSA^{T} D.4026, 155a6–b1; Q.5527, 165b8–166a2.

sence of self is not an idea found in Buddha-nature texts that we have so far discussed, but does play an important role in how the *ātmavādin* language of earlier *tathāgatagarbha* tradition was explained by later works in this tradition. Material that is very close to the passage above is preserved in the Chinese translation of the RGVV (see 7.3), and there explains the manner in which the *dharmakāya* can exhibit the "perfection of self" (*ātmapāramitā*) that we first encounter in the ŚDS (see 5.3).

In the passage of the MSABh above we read that the Buddha's supreme self refers to his achievement of (*ātma*)*māhātmya,* which Ruegg (1989b: 305) understands to mean the Buddha's "magnanimity of self." In support of Ruegg's reading, we find that the MSA elsewhere (14.37) employs the term *mahātman* to mean something like a "great character," that is, celebrating the status of the Buddha without intending any caveat to teachings about things not being the self: "Having come to understand the world to be nothing but constructions—without a self, merely a wealth of suffering—and having abandoned the view of the self that is without meaning, one relies on the view of the great self (*mahātman*) that is the great meaning (*mahārtha*)."[58] Here the accompanying commentary of MSABh is again instructive: "The view of the self that is without meaning is the afflicted view of a worldly self (*satkāyadṛṣṭi*). The view of a great self, which is the great meaning, is the view of self that is attained by the mind that sees sameness between [one's] self and all sentient beings. This is the great meaning, due to its being the cause of actions for the sake of all sentient beings."[59] In other words, the end result of understanding absence of self is the superlatively compassionate perspective of a Buddha, in which one sees no distinction between oneself and others. Enigmatically this is called the "great meaning" (*mahārtha:* alternatively "great purpose"), an expression used throughout MSA(Bh) to describe teachings proper to the Mahāyāna.[60] Though this "great self" has its basis in correct insight (i.e., correct understanding of teachings about absence of self), the expression *mahātman*

---

58. Lévi 1907: 95: *saṃskāramātraṃ jagad etya buddhyā nirātmakaṃ duḥkhavirūḍhimātraṃ / vihāya yānarthamayātmadṛṣṭiḥ mahātmadṛṣṭiṃ śrayate mahārthāṃ //* Compare MSA^{C} 625c29–626a1; MSA^{T} D.4026, 193b2–3; Q.5527, 210a1–2.

59. Lévi 1907: 95: *anarthamayātmadṛṣṭir yā kliṣṭā satkāyadṛṣṭiḥ / mahātmadṛṣṭir iti mahārthā yā sarvasatveṣv ātmasamacittalābhātmadṛṣṭiḥ / sā hi sarvasatvārthakriyāhetutvāt mahārthā /* Compare MSA^{C} 626a4–7; MSA^{T} D.4026, 193b5–7; Q.5527, 210a6–7.

60. A primary concern of the MSA (especially its second chapter) is the legitimacy of the Mahāyāna as a program of authentic teachings by the Buddha. It is possible that "*mahā-*" of *mahātman* (and indeed *mahārtha*) is employed in a manner similar to what I hypothesize regarding "*pāramitā*" in the *ātmapāramitā* of the ŚDS (5.3n38). Just as the ŚDS brands its account of the self as somehow the "perfection" of it—in accordance with the bodhisattvas' path of perfections—so too might the MSA intend its *mahātman* to be an account of the self that is proper to the "great vehicle" and to its "great meaning(s)." A similar device is used in a later Indian context by authors of Buddhist tantric materials, in which the prefix *vajra-* ("diamond"; "adamantine") comes to be used as a means of identifying some or other concept , instrument, or deity as proper to the Buddha's own "adamantine vehicle" (Vajrayāna).

refers not, it seems, to anything metaphysical so much as to the superior person of the bodhisattva or Buddha, who works for the benefit of all sentient beings.

To summarize, this material is likely not directly related to the *ātmavādin* enterprise of some *tathāgatagarbha* sources—that is, that Buddha-nature constitutes the presence of an enduring, somehow powerful "self." But given that chapter nine of the MSA also reflects awareness of the expression *tathāgatagarbha,* the MSA(Bh) may have intended a clarification that declarations about "the self of the Buddha," as exhibited in various sources for understanding the expression *tathāgatagarbha,* should not be thought to contradict central Buddhist teachings about emptiness or absence of self; what is being taught, in the end, is the "greatness" (*māhātmya*) of a Buddha, due to his being, and knowing, absence of self.

Both the MSA and MSABh sit only on the periphery of texts concerned with teaching about Buddha-nature, but may reflect an outsider's perspective (though still clearly Mahāyānist) on the *tathāgatagarbha* tradition and the contentious language it was known to have employed. While aware of teachings about *tathāgatagarbha,* and perhaps also its association with discourse about the self, the MSA understands any reference to the "self" of the Buddha to refer only to his comprehension that nothing is worthy of being called the self, or otherwise—in accordance with teachings of the *prajñāpāramitā* tradition—that all phenomena are by nature "empty." It is then curious that this material of MSABh, concerned with the Buddha's "great self" and to what this must refer, is also found in one version of the long and influential treatise on Buddha-nature teaching, the *Ratnagotravibhāgavyākhyā,* to which we turn next.

CHAPTER 7

The *Ratnagotravibhāga* and the Self That Is No Self

7.1 The Text

We arrive now at perhaps the most influential text of the *tathāgatagarbha* tradition, which sits at the culmination of what Jikidō Takasaki supposed to be the main trajectory of works in this corpus of literature (see 1.2). This is the *Ratnagotravibhāga* (RGV), a verse text that is normally considered together with its prose commentary (commonly called the *Ratnagotravibhāgavyākhyā;* henceforth RGVV).[1] The text has several discernable strata, and we require some analysis of its likely composition if we are to assess how its understanding of Buddha-nature, over successive stages of the RGVV's development, related to discourse about the self.

The RGVV in its complete form was known also as the *Mahāyānottaratantraśāstra-vyākhyā,* "a commentary upon the treatise that is the later/higher teaching (*uttaratantra*) of the Mahāyāna"; it is accordingly something of a compendium of Mahāyānist doctrine, and one that privileges an account of *tathāgatagarbha.*[2] Content of the RGVV is indebted to at least three *sūtras* that we have already discussed—the TGS, ŚDS, and AAN—and exhibits knowledge also of the MPNMS. Much has been written about the RGVV, its history in India, and its interpretation in Tibet.[3] We are fortunate to have Sanskrit manuscripts of the Indian text.[4] This chapter will rely on the 1950 edition of the RGVV by E. H. Johnston (RGVV^{S}), though will take into account emendations to it suggested by several other authors.[5] Available also are the Tibetan translation (e.g., D.4025; Q.5526: *Theg pa*

1. Regarding attested titles for the RGVV, see Kanō 2016: 19n6.

2. It seems that Indo-Tibetan commentators preferred the title *Mahāyānottaratantra* (regarding which see more below); see also ibid., 27nn40–41.

3. Regarding reception of the RGVV in India and into Tibet, see Kanō 2016. Other studies of the RGVV in Tibet include Mathes 2008; Brunnhölzl 2014; and T. Wangchuk 2017.

4. Regarding details of our two virtually complete manuscripts, see—most recently—Kanō 2016: 17. Also Johnston (1950) 1991: v–x.

5. Takasaki 1966; de Jong 1968; Schmithausen 1971.

chen po rgyud bla ma'i bstan bcos rnam par bshad pa; henceforth RGVV^{T}), together with a Tibetan version of the verses of the RGV that appear to have been extracted from the prose commentary (D.4024; Q.5525: *Theg pa chen po rgyud bla ma'i bstan bcos*), the translation of which is by rNgog Blo ldan shes rab, together with the Indian master Sajjana, in the eleventh century.[6] But our earliest witness to the Indian text is the Chinese translation of the RGVV (T.1611: *Jujing yisheng baoxing lun* 究竟一乘寶性論; henceforth RGVV^{C}), the production of which is ascribed to Ratnamati 勒那摩提, between 511 and 515 CE.[7]

The authorship of the RGV(V)—both the verses and prose commentary—is unclear. Our earliest source (RGV[V]^{C}) names no author.[8] Chinese tradition of the late sixth century onward attributed the RGVV as a whole to one Jianyi 堅意, likely rendering the Sanskrit Sāramati, or possibly Sthiramati, an author to whom is ascribed also the doctrinally similar **Mahāyānadharmadhātunirviśeṣa*.[9] But Tibetan tradition has long held the RGV to be one of five texts delivered by the bodhisattva Maitreya, and attributes the RGVV to his amanuensis, Asaṅga.[10] Evidence of association between the RGV and some Maitreya (or Maitreyanātha) dates back to the early eighth century, preserved in a Khotanese fragment of the RGV found at Dunhuang.[11] From the eleventh century, when it appears that there was a resurgence of interest in the RGV in India, tradition there ascribed authorship of both it and the RGVV to Maitreya.[12] The colophon of RGVV^{T}—also from the eleventh century—adds that the prose commentary is the work of Asaṅga, which is how this material has been understood in Tibet since.[13]

The longest study of the content and composition of the RGV(V) remains that of Takasaki (1966).[14] Further analysis by Lambert Schmithausen (1971, 1973) built upon Takasaki's attempts to identify the likely earliest material—"basic" verses—from among the verses of the RGV. Other significant studies of the RGVV have been produced by David Seyfort Ruegg

6. A Tibetan edition of RGVV^{T} is that of Zuiryū Nakamura (1967), which is referenced throughout this chapter. Its most influential English translation remains that by Obermiller (1931) 1991.

7. Ui 1959 (cited in Kanō 2016: 21n12). Silk (2015b: 7–9) puts this date several years later, based on the observation that Ratnamati shows familiarity with the Chinese translation of the AAN (made in 520 CE). Regarding another recorded Chinese translation of the RGVV, attributed to Bodhiruci (which may well not have existed), see Kanō 2016: 21n15.

8. Kanō 2016: 21–22.

9. Kanō 2016: 22–24; Silk 2015b: 149–157.

10. See Ruegg 1969: 39–55.

11. Bailey and Johnston 1935; Kanō 2016: 24–27.

12. Kanō 2016: 97–154.

13. Kanō 2016: 20–31 provides an excellent, detailed assessment of different hypotheses concerning authorship of the RGV(V).

14. Addressed again throughout Takasaki 1974 (in the first instance, pp. 19–36); see this together with various later articles, many of which are collected in Takasaki 2014.

(e.g., 1969, 1989a), who has focused on the interpretation of the RGVV as a complete and coherent commentarial work, as well as its influence in India and in Tibet. The most recent study of the RGVV, its production and transmission is that by Kazuo Kanō (2016), which includes a valuable account of the text's history and reception across both India and Tibet. A recent re-evaluation of how the RGV(V) was produced, and how its ideas developed across its composition, is by Klaus-Dieter Mathes (2015).

This chapter will confront three aspects of the RGVV: (1) Buddha-nature teaching as reflected by the "root" (*śloka/mūla*) verses of its first chapter, among which are likely the earliest, or "basic," materials in the composition of the text (see 7.2); (2) the manner in which the commentarial RGVV interprets the difficult expression *ātmapāramitā*—the "perfection of self," attributed to the *dharmakāya*—which is found in one of these root verses (7.3); and (3) the manner in which the RGVV attends specifically to the idea that *tathāgatagarbha* teaching sails close to a Buddhist account of the self (7.4). We will see that the earliest material of the RGV contains language reminiscent of the MPNMS-group of texts but is indebted also to the ŚDS, which focused solely on the expression *tathāgatagarbha,* and conspicuously avoided any reference to some "essence" (*dhātu*) that is somehow "within" sentient beings (5.2). The commentarial RGVV displays a preference for the doctrine of the ŚDS, and otherwise features ideas and terminology associated with the Yogācāra-Vijñānavāda tradition of Indian philosophy; the purification of the *tathāgatagarbha* is described as an "inversion of the basis" (*āśrayaparivṛtti*) that underlies transmigration, which is language more commonly used to refer to the transformation of the substratum consciousness (*ālayavijñāna*)—a central teaching of the Yogācāra-Vijñānavāda system—at the achievement of awakening.[15]

The matter of the composition of the RGV(V) is more complex than just a distinction between verse and prose material. The RGVV recognizes some verses of the RGV to be more fundamental than others, and calls these "*śloka*s," upon which other verses depend. We know later Indian tradition to have discerned "root" verses (*mūla*s) of the text from "commentarial" verses (*vyākhyāśloka*s).[16] What I shall henceforth call "root" verses for the most part correspond to those preserved in a short, verse-only form

15. See e.g., Johnston (1950) 1991: 80.15–19, 82.5–9; also Ruegg 1969: 421–424; Mathes 2015: 126–136; Radich 2016: 286–288. Schmithausen (1973: 124–127) contends that because the RGVV seems to owe a debt to Yogācāra-Vijñānavāda works (such as the *Mahāyānasūtrālaṃkāra;* see 7.3), its commentarial prose cannot have originated earlier than the late fourth century; the antiquity of basic verse material of the RGV—some verses of which may have known the ŚDS and AAN (see 7.2)—is another matter.

16. This language is used in the commentary on the RGVV (*Mahāyānottaratantraṭippaṇī*) by Vairocanarakṣita (eleventh–twelfth century; see Kanō 2016: 19n5). For more on this author, and on reception of the RGVV more broadly, see various publications by Kanō (listed in ibid., 441–443).

of the RGV found at the start of RGVV^C.[17] Takasaki called these the "*kārikās*" of the RGV, which he took to be a guideline to what must have been the most basic materials in the composition of the text, or what Takasaki termed the "the collection of [its basic] verses" (*ślokagrantha*). Close reading of the RGV(V) reveals doctrinal development between (1) root verses of the RGV, some of which seem to be more "basic" to its composition than others; (2) its commentarial verses, and then between these verses; and (3) the prose RGVV, which exhibits influence by the Yogācāra-Vijñānavāda tradition.[18]

We are foremost concerned with the manner in which the RGV(V) received and developed the Buddha-nature idea, and there is much to be learned by attempting to identify its earliest component verses. In some detail, Takasaki justifies why we can consider only the first chapter of the RGV—that concerned with Buddha-nature—to contain its earliest materials, and concluded that among its root verses we can discern the basic form of the RGV, composed of a total of only twenty-seven "basic" verses.[19] Ruegg contended that Takasaki's analysis has the repercussion of excluding from these supposed earliest materials any verse that makes reference to the source (*gotra*) of the three "jewels" of Buddhist authority (*ratnas*; i.e., Buddha, dharma, and sangha), which would allow for the text to be called an analysis (*vibhāga*) of this.[20] A likely hypothesis (as Ruegg himself suggests) is that earlier Indian audiences knew the oldest form of the RGV by its alternative title, the *Mahāyānottatantraśāstra*.[21] After Takasaki, Schmithausen (1971) suggested a still shorter set of basic verses, whittling a hypothetical "basic RGV" down to a mere fifteen verses. Among these we find the expression *tathāgatagarbha* understood to refer to the "lineage" (*gotra*) for awakening (RGV 1.27, discussed below), though this occurs fleetingly in an otherwise terse set of explanations of what it means for all sentient beings to possess the nature of a Buddha.[22]

17. RGVV^C 813a8–820c20. This material features a total of eighteen verses that are not preserved in any version of the RGVV proper, and that Takasaki (1966: 10–11) took to be contributions by its Chinese translator.

18. A complication is that the prose RGVV contains verses that have been on occasion conflated with earlier, "true" commentarial verses of the RGV; see Kanō 2016: 20n9 for an example of this. Like Kanō, and due to their wide acceptance by many authors (in spite of errors), I still follow Johnston's numbering of the verses proper to the RGV.

19. Takasaki 1966: 10–19.

20. Takasaki included among his basic verses RGV 1.27, though Ruegg (1976: 349–351) deftly shows that this contravenes Takasaki's criteria for inclusion in his "basic" text.

21. Ibid., 350; see also Kanō 2016: 27, 34–70.

22. See Ruegg 1976: 344–348. Where the RGV understands *tathāgatagarbha* in the sense of *gotra*, this must be proper to all sentient beings, and cannot be the diverse "lineages" taught in works of the Yogācāra-Vijñānavāda tradition (e.g., in the MSA; see 6.3n41). See also Ruegg 1969: 73–78, 123f, 177f; Hara 1994: 52–55; also Schmithausen 2009: 107–109. Note, however, that a commentarial verse of the RGV (1.41) holds that some sentient beings lack any lineage (*agotra*) for liberation, and that this view is repeated in the RGVV; see below, 7.3; also 9.1.

Portions of this chapter will be quite technical—unavoidable if we are to tease apart the development of Buddha-nature thinking across the growth of the RGVV.[23] Amid its strata, and beneath layers of accrued commentary and exposition, we find in the RGV ideas and language reminiscent of a variety of *tathāgatagarbha* sources that we have so far discussed, including allusions to Buddha-nature as taught in the MPNMS-group, and in relation to discourse about the self. At the other end of its composition—when we come to consider the completed, mature RGVV—we deal with the most sophisticated exposition of Buddha-nature thinking produced in India, and witness difficulties that its authors faced when reconciling this idea, and its associations with the language of selfhood, with *nairātmyavāda* discourse, and with Mahāyānist teaching concerned with the perfection of insight (*prajñāpāramitā*) specifically.

7.2 Buddha-nature and the "Basic" RGV

This section concerns probable "root" verses of the RGV (a total of fifty-nine), and will privilege those that Schmithausen took to be most "basic" among them (a total of fifteen),[24] and so contenders for the earliest materials in the text. Within the root verses of the RGV we can discern several "strings" of verses that deal with subtly different aspects of Buddha-nature teaching, and may even represent different literary traditions from which the author(s) of the RGV drew inspiration. In the structure of the mature RGVV these strings are punctuated by commentarial verses and/or prose exposition, but if we read these privileged verses without interval, they reveal a coherent text, and one that exhibits acquaintance with a wealth of ideas concerning Buddha-nature.

The accompanying table organizes all (contested) fifty-nine root verses of the RGV: that is, those recognized by the RGVV as its *śloka*s, and which are also presented in isolation at the start of RGVV^{C} (see 7.1). Table 1 presents (1) Takasaki's (1966) numbering of supposedly root verses (his "*kārikā*s"), together with (2) their place among Johnston's ([1950] 1991) numbering of all verses in the RGV (widely used, and to which I shall refer frequently), that is, those that are both "root" and "commentarial" taken together. I agree with Schmithausen's identification of a set of fifteen "basic" root verses among these—perhaps the very earliest content of the RGV—which are numbered in bold. Finally, I present also (3) my own synopsis of the

23. A convenient, synoptic presentation of the RGVV—including Johnston's RGVV^{S} (minus emendations), Takasaki's translation of it, RGVV^{C}, and RGVV^{T}—is available online via the University of Oslo Faculty of Humanities' *Bibliotheca Polyglotta: Thesaurus Literaturae Buddicae* available at https://www2.hf.uio.no/polylgotta.

24. Schmithausen 1973: 126–129; a recent translation and reevaluation of these verses is that by Mathes 2015: 119–126. A separate discussion of these proposed "strings" of verses is Jones 2020: 68–73.

Table 1 Root verses of the RGV and their thematic content.

RGV root (*mūla*) verse numbers (from Takasaki 1966)	**RGV verse number (from Johnston's 1950 numbering of all verses; basic root verses, after Schmithausen 1971, are in bold)**	**Summary of verses' content in regard to Buddha-nature / *tathāgatagarbha***
1–3	1.4; 9; 13	Introductory verses, which praise (*namaskāra*) the three jewels/refuges (Buddha, dharma, sangha).
4	1.23	Outlines content of the four chapters of the RGVV.
5–10	**1.27**; **30**; **35**; **42**; **45**; **47** (henceforth "String A")	Concern *buddhagarbha/jina-garbha,* including its presence "within" all sentient beings, its superlative qualities, and its relation to a commonality between sentient beings, bodhisattvas, and Buddhas.
11–26	1.**49**; **52–54**; 55–63; **66**; **79**; **84** (henceforth "String B")	Concern *dhātu,* a "nature" of sentient beings, explained in terms of the intrinsically pure mind.
27–57	1.96–126 (henceforth "String TG")	Concern (primarily) (*tathāgata*) *dhātu;* reproduce the nine similes found otherwise in the TGS.
58–59	**1.156–157** (henceforth "String C")	Concern *buddhadhātu:* two verses on the value of teaching about Buddha-nature to sentient beings, and how this relates to teachings about the "illusory" status of *dharmas*.

content of each discernable "string" of root verses. We will not address the fourth root verse (RGV 1.23), which recounts the four primary topics of the RGV(V) as a whole, and which neither Takasaki nor Schmithausen take to be a basic verse of the RGV. We can also follow Schmithausen and set aside the initial *namaskāra* verses that laud the Buddha, dharma, and sangha, and say nothing about any account of Buddha-nature.[25]

25. Regarding rejection of these from "basic" verses on metrical grounds, see Schmithausen 1971: 129. Mathes (2015: 121–122) is, however, right to defend the appropriateness of the content of these three verses given the themes explored by the rest of the RGV(V).

The first verse in Schmithausen's "basic" text (RGV 1.27)—and the beginning of what I am calling "String A"—stands out among the root verses of the RGV due to its use of the expression *buddhagarbha,* which is likely intended as an exocentric (*bahuvrīhi*) compound: "Because 1) the gamut of sentient beings is within the knowledge of the Buddha, 2) of the natural non-duality of its purity, and 3) the fact that its fruit (i.e., buddhahood) is used metaphorically to refer to the lineage of a Buddha, all corporeal beings are said to contain a Buddha (*sarve dehino buddhagarbhāḥ*)."[26] This sets up much of the commentarial material found in the RGVV, to which we will turn later (7.3). Curiously, the location of this verse in RGVV^{C} and RGVV^{T} differs to its position within the prose of RGVV^{S}; it is also accompanied by a commentarial verse (RGV 1.28) that essentially repeats the same content using slightly different terminology, and runs as follows:[27] "Because 1) of the pervasiveness of the body of the Buddha, 2) reality is undifferentiated, and 3) of the lineage [of the Buddha], all corporeal beings always contain a Buddha (*sarve buddhagarbhāḥ śarīriṇaḥ*)."[28] The root verse associates *buddhagarbha* with the pervasiveness of the knowledge of the Buddha (*buddhajñāna*),[29] though the commentarial verse refers instead to the pervasiveness of the *dharmakāya.* At this juncture, both the RGV and the commentarial RGVV hold that *tathāgatagarbha* (though this exact term is not used) refers to sentient beings themselves, reminiscent of the TGS (see 6.2), though other basic verses of the RGV present a more complex picture.[30]

26. RGV 1.27, Johnston (1950) 1991: 26.1–4: *buddhajñānāntargamāt sattvarāśes tannairmalyasyādvayatvāt prakṛtyā / bauddhe gotre tatphalasyopacārād uktāḥ sarve dehino buddhagarbhāḥ //* See also Ruegg 1969: 272–273.

27. Takasaki 1966: 197n2.

28. RGV 1.28, Johnston (1950) 1991: 26.5–6: *saṃbuddhakāyaspharaṇāt tathatāvyatibhedāt / gotrataś ca sadā sarve buddhagarbhāḥ śarīriṇaḥ //*

29. This is more reminiscent of the *Tathāgatotpattisaṃbhavanirdeśa,* preserved independently in Chinese (e.g., T.291) and as a constituent chapter of the compendious *Buddhāvataṃsaka* (e.g., T.278, T.279), regarding which see Hamar 2007. The *Tathāgatotpattisaṃbhavanirdeśa* preserves one reference to the *tathāgatagarbha* (T.291[10]605c12), though its focus throughout is the pervasiveness in all sentient beings of specifically the Buddha's knowledge (*buddhajñāna*). Takasaki (1958; 1966: 35–37; 1974: 507–602) considered this text to be an important precursor to the *tathāgatagarbha* tradition; more recently, Shirō Matsumoto (2014: 287–288) relies on this to explain the origins of the Buddha-nature idea in the TGS (understood, in the context of his article, to be the earliest text of the *tathāgatagarbha* tradition): that the pervading knowledge of the Buddha became reified into the presence of an awakened being. While the position of the *Tathāgatotpattisaṃbhavanirdeśa* is similar to the fully developed Buddha-nature idea (and, indeed, this text is quoted by the RGVV in a gloss on the expression *buddhajñāna;* Johnston [1950] 1991: 22.10–24.8), this is nonetheless still a statement about the Buddha's knowledge pervading all sentient beings, which is subtly different from the position—evident especially in the MPNMS-group—that each sentient being possesses, for their own part, the fully realized character or "body" of a Buddha hidden beneath afflictions. See also Zimmermann 2002: 53–54.

30. Commentarial prose of RGVV^{S} keeps what looks like an exocentric rendering of *tathāgatagarbha* (Johnston [1950] 1991: 26.7: *sarvasattvās tathāgatagarbhā*), but RGVV^{C} instead communicates the "presence" of **tathāgatagarbha* (828b1–2: 一切眾生有如來藏).

Commentarial verses explain these three meanings of *tathāgatagarbha* at some length, and relate them to different similes drawn from the TGS.[31] The rest of String A (i.e., RGV 1.30, 35, 42, 45, 47) presents a densely packed catalogue of ideas pertaining to Buddha-nature. With commentarial materials extracted, the remaining five verses of String A run as follows:

> Always, by nature, unafflicted; like a clear jewel, the sky, or water; it follows from faith in the dharma, superior insight, concentration and compassion (30);[32] [its] results are the perfected qualities of purity, selfhood, bliss, and permanence, with the functions that are aversion to suffering and the appetite and aspiration for the achievement of peace (35); like the ocean, being an inexhaustible store of treasured qualities, and like a lamp, being naturally conjoined with qualities that are inseparable from it (42).[33]
>
> What is taught by those who perceive reality is the distinction between ordinary persons, noble persons and Buddhas in terms of reality (*tathatā*): hence is it taught that this womb/chamber for a victor exists in sentient beings (*sattveṣu jinagarbho 'yaṃ*) (45); [depending on whether this reality is] impure, impure yet pure or perfectly pure, it refers to the realm of sentient beings,[34] the bodhisattva or the Tathāgata [respectively] (47).[35]

The first three verses lack a named grammatical subject; what must be meant is the "womb/chamber for a victor" (i.e., Buddha: *jinagarbha*) that occurs in the second portion of this string. Hence the rest of String A concerns some entity—called (*tathāgata*)*garbha*—that resides "within" sentient

31. RGV(V) 1.144–152; Johnston (1950) 1991: 69–72: the first sense (regarding the *dharmakāya*) is taught by examples 1 through 3, the second by example 4, and the third by examples 5 through 9 (see 6.2).

32. My reading differs from that of Mathes (2015: 122n19), and agrees with that of Takasaki (1966: 200n11). Here MPNMS^{T} renders -*anvaya* (see next note) as *las byung ba*, meaning that "*x*-quality is realized after (faith etc.)"; the meaning is also reflected in the commentarial RGVV (1.35), which understands faith and such to be "causes of purity" (*śuddhihetu;* see 7.3); that is, factors that lead to a realization of Buddha-nature, already present.

33. RGV 1.30, 1.35, 1.42: *sadā prakṛtyasaṃkliṣṭaḥ śuddharatnāmbarāmbuvat / dharmādhimu ktyadhiprajñāsamādhikaruṇānvayaḥ // ... śubhātmasukhanityatvaguṇapāramitāphalam / duḥkhanirvicchamaprāpticchandapraṇidhikarmakaḥ // ... mahodadhir ivāmeyaguṇaratnākṣayākaraḥ / pradīpavad anirbhāgaguṇayuktasvabhāvataḥ //* See Johnston (1950) 1991: 26–37.

34. Though RGV^{S} has *sattvadhātu,* both translations omit any sign of *dhātu* and refer only to "sentient beings" (i.e., Ch. *zhongsheng* 眾生; Tib. *sems can*). I opt to translate in the same way, such that -*dhātu* in RGV^{S} does not intend any "essence" but rather sentient beings in their totality (i.e., the "realm" of them). See also Takasaki 1966: 231; Mathes 2015: 123.

35. RGV 1.45, 1.47; Johnston (1950) 1991: 39.10–11, 40.7–8: *pṛthagjanāryasaṃbuddhatath atābhinnavṛttitaḥ / sattveṣu jinagarbho 'yaṃ deśitas tattvadarśibhiḥ // ... aśuddho 'śuddhaśuddho 'tha suviśuddho yathākramam / sattvadhātur iti prokto bodhisattvas tathāgataḥ //* Minor emendations follow Schmithausen 1971: 147–148.

beings.[36] With echoes of the ŚDS, we also encounter the four "perfected" qualities (*pāramitā*)—purity, selfhood, bliss, and permanence (see 5.3)—together with what RGVV will later call four "causes of purity" (*śuddhihetus*; see 7.3). We also find sentient beings, bodhisattvas, and Buddhas described in terms of their relative purity, which is reminiscent of the AAN (see 6.1).

All of these ways of explaining the *tathāgatagarbha* want for further exposition, which they receive in both commentarial verses and in the prose of the RGVV. But conspicuously, if we stay with likely *basic* verses of the RGV (see table 1, above), this is where attention to *tathāgatagarbha* (or *buddhagarbha/jinagarbha*), by name, ends. Remaining basic verses discuss instead the *(buddha)dhātu,* reflected also by RGV^{C} (with an abundance of *xing* 性 over *zang* 藏) and RGV^{T} (with greater use of *dbyings* over *snying po* [*can*]). All other basic verses (proper to Strings B and C), and other verses that echo the similes of the TGS (String TG), understand *tathāgatagarbha* to refer to the presence of some *(buddha)dhātu* in all sentient beings. As we have seen in previous chapters, we find no reference to Buddha-nature understood as the presence of some *buddhadhātu* in either the ŚDS (see 5.2) or AAN (6.1), which become the primary sources for most of the commentarial RGVV, but of course it was this language that was so central to Buddha-nature teaching found in the MPNMS-group, our likely earliest sources in the *tathāgatagarbha* literary tradition.

This being said, the "essence" or "nature" (*dhātu*) explored throughout String B of root verses is not simply the *buddhadhātu* transposed from any of the MPNMS-group of texts. In language again more reminiscent of the ŚDS, this "nature" is taken to refer to "the intrinsically stainless nature of the mind" (*cittaprakṛtivaimalya*). The first verse of String B (RGV 1.49) reads as follows: "Just as the sky, being of indiscriminative character, pervades everywhere, so is the nature (*dhātu*) that is the intrinsically stainless nature of the mind, all-pervading."[37] Nowhere in any *ātmavādin* account of Buddha-nature is the *(buddha)dhātu* said to be "all-pervading," nor is it taught to mean the intrinsic nature of the mind (see 9.3). On first impression, this notion of *dhātu* cannot be the same kind of "nature" explored by the MPNMS-group of *sūtras*. And yet in the very next verse (1.52) we encounter a tantalizing allusion to the belief that Buddha-nature teaching bears a resemblance to wider Indian discourse about the self and, very specifically, to the all-pervading *ātman* taught by the *Bhagavadgītā*.[38] For comparison, we should consider this Buddhist verse (RGV 1.52) side by side with the relevant verse of the *Bhagavadgītā* (v.13.32):

---

36. RGVV^{T} 77.1: *sems can la rgyal pa'i snying po 'di bstan no*; more ambiguous is RGVV^{C} 831c22: 眾生如來藏.

37. RGV 1.49, Johnston (1950) 1991: 41.7–8: *sarvatrānugataṃ yadvan nirvikalpātmakaṃ nabhaḥ / cittaprakṛtivaimalyadhātuḥ sarvatragas tathā //*

38. V. V. Gokhale 1955: 90–91; also Kanō 2016: 31–32.

Bhagavadgītā 13.32 In the manner that all-pervading space, due to its subtle nature, cannot be tainted, likewise the self (*tathātma*), everywhere situated within a body (*dehe*), cannot be tainted.[39]

RGV 1.52 In the manner that all-pervading space, due to its subtle nature, cannot be tainted, likewise this (*tathāyaṃ*, i.e., the *dhātu*), everywhere situated within a sentient being (*sattve*), cannot be tainted.[40]

Both verses consider their grammatical subject to reside "within" living beings (*Bhagavadgītā: dehe;* though RGV: *sattve*). The subject of the *Bhagavadgītā* verse is *ātman,* which in that text is revealed to be the permanent, enduring presence of the supreme deity in all created beings; in the RGV the subject is simply "this" (*ayam*). $\mathrm{RGV^C}$ clarifies what is evident from the grammar of the Sanskrit text: that "this" must refer to the *dhātu* (*foxing* 佛性) of the preceding root verse (RGV 1.49). Whereas the *Bhagavadgītā* concerns the pervading, embodied self, the verse of the RGV concerns the similarly pervading, also embodied, (*buddha*)*dhātu.*

The remaining verses of String B understand this *dhātu* to again refer to the intrinsic nature of the mind (*cittaprakṛti*). This *dhātu* is called the ground for irrational thought (*ayoniśomanaskāra*), which in turn is the basis for the component factors of experience in transmigration (*skandhāyatanadhātavaḥ*); it is the luminous nature of the mind that is, like space, unchanging, and apart from afflictions that are born from false conceptualization.[41] But Schmithausen demonstrates that verses explaining this interrupt the trajectory of what was in likelihood a trio of properly basic verses in this string (RGV 1.53, 54 and 79),[42] which when presented together read, more simply, as follows:

Just as the worlds everywhere have their origin and destruction in space (*ākāśa*), so do the sense-organs have their destruction and origination in this unconditioned *dhātu* (53). Just as space is not burnt by fire, likewise is this [*dhātu*] not burnt by the fires of death, disease or age (54).[43]

39. Sargeant 2009: 560: *yathā sarvagataṃ saukṣmyād ākāśaṃ nopalipyate / sarvatrāvasthito dehe tathātmā nopalipyate //*

40. Johnston (1950) 1991: 42.6–7: *yathā sarvagataṃ saukṣmyād ākāśaṃ nopalipyate / sarvatrāvasthitaḥ sattve tathāyam nopalipyate //* Compare $\mathrm{RGVV^C}$ 832c4–5 (also 814a18–19); or $\mathrm{RGVV^T}$ 81.18–21.

41. Johnston (1950) 1991: 42.12–43.8, 43.11–12.

42. Schmithausen (1971: 128–129) demonstrates that embedded within String B is a shorter series of verses (RGV 1.55–63) that provide an extended gloss on the two basic verses that precede them (RGV 1.53–54). The explanatory verses, he notes, resemble content of the *Gaganagañjaparipṛcchā*, one of the Mahāyānist works cited by the RGVV when it explains the manner in which the mind of a sentient being is intrinsically pure (see 9.3).

43. RGV 1.53–54, Johnston (1950) 1991 42.8–11: *yathā sarvatra lokānām ākāśa udayavyayaḥ / tathaivāsaṃskṛte dhātāv indriyāṇāṃ vyayodayaḥ // yathā nāgnibhir ākāśaṃ dagdhapūrvaṃ kadācana / tathā na pradahaty enaṃ mṛtyuvyādhijarāgnayaḥ //*

> This [*dhātu*] is of unchanging character, due to its conjunction with inexhaustible qualities; it is the refuge of the world, due to it having no limit ahead of it; it is always non-dual, due to being without discrimination; it is also characterized as indestructible, as its nature is uncreated (79).[44]

These verses draw together a number of themes from across Buddha-nature teaching, to which we will return later in this study (10.2). After them we are left with only one remaining root verse in String B (RGV 1.84), which must continue to take this same *dhātu* as its grammatical subject: "Hence [the *dhātu*] is the *dharmakāya;* it is the Tathāgata; it is the truth of the noble ones; it is the ultimate liberation (*paramārthanivṛtti*). Hence, it not being separate from its qualities—in the manner of the sun and its rays—there is no liberation apart from buddhahood."[45] The commentary of the RGVV that accompanies this verse quotes extensively from both the ŚDS and AAN (as well as from a third text, the *Jñānālokālaṅkārasūtra*).[46] But what we see in the root verses themselves—and those among them that are most "basic" to the RGV—is a unique articulation of the Buddha-nature idea, articulated in terms of some universally present *dhātu* that is identifiable with both the Buddha himself (language reminiscent of the MPNMS-group) as well as the nature of the mind (more reminiscent of the ŚDS). These verses bridge differences in vocabulary and doctrine exhibited by the two distinct traditions of Buddha-nature teaching that we have observed in earlier chapters. To what these verses are committed, moreover, is the notion that liberation can mean only the achievement of buddhahood, a passing agreement with the teaching of the SP, and the single vehicle paradigm that has informed all *tathāgatagarbha* sources that we have so far addressed (see also 9.1).

Particularly interesting is of course the verse reminiscent of the *Bhagavadgītā,* which presents the (*buddha*)*dhātu* as having a superficial resemblance to discourse about the self as taught by a non-Buddhist tradition (call it Brahmanical, Bhāgavata, or Vaiṣṇava).[47] Whoever adapted this verse—from the *Bhagavadgītā,* or possibly another source—tacitly acknowledged that the (*buddha*)*dhātu* bears some functional resemblance to what

44. RGV 1.79, Johnston (1950) 1991: 53.10–13: *ananyathātmākṣayadharmayogato jagaccharaṇyo 'naparāntakoṭiḥ / sadādvaya 'sāv avikalpakatvato 'vināśadharmāpy akṛtasvabhāvataḥ //*

45. RGV 1.84, Johnston (1950) 1991: 55.3–6: *sa dharmakāyaḥ sa tathāgato yatas tad āryasatyaṃ paramārthanirvṛttiḥ / ato na buddhatvam ṛte 'rkaraśmivad guṇāvinirbhāgatayāsti nirvṛtiḥ //*

46. Johnston (1950) 1991: 55–57. Regarding other texts quoted in this portion of the RGVV (the sources for which have proved difficult to identify), see Takasaki 1966: 259–261.

47. V. V. Gokhale (1955) contends that this verse reflects later "more Vedāntic" content of the *Bhagavadgītā,* such that the RGV may have instead known a third source upon which both texts drew. Either way, it is undeniable that the root verse of the RGV exhibits language that was drawn from a source concerned with discourse about *ātman.* See also 10.3.

was elsewhere, by some other tradition, called *ātman*.[48] Though this "pervading" *dhātu* of the RGV does not seem conceptually reminiscent of Buddha-nature in the MPNMS-group, the evocation of a non-Buddhist verse concerned with nothing other than the self "within sentient beings" continues a theme that we observe through the MPNMS and AMS in particular (see also 9.6).

Further evidence that basic verses of the RGV knew the MPNMS-group continues in "String C" (see again table 1), which consists of the two verses that conclude the basic RGV as imagined by both Takasaki and Schmithausen (RGV 1.156–157). These refer to the *buddhadhātu* specifically, and the seemingly problematic relationship between this and Buddhist teachings about emptiness: "It has been said that all things everywhere should be known to be empty, in the manner of clouds, dreams or illusions; why then has the Buddha taught here that in all sentient beings there exists Buddha-nature (*buddhadhātu*)?[49] It has been taught because of five defects [that might be remedied]: the depressed mind; contempt for inferior sentient beings; attachment to what is unreal; criticism of the real dharma, and having affection for one's self."[50] These verses understand Buddha-nature teaching to be something of a corrective to miscomprehension about emptiness (*śūnyatā*), which in sources of the *prajñāpāramitā* tradition is explained to mean that phenomena which appear substantial are in fact "like illusions" (*mayopama*).[51] But use of the expression *buddhadhātu* also evokes (at least for us) *tathāgatagarbha* as expounded by the MPNMS-group of texts, which understand teachings about Buddha-nature to either qualify or even surpass teachings about emptiness (see 9.5; also 4.5). That these verses may have referred to Buddha-nature as taught in the MPNMS specifically is supported by a commentarial verse that follows soon after, which refers to the RGV as the "higher teaching" (*uttaratantra*) of the Buddha.[52] On the one hand, this may be the earliest source for the RGV understood as the "*Mahāyānottaratantra*" (see 7.1); on the other, this epithet is found also in the MPNMS, which also refers to itself as embodying the "higher

48. Kanō (2016: 32) writes that this material suggests that the RGV was on one level "claiming that the Buddha-nature is a true *ātman*."

49. RGVV^C agrees that the subject is **tathāgatadhātu* (892c13: 皆有如來性), though RGVV^T (151.18) suggests instead *buddhagarbha* (*sangs rgyas snying po*).

50. RGV 1.156–157, Johnston (1950) 1991: 77.12–19: *śūnyaṃ sarvaṃ sarvathā tatra tatra jñeyaṃ meghasvapnamāyākṛtābham / ity uktvaivaṃ buddhadhātuḥ punaḥ kiṃ sattve sattve 'stīti buddhair ihoktam // līnaṃ cittaṃ hīnasattveṣv avajñābhūtagrāho bhūtadharmāpavādaḥ ātmasnehaś cādhikaḥ pañca doṣā yeṣāṃ teṣāṃ tatprahāṇārtham uktam //*

51. Expressed particularly clearly in a closing verse of the *Vajracchedikā-prajñāpāramitā* (e.g., Schopen 1989: 107 [12b1–2]; also 113) and otherwise observable in the *Aṣṭasāhasrikā-prajñāpāramitā* (Vaidya 1960: 20.11–25), in which all things, including the Buddha and *nirvāṇa*, are compared to illusions (*māyopama*) or dreams (*svapnopama*).

52. RGV 1.60, Johnston (1950) 1991: 78.5–6: *pūrvam evaṃ vyavasthāpya tantre punar ihottare.*

teaching" of the Mahāyāna.[53] In short, the authors of the RGV may have held that their verses present the authoritative account of the Buddha's higher teaching, which takes priority over (or at least correctly explains) earlier accounts of Buddha-nature and its meaning.

Finally, we should mention also a string of root verses that are likely not "basic" in the composition of the RGV but which still predate commentarial materials within which they are embedded. "String TG" (RGV 1.96–126; see again table 1) consists of the similes found also in the TGS.[54] But in contrast to the diversity of expression that these similes exhibit across surviving versions of the TGS (see 6.2), the similes preserved in the RGV consistently refer to that which resides in all sentient beings as some "essence" (*dhātu*).[55] Commentarial verses that follow this string (RGV 1.127–129) explain these root verses to be in accord with what we are calling String B: that is, that they concern "the intrinsically stainless nature of the mind (*cittaprakṛtivaimalya*)" that is plagued by afflictions that are adventitious to it.[56] But this is not clear from the verses of String TG themselves, which concern simply the *(buddha)dhātu,* without any clear reference to this as an epithet for the mind.[57]

This analysis of likely "basic" materials in the RGV—together with verses reminiscent of the TGS, which are likely not late in the composition of the RGV—demonstrates that we cannot easily align this short, reconstructed text with either the MPNMS-group or something like the reinvention of the expression *tathāgatagarbha* exhibited by the ŚDS and AAN. The earliest materials in the RGV appear to be a unique collection of thoughts about Buddha-nature, amid which are traces of an *ātmavādin* heritage as well as the sense that the nature of a Buddha, proper to all sentient beings, refers to the mind and its intrinsic purity. These ideas receive a satisfying explanation only in the RGVV, a full exploration of which exceeds the aims of this chapter. However, we must give due attention to what the RGVV acknowledges to be a particularly difficult matter, inherited from the ŚDS and no doubt related to the MPNMS before it: the *dharmakāya* understood in terms of the perfection of self.

53. See Radich 2015a: 48–49; also Hodge 2010/2012: 56–59; Habata 2007: 105n3; Takasaki 1974: 132–136. This epithet is particularly clear in MPNMS^{T} (e.g., §85.5, §498). Regarding *uttaratantra* as a medical (i.e., *āyurveda*) category, see Habata 1989.

54. Johnston (1950) 1991: 59.16–66.10. Note that the title *Tathāgatagarbhasūtra* appears in the commentarial RGVV, and not the verses of the RGV themselves (Johnston [1950] 1991: 66.18).

55. We encounter *dhātu* in RGV verses 1.97, 98, 103, 116 (here *śubhadharmadhātu*), 120, 122, 129 (here *sattvadhātu*); also *saṃbuddhagarbha* in 1.101. In RGVV^{C} (814b22–816a18) the content of a sentient being is called throughout either 如來藏 or 如來性; RGVV^{T} (117–129) agrees with our Sanskrit text and shows a marked preference for *khams* (i.e., *dhātu*) over, for example, *snying po* (i.e., *garbha*). See also Jones 2020: 72–73.

56. Johnston (1950) 1991: 66.16–17.

57. A possible exception—though ambiguous—is RGV 1.125 (Johnston [1950] 1991: 66.3–6), in which there is a "natural luminosity" present but no mention of "the mind" (e.g., *citta*).

7.3 "Perfection of Self" in the RGVV

Leaving to one side what may be the earliest or "most basic" content of the RGV(V), we turn to the RGVV as a mature treatise. In terms of sheer length and density of exposition, the verses to which the RGVV gives the most attention are those that unpack String A, discussed above (see also table 1). The RGVV supplies a lengthy account of the *dharmakāya* in terms of the four perfections (*pāramitā*) that feature in RGV 1.35, and which—expressed as such—may have been innovations of the ŚDS (5.3). One of these perfections is of course the "perfection of self" (*ātmapāramitā*), predicated of the *dharmakāya* (rather than the *tathāgatagarbha* that is its afflicted antecedent), and among what the RGVV calls the four "perfected" qualities (*guṇapāramitā*). As already discussed, these positive articulations of the Buddha's transcendent mode of being are likely heirs to the "inversions" of the four distortions (*viparyāsas*) seen in the MPNMS (2.2). Whereas the ŚDS is silent on the interpretation of these perfected qualities, the RGVV provides a thorough account of to what they must refer, in which the RGVV creatively (re)defines *ātmapāramitā* as nothing other than absence of self (*nairātmya*).[58]

The explanation of *ātmapāramitā* in the RGVV requires careful contextualization, as it is embedded in other important statements regarding the *dharmakāya,* selfhood, and the failings of non-Buddhist "*ātmavādin*" teachers. In a significant root verse (RGV 1.35, of "String A," translated above in 7.2), the four "perfected qualities" are described as results (*phala*) of the *tathāgatagarbha*. In the root verse that precedes this (i.e., RGV 1.30, again translated in the previous section), we encounter what the RGVV calls four "causes of purification" (*śuddhihetu*), or those factors that allow for the *tathāgatagarbha* to be "cleansed" into the *dharmakāya,* namely, (1) faith in the dharma (*dharmādhimukti*), (2) superior insight (*adhiprajñā*), (3) concentration (*samādhi*), and (4) compassion (*karuṇā*). Commentarial verses (RGV 1.32–33) and accompanying prose explain how these causes relate to particular obstructions to bodhisattva practice, and to categories of persons who suffer from them:

> Obstruction [to liberation] is fourfold: 1) hostility towards the dharma, 2) perception of a self, 3) fear of suffering in transmigration, and 4) indifference to sentient beings (32).

58. See Ruegg 1969: 250–251, 370–380; Eltschinger and Ratié 2013: 53–58; Kanō 2014: 239–241; also S. King 1991: 177–181, who attends to the *Foxing lun* (see 1.4) and its reproduction of material from the RGVV. King focuses on the use of positive language in these *pāramitās* as a form of pedagogical strategy (*upāya*) for certain audiences. Historically speaking, I believe that the authors of the RGVV inherited positive expressions such as *ātmapāramitā* from an earlier source—the ŚDS, after the MPNMS—and were compelled by their commitment to more conventional Buddhist teaching (including that of the *prajñāpāramitā* tradition) to gloss *ātmapāramitā* in terms of precisely *anātman/nairātmya*.

> There are four causes of purification, beginning with faith in the dharma, which belong to 1) *icchantika*s, 2) *tīrthya*s, 3) *śrāvaka*s and 4) *pratyekabuddha*s [respectively] (33).[59]

Attending to these last four, the RGVV categorizes sentient beings in terms of their status either "inside" or "outside" of the sangha, and then—across both—whether or not they can be said to have any desire for liberation. Some who are "outside of the dharma" desire transmigration over any end to it, and so by soteriological "lineage" are declared to be "not for *nirvāṇa*" (*aparinirvāṇagotraka*).[60] Some persons "within the dharma" (*ihadhārmika*) have succumbed to this also, and show hostility to the Mahāyāna, so face terrible future existences.[61] Some who seek liberation have no means for it (*anupāyapatita*), among whom are non-Buddhists, extraneous to the dharma (*itobāhya … anyatīrthya*), whom we have seen to be a recurring preoccupation of earlier Buddha-nature works also. In RGVV^{S} these "outsiders" are listed as *caraka*s, *parivrājaka*s, and *nirgrantha*s (in RGVV^{T}: *tsa ra ka, kun tu rgyu, gcer bu pa*): perhaps (very loosely) "ascetics, wanderers and mendicants."[62] RGVV^{C} supplies different details, and glosses these non-Buddhists (*waidao* 外道: **tīrthya*s) to be, by name, Sāṃkhyas (*sengqia* 僧佉), Vaiśeṣikas (*weishishi* 衛世師), and Nirgrantha-Jñātiputras (*niqiantuo ruotizi* 尼揵陀若提子), in which the last must refer to exponents of Jainism.[63]

Others who "have no means" for liberation are said to be within the dharma; they have erroneous views and behave "like those [teachers or adepts of other systems]" mentioned above.[64] Some of these persons cling to views of personhood (*pudgaladṛṣṭi*), and "lack faith in what is ultimate" (*paramārthānadhimukta*); some have no inclination toward teachings about emptiness (*śūnyatānadhimukta*), and so are said to be no different from persons affiliated with non-Buddhist systems.[65] At another extreme, some are

59. RGV 1.32–33, Johnston (1950) 1991: 27.13–16: *caturdhāvaraṇaṃ dharmapratigho 'py ātmadarśanam / saṃsāraduḥkhabhīrūtvaṃ sattvārthaṃ nirapekṣatā // icchantikānāṃ tīrthyānāṃ śrāvakāṇāṃ svayaṃbhuvām / adhimuktyādayo dharmāś catvāraḥ śuddhihetavaḥ //*

60. See 7.1n22, above; also 9.1.

61. RGVV 1.33, Johnston (1950) 1991: 28.2–4: *tamasas tamo 'ntaram andhakārān mahāndhakāragāminas tamobhūyiṣṭhā iti vadāmi* / This is a quotation of the AAN, though our surviving version of the AAN adds that these condemned persons are called *icchantika*s (Silk 2015b: 127–128, §21ii). This detail is absent from the quotation in the Sanskrit RGVV, but present in RGVV^{C} (828c15–16), which leads Silk (2015b: 9) to suggest that the translator(s) or redactor(s) of RGVV^{C} knew the Chinese translation of the AAN.

62. Johnston (1950) 1991: 28.6–7; RGVV^{T} 53.12–13. See also Schmithausen 1971: 142. Similar lists appear in, for example, the SP (276.2–3), and *Vimalakīrtinirdeśasūtra* (Taishō University 2006: 33 [20a1]).

63. That is, disciples of the teacher Nigantha Nātaputta, who features in texts including the *Sāmaññaphalasutta*; see MacQueen 1988: 148–168.

64. Johnston (1950) 1991: 28.7–8: *ihadhārmikāś ca tatsabhāgacaritā eva śrāddhā api durgṛhītagrāhiṇaḥ /*

65. Johnston (1950) 1991: 28.9. RGVV^{C} provides another interesting variation, as it mentions by name "Vātsīputra" (828c22: *duzi* 犢子), likely intending the Vātsīputrīyas, a school of the Śrāvakayāna tradition that accepted a form of *pudgalavāda* teaching (see 1.2).

"intoxicated by emptiness,"[66] of which the RGVV retorts that this is no better than holding erroneous views about personhood.[67] Apart from all of these sit those who are true to the vehicles of the *śrāvaka* or *pratyekabuddha*, and beyond them the bodhisattvas—who transcend the desire for either existence or nonexistence—are on the path to comprehending the identity of transmigration and liberation from it, and strive for "the non-abiding *nirvāṇa*" (*apratiṣṭhitanirvāṇa*) that is proper to a Buddha.[68]

From among these categories, and in accord with the commentarial verses translated above, the RGVV highlights the *icchantika*s—that is, those who show hostility to the Mahāyāna—the non-Buddhists (*tīrthya*s), *śrāvaka*s, and *pratyekabuddha*s, and to each ascribes a particular obstruction (*āvaraṇa*) that stands in the way of their liberation, as well as a remedy for this (*śuddhihetu*) drawn also from commentarial verses of the RGV:

1. Regarding *icchantika*s, "faith in the dharma" (*dharmādhimukti*) remedies aversion to the dharma (*dharmapratigha*).
2. Regarding *tīrthya*s, "higher insight" (*adhiprajñā*) remedies (false) views of the self (*ātmadarśana*).
3. Regarding *śrāvaka*s, "concentration" (*samādhi*) remedies fear of suffering through transmigration (*saṃsāraduḥkhabhīrūtva*).
4. Regarding *pratyekabuddha*s, "compassion" (*karuṇā*) remedies indifference to sentient beings (*sattvārthaḥ nirapekṣatā*).[69]

A commentarial verse (1.36) states that the results of these causes—that is, the four perfected qualities—are "remedies to the fourfold distortions," and come about by inversion of erroneous thinking about the *dharmakāya*.[70] The RGVV reminds us that the four distortions—seeing permanence where there is impermanence, self where there is none, etcetera—still hold in regard to entities composed of the heaps of experience (*skandha*s), and that inversion of them results in a fourfold "non-distortion" (*aviparyāsa*). But these nondistortions—impermanence, not-self, etcetera—can themselves be considered erroneous in regard to the *dharmakāya*, which is characterized by "perfected" permanence, selfhood, etcetera.[71] In summary, and much like after the example of the dizzied man in MPNMS-dhk (see 2.2), the RGVV recognizes that conceiving (1) permanence, selfhood, etcetera are distorted views in regard to worldly phenomena, but also that (2) the *correction* of these views must be modified again in consideration of the

66. Johnston (1950) 1991: 28.10–11. See also Schmithausen 1971: 142.

67. Johnston (1950) 1991: 28.11–12. This quotes the *Kāśyapaparivarta*, regarding which see Vorobyova-Desyatovskaya 2002: 26–27 (§65).

68. Johnston (1950) 1991: 28.12–18. Regarding *apratiṣṭhitanirvāṇa*, see Nagao 1991: 23–29.

69. These correspondences are presented also in Ruegg 1969: 368.

70. RGV^{S} 1.36, Johnston (1950) 1991: 30.7–8: *phalaṃ eṣāṃ samāsena dharmakāye viparyayāt / caturvidhaviparyāsapratipakṣaprabhāvitam //* Regarding curiosities in the form of this verse as reflected by both RGVV^{C} and RGVV^{T}, see Takasaki 1966: 208n72.

71. RGVV^{S} 1.36, Johnston (1950) 1991: 30.11–17.

dharmakāya, the supermundane mode of being proper to a Buddha, which is fundamentally different from anything worldly.

As a final step, the RGVV maps the four perfected qualities onto the correspondences between categories of persons, their respective obstructions, and the remedies prescribed to them, as outlined above. It is not for us to consider each of these correspondences in turn.[72] Our priority is of course the *dharmakāya* understood as *ātmapāramitā,* which we are told is the aspect of the *dharmakāya* arrived at by those commonly associated with ideas of a self: non-Buddhist teachers or adepts (*tīrthyas*). To recap, to these non-Buddhists the RGVV prescribes cultivation of superior insight (*adhiprajñā,* a synonym, as the passage below shows, for *prajñāpāramitā*) in order to remedy their attachment to views about a self, and so arrive at the perfection of self realized in the *dharmakāya.* The RGVV explains this as follows:

> The acquisition of the perfection of the supreme self (*paramātmapāramitā*) should be understood to be the result of the cultivation of the perfection of insight, by an inversion of delight in attachment to an unreal self that is proper to the those of other systems, who have a view of the self among the five heaps of experience, the nature of which is no such thing; the entity at which they have grasped in just such a way, due to it contradicting the characteristics of the self (*ātmalakṣaṇa*), is not ever the self.
>
> But the Tathāgata, due to having knowledge of things as they are, has attained the pinnacle of absence of self in respect to all phenomena; this absence of self that he perceives, as it conforms to the character of what is not the self (*anātmalakṣaṇa*), at all times is affirmed as the self, in which "the self" has the sense of precisely absence of self, as in the phrase "standing by means of not standing."[73]

72. Worth noting is that the error of the *icchantika* is a "lack of faith in the dharma." The aspect of the *dharmakāya* at which they arrive is the perfection of purity (*śubhapāramitā*), which remedies their delight in transmigration. This does not appear to be the sense of *icchantika* encountered in the MPNMS-group (see 2.7n126) and instead understands *icchantika* to refer to someone desirous (after the Sanskrit root √*iṣ*) for continued existence (whom the RGVV calls a *bhavābhilāṣin*). The RGVV does not consider the *icchantika* incapable of attaining liberation, otherwise it would not prescribe faith in the dharma as a remedy to their flaw.

73. RGVV[S] 1.36, Johnston (1950) 1991: 31.10–16: *pañcasūpādānaskandheṣv ātmadarśinām anyatīrthyānām asadātmagrahābhirativiparyayeṇa prajñāpāramitābhāvanāyāḥ paramātmapāramitādhigamaḥ phalaṃ draṣṭavyam / sarve hy anyatīrthyā rūpādikam atatsvabhāvaṃ vastv ātmety upagatāḥ / tac caiṣāṃ vastu yathāgraham ātmalakṣaṇena viṣaṃvāditvāt sarvakālam anātmā / tathāgataḥ punar yathābhūtajñānena sarvadharmanairātmyaparapāramiprāptaḥ*[a] */ tac cāsya nairātmyam anātmalakṣaṇena yathādarśanam avisaṃvāditatvāt*[b] *sarvakālamātmābhipreto nairātmyaṃ evātmana iti*[c] *kṛtvā / yathoktaṃ sthito 'sthānayogeneti* / See also Ruegg 1989a: 24–26.

[a] Emended after Takasaki 1966: 210n91: *-parapāram abhiprāptaḥ* to *-parapāramiprāptaḥ*

[b] Emended after Schmithausen 1971: 143: *avisaṃvāditvāt* to *avisaṃvāditatvāt*

[c] Emended after Schmithausen 1971: 143: *ātmanti* to *ātmana iti.*

Here the RGVV refers to not only the perfection of self but also "the supreme self" (*paramātman*), which describes the *dharmakāya*.[74] This is not any self amid the heaps of experience but something realized at the apex of comprehending *absence* of self in all phenomena (*dharmanairātmya*), in other words what is taught by the perfection of insight tradition. Although this perfection of self is called a "quality" (*guṇa*) of the *dharmakāya*, the RGVV takes this to refer to the Buddha having realized absence of self to its full extent, which is a corrective prescribed for persons who remain wedded to any views about a self, foremost among whom are non-Buddhists. The passage ends with material that echoes the *Aṣṭasāhasrikā-prajñāpāramitā:* in the manner that the correct view of the bodhisattva is to eschew all views—akin to "standing by not standing"—so too must all affirmative statements about the Buddha's self ("supreme" or otherwise) refer, in the final analysis, to absence of self.[75] In summary, the RGVV strives to reconcile the notion of a "perfected" self, apropos of the *dharmakāya,* with the *nairātmyavādin* discourse of wider Buddhist literature, here taken to be the bodhisattva's understanding that no phenomenon has to it a substantial nature, and that all elements of our experience should be thought of as being like illusions.

This material is challenging enough, but the equivalent prose of RGVV^C^—our earliest witness to the Indian RGVV—presents us with some intriguing differences. This version ceases to follow the trajectory of the others after having declared that "self" should be taken to in fact mean "absence of self."[76] RGVV^C^ instead affirms that absence of self must mean absence of *erroneous* notions of selfhood to which non-Buddhists remain attached, but *ātman* can *correctly* refer to the achievement of a "powerful" or "sovereign" self (*zizaiwo* 自在我).[77] This marks the beginning of a line of thinking unique to the Chinese version of the RGVV. In place of the statement reminiscent of the *Aṣṭasāhasrikā-prajñāpāramitā,* we find the following verse: "Having attained the pinnacle of absence of self—which is like pure, real emptiness—the Buddhas attain the pure nature (*jingti* 淨體): hence is it said that they attain a "great body/person" (*dashen* 大身)."[78] This last expression, as we shall see below, may well have reflected something like the Sanskrit *mahātman*. RGVV^C^ comments on this verse at length, focusing on the expression "great person," and otherwise using terminology distinct from the rest of the RGVV:

74. Compare RGVV^C^ 829c17 (第一我波羅蜜) and RGVV^T^ 59.21 (*bdag dam pa'i pha rol pa phyin pa*). Of the other three *guṇapāramitā*s, only bliss (*sukha*) also uses the expression *parama-*, and only in RGVV^T^ (61.7: *bde ba dam pa'i pha rol pa*). See also Ruegg 1989b: 305–306.

75. Vaidya 1960: 4.25: *susthito 'sthānayogena*.

76. RGVV^C^ 829c23–24: 以即無我名爲有我

77. RGVV^C^ 829c24–25.

78. RGVV^C^ 829c26–27: 如[a]清淨真空，得第一無我，諸佛得淨體，是名得大身。

[a] T 如 = Song/Yuan/Ming/Palace 知

> Attaining the great person means that the Tathāgata attains the highest, pure reality of the *dharmakāya;* this is the true self of the Buddha-Tathāgatas, because they have attained a nature that is sovereign, and attained the supremely pure body. Because the verse [above] teaches that Buddhas have attained the pure nature, Buddhas are said to have attained purity and sovereignty. Because the verse states that they have attained the great person, there is the sense that all Buddha-Tathāgatas attain, in the untainted realm, the supremely sovereign self.
>
> Moreover, based on what is meant [above], the *dharmakāya* of the Tathāgata is not called a "being" (*you* 有). Lacking the characteristic(s) of a self (*wuwoxiang* 無我相: *anātmalakṣaṇa*), or of any *dharma* (*wufa* 無法相: **adharmalakṣana*), he cannot be said to be existent; having such a character, he is therefore non-existent. Moreover, based on what is meant [above], the *dharmakāya* of the Tathāgata is not a "non-being" (*wu* 無), simply because his identity is reality itself (*zhenruwoti* 真如我體); hence it cannot be said that there is no *dharmakāya* as, having such a character, [the *dharmakāya*] exists. For this reason, when non-Buddhists asked "After he has died, does the Tathāgata possess a body, or does he not?" about such things the Buddha did not explain or respond.[79]

It has been acknowledged before that the initial verse above is highly reminiscent of one that is found in the MSA (9.23), and the ensuing prose similar to what follows in its commentary, the MSABh (see 6.3).[80] It is then plausible that an underlying form of the Indian RGVV concerned the pure self (*śuddhātman,* corresponding to RGVV^{C} *jingti* 淨體) and what is meant by the Buddha's great person is his "great self" (**mahātman*) in the sense, perhaps, of a superior kind of character.[81] It is likely that this material in RGVV^{C} postdates what is preserved in the MSA(Bh); it is not only conspicuously absent from other versions of the RGVV but also includes reference to the Buddha's power or "sovereignty" (*zizai* 自在; **aiśvarya*), which is absent from the MSA(Bh). Also differing from any form of the MSABh is the concluding discussion about the Buddha as neither a "being" nor "non-being," which evokes the "unexpounded" (*avyākṛta*) questions known from earlier Buddhist literature.[82] This is particularly reminiscent of material exclusive

79. RGVV^{C} 829c28–830a11: 得大身者謂如來得第一清淨真如法身；彼是諸佛如來實我，以得自在體，以得第一清淨身。偈言諸佛得淨體故，以是義故諸佛名得清淨自在。偈言是名得大身故，以是義故依於此義諸佛如來於[a]無漏界中得為[b]第一最自在我。又復即依如是義故，如來法身不名為有，以無我相無法相故，以是義故，不得言有，以如彼相如是無故。又復即依如是義故，如來法身不名為無，以唯有彼真如我體，是故不得言無法身，以如彼相如是有故。依此義故，諸外道問「如來死後為有身耶？為無身耶？」有如是等，是故如來不記不答。

[a] Song/Yuan/Ming/Palace omit 於

[b] Song/Yuan/Ming/Palace omit 為

80. Tsukinowa 1938: 135–136; Takasaki 1966: 211–212.

81. See Zacchetti 2004: 202n28; also H. Nakamura 1980: 922d.

82. For example, the *Aggivacchagottasutta* (MN.I.483); see Anālayo 2011: 389–399; also 1.1.

to Dharmakṣema's influential Chinese translation of the MPNMS (i.e., MPNMS^{D}+; see 2.1), which also understands the Buddha's "great self" (*dawo* 大我) in terms of his "sovereignty," and otherwise reflects on liberation as neither "*x* nor not-*x*" (see 2.7). In short, this material unique to RGVV^{C} reflects a variant interpretation of how the Buddha can be said to possess a "great self," shaped perhaps by the MSA, but consistent also with the language and doctrine of (the Chinese) MPNMS^{D}(+).

To recap, both RGVV^{S} and RGVV^{T} redefine what appears to be a kataphatic account of the Buddha's *dharmakāya*—in terms of the perfection of self—into an apophatic account of absence of self with respect to all phenomena, an expression of the more established *nairātmavāda* discourse of wider Buddhist tradition, and particular to teachings about the perfection of insight.[83] Teaching about perfection of self is couched as a remedy for (predominantly *ātmavādin*) non-Buddhist teachers, but must refer—in the end—to nothing less than teachings about absence of self. In RGVV^{C} we find other material, evocative of both the MSA and MPNMS^{D}+, that explores this matter differently, but once again seems invested in explaining the language of selfhood, apropos of the Buddha or the *dharmakāya*, to be a means of articulating a reality that is in fact bereft of anything worthy of being called the self.

All three versions of the RGVV go on to clarify that the attainment of *ātmapāramitā* comes about by the cultivation of the perfection of insight, the content of which is the full realization that nothing in either sentient beings or the world deserves to be thought of as possessing any self.[84] In this context it could not be much clearer that *ātmapāramitā* refers to nothing about the Buddha's power or permanence so much as the Buddha's perception of *absence* of self with respect to all phenomena. The instrument of this is the perfection of insight, focused—as is well-known—on an appreciation of the fundamental emptiness, or otherwise absence of self, of all phenomena: teachings that were downplayed in earlier Buddha-nature texts, but which were a lodestar for Mahāyāna Buddhism in general (see 4.5, 9.5).

Before leaving this portion of the RGVV, we should consider a final pair of commentarial verses (RGV 1.37–38) that provide some closing detail on the matter of *paramātman:*

> Indeed this [*dharmakāya*] is pure because of its intrinsic purity and because of the removal of impressions; having calmed the false conceptualizations of self and absence of self, it is the supreme self (*paramātman*)

83. Regarding what might be termed "kataphatic" as opposed to "apophatic" articulations of Buddhist teaching (the latter, par excellence, represented by the Madhyamaka tradition), see Gimello 1976; also, apropos of Buddha-nature teaching specifically, Ruegg 1989a: 36–44; Radich 2015a: 211–214.

84. Johnston (1950) 1991: 32.9–10: *prajñāpāramitābhāvanayā ākāśopamasattvabhājanalok anairātmyaniṣṭhāgamanād.* Compare RGVV^{C} 830a22–24; RGVV^{T} 63.3–5.

> (37); it is bliss due to the removal of the mind-made heaps (*skandhas*) and their causes;[85] it is permanent due to the realization of the equality of *saṃsāra* with *nirvāṇa*. (38)[86]

Here the *dharmakāya* understood as *paramātman* is that which is beyond both self and its absence, an interpretation that we saw also, in passing, in the MPNMS (see 2.6). The prose commentary following these verses states that this teaching corrects the errors of both (1) non-Buddhists (*tīrthyas*), who falsely impute a self, and (2) Buddhist *śrāvakas*, who subscribe to a false view about absence of self.[87] This is consistent with what we have seen in our *ātmavādin* Buddha-nature texts, but with an important twist: whereas the MPNMS-group of texts reject both the self taught by the non-Buddhist and total negation of any self as accepted by the *śrāvaka*, they also contend that the apex of the Buddha's dharma is an account of the self, taught by the expression *tathāgatagarbha*. By contrast, the RGVV teaches that correcting the *śrāvaka* with teaching about the "supreme self" must still, when understood correctly, refer to what is taught by the *prajñāpāramitā* literature: absence of self with respect to all phenomena.

Of all of the sources for Buddha-nature teaching that we have so far addressed, the RGVV exhibits the clearest influence by the *prajñāpāramitā* tradition, and works to reconcile Buddha-nature thinking with the language and priorities of that literature. Its understanding of the *dharmakāya* and any "selfhood" predicated of it attempts to bring this into accord with teachings about how all things are empty of self, and downplays tensions between these lines of thought that are easily discernable in the MPNMS-group of texts (see also 9.5). Across all extant versions of it, the RGVV has traveled far from the tone of *sūtras* that promoted Buddha-nature, and before it the nature of the Buddha himself, in terms of selfhood.

---

85. The RGVV (Johnston [1950] 1991: 33.4–14) clarifies that this cause is the "basis of ignorance" (*avidyāvāsabhūmi*) that underpins the continued existence of arhats, *pratyekabuddhas*, and bodhisattvas "who have attained power" (*vaśitāprāpta*); due to false conceptualization, which obstructs the perfection of self, these individuals continue to exist as "mind-made bodies" (*manomayakāya*). This essentially follows the ŚDS (see 5.4), though the ŚDS does not clearly relate its account of the *avidyāvāsabhūmi* and so on to the perfection of self. De Jong (1968: 44), with reference to the *Daśabhūmikasūtra* and *Mahāyānasūtrālaṃkārabhāṣya* (Lévi 1907: 26.1–2), clarifies that these bodhisattvas "with power" must refer to those who have achieved at least the eighth stage (*bhūmi*) of bodhisattva practice.

86. RGV 1.37–38, Johnston (1950) 1991: 34.8–11: *sa hi prakṛtiśuddhatvād vāsanāpagamāc chuciḥ / paramātmātmanairātmyaprapañcavyupaśantitaḥ*[a] *// sukho manomayaskandhataddhetuvini vṛttitaḥ / nityaḥ saṃsāranirvāṇasamatāprativedhataḥ //*

[a] Emended following Schmithausen 1971: 143: *-ātmanairātmyaprapañcakṣayaśāntitaḥ* to *-ātmanairātmyaprapañcavyupaśāntitaḥ*.

87. Johnston (1950) 1991: 34.13–15.

7.4 *Tathāgatagarbha* as, Once Again, the Self

So ends the bulk of the material, in both the verse RGV and prose RGVV, concerned with discourse about the self. However, elsewhere in the RGVV—where the text provides a rare quotation of the MPNMS—it provides a few more thoughts on how teaching about the *tathāgatagarbha* does or does not relate to ideas about selfhood. In this instance the RGVV leans closer to the position of the MPNMS: that positive attributes applicable to the Buddha (or *dharmakāya*) can also be ascribed, in some enigmatic sense, to that which endures over the successive lives of sentient beings. An important nuance in both the ŚDS and the RGVV is that the expression *ātmapāramitā* does not predicate the (afflicted) *tathāgatagarbha*—that is, that which is proper to transmigrating beings—but rather the (purified) *dharmakāya*. Most of the RGVV acknowledges a subtle difference between the "purified reality" (*nirmalā tathatā*) that is the accomplishment of the Buddha, and the "impure reality" (*samalā tathatā*) that describes sentient beings while they are plagued by afflictions, and still bound to transmigration.[88] In other words, the "perfected qualities" (*guṇapāramitā*) are reserved for describing the true mode of a Buddha's existence—the "result" of the *tathāgatagarbha* (see 7.2)—rather than the aspect of a sentient being that constitutes its cause or basis, which would be called the *tathāgatagarbha*.

However, toward the end of its first chapter (that which is concerned with Buddha-nature teaching), the RGVV appears to disregard this distinction. The RGVV interprets *tathāgatadhātu* to refer to the "cause" (*hetu*) of the Buddha's different modes of existence, and in an interesting verse (notably absent from RGVV^{C}) claims that it resides either "as an embryo," or at least is something "within a womb/chamber" (*garbhagata*), in all sentient beings.[89] A commentarial verse (RGV 1.153) first states that what is ultimate can be known only by faith, and with echoes of the MPNMS the RGVV then tells us that persons incapable of seeing the *tathāgatagarbha* are ordinary people (*pṛthagjanas*), *śrāvakas*, *pratyekabuddhas*, and bodhisattvas "newly entered into the [great] vehicle" (*navayānasaṃprasthita*).[90] The RGVV quotes the ŚDS, and states that the faults leading to the limitations of these beings are (1) the view of a worldly self, (2) conceptual distortions (*viparyāsas;* see 2.2), and (3) a mind "bewildered by emptiness" (*śūnyatāvikṣipta;* see 5.1).[91] Ordinary persons cling to worldly notions of the self (*satkāyadṛṣṭi*), while

88. It is this language that has led to interpretations of the RGVV as a "monistic" text; see Obermiller (1931) 1991: 104–105; also S. King 1991: 99–115; Matsumoto 1997.

89. Johnston (1950) 1991: 72.11–12: *tatra ca sattve sattve tathāgatadhātur utpanno garbhagataḥ saṃvidyate na ca te sattvā budhyanta iti.* See also Takasaki 1966: 290.

90. Johnston (1950) 1991: 74.1–2, 74.3–5. In further agreement with the MPNMS (see 2.3), the RGVV goes on to state that the *tathāgatagarbha* can indeed be seen "in part" (*īṣat paśyanti*) by bodhisattvas at the tenth stage of progress (ibid., 77.3–4).

91. Ibid., 74.5–19. The third of these is associated with the "novice" bodhisattvas, some of whom are said to understand emptiness in an annihilationist sense, while others reify it into something apart from the *skandhas*.

novice bodhisattvas struggle to understand teachings about emptiness. But the second fault—proper to *śrāvaka*s and *pratyekabuddha*s—refers to a failure to mentally cultivate *tathāgatagarbha* to mean the self in some "higher sense" (*uttaribhāvayitavya*), and is proper to those who rely only on the Buddha's teachings about absence of self.[92] The same is said about comprehension of the other four distortions, mutatis mutandis. With echoes of the MPNMS-group, the RGVV refers to that which is beyond the knowledge of *śrāvaka*s and *pratyekabuddha*s as the nature (*dhātu*) that is characterized by supreme (*parama*) permanence, bliss, selfhood, and purity.[93] If this *dhātu* refers also to the *tathāgatagarbha*—as surely it must—then the RGVV acknowledges that some "higher" notion of selfhood, etcetera, is indeed appropriate for the *tathāgatagarbha* (the condition of the *dharmakāya* while it is still afflicted), and presumably then that bodhisattvas are correct if they understand something of sentient beings—their (*buddha*)*dhātu*—to warrant designation as the ("higher") self.

The RGVV does not develop this explanation further, but does quote a relevant source: a passage from the MPNMS (specifically, MPNMS-dhk) that justifies the language of permanence, selfhood, etcetera in reference to the liberated status of a Buddha. The passage that the RGVV reproduces is the example of the merchants diving for a lost, radiant beryl stone, which we have discussed in its original context in an earlier chapter (see 2.2). This simile, the RGVV tells us, explains how a bodhisattva must disregard what is mundane and instead appreciate "the reality of the supreme dharma(s)" (*paramadharmatattva*), though in the context of the MPNMS(-dhk) this seems to have intended the qualities of the Buddha, or of liberated reality, rather than anything about Buddha-nature proper to sentient beings.[94]

Elsewhere in the RGV(V)—and in the ŚDS—we observed some precision regarding to what the expression *ātman*, or rather *ātmapāramitā* (or, indeed, *paramātman*) must refer. Though the ŚDS and RGV(V) accept that the *tathāgatagarbha* can be identified with the *dharmakāya*, the "perfection of self" has been presented as a quality of the *dharmakāya* specifically, which in likelihood intended a distancing from the implication that there is something about sentient beings themselves that is worthy of being called the self. Whereas our *ātmavāda tathāgatagarbha* sources were bold enough to declare that sentient beings have about their person something that warrants calling the self, both the ŚDS and RGVV otherwise restrict this kind of language to the *dharmakāya,* rather than anything proper to sentient beings during the course of their transmigration. Here, however,

92. Ibid., 74.14–15: *ātmani tathāgatagarbhe saty uttaribhāvayitave tadātmasaṃjñābhāvanā viparyayeṇa anātmasaṃjñābhāvanābhiratāḥ.*

93. Ibid., 74.18–19: *sa paramanityasukhātmaśubhalakṣaṇo dhātur ity uktam.*

94. Presumably authors of the RGVV knew the MPNMS only in its fully developed form, apart from the kind of textual archaeology in which we have been engaged, and so did not recognize some of its material about *ātman, nitya,* etcetera, to not concern (explicitly, at least) something proper to sentient beings (Buddha-nature) so much as the figure of the Buddha.

the RGVV agrees that the *tathāgatagarbha* itself exhibits, in some "higher sense," *ātman*, etcetera, and that this should be taught to correct some wrong-minded understanding of teaching about not-self that is found among *śrāvaka*s and *pratyekabuddha*s.

We should note that this claim occurs both where the RGVV quotes the MPNMS and, moreover, in proximity to "String C" of our basic verses, which concern the *buddhadhātu* and the benefits of teaching about it to sentient beings (see 7.2 above). We also must keep in mind that according to the RGVV—and, indeed, the ŚDS and AAN before it—the expressions *tathāgatagarbha* and *dharmakāya* must refer to the same reality that underlies the lives of sentient beings and the liberation of Buddhas. Some further commentarial verses (RGV 1.154–155) stress the lack of distinction between this underlying reality in its both "pure" and "impure" states:

> Here is nothing to be removed, and nothing to be added; reality should be seen as it is, and he who sees reality is liberated (154).[95]
>
> The *dhātu* is empty of adventitious afflictions, which are separate from it; it is not empty of the superior qualities that are inseparable from it (155).[96]

The RGVV identifies this *dhātu* with the *tathāgatadhātu,* and calls it also the *tathāgatagarbha.*[97] Whereas the ŚDS also testifies to the "not-empty" status of the *tathāgatagarbha*—that is, its possession of the qualities of a Buddha (see 9.5)—it had not gone so far as to declare that *tathāgatagarbha* could be expressed in terms of the self; it was more concerned, as we have seen, with clarifying that *tathāgatagarbha* was nothing like an account of the self so much as an enduring foundation to birth, rebirth, and (eventually) liberation (5.1). In contrast, the RGVV seems to fleetingly acknowledge a contribution from the MPNMS: the notion that the *tathāgatagarbha,* or that which is enduring and most precious about any sentient being, could be taught as the self—or rather a "higher" notion of the self—in order to laud the supermundane character of the *dharmakāya* both after its purification but also, though hidden beneath afflictions, present throughout the successive lives of every sentient being.

In summary, though most of the RGVV follows the ideas and terminology of the ŚDS, some of its content still draws on the MPNMS and preserves a trace of the idea that the *tathāgatagarbha* can indeed be conceptualized in terms of a ("higher") notion of the self. This trace of the MPNMS and its

---

95. For other occurrences of this verse in other Mahāyānist sources, see Takasaki 1966: 300n53; also Sferra 2003: 76n40, who notes a similarity between this verse and one found in the Brahmanical *Gauḍapādīyakārikā*; see 9.6n90.

96. Johnston (1950) 1991: 76.1–4: *nāpaneyam ataḥ kiṃcid upaneyaṃ na kiṃcana / draṣṭavyaṃ bhūtato bhūtaṃ bhūtadarśī vimucyate // śūnya āgantukair dhātuḥ savinirbhāgalakṣaṇaiḥ / aśūnyo anuttarair dharmair avinirbhāgalakṣaṇaiḥ //* See also 9.5.

97. Ibid., 76.5–77.4.

ātmavādin orientation appears in a context where its perspective on Buddha-nature had otherwise been eclipsed; the RGVV does not consider *tathāgatagarbha* to refer to anything "hidden" or about which the Buddha taught cryptically, but instead understands Buddha-nature to give a different perspective on teachings about the intrinsically pure nature of the mind. After the ŚDS, it is this understanding of *tathāgatagarbha* that seems to have triumphed in India, even if, here or there, we find the occasional recollection that this expression had been used also to refer to something more doctrinally contentious.

7.5 Conclusions

Much has been written about the RGV, the RGVV, the manner of their composition, and their authorship, transmission, and—of course—doctrinal content. This chapter could not attend to all of these issues in great depth, but has provided some overview and analysis of the Buddha-nature idea discernable in basic materials of the RGV, including verses that might be "most basic" amid these. Our focus has been the way(s) in which the RGVV unpacks the categories *tathāgatagarbha* and *dharmakāya*, and their relationship to discourse about the self. Early material in the composition of the RGV reflects different aspects of Buddha-nature teaching. Its author(s) may well have known the ŚDS (and its "perfected qualities"), the AAN (regarding degrees of purity), and the *(buddha)dhātu* understood as a teaching that both (1) bore resemblance to non-Buddhist discourse about the self, and also (2) offered reassurance to audiences uneasy with teachings about emptiness. Where the RGV reproduces material known from the TGS, it acknowledges Buddha-nature to refer still to the presence of some "essence" of the Buddha that resides "within" the constitution of a sentient being. But other very early content of the RGV has understood that the *(buddha)dhātu* refers to the intrinsically pure status of the mind, and so can be more easily reconciled with wider Buddhist teaching concerned with this same, older idea (see 9.3).[98]

The commentarial RGVV inherits concern with the language of selfhood from its root verses, and strives to make sense of the claim that the *dharmakāya* exhibits "the perfection of self." Apart from in material found only in RGVV[C], the RGVV does not attempt to explain the perfection of self in terms of the Buddha's enduring existence or power—that is, it does not understand the Buddhist self in the manner of the MPNMS-group—but instead interprets *ātmapāramitā*, or *paramātman*, to refer to a state in which one comprehends absence of self in respect to all entities, the end of the perfection of insight. In other words, the perspective of the RGVV is that which is common to more conventional modes of Mahāyānist discourse: Buddhist "selfhood" must refer to teaching about absence of self,

98. Regarding this important theme in the mature RGVV, see Ruegg 1969: 417–424.

and where the Buddha seems to have taught otherwise this is still, somehow, a means of leading sentient beings to abandon the thought that any phenomenon is worthy of calling the self (see 1.1).

We have seen that in one instance the RGVV does hold that selfhood (and other positive qualities) can describe the *tathāgatagarbha* (see 7.3). This passage may relate to the root verses of the RGV that are most proximate to it ("String C"; see 7.1): those that explain teaching about the *buddhadhātu* to be a corrective to erroneous thinking about emptiness and its deleterious effects on certain audiences. This corrective can apply to both the *śrāvaka* (who misunderstands absence of self) and also, crucially, to the non-Buddhist teacher or adept (*tīrthya*), whose defining flaw is attachment to thoughts about the self. If the Buddhist account of a perfection of self is taught specifically to counteract the "self-obsession" of non-Buddhists, whose attraction is to liberation understood as the realization or enjoyment of the self, this puts a different spin on how Buddha-nature teaching relates to non-Buddhist teachings. In our *ātmavāda tathāgatagarbha* sources, the Buddha introduced his account of Buddha-nature only after teaching about absence of self, which was employed to undermine notions of the self already in the world; in the apologetic account of the RGVV the Buddha's allusions to *ātmavāda* do not succeed teachings about not-self so much as guide one audience or another *back* to correct comprehension of it.

In summation, the RGVV does not understand Buddha-nature teaching to be as radical or revelatory as it was presented in the MPNMS-group of texts, where *tathāgatagarbha* is introduced as the Buddha's account of the self of sentient beings. Instead, the *tathāgatagarbha-dharmakāya* is presented as a kataphatic spin on more established Buddhist teachings about universal emptiness or absence of self. The RGVV is a challenging text, not least because it attempts the difficult task of reconciling Buddha-nature tradition—with its affirmations of what is permanent, precious, and unchanging—with the apophatic orientation of the *prajñāpāramitā* tradition. On the one hand, Buddhist liberation is described in the most kataphatic, even apotheotic, terms imaginable: "And because of [the four perfected qualities], it is said that the Tathāgata is the pinnacle of the nature/realm of phenomena (*dharmadhātuparama*), reaching to the limit of the element of space (*ākāśadhātu*), lasting until the very end [of time]."[99] On the other hand, the RGVV does not privilege the sense that the Buddha, or the *tathāgatagarbha,* constitutes *ātman, paramātman, ātmapāramitā,* or otherwise; these are all expressions that must be explained further, and with recourse to the RGVV's preferred highest principles, such as the nature of phenomena (*dharmadhātu*) or things as they really are (*tathatā*). In short, if the RGV(V) understood itself to embody the "higher teaching of the Mahāyāna"

---

99. Johnston (1950) 1991: 32.7–8: *ābhiś ca tathāgato dharmadhātuparamākāśadhātupary asāno 'parāntakoṭiniṣṭha ity ucyate.* Regarding this verse, reminiscent of material in the *Daśabhūmikasūtra,* see Takasaki 1966: 213n102.

(*Mahāyānottaratantra*), its focus is certainly not a Buddhist account of the self so much as a justification of how discourse about a "higher" or "perfected" self can play an important part in the development of certain sentient beings. Buddhist discourse about the self—in reference to either liberation or that which prefigures it—has been interpreted as a device or strategy, an approach found also in the next text to which we must attend, the *Laṅkāvatārasūtra*.

CHAPTER 8

The *Laṅkāvatārasūtra* and Rejecting the Buddhist Self

8.1 The Text

A final text that we must consider is something of an outlier from our core *tathāgatagarbha* literature, in that it does not consider *tathāgatagarbha* to be a definitive articulation (i.e., "*nītārtha*") of the Buddha's teaching but is instead in need of further exposition. This is the *Laṅkāvatārasūtra* (LAS), "the discourse about the appearance (of the Buddha) on Laṅkā,"[1] which—though certainly distinct from the *tathāgatagarbha* corpus so far discussed—provides important insights into how the Buddha-nature idea, and its relationship to teachings about a self, was received by later Mahāyānist authors.

Appreciation of the LAS, especially in the West, has for a long time been shaped by the work of D. T. Suzuki (e.g., 1930; 1932), whose influential English translation of the text is informed by its reception in Japan. We once again have valuable studies of the LAS by Jikidō Takasaki (e.g., 1980; 1981; [1981] 2014; [1982] 2014). Philosophical treatments of its ideas (generous, in places, to the abstruseness of the text) include those by Brian Edward Brown (1991) and Florin G. Sutton (1991). The LAS remains extant in Sanskrit, and this chapter relies on the 1923 edition of Bunyio Nanjio.[2] Three translations survive in Chinese (a fourth, by Dharmakṣema, is lost to us). The first is attributed to Guṇabhadra, from 443 CE (T.670: *Lengqie abaduoluo bao jing* 楞伽阿跋多羅寶經; henceforth LAS^{C1}); the second to Bodhiruci 菩提流支, from 513 CE (T.671: *Ru lengqie jing* 入楞伽經; henceforth LAS^{C2}), and the third to Śikṣānanda 實叉難陀, dated 700 CE (T.672: *Dasheng ru lengqie jing* 大乘入楞伽經; henceforth LAS^{C3}). We have available also two Tibetan translations, the first of which dates from the middle of the ninth century (e.g., D.107; Q.775, *Lang kar gshegs pa theg pa chen po'i mdo;*

1. Alternatively, as preserved in the surviving Sanskrit text, *Saddharmalaṅkāvatārasūtra* (Nanjio 1923: 375.15).

2. The later edition of the text by Vaidya (1963) adds nothing to that of Nanjio. A thorough bibliography of scholarship pertaining to the LAS is Deleanu 2018.

henceforth LAS^{T}) and is attributed, in some editions, to the Dunhuang scholar Chos grub (c. 750–850). The second (e.g., D.108; Q.776: *Lang kar gshegs pa rin po che'i mdo las sangs rgyas thams cad kyi gsung gi snying po zhes bya ba'i le'u*), which will not be considered here, is likely a rendering of Guṇabhadra's Chinese translation, and is again recorded as being a work by Chos grub.[3] Contemporary scholarship generally holds that Guṇabhadra's version, LAS^{C1}, reflects an earlier form of the Indian *sūtra* than those preserved in our other extant translations.[4]

We can be sure that the LAS is comparatively late in the chronology of Indian Buddha-nature literature, and appears to be something of a patchwork. When introducing an account of *tathāgatagarbha* it mentions by name the ŚDS, and approves its understanding of how this expression should be understood (see 8.2). The eighth chapter of the LAS is notable for its endorsement of vegetarianism, in which it cites both the MPNMS and AMS as other authoritative texts on that issue (see also 3.6).[5] Finally, there is no trace of the LAS in the compendious RGVV; seeing as the RGVV otherwise reflects awareness and approval of some Yogācāra-Vijñānavāda terminology, it was perhaps not aware of the LAS and its account of *tathāgatagarbha* in terms of the functions and character of the mind (i.e., *vijñānavāda*).[6] This

3. See Deleanu 2018: 18–20. Two commentaries on the LAS survive in Tibetan: that by Jñānaśrībhadra (eleventh century) and by Jñānavajra (twelfth century), regarding which see ibid., 25.

4. Regarding these details—and much more regarding the LAS besides—see Jia 2015.

5. Nanjio 1923: 258.4–5 (including *nirvāṇāṅgulimālīke*). However, our oldest version, LAS^{C1} (514b6–7), lacks mention of the MPNMS, whereas LAS^{C2} (564b20–21) replaces the AMS with mention of the ŚDS (a *sūtra* that makes no reference to vegetarianism); all versions of the LAS list also the *Hastikakṣyasūtra* and *Mahāmeghasūtra*; see 3.1n5; also Takasaki (1982) 2014: 131–132. In its chapter on the consumption of meat (*Māṃsabhakṣaṇaparivarta;* see Nanjio 1923: 244–259), the LAS provides several reasons why a bodhisattva should practice vegetarianism. As in the AMS (see 3.6), we find the claim that all sentient beings have been, in past lives, relatives. But the LAS is also very concerned with the "love of purity" (*śucikāma*), and that the bodhisattva not scare other sentient beings by coveting meat, evidence of societal or cultural motivations for abstaining from it. Moreover, the entire chapter is initiated by a recognition that even followers of other religious systems (*anyatīrthikas*) and persons sunken into the views of "worldly thinkers" (*lokāyatas*) abstain from meat (see also 3.7), and that this must be the case in the Buddha's teaching also (Nanjio 1923: 244.12–14). Similar arguments—which refer to the terrifying impression made by persons who eat meat—are found also in the MPNMS (MPNMS^{F} 869a8–17; MPNMS^{D} 386a28–b14; MPNSM^{T} §175). Regarding all of these texts, see Schmithausen 2002: 315–323, who observes that similar concerns about the purity of meat are found in the *Mahābhārata* (13.117.12); see also further discussion of Buddhist vegetarianism in Schmithausen forthcoming. Regarding the position(s) of the *dharmaśāstra* tradition on meat, see Olivelle 2018b: 189–196.

6. I intend "*vijñānavāda,*" in a broad sense, to refer to Buddhist discourse that explains sentient beings, and the transmigration that they experience, in terms of consciousness (*vijñāna*) and its operations. This is an orientation proper to the Yogācāra-Vijñānavāda school of philosophy, which takes all phenomena to be "mind-only" (*cittamātra*). Takasaki ([1982] 2014: 147–148; 152–155) stresses that the LAS was not an orthodox Yogācāra-Vijñānavāda work, not featured in the works of Maitreya/Asaṅga and Vasubandhu. Regarding

need not lead us to conclude that the LAS is necessarily later than the RGVV, though if we are interested foremost in a *conceptual* trajectory of the Buddha-nature idea, then all evidence points to the LAS departing further from the ideas of the ŚDS and AAN, and their exposition in the RGVV.

We can consider apart from the core LAS the so-called *Sagāthaka*, the verse-only tenth chapter of the text that is absent from LAS^{C1}, and so likely a later addition. Constituent verses of the *Sagāthaka* include many that are repeated from earlier in the text (with the exception of any found in chapters 1, 5, 7, 8, and 9, suggesting a later date for material in those chapters), summarizations of ideas found earlier in the prose LAS, and many verses unique to it that represent and refute the views of non-Buddhist philosophical schools, including—by name—the Sāṃkhyas and Vaiśeṣikas.[7] The *Sagāthaka* is long and ostensibly contradictory, but as we will see includes approval of distinctly *ātmavādin* Buddhist discourse and some verses that related this to teaching about *tathāgatagarbha*. Otherwise the main portions of the LAS that deal with *tathāgatagarbha* are its second and sixth chapters, which likely belong to some of its earliest content. Two main concerns of its authors, as reflected in these chapters, were the rejection of an *ātmavādin* interpretation of Buddha-nature and, perhaps later than this, the appropriation of the expression *tathāgatagarbha* conceptualized in distinctly *vijñānavādin* terms.

8.2 *Tathāgatagarbha* and Absence of Self

The LAS clarifies, in no uncertain terms, that *tathāgatagarbha* properly refers to nothing like the self taught in other Indian religious systems. It is worth presenting the most influential portion of this material in full, voiced in the text by the bodhisattva Mahāmati:

> In the pronouncement of his discourses (*sūtras*) the Lord has explained also the *tathāgatagarbha*. The Lord has explained it to be pure in its intrinsic luminosity, pure from the start, endowed with the thirty-two characteristics [of a superior being]; present within the body of every sentient being; concealed within the cloth of the heaps (*skandhas*), elements of experience (*dhātus*), and bases of sensory activity (*āyatanas*) [that constitute worldly experience], like a jewel of great value wrapped in a dirty garment, soiled by the filth of passion, aversion, delusion and false imagination; permanent, lasting, calm, enduring.

---

material common to both the LAS and Vasubandhu's *Triṃśikā*—a very influential Yogācāra-Vijñānavāda text, from likely the fifth century—see Schmithausen 1992.

7. This is found also in chapter two of the LAS (v. 2.172; Nanjio 1923: 116.7–8), as well as throughout the *Sagāthaka* (e.g., v.10.118, 10.627). See also Kunst 1980.

> Lord, how is discourse about *tathāgatagarbha* not comparable to discourse about the self, which belongs to non-Buddhist teachers (*tīrthakaras*)? Lord, non-Buddhist teachers expound doctrines about a self that is permanent, agentive, without qualities, pervasive and imperishable.[8]

This passage refers to the *tathāgatagarbha* understood as some entity that resides "within" the bodies of sentient beings (*sarvasattvadehāntargata*).[9] This, as we have by now established, is not the manner in which *tathāgatagarbha* is explained in either the ŚDS or AAN, but accurately reflects the corporeal tone of Buddha-nature teaching encountered throughout the MPNMS-group. This is clearest when the LAS presents a contrast between the *tathāgatagarbha* and that within which it dwells: the *skandhas*, *dhātus*, and *āyatanas*. We have seen that versions of the MPNMS present an opposition between the **buddhadhātu* and the *skandhas*, or otherwise the "external" elements that are apart from their Buddha-nature (see 2.4). This is what may have been implied wherever in the MPNMS this **buddhadhātu* is said to be "within" the body: it is some element that exists amid, but apart from, that which otherwise describes the constitution of a sentient being (*skandhas* or *dhātus*).

It is then very likely that the LAS intended to evoke the *tathāgatagarbha* as expounded in the MPNMS-group, though this does overlook the fact that the LAS also describes the *tathāgatagarbha* in terms of an intrinsic luminosity (*prakṛtiprabhāsvara*).[10] This specific attribute usually refers to Buddha-nature understood in terms of the intrinsic nature of the mind, an idea absent from the MPNMS and MBhS,[11] and mentioned only in passing in

8. Nanjio 1923: 77.13–78.4: *tathāgatagarbhaḥ punar bhagavatā sūtrantapāṭhe 'nuvarṇitaḥ / sa ca kila tvayā prakṛtiprabhāsvaraviśuddhyādiviśuddha eva varṇyate dvātriṃśallakṣaṇadharaḥ sarvasattvadehāntargato, mahārghamūlyaratnaṃ malinavastupariveṣṭitam iva skandhadhātvāyatanavastuveṣṭito rāgadveṣamohābhūtaparikalpamalamalino nityo dhruvaḥ śivaḥ śāśvataś ca bhagavatā varṇitaḥ / tat katham ayaṃ bhagavaṃs tīrthakarātmavādatulyas tathāgatagarbhavādo na bhavati / tīrthakarā api bhagavan nityaḥ kartā nirguṇo vibhūr avyaya ity ātmavādopadeśaṃ kurvanti //* Compare LAS^{C1} 489a25–b3; LAS^{C2} 529b18–26; LAS^{C3} 599b9–15. LAS^{T} D.107, 85b7–86a4; Q.775, 94a5–96b2. Whereas LAS^{T} agrees with the surviving Sanskrit text, our Chinese translations vary in some details: LAS^{C3} suggests that the *tīrthakaras* (*waidao* 外道) teach a self that is sovereign (*zizai* 自在), and both LAS^{C1} and LAS^{C2} refer to its universality (*zhoubian* 周遍).

9. Also, for example, LAS^{C1} 於一切眾生身中; LAS^{T} *sems can thams cad kyi lus la mchis par brjod.*

10. LAS^{C1} 自性清淨; LAS^{T} *rang bzhin gyis rnam par dag pa.*

11. A possible exception is found at MPNMS^{D} 414a24–27. This comes at the culmination of an excursus into the nature of letters (*akṣaras*), immediately following the parable of the lost sword (see 2.5). The MPNMS declares that the nature of the Buddha is not like a verbal designation that might become pure but is rather "pure originally" (*xingbenjing* 性本淨). This line is absent from MPNMS^{F} (888c22–24)—our most concise version of the text—while MPNMS^{T} (§435.5–6) instead discusses the "*dhātu* of the body" (*lus kyi khams*) that is identified with the lips, teeth, and so forth (*lce dang so la sogs rnams*), which is called intrinsically pure (*rang bzhin gyis yongs su dag pa: *prakṛtipariśuddha*). This material requires further study but does not challenge the fact that "intrinsic/original purity" does not seem to have

the AMS (see 9.3). The mind that is intrinsically pure is more prominent in both the ŚDS and AAN, and as we saw in the last chapter occurs in materials that may be very early in the composition of the RGV (see 7.2). Hence the above synopsis of how the Buddha had previously explained *tathāgatagarbha* may well not intend reference to the MPNMS-group directly but rather a broad sketch of Buddha-nature understood in terms of an abiding, precious essence.[12]

At any rate, the LAS understands some previous articulations of *tathāgatagarbha* to be dangerously reminiscent of what is taught by so-called *tīrthakaras*, a term that is all but synonymous with the expression *tīrthika* (Ch. *waidao* 外道; Tib. *mu stegs can*), in other words, teachers or adepts belonging to non-Buddhist religious systems.[13] In the passage above the LAS provides a list of qualities associated with non-Buddhist *ātmavādin* tradition(s) as if these were proper to Buddha-nature teaching also, but of these, agency (*kartṛ*), absence of qualities (*nirguṇa*), and pervasiveness (*vibhū*) do not describe Buddha-nature in any *tathāgatagarbha* source available to us.[14] All of this suggests that the authors of this critique were not interested in accurately presenting the *ātmavādin* form of Buddha-nature teaching as we have seen it in any other surviving source, but rather conflate this with ideas found in non-Buddhist accounts of the self, for example, the Brahmanical *Śvetāśvatara-upaniṣad* (v.6.11): "The one god hidden in all beings, all-pervading, the inner self of all beings; the beholder of actions who dwells in all beings; the witness, the observer, alone and without qualities."[15]

By now we are well acquainted with the concern—predominantly from *ātmavādin tathāgatagarbha* works themselves—that teaching about Buddha-nature could indeed be confused for non-Buddhist ideas about the self. But whereas those texts understood the Buddha's to be the true account of the self, the LAS reduces this to an expedient teaching, for those audiences who required a teaching that takes an *ātmavādin* form. In response to his lengthy question, the Buddha clarifies to Mahāmati that the *tathāgatagarbha* properly understood is nothing like what is taught by non-Buddhists but should instead be understood in the sense of "emptiness, the limit of reality,

been an important aspect of Buddha-nature teaching recorded by the MPNMS. See also Habata 2015b: 191.

12. See Takasaki (1982) 2014: 137–138.

13. See Jones: forthcoming. The LAS may intend nothing more than followers or advocates of non-Buddhist systems, though *tīrthakara* more accurately denotes a "producer" (*-kara*) of a non-Buddhist account of liberation (*tīrtha-*).

14. The AMS in particular keeps a clear distinction between the *tathāgatagarbha* and the performer of actions; for example, in the simile of the negligent ascetic boy (see 3.5). Moreover, a central declaration in all *sūtras* that we have so far addressed is that the *tathāgatagarbha* possesses the characteristics of a Buddha, which rules out its being "*nirguṇa*" also. The sense of "pervasiveness" (*vibhū*) is unclear, though we find suggestions of something like this in the AMS (see 3.6), AAN (see 6.1), and RGV (see 7.2).

15. Olivelle 1998: 430–431: *eko devaḥ sarvabhūteṣu gūḍhaḥ sarvavyāpī sarvabhūtāntarātmā / karmādhyakṣaḥ sarvabhūtādhivāsaḥ sākṣī cetā kevalo nirguṇaś ca //*

nirvāṇa, the unborn, signless, without intention."[16] The LAS understands prior teaching about *tathāgatagarbha* to require further clarification, and rather than refer to any mystery that the Buddha reveals only late in his ministry—a theme prominent throughout the MPNMS-group (see 9.2)—it must simply refer to more conventional categories from more established Mahāyānist tradition, for example, the three "gates to liberation" (*vimokṣamukha*) that are emptiness (*śūnyatā*), signlessness (*animitta*), and absence of intention (*apraṇihita*). The LAS meanwhile denies that teaching about *tathāgatagarbha* could ever mean an account of the self: "The Tathāgatas—reverend, and completely awakened—by means of the gateway [into the dharma] that is the *tathāgatagarbha,* in order to remove fear regarding [teachings about] absence of self among those who are ignorant, teach the sphere of neither imagination nor conceptualization. Regarding this, Mahāmati, the venerable bodhisattvas, in the present and future, should not adhere to [notions of] the self."[17] Clearly this is at odds with how Buddha-nature teaching is explained in the MPNMS-group. All sources that we have discussed so far understand their account of *tathāgatagarbha* to be definitive, and those texts that understood this to constitute the Buddha's teaching about the self took this to be a valuable dimension of what should be understood by Buddha-nature. But in the LAS—and with some similarity to what we find in the RGVV (see 7.3)—what is taught by the name *tathāgatagarbha* must accord with the *prajñāpāramitā* tradition, and moreover with the *vijñānavāda* or consciousness-oriented perspective promoted throughout the LAS. Where teaching about *tathāgatagarbha* resembles something like a self, this can only be to allay the fears of certain audiences.

After this the LAS introduces the example of a potter who employs different tools to produce different vessels; similarly the Buddha, in accordance with his skill-in-methods (*upāyakauśalya*), shares teachings either about *tathāgatagarbha* or about absence of self with respect to all phenomena (*dharmanairātmya*), "by means of various terms, expressions and synonyms," in order to teach different sentient beings.[18] On first impression this could suggest that the LAS understands both of these teachings to be expediencies. However, the LAS concludes the matter by making explicit that any resemblance that the *tathāgatagarbha* may have to a doctrine of the self can be only for the benefit of persons attached to discourse concerning the self

16. Nanjio 1923: 78.6–8: *śūnyatābhūtakoṭinirvāṇānutpādānimittāpraṇihitādyānāṃ mahāmate padārthānāṃ tathāgatagarbhopadeśaṃ kṛtvā.* Compare LAS^{C1} 489b3–7; LAS^{C2} 529b26–29; LAS^{C3} 599b15–17; LAS^{T} D.107 86a4–5; Q.775, 94b2–3.

17. Nanjio 1923: 78.8–12: *tathāgatā arhantaḥ samyaksaṃbuddhā bālānāṃ nairātmyasaṃtrās apadavivarjanārthaṃ nirvikalpanirābhāsagocaraṃ tathāgatagarbhamukhopadeśena deśayanti / na cātra mahāmate anāgatapratyutpannaiḥ bodhisattvair mahāsattvair ātmābhiniveśaḥ kartavyaḥ //* Compare LAS^{C1} 489b7–10; LAS^{C2} 529b29–c4; LAS^{C3} 599b17–20; LAS^{T} D.107, 86a5–7; Q.775, 94b3–6. See also Kanō 2016: 7.

18. Nanjio 1923: 78.17. Compare LAS^{C1} 489b10–15; LAS^{C2} 529c5–11; LAS^{C3} 599b20–24; LAS^{T} D.107, 86a7–b2; Q.775, 94b6–95a1.

and its liberation, and that the definitive teaching of the Buddha is indeed, yet again, aimed at relinquishing notions of the self:

> Mahāmati, teaching *tathāgatagarbha* is for the purpose of attracting non-Buddhist teachers, who are attached to discourse about the self; those whose minds had fallen into the false view of an unreal self, having arrived at the sphere of the three [gates] of liberation, quickly attain supreme, complete awakening ... hence, that [*tathāgatagarbha*] is not similar to the view of the self that belongs to non-Buddhist teachers. Therefore, Mahāmati, for the purpose of relinquishing the views of non-Buddhist teachers you should practice in conformity to the teaching about *tathāgatagarbha* that is absence of self.[19]

The translation above communicates the sense that *tathāgatagarbha* refers in fact to absence of self, but is sometimes taught otherwise in order to attract non-Buddhists who concern themselves with discourse about the self.[20] A bodhisattva must know better, and abandon this meaning in favor of understanding *tathāgatagarbha* in a fashion that accords with Buddhist *nairātmyavāda* discourse.

It seems beyond doubt that the authors of the LAS knew of some form of specifically *ātmavādin tathāgatagarbha* doctrine—perhaps, as it mentions them elsewhere (in the eighth chapter), those reflected by the MPNMS and/or AMS.[21] The LAS is aware that *tathāgatagarbha* has been taught by the Buddha in such a fashion that it resembles the *ātman* of non-Buddhist systems, and finds this to be in need of explanation: such a thing could only have been taught in order to lure "self-obsessed" non-Buddhists into the Buddha's teaching, so that they might later be educated regarding absence of self with respect to all phenomena. For the bodhisattva, any *ātmavādin* account of the *tathāgatagarbha* could, but should not, be misleading: it is not for them.

On the one hand, the LAS declares that *tathāgatagarbha* is taught specifically to attract non-Buddhist teachers (or, surely, for the sake of

19. Nanjio 1923: 79.1–9: *evaṃ hi mahāmate tathāgatagarbhopadeśam ātmavādābhiniviṣṭānāṃ tīrthakarāṇām ākarṣaṇarthaṃ tathāgatagarbhopadeśena nirdiśanti / kathaṃ batābhūtātmavikalpad ṛṣṭipatitāśayā vimokṣatrayagocarapatitāśayopetāḥ kṣipram anuttarāṃ samyaksaṃbodhim abhisaṃbudhyerann iti / etadarthaṃ mahāmate tathāgatā arhantaḥ samyaksaṃbuddhās tathāgatagarbhopadeśaṃ kurvanti / ata etan na bhavati tīrthakarātmavādatulyam / tasmāt tarhi mahāmate tīrthakaradṛṣṭivinivṛttyarthaṃ tathāgatanairātmyagarbhānusāriṇā ca te bhavitavyam //* Compare LAS^{C1} 489b15–20; LAS^{C2} 529c11–18; LAS^{C3} 599b24–28; LAS^{T} D.107, 86b2–5; Q.775, 95a1–6. See also Kanō 2016: 7.

20. The curious expression *tathāgatanairātmyagarbha* is typical of unusual compounds found throughout the Sanskrit LAS (see Jia 2015: 138); our other versions of the text clarify that *tathāgatagarbha* should be taken to mean absence of self; for example, LAS^{C1} 當依無我如來之藏; LAS^{T} *de bzhin gshegs pa'i snying po bdag med pa'i rjes su 'jug par bya;* see previous note for references.

21. See 8.1n5.

any who have succumbed to their arguments), but on the other, it declares that for a bodhisattva *tathāgatagarbha* must be understood differently.[22] There are clear similarities between this material of the LAS and the *nairātmyavādin* interpretation of the "perfection of self" encountered in the RGVV: both texts associate *tathāgatagarbha* with the education of non-Buddhist opponents (see 7.3) but interpret kataphatic discourse about the self to in fact refer, in the end, to absence of self. But while the RGVV wants to preserve some of the *ātmavādin* flavor of Buddha-nature teaching, the LAS is more intent on drawing a line under any association between *tathāgatagarbha* and the language of selfhood. For later Buddhist authors, this was an influential move indeed (see 8.6).

8.3 The "*Ālayavijñāna-Tathāgatagarbha*"

According to chapter 2 of the LAS, any final resemblance between the *tathāgatagarbha* and a Buddhist account of the self must be denied. With some similarity to what we find in the RGVV, discussion of the Buddha or sentient beings in terms of the self is (re)interpreted to refer to nothing other than absence of self, in conformity with more conventional Buddhist teaching. The LAS does not outright dismiss the *ātmavādin* form of the Buddha-nature idea so much as relegate its status to a provisional teaching for the benefit of persons affiliated to, and who may be converted from, non-Buddhist systems. When understood apart from its *ātmavādin* articulation, *tathāgatagarbha* must be understood in such a fashion that it accords with wider Mahāyāna thought, and with the language and teachings of the Yogācāra-Vijñānavāda tradition specifically.

In its sixth chapter, regarding "transience" (*Kṣaṇikaparivarta*), the LAS revisits what it understands by the expression *tathāgatagarbha*. The bodhisattva Mahāmati inquires about the origination of the *skandha*s, *dhātu*s, and *āyatana*s, three categories for the constituent experiences of a sentient being, which back in chapter 2 of the LAS were contrasted with the *tathāgatagarbha* when it is taught in an *ātmavādin* mode (see 8.2 above). These three categories of existents were said to be like a cloth that hides the *tathāgatagarbha,* but the Buddha now explains to Mahāmati that the *tathāgatagarbha* is in fact the causal basis for all of these elements, or otherwise all that is wholesome and unwholesome (*kuśalākuśalahetuka*), and so all forms of birth (*sarvajanmagati*). The *tathāgatagarbha* is compared to a performer (*naṭa*) who takes on different guises, but—if there is still any confusion—is certainly apart from any notion of the self and what is of the

22. A verse at the end of this discussion (Nanjio 1923: 79.11–12) interprets all that came above through an undeniably Yogācāra-Vijñānavāda lens: *pudgalaḥ saṃtatiḥ skandhāḥ pratyayā aṇavas tathā / pradhānam īśvaraḥ kartā cittamātraṃ vikalpyate //* (A person, a continuum, the heaps of experience, conditions, atoms, a supreme, a lord, a creator: all are imagined, being nothing but the mind" [*cittamātra*]). Compare LAS^{C1} 489b22–23; LAS^{C2} 529c19–20; LAS^{C3} 599c1–2; LAS^{T} D.107, 86b6; Q.775, 95a6–7. See also Lindtner 1992: 263.

self (*ātmātmīyavarjita*).[23] When someone is not awakened, a convergence of causes and conditions sustains their ongoing transmigration, which non-Buddhists (*tīrthyas*) mistake for a single cause (*kāraṇa*) to successive rebirths: they impute, erroneously, some *ātman* that is the subject of transmigration.[24]

In place of this account, the LAS teaches the existence of a substratum consciousness (*ālayavijñāna*) that underpins the experience of death and rebirth, together with the different modes of consciousness (aligned with different modes of perception, including thought) that depend upon it. It reveals that the substratum consciousness should be identified with the *tathāgatagarbha:* "Mahāmati, venerable bodhisattvas who desire for excellence should purify the *tathāgatagarbha,* which is a name for the substratum consciousness."[25] Without this "*ālayavijñāna-tathāgatagarbha,*" we read, there would be neither the occurrence (*pravṛtti*) nor cessation (*nivṛtti*) of persons ignorant (*bāla*) or noble (*ārya*), but comprehension of this is beyond the speculative theories of *śrāvakas* and *pratyekabuddhas*, let alone non-Buddhist teachers.[26] There is little doubt that insofar as the LAS approves of teaching about *tathāgatagarbha,* it is in reference to some substratum that runs through or "beneath" transmigration, and can be considered an epithet for the fundamental stratum of the mind developed in other sources of Yogācāra-Vijñānavāda teaching.

In lines that follow this identification the LAS associates its account of the *tathāgatagarbha* with what is taught in the ŚDS.[27] The LAS understands the ŚDS to have taught—as we encountered earlier (see 5.2)—the *tathāgatagarbha* in conjunction with seven modes of consciousness. However, the LAS contends that this in fact refers to the *ālayavijñāna,* and that otherwise—without any firm basis in the ŚDS as we know it—that Queen Śrīmālā exposited her teaching about *tathāgatagarbha* for the benefit of *śrāvakas*, and for teaching about absence of self with respect to all *dharmas* (*dharmanairātmyapradarśanārtha*). The LAS provides some indication of how to square the absence of the *ālayavijñāna* in the ŚDS: the audience of the ŚDS, we read, were *śrāvakas*, *pratyekabuddhas*, and non-Buddhists, who are all attached to texts in their literal phrasing (*yathārutadeśanāpāṭhābhini*

---

23. An image found also in the AMS, and reminiscent of the *Sāṃkhyakārikā;* see 3.6n70.

24. Nanjio 1923: 220.9–13 (alternatively Takasaki [1981] 2014: 19–20). Compare LAS^{C1} 510b4–8; LAS^{C2} 556b22–29; LAS^{C3} 619b29–c4; LAS^{T} D.107, 142b3–4; Q.775, 156a7–8.

25. Nanjio 1923: 222.6–8: *mahāmate tathāgatagarbha ālayavijñānasaṃśabdito viśodhayitavyo viśeṣārthibhir bodhisattvair mahāsattvaiḥ* // Compare LAS^{C1} 510b26–27; LAS^{C2} 556c26–28; LAS^{C3} 619c23–24; LAS^{T} D.107, 143b1–2; Q.775, 157a5–6. Kanō (2016: 7n21) notes that the *Ghanavyūhasūtra* echoes the reduction of the *tathāgatagarbha* to the *ālayavijñāna* (see, for example, T.681[16]747a17–19: 佛說如來藏 / 以爲阿賴耶); compare its Tibetan version: D.110, 55b1–2; Q.778, 62b1–2.

26. Nanjio 1923: 222.9–18. Compare LAS^{C1} 510b27–c4; LAS^{C2} 556c28–557a6; LAS^{C3} 619c24–620a1; LAS^{T} D.107, 143b2–5; Q.775, 157a6–b2.

27. Nanjio 1923: 222.19 (which names *śrīmālāṃ devīm*). See next footnote for full references to other versions of the LAS.

viṣṭa), whereas the "*ālayavijñāna-tathāgatagarbha*" is known only to bodhisattvas who understand teachings in accordance with their meaning (*arthapratiśaraṇa*), endowed as they are with "subtle and sharp intelligence" (*sūkṣmanipuṇamatibuddhi*).[28]

Let us take stock of what this portion of the LAS accepts *tathāgatagarbha* to mean. Its authors were aware of the ŚDS, and observe that it taught *tathāgatagarbha* in relation to separate modes of consciousness, which is also appropriate for an account of the substratum consciousness that is important to the *vijñānavāda* orientation of the LAS. What non-Buddhists may confuse for a self is in fact the most fundamental layer of consciousness that persists throughout, or "beneath," instances of rebirth. It is certainly not any discrete, transmigrating *ātman* as valued by non-Buddhist systems, or indeed—as critiqued earlier in the LAS (see 8.2)—as taught by other, earlier works of the *tathāgatagarbha* tradition.

A thorough study of the *ālayavijñāna*—"the basic, subliminal, subconscious layer of the mind, forming a continuous, uninterrupted flow [until liberation]" (Schmithausen 2017: 265)—is beyond the scope of this volume.[29] In the LAS it is compared to a great ocean that is undisturbed by waves, which are akin to the seven modes of consciousness that cross its surface.[30] This brings to mind not only the similar account of the *tathāgatagarbha* in the ŚDS—called there a basis or foundation for transmigration, unaffected by its content—but also the AAN and its account of an "ocean of beings" that has the *tathāgatagarbha-dharmakāya* as its common foundation (see 6.1).[31] At any rate, the account of the *tathāgatagarbha* "approved" in chapter 6 of the LAS is imagined very differently from the "enshrouded," *ātmavādin* articulation of this same expression that is explained, and undermined, in its second chapter.

At the end of its seventh chapter the LAS returns briefly to the *tathāgatagarbha*, and claims that it transmigrates (*saṃsarati*), unlike the seven modes of consciousness; it is the causal ground of joy, suffering, and *nirvāṇa* (*nirvāṇasukhaduḥkhahetuka:* see also 5.2). The LAS concludes that this teaching is not understood by fools who are bewildered by emptiness,

28. Nanjio 1923: 222.19–223.13. LAS^{C1} 510c4–c12; LAS^{C2} 557a6–557a14; LAS^{C3} 620a1–a9; LAS^{T} D.107, 143b6–144a3; Q.775, 157b2–7. The seven modes of consciousness mentioned in this passage are the six associated with the senses—including the mind—as well as the distinct seventh "mental faculty" (*manas*). Takasaki (1981) contends that the *manas* of the LAS is not clearly the more developed "afflicted mind" (*kliṣṭamanas*) known from classical Yogācāra-Vijñānavāda doctrine.

29. Authoritative studies of the *ālayavijñāna* are those by Schmithausen (e.g., 1987; 2014: part 1). For a valuable digest of that author's arguments regarding the early life of the *ālayavijñāna* idea, see Schmithausen 2017: 272–275. A fine introduction to this topic otherwise is Williams 2009: 97–100.

30. Nanjio 1923: 220.15–16: *mahodadhitaraṃgavan nityamavyucchinnaśarīraḥ*. Also LAS^{C1} 497c25–26; LAS^{C2} 538c8–9; LAS^{C3} 607b29–607c1; LAS^{T} D.107, 142b5; Q.775, 156b1–2. See also Radich 2016: 274–275.

31. Silk 2015b: 59 (§2); AAN 466a20: *zhongsheng hai* 眾生海.

which here refers to the emptiness of subject-object duality that is the primary characteristic of the substratum consciousness.[32] As a final detail, this brief digression back into discussion of *tathāgatagarbha* is embedded in material that critically reevaluates the single vehicle (*ekayāna*) teaching of the SP, which we have seen to have been influential for virtually all Buddha-nature works discussed thus far. The ambivalence that the LAS shows toward the SP, which highlights the status of the LAS on the periphery of the *tathāgatagarbha* tradition proper, will be examined later (9.1).

The LAS is a confusing and, in places, seemingly contradictory text. In its core content we observe two separate accounts of the *tathāgatagarbha*. At first, *tathāgatagarbha* teaching is relegated to an expedient teaching insofar as it is imagined to reveal some concealed element, easily confused for a self, and reminiscent of what we find in the MPNMS-group; but later *tathāgatagarbha* is approved if taken to refer to the untroubled basis for successive rebirths, identified now with the *ālayavijñāna*, and associated with what is taught by the ŚDS. In its second chapter, in which an *ātmavādin* articulation of the *tathāgatagarbha* is criticized, the LAS does not relate the *tathāgatagarbha* to the *ālayavijñāna*, though that chapter mentions both concepts.[33] This suggests that some of the material of chapter 8—in which the *tathāgatagarbha* is identified with this central *vijñānavādin* category—may have been a marginally later development, and an attempt to make further use of Buddha-nature thought apart from its contentious *ātmavādin* heritage.

8.4 Selfhood in the *Sagāthaka*

The two interpretations of *tathāgatagarbha* teaching that we have discussed so far appear in "core" material of the LAS (i.e., chapters 2 and 8), represented in all surviving versions of the text.[34] However, in the many and challenging verses of its so-called *Sagāthaka*—an "appendix" to the main text, absent from LAS^{C1}—we find further mention of *tathāgatagarbha* and its relationship to discourse about the self, some of which does not easily fit with what we have observed in the main text.

---

32. Nanjio 1923: 242.2–6; compare LAS^{C1} 513a27–29; LAS^{C2} 560c17–23; LAS^{C3} 622c4–7; LAS^{T} D.107, 151b7–152a2; Q.775, 166a8–b1.

33. See, for example, Nanjio 1923: 38–39.

34. One could argue that the first chapter of the LAS also contains a fleeting mention of discourse about the self. Here the King Rāvaṇa, the Buddha's host in the LAS, lauds the Buddha's teaching about "one's innermost self, the basis for buddhahood that is the chamber/womb of the Tathāgata" (*tathāgatagarbhabuddhabhūmyadhyātma-*). The expression "*adhyātma-*"—as reflected in my translation—makes a vague point about Buddha-nature as an account of "one's innermost self/character," which may not intend anything like Buddha-nature taught in the MPNMS-group of *sūtras*. See Nanjio 1923: 10.1. Compare LAS^{C2} 516c11–12; LAS^{C3} 588c15–16; LAS^{T} D.107, 58b7–59a1; Q.775, 63b8–64a1.

One of the nearly nine hundred verses in the *Sagāthaka* (10.746) identifies the expression *tathāgatagarbha* with some notion of *ātman,* but also distinguishes this from the views of non-Buddhist philosophers (*tārkika*s): "The *ātman* that is characterized by purity is attained by self-realization; this is the *garbha* of the Tathāgatas, which is not the domain of (worldly) philosophers."[35] The verses that follow (beginning with 10.747–754) present us with some challenges. These state that non-Buddhists take the *ālaya* (*vijñāna*) under the guise of (*tathāgata*)*garbha* to be "the mind conjoined with the self," but that this is not the position proper to Buddhist dharma.[36] What *is* the position of the dharma, we read, is the equivalence of the (*tathagata*)*garbha* to the mind that is intrinsically pure (*prakṛtiprabhāsvaraṃ cittam*), free from limit or absence of limit, but which can nevertheless become an object of attachment for wrong-minded sentient beings.[37] The Buddha, meanwhile, is himself neither a person (*pudgala*) nor "heaps" of experience (*skandha*s), but is himself the knowledge that is without impurities (*anāsrava*), always tranquil (*śānti*), to whom one should go for refuge.[38] Again, this material accords well with the ŚDS, but with the qualification that what is taught in the ŚDS is superseded by an understanding that *tathāgatagarbha* means nothing other than the *ālayavijñāna.*

As already acknowledged by Suzuki, the next verses (10.755–766) seem to contradict the more conventional *nairātmyavāda* orientation of the rest of the LAS.[39] Though these make no explicit mention of the *tathāgatagarbha,* it is likely that they were intended to evoke imagery found in precisely *ātmavādin* articulations of this teaching, as we saw confronted back in chapter 2 of the core LAS (see 8.2): "The self that is luminous is afflicted, without beginning, by adventitious afflictions. Thus afflicted, what is added can be cleansed, like a garment. Just as when a garment is cleansed of dirt, or when gold is rid of its impurities, these [primary entities] are not destroyed; likewise is the self freed from its deficiencies."[40] The *Sagāthaka* then compares the lasting presence of a self to the sound of a lute, conch,

35. Nanjio 1923: 357.14–15: *pratyātmagatigamyaś ca ātmā vai śuddhilakṣaṇam / garbhas tathāgatasyāsau tārkikāṇām agocaraḥ //* Compare LAS^{C2} 583a10–11; LAS^{C3} 637b22–23; LAS^{T} D.107, 186a6–7; Q.775, 203a3–4.

36. Nanjio 1923: 357.16–17: *ālayaṃ garbhasaṃsthānaṃ mataṃ tīrthyānuvarṇitam / ātmanā saha saṃyuktaṃ na ca dharmāḥ prakīrtitāḥ //* Compare LAS^{C2} 583a14–15; LAS^{C3} 637b26–27; LAS^{T} D.107, 186a7–b1; Q.775, 203a4–5.

37. Nanjio 1923: 358.5–6: *prakṛtiprabhāsvaraṃ cittaṃ garbhaṃ tāthāgataṃ śubham / upādānaṃ hi sattvasya antānantavivarjitam //* Compare LAS^{C2} 583a16–19; LAS^{C3} 637b28–c2; LAS^{T} D.107, 186b1–2; Q.775, 203a5–6.

38. Nanjio 1923: 358.9–10. Compare LAS^{C2} 583a22–23; LAS^{C3} 637c5–6; LAS^{T} D.107, 186b2–3; Q.775, 203a6–7.

39. See D. T. Suzuki 1932: 283–284.

40. Nanjio 1923: 358.15–359.3: *āgantukair ānādyaiś ca kleśair ātmā prabhāsvaraḥ / saṃkliśyate upetaś ca vastravat pariśudhyate // malābhāvād yathā vastraṃ hemaṃ vā doṣavarjitam / tiṣṭhanti na ca naśyante ātmā doṣais tathā vinā //* Compare LAS^{C2} 583a28–b2; LAS^{C3} 637c11–14; LAS^{T} D.107, 186b3–5; Q.775, 203a8–b1.

or drum, and criticizes those who seek to "see" the self amid the *skandhas*, as if it were a jewel in a treasure-store (10.757–762).[41] However, this string of verses focuses repeatedly not on *ātman* but rather—according to the Sanskrit LAS^S^—to some "person" that is amid the "heaps" of experience (*skandheṣu pudgalam*). It is plausible that this is not a reference to *tathāgatagarbha* teaching at all, and may have instead targeted the *pudgalavāda* tradition and its account of the "person" that is neither "amid" nor "apart from" the *skandhas*.[42]

The expression *ātman* does feature in verse 10.760, in which perception of the self is compared to the womb (*garbha*) of a woman who is pregnant, who knows herself to be so but cannot see the unborn child that she carries; similarly, one who lacks insight (*ayuktijña*) cannot see the self that is somehow among the heaps of their experience.[43] Two more verses (10.761–762) refer by name to some "person" amid the *skandhas* (compared to, among other things, fire amid kindling, an image used by *pudgalavādin* sources).[44] A further verse (10.763) then articulates that without the existence of the self (*asatyātmani*) there could be no stages of accomplishment (*bhūmi*), no mastery (*vaśitā*), no powers (*abhijñā*), no "anointment" (*abhiṣeka*) to the stage of buddhahood, and no higher states of concentration (*uttara samādhi*s) proper to this status.[45] The *Sagāthaka* then tells us how to confront a nihilist (*vaināśika*) who objects that he cannot see the self: he should have it pointed out to him that he also cannot "see" his own faculty of discrimination (*svavikalpa*), and so he has failed to understand to what teaching about *ātman* must refer (10.764).[46] The final verses in this sequence (10.765–766) conclude with a striking admonishment of, by name, the *nairātmyavāda* orientation that characterizes most Buddhist teaching, including—as we have seen—much of the LAS itself: "Those who hold to discourse concerning absence of self should be ignored, excluded from the activities of monks: they are opponents to the Buddha's dharma, and possess [erroneously] oppositional views of being and of non-being. This teaching about the self (*ātmavāda*) shines powerfully, like the great conflagration at the end of the

41. Nanjio 1923: 359.4–15. Comparison of the self to the sounds made by instruments is reminiscent of the *Bṛhadāraṇyaka-upaniṣad* (4.5.8); see Olivelle 1998: 68–69.

42. See Priestley 1999: 53–80; also 1.1n28.

43. Nanjio 1923: 359.10–11: *yathā hi garbho garbhinyāṃ vidyate na ca dṛśyate / ātmā hi tadvat skandheṣu ayuktijño na paśyati //* Compare LAS^C2^ 583b9–10; LAS^C3^ 637c21–22; LAS^T^ D.107, 186b7–187a1; Q.775, 203b1–3. Here the dual sense of *garbha*—as "womb" or "embryo"—presents an ambiguity: our two Chinese versions suggest that a woman cannot see her womb, whereas LAS^T^ states that what cannot be seen is the woman's unborn child (*bu*).

44. Nanjio 1923: 359.12–15. Compare LAS^C2^ 583b11–12; LAS^C3^ 637c23–24; LAS^T^ D.107, 187a1; Q.775, 203b4–5. See also Priestley 1999: 165–186.

45. Nanjio 1923: 359.16–17. Compare LAS^C2^ 583b13–18; LAS^C3^ 637c25–28; LAS^T^ D.107, 187a1–2; Q.775, 203b5.

46. Nanjio 1923: 360.1–2. Compare LAS^C2^ 583b19–20; LAS^C3^ 637c29–638a1; LAS^T^ D.107, 187a2–3; Q.775, 203b5–6.

age: it is free from the faults of non-Buddhist systems (*tīrtha*s), burning up the thicket that is absence of self (*nairātmya*)."[47]

As observed by Arnold Kunst (1980), a great deal of seemingly contradictory material in the *Sagāthaka* is explained by the hypothesis that it contains articulations of teachings and responses to them that are not always clearly distinguishable in the text as we read it today.[48] The verses above may preserve a critique of both *pudgalavādin* and Buddha-nature thought woven together: where we find womb imagery (and indeed the expression *garbha*), or otherwise *ātman,* we are likely to be in the midst of material concerned, albeit obliquely, with *tathāgatagarbha*. There is no doubt that on some level the *Sagāthaka* praises the correction of *nairātmyavāda* discourse by some Buddhist account of the self; the sight of which, we are told (10.768), constitutes liberation.[49]

In summary, the *Sagāthaka*—taken either as an independent work, or as an adjunct to the prose LAS—is challenging material to unpack. Its author(s) take aim at more than one wrong-minded form of what could have been understood as Buddhist *ātmavāda,* both some manner of *pudgalavādin* position—evident where we find reference to the *pudgala* that is imagined in relation to the *skandha*s—but also the *tathāgatagarbha* tradition, associated with the expressions *ātman* and *garbha*. But the closing verses cited above still explicitly approve a kind of Buddhist *ātmavāda,* and with reference to that which can be "seen" by an awakened being, a view at odds with what we see in material proper to the earliest content of the "core" LAS, but very reminiscent of our sources for a Buddhist *ātmavāda*.

8.5 Conclusions

While the diverse and seemingly contradictory verses of the *Sagāthaka* remain something of an enigma, and are definitely a rich vein for further study, we can draw firm conclusions regarding the perspective on Buddha-nature teaching approved in the main body of the LAS. In accordance with Yogācāra-Vijñānavāda teaching about the substratum consciousness

47. Nanjio 1923: 360.3–6: *nairātmyavādino 'bhāṣyā bhikṣukarmāṇi varjaya / bādhakā buddhadharmāṇāṃ sadasatpakṣadṛṣṭayaḥ // tīrthadoṣair vinirmuktaṃ nairātmyavanadāhakam / jājvalatyātmavādo 'yaṃ yugāntāgnirivotthitaḥ //* Compare LAS^{C2} 583b21–26; LAS^{C3} 638a2–5; LAS^{T} D.107, 187a3–4; Q.775, 203b6–7.

48. It would be helpful to know who is meant to be speaking throughout the *Sagāthaka*. In v.798–803 we are told that the speaker of some verses is the "victor" (*jina:* i.e., Buddha) Viraja, who taught with three other Buddhas (Kāśyapa, Krakucchanda, and Kanaka/Koṇāgamana) prior to Śākyamuni (and a host of named non-Buddhist teachers), that is, operating in the "ideal" period (*kṛtayuga*) of our current eon, whereas Śākyamuni taught in our period of decline (*kaliyuga;* see Eltschinger 2010: 460–462). This is not enough, however, to make sense of the confusing content throughout the *Sagāthaka,* including where it alludes to Buddha-nature.

49. Nanjio 1923: 360: 9–10: *vidvān dṛṣṭvā vimucyate*. Compare LAS^{C2} 583b29–c1; LAS^{C3} 638a8–9; LAS^{T} D.107, 187a4–5; Q.775, 203b7–204a1.

(*ālayavijñāna*), and making good use of *tathāgatagarbha* articulated as a basis or foundation, drawn from the ŚDS, the LAS understands Buddha-nature to again refer to some subliminal nature of the mind that runs across successive rebirths. But whereas the ŚDS simply distanced its teaching from *ātmavādin* models of Buddha-nature teaching, the LAS goes so far as to actively confront the problem of the Buddha having declared, in some discourses attributed to him, that *tathāgatagarbha* constitutes his account of the self.

It would be wrong to consider the LAS to have followed the ŚDS in all regards. One difference between the two is the refusal on the part of the LAS to accept the single vehicle paradigm known from the SP (to which we shall return later; see 9.1). Moreover, the LAS declares that what was taught by Śrīmālā was still something of an expediency, for the benefit of *śrāvaka*s who could not know that the real referent of this teaching was the substratum consciousness (see 8.3). For all of its interest in the expression *tathāgatagarbha*, the core LAS (i.e., excluding the slippery content of the *Sagāthaka*) attempts to accommodate the Buddha-nature idea in an account of this basic stratum of the mind, and so a fundamentally mentalistic model of how to understand both transmigration and its possible end.

8.6 Postscript: After the LAS

The circulation of the LAS may have marked a downward turn in the popularity of a discernible (if heterogeneous) tradition of Buddha-nature thought in India; after it we have no other Indian texts that make any significant commitment to explain to what the expression *tathāgatagarbha* must refer.[50] It is not the intention of this study to pursue reception of the Buddha-nature idea outside of the Indian subcontinent. Our focus must remain the *tathāgatagarbha* in India, imagined as either a Buddhist teaching about the self, or otherwise an account of some commonality between sentient beings and Buddhas that steered strategically away from being understood in *ātmavādin* terms. While it is clear that what may be early Buddha-nature

50. Buddha-nature raises its head again in a number of tantric compositions. Perhaps earliest is the *Adhyardhaśatikā-prajñāpāramitā* (see Zacchetti 2015: 201–202), relevant content of which survives in Bodhiruci's translation of 693 CE (T.240[5]777c9–10). Our surviving Sanskrit text states that "all sentient beings are *tathāgatagarbha* (*sarvasattvās tathāgatagarbhāḥ* ...) by virtue of their identity with the great bodhisattva Samantabhadra (... *samantabhadramahā bodhisattvasarvātmatayā*)"; see Toganō (1930) 1982: 6.18–19. A particularly fascinating reference to *tathāgatagarbha* occurs in the *Mahāpratisarā-mahāvidyārājñī* (sixth century, at latest), which states that an observer of this text and its teachings can be empowered by all Tathāgatas, obtain their body that is a *vajrakāya* (see 2.1n15), and has within himself (*garbha*) the *dhātu* of all Tathāgatas (*sarvatathāgatadhātugarbha*), language that evokes Buddha-nature teachings of the MPNMS specifically (see Hidas 2012: 133.1–5l; I thank Kazuo Kanō for bringing this to my attention). Regarding these and other (likely) later tantric discussions of Buddha nature, see Kanō 2016: 6n17; 2017: 32n34. In these later instances, associations between *tathāgatagarbha* and discourse about the self seem to have been left behind.

texts—that is, those of the MPNMS-group—subscribed to the former view, Indian commentators seem to have been influenced instead by the ŚDS and LAS, which reject associations between *tathāgatagarbha* and discourse about the self. Prior to what seems to have been a rediscovery of the RGVV in the early second millennium (see 7.1), other Indian commentarial works cited the LAS in particular as having articulated the most authoritative account of the *tathāgatagarbha* and to what this expression must refer.

Despite its obvious Yogācāra-Vijñānavāda leanings, Buddhist authors who referred to the LAS as a source for *tathāgatagarbha* teaching included important exponents of the Madhyamaka, a philosophical tradition that would have struggled to reconcile its interpretation of emptiness (*śūnyatā*), or the universal absence of independent nature (*niḥsvabhāva*) in all phenomena, with the notion of some enduring, underlying basis to transmigration. Mādhyamika authors including Bhāviveka (c.490–570), Candrakīrti (c.600–650), and Kamalaśīla (c.740–795) all seem to know the LAS as a text that clarified the expression *tathāgatagarbha,* to what it refers, and its distinction from anything like an account of the self.[51]

In chapter 4 of his *Tarkajvāla,* which survives only in Tibetan translation, Bhāviveka responds to various objections by exponents of "mainstream" or Śrāvakayāna Buddhism who challenge the authenticity of Mahāyānist teachings, regarding Buddha-nature and otherwise. Bhāviveka groups together a set of objections that seem to be associated with the *tathāgatagarbha* tradition specifically: teaching about the permanence of the Tathāgata, we read, contradicts the declaration that all conditioned things are impermanent, whereas teaching the pervasiveness of *tathāgatagarbha* (Tib. *khyab pa nyid:* **vyāpti*), and about the receiving consciousness (*ādānavijñāna*; a common epithet for the *ālayavijñāna*), does not overcome grasping to the self (*ātmagrāha*).[52] A final objection is that it is an affront to the dharma to teach that the Buddha "has not obtained *nirvāṇa,*" which clearly has in mind the notion of the Buddha's projected display of his death, encountered throughout *tathāgatagarbha* literature specifically.[53] The imagined objector in the *Tarkajvāla* contends that these doctrines are counterproductive to relinquishing notions of selfhood. In his responses, Bhāviveka cites the LAS, by name, as a source that explains the Buddha's perma-

51. For more, see also Kanō 2016: 7–11; also Ruegg 1989a: 26–35. Śāntideva—another Mādhyamika, of the eighth century—mentions the LAS in his *Śikṣāsamuccaya* (Bendall [1897–1902] 1970: 133.4; also 131.13–14, 135.5) as a source for teaching about vegetarianism, together with the *Hastikakṣayasūtra, Mahāmeghasūtra,* MPNMS, and AMS (i.e., the four texts cited by the LAS on the same theme: see 3.1n5). Regarding all of these Mādhyamika authors, see relevant chapters in Ruegg 1981.

52. Eckel 2008: 319: *de bzhin gshegs pa rtag pa nyid du ston par byed pas 'dus byas thams cad mi rtag pa zhes bya ba dang 'gal ba'i yang phyir ro // de bzhin gshegs pa'i snying pos khyab pa nyid dang / len pa'i rnam par shes pa ston par byed pas bdag tu 'dzin pa ma spangs pa'i yang phyir ro //* For Eckel's translation, see ibid., 126.

53. Ibid., 126; also (for Eckel's edition) 319.

nence, which he takes to refer to the Buddha's existence as some continuum (*rgyun: santāna*), so not a static entity, devoid of change.[54] Bhāviveka then clarifies that the pervasiveness of the Tathāgata (not explicitly the *tathāgatagarbha,* though this may have been implied) refers to the knowledge of the Buddha pervading all objects of cognition, but "not pervading all things in the manner of Viṣṇu."[55] Turning to the expression *tathāgatagarbha* itself, he writes that it refers to emptiness, signlessness, and absence of intention: the three gates of liberation associated with *tathāgatagarbha* in the LAS (see 8.2), which permit entry to *nirvāṇa.* Bhāviveka is also explicit that this is not like a permanent or enduring person (*skyes bu: puruṣa*) that resides "inside" sentient beings, "permanent and all-pervading." The *ādānavijñāna,* he concludes, is the ground for the ebb and flow of transmigration, akin to a great river, the character of which is momentariness: "It is not like a self, hence does not contradict the seal of the dharma that is absence of self."[56]

Here the Buddha's pervading knowledge (**buddhajñāna*) evokes what we find in the RGV (see 7.2) and similes of the TGS (6.2), and perhaps also works on the periphery of the *tathāgatagarbha* tradition, such as the *Tathāgatotpattisaṃbhavanirdeśa.*[57] Also interesting is that Bhāviveka makes explicit reference to Vaiṣṇavism and—in his rejection of a pervading *puruṣa* across all living beings—may have been evoking Sāṃkhya teaching, or otherwise the supreme *puruṣa* as taught by some principle Upaniṣads (see 9.6; also 10.4).[58] Showing awareness of non-Buddhist discourse about the self, Bhāviveka contends that to what both *tathāgatagarbha* and *ādānavijñāna* must refer—some basis to the experience of transmigration and liberation from it—does not contradict conventional Buddhist teaching about absence of self. His scriptural authority for all of this is the LAS, though Bhāviveka stops short of identifying the *tathāgatagarbha* and *ādānavijñāna* as names for the same substratum—evidence, perhaps, that he was well

---

54. Ibid., 154–155.

55. Ibid., 339 (... *khyab 'jug dang 'dra bar thams cad du gnas pa nyid ni ma yin no*). Compare, for example, *Bhagavadgītā* 11.38–40 (e.g., Sargeant 2009: 490–492).

56. See Eckel 2008: 339, which concludes (regarding selfhood): *bdag dang 'dra bar ni ma yin pa'i phyir bdag med pa'i chos kyi phyag rgya dang mi 'gal lo //* (This [*tathāgatagarbha*] is not like a self, so does not contradict the seal of the dharma that is absence of self). For Eckel's translation of this material, see ibid., 154–155.

57. See 7.2n29.

58. In its eighth chapter, Bhāviveka's *Tarkajvāla* (and his verse text, the *Madhyamakahṛdayakārikā,* upon which it elaborates) also provides us with likely our earliest surviving Buddhist confrontation with (seemingly Advaita) Vedānta, and confronts teaching about a self that is a single substance pervading many sentient beings (Qvarnström 1989). In its chapter defending the authenticity of the Mahāyāna, the *Madhyamakahṛdayakārikā* contests that what appears to be "well spoken" (*sūkta*) in Vedānta is so because it has been taught already by the Buddha (ibid., 103), and—as the *Tarkajvāla* clarifies—by various manifestations (*sprul pa: *nirmāṇa/nirmita*) produced by him (Eckel 2008: 199, 376), a feature of our early Buddha-nature sources (see 2.5, 3.7), to which we return later (10.4).

aware that apart from their equation in the LAS these expressions belong to two separate traditions of Buddhist literature.

A still clearer reliance on the LAS is found in Candrakīrti's *Madhyamakāvatārabhāṣya* (commenting on verse 4.95 of the root text, by the same author). Candrakīrti quotes the LAS regarding the intention of the Buddha when he taught about *tathāgatagarbha* (see 8.2), in order to allay the fears of audiences who are incapable of accepting absence of self, and for the sake of attracting non-Buddhists. For Candrakīrti, this demonstrates that the *tathāgatagarbha* is necessarily a provisional teaching (*neyārtha*); his position is that *vijñānavāda* teachings as a whole—what the LAS advances as definitive or final teachings of the Buddha (*nītārtha*)—are themselves only provisional.[59] Hence Candrakīrti accepts the presentation of *tathāgatagarbha* in the LAS, that it is (1) in some instances articulated as something like a self, which is for some expedient purpose, and is (2) properly an epithet for the *ālayavijñāna*. But both teachings must be secondary to the stance of the Madhyamaka, for which everything down to the mind itself must be empty of an independent nature, and so cannot be taken to be any foundation for knowledge.

Finally, the same material of the LAS is again quoted by Kamalaśīla in his *Madhyamakāloka*.[60] Kamalaśīla associates Buddha-nature with a markedly Mādhyamika interpretation of teaching about the single vehicle: "That all sentient beings are *tathāgatagarbha* is the teaching that all [of them] are able to attain the state of supreme, complete awakening, because the expression 'Tathāgata' means the nature/realm of *dharma*s (Tib. *chos kyi dbyings*: *dharmadhātu*), which has as its character absence of self with respect to both persons and phenomena, as it is said to be intrinsically luminous (*rang bzhin gyis 'od gsal ba: prakṛtiprabhāsvara*)."[61] Kamalaśīla cannot conceive of Buddha-nature in any substantial sense, that is, in the sense of the Buddha's abiding "essence" that is "within" sentient beings. According to Kazuo Kanō (2016: 10–11), Kamalaśīla instead understands *tathāgatagarbha* to mean *dharmadhātugarbha*, an equation found otherwise in the ŚDS (see 5.2), and which understands that the true nature of phenomena can be discerned "within" sentient beings, insofar as each is already the locus for realizing the real status of things. Whereas the LAS equates *tathāgatagarbha* with its

59. See La Vallée Poussin 1912: 198.13–15: *de'i phyir de ltar na rnam pa de lta bu'i mdo ste rnam par shes par smra ba rnams kyis nges pa'i don nyid du khas blangs pa thams cad drang ba'i don nyid yin par lung 'dis mngon par gsal par byas*. See also Kanō 2016: 9n29–30.

60. For more regarding Kamalaśīla, see Ruegg 1981: 95–96.

61. *Madhyamakāloka*, D.3887, 242b4–b6; Q.5287, 272a8–273a2: *sems can thams cad ni de bzhin gshegs pa'i snying po can no zhes bya ba 'dis kyang / thams cad bla na med pa yang dag par rdzogs pa'i byang chub kyi go 'phang thob par rung ba nyid du yongs su bstan te / de bzhin gshegs pa'i sgra ni chos kyi dbyings gang zag dang chos la bdag med pa'i mtshan nyid rang bzhin gyis 'od gsal ba yin par brjod par bzhed pa'i phyir ro //* A paraphrase of Kamalaśīla's position, preserving *tathāgatagarbha* as an exocentric compound (i.e., *tathāgatagarbhāḥ sarvasattvāḥ*), survives in the Sanskrit of the *Munimatālaṃkāra* by Abhayākaragupta (eleventh–twelfth century), regarding which see Ruegg 1977; also Kanō 2016: 10n34.

own account of some substrate that is a basis for both birth and (eventually) liberation, Kamalaśīla understands *tathāgatagarbha* to refer to simply the true nature of all phenomena, their emptiness, which—being the same in all sentient beings—assures a universal ability to attain the status of a Buddha.[62] Notably this does not preserve the way that emptiness seems to be explained in virtually all works concerned with *tathāgatagarbha*, in which it is taught to refer to an absence of something "other"—namely adventitious afflictions (*āgantukakleśa*s)—with respect to what is supermundane, including Buddha-nature (see 9.5)

These Mādhyamika authors all understand Buddha-nature teaching to have been a kind of strategy or expediency, taught—as the LAS contends—for the benefit of certain audiences who could be led to the dharma by something that appears to be a Buddhist teaching about the self. We are, by now, a long way from those texts to which the LAS seemed to respond, which predate the mentalistic or "*vijñānavādin*" interpretation of *tathāgatagarbha* proper to both the ŚDS and the root verses of the RGV. Before all of these were *sūtra*s that did indeed understand *tathāgatagarbha* in terms of the Buddha's account of the self, and which likely did not—as later apologists contended—consider their articulations of the dharma to be either expedient or intentional, so much as the revelation of a mysterious "higher" teaching about that which is beyond the faculties of regular sentient beings.

In the next chapter we will revisit other themes and developments observable across the *tathāgatagarbha* literature, in order to defend the hypothesis that our earliest accounts of Buddha-nature teaching are indeed those that articulate *tathāgatagarbha* as the Buddha's account of the self. If we can indeed establish that the *ātmavādin* mode of the Buddha-nature idea is earlier than other accounts of *tathāgatagarbha*, a remaining task will be to offer our own explanation—apart from the creative hermeneutic employed by the LAS—of why sources for Buddha-nature teaching promoted a kind of Buddhist *ātmavāda*. We must attempt this with recourse not to the intentions or strategies of the Buddha, but rather the interests and ambitions of Mahāyānist authors who were operating, and innovating, in the early centuries of the Common Era.

62. Kamalaśīla's interpretation is inherited by later Mādhyamikas. Dharmamitra (eighth-ninth century) draws upon the *Adhyardhaśatikā-prajñāpāramitā* (see note 50 above) but also refers to the Buddha having previously taught the existence of a self (*ātman*), person (*pudgala*) or some "essence" (*dhātu*) as only expediencies (see Ruegg 1977: 292). Abhayākaragupta (eleventh-twelfth century; see Ruegg 1977; Kanō 2016: 108–123), in his *Munimatālaṃkāra*, preserves close ties between *tathāgatagarbha*, *dharmadhātu*, and *ekayāna* teachings, and (presumably following Kamalaśīla) quotes the ŚDS and its account of the "death that is an inconceivable transformation" (Kanō 2016: 110; see also 5.1n2, 5.4n53). Jayānanda (eleventh-twelfth century; see Kanō 2016: 148–152), commenting on Candrakīrti's *Madhyamakāvatārabhāṣya*, explains both *tathāgatagarbha* and the *ekayāna* in terms of the ubiquity of emptiness.

PART III

Buddha-nature Reconsidered

CHAPTER 9

Recurring Themes and Motifs

At this stage we have dealt with all of the texts most relevant to the guiding and intertwined themes of this study: the expression *tathāgatagarbha* and Buddhist discourse about the self, used in relation to either something about the nature of sentient beings or, in some instances, the supermundane status of a Buddha. An objective of the final part of this volume is to defend its central thesis: that the expression *tathāgatagarbha* was in the first instance promoted as a Buddhist account of the self (reflected in works addressed in part 1), and only after this was reimagined apart from its contentious "*ātmavādin*" heritage (evident in works addressed in part 2). While chapter 1 presented some initial justification for this hypothesis—namely the claim that the *Mahāparinirvāṇamahāsūtra* is our best contender for earliest source concerned with *tathāgatagarbha* (see 1.3)—we will here review other prominent themes that are common to constituent texts of the *tathāgatagarbha* corpus, and attend to how these support a reassessment of the early trajectory of Buddha-nature teaching in India.

9.1 The Single Vehicle

Following Michael Radich (see 1.2–3), this study has taken the *Mahāparinirvāṇamahāsūtra* (MPNMS) to be our likely earliest source for the expression *tathāgatagarbha* and the teaching(s) for which it stands. One of the few texts mentioned by name in the MPNMS, and with no lack of clarity about what text is intended, is the *Saddharmapuṇḍarīka* (SP), or frequently today called simply the *Lotus Sūtra* (see 2.1). At the heart of the SP is the Buddha's revelation that there exists only a single vehicle (*ekayāna*), such that the "vehicles" or soteriological pathways proper to the *śrāvaka* and *pratyekabuddha*—commonly held to be distinct from that of the bodhisattva (i.e., the Mahāyāna)—are in fact expediencies. Absent from older and more conventional Buddhist thought (Mahāyānist and otherwise), the *ekayāna* is a soteriological paradigm that imagines the Mahāyāna to be the single, exhaustive vehicle in which the other vehicles of Buddhist teaching and practice are included, and which aims to lead all sentient beings to the status of a Buddha.[1] The single vehicle is mentioned throughout the *Aṅgulimālīyasūtra* (AMS; see, e.g., 3.7), whereas the **Mahābherīhārakasūtra* (MBhS) affirms commitment to the single vehicle and repeats at length two parables found otherwise in the SP (see, e.g., 4.1). Material exclusive to Dharmakṣema's version of the MPNMS (i.e., MPNMS^{D}+), unlike the core MPNMS, mentions the single vehicle frequently. All three of these texts, proper to the "MPNMS-group" of *sūtra*s, exhibit some awareness of, or debt to, the SP.

The *Śrīmālādevīsiṃhanādasūtra* (ŚDS), for all of the differences observable between its doctrine and the ideas of the MPNMS-group (see 5.2), is also committed to the *ekayāna*. The ŚDS refers repeatedly to the single vehicle, and goes beyond the SP by articulating the manner in which arhats and *pratyekabuddha*s continue to transmigrate—via "mind-made bodies" (*manomayakāya*), experiencing "a death that is an incomprehensible transformation" (*acintyā pāriṇāmikī cyuti*)—up to the point at which they can finally achieve the liberation of a Buddha (see 5.4). Meanwhile, the model of a single nature of reality, or "nature/realm of *dharmas*" (*ekadharmadhātu*), found in the *Anūnatvāpūrṇatvanirdeśaparivarta* (AAN), understands all sentient beings to have the same underlying nature as bodhisattvas and Buddhas, so implicitly—though it is not mentioned—presumes the single vehicle paradigm also (see 6.1). Finally, Michael Zimmermann has addressed structural as well as doctrinal similarities between the *Tathāgatagarbhasūtra* (TGS), previously held to be our oldest Buddha-nature source, and the SP (see 6.2).[2] Hence the core *sūtra* literature of the *tathāgatagarbha* tradition acknowledges that if all sentient beings possess the nature of a Buddha,

1. A classic discussion of *ekayāna* is Fujita 1975. Nattier (2007; also 2003: 174–176) contests that there is little evidence that what I am calling the single vehicle paradigm was a majority position among the authors of Mahāyānist *sūtra*s, and certainly does not feature in materials that represent our earliest sources for the Mahāyāna (e.g., Chinese translations attributed to Lokakṣema, or surviving Gāndhārī materials dated to the early Common Era). It was more commonly the case that Mahāyānist *sūtra*s took the *nirvāṇa* of the arhat to be an alternative achievement that the bodhisattva opts (and must take care) to avoid. See also Kunst 1977; D. Wangchuk 2007: 111–121. Inscriptional evidence suggests gradual acceptance of what Nattier calls "bodhisattva universalism" (2003: 174–176), to which teaching about a single vehicle is an obvious complement. The Govindnagar Brāhmī inscription, from near present-day Mathurā and dated to the reign of the Kuṣāṇa king Huveṣka/Huviṣka (mid-second century, perhaps 153 CE), includes the wish that *all* sentient beings might attain the knowledge of a Buddha (Schopen [1987] 2005), an expression that becomes more prominent in inscriptions from the Gupta period (mid-fourth century) onward; see Ruegg 2004: 13–16. It is also clear that exponents of the Madhyamaka tradition (perhaps Nāgārjuna himself; see note 22 below) accepted and defended the single vehicle paradigm, even if their works do not make frequent reference to the SP itself (see 8.6, especially note 62).

2. Of particular note is a simile in the SP that would be at home in any of our *tathāgatagarbha* sources: a man may not know that he possesses a precious jewel in the hem of his garment, and so is like the arhats who do not know that they have made vows—long ago—to be bodhisattvas (SP 210.5–212.2; Kern 1884: 201–202). See also Zimmermann 1999: 161–165, especially note 48.

then liberation must surely refer to the realization of precisely his status; the status of an arhat or *pratyekabuddha* cannot be the end of any religious career, if in each of these persons there remains still the dormant essence or qualities of a fully realized Buddha.

Ties between the *ekayāna* and *tathāgatagarbha* are visible in another Indian *sūtra* text that is worthy of passing consideration. This is the impressively titled *Bodhisattvagocaropāyaviṣayavikurvāṇanirdeśa* (*sūtra*) (henceforth BGVNS), which likely also circulated India under the title *Satyakaparivarta*.[3] Our earliest version of the text is a Chinese translation produced by Guṇabhadra in the early fifth century (T.271), and our most detailed is the Chinese of Bodhiruci 菩提流支 from a century later (T.272, *Dasazhe niqianzisuo shuo jing* 大薩遮尼乾子所說經; henceforth BGVNS^{B}).[4] The surprising "guest teacher" in the BGVNS (akin to Aṅgulimāla in the AMS, or Queen Śrīmālā in the ŚDS) is a non-Buddhist renunciant (*nirgrantha*) named Satyaka, who is the same Satyaka (or Pāli Saccaka) known from earlier Buddhist discourses.[5] The BGVNS provides an enthusiastic espousal of single vehicle teaching, and records that five hundred monks of the Śrāvakayāna who witnessed the Buddha's teaching about it generated the aspiration for complete awakening.[6] BGVNS^{B}—that is, our longer recension of the text—includes also several similes that describe the *tathāgatagarbha*.[7] "Know that amid the store of all afflictions and impurities there exists, calmly realized, the nature of the Tathāgata: like gold within stone; fire within wood; water beneath the earth; yoghurt in milk; oil in hemp; a sprout within a seed; riches within a treasury; an icon within a mold; a fetus within the womb; the sun behind cloud. For this reason do I teach that within the body that is afflicted there exists the *tathāgatagarbha*."[8] Though not "core" material of the BGVNS—that is, not common to all surviving versions of it—this curious set of similes is reminiscent of Buddha-nature taught by the MPNMS-group,

3. Named in Śāntideva's *Śikṣāsamuccaya*, see Bendall [1897–1902] 1970: 165.17: *āryasatyake parivartte;* see also Silk 2013: 158–160. The BGVNS was also considered by Takasaki (1974: 254–274), and in association with the MPNMS-group of *sūtras*.

4. We have also a Tibetan translation produced in the ninth century, the subject of a study and English translation by Jamspal 2010; see also Silk 2013.

5. The *Cūḷasaccakasutta* (MN.I.227) and *Mahāsaccakasutta* (MN.I.237). In these Satyaka is referred to as a *nirgrantha* but also as a *paṇḍitavādin,* something akin, perhaps, to a sophist.

6. See, for example, BGVNS^{B} 327a3–5; also (in Guṇabhadra's translation) T.271(9)306a10–11. See also Takasaki 1974: 262–264.

7. Regarding other material unique to this version, see Zimmermann 2000.

8. BGVNS^{B} 359a28–359b3: 當知一切煩惱諸垢藏中有如來性湛然滿足：如石中金；如木中火；如地下水；如乳中酪；如麻中油；如子中芽[a]；如藏中寶；如模[b]中象；如孕中胎；如雲中日。是故我言煩惱身中有如來藏。

[a] T 牙 = Yuan/Ming 芽

[b] T 摸 = Yuan/Ming 模

and evinces further that for Indian authors the *ekayāna* and *tathāgatagarbha* were understood to be complementary teachings.[9]

But in contrast to these "ekayānist" sources, other works we have discussed either confront or develop Buddha-nature teaching at its intersection with the Yogācāra-Vijñānavāda tradition. As exemplified most clearly in the *Mahāyānasūtrālaṃkāra* (MSA; see 6.3), the Yogācāra-Vijñānavāda held to the principle that there exist three discrete vehicles of Buddhist teaching and aspiration (of the *śrāvaka*s, *pratyekabuddha*s, and bodhisattvas), as well as individuals who have "no lineage" (*agotra*), that is, no capacity for liberation, and so will never achieve any form of escape from rebirth at all.[10] The *Ratnagotravibhāga* (RGV; i.e., the verse text) is ambiguous on this issue: some verses certainly suggest an *ekayāna* orientation (see 7.4), but a verse preserved only in our Chinese version of the text (i.e., RGV^{C}; see 7.1) acknowledges that there are three vehicles leading to three separate kinds of liberation.[11] A commentarial verse of the RGV (1.41) refers to some sentient beings as having no lineage at all (*agotra*).[12] Finally, the prose *Ratnagotravibhāgavyākhyā* (RGVV)—no doubt the product of some later author(s)—also mentions persons who are "not for *nirvāṇa*" (see 7.3). A later chapter of the RGVV also mentions the SP by name but states that the Buddha delivered its content in order to convert to the Mahāyāna his disciples who had entered the "path to peace" (*śāntimārga*), and so seems to understand the *ekayāna* to be a provisional teaching intended only for certain audiences.[13]

A still more complicated picture is visible in the *Laṅkāvatārasūtra* (LAS). At the end of its second chapter (lines after the text has confronted *tathāgatagarbha* as something like an account of the self; see 8.2), the LAS clarifies that the Buddha must teach three vehicles because there is no fashion by which *śrāvaka*s and *pratyekabuddha*s can attain liberation "by

9. A further curiosity is the Chinese *Miaofa lianhua jing youboiishe* 妙法蓮華經憂波提舍 (T.1519: **Saddharmapuṇḍarīkasūtropadeśa*), translated by Bodhiruci 菩提流支 and Tanlin 曇林 between 508/509 and 535 CE, and in another instance by Ratnamati and Senglang 僧朗 in 508 CE (the essentially identical *Miaofa lianhua jing lun youbotishe* 妙法蓮華經論憂波提舍, T.1520; see Abbott 2013: 89–90; also 1985: 82–98). This is the only surviving commentary of the SP that has any claim to Indian provenance. It teaches also about *tathāgatagarbha;* associates this with the *dharmakāya* (T.1519[26]6a12–13), with a *nirvāṇa* that is permanent, quiescent, and changeless (9b17–18), and with the *sattvadhātu* (9b20–21); and moreover appears to represent *tathāgatagarbha* in terms of the **buddhadhātu* (9a14: 眾生皆有佛性). The commentary is attributed to Vasubandhu, though does not exhibit any hallmarks of the *vijñānavāda* orientation that is characteristic of his widely accepted Mahāyānist writings, and instead teaches faithfully—and with some complexity—the single vehicle doctrine of the SP. As we lack any solid evidence of its existence in India, it remains very possible that the text is a Chinese creation. See also Takasaki 1974: 419; Abbott 1985: 102–108; Mochizuki 2017.

10. See 6.3nn41–42.

11. RGV^{C} 813a17: 順三乘菩提. See also Kanō 2016: 36–37; also 259.

12. Johnston (1950) 1991: 36.8–9.

13. Ibid., 88.7–8.

themselves." The LAS then states that arhats and *pratyekabuddhas* have not comprehended absence of self in all *dharmas*, nor achieved "the death that is an inconceivable transformation" (*acintyapariṇāmacyuti*). This is the mode of rebirth described also in the ŚDS, and proper to those who have achieved limited freedom from the bonds of transmigration (see 5.4), but who according to the LAS are yet to realize "the power of the inconceivable *dharmakāya* (*acintyadharmakāyavaśa*)," and so full awakening.[14] This may seem to endorse a form of teaching about the single vehicle, but verses of the LAS (2.201–204) pose something of a contradiction: the Buddha explains that talk of vehicles, at all, is expedient.

> I speak of the vehicles of the gods (*devas*), of the *brahma* gods and also those of the *śrāvaka*, the Tathāgata and *pratyeka*[*buddha*] (201), but there is no completion of any vehicle so long as the mind continues to operate; when the mind ceases to do so there is no vehicle, nor any who rides in it (202)! There is no establishment of any vehicles, hence do I speak of the one vehicle;[15] for the sake of leading those who are ignorant, I speak of different vehicles (203).
>
> There are then three [kinds of] liberation, and all *dharmas* are without self; knowledge and afflictions are said to be of the same nature, and are abandoned when one is liberated (204).[16]

The LAS goes so far as to present a "five vehicle" model of Buddhist teaching, extending to those who follow the "vehicles" for gods (*devas*) and greater deities still (*brahmans*), which may have struck audiences as irregular (see also 9.6 below).[17] Here and elsewhere the LAS criticizes unnecessary argument over the number of vehicles taught by the Buddha, and privileges a "no vehicle" teaching that is proper to those who understand all things to

---

14. Nanjio 1923: 134.3–15. Compare LAS[C1] 497b9–22; LAS[C2] 540a7–21; LAS[C3] 607a14–a27; LAS[T] D.107, 108b4–109a2; Q.775, 119b8–120a6.

15. I here alter Nanjio's edition *yānabhedaṃ* to *yānam ekam*, which agrees with the reading of all Chinese and Tibetan translation of the passage, and indeed makes better sense in the verse. See the next note for full references.

16. Nanjio 1923: 134.16–135.7: *devayānaṃ brahmayānaṃ śrāvakīyaṃ tathaiva ca / tāthāgataṃ ca pratyekaṃ yānān etān vadāmy aham // yānānāṃ nāsti vai niṣṭhā yāvac cittaṃ pravartate / citte tu vai parāvṛtte na yānaṃ na ca yāninaḥ // yānavyavasthānaṃ naivāsti yānam ekam*[a] *vadāmy aham / parikarṣaṇārthaṃ bālānāṃ yānabhedaṃ vadāmy aham // vimuktayas tathā tisro dharmanairātmyam eva ca / samatājñānakleśākhyā vimuktyā te vivarjitāḥ //*

[a] See previous note.

Compare LAS[C1] 497b23–497c1; LAS[C2] 540a22–29; LAS[C3] 607a28–608b6; LAS[T] D.107, 109a2–4; Q.775, 120a6–8. D. Wangchuk (2007: 116) relates this material to a passage of the *Akṣayamatinirdeśasūtra*.

17. See also D. Wangchuk 2007: 116, 119–120. Regarding "no vehicle" teaching, see Ruegg 2004: 9, 57–58n103. Though not reflected in our translations, it is also plausible that the Indian LAS intended *deva* in the sense of royalty, and/or *brahman* in the sense of Brahmanas.

be mind-only.[18] And yet the verses of the LAS translated above also tell us, in accordance with its Yogācāra-Vijñānavāda leanings, that it still accepted discrete forms of liberation.[19]

The *gotra* model of Buddhist soteriology holds that only some beings can attain complete awakening, some only lower forms of liberation (of the arhat or *pratyekabuddha*), that others are "undetermined" in their capacities, and that some are destined to transmigrate forever. Though in its systematized form this teaching is associated with the Yogācāra-Vijñānavāda tradition, it also underpins the more conventional "three vehicle" (*triyāna*) model of liberation(s) presumed by earlier Mahāyānist sources.[20] Indeed, the SP presented its account of the *ekayāna* as a radical and challenging reimagination of Buddhist soteriology (see 9.2, below) and while its new paradigm seems to have been a minority position in (surviving) Mahāyānist *sūtras*, it seems to have been a pronounced influence upon the *tathāgatagarbha* tradition.[21]

The fact that most "true" *tathāgatagarbha sūtras*—the MPNMS, AMS, MBhS, ŚDS, AAN, and TGS—all exhibit at least some influence by the SP requires further consideration. We should first attend to what distinguishes the *ekayāna* from teaching about Buddha-nature. The revelation of the *ekayāna* by the SP addresses the status of the *śrāvaka* (including anyone who may have been considered to be an arhat). The SP promises that all sentient beings who have accepted Buddhist dharma, in some form or other, are already on the singular path toward attaining the liberation proper to a Buddha;[22] its provocative position is that non-Mahāyāna

18. For example, Nanjio 1923: 65.11–12 (v.2.131); also 62.2–4.

19. Ibid., 63–65; also D. T. Suzuki 1930: 358–361. The LAS also mentions *icchantikas*, and identifies them as persons who have abandoned all of the roots of wholesome activity (*sarvakuśalamūlotsarga*) but who can, under the influence of the Buddha, find their way back on track toward some mode of liberation from rebirth (Nanjio 1923: 65.17–66.9).

20. See 9.1n1.

21. This is not to ignore other types of Mahāyānist literature—that is, works not presented as discourses by the Buddha—that show commitment to, or at least awareness of, teaching about the single vehicle. A fascinating example of this is the *Ratnāvalī*, traditionally attributed to Nāgārjuna (c. second century), which instructs that "because it is not easy to comprehend the intentional/allusional (*abhisandhi*) speech of the Buddha, with equanimity guard yourself from speech regarding the single vehicle and the three vehicles (Tucci 1936: 251 [v.4.88]: *tathāgatābhisandhyoktāny asukhaṃ jñātum ity ataḥ / ekayānatriyānoktād ātmā rakṣya upekṣayā //*). This may not demonstrate the author's approval of the *ekayāna* (a mark of later Mādhyamika authors; see 8.6), but does acknowledge two different models of Buddhist soteriology. Other evidence of Buddha-nature thinking in work attributed to Nāgārjuna has been observed in the *Niraupamyastava* (Mitrikeski 2009), a text that accepts that there is only a single vehicle (v.21), that the Buddha's *parinirvāṇa* was only a docetic show, and that the Buddha's (true) body is permanent (*nitya*), lasting (*dhruva*), and tranquil (*śiva*) (v.22); see Tucci 1932; also Harrison 1982: 224; Shimoda 1994: 25–26. See also 10.2n7. Regarding the matter of what works may or may not have been composed by Nāgārjuna, see Ruegg 1981: 9–50.

22. SP 81.11–82.1; Kern 1884: 81–82. The Buddha clarifies that he does not teach different modes of liberation but leads all sentient beings to the *parinirvāṇa* proper to a Buddha. See also SP 90.7–10 (v.3.90–91); Kern 1884: 88–89.

Buddhists—*śrāvaka*s, or those of the "lesser vehicle" (Hīnayāna)—are still "passengers" of the Mahāyāna, the Buddha's teachings aimed at the achievement of complete awakening.[23] Teaching about Buddha-nature provides something of a doctrinal buttress for this new paradigm: if all sentient beings—animals, deities, and indeed rivals to the Buddha's teachings (i.e., *tīrthika*s)—possess the nature of a Buddha, then this all-encompassing Mahāyāna, which aims to lead *every* sentient being to the status of a Buddha, by innumerable kinds of teachings, should extend to all of them.[24]

Though the MPNMS does not refer to the single vehicle directly, it both mentions the SP by name and otherwise shares the kind of docetic Buddhology promoted by it (see 1.3, also 10.2). Both texts promote the view that Buddha Śākyamuni exceeds what is seen of him in the world, and only projects events of his life—his final birth, (apparent) awakening, teaching, and death—in conformity with the world (*lokānuvartana*) in order to instruct sentient beings. The absence of any mention of the single vehicle paradigm in the MPNMS is curious: although the MPNMS refers to *śrāvaka*s, *pratyekabuddha*s, and Buddhas as all having the same essential nature (*dhātu*), we are not told what becomes of the arhat—having achieved the goal of the Śrāvakayāna teaching—who has not yet realized his Buddha-nature.[25] The notion of a single vehicle—which understands that the arhat can and must progress further toward the status of a Buddha—would be a logical complement to this idea, and indeed the AMS, MBhS, and ŚDS (as well as material added to the core MPNMS, i.e., MPNMS^{D}+) all actively promote the *ekayāna* by name. This gives the impression that it was only after the production of the MPNMS, and perhaps the very invention of the expression *tathāgatagarbha*, that a full marriage of these two teachings took place; the prospect that anyone can be directed toward the liberation of a Buddha is confirmed by the revelation that they all, already, possess what is essential to him.

Another important corollary of there being only a single vehicle is that there can in the end be only *one definitive type of liberation;* the *ekayāna* does not simply belittle the supposed liberation of the arhat but denies that such

23. See Nattier 1997; Hubbard 1995: 128–132, both in response to the unpersuasive reading of the SP that it approves—rather than condescends to—teachings proper to the Śrāvakayāna tradition. See also Kunst 1977: 316–317.

24. This relates also to the Buddha's use of his profound "skill in means" (*upāyakauśalya*) when teaching (see, e.g., Pye 2003), a prominent theme in the SP but less visible in the *tathāgatagarbha* literature, in which there is a greater focus on the fact that the Buddha's teachings can be cryptic and may even appear to contradict one another (see 9.2 below).

25. This undifferentiated nature is explained at MPNMS^{F} 895a20–b15; MPNMS^{D} 422c20–423b1; MPNMS^{T} §520–523. Of these, MPNMS^{D} alone (423a2–3) takes this nature to be a challenge to the idea of three vehicles, so that "all arhats will attain *mahāparinirvāṇa*" (423a23–24: 諸阿羅漢悉當得是大涅槃). A Sanskrit fragment that preserves some of this material (no. 22.8) reflects what Habata (2019: 170–171) reconstructs as *tathāgata{ḥ}pratyekabud dhaśrāvakabodhisatvadhātunirnnā[n]ākaraṇaṃ* (the lack of distinction between the essence [*dhātu*] that is proper to Tathāgata, *pratyekabuddha, śrāvaka* and bodhisattva).

a thing truly exists.[26] In full accord with this alternative soteriological paradigm, the Buddha-nature idea presents a distinctive model of what it means to achieve liberation, such that all sentient beings are reimagined to have some dormant awakened nature that requires—through diligent practice—cleansing from innumerable (but adventitious) afflictions. The revelation of this nature, and the discovery of a distinctively Buddhist "self" hidden beneath afflictions, becomes the Buddha's definitive account of how liberation should be understood, such that prior teaching about *nirvāṇa*(s), or other talk about liberation besides (see 10.4), can be considered expedient articulations of what is taught by the *ekayāna,* or otherwise the single and exhaustive account of how any sentient beings can achieve release from rebirth.

We proceed having established one simple fact: that teachings about the *tathāgatagarbha* and about the single vehicle appear to have been intertwined in the development of Mahāyānist *sūtra* literature. Though later works of the *tathāgatagarbha* corpus—namely the RGVV and LAS, both influenced by the Yogācāra-Vijñānavāda tradition—exhibit commitment to the older three vehicle model of liberation(s), earlier texts concerned with Buddha-nature embrace a soteriological paradigm that was likely first promoted by the SP. Liberation, from this perspective, is of only one kind: it is the realization of what is proper to every sentient being—*śrāvaka,* bodhisattva, or otherwise—and which prefigures the status of complete awakening that is embodied in a Buddha.

9.2 "Cryptic" Utterances

Another important theme ties the SP not to the *tathāgatagarbha* corpus as a whole but specifically to the MPNMS-group that includes likely its earliest constituent text(s). The SP refers to the single vehicle as the Buddha's explanation of his *saṃdhābhāṣya,* a tricky expression that intends some reference to the meaning or purpose behind the Buddha's pronouncements that is not transparently clear, hence his use of what can be called "cryptic," "secretive," "oblique," or "allusive" utterances.[27] In Sanskrit fragments

---

26. As expressed in the SP and its parable of the magically conjured city (SP 187.4–189.11; Kern 1884: 181–183), which is repeated in the MBhS (see 4.5n50).

27. See, for example (in its first occurrence), SP 34.2–5; also, for example, ibid., 39.9–11; 59.3–6 (where we find *saṃdhāvacana*). Otherwise SP verses 3.36–37 (ibid., 70.5–8), in which *saṃdhābhāṣya* refers to the Buddha's prediction of buddhahood for the arhat Śāriputra, or later (ibid., 199.1–4) where Pūrṇa reflects on predictions made about other arhats, and so has heard "the explanation of the Buddha's *saṃdhābhāṣya*." Elsewhere the SP relates use of *saṃdhābhāṣya* to the Buddha's "secret" (ibid., 233.11–13: *nigūḍha*). Kern (e.g., 1884: 35, 59, 70, 121) translates this expression in terms of "the mystery(s) of the Tathāgata(s)." See also Ruegg 1989b: 309–310. Another informative reference to *saṃdhābhāṣya* is in the *Vimalakīrtinirdeśasūtra,* in which the Buddha is said to appear to practice fraudulence and boastfulness (*kuhanalapana*), but he is instead worthy of praise due to his skill-in-means (*upāyakauśalya*) and his proficiency in the use of cryptic utterance (*saṃdhābhāṣyakuśala;*

of the MPNMS we find repeated reference to the Buddha having just expounded his *sandhāvacana,* which (together with the synonymous *saṃdhābhāṣya*) features frequently throughout the SP.[28] In the SP the truth of the Buddha's teaching, to which his uses of *saṃdhābhāṣya* enigmatically direct, is the single vehicle. In the MPNMS the equivalent revelations are the permanence of the Buddha and the ubiquity of Buddha-nature in all sentient beings—truths not heard before, but revealed now to be that to which the Buddha has been skillfully leading his disciples, in accordance with their dispositions, all along.[29]

The MBhS declares that the "cryptic utterance" of the Buddha (*yinfushuo* 隱覆説; *dgongs pa'i tshig: *sandhāvacana*) refers to his permanent existence beyond his apparent *parinirvāṇa* (see 4.1). The AMS is more creative still, and refers repeatedly to cryptic teaching/utterances (*mijiao* 密教; *ldem po ngag: *sandhāvacana*) that express somewhat codedly what a learned audience should draw from the dharma.[30] For example (and rather perversely), we saw earlier that Aṅgulimāla takes "what the Buddha did not discern" among sentient beings to mean not simply the absence of any worldly notion of the self but also the presence of the *tathāgatagarbha* (see 3.2). Such an interpretation could not have been known to Aṅgulimāla's interlocutor, Pūrṇa—nor, surely, to any real-world audience of the AMS—until its proclamation by Aṅgulimāla. Perhaps the most colorful example

---

Taishō University 2006: 77 (46a7), two traits central to the revelatory tone of the SP, and the notion that the meaning or purpose behind some of the Buddha's pronouncements is not so clear to his audience.

28. See Hoernle 1916: 95; also Takasaki 1974: 770–771; Habata 2019: 160–161; also 2009: 580 (concerning Sanskrit fragment no. 21.2, which Habata reconstructs to include "*(mah)ās(ū)tre saṃdhāvacanam śrutvā*"). Other occurrences of this expression—collated by Radich (2015a: 177–192)—are discussed in greater detail by Habata (2019: 154–155, 160–161), whose hypothesis (supported by MPNMS fragment no. 20.5, also no. 21.2) is that *sandhāvacana* is used in the sense of "salvific speech" ("die heilvollen Worte"), referring to that which is "beneficial/wholesome" (*kalyāṇa*), and relates to the use of medicinal metaphor that runs through the MPNMS. See also note 34 below.

29. In MPNMS-dhk (i.e., in material concerned with the permanence of the Buddha) the Buddha's *sandhāvacana* constitutes secret (*guhya*) entries into the dharma, comparable to a physician's range of medicinal treatments (see Habata 2007: 74–75, concerning Sanskrit fragment no. 12, which corresponds to, for example, MPNMS^{T} §166). Regarding the prevalent use of medicinal metaphor in the MPNMS, see Habata 1989; 2019: 27–38.

In MPNMS-tg *sandhāvacana* refers to the Buddha's teachings about permanence (e.g., MPNMS^{F} 886a5–10; MPNMS^{D} 410c5–11; MPNMS^{T} §397), to contradictions between monastic instructions (e.g., MPNMS^{F} 878c16–29; MPNMS^{D} 410c4–17; MPNMS^{T} §323), but also—crucially—the existence of the self, in spite of the Buddha having previously taught at length about absence of self (e.g., MPNMS^{F} 883c29–884a7; MPNMS^{D} 408b27–c3; MPNMS^{T} §383.1–13: translated above, see chapter 2.4). Regarding these passages, see also Radich 2015a: 193–194.

30. T. Suzuki (1999a) argues that this is an innovation of the AMS: that many of the Buddha's earlier utterances are characterized by different instances of **saṃdhābhāṣya,* such that, for example, "absence of self" has the "hidden meaning" that is precisely the presence of the *tathāgatagarbha*. See also Kanō 2000: 70; 2016: 4n11.

of this trope in the AMS, relating again to the Mahāyāna as a single vehicle, runs as follows: "In the discourses of the exalted Buddha are taught innumerable cryptic utterances (**sandhāvacana*): in these there is [only] a single path; the Tathāgata is the pursuit of a single vehicle, a single refuge, a single truth; a single nature (*khams: *dhātu*), a single progress, a single countenance. For this reason there is said to be a single vehicle; the others are strategies (*thabs: upāya*)."[31] It is beyond reasonable doubt that the texts proper to the MPNMS-group, in their Indic forms, employed some variation of the Sanskrit "*saṃdhā/sandhā-bhāṣya/vacana*"; in each instance the sense is that the meaning or intention behind some of the Buddha's teachings are not transparent to his audience. While Chinese translations of these texts seem to understand the Buddha to have been strategically "hiding" something (*yinfu* 隱覆; *mi* 密),[32] Tibetan translations lean toward the sense that what the Buddha teaches is "allusive" (e.g., *dgongs pa'i tshigs; ldem po ngag*). However, in each instance the Buddha reveals some truth that was not already explicit or even knowable, and that sits—like the single vehicle that is "revealed" by the SP—in undeniable tension with the dharma as it had so far been received.[33] Likely related to this motif is the awareness throughout all three texts of the MPNMS-group that their teachings will be opposed or challenged, and that a bodhisattva who promotes *tathāgatagarbha* will face difficult opposition for daring to do so. We can safely assume that the Buddha-nature idea—especially presented as the Buddha's account of the self—would have been contentious, and that its tension with teachings about absence of self could be permissible only if the *tathāgatagarbha* constituted some "secret" that the Buddha reveals just to certain audiences who were ready to receive it.[34]

---

31. AMS^{T} D.213, 169a6–7; Q.879.48, 176a8–b1: *sangs rgyas bcom ldan 'das ni mdo sde mtha' yas pa ldem po ngag tu ston pa'o // 'di ni lam gcig po ste / de bzhin gshegs pa ni theg pa gcig / skyabs gcig / bden pa gcig gi phyir 'brang ba / khams gcig pa / 'gro gcig pa / kha dog gcig pa ste / de bas na theg pa gcig ces bya'o // gzhan ni thabs kyi bya ba'o //* Compare AMS^{C} 532b8–12.

32. Blum's 2013 translation of MPNMS^{D} translates this as "recondite speech." Hoernle (1916, following Kern apropos of the SP; see note 28 above) refers to "mysterious sayings."

33. For more regarding this terminology, see Ruegg 1989b. Though Sanskrit expressions such as *saṃdhāya* frequently understand the Buddha to employ "oblique" or "intentional" utterances (see, for example, text in 2.6n120), this does not do justice to the sense in the MPNMS (and SP; see note 28 above) that the Buddha's *sandhāvacana* (perhaps a more technical expression) entails something close to a secret (Tib. *gsang ba:* Skt. *guhya*), and marks some tension between what the Buddha ostensibly taught (e.g., three vehicles; not-self) and the explanation that comes as something of a surprise to his audience (one vehicle; Buddha-nature). See especially MPNMS^{T} §219–221 (with corresponding material at MPNMS^{F} 872a25–b7; MPNMS^{D} 390b15–c24), which confronts the implication that the Buddha seems to have withheld teachings from his disciples in a manner comparable to an illusionist. See also Radich 2015a: 193–197.

34. Hodge (2010/2012: 48–60) has suggested that the *tathāgatagarbha* content of the MPNMS was initially some kind of esoteric doctrine, and not for audiences that would be unable to appreciate the revelation of a Buddhist self; see also 10.3. It is notable that the one mention of the *tathāgatagarbha* in the *Mahāmeghasūtra*—the fourth text (though likely not

However we interpret this motif, the issue of the Buddha's use of "cryptic" speech—his intentions not being clear to ignorant audiences—is found throughout the SP and MPNMS-group but is otherwise conspicuously absent from other *tathāgatagarbha* works, making no discernable appearance in surviving forms of the ŚDS, AAN, TGS, or RGV(V). Though the ŚDS states that *tathāgatagarbha* is something difficult for its audience to grasp, neither the Buddha nor Śrīmālā refer to use of "*saṃdhā-*" utterances, let alone anything "hidden" from earlier audiences.[35] What is presented in the MPNMS as new, mysterious, and clearly contentious is for the ŚDS no less difficult to comprehend, but not quite so novel as to warrant the same revelatory tone. With this in mind, if the ŚDS *did* predate the notion that the *tathāgatagarbha* was in any way something "secret," or expressed cryptically by the Buddha in order to accord with the understanding of its audience, it would be hard to imagine why any *later* text would introduce the air of mystery that we encounter throughout the MPNMS-group. It is therefore much more likely—as I have argued above (e.g., 5.2–3)—that the MPNMS-group of *sūtra*s reflects an earlier understanding of the *tathāgatagarbha*, whereas the authors of the ŚDS strove to reinvent *tathāgatagarbha* away from its evidently problematic, explicitly *ātmavādin* form.

The air of revelation in the MPNMS-group supports closer ties still between these works and the SP, but also a distance between these and the ŚDS, in which *tathāgatagarbha* appears to have been reimagined away from an earlier, more controversial context.[36] In place of any account of the Buddha's use of cryptic utterances, the ŚDS, AAN, and RGVV all affirm that acceptance of the *tathāgatagarbha* requires faith (*śraddhā*), testament still to the sense that this teaching is difficult for audiences to comprehend, even if it is not so clearly an affront to prior Buddhist teaching about, for example, absence of self.[37] In spite of its still challenging character, all three of these later texts evince a reconciliation between the expression

latest; see T. Suzuki 2001) of the MPNMS-group—occurs just after fleeting mention of the Buddha's "secret" (e.g., Ch. T.387[12]1102b19–21: *mizang* 密藏; Tib. D.232, 195a6–7: *gsang ba*), in what appears to be an allusion to more sustained discussion of this topic in other literature (perhaps the MPNMS).

35. Regarding a trace of this language preserved in the ŚDS, see 5.1n10.

36. Radich (2015a: 47n90) identifies that a possibly related and very relevant text may be the *Tathāgataguhyasūtra*, first translated into Chinese by Dharmarakṣa 竺法護, c. 280 CE (text no. 3 in T.310: *Miji jingang lishi hui* 密迹金剛力士會). This and other versions of the same text refer to the Buddha's "secret(s)" (*miyao* 祕要: **guhya*) and his body that is "like diamond (*vajra*)" (310[11]55a29–b9), as well as—with echoes of the *Tathāgatotpattisaṃbhavanirdeśa* (see 7.2n29)—the pervasiveness of the Buddha's knowledge (**buddhajñāna*) in the bodies of sentient beings (65c20: 如來至慧入我身中). Regarding reference to the *Tathāgataguhyasūtra* in the LAS, see Takasaki (1982) 2014: 133–134. The relation of this text to the Buddha-nature tradition requires further attention.

37. Regarding "faith" in the ŚDS, see, for example, ŚDS^{C1} 222a21–22. Regarding the AAN, see Silk 2015b: 92 (§10ii). Regarding the RGV(V), see Johnston (1950) 1991: 74.1–2 (v.1.153). See also Zimmermann 2014a: 522–525.

tathāgatagarbha and more widely accepted Buddhist teachings, including those that concern the intrinsically pure nature of the mind.

9.3 The Intrinsically Pure Mind

We have observed that the ŚDS, AAN, RGV(V), and LAS all understand *tathāgatagarbha* in terms of the intrinsically pure mind (*prakṛtipariśuddhacitta*), or the mind that is intrinsically luminous (*prakṛtiprabhāsvaracitta*).[38] This category dates back to early discourses preserved, for example, in the *Aṅguttaranikāya* of the Pāli canon, which contrast the intrinsic luminosity of the mind to afflictions that are adventitious to it (AN.I.70).[39] The same notion appears in earlier Mahāyānist sources, for example, in passing, in the *Aṣṭasāhasrikā-prajñāpāramitā*,[40] as well as in other, more developed literature such as the *Suvikrāntavikrāmiparipṛcchā-prajñāpāramitā*,[41] as well as a host of other *sūtra*s, including several that are quoted, at some length, by the RGVV.[42] An association between Buddha-nature and the fundamental nature of the mind is quite natural; both are usually contrasted with the myriad vices or afflictions (*kleśa*s)—passion, aversion, delusion, and so on—that are the enemies of Buddhist practice.[43] It is, however, revealing that the TGS and the works of the MPNMS-group, which likely reflect an older mode of Buddha-nature thinking, make virtually no mention of the mind in something like its "natural" state, and even then do not ever privilege this as an explanation of to what the expression *tathāgatagarbha* must refer.

Approval for an association between these two teachings is found in the ŚDS, which mentions the pure mind at the end of its account of the *tathāgatagarbha,* and reflects on the twin mysteries of its existence (apart from normal mental functions) and the manner in which this mind becomes tainted with afflictions (see 5.2). While the ŚDS does not explicitly identify the pure mind with the *tathāgatagarbha,* the sense that both are plagued by afflictions would leave no audience in any doubt that these are two perspectives on the same teaching. The AAN repeats the identification

---

38. Regarding how these expressions were rendered in Chinese translation (without clear distinction between them), see Silk 2015b: 135–140.

39. See also Anālayo 2017. Perhaps the most thorough discussion of the luminous mind—its basis in *sūtra* literature and development in later Buddhist works—remains Ruegg 1969: 409–437; see also Takasaki 1974: 704–721; Radich 2016: 256–262, 268–279.

40. Vaidya 1960: 3.18.

41. Hikata 1958: 85.15–86.13; for further sources, see Radich 2016: 270.

42. The RGVV draws from the *Sāgaramatiparipṛcchā* (T.397[13]67b5–74c10, text number 5) and *Gaganagañjaparipṛcchā* (T.397[13]122a3–128a2, text number 8); see Takasaki 1966: 34–35; 1974: 673–704. Interpretation of *tathāgatagarbha* in the RGVV in terms of the intrinsically pure mind was an important feature of the text's interpretation by the eleventh-century Kashmiri master Sajjana, regarding whom see Kanō 2016: 135–139, 154, 211–228.

43. See, for example, Zimmerman 2002: 294. Regarding these in Pāli tradition, see Harvey 1995: 166–168.

of *tathāgatagarbha* with the intrinsically pure mind but is even more concerned with *tathāgatagarbha* as a designator for the single (*eka-*), or indeed "pure" (*viśuddha*) *dharmadhātu,* that is, the single reality or "nature/realm of *dharmas*" common to both transmigrating and liberated beings. This identification is crucial for the AAN, and—in accordance with its preoccupation with "reality" properly conceived—may reflect a subtly different take on *tathāgatagarbha* as some metaphysical basis to different modes of being (see 6.1).

Otherwise the mind that is intrinsically pure is a key element of early verses in the composition of the RGV; as far back as one of its basic root verses (1.149, at the beginning of "String B": see 7.2) the RGV identifies the (*buddha*)*dhātu* with the intrinsically stainless mind (*cittaprakṛtivaimalya*). The commentarial RGVV develops this at some length, and uses a number of other Mahāyānist *sūtras*—associated with the **Mahāsaṃnipāta* collection of texts—to flesh out the manner in which *tathāgatagarbha* must refer to the intrinsically pure mind, that is, a notion familiar from wider Mahāyānist teaching.[44] The position of the LAS is more developed still: the identification of the *tathāgatagarbha* with the mind—pivotal in the ŚDS—opens the door to a full-throated equation of the *tathāgatagarbha* with the *ālayavijñāna,* the subliminal stratum of consciousness taught in the Yogācāra-Vijñānavāda tradition, which must run across successive lives (see 8.3).

In contrast to all of this, the texts of the MPNMS-group show little or no interest in Buddha-nature understood in mentalistic terms. Neither the MPNMS nor MBhS make any clear reference to Buddha-nature in terms of the intrinsically pure mind. This should not, given what we have seen otherwise, surprise us; for these texts, the *tathāgatagarbha* constitutes the presence of the corporeal essence of the Buddha somehow "within" one's person, language that does not so easily describe something "mental." Though both the MPNMS and AMS critique the search for the *tathāgatagarbha* in the physical body (see 2.3–4, 3.3–4), it is clear that this is taught as something like an essential component of a sentient being, and exists in some imperceptible opposition to the "heaps" of experience (*skandhas*), physical elements (*dhātus*), and—most frequently—afflictions of character that obscure it.[45]

One very intriguing mention of the pure mind does feature, rather fleetingly, in the AMS. However, close attention to this material suggests agreement with neither the ŚDS nor RGV(V). At one point in the AMS, the Buddha explains to the bodhisattva Mañjuśrī the cryptic meaning (see 9.2

44. Ruegg 1969: 417–424; see also note 39 above.

45. I tentatively suggest that the texts of the MPNMS-group do not present afflictions—desire, anger, delusion, etcetera—as strictly *mental* phenomena so much as afflictions of *character.* The difference is on one level trivial, but the *ātmavādin* mode of *tathāgatagarbha* teaching wants for an end to afflictions without focusing on their presence "in the mind," and attends instead to the obscuration of the superlative character, and accompanying activities, of a future Buddha.

above) of two plausibly famous verses, preserved in the *Dhammapada,* which the AMS understands must refer to the mind that is intrinsically pure (*zixing qingjingyi* 自性清淨意; *yid rang bzhin gyis dag pa: *cittaprakṛtiviśuddhi*). The first verse cited is clearly the second verse of the *Dhammapada,* which states that happiness accompanies "like a shadow" whoever thinks and acts in a pure fashion.[46] The Buddha states that this teaching was for the benefit of the Śrāvakayāna—that is, pursuit of the status of an arhat—and that the mind that is intrinsically pure refers to the *tathāgatagarbha.*[47] The mind without afflictions, we are told, reveals one's own true nature (**ātmadhātu;* see 3.2); when a bodhisattva performs the actions of a Buddha, he "sees the *tathāgatagarbha*" in the actions of the bodhisattva, "like a shadow."[48] The Buddha then clarifies the very first verse of the *Dhammapada,* which reflects on how suffering follows those who are wicked in the fashion that the wheels of an ox-cart follow the ox; the cryptic referent, we are told, is the *tathāgatagarbha* and its acquisition of afflictions.[49]

In both instances the AMS takes the purity of the mind to refer to the *tathāgatagarbha,* the inverse of what seems to be the position of the ŚDS. In the AMS the intrinsically pure mind is presented as something that was taught for the benefit of *śrāvaka*s, and with reference to a text (the *Dhammapada*) representative of earlier or "mainstream" Buddhist teachings, whereas the audience of the AMS should know that this in fact refers to the Buddha's cryptic meaning that is revealed now, to those who are superior, in the Mahāyāna. Hence it is quite possible that the authors of the AMS knew of a mentalistic interpretation of *tathāgatagarbha* exhibited in works such as the ŚDS (see 5.4) but did not approve this interpretation, and taught instead that an account of the intrinsic purity of the mind is superseded by revelation of the *tathāgatagarbha,* or otherwise the enduring nature of a Buddha ready to act in the world, as affirmed in its own lines.

In summary, interpretation of the *tathāgatagarbha* in terms of the intrinsic purity of the mind, or indeed some stratum or undercurrent of the mind that runs through successive births, does not seem to belong to our earliest articulations of Buddha-nature teaching.[50] By contrast, the Buddha-nature idea articulated in the language of the MPNMS-group is a quite different thing: the abiding essence of the Buddha—otherwise one's true

46. *Dhammapada* v.2 (von Hinüber and Norman 1994: 1): *manopubbaṅgamā dhammā manoseṭṭhā manomayā, manasā ce pasannena bhāsatī vā karoti vā tato naṃ sukham anveti chāyā'va anapāyinī.*

47. AMS^{C} 540a3–4: 我爲聲聞乘説此偈。意者謂如來藏義。若自性清淨意，是如來藏。Compare AMS^{T} D.213, 194b5–7; Q.879, 202a3–4.

48. AMS^{C} 540a4–8. Compare AMS^{T} D.213, 194b5–7; Q.879, 202a4–6.

49. AMS^{C} 540a9–17. Compare AMS^{T} D.213, 194b7–195a3; Q.879, 202a4–b1; see also *Dhammapada* v.1 (von Hinüber and Norman 1994: 1).

50. Regarding some accounts of what happens to the mind after its purification, with reference to the **amalavijñāna* or "stainless consciousness" that is developed in works associated with Paramārtha, see Frauwallner 1951; Radich 2016.

self—that resides enigmatically "within" the constitution of a sentient being, and surpasses anything taught to followers of the Śrāvakayāna, or mainstream Buddhist tradition.

9.4 "Sarvalokapriyadarśana"

Another curious feature common to the SP, AMS, and MBhS is the appearance of a bodhisattva whose name translates as something like "A Sight Dear to All Sentient Beings."[51] In the SP this is Sarvasattvapriyadarśana, but in both the AMS and MBhS he seems to be *Sarvalokapriyadarśana (e.g., AMS 一切世間現; *'jig rten thams cad kyis blta na sdug pa*; MBhS 一切世間樂見; *'jig rten thams cad kyis mthong na dga' ba*). In the SP, Sarvasattvapriyadarśana is first used as the name of a Buddha—the future awakened form of the Buddha's stepmother, Mahāprajāpatī—but in a later chapter is also the name of a bodhisattva who had revered a previous Buddha by setting himself alight; a superlative offering that acquired for him a tremendous quantity of merit.[52]

In the AMS, *Sarvalokapriyadarśana is the birth name given to the Brahmana who becomes a notorious killer and adopts the mantle Aṅgulimāla.[53] At the end of the text Aṅgulimāla is revealed to be a strategic creation by a Buddha who resides in a distant world, who is named "Superior Great Exertion, the Sight of Whom Is Dear to All the World," perhaps *Sarvalokapriyadarśana-Abhyudgatamahāvīrya.[54] This revelatory climax to the AMS associates Aṅgulimāla's (displayed) birth name—perhaps one that was very meaningful to some Indian audiences—with allusion to the idealized bodhisattva's superhuman toil if (s)he is ever to ascend to the status of a Buddha, a theme common to both the AMS and to the self-immolation episode of the SP.

Meanwhile in the MBhS *Sarvalokapriyadarśana is a young bodhisattva from the high-born Licchavi clan, who alone among the Buddha's congregation is able to see and ensnare the insidious deity Māra hiding among the assembly.[55] The Buddha predicts that in the final eighty years of the dharma's presence in the world, the MBhS will be proclaimed and defended by this same bodhisattva, who will be born and reign as a king in "the South."[56] The same figure appears in similar circumstances in the

51. See Takasaki 1974: 295–296; T. Suzuki 1996b; 1999b; Hodge 2006; Radich 2015a: 199–202 (especially 199n481).

52. SP 268.6–269.5, then later 404.9–415.9; also Kern 1884: 255–258, 376–379; Benn 2009.

53. See, for example, AMS^{C} 512b16–18.

54. AMS^{C} 543a18 (一切世間樂見上大精進); AMS^{T} D.213, 204a2; Q.879, 211b7–8 (*'jig rten thams cad mthong na dga' ba mngon par 'phags pa brtson pa chen po*).

55. MBhS^{C} 298b24–299a12; MBhS^{T} D.222, 118a5–125b4; Q.888, 124a2–132b3.

56. See 4.5n66. The prophecy of the MBhS specifically is a focus of Dol po pa's RC (Hopkins 2006: 182–184).

Mahāmeghasūtra, the fourth text of the MPNMS-group, otherwise absent from this study due to its relative lack of interest in teachings about Buddha-nature.[57] Though no figure by this name appears in the MPNMS, Stephen Hodge (2006) has argued that a mysterious bodhisattva "of the family of Mahākāśyapa" may be a coded reference to *Sarvalokapriyadarśana also.

Hodge's further argument—developed also by Michael Radich—is that the name *Sarvalokapriyadarśana ties the prophecy complex common to the MPNMS-group (in which the dharma disappears seven hundred years after the Buddha's *parinirvāṇa*) to the reign of the Śātavāhana dynasty, in the second century of the Common Era, and in the Andhra region of South India (see also 10.2).[58] There is otherwise an argument that this figure may be a reference to the philosopher Nāgārjuna, who has long been associated with the Śātavāhanas in this period.[59] Whether or not *Sarvalokapriyadarśana was intended to allude to a real-world personage, and perhaps someone still known to modern scholarship, the fleeting but perhaps at one time significant mention of this figure throughout the MPNMS-group evinces further ties between these *sūtra*s and, prior to them, the SP.

9.5 Emptiness and Nonemptiness

Another recurring theme that we encounter throughout the *tathāgatagarbha* literature is how an account of Buddha-nature—which entails the persistence of some entity or principle, called *ātman* or otherwise, across successive lives—should be understood in light of more established Buddhist and particularly Mahāyānist teachings about the emptiness (*śūnyatā*) of all phenomena. Mahāyānist literature frequently relies on an apophatic mode of discourse that, by one interpretation, is an extension of not-self teaching that discourages grasping to any entity as if it were reliably, foundationally "real" (see 1.2). Indeed, literature concerned with the "perfection of insight" (*prajñāpāramitā*)—which is particularly focused on emptiness as absence of independent nature (*niḥsvabhāva*) or indeed of any "self" to phenomena (*dharmanairātmya*)—was profoundly influential for the Mahāyānist imagination from an early stage. Jikidō Takasaki devoted a chapter of his *Nyoraizō shisō no keisei* to the *prajñāpāramitā* literature and its influence on the

57. T.387(12)1100a2–7. See also 2.2n22. The passage concerning Sarvalokapriyadarśana in the *Mahāmeghasūtra* is reproduced in the *Suvarṇaprabhāsasūtra* (surviving also in Sanskrit); see 10.4n69.

58. See Hodge 2006 (which anticipates as yet unpublished research by the same author); also Radich 2015a: 59–99 (especially 61n126); 199–205. Regarding Indian Buddhist "eschatology" more broadly, see Nattier 1991; Watanabe 2009.

59. Walser 2005: 71–73. For further references, see also Radich 2015a: 199n481. See also above 9.1n22.

tathāgatagarbha tradition.[60] However, Takasaki's focus in that chapter was the RGVV, and not the influence of the *prajñāpāramitā* tradition visible upon *sūtra* texts concerned with Buddha-nature—that is, works earlier than the RGVV—that have been the primary concern of this study.

Takasaki's understanding of the *tathāgatagarbha* literature prioritized (in his ordering) the TGS, AAN, and ŚDS as likely the earliest and most formative texts in this tradition. Of these, neither the TGS nor AAN show any marked interest in teachings about emptiness. But most other sources for Buddha-nature teaching are notable for having attempted to situate *tathāgatagarbha*—a kataphatic account of that which is permanent, lasting, and enduring across successive lives—in relation to one or other understanding of emptiness. The LAS, we have seen, understands *tathāgatagarbha* to be an entry into comprehension of emptiness, signlessness, and absence of intention, three central teachings of the *prajñāpāramitā* tradition (see 8.2).[61] The RGVV invokes *prajñāpāramitā* teaching when interpreting the enigmatic expression *ātmapāramitā;* "perfection of self" refers to knowing absence of self, at which one arrives through the perfection of insight (see 7.3). However, the basic root verses of the RGV acknowledge a tension between the *buddhadhātu* and the claim—reminiscent of *prajñāpāramitā* teaching—that all phenomena should be thought of as like clouds, dreams, or illusions (see 7.2); insofar as this might have intended a reference to earlier teaching about *tathāgatagarbha,* the RGV likely remembered the unease that some Buddha-nature texts exhibited regarding emptiness and its implications for certain audiences (see below).

The RGVV understands knowledge of the *tathāgatagarbha* to be the knowledge of emptiness that is proper to the Buddhas.[62] However, the content of this knowledge has been much disputed. In Tibet the RGVV was at the center of debate over the correct interpretation of emptiness, concerned with whether in the final instance this refers to an emptiness of some "other" (*gzhan stong*) from the awakened mind—as implied by the ŚDS, RGVV, and other Buddha-nature works—or better the universal "emptiness of itself" (*rang stong*) that accords better with declarations made by the *prajñāpāramitā* tradition.[63] The most influential declaration about

60. Takasaki 1974: 370–411.

61. Regarding "emptiness of other" in the LAS, see Mathes 2012: 195–198. Closer inspection of different interpretations of emptiness in the LAS (see Nanjio 1923: 73.11–77.1) exceeds what it is possible to discuss in this chapter.

62. Johnston (1950) 1991: 76.15: *tathāgatagarbhajñānam eva tathāgatānāṃ śūnyatājñānam.*

63. Regarding reception of the RGVV as a source for the *gzhan stong* position, see Ruegg 1969: 319–346; Hookham 1991; D. Wangchuk 2004: 172–174n3; Mathes 2004; 2008: 45–48; 2011 (2012); 2015; T. Wangchug 2017. Tibetan teachers who favored this interpretation include representatives of the Jonang pa tradition, such as Dol po pa (see, e.g., Stearns 2010; Hopkins 2006) and the celebrated historian Tarānātha (1575–1635). See also Burchardi 2007; Williams 2009: 112–115; and contributions to Mathes and Sheehy 2019.

In an Indian context, Mathes (2012: especially 191–194) finds the "emptiness-of-other" position of the RGVV to accord with Yogācāra-Vijñānavāda accounts of emptiness prominent

emptiness in the RGVV is drawn from the ŚDS, which held that sentient beings cannot know *tathāgatagarbha* due to having minds that are confused or bewildered by teachings about emptiness (see 7.4). Though the ŚDS makes no mention of the *prajñāpāramitā* literature, its authors likely had this tradition in mind when clarifying that *tathāgatagarbha* is simultaneously both empty, of what is not proper to it, and not empty of its real attributes:

> Lord, there are two kinds of knowledge of the emptiness of the *tathāgatagarbha*. Lord, the empty *tathāgatagarbha* is separate from, apart from, other to its covering by afflictions. Lord, the not empty *tathāgatagarbha* is not separate from, apart from, or other to the inconceivable qualities of a Buddha, which surpass in number the sands of the Ganges.[64]

This passage is repeated by the RGVV, which applies this same language to the *(buddha)dhātu,* or otherwise (in this text) the intrinsically pure nature of the mind.[65] While this certainly does not constitute a rejection of teachings about emptiness, the authors of the ŚDS clearly held that the meaning of emptiness teachings had to be reassessed when it comes to the *tathāgatagarbha,* which—if it is to mean anything—must be the very real, enduring, and moreover valuable presence of qualities proper to liberation in respect to every sentient being.

However, the ŚDS was likely not the first text of the *tathāgatagarbha* tradition to espouse something like the "nonemptiness" of liberation. All three texts of the MPNMS-group challenge prior understandings of emptiness teachings, and espouse what the LAS would later call teachings about "emptiness of one thing from another" (*itaretaraśūnyatā*).[66] We have seen already that the MPNMS makes only passing reference to the *prajñāpāramitā* literature, and there in the context of the supposed "nonduality" of *ātman* and *anātman* (see 2.6). However, outside of its account of Buddha-nature, the MPNMS offers a fuller exposition about emptiness and how it relates to the liberated state of the Buddha. The MPNMS criticizes the idea that

---

in other works attributed to Maitreya, foremost the *Madhyāntavibhāgakārikā* (v.1.20–22; see Nagao 1964: 26.9–27.20), in which we find emptiness understood in terms of the intrinsically luminous mind, free of adventitious afflictions. Mathes considers the *Madhyāntavibhāgakārikā* to have been influenced by the RGV(V), which itself—we observe—follows a longer tradition of understanding emptiness in extrinsic terms.

64. ŚDS^{C1} 221c16–18: 世尊，有二種如來藏空智。世尊，空如來藏若離、若脱、若異，一切煩惱藏。世尊，不空如來藏，過於恒沙，不離、不脱、不異、不思議佛法。 Compare ŚDS^{C2} 677a22–25; ŚDS^{T} 130.13–132.4. The latter portion of this passage is preserved by the Sanskrit RGVV (Johnston [1950] 1991: 55.14–15): *aśūnyo bhagavaṃs tathāgatagarbho gaṅgānadīvālukāvyativṛttair avinirbhāgair amuktajñair acintyair buddhadharmair iti* / Regarding the expression *amuktajña,* see Ruegg 2015: 320–325; Silk 2015b: 141–148.

65. Johnston (1950) 1991: 76.1–4. See also Takasaki 1966: 302n62.

66. See, for example, Nanjio 1923: 75.10–19; also Mathes 2012: 195–198. Regarding "not-empty" teachings in the MPNMS-group, see also T. Suzuki 2000a.

"emptiness" refers to "nothing whatsoever" (*wusuoyou* 無所有; *ci yang med pa: *ākiṃcanya*), which we are told is something proper to non-Buddhist renunciants.[67] Just as vessels can be "empty" of some content but are also not empty by virtue of still having attributes, liberation can be called empty and also not empty:

> Liberation, in that way, is not empty. Liberation also has form and excellent color; in the manner that a yoghurt pot is not empty, yet when lacking yoghurt is called empty, likewise liberation also is not empty but is called empty. While it has form, how can it be called empty? "Empty" means absence of the many afflictions, of the twenty-five existences, of suffering, of worldly creeds, rites and activities; hence, like absence of yoghurt from a yoghurt pot, liberation is called empty. Here, just as the form of a pot remains consistent, [liberation] is very pleasant, joyous, permanent, lasting, enduring, and is characterized by supermundane creeds, rites and activities. Like the form of the pot liberation is permanent, lasting and enduring, but the pot can be broken if it is so much as dropped, whereas liberation, because it is not something that is made, cannot be broken. That which is liberation is the uncreated essence (*bcos ma ma yin pa'i khams: *akṛtrimadhātu*), which is precisely the Tathāgata.[68]

Both Chinese versions of this passage conclude without apparent mention of any *dhātu*, but agree that this liberation is the state of the Tathāgata. All three versions of this material teach that liberation is both empty—that is, "without" afflictions, rebirth, suffering, and many more "worldly" phenomena—yet is also *not* empty by virtue of still having some "form" (*su* 色; *gzugs: rūpa*), so cannot be "nothing whatsoever."

We have seen that liberation having "form" was important also to the MBhS, in which the Buddha warned that audiences unprepared for teachings

67. MPNMS^{D} (395b15–16) states that "*nirgrantha*s think of liberation as nothing whatsoever," but this translation perhaps obscures wordplay intended by the Indic text: the *nirgrantha* is someone who has forsaken all possessions or bonds (*nis-grantha*), and so sees pursuit of liberation in terms of having "nothing whatsoever."

68. MPNMS^{T} §280.10–27: *thar pa ni de lta bur stong pa ma yin te / thar pa la ni gzugs dang kha dog phun sum tshogs pa yang yod na / ji ltar zho'i bum pa stong pa ma yin du zin kyang zho med pa'i phyir stong pa zhes bya ba bzhin du thar pa yang stong pa ma yin bzhin du stong pa zhes bya ba ste / gzugs yod bzhin du ji ltar stong pa zhes bya zhe na / stong pa zhes bya ba ni nyon mongs pa'i rnam pa dang / srid pa'i tha snyad nyi shu rtsa lnga dang / sdug bsngal dang / 'jig rten gyi chos lugs dang / cho ga dang / spyod yul 'byung ba rnams med pa'i phyir zho'i bum pa zho med pa bzhin du thar pa la stong pa zhes bya ba ste / de la ni bum pa'i gzugs mi g.yo ba bzhin du shas cher bde ba dang / dga' ba dang / rtag pa dang / brtan pa dang / ther zug dang / 'jig rten las 'das pa'i chos dang / cho ga dang / spyod yul rnams yod do // thar pa ni bum pa'i gzugs bzhin du rtag pa dang / brtan pa dang / ther zug pa ma yin gyi / bum pa ni chag par 'gyur te / rgyu'i sgo nas bzhag pa tsam du zad do // thar pa ni byas pa ma yin pa'i phyir chag par mi 'gyur la / thar pa gang yin pa de ni bcos ma ma yin pa'i khams yin te / de ni de bzhin gshegs pa'o //* Compare (including the introduction to this passage) MPNMS^{F} 875a10–20; MPNMS^{D} 395b14–c2. This material is referenced in Dol po pa's RC (Hopkins 2006: 213–214).

about the *tathāgatagarbha* would retreat into an annihilationist interpretation of emptiness. Indeed, the MBhS goes so far as to devalue teachings about emptiness to "intentional" (*ābhiprāyika*) status, and so are superseded by teachings about Buddha-nature (see 4.5). The notion that emptiness designates "nothing whatsoever" or an absence of qualities (*wuwu* 無物; *ci yang med pa: *ākiṃcanya*) features also in the AMS, which reflects similar language to that which we see in the MPNMS (above). At one stage in the AMS, the bodhisattva Mañjuśrī compares the Buddha and his liberation to space (*ākāśa*), due to their absence of characteristics, origination, and form; Aṅgulimāla, Mañjuśrī concludes, cannot know the manner in which emptiness refers to "nothing whatsoever."[69] Aṅgulimāla responds with a simile, in which a foolish man treasures a hailstone that he takes to be a precious jewel. The foolish man stores the hailstone in a jar and, as it melts, thinks it to be worthless; Mañjuśrī is like someone who would take all jewels to be like hailstones, so considers all *dharma*s to be empty (in the sense, it seems, of being "unreal"), when some are in fact "not-empty," and worth treasuring.[70]

Aṅgulimāla then provides his own account of emptiness, which clearly understands the concept in extrinsic terms—that is, "*x* is empty of *y*"—and takes emptiness to mean houses empty of people, rivers bereft of water, and so on. He concludes as follows, presenting emptiness in a manner very reminiscent of what we read in the ŚDS:

> The true liberation of the Tathāgata is not empty, in just this way.
> Being apart from all faults, liberation is said to be empty.
> The Tathāgata is really not empty, [but] is apart from all afflictions,
> Including the heaps [of experience] proper to gods and men, so is called "empty."[71]

All texts of the MPNMS-group are invested in denying that emptiness teachings refer in some manner to the nonexistence of the Buddha, and—by extension—the presence of Buddha-nature in all sentient beings. Though there is little doubt that their authors recognized the authority of teachings about emptiness, they reject these insofar as they were understood to provide a universal truth about all phenomena, including those that are supermundane or, in other words, characteristic of liberation. For the early Buddha-nature tradition, the definitive teaching of the Buddha—something that had been expressed cryptically, or even kept "secret"—is a

69. AMS^C 527b7–15; AMS^T D.213, 159b3–5; Q.879, 167a1–4.

70. An English translation of this material, following AMS^T, is Brunnhölzl 2014: 20–21; see also use of this material in Dol po pa's RC (Hopkins 2006: 210–212).

71. AMS^C 527c10–13: 如來真解脱 / 不空亦如是 / 出離一切過 / 故說解脱空 / 如來實不空 / 離一切煩惱 / 及諸天人陰 / 是故說名空。Compare AMS^T D.213, 160a7–b1; Q.879, 167b5–2 (in which there is no reference to the "heaps" of experience [Ch. *yin* 陰: Skt. *skandhas*]).

distinctly kataphatic articulation of liberation and the propensity for achieving it. Though an account of the "not-empty" nature of the *tathāgatagarbha* survives in the ŚDS, it is in the MPNMS and AMS that this contentious idea receives greater attention and justification—further evidence, it is likely, of the relative antiquity of these two, more unconventional Buddhist texts.

When Aṅgulimāla admonishes Mañjuśrī for his poor grasp of emptiness, he states that followers of other systems also practice in accordance with "emptiness," and that non-Buddhist renunciants (*nirgrantha*s)—to whom Mañjuśrī is unfavorably compared—must be silent about such things.[72] In the MPNMS, when the Buddha clarifies the meaning of the four truths, he states that were cultivation of total emptiness to lead to the cessation of suffering, then practitioners of non-Buddhist systems would know this also.[73] An interest in what non-Buddhists have to say about emptiness leads us to a final and very important theme that runs through the Indian Buddha-nature tradition: the resemblances and differences between Buddhist and non-Buddhist accounts of liberation, and the sense that teachings about Buddha-nature surpass, but also help to explain, all manner of other religious teachings found in the world.

9.6 Non-Buddhists and Their Teachings

Later works of the *tathāgatagarbha* corpus—namely the RGVV and LAS—understand any association between the *tathāgatagarbha* and the language of selfhood to have intended the conversion or development of non-Buddhists: those commonly referred to by some or other variation on the Indic expression *tīrthika*. This denotes advocates of any rival Indian tradition of thought and practice that espoused some alternative account of transmigration and liberation from it.[74] As we see in both the RGVV and LAS, non-Buddhists were commonly associated with false notions of the self; theirs could not be reliable accounts of transmigration and its end, as they could not get as far as the fundamental Buddhist teaching that occupation with the notion of an enduring self (*ātman*) is detrimental to pursuit of liberation. Both the RGVV and LAS teach that if the Buddha seemed to employ an account of a self (or in the RGVV, after the ŚDS, "the perfection of self"), this could have been only a strategy for appealing to and

72. AMS^{C} 527c15 (外道亦修空). AMS^{T} (D.213, 160b1–2; Q.879, 167b6–7) states more clearly that "*nirgrantha*s also cultivate [the idea of] everything as being empty" (*gcer bu pa yang thams cad stong par sgom ste*).

73. MPNMS^{F} 883a4: 彼諸外道相違義者，亦修行空得滅諦耶? Compare MPNMS^{D} 406c10–11; MPNMS^{T} §369.3–5. MPNMS^{T} here refers to "the adverse account of emptiness, proper to non-Buddhist sectarians (*pāṣaṇḍa*s)" (§369.3–5: *ya mtshan can thams cad la yang don dang 'gal ba'i stong pa nyid*).

74. Certainly not what is commonly denoted by the English "heretic," with which this expression is often translated; see Jones forthcoming.

then correcting rivals of Buddhist dharma, who require such a notion in order to begin to accept the Buddha's teachings about absence of self (*nairātmya*), or not-self (*anātman*) with respect to all phenomena.

This is how the *tathāgatagarbha* and its relation to discourse about the self seem to have been remembered both in India and in much modern scholarship.[75] According to the LAS (as well as authors influenced by it; see 8.6), the sense that the *tathāgatagarbha* constitutes something like a self can only be an instance of the Buddha's pedagogical strategizing, or skill-in-methods (*upāyakauśalya*); the Buddha cannot have genuinely departed from teaching about transmigration and its end that eschews any notion of the self (what we have called the *nairātmyavāda;* see 1.1). But this is a long way from bold assertions made in the MPNMS-group of texts: that the Buddha taught about not-self only in order to combat erroneous notions of the self, associated with non-Buddhist teachings about liberation (see 2.2, 3.3, 4.5), and *not* because there is nothing on the supermundane level that warrants calling the self. If we take at face value what is said by the MPNMS, AMS, and MBhS themselves, we are left in little doubt that authors of these texts meant to present *tathāgatagarbha* as nothing less than the correct account of the self, in opposition to what was found in the teachings of non-Buddhists systems.

Throughout the Buddha-nature tradition—and with unusual detail for Mahāyāna *sūtra* literature—we encounter a great deal of attention to the content and status of non-Buddhist ideas and practices, especially (but unsurprisingly) apropos of the self. We benefit from reviewing non-Buddhist ideas that seem to have been known to the authors of the MPNMS and AMS in particular, in order to identify what forms of *ātmavādin* teachings were known to them, and with which the *tathāgatagarbha* was held to be at least superficially similar. Most noticeable in the MPNMS-group are language and imagery reminiscent of the Brahmanical tradition, the Upaniṣads in particular, and—even more specifically—imagery found in "middle period" Upaniṣads that were likely produced in the later centuries of the first millennium BCE (and so, we note, after the earliest intellectual context for Buddhist rejection of discourse about the self, several hundred years earlier).[76] Both the MPNMS and AMS oppose ideas about the self—including its location in the heart, some sense organ, or elsewhere in the body—that invite comparison to the *Chāndogya-*, *Kaṭha-*, and *Śvetāśvatara-upaniṣads* (see 2.4 and 3.3). The MPNMS affirms that there is neither "killer" nor "killed" amid what is proper to a sentient being, with strong echoes

75. Explored eloquently by Ruegg (1989a: 17–55), who provides a sophisticated discussion of *ātmavāda* discourse as unpacked by the RGVV and the LAS in particular.

76. See Olivelle 1998: 12–13. These "middle period" Upaniṣads include the *Īśā-*, *Praśna-*, *Muṇḍaka-*, *Kaṭha-*, *Śvetāśvatara-*, and *Kena-upaniṣads*, regarding which see relevant chapters in Cohen 2018 (especially Killingley 2018b). We return to the significance of these apropos of early Buddha-nature thought in the next chapter (10.4).

of the *Katha-upaniṣad* (and, moreover, the *Bhagavadgītā*).[77] At a greater stretch, the account of the "single nature" (*ekadhātu*) in the AMS—as well as injunctions against eating meat found in both this and the MPNMS (see 3.6)—bears resemblance to what is taught by the theologically developed *Īśā-upaniṣad*, which declares that the self exhibits "oneness" (*ekatva*) across its different, embodied expressions, such that one should "eat [only] what has been abandoned," and "not kill what is the self."[78]

The AMS is aware of the idea that the self, were it to be found, might exhibit some color (see 3.3). Our Upaniṣadic comparison here is the *Muṇḍaka-upaniṣad*, which agrees with the AMS that the self cannot have any color to it.[79] A Brahmanical account of colors of the self appears in a portion of the *Mahābhārata* (12.271.33–55), in which the sage Bhīṣma explains *karma* to be a material substance that clings to and discolors the intrinsically pure status of the self.[80] Again an exceptional occurrence, the third- or fourth-century **Satyasiddhiśāstra* (T.1646: *Chengshi lun* 成實論) of Harivarman gives a Brahmanical account of selfhood similar to that represented in the AMS, in which colors are clearly associated with the respective *ātman* of each *varṇa* (which also brings to mind criticism about erroneous *ātmavāda* teaching found in the MPNMS; see 2.4).[81] By comparison, the idea that the self exhibits some or other color is much better established in Jain doctrine, in which different colors (*leśyā*s) of the self correspond to levels of spiritual development, itself perhaps indebted to the more ancient account of colorings (*abhijāti*s) taught by the Ājīvikas.[82]

There is clearly some similarity between the model of Buddha-nature found in the MPNMS-group and the Jain and (though our sources are sparse) Ājīvika teachings about selfhood, in which what is proper to one's self (*jīva*, but in many Jain sources also *ātman*) transmigrates due to some manner of affliction accidental to what one truly is. In Jainism these are the "channels" (*āsrava*s) through which karmic residue accrues, which in

77. Olivelle 1998: 384–385 (v.2.19); see also 2.4n88.

78. See Olivelle 1998: 405–411 (especially v.1, 3, 6 and 7).

79. Ibid., 444–445 (v.1.1.6). The *Muṇḍaka-upaniṣad* makes special mention of the value of renunciation (*saṃnyāsa*) and of asceticism (*tapas*) over the performance of ritual (1.2.11–12). This text may have had origins that were especially close to developments in Brahmanical renunciation, and understandably shows greater concern with ideas and activities proper to the Buddhist and Jain traditions (Cohen 2008: 179–180; 2018: 312–313).

80. See also H. Nakamura 1955: 86–88; Bedekar 1968; Brockington 2002: 106. The self (here *jīva*) is also compared to gold purified in a furnace, an image familiar from the MBhS (see 4.4), and found also in Jain accounts of liberation (Jaini 1977: 97–100).

81. T.1646(13)316b4–8. See also H. Nakamura 1955: 82.

82. See Balcerowicz 1997: 208n31; Dundas 2002: 43. Both authors attend to a passage in the Jain *Āyāraṅgasutta* (1.5.6.4: Jacobi 1882: 26), which states that the liberated *jīva* lacks shape, color, odor, taste, etcetera. It is plausible that the qualities of the self were a point of dispute between the Jains and Ājīvikas, though this may have been quite ancient by the time of our Mahāyānist sources. See also Basham 1951: 243–245; Wiley 2000.

turn obstructs the *jīva*'s natural omniscience.[83] An important difference is that Jainism understands the *jīva/ātman* to be also an agent (*kartṛ*) and recipient (*bhoktṛ*) of karmic results;[84] insofar as this intends the performer of actions or "worldly" agent, the *tathāgatagarbha* tradition is quite clear that Buddha-nature sits apart from this process (see, e.g., 3.5). Michael Zimmermann has also observed similarities between Buddha-nature teaching (in the context of the TGS) and the model of liberation proper to Pāśupata Śaivism: the manifestation (*abhivyakti*) of qualities proper also to Śiva, apart from impurities (*mala*).[85] The Pāśupata conception of the relationship between the supreme deity (Maheśvara/Rudra, or simply *pati*) and the self (*paśu,* "one who is bound") is such that the latter can come to exhibit the perfect qualities of the former, realizing a liberated state characterized by omniscience, superlative power, and so on.[86]

Our early *tathāgatagarbha sūtra*s also show familiarity with the habits and practices of non-Buddhist renunciants—according to the AMS, those called, for example, *brāhmaṇa*s, *pravrājya*s, *nirgrantha*s, and even **pāśupata*s (see 3.7)—who would have likely considered the self and the search for it a central aspect of their religious vocation. The MPNMS voices concern that non-Buddhist practices—staying still for great lengths of time, leaping from cliffs, lying in ashes, use of spells, and so forth—should not be confused for what has been taught by the Buddha to his bodhisattvas.[87] Both the MPNMS and AMS were remembered by the LAS as sources for teachings about vegetarianism (see 8.1), but are also careful to distinguish their dietary proscriptions from more austere or "vegan" avoidance of all animal produce or remains altogether (see 3.6).[88] Finally, as we saw above (9.5), both the MPNMS and AMS feature the curious suggestion that there are non-Buddhist teachers who espouse doctrines about emptiness, referring to the position that there exists "nothing whatsoever." A possibility is that these are references to something like Cārvāka tradition, which held the view that no entity survives its present life, and accordingly that pursuit of liberation is a pointless enterprise.[89] We also cannot exclude the possibility that what our authors had in mind was some non-Buddhist tradition(s),

83. See Dundas 2002: 88–89. The MPNMS and AMS are also aware of selfhood conceived as something that pervades the body, in the manner classically associated with the *jīva;* see Jain 1935.

84. Jhaveri 1977: 238–239.

85. Zimmermann 2002: 67.

86. Indeed, this is the basic model for liberation common to many forms of Śaivism that were influenced by the Pāśupata tradition; see Acharya 2014: 9–14; also Sanderson 1988: 664–665. I am grateful to Diwakar Acharya for valuable discussion about this matter.

87. See MPNMS^F 882b19–25; MPNMS^D 406a16–25; MPNMS^T §364.

88. See MPNMS^F 869a8–17; MPNMS^D 386a28–b14; MPNMS^T §175.

89. See Bronkhorst 2007: 309–328, 363–366; R. Bhattacharya 2011; also 1.1n14.

about which we know even less, that employed teachings concerned with, by name, emptiness.[90]

Whereas all of these references to non-Buddhist ideas and practice are proper to the MPNMS and AMS—likely our earliest sources for Buddha-nature teaching—it is worth acknowledging that later sources in the *tathāgatagarbha* corpus reference non-Buddhist traditions or systems that are not named in earlier Buddha-nature texts. Mention of the Sāṃkhya tradition, for example, is found only in RGVV[C] and in the LAS (8.1).[91] Bhāviveka's defense of *tathāgatagarbha* teaching raises the interesting comparison with Vaiṣṇava theology (see 8.6), but our early Buddha-nature works do not exhibit any evidence of knowing anything about Vaiṣṇavism per se (with the exception, perhaps, of the *Bhagavadgītā* in verses of the RGV; see 7.2). It is nevertheless important that Upaniṣadic materials evoked by both the MPNMS and AMS—the *Kaṭha-* and *Śvetāśvatara-upaniṣad*s in particular—are early sources for discourse about the self that understood this to be the presence about one's person of a supreme deity, or a higher reality that is distinctly personal and a worthy object of reverence, a fact to which we must return in the next chapter (see 10.3–4).

To sum up, the authors of the MPNMS and AMS in particular were familiar with different ideas and practices common to other Indian traditions of renunciation, and in particular with non-Buddhist musings on the self that resembled (even in some superficial manner) teachings about

90. We find a tantalizing suggestion of such a thing in the *Gauḍapādīyakārikā* of Gauḍapāda, the (perhaps) sixth-century antecedent of the great Brahmanical philosopher Śaṅkarācārya, and possible founder of the Advaita Vedānta tradition. These verses likely postdate our Buddha-nature sources, but suggest that teachings about emptiness were not a uniquely Buddhist preoccupation. The fourth section (*prakaraṇa*) of the *Gauḍapādīyakārikā*—which Vetter (1978: 108) argued must preserve its earliest material—affirms that the mind and its object are both empty of characteristics (*lakṣaṇaśūnya*) and can be grasped only through their dependence upon one another. The same text makes approving allusion to the *agrayāna*—"the superior vehicle"—which is an expression found also in Mahāyānist sources, including the SP (e.g., 61.6–7, 82.5–6) and *Vajracchedikā-prajñāpāramitā* (Harrison and Watanabe 2006: 129 [§15b, fol.45v1]); see R. King 1995a: 185–186. Elsewhere in his study of the *Gauḍapādīyakārikā,* Richard King (1995a: 205–234) argues that Gauḍapāda's text could reflect influence by ideas found in the *tathāgatagarbha* tradition specifically. See also Isayeva 1993: 11–15, 172–198; Comans 2000: 88–124.

91. With the exception of the LAS (and a passing mention in RGV[C]; see 7.3), I am not convinced that any of our sources—especially those of an *ātmavādin* orientation—knew the sophisticated metaphysics of the Sāṃkhya tradition. Early sources for forms of Sāṃkhya, which is itself a very vague designator (referring to "enumeration" or "discrimination" of entities and attributes), include component books of the *Mahābhārata,* in which Sāṃkhya is associated with a variety of metaphysical speculations that are distinguishable from the "classical" Sāṃkhya of the *Sāṃkhyakārikā,* produced in perhaps the fourth century (Brockington 1999; 2002; Bronkhorst 2006.). While some Sāṃkhya authors may have been contemporaneous with our early Buddha-nature literature, I see no evidence that our earliest sources regarding Buddha-nature were influenced by this tradition specifically (see also 3.6n70). An erudite consideration of how *tathāgatagarbha* sources excluding the MPNMS-group compare to Sāṃkhya teachings is Khosla 2015.

Buddha-nature. The MPNMS-group of texts all understand Buddha-nature in terms of some revelation in the Buddha's teaching—very much like that of the single vehicle, announced by the SP—and as something like a caveat to teachings about emptiness, or indeed absence of self. Our *ātmavāda tathāgatagarbha* sources evince that their account of Buddha-nature is something conceptually older—creative, contentious, and noticeably more "self"-conscious—than what we can take to be the reinvention of the expression *tathāgatagarbha* reflected in other, better-remembered sources of this tradition, including the ŚDS and RGVV.

All of the themes explored above support the relative antiquity of our *ātmavāda tathāgatagarbha* sources, and behind these the looming influence of the SP and its radical recharacterization of the Mahāyāna in terms of the single vehicle. With the benefit of all that we have seen, the final chapter of this study will trace again the development of the expression *tathāgatagarbha* through Indian sources for it, and attempt to make sense of the most pressing question with which we are still confronted: why some Buddhist authors, in an unconventional corner of the Indian Mahāyāna, went so far as to articulate the apex of the Buddha's teaching as an account of an enduring, indestructible self.

CHAPTER 10

Evolution of the Buddhist Self

All living things are the residence of that which dwells in hiding,
which cannot be killed and is without stain.
What is immovable but inhabits that which moves,
those who venerate this attain immortality.

—*Āpastamba-dharmasūtra*

The previous chapter examined several themes that run through the *tathāgatagarbha* literary corpus and that support a revised relative chronology of texts within this tradition. This chronology is shaped by the hypothesis that teaching about *tathāgatagarbha* began as nothing less than a Buddhist account of the self, but in time came to be divorced from its "*ātmavādin*" form and was reinvented to better accord with other aspects of Buddhist teaching. This final chapter will attend to the remaining and very pressing question of why early authors in this tradition—those responsible for the so-called MPNMS-group of texts—opted to present their account of an internalized, universal Buddha-nature as a teaching at odds with prevailing Buddhist discourse concerned with absence of self (*nairātmyavāda*). We begin by reviewing what we have observed over the preceding chapters, and trace the trajectory of the Buddha-nature idea—commonly taught with recourse to the expression *tathāgatagarbha*—through the Indian sources that have concerned us.

10.1 The Course of Buddha-nature Teaching

In order to investigate the development of teaching about *tathāgatagarbha* and its relationship to *ātmavāda* discourse, we were required to presume an order of relevant materials. This took as its starting point Michael Radich's contention that it is the *Mahāparinirvāṇamahāsūtra* (MPNMS) that is our

Epigraph: Āpastamba-dharmasūtra 1.22.4 (Bühler 1932: 39.3–5): *pūḥ prāṇinaḥ sarva eva guhāśayasya / ahanyamānasya vikalmaṣasya / acalaṃ calaniketaṃ ye 'nutiṣṭhanti te amṛtāḥ* / Translation modified from that of Olivelle 1999: 33. See references at 10.3n44–45.

best contender for earliest available source for the expression *tathāgatagarbha,* and with it the Buddha-nature idea that is expressed by it (see 1.3). Radich's analysis of the MPNMS develops Masahiro Shimoda's understanding that the text was likely composed in (at least) two stages. Earlier material of the MPNMS concerns the Buddha's true and permanent mode of existence apart from his physical body, or *dharmakāya* (material that we have called "MPNMS-dhk"), which likely predates content that teaches the presence of the *tathāgatagarbha* in all sentient beings ("MPNMS-tg"; see 2.1). This *tathāgatagarbha* signifies the presence of the *buddhadhātu,* the enduring essence or nature (*dhātu*) of a Buddha that evokes what was commonly held to reside at a *stūpa* (1.3). Hence the MPNMS—an account of the (apparent) demise of the Buddha—reimagines the distribution of his relics into the revelation that in all sentient beings there endures the precious nature of a Buddha.

This notion—that all sentient beings possess some permanent, indestructible essence—is irregular enough given the importance of discourse about absence of self in earlier Buddhist teaching (see 1.1). But the MPNMS, in both stages of its composition, approves that its teachings refer to what can be called the self (*ātman*). In MPNMS-dhk, the Buddha contrasts his own teaching about the self with erroneous ideas about such a thing found in the world. In this material the expression *ātman* does not yet refer to anything about sentient beings themselves so much as the enduring, enjoyable state of liberation that is known to a Buddha. Beyond the body that he merely displayed in the world, the Buddha is not only permanent (*nitya*) but "is," or perhaps "experiences," the self (see 2.2). MPNMS-dhk teaches that the Buddha taught his disciples to cultivate absence of self in order to lead them away from erroneous notions of worldly selfhood, that there is nothing about them that is apart from conditioned existence in transmigration, so nothing worthy of pursuit or attachment. Only now does the Buddha reveal that the self is enjoyed at the achievement of Buddhist liberation, something that non-Buddhist teachers—though they may teach other accounts of a self, its qualities, and whereabouts—cannot know.

That things supermundane can be predicated in these positive terms—as permanent, the self, blissful, and pure, a direct inversion of the way that one should understand all worldly, conditioned phenomena—is an important innovation in and of itself. But according to MPNMS-tg, and in greater agreement with what is taught in non-Buddhist systems, a self is also located "within" sentient beings. If, as we are told, all sentient beings possess what is essential to a Buddha (*buddhadhātu*), in the "chamber" or "womb" for a Buddha that is, invisibly, part of their constitution (*tathāgatagarbha*), then each must possess some enduring, indestructible nature, or otherwise the internalized trace of the Buddha, which warrants designation as the self. This nature possesses already the characteristics of liberated existence but is concealed by a wealth of afflictions (worldly desire, aversion, delusion, and so forth) that prevent it from being "seen." Though only a

Buddha can see this self, it is still somehow a component part of a sentient being's "body" (see 2.3); from the awakened perspective of a Buddha, every sentient being is a dormant Buddha hidden beneath afflictions that are adventitious to him.[1]

As far as MPNMS-tg is concerned, the existence of the *buddhadhātu,* otherwise the *tathāgatagarbha,* is the Buddha's account of the existence of the self, expressed cryptically (*sandhāvacana*) and fully explained only at the end of his teaching (see 9.2). Elsewhere the MPNMS reminds us that the Buddha stands by his teaching that there is no worldly phenomenon that deserves to be considered the self, but this does not undermine the revelation of the *true* self—the Buddhist self—that is supermundane and somehow proper to all sentient beings. The existence of such a thing can be perceived only by a Buddha (or, imperfectly, by someone advanced along the path of the bodhisattva), and is otherwise accessible only through the Buddha's pronouncements. To borrow an image from the MPNMS, that a regular person cannot see the trail left by a bird in the sky does not mean that such a trail does not exist, and could still, in theory, be seen by someone with superhuman faculties (see 2.6; also 3.4).

It is clear that a Buddhist account of the self was contentious from the start; versions of MPNMS-tg go to great lengths to confront objections to what the Buddha seems to be teaching (see 2.4). The MPNMS concludes its defense of the *tathāgatagarbha* by addressing the issue of how this relates to similar teachings about selfhood that are found in other systems (2.6) and provides two different responses. For one, extraneous teachings about the self may have misunderstood what was taught by some bodhisattva already; the Buddhist self could be "misremembered," and so have begun all manner of inaccurate theories and arguments. But we also read that discourse about the self can be purposefully circulated by bodhisattvas—or emanations (**nirmāṇa/nirmita*) by them—and that any number of religious utterances that can be found in the world owe their existence to the influence and stratagems of the Buddha and his agents.[2] Where non-Buddhist accounts of the self are persuasive, or reminiscent of a truly supermundane self as propounded by the MPNMS, these must be a product of some bodhisattva, who teaches what is, in the end, the universal presence of Buddha-nature.

---

1. The MPNMS states that the *tathāgatagarbha* possesses all of the marks of a Buddha, or superior man (*mahāpuruṣa;* see 2.3n49), and so what is most proper and enduring in all sentient beings—according to this text at least—would most naturally be discussed in male terms.

2. Similar arguments are employed in texts related to the Buddha-nature tradition, such as the *Saddharmapuṇḍarīka* and BGVNS, and beyond into later Mahāyāna *sūtras* and *tantras*: see 10.4 below. A further instance of this kind of thinking is found in Bhāviveka's *Tarkajvāla,* which explains away any persuasiveness that might be attributed to the (Advaita) Vedānta tradition; see 8.6n58.

After the MPNMS, two other texts—the *Aṅgulimālīyasūtra* (AMS) and **Mahābherīhārakasūtra* (MBhS)—developed further this *ātmavādin* model of Buddha-nature teaching. The AMS continues to understand the expression *tathāgatagarbha* to refer to some enduring essence (*dhātu*) that is proper to sentient beings ("one's own essence/nature": **ātmadhātu; *svadhātu*—see 3.2) and which again persists imperceptibly "within" one's constitution (3.3). While the AMS (mostly) avoids referring to this as "the self," it is clear that the *tathāgatagarbha*—otherwise something "essential," and even some "secret" aspect of the Buddha's teaching—is presented as a corrective to how teachings about absence of self had been previously received. The revelation of Buddha-nature is not cause for the bodhisattva to weaken in his diligence, although apart from the wholesome or unwholesome actions that affect the transmigrating individual (3.5), it is the reason why practices like celibacy and dietary restrictions, in the pursuit of purity, are integral to the Mahāyāna as the AMS understands it (3.6). Where these practices resemble the activities of non-Buddhists, such things are either erroneous recollections of Buddhist teaching, or are again generated, for some enigmatic, strategic purpose, by bodhisattvas (3.7).

By comparison, the MBhS is less troubled by complaints that a Buddhist account of the self is problematic; whereas some audiences may retreat from it, this is only because they have failed to accept the *tathāgatagarbha* as a revelation that succeeds teachings about emptiness (*śūnyatā*) or, indeed, absence of self (4.5). The MBhS is more direct than the AMS in its insistence that the *tathāgatagarbha* constitutes, by name, the true self: that which survives throughout transmigration and which, once it has been cleansed of adventitious afflictions, enjoys a state of enduring freedom (4.2–4). Whereas the MBhS lacks attention to the arduous career of the bodhisattva—a theme visible throughout both the MPNMS and AMS—it does concisely present logic that underpins Buddha-nature thinking in general: if the status of a Buddha can be accurately described in terms of selfhood (as we see in MPNMS-dhk), and if, by definition, no permanent, enduring element of experience (i.e., *ātman*) can come into existence, then any sentient being capable of attaining such a status must have about them, already, something that warrants designation as the self (4.2).

All three of these texts exhibit some influence by another radical (though by no means "early") Mahāyānist text, the *Saddharmapuṇḍarīka* (SP). With relatively little attention to the manner in which the bodhisattva cultivates insight into the real nature of phenomena, all three texts of the MPNMS-group follow the SP in celebration of the enduring existence of the Buddha, his existence beyond his appearances in the world, the potential of the aspirant bodhisattva to achieve a similar status, and the Buddha's explanation of such things—the content of his "cryptic" or "secretive" pronouncements—only at a late stage in his teaching. All of these elements, according to both the AMS and MBhS, are characteristic of the Mahāyāna imagined as the single vehicle (*ekayāna*), the comprehensive apparatus by which all sentient beings approach the only form of liberation that is possible, of which teachings proper to mainstream (or Śrāvakayāna) Buddhist tradition are only expediencies or devices (9.1).[3]

The SP continues to influence other *tathāgatagarbha* texts apart from the MPNMS-group, most significant of which must be the *Śrīmālādevīsiṃhanādasūtra* (ŚDS). But while it accepts the single vehicle paradigm that was integral to the SP, the ŚDS also exhibits a resolution that what is taught by the expression *tathāgatagarbha* should not make any positive recourse to discourse about a self. The ŚDS marks the beginning of a second phase of Buddha-nature literature—still with a clear debt to the MPNMS-group, and knowledge of its *ātmavādin* orientation—in which the enigmatic label *tathāgatagarbha* does not refer to an enduring essence that is some constituent of sentient beings, so much as to a beginningless basis (*niśraya*), support (*ādhāra*), and foundation (*pratiṣṭhitā*) that underpins both transmigration and a liberated status beyond it (5.2).

In what is likely our earliest source for such an interpretation, the ŚDS reimagines *tathāgatagarbha* to refer to some enduring aspect of sentient beings expressed in mentalistic terms: Buddha-nature refers to the mind that is intrinsically pure (*prakṛtipariśuddhacitta*), which sits "beneath" the modes of consciousness that account for the entirety of normal worldly experience. While the MPNMS-group espouses Buddha-nature in terms of the realization of new Buddhas active in the world, the ŚDS focuses on the *tathāgatagarbha* as that which prefigures the Buddhas' true mode of being apart from any physical appearance in the world: the *dharmakāya*, understood as a collection of inconceivable, supermundane qualities. Whereas the ŚDS is adamant that *tathāgatagarbha* cannot refer to anything that resembles a self (indeed, its understanding of Buddha-nature resembles nothing of the sort), the *dharmakāya* that is the *tathāgatagarbha* purged of afflictions can still somehow exhibit "the perfection of self" (*ātmapāramitā*). Such a claim reflects acquaintance with the ideas of the MPNMS specifically (5.3; see also 2.2), and though the ŚDS offers nothing more regarding what this "perfection of self" intends, it is not the discovery of any abiding "essence" (*dhātu*) that passes through transmigration.

Although it continues to understand *tathāgatagarbha* in accordance with the single vehicle teaching of the SP (with curious parallels to the AMS; see 5.4), the ŚDS no longer understands *tathāgatagarbha* to refer to some problematic revelation that sits in tension with the Buddha's otherwise fundamental teachings about absence of self. Rather, *tathāgatagarbha* is that locus

3. The Mahāyāna understood as the single vehicle is also a prominent theme in material found only in Dharmakṣema's translation of the MPNMS ("MPNMS^{D}+"), which wants for further study distinct from core material of the MPNMS. We cannot currently be sure that MPNMS^{D}+ had origins in India, and so ideas unique to it—including greater caution about Buddha-nature articulated in terms of the self—cannot further influence our account of the demonstrably Indian *tathāgatagarbha* tradition (see 2.8).

(*garbha*), proper to a sentient being, at which can be "found" or "realized" the true body of the Buddha (*dharmakāya*), the true nature of phenomena (*dharmadhātu*), and qualities that are intrinsically pure (*prakṛtipariśuddha-dharma*). This model of Buddha-nature teaching is found also in the *Anūnatvāpūrṇatvanirdeśaparivarta* (AAN), which again relies on the identification of the *tathāgatagarbha* and *dharmakāya,* but now with a greater focus on these as epithets for the single nature or realm of phenomena (*ekadharmadhātu*) that is a common metaphysical basis for sentient beings, bodhisattvas, and Buddhas alike (6.1). Their differing emphases aside, the ŚDS and AAN share a more systematic tone than we encounter in the colorful, narratively rich material of the MPNMS-group—reason, in all likelihood, that they were important influences in the composition of the most detailed expositional work in the *tathāgatagarbha* tradition, the *Ratnagotravibhāgavyākhyā.*

Somewhere along this trajectory—as the Buddha-nature idea emerged, developed and was then distanced from its *ātmavādin* origins—some author(s) collated the set of nine similes that comprise the *Tathāgatagarbhasūtra* (TGS). As Michael Zimmermann has recognized already, it is possible that the expression *tathāgatagarbha* was only a late addition to the structure of this text, and that earlier in the life of its component similes the TGS was concerned with articulating ideas about Buddha-nature without reference to this specific, enigmatic, and even contentious expression (6.2). At any rate, the similes of the TGS were known to whoever produced or at least assembled the verses of the *Ratnagotravibhāga* (RGV; see 7.2), who either knew or redacted their content to reflect a set of poetic musings on the (*buddha*)*dhātu* that resides "within" sentient beings, with overtones of what we read in the MPNMS-group of *sūtra*s. Lack of clear influence over other specific works of the *tathāgatagarbha* corpus makes it difficult to determine the antiquity of the TGS relative to other *sūtra*s in this tradition, though its articulation of Buddha-nature in more like corporeal terms is certainly more reminiscent of the MPNMS-group than it is of mentalistic *tathāgatagarbha* expounded in, for example, the ŚDS.

Also difficult to situate in this trajectory are "basic" materials in the RGV itself (what may have originally been known as the "*Mahāyānottaratantra*"; see 7.1). Its earliest content concerning Buddha-nature—perhaps comprised of no more than fifteen "basic" verses—reflects awareness of ideas found in the ŚDS and AAN, but also has traces of the MPNMS-group and its account of the abiding, enduring *buddhadhātu.* While some verses of the RGV are densely packed with terminology reminiscent of both the ŚDS and AAN (what I called "String A"), its remaining verses ("Strings B and C," and the perhaps marginally later "String TG") teach the existence of a pervading nature (*dhātu*) that is both the intrinsic purity of the mind but also, it is implied, something that bears a superficial resemblance to the self as it is explained in the Brahmanical *Bhagavadgītā* (see 7.2). Though the earliest form of the RGV remains difficult to finally determine—buried, as it is, beneath layers of accrued commentarial material—it likely on its own terms reflected an original perspective on the Buddha-nature idea, certainly distinct from what is unpacked in the detailed and technical exposition of its commentary, the *Ratnagotravibhāgavyākhyā* (RGVV).

The RGVV is considered the definitive treatise on teaching about *tathāgatagarbha*. Its foundational materials are both root and commentarial verses of the RGV, as well as lengthy passages drawn from the ŚDS, AAN, and various other Mahāyānist sources besides, together with the similes of the TGS. Doctrinally the RGVV is particularly indebted to the ŚDS, and provides an exposition of what is meant by the "perfection of self," proper to the *dharmakāya*, that we find lacking in the ŚDS itself (7.3). According to the RGVV, both the perfection of self and the "supreme self" (*paramātman*) of the Buddha must refer, after all, to his perfection of insight, such that he in fact perfectly comprehends *absence* of a self among all phenomena. Hence the Buddha's teaching about selfhood is interpreted to be a teaching about absence of self, a reading that jars with what the Buddha himself voices about his methods in the MPNMS-group of texts. Our Chinese version of the RGVV (RGVV^{C}) preserves a little more of the character of this earlier, *ātmavādin* tradition. In material that may have been drawn from the *Mahāyānasūtrālaṃkāra* and its commentary (MSA[Bh]; see 6.3), RGVV^{C} retains the sense that the Buddha achieves a "great self" (*mahātman*), perhaps indicative of his "majesty" (*māhātmya*) apart from the world of conditioned phenomena. However, even this material, consistent with other content of the RGVV, shies from understanding the Buddha as having taught an account of the self that in a way succeeds teachings about absence of self. The RGVV tells us that where the Buddha employed seemingly *ātmavādin* pronouncements, these were intended to instruct individuals who were particularly attached to notions of the self (7.3–4), exponents or adepts of non-Buddhist systems (*tīrthyas*/*tīrthikas*), whose flaw is a futile preoccupation with discovering anything in the world that deserves to be known, and so treasured, as *ātman*.

Like the ŚDS, the RGVV also understands *tathāgatagarbha* in mentalistic terms, and evinces influence by the Yogācāra-Vijñānavāda tradition. It understands liberation as transformation of the mind at its basis, and does not accept the single vehicle paradigm that was so important for earlier authors concerned with Buddha-nature (9.1). Influences by the Yogācāra-Vijñānavāda tradition—which reduce the experience of transmigration to phenomena produced from a subliminal layer of the mind (such that all is ultimately "mind-only," *cittamātra*)—are yet more pronounced in the *Laṅkāvatārasūtra* (LAS). According to the LAS, the *tathāgatagarbha* had indeed been taught as something like a doctrine of the self, but only for the purpose of attracting teachers of non-Buddhist systems (*tīrthakaras*), to whom such a thing might appeal (8.2). There is an asymmetry between this and what we read in the MPNMS-group of texts, in which the Buddha is said to have avoided revealing the self so that he might first quash erroneous teachings about the self that prevailed in the world; in the LAS, a Buddhist account of the self can only have been taught in order to appeal to those who espouse these erroneous views. This seemingly revisionist interpretation of the *tathāgatagarbha* and its function seems to have won the approval of later Buddhist authors, including those who otherwise did not privilege the *vijñānavāda* orientation of the LAS over other traditions of Mahāyānist thought (8.6).

Elsewhere in its content the LAS cites the ŚDS as a source for a more "definitive" account of to what the expression *tathāgatagarbha* must refer, though this too is a creative reinterpretation of what the ŚDS had earlier disclosed. According to the LAS, *tathāgatagarbha* refers to nothing other than the "substratum consciousness" (*ālayavijñāna*) that underlies all experience, a foundational teaching in the Yogācāra-Vijñāna tradition (8.3). But apart from this, verses in the long and challenging "appendix" to the LAS—the *Sagāthaka*—refer to Buddhist *ātmavādin* teachings with approval ("free from the faults of non-Buddhist systems, burning up the thicket that is absence of self"), and again contrast this with erroneous notions about worldly selfhood (8.4). The final position of the *Sagāthaka* (if these verses were intended to present one) is difficult to pin down, but the core chapters of the LAS are clear that Buddha-nature as a kind of *ātmavāda* could only be a kind of expediency. Though this is a reasonable hermeneutic by which the LAS could interpret Buddhist teachings about the self, we cannot shake the fact that authors of the MPNMS-group of texts surely did not imagine the revelation of the true self to be anything but a definitive articulation of Buddhist dharma.

It is quite clear that the SP had a profound influence on all of these *tathāgatagarbha* works. But themes shared by the SP and the MPNMS-group of texts reflect an earlier stage in the life of the Indian Mahāyāna, quite different from the more philosophically sophisticated adaptations of the Buddha-nature idea found in the ŚDS, AAN, RGVV, and LAS. The latter have the hallmarks of a more "mature" Mahāyāna: they are less concerned with the unforgiving career of the bodhisattva, hampered by abuse wherever he teaches about *tathāgatagarbha,* or with affirming the continuing and transcendent influence of the Buddha; indeed, they articulate a Buddhology—focused on the *dharmakāya* that is identifiable with reality itself—that places comparatively less emphasis on Buddha(s) as personal entities that emerge and influence the world. Though it is difficult to prove conclusively, the poetic musings on Buddha-nature found in the TGS (and preserved in the RGV as, specifically, an exploration of the *dhātu* of the Buddha) may sit between these two groups of texts, with less to say about the austerity of bodhisattva practice evinced in the former, but apart from the mentalistic reinvention and systematization of the expression *tathāgatagarbha* that is so evident in the latter.

To sum up, we can trace the transformation of the Buddha-nature idea from (1) the affirmation of the enduring essence of the Buddha in all sentient beings to (2) an account of an underlying nature of sentient beings that possesses his transcendent qualities. The former understands *tathāgatagarbha* to refer to something like an account of a properly awakened *subject,* the figure of the Buddha, or vital essence of him, that lies hidden throughout transmigration, an imperceptible presence in one's constitution, and what can hence be legitimately called *ātman.* The latter, by contrast, is an account of a properly awakened *substrate,* a basis for transmigration and liberation, or otherwise the basic nature of the mind, and that which the bodhisattva seeks to cleanse of its myriad vices and failings. These two glosses on how the term *tathāgatagarbha* is used, by the two strains of this literature that we have discerned, share a common element: in both, *tathāgatagarbha* refers to what is "beneath" (*sub-*) the elements of conditioned existence that comprise transmigration—in the first model hidden "within," and in the second properly "underpinning" rebirth, and after it liberation, in the sense of some basis or foundation.

Both models of Buddha-nature teaching—or otherwise that to which the expression *tathāgatagarbha* refers—are contentious. In each instance Mahāyānist authors are agreed that something permanent (*nitya,* otherwise *dhruva,* or *śāśvata*) persists through this life and the successive lives of a sentient being, either in "essence" (*dhātu*) or "intrinsically" (*prakṛti*).[4] The difference, as should by now be clear, is that only later in the life of the Buddha-nature idea—though still relatively early in the history of Mahāyāna Buddhism—was the expression *tathāgatagarbha* taken to refer to a beginningless basis of experience that is the mind. Prior to this, we are witness to something even more irregular, with which it is quite evident that some Indian audiences were not so comfortable: an account of sentient beings having in their person a trace of what is supermundane; a reality that is unchanging, indestructible, of superlative value, and so worthy of being called the self.

10.2 Origins of the Buddha-nature Idea

If we are to address the conditions under which Mahāyānist authors began to espouse a Buddhist teaching of the self, we should also address the possible origins of the Buddha-nature idea in general, and of the expression *tathāgatagarbha* that stood for it. Once again, the Buddha-nature idea is *that something proper to all sentient beings across their successive births and deaths is, at all times, that which is proper also to a Buddha* (see 1.2). We have observed that there were at least two broad types of Buddha-nature teaching in India. One, which I have argued is the older, imagines something like an enduring *subject* (*ātman*) that suffers transmigration and enjoys liberation from it—and hence is articulated in terms of a self ("*ātmavāda*"). The other postulates an enduring mental *substrate,* a contribution to discourse about the

4. To bring us full circle, see again the notions of the liberated self that are opposed in the *Alagaddūpamasutta* (1.1n21).

mind and its composition ("*vjñānavāda*"), which in some manner underpins transmigration and—textual evidence suggests—proved not quite so objectionable to Indian Buddhist authors and their audiences.

We should also determine some ballpark period within which to situate the production of our texts. Our likely latest source in the *tathāgatagarbha* corpus is the LAS, our *terminus ante quem* for which is the production of Guṇabhadra's translation (LAS^{C1}; see 8.1) in 443 CE. The LAS is not mentioned in any works of the Yogācāra-Vijñānavāda tradition attributed to Maitreya/Asaṅga, including the MSA or RGVV, so was probably not produced earlier than the fourth century.[5] Our earliest form of the LAS knows of both the AMS and ŚDS. Though the relative dating of these two works is a tricky issue (see 5.4), the ŚDS gives the impression of being further from the contentious "revelation" of teaching about *tathāgatagarbha,* so may be later. If we permit for some passage of time between the composition of any two related texts—it being unlikely that any was produced as an immediate response to another—we can presume that both the AMS and ŚDS belong to the third or fourth century at latest.

At the other end of this chronology, Radich develops a detailed argument for the dating of the MPNMS.[6] Both the MPNMS and *Mahāmeghasūtra* (see 9.4) exhibit what may be knowledge of the Śātavāhana dynasty in Andhra, and specifically of the king Gautamīputra Śātakarṇi (reigned c. 86–110 CE). Analysis of the prophecy complex common to these and the other texts of the MPNMS-group leads Radich to conclude that MPNMS-tg may have been produced in the Andhra region, in "the late first to mid-second century CE."[7] Even if Radich's hypothesis concerning the MPNMS puts its composition too early, we could still comfortably suppose that the

5. See also 8.1n6. Regarding the (improbable) hypothesis that some form of the LAS was known to Nāgārjuna, and hence may have existed as early as the second century, see Lindtner 1982; 1992.

6. Radich 2015a: 59–85; also Hodge 2006.

7. The *Mahāmeghasūtra* refers to the Śātavāhanas by name (T.387[12]1099c23: 娑多婆呵那); both it and the MPNMS refer to geographical features of the Andhra region (in "the South") as well as, perhaps, epithets for Gautamīputra Śātakarṇi himself (see references in the previous note for more). Both of these texts prophesy that a decline in the dharma will take place seven hundred years after the Buddha's (apparent) death, which may accord with the period during or after Śātakarṇi's rule. See Radich 2015a: 74–75 (also pages indicated in the note above) and Hodge 2006.

The Andhra/Śātavāhana thesis also supports the much-discussed association between *tathāgatagarbha* and the Mahāsāṃghika tradition—which was resident in the Andhra region—proposed by Wayman (1978) and supposed by Barber (2008: both with reference to the ŚDS specifically: see 5.1nn6, 8), and supported by ties between the MPNMS and Mahāsāṃghika that have been observed by Shimoda (e.g., 1994; 2014: 74–84). See also Radich 2015a: 55n114. For overviews of Mahāsāṃghika(-Lokottaravāda) doctrine, preserving ideas common to the Buddha-nature tradition, see Bareau 1955: 55–77; Westerhoff 2018: 45–49. Regarding the need for caution in any attempt to discern affiliation between Mahāyānist texts and schools (*nikāyas*) of Buddhist ordination, see Harrison 1995a: 56–57. A further curiosity is the tradition that Nāgārjuna may have had as his patron a king of the

MPNMS, AMS, and MBhS—representing the earlier, *ātmavādin* mode of Buddha-nature thinking—were produced some time between the second and third centuries CE.[8] All of these texts show some degree of influence by the SP (see 9.1), which was likely produced in the first quarter of the first millennium CE.[9] It should be stressed that the single vehicle paradigm to which our Buddha-nature sources are indebted does not feature among our supposedly "early" literary sources for Mahāyāna Buddhism, which presume the Mahāyāna (or *bodhisattvayāna*) to be reserved for an elite few, whereas other sentient beings can, at best, aspire to achieve the status of an arhat.[10] In short, sources for the early history of the Buddha-nature idea likely originated late in the first quarter of the first millennium CE, perhaps across the late second and early third century, by which time some corner of Mahāyāna Buddhism, represented by the SP, had proposed that liberation can mean only the status achieved by a Buddha, toward which the "great vehicle" of the Mahāyāna is the only conveyance. Whereas the SP makes this goal available for anyone willing to accept its teachings, the authors of the MPNMS go further, and explain how buddhahood is achievable by anyone who will commit to eventually realizing, for the sake of all sentient beings, their ever-present Buddha-nature.

The dates proposed above can only ever be reasonable hypotheses. Moreover, the production of any of our sources could, in theory, postdate years of discussion and argument regarding the ideas that they promote.[11] But we will proceed supposing that by the middle of the third century of the Common Era, Buddhist authors had developed from a fantastical account of the Buddha's apparent death (in MPNMS-dhk) a creative reimagining of the distribution of his relics—his superlatively precious, enduring essence—now in all sentient beings (MPNMS-tg), such that they can be understood to possess at all times, though lying unrealized, the full gamut of the Buddha's qualities. In tandem with this, the liberation proper to a Buddha—that is, the uncovering of one's own Buddha-nature—was articulated

---

Śātavāhana dynasty (Walser 2005: 61–87; Yamano 2008), and evidence of awareness of *tathāgatagarbha* and *ekayāna* teachings in works attributed to him; see also 9.1n21.

8. A later dating—recorded by H. Nakamura ([1980] 1987: 212); Williams (2009: 109); and Verardi (2011: 128)—takes the MPNMS to have been produced around the dawn of the Gupta Empire (mid-fourth century CE), and assumes that its "prophecy" referred to the renewed political fortunes of Brahmanism, at the expense of Buddhism, in that period.

If the composition of the MPNMS is as early as Radich has argued, Zimmermann's (2000: 77–79) position that the TGS was produced in the second half of the third century remains very plausible.

9. Our terminus for the SP is its first translation into Chinese, the *Zhengfahua jing* 正法華經 (T.263), by Dharmarakṣa 竺法護 (fl.265–313 CE), in 286CE.

10. Regarding accurate use of (or abstention from) the designation "early Mahāyāna," see Harrison 1995a: 55–56; 2018a: 12–13. Regarding the *ekayāna*, see also 9.1n1.

11. A point made by Harrison (1995a: 55–56), who acknowledges that the Chinese translations of Lokakṣema do not necessarily provide access to the "early" Indian Mahāyāna so much as what are, for us, relatively early sources for it.

in terms of the discovery of this essence, or otherwise one's self, which refers to both the supermundane status of the Buddha and the presence of that which is proper to him in every sentient being (see 1.3).

In the next section we will turn to the matter of why early advocates of the Buddha-nature idea promoted their teaching as an account of the self, such that later inheritors of the expression *tathāgatagarbha* had to wrestle with what I am claiming are its (authentically Buddhist) "*ātmavādin*" roots. But it should first be clarified that the origins of Buddha-nature teaching surely do not lie exclusively in a desire to promote a teaching about, by name, the self. It is unlikely that we can identify any one comprehensive reason why Mahāyānist authors began to promote the idea of an enduring, indestructible Buddha-nature, and the search for a single cause behind its development is likely a flawed endeavor.[12] Before we attend to our primary interest--why the *tathāgatagarbha* was ever articulated in terms of selfhood—we should consider what function(s) teaching about Buddha-nature may have served in the interests of Mahāyānist authors and audiences in the early centuries of the Common Era.[13]

If the earliest context for Buddha-nature teaching is indeed visible in the MPNMS—which, we should remember, is ostensibly an account of the Buddha's death—then it is to this text in particular that we must attend. A very relevant concern of Indian Buddhism, dating back to the generations immediately after the Buddha's death, was the absence from the world of the Buddha himself. Arguably this problem is all the more pronounced for the Mahāyāna tradition, in that pivotal moments in the career of a bodhisattva include forming the vow to become fully awakened, usually believed to be made in the presence of a living Buddha, and the prediction (*vyākaraṇa*) by a Buddha that this bodhisattva will, eventually, succeed in that endeavor.[14] As outlined in the first chapter of this volume (1.3), the veneration of the Buddha's relics, or otherwise the *stūpa* in which they reside, constituted one means by which the Buddha or some trace of him was believed to remain present and accessible in the world. In tension with the veneration of the Buddha's very physical remains sits the development of what has been called docetic Buddhology: the understanding that the Buddha did not truly depart from the world because all that was seen of his physical person were merely "displays" from beyond it, and hence that his involvement in human affairs need not have come to an end. The *tathāgatagarbha* tradition adopts the language of the former to explore the implications of the latter: that the enduring, valuable essence of the Buddha is housed not in a cold stone reliquary but resides somehow, mysteriously, in sentient beings themselves.

---

12. See Zimmermann 2002: 75; also Radich 2015a: 157.

13. Regarding the challenges we face if wanting to discern the origins of doctrinal concepts such as *tathāgatagarbha,* see Radich 2015a: 101–104, after Schmithausen 1987: 1–7.

14. See Drewes 2019.

Among our earliest sources for docetic Buddhology is Lokakṣema's Chinese translation of the *Lokānuvartanasūtra,* produced in the late second century (see again 1.3), in which are recorded a great many examples of the Buddha's "displayed" activities from some status beyond the physical world: that the Buddha only "appeared" to be born, mature, experience suffering, and eventually die.[15] As Radich has argued, the expression *tathāgatagarbha* served as a "positive corollary" to docetic Buddhological developments in the early Common Era, which are very evident in MPNMS-dhk (see 2.2). With MPNMS-dhk as its foundation, MPNMS-tg affirms the existence of the *tathāgatagarbha*—transforming, as Radich had written, the "tomb" of the (seemingly) departed Śākyamuni into the "womb" for a future Buddha—to explain how a newly awakened being can be realized in the world if, as a docetic account of the Buddha would hold, he exists beyond not only his apparent awakening but also his final conception, gestation, and birth (see 1.3).[16] In whatever fashion the expression *tathāgatagarbha* is employed, be it somehow corporeally (in the MPNMS-group) or mentalistically (in the ŚDS and otherwise), it communicates that the creation of a Buddha culminates in a kind of "self"-revelation, of something apart from the physical processes of birth, aging, and death observable in the world, what Zimmermann (2014a) has referred to as a "disclosure" of a liberated state that is already present.

As previous scholarship has acknowledged, the notion of an internalized Buddha-nature also plays into other important themes in the development of the Indian Mahāyāna, such as visual encounter (*darśana*) with the Buddha.[17] Notably the status of the Buddha-nature as something one might "see" is not prominent in the ŚDS, AAN, or RGV(V), but is found repeatedly throughout the MPNMS-group (see, e.g., 2.3, 3.4, 4.4). As the Buddha's essence/relic at the *stūpa* is functionally equivalent to the Buddha himself, to behold such a thing is to encounter the Buddha; similarly, to "see" one's *tathāgatagarbha,* or the womb/chamber for the Buddha(*dhātu*), is to see the Buddha within oneself.[18] Visual encounters with a Buddha—by

15. Harrison 1982; 1993: 159–161; also Radich 2007: 593–684.

16. Radich 2015a: 165. An account of the "postmortem" dimension of a docetic Buddhology (i.e., that the Buddha "did not really die") is Radich 2012a. A central contention of Radich's study of the MPNMS (2015a: 105–157) is that *tathāgatagarbha* doctrine presents a "prenatal" complement to this (i.e., the Buddha "was not really born"), which explains the manner by which a Buddha might emerge in the world—from amid afflictions, cleansed by the bodhisattva who prefigures him—while being utterly apart from the polluted process of being born in a regular, "worldly" fashion; see Sasson 2008; Langenberg 2017.

17. See Zimmermann 2014a; Radich 2015a: 212–213; also Shimoda 2014: 61–66. Regarding the importance of *darśana* in Buddhism, in particular in the centuries associated with the emergence of the Mahāyāna, see Rotman 2009: 185–192.

18. Schopen (1988: 531) draws attention to a passage in the Pāli *Mahāvaṃsa,* in which Mahinda—the missionary son of Aśoka—instructs King Devānaṃpiya of Laṅkā that "when the relics are seen, the victor (i.e., Buddha) is seen" (*dhātusu diṭṭhesu diṭṭho hoti jino iti*). See also N. Falk 1977.

meditative practices focused on him (*buddhānusmṛti*), or the pursuit of other worlds in which Buddhas are currently teaching (*buddhakṣetras*)—were important preoccupations of some of our probably oldest Mahāyānist literature, which attests to the desirability of an immediate, undeniable encounter with a living, teaching Buddha.[19]

The novel innovation in the *tathāgatagarbha* literature is to situate the Buddha, or what is essential to him, within one's own constitution; the bodhisattva is reassured that the glorious, fully-formed person of the liberated being resides in his own body, across this and successive lives. But especially where *tathāgatagarbha* is taken to refer to the self, and in order to square this claim with wider *nairātmyavāda* discourse (in which nothing discernible in one's experience qualifies to be called the self; see 1.1), Buddha-nature must refer to something that is commonly indiscernible: always in one's own constitution but knowable only to a Buddha until there is, visible in the world, another fully realized Buddha. The *tathāgatagarbha* literature at once promises the presence of Buddha(-nature) while denying perception of it to anyone below the status of advanced bodhisattvas, who themselves can perceive it only imperfectly (see 2.3). Our Buddha-nature sources offer no program of introspection by which such an encounter might be possible, and if anything may have frustrated audiences who would want there to be some means by which this precious entity could be accessed (apart from, as our sources teach, by commitment to texts of the Buddha-nature tradition).[20] The point, however, is encouragement: *tathāgatagarbha* works stress the imperceptibility of Buddha-nature up until a bodhisattva becomes, through great exertion, a Buddha himself, at which point what is proper to a Buddha—indeed, "Buddha-nature"—is visible for all to see.

This brings us to what may be the most pressing concern behind teaching regarding *tathāgatagarbha*, at least in our MPNMS-group of texts: the maintenance in the world of the three jewels or refuges (Buddha, dharma, and sangha), and the bodhisattva's role in the continuing production of Buddhas that are the fountainhead of the other two.[21] This is particularly evident in the theme of a "single refuge" that is observable, in more or less detail, across the MPNMS, AMS, ŚDS, and RGV (see, especially, 5.4), which

---

19. Harrison (1992b: 225–228) explores the manner in which what is often abbreviated to the *Pratyutpanna-sūtra* (e.g., T.418: *Panchou sanmeijing* 般舟三昧經, a text listed among Lokakṣema's corpus of translations) describes "visualization" (*anusmṛti*) of a Buddha as an invocation and internalization of the Buddha's presence, which invites identification with the visualized Buddha and a transformation of the observing subject. That "visualization of" leads to "identification with" is a prominent feature of developments in tantric Buddhism, but in a period closer to that of the *Pratyutpanna-sūtra*, our *tathāgatagarbha* sources seem to invert this process: "identification with" a Buddha—which must be accepted on faith—prefigures an eventual visual encounter with our ever-present, concealed Buddha-nature.

20. Regarding an exceptional passage in MPNMS^{D}+, see 2.7n135.

21. See Skilling 2018: 35–45, 53–56.

all stress the primacy of the Buddha over the other two refuges, and by implication the importance of a bodhisattva as the precursor to another, future Buddha. Already in the MPNMS we find the notion that by knowing his Buddha-nature a bodhisattva understands himself to be a site of worship as if he were a Buddha already (2.2); the AMS goes so far as to declare that bodhisattvas are, in a sense, Buddhas (3.4), and that acting like a Buddha betrays the presence of the *tathāgatagatbha* (9.3). Such identifications are defensible insofar as bodhisattvas know themselves to have the nature of the Buddha about them, and are by their efforts contributing to the future in the world of the three refuges.[22]

For the Mahāyāna, the path of the bodhisattva is integral to the continuity of Buddhism in the world. This would be especially pertinent for authors like those of the MPNMS-group, who record (or "predict") a decline in the discipline of the sangha and in the influence of Buddhist teaching long after the (flesh-and-blood) disappearance of the Buddha.[23] The Buddha-nature idea reassures both the bodhisattva and perhaps also his patrons—lay devotees, whose gifts would support renunciants or communities of them—that the efforts of an adept who is true to the Mahāyāna are not in vain, and that each bodhisattva constitutes the presence (or at least promise) of a new, fully formed Buddha. In this role the bodhisattva surpasses the supposed presence of the Buddha at the *stūpa;* while the relic-chamber was held to retain the trace of a Buddha's physical presence, the *tathāgatagarbha* marks the transcendental locus—immanent yet imperceptible, "in" the body but not of it—from which a future Buddha can someday emerge. Insofar as the bodhisattva is one who strives to reveal this hidden nature, (s)he is the most valuable object of reverence: the dynamic site of a new Buddha, to be contrasted with the cold burial mound of the previous Buddha (who never, we should add, really died).

A final very significant factor behind the development of Buddha-nature thinking is the account of Buddhist liberation observable in our earliest sources for this idea. Material in MPNMS-dhk articulates that what is beyond the world of transmigration can be characterized by permanence, purity, bliss, and—most contentiously—"selfhood" (see 2.2). This material of the MPNMS does not yet propose that *ātman* can describe anything about lowly, transmigrating sentient beings (an error, we are initially told, that is proper to non-Buddhist systems), and yet this certainly invites an

22. Zimmermann (2014a: 525) observes that a recurring feature in the similes of the TGS is the claim that the bodhisattva can perform all of the tasks of a Buddha. The concept of perceiving the bodhisattva (or other figures) as a Buddha—specifically "as the teacher" (*śāstṛsaṃjñā*)—dates further back in the history of Mahāyānist literature, and is visible in, for example, the *Kāśyapaparivarta* (Vorobyova-Desyatovskaya 2002: 5 [§4]) and the SP (286.1; Kern 1884: 271); see Skilling 2009; 2018.

23. We see this, for example, where the MPNMS condemns monks who keep prohibited items and engage in worldly arts or practices: MPNMS^{F} 869a17–869b7; MPNMS^{D} 386b14–386c5; MPNMS^{T} §176–177.

extension of this language to sentient beings themselves, which in MPNMS-tg is the localization of the Buddha's "essence" in every one of them. Following our Tibetan translation of this material, MPNMS-dhk records that the Buddha is permanent (*rtag pa:* Skt. *nitya*), enduring (*ther zug: śāśvata*), unconditioned (*'dus ma byas pa: asaṃskṛta*), and lasting (*brtan pa: dhruva*).[24] Three of these expressions—explaining the Buddha's temporal extension—are by now very familiar to us; but all versions of the MPNMS also confirm that the Buddha is unconditioned or "uncreated"; he is different from all worldly entities, because he is not a product of, or dependent upon, worldly causation.

In earlier Buddhist teaching, that which is unconditioned or uncreated (*asaṃskṛta*) refers to *nirvāṇa,* the experience realized by arhats and Buddhas alike, and apart from the process of transmigration.[25] But in the MPNMS this language describes the transcendent existence of a Buddha, whose status is beyond *nirvāṇa* as imagined in mainstream (i.e., non-Mahāyānist) teaching: "Regarding the expression 'uncreated,' take the example of a potter making a pot, and then breaking it: liberation is not like that.[26] Liberation has neither an origin nor cessation; that which is liberation is the Tathāgata, [who is] without origination, without death. That which is without origination, without destruction, without ageing, without death, which is uncreated, is the Tathāgata; therefore [it is said that] he goes to *mahāparinirvāṇa.*"[27] The Buddha's liberation is expressed in terms of a separation from that which characterizes all worldly phenomena (origination and cessation), and the experiences proper to the normal lives of sentient beings (aging and death). If the deathless state enjoyed by a Buddha "comes" from nowhere—that is, it is uncreated—some basis for this state should exist already, and must pertain to any sentient being who is capable of becoming a Buddha. If that which is transcendent and unconditioned can, in contrast to all worldly things, be called *ātman,* then a thing by the same name must exist already at the place from which a Buddha can

---

24. MPNMS^{T} §65.1–5. Compare MPNMS^{F} 860a27–28 (如來常住、無爲、非變易法) and MPNMS^{D} 374b18–20 (如來是常住法、不變異法、無爲之法).

25. Explained, for example, in the *Asaṅkhatasaṃyutta* (SN.IV.359–373), or—from likely a very early stage in Buddhist teaching—the *Udāna* (8.3; Steinthal 1885: 80–81). See also, apropos of *tathāgatagarbha* teaching specifically, Grosnick 1981. Regarding abhidharmic debate over what is unconditioned—together with early Buddhist sources that discuss the ontological status of *nirvāṇa*—see Dhammajoti 2009: 471–485. Crucially, early Buddhist literature, such as the discourses of the Pāli *Suttapiṭaka,* is careful not to promote the idea that *nirvāṇa,* though unconditioned, deserved to be called the self; see Collins 1998: 138–142.

26. Regarding the pot imagery apropos of emptiness teaching in the MPNMS, see 9.5.

27. MPNMS^{T} §232.1–9: *'dus ma byas 'dus ma byas zhes bya ba ni / ji ltar rdza mkhan gyis snod byas nas / de'i og tu zhig par 'gyur ba bzhin du / thar pa ni de lta ma yin no // thar pa ni skye ba yang med / 'gag pa yang med do // thar pa gang yin pa de ni de bzhin gshegs pa ste / skye ba yang med / 'chi ba yang med do // gang ma skyes pa dang / ma zhig pa dang / rga ba med pa dang / 'chi ba med pa dang / 'dus ma byas pa de ni de bzhin gshegs pa ste / de bas na de bzhin gshegs pa ni yongs su mya ngan las 'das pa chen por 'gro ba'o //* Compare MPNMS^{F} 873a15–20; MPNMS^{D} 392a25–29.

emerge, hidden somehow within the otherwise ephemeral constitution of any sentient being. This trace of what is unconditioned must endure apart from worldly activities, survive successive births and deaths, be superlatively valuable, and is hence—in agreement with wider Indian discourse—that which one might naturally call the self.

And yet, as the MPNMS itself acknowledges, to refer to this enduring Buddha-nature as the self was a departure from standard Buddhist discourse, and invited consternation. It is clear that later authors in the *tathāgatagarbha* tradition were at pains to distance teaching about Buddha-nature from anything that should be explained in *ātmavādin* terms, and so from the implication that the *tathāgatagarbha* constitutes a caveat to, if not outright departure from, teachings about absence of self. The MPNMS, AMS, and MBhS all commit to the idea that the nature of the Buddha constitutes the Buddha's account of the self, and therefore that Buddhist teaching culminates in the realization of just such a thing. The remaining sections of this volume will attempt to explain motivations behind the doctrinal "experiment" that was Buddha-nature teaching articulated as a form of Buddhist *ātmavāda,* prior to its reinvention in terms that proved to be more palatable for wider Indian Buddhist audiences.

10.3 Liberation and the Self

We have seen that although later works concerned with *tathāgatagarbha* salvaged this expression from its *ātmavādin* heritage, relatively early articulations of Buddha-nature teaching were certainly framed as the Buddha's account of the self. This was in apparent contravention of prior Buddhist teaching about the redundancy of a conception of the self in a correct (or at very least soteriologically advantageous) understanding of transmigration and escape from it. If we accept that teaching about Buddha-nature began with the internalization of a Buddha's essence (*dhātu*), which understands any sentient being to possess the chamber/womb for the presence of a Buddha (*tathāgatagarbha*), then although this is clearly an account of something enduring and valuable, there is no strict need to couch this as a teaching about the self, and so to court controversy in the manner that the texts of the MPNMS-group all concede that they do. And yet these texts both promote and defend the *buddhadhātu,* or *tathāgatagarbha,* articulated as the Buddha's definitive contribution, and so conclusion, to discourse about the self.

With the benefit of all that we have seen in earlier chapters—and especially with respect to the MPNMS and AMS—I suggest two interrelated explanations for this excursion into what has sometimes been seen to be "un-Buddhist" doctrinal territory or, at very least, nomenclature. The first, addressed in this section, situates teaching about Buddha-nature in the wider religious landscape of India in the first two or three centuries of the Common Era; the second, addressed in the next section, considers

Buddha-nature thinking as a development within a particular strain of Mahāyāna Buddhist thought that likely originated in this same period.

As reviewed already in this chapter, the groundwork for a Buddhist *ātmavāda* was laid by MPNMS-dhk: material of the MPNMS that does not concern the status of sentient beings themselves but does find it appropriate to call the Buddha, or the liberated state that he enjoys, "the self." Establishing the precious nature of the Buddha in every sentient being went a step further, and led to the promotion of a true *ātmavāda:* an account of the enduring, precious "central something" of every sentient being, in which is invested power and longevity, and which was a well-established desideratum for Indian religious authors and adepts in general (see 1.1). In likely later texts such as the ŚDS and AAN, and—more clearly still—the RGVV and LAS, we find what read like clarifications about Buddha-nature teaching, in which *tathāgatagarbha* and that to which it refers is not "revealed" so much as explained in a fashion that shores up and defends a place for it in wider Buddhist thought.[28] While they certainly attempt to persuade audiences about the Buddha's account of the self (see 2.4, 3.5, 4.2), the *sūtra*s of the MPNMS-group lack these more systematic explanations of *tathāgatagarbha* and its relation to other Buddhist teachings. By contrast, our *ātmavāda* sources explain *tathāgatagarbha* with recourse to the Buddha's use of cryptic utterances (see 9.2); the Buddha taught first, for the benefit of the world, in terms of absence of self, but this prefigured his account of the true self, hidden from view, that is Buddha-nature.

We should here acknowledge that our Buddha-nature authors were part of a broader religious landscape, in which debate about liberation—what it was, and how it could be achieved—was still occupied with questions about the self, and understood the self to be that by which one could engage with a reality higher than anything in the everyday world. We could venture to think more about this landscape and the place that our authors occupied in it.

If our earliest Buddha-nature sources belong to the first three centuries of the Common Era, theirs was likely not yet a world within which the many and varied innovations of Mahāyānist *sūtra*s had been thoroughly scrutinized or systematized, neither for the benefit of Buddhist audiences nor for the purposes of engagement with the doctrines of non-Buddhist authors (concerned with the self or otherwise). Moreover, where our early Buddha-nature *sūtra*s laud the supermundane status of the Buddha, they are interested not in what David Drewes has called "the thin, this-worldly religious experience of modern apologists" but rather, Drewes continues,

28. A good example is exposition of the single vehicle by the ŚDS, and its creative endeavors to explain the manner in which arhats and *pratyekabuddha*s are not yet liberated (5.4). But there are no "secrets" explained by the ŚDS; it provides simply an account of transmigration and liberation that is informed by its interpretation of what is meant by *tathāgatagarbha*.

"a state of omniscience and nearly infinite power and glory to be attained in another world after death;"[29] what Paul Harrison has described (and in the context of "docetic" Buddhology specifically) as "the ideal or dream or fantasy of becoming superhuman, of triumphing over all limitations of time and space—an idea whose realization calls for extraordinary asceticism."[30] Our earliest Buddha-nature sources are concerned with the acquisition of something like this status, a kind of apotheosis, described as permanent, pleasant, pure, and powerful; apart from conditioned existence, and unlike anything known in the world. The authors of MPNMS-dhk declared that the Buddha—who enjoys just such a state—could be referred to as the self, distinguishing his liberation from all worldly experience (impermanent, unpleasant, impure, and impotent). As explained in the parable of the woodworm (2.2), it is about this that other religious systems may seem to speak, but resemblances between their ideas and the liberation proper to a Buddha are superficial. Though the Buddha had taught that nothing worldly qualifies as the self, the terminus of the bodhisattva path is that which eludes the renunciant practitioner—Buddhist, Brahmanical, or otherwise—throughout any career of meditative introspection. In short, liberation is presented as the discovery of that which earlier Buddhist teaching would have held in high regard *if* the Buddha had revealed that such a thing could be found: one's self, or an enduring nature invested with liberated power, and very worthy of discovery.

Hence Buddha-nature teaching—at least in its *ātmavādin* mode—brings this corner of the Mahāyāna into a new relationship with wider Indian discourse about the self, its qualities, and value. As we observed in the first chapter, the self and its whereabouts were a central and long-standing concern of non-Buddhist and particularly Brahmanical inquiry; according to the *Bṛhadāraṇyaka-upaniṣad,* the self is "what one should see and hear, consider and reflect upon … [by which] one knows all."[31] But we have acknowledged also that the MPNMS and AMS may have been aware of developments in Upaniṣadic *ātmavāda* that belong to the centuries closer to the dawn of the Common Era, in which discourse about the self—and moreover *the higher reality that might be known by it*—had developed beyond what is found in some early Upaniṣadic works, and which may not have been known (or at least well-known) to Buddhist literature that originated before the emergence of the Mahāyāna (see 9.6).

29. Drewes 2018: 87.

30. Harrison 1995b: 21; elsewhere, "a dream … of unlimited power, bliss and freedom from the shackles of our ordinary reality, of purity and perfection" (Harrison 2003: 146). In this respect many Mahāyānist texts are in accordance with a wider Indian preoccupation with the acquisition of "complete control over one's environment … even control of the physical sources of power in the universe," as characterized by Potter (1963: 3).

31. BĀU 2.4.5: *ātmā vā are draṣṭavyaḥ śrotavyo manatavyo nididhyāsitavyo … ātmano vā are darśanena śravaṇena matyā vijñānenedaṃ sarvaṃ viditam //* (Olivelle 1998: 67–69; see also 1.1).

We benefit from returning to the diversity of *ātmavādin* utterances found in the Upaniṣads. Composed over many centuries, the "classical" Upaniṣads are not of one voice regarding their two primary themes: how best to understand that which is proper to one's own existence (i.e., the self, or *ātman*), and how the self relates to that which seems to exceed it, called *brahman* or otherwise.[32] While the *Bṛhadāraṇyaka-upaniṣad* does indeed focus on the discovery of the self (see 1.1), it and later Upaniṣads associated with the Atharvaveda tradition (the *Praśna-* and *Muṇḍaka-upaniṣads*) focus on the self as the means by which one can come to know *brahman.*[33] Famous passages of the *Chāndogya-upaniṣad* are focused on the self as that which survives death, and celebrate it as the route to knowledge of *brahman,*[34] the sense also of the particularly terse *Māṇḍūkya-upaniṣad.*[35] In the *Kauṣītaki-upaniṣad* the self is the enduring essence of any living being: unaging, immortal, and again identifiable with *brahman.*[36] However, in the *Aitareya-upaniṣad* there is virtually no mention of *brahman; ātman* is at once the creator, that which is the abiding essence of every living being, and equated with the power of cognition.[37] Also with markedly less emphasis on *brahman,* the *ātman* is also the principle concern of the *Kaṭha-*,[38] *Taittirīya-, Maitrī-*, and *Śvetāśvatara-upaniṣads,* and to different degrees passages of these works understand the self to be the means by which one knows the divine "person" (*puruṣa*) beyond the world,[39] which the *Īśā-upaniṣad* knows as "the Lord" (*īś*).[40]

In short, different traditions of Vedic knowledge (*śākhās*), all of which produced and preserved their own discrete Upaniṣad(s), held *ātman* to denote that which is supremely valuable in oneself, and moreover believed that this provides a route to that which is more valuable still, matters about which Brahmanical sages pondered and, importantly, contested.[41] Notably it is "middle-period" Upaniṣads—composed in centuries closer to the start of the Common Era—that begin to show traces of theism: *brahman* or the Brahmanical "summum bonum," of which the self provides some knowledge or access, is either equated with or eclipsed by some personal reality

32. Cohen 2018: 11–17; Black 2007: 30–58; also Brereton 1990, who acknowledges that *brahman* itself serves as an "open concept" in this literature, standing for "whatever principle or power a sage believes to be behind the world to make the world explicable" (Brereton 1990: 188). A recent and excellent discussion of *ātman* across the Upaniṣads is Suthren Hirst 2018.

33. Cohen 2018: 305–306, 310–312.

34. Brereton 1990: 124–125; Black 2007: 30–46.

35. Olivelle 1998: 473–477; Cohen 2018: 352–355.

36. Cohen 2018: 278–279. The inverse is true of the *Kena-upaniṣad,* which gives hardly any attention to *ātman* at all (ibid., 338–339).

37. Cohen 2008: 134–135; 2018: 269–273.

38. See Schiltz 2018.

39. Cohen 2018: 288–291, 344–346, 327–330.

40. Cohen 2018: 294–295.

41. Black 2007: 59–101.

who is beyond, yet responsible for, the world.[42] These middle-period sources include the *Īśā-, Kaṭha-,* and *Śvetāśvatara-upaniṣads,* ideas and imagery of which appear also in the MPNMS and AMS (see 9.6). More developed still—and perhaps tripping over into the early Common Era—are Upaniṣads more clearly aligned to the worship of named gods (e.g., the *Kaivalya-* and *Mahānārāyana-upaniṣads*), and with them the *Bhagavadgītā* also, which understand the self to be that by which one knows the supreme deity (*adhidaiva*).[43] These theistic texts evince the congruence of a central Brahmanical principle—that the self constitutes a means of access to that which lies *beyond* the world—with the acknowledgment, in later centuries, that this supreme principle can be identified with one or other personal deity venerated by people *in* the world. This diversity of Brahmanical expression across the Upaniṣads and into Brahmanical theism does not diverge from a simple premise: knowledge of one's self is supremely valuable because it is the key to that which is supreme, called *brahman, puruṣa,* or *adhidaiva.*

We cannot, by reference to the Upaniṣads alone, confirm that interest in the self remained paramount to the Brahmanical tradition in the first quarter of the first millennium CE, the period in which we are locating Buddha-nature sources that exhibit familiarity with language and imagery found in certain Upaniṣads (see 10.2). We might also consider other Brahmanical literature, for example, the *Āpastamba-dharmasūtra* (perhaps third or second century BCE),[44] from which is drawn the verse that began this chapter. The *Āpastamba-dharmasūtra* introduces that verse as follows: "[The Brahmana] should practice forms of discipline that are proper to one's innermost self (*adhyātmika*), which have assured consequences and do not pertain to distraction. There is nothing higher than acquisition of the self (*ātmalābha*)."[45] The self mentioned in the verse at the start of this chapter is that which dwells "in hiding" (*guhāśaya*), in terms familiar from "middle-period" Upaniṣads: indestructible, stainless, immovable, and that which—if known and venerated—is the route to immortality.[46] This is reminiscent of how Buddha-nature is presented in our early *tathāgatagarbha* sources, to the extent that the MPNMS and AMS both teach that one might "make an

42. See Killingley 2018b.

43. Cohen 2018: 379–380, 359–367. The *Bhagavadgītā* understands that what Arjuna has had revealed to him is "the secret, known as one's innermost self" (v.11.1: *guhyam adhyātmasaṃjñitam;* e.g., Sargeant 2009: 453), the specific content of which is the revelation that one's true self is none other than the presence of Kṛṣṇa-Vāsudeva, the supreme deity abiding in all living beings (Sargeant 2009: 430, v.10.20: *aham ātmā … sarvabhūtāśayasthitaḥ*). See also Brockington 1998: 267–277; Malinar 2007: 113–120.

44. Olivelle 2018a: 21.

45. *Āpastamba-dharmasūtra* 1.22.1–2 (Bühler 1932: 38.19–39.1): *adhyātmikān yogān anutiṣthen nyāya saṃhitān anaiścārikān / ātmalābhān na paraṃ vidyate //* Translation modified from that of Olivelle 1999: 32–33. The *Āpastamba-dharmasūtra* is not an enthusiastic advocate of renunciation, but acknowledges that the self is that which the contemplative Brahmana endeavors to know.

46. Most noticeably the *Kaṭha-upaniṣad;* see references in 3.3n34.

offering" to their own *(buddha)dhātu* (see 2.3, 3.8): that is, the internalized "essence" of the Buddha, apart from all that is conditioned and can die, and the presence in oneself of that which surpasses all that is mundane and ephemeral.[47]

A particularly valuable source for us is the *Mānava-dharmaśāstra* (commonly "*The Laws of Manu*"; henceforth MDh): among the most historically influential treatises on the subject of Brahmanical dharma, which Patrick Olivelle (2018a: 20–21) has dated to the first two or three centuries of the Common Era. Though the MDh devotes greater attention to the duties of a householder, it also prescribes the career of the renunciant Brahmana and his desire for personal purity (*ātmasaṃsiddhi*), which entails observances including celibacy and abstention from meat,[48] as well as private recitation of the Upaniṣads.[49] The renunciant should otherwise reflect on the supreme self (*paramātman*), which inhabits all manner of different bodies as it transmigrates.[50] Though it is difficult for those who are not practiced,[51] the Brahmana must observe the self through meditative discipline (*dhyānayoga*); one who does not know the self (*adhyātman*) through this method cannot reap the benefits of ritual.[52] Verses that conclude the entire MDh reveal that the "highest secret" (*paramaṃ guhyaṃ*) of Brahmanical dharma is knowledge of the self:[53] "One's mind collected, one should see everything in the self, both existent and non-existent; for when one sees everything in the self, one's mind goes not to what contradicts (Brahmanical) dharma. All deities are simply the self; all that exists abides in the self; it is the self, in all embodied beings, that gives rise to the performance of actions."[54] This self is otherwise said to be smaller than an atom, lustrous like gold, but also the supreme person that moves from one life to another: "Hence when one sees, by the self, the self that is all beings, one becomes equal towards all and reaches *brahman*, the highest state."[55]

---

47. Notably the MPNMS understands teaching about the *(buddha)dhātu* to be akin to "ambrosia" (*amṛta*), which in Indic language can be indistinguishable from "immortality" itself; see MPNMS^F 884a26–b15; MPNMS^D 409a19–b18; MPNMS^T §386–387. This nuance lends itself to Habata's focus on the use of medicinal imagery running through the MPNMS (1989; also 2019: 27–38), but no doubt also invites comparison to wider Indian interest in the self as that which provides a means to end (repeated) death.

48. MDh 6.29 (Olivelle 2005: 149, 599).

49. MDh 6.83 (ibid., 152, 609): specifically, the renunciant should recite "those [texts] called *vedānta*"; see ibid., 292; also Olivelle 2018b: 196.

50. MDh 6.65 (ibid., 151, 606). One might consider the objections voiced in the MPNMS; see 2.4.

51. MDh 6.73 (ibid., 152, 608).

52. MDh 6.82 (ibid., 152, 609).

53. MDh 12.117 (ibid., 236, 911).

54. MDh 12.118–119: *sarvam ātmani saṃpaśyet sac cāsac ca samāhitaḥ / sarvaṃ hy ātmani saṃpaśyan nādharme kurute manaḥ // ātmaiva devatāḥ sarvāḥ sarvam ātmany avasthitam / ātmā hi janayaty eṣāṃ karmayogaṃ śarīriṇāṃ //* (ibid., 236, 911).

55. MDh 12.122–125, which concludes: *evaṃ yaḥ sarvabhūteṣu paśyaty ātmānam ātmanā / sa sarvasamatām etya brahmābhyeti paraṃ padam //* (ibid., 236, 912–913).

If this self is indeed some manner of "secret," the MDh nonetheless understands that teachings about it have an audience wider than simply renunciants; in its chapter on the instruction of kings, we read that a king must learn "the science of the self" (*ātmavidyā*), and that his instructors must be those "learned in the three Vedas," that is, they must be Brahmanas.[56] Knowledge of the self (*ātmajñāna*) is valued above all else, and its acquisition the focus of the kind of learning that leads to immortality.[57] Hence the secrecy associated with teachings about the self is indicative of the special status given to knowledge about it, rather than any sense that this must be kept strictly within Brahmanical circles; persuasive discourse about the self was a commodity, and a valuable one, that the Brahmana was able to offer to an influential donor or patron.[58]

In these passages the MDh attests to the continuing importance of discourse about the self in the earliest centuries of the Common Era, when erudite exposition about the self was attractive not only to renunciants but also, in the eyes of the Brahmanical tradition, to persons of wealth and influence whose support could make or break the fortunes of a religious sect or community. The MDh does not reflect the prominence of any one account of the self but rather the importance of discourse about it (i.e., *ātmavāda*), which—whatever its content—denotes a secret about beings in general, to which only the Brahmana is supposed to have access. By the early centuries of the Common Era some Brahmanical accounts of the self were of an avowedly theistic nature, as epitomized by the *Bhagavadgītā:* the "secret" of the self is that the valuable center of every sentient being can also be he who is the focus of all manner of rites, offerings, and other religious practices. In at least some Brahmanical contexts, an account of the self was an account also of the supreme deity, by whatever name, who resides beyond, but acts upon, the world.[59]

The formal similarities between this and our earliest accounts of Buddha-nature—that is, an internalization of something supermundane, a trace of a Buddha who exists beyond worldly appearance—are clear. Insofar as *tathāgatagarbha* designates that which is permanent, indestructible, and superlatively valuable, and moreover points outside of oneself to the timeless, higher reality that is the Buddha, this resembles an account of the self typical of theistic Upaniṣads specifically or, indeed, the *Bhagavadgītā*. Importantly, the more fitting comparison is not between the Buddha and the abstract *brahman* of earlier Upaniṣadic discourse (however *brahman* is understood in different literary contexts), but what we might call theistic modes of *ātmavāda* that developed in India in the centuries either side of

56. MDh 7.43 (ibid., 156, 619). Regarding the content of *ātmavidyā*, see MDh 12.12–25 (ibid., 230–231, 891–894; also 348). Regarding the economic and political value of *ātmavidyā* evinced by the Upaniṣads, see Black 2007: 88–92, 119–121.

57. MDh 12.85 (Olivelle 2005: 234, 905).

58. Black 2007: 24, after Urban 2001: 12.

59. See note 43 above.

the Common Era.[60] What our earlier Buddha-nature literature offers—couched in terms of something like the Buddha's "secret" revealed only late in his teaching—is something that Brahmanical sources such as the MDh acknowledge to have been of value to both renunciants (in their disputations) or to their donors (in their deliberations regarding who or what is worthy of patronage).[61]

In the first quarter of the first millennium, Mahāyānist authors opted to present an expressly Buddhist account of the self and that toward which it points, and declared this to be knowable only to a Buddha and "revealed" as something like the culmination of his teachings. Knowledge of Buddha-nature—"the Buddhist self"—is the preserve of the Buddha and those who know his pronouncements about it, a revelation that speaks to sentient beings in universal terms, but available only to those who attend to Buddhist teachings, and those of the Mahāyāna specifically. It was perhaps further developments in non-Buddhist discourse about the self, beyond the boundaries of what was opposed by earlier Buddhist teaching, that motivated some account of "the Buddha as a (supermundane) self," and with this "the Buddha as one's self," perhaps spurred by the creeping success of theistic modes of *ātmavāda* in the early Common Era. Our authors ventured to contest that it is in Buddhist liberation that one finds that with which other Indian religious traditions—Brahmanism in particular—were still occupied: not just escape from rebirth, but this imagined as the discovery of something enduring, incorruptible, and immortal. The *tathāgatagarbha*—an

60. Crucially, the comparison I am drawing is between our *ātmavāda tathāgatagarbha* sources—which explicitly articulate Buddha-nature as an account of the self—and increasingly creative (including theistic) forms of *ātmavāda* discourse in India proper to the turn of the Common Era. This is apart from the question of how far later *tathāgatagarbha* texts—for example, the ŚDS or RGVV, which are noticeably uncomfortable with the prospect of a Buddhist *ātmavāda*—exhibit a conceptual similarity to some Upaniṣads (especially those concerned with the equation of *ātman* to the abstract, impersonal *brahman*) or to a form of (Advaita) Vedānta. Regarding the relationship between some *tathāgatagarbha* teaching and monism see, for example, Takasaki 1966: 28, 61–66; 1974: 762; Nagao 1978: 81n35; Ruegg 1989a: 42n63; S. King 1991: 99–100 (citing Obermiller ([1931] 1991: 82); Matsumoto (for example) 1997: 171.

61. The supposedly sacred relationship between Brahmanas and kings—or "*brahman* and *kṣatra*"—is a central theme throughout the *Mahābhārata*, which may have also achieved a mature form in the early centuries of the Common Era. Fitzgerald (2006: 282–283) reflects on the epic as a defense of Brahmanical courtly influence; books including the *Mokṣadharmaparvan* work to persuade a patron that "brahmins had as much of the newer nonesoteric wisdom to teach as did the *nāstika* favorites" of earlier rulers (Mauryan, Kuṣāṇas, or otherwise), that is, Buddhists or Jains. It is perhaps revealing that besides the example of the woodworm (see 2.2), MPNMS-dhk tells us that when the Buddha subjugates other systems of thought he "pleases many kings" (MPNMS^{T} §107.7: *rgyal po du ma mgu bar mdzad*; compare MPNMS^{F} 863a5–7; MPNMS^{D} 378c20–22). Our Buddha-nature sources, which argue for the Buddhist origins of discourse about the self, as well for religious utterances (spells, treatises, etc.) in general, may reflect a Mahāyānist riposte in this exchange: that anything Brahmanism has to offer has origins in the Buddha, his Mahāyāna, and its diverse range of teachings and stratagems.

expression that is as much charged with "hiddenness" as it is pregnant with promise—equipped Mahāyānist authors with an affirmative response to wider discourse about liberation as a process of "self"-realization. That persons inferior to advanced bodhisattvas cannot themselves perceive this nature is of little consequence; the scriptural revelation of Buddha-nature acknowledged as the self—that which, in all sentient beings, points beyond itself—makes an ambitious contribution to an intersectarian debate in which Indian authors and audiences continued to invest importance.

In conclusion, we might characterize the *tathāgatagarbha,* presented as the Buddha's teaching about the true self, as the strategic adoption of a mode of discourse that was beyond the parameters of conventional Buddhist thought and expression, a teaching that does not reject prior Buddhist teaching about things in the world, or indeed the Buddha present beyond it, so much as supplement it with the Buddha's authoritative account of what *can,* unlike all things worldly, be called the self. Teaching about *tathāgatagarbha,* as a relocation of the abiding presence of buddhahood, is continuous with themes and concerns proper to the Indian Buddhist imagination, and serves also to develop a Buddhology that elevates the status of Buddhas—and the bodhisattvas who become them—further above all that is worldly. But we must still account for what could permit this level of innovation (critics might say "deviation") in this period of Indian Buddhist intellectual history, given that other Buddhist sources, from this era and later, remained committed to an ancient and highly productive discourse concerned with absence of self. To address this we must contextualize Buddha-nature teaching as not only Buddhist, or even Mahāyānist, but as an expression of one particularly bold strain of the Mahāyāna that emerged in association with the SP, which we can call "ekayānist."

10.4 Buddhist Selfhood and the Mahāyāna

We have seen that Brahmanical sources, including many Upaniṣads, reflect a variety of perspectives regarding to what the expression *ātman* must refer and what higher principle or reality it makes knowable (see 9.6). The MDh evinces that in the early centuries of the Common Era the self and discussion about it remained important for both the Brahmanical renunciant (intent on liberation) and courtier (intent on patronage). But it is not so clear that Brahmanical tradition had reached any consensus regarding the self, only that a Brahmana should be acknowledged as one who has expertise regarding its qualities, location, and the supermundane reality in which it somehow participates. It was debate about these questions that earlier (indeed, likely the earliest) Buddhist teachers had eschewed, and that is still challenged wherever our *tathāgatagarbha* sources deny the existence of this or that erroneous notion of selfhood. But the MPNMS, AMS, and MBhS reject wrong-minded thinking about the self while advancing the Buddha's own account of that which deserves this label; their rejection of non-Buddhist teaching about the self is no longer an outright dismissal of this debate but features some participation in it. The true self of any sentient being is the nature of the Buddha, or the presence of the *tathāgatagarbha.* If the status of the Buddha, contrary to any worldly phenomenon, could be understood as the discovery of the self, and if the essence of a liberated being lies imperceptibly in one's own constitution, then Mahāyānist authors arrive at their own answer to a perennial Indian concern: Buddhist dharma has its own account of the self.

If we pay careful attention to our earliest Buddha-nature sources we observe that they do not simply promote a rival account of the self, but also venture to accommodate discourse about the self in general within the parameters of the Buddha's influence. Both the MPNMS and AMS—our two most thorough and detailed sources of a Buddhist *ātmavāda*—propose that non-Buddhist discourse about the self owes its existence to the activities of the Buddha or bodhisattvas; either through miscomprehension or, more creatively, by design (see 2.5, 3.7). The account of the self that our authors innovate constitutes entry into a debate about to what this label should refer, and in the process explains that all other discourse about a self that is supermundane derives from the definitive teaching about it that is revealed, finally, in the Mahāyāna. Remembering that possession of the *tathāgatagarbha* extends to *all* sentient beings regardless of status or orientation, non-Buddhist teachings about the self are included within the domain of the Buddha's many and varied teachings and activities, regardless of from where they appear to have arisen. Put crudely, Buddha-nature is not simply a teaching about the self, but teaching about the self—where it points to what is supermundane—is always, in the end, about Buddha-nature (see, again, 2.5).

Anticipating further discussion of these categories in the pages that follow, we could suppose that by adopting the language of selfhood our Buddha-nature authors attempted something like a strategy of inclusion or accommodation, aimed at Indian religious discourse that was previously beyond the limits of what could be imagined to have been taught by the Buddha. Both the MPNMS and AMS explain how non-Buddhist discourse about the self is a product of the Buddha and of his bodhisattvas, the work of emanations (*nirmāṇa/nirmita*) that only appear to originate outside of the Buddhist sphere of influence. A similar phenomenon is described in a text on the periphery of the main *tathāgatagarbha* tradition, the BGVNS, which we acknowledged above shows strong ties to the SP and in one of its recensions teaches about *tathāgatagarbha* (see 9.1). As its title suggests, the BGVNS is concerned with the range of methods that are employed by bodhisattvas (*bodhisattvagocaropāya*) in their efforts to teach sentient beings. These extend to the revelation that all manner of non-Buddhist teachers—those called *tīrthikas*, *nirgranthas*, or otherwise—are in fact sustained by the Buddha's power, or are otherwise evidence of bodhisattvas covertly teaching ideas and practices that lead sentient beings toward Buddhist dharma.[62] In a logical development of the single vehicle paradigm, and thematically very similar to what we find in our earliest sources for Buddha-nature teaching, the BGVNS declares not only that all Buddhist teachings guide in the direction of complete awakening but that *all* discourse about liberation, no matter its apparent origins or affiliation, is somehow discourse about buddhahood specifically.[63]

The similarities between what is taught in the BGVNS and claims made in the MPNMS and AMS are, I believe, quite clear. I have contended above that even though core material of the MPNMS does not use the expression, all three of these texts are "ekayānist" in type (9.1), and so teach that liberation can only mean achieving the status of a Buddha. This can be true, as the SP explains, only if the Buddha's earlier teachings about different kinds of achievement (the liberations of the arhat or *pratyekabuddha*) were expediencies taught so that all manner of beings could be led, often very gradually, to realize the complete awakening of a Buddha. A dominant theme in the SP is the revelation that the Buddha's activities exceed what was previously believed: Śākyamuni is not limited to his final (apparent) birth and death but is himself also responsible for the activities of previous Buddhas "from Dīpaṃkara onwards."[64] Otherwise two whole chapters of the SP (likely later additions to its final form) are devoted to the works and worship of named bodhisattvas—Gadgadasvara and Avalokiteśvara—who teach sentient beings by taking on the forms of deities, including Brahmā, Rudra, Śakra, Īśvara, and Maheśvara.[65] This is all for the benefit of those sentient beings who might be developed by precisely these forms; the adoration of deities ostensibly apart from Buddhist dharma is in fact the veneration of a bodhisattva, whether a devotee understands this or not.[66]

This same soteriological paradigm is promoted by our early *tathāgatagarbha* literature, in which all discourse about liberation can be considered expressions by Buddhas or bodhisattvas, whose true forms and intentions are concealed but who can be considered responsible for any

62. BGVNS^{B} 326c23–327a2, in which we read about the Buddha's "sustaining power" (*zhchili* 住持力: **adhisthāna*) over all "non-Buddhist" systems; see also C. V. Jones 2016a: 144–153.

63. Indeed, the revelation late in the BGVNS is that the seemingly not Buddhist Satyaka is himself an advanced bodhisattva, who merely takes the forms of non-Buddhist adepts to help liberate innumerable sentient beings; see BGVNS^{B} 361b10–24.

64. SP 317.10–13 (Kern 1884: 300, including note 2): *dīpaṃkaratathāgataprabhṛtayaḥ … upāyakauśalyadharmadeśanābhinirhāranirmitāni.* See also Radich 2012a: 242. This understands prior Buddhas, who did not reveal the great "secret" of the single vehicle—and so the comprehensive nature of the Mahāyāna—to have been only emanations (*nirmita*) by Śākyamuni.

65. SP 442.5–445.10 (Kern 1884: 410–412). See also Ruegg 2008: 32–33.

66. See excellent discussion by Ruegg (2004: 32–33; 2008: e.g., 41–44, 69–74, 131–134) regarding the reduction of worldly (*laukika*) "ectypes" to the activities or productions of supermundane (*lokottara*) "archetypes," and the means by which Buddhist authors claimed authority over the former by privileged knowledge of the latter.

number of ostensibly non-Buddhist ideas, practices, and authorities. Authors who embraced this picture of Buddhist soteriology may have still understood the path of the bodhisattva to be reserved for an elite few, but they affirm that preparatory stages for this journey extend into teachings given to *śrāvaka*s and *tīrthika*s, and to the worship of worldly deities. Equipped with an account of the Buddha as an enduring and supermundane orchestrator of worldly events, who with a host of bodhisattvas produces any number of doctrines and practices aimed at directing all sentient beings to a single goal, our Buddha-nature authors were part of an enterprise to expand the perceived horizons of (Mahāyānist) Buddhism further than had been previously known. In the process, they affirm the authority of the Mahāyāna—a single, comprehensive vehicle that is taught by the myriad devices of a transcendent, godlike Buddha—over the wider Indian religious landscape.[67] In summation, it benefits us to appreciate that earlier *tathāgatagarbha* literature—and earliest within it those *sūtra*s that present Buddha-nature as a teaching about the self—is not only Mahāyānist in orientation but represents a particular strain of Mahāyānist innovation informed by the SP, which aspires to universalize the Mahāyāna into a comprehensive treasury of all teachings about liberation regardless of their apparent origin.

Later authors in the *tathāgatagarbha* tradition wished to preserve the central Buddha-nature idea but did not pursue any advantages there may have been to articulating this as an account of the self; this was, textual evidence suggests, too much of a departure from wider Buddhist commitment to its normative *nairātmyavādin* orientation. But it is beyond doubt that other Mahāyānist literature continued to push at the boundaries of what audiences took to be the Buddhist sphere of influence, and in this sense our early Buddha-nature authors were, perhaps, pioneers. Pertinent examples include versions of the *Suvarṇaprabhāsasūtra,* which justifies the practice of worldly rituals, and the evocation of deities associated with them, as proper to the Mahāyāna.[68] Core material of this work, which existed in some form by the early fifth century, includes instructions for ritual

67. It is also plausible—as argued by, for example, Verardi (2011: 105–106)—that docetic Buddhism as espoused by the SP functioned (in part) as a response to the growing influence of theistic movements, focused on Viṣṇu or Śiva, that were burgeoning at the start of the Common Era, and which utilized forms of theistic *ātmavāda* discussed above (10.4). It is likely in portions of the *Mahābhārata* that we have our earliest evidence of Brahmanism teaching that deities beyond the world produce something like manifestations (*prādurbhāva*; *avatāra*) within it; see Brockington 1998: 277–289; also, apropos of the *Bhagavadgītā* in relation to these themes (aspects of its "cosmological monotheism"), see Malinar 2007: 232–241.

68. See, for example, T. Suzuki 2003; 2004; 2005; 2006; 2007; 2008. Our terminus for core material of the text is the production of Dharmakṣema's translation, the *Jin guangming jing* 金光明經 (T.663), in perhaps 420 CE. Regarding the continued growth of the text beyond India, see Radich 2014, 2015c. An excellent discussion of the *Suvarṇaprabhāsasūtra* and its complex textual history is Gummer 2015.

bathing, as well as rites conducive to eloquence, prosperity, protection, and agricultural success (invoking the deities Sarasvatī, Śrī, the four Lokapālas, and the earth goddess Dṛḍhā, respectively).[69] As Takayasu Suzuki has argued, reinterpretation of these phenomena as being within the remit of Buddhist authority does not constitute some "depravation" of Buddhism but is rather evidence of Buddhist authors "emphasizing the value, usefulness and *completeness* of [Mahāyāna] Buddhism" (my italics), which—the *sūtra* reveals—has at its disposal all manner of ritual activities that an intended audience may not have naturally considered "Buddhist."[70] In another literary context, from perhaps the fifth or sixth century, Mahāyānist authors contested with mythic narratives that became component stories in the Brahmanical Purāṇas.[71] As Alexander Studholme has demonstrated, the fantastical narratives of the *Kāraṇḍavyūhasūtra* reimagine deeds better associated with the deities Viṣṇu and Śiva as activities of the bodhisattva Avalokiteśvara, and develop Mahāyānist "creation" myths to compete with those that celebrated non-Buddhist deities.[72] Ritual and mythic structures, and the deities associated with them, are reimagined as the property of Buddhism. All of this is possible because of the inherently innovative nature of Mahāyānist *sūtra* composition, which became increasingly inventive—especially in its responses to the wider Indian intellectual-religious landscape—as Buddhism began to develop elaborate forms of tantrism in the second half of the first millennium (see below).[73]

How, though, to characterize the adoption of an entire mode of discourse, a form of *ātmavāda,* which earlier Buddhist tradition—and very

---

69. This is explored across publications by T. Suzuki (see previous note), and summarized in Suzuki 2008: 69–73. Suzuki (1996b; 1998) has also demonstrated that the *Suvarṇaprabhāsasūtra* borrows material from the *Mahāmeghasūtra*—our fourth member of the MPNMS-group—that is concerned with the superficial nature of the Buddha's physical relics, and features also the enigmatic figure Sarvalokapriyadarśana (Nobel 1937: 12.6–19.4; Emmerick 1970: 6–7; compare *Mahāmeghasūtra* T.387[12]1096c4–1097a27; 1099a9–14; see also 9.4). This material preserves a verse that the *Mahāmeghasūtra* appears to have in common with the AMS; see 3.1n13 (translated at 3.1n11; compare Nobel 1937: 18.6–7 (v.2.27); Emmerick 1970: 7).

70. T. Suzuki 2006: 46.

71. A thorough survey of the Purāṇas, and their content and composition, is Rocher 1986.

72. See Studholme 2002: 11–35; see also Ruegg 2008: 31–33; Eltschinger 2014: 82–85.

73. The matter of Mahāyānist *sūtra* production, and by it the broadening of what could be considered to be "utterances by the Buddha" (*buddhavacana*), is too complex to explore here. However, we should recall the observation of MacQueen (1982) that the SP—in contrast to other works of Mahāyānist literature—relies on what he calls a "theistic" authorization of texts, by assurance of the Buddha's enduring presence throughout the revelation/production of what are discernibly novel and innovative articulations of Mahāyāna Buddhism. MacQueen is no doubt correct that this is typical of "newer developments in Indian religion" such as "devotionalism and *avatāra* mythology" (1982: 62), which we should imagine to be the backdrop against which the attitudes and aspirations our earliest Buddha-nature texts, alongside the SP, had provenance.

plausibly the founder of the tradition himself—had very purposefully rejected?[74] One option, alluded to above, would be to understand the Buddhist self in terms of Paul Hacker's definition of "inclusivism." This, in short, refers to instances in which one religious system finds approval within its worldview for ideas or practices more conventionally understood to belong to another, and in such a fashion that subordinates what is foreign in the shadow of that which is one's own.[75] In spite of various criticisms of his work, Hacker's central observation—that authors within one tradition may lay claim to extraneous phenomena, and so reduce them to peripheral or subsidiary elements of one's own system—remains valuable. But in the instance of a Buddhist *ātmavāda* we have a problem: in order to "include" non-Buddhist discourse about the self on the periphery of Buddhist teaching (e.g., as expedient works by bodhisattvas), something at the heart of Buddhist teaching is also altered, such that the highest truth becomes—to the surprise of any Buddhist audience—an account of the self.[76] This looks like inclusion of the other at the expense of the integrity of one's own central teachings: *nairātmyavāda* is superseded by a form of *ātmavāda,* which for at least some Buddhist audiences threatened the integrity of the dharma, and the cornerstone of its identity that is teaching about absence of self.

To make sense of the kind of enterprise in which our *ātmavādin* authors were engaged, we might consider another, later adaptation of Buddhist dharma that was a good deal more successful, at least in Buddhism's South Asian homeland. In the latter half of the first millennium, Mahāyānists took to producing texts that justified Buddhist expansion into the world of tantric ritualism. The *Mahāvairocanābhisaṃbodhi,* which was extant in some form before the late seventh century,[77] warns its audience that some within the Buddhist community will think that its program of ritual procedures that aim at progressing faster toward the status of a fully awakened being—esoteric initiations (*abhiṣeka*), fire oblations (*homa*), and so forth—is the

74. A learned discussion of this matter is by Ruegg (1989a: 17–55), though with some notable differences from my own. Ruegg offers comparatively less attention to *sūtra* materials—most significantly, those that advance an account of the *tathāgatagarbha* in terms of the self—and instead attends to how the Buddhist hermeneutical tradition (beginning, in this instance, with the RGVV and LAS) makes sense of teachings about some "immanent absolute."

75. Oberhammer 1983: 12. Apart from contributions to Oberhammer 1983, see also Schmithausen 1981: 223; Ruegg 1989a: 7–10, 50–55; 2008: 98. Regarding Hacker's publications on this theme, see Halbfass 1995; also Olivelle 1986. Polemical "inclusivism" should be distinguished from the same term taken to refer to pluralistic enterprises in interreligious dialogue, as explored more thoroughly by Kiblinger 2005.

76. This problem is acknowledged by Ruegg (1989a: 7–10): that teachings about Buddha-nature are not understood to be "expedient" (*neyārtha*) by our primary sources for this tradition, nor by a great number of later receptions of Buddha-nature teaching, and hence something other than "inclusion"—classically understood—seems to have been at play.

77. Hodge 2003: 14–15.

kind of thing that belongs to the teachings of non-Buddhist systems.[78] Employing a by now familiar response, the *Mahāvairocanābhisaṃbodhi* explains that deities such as Maheśvara, Brahmā, Nārāyana, and others, all of whom were venerated in non-Buddhist tantric systems, are in reality productions by the Buddha Vairocana, who is the source of any ritual system that resembles what is found in its pages.[79] This strategy legitimizes emulation of the ritual and iconographic repertoires of non-Buddhist traditions, such that later Buddhist *tantra*s—such as the *Laghuśaṃvara* and *Hevajratantra,* now undeniably influenced by Śaiva ritualism specifically—can be explained to audiences in terms of a debt that *non*-Buddhist systems owe to the many and varied methods and instruments of Buddhas and bodhisattvas.[80] Ritual motifs and mechanisms that were surely conspicuously reminiscent of non-Buddhist phenomena are reinterpreted as authoritative, definitive expressions of Buddhist power.[81] Where such things are visible in non-Buddhist systems, these are reduced to derivations from that which the Buddha(s) or bodhisattvas are understood to have taught.

Our Buddhist attempt at *ātmavāda* is, I believe, comparable to what can be observed in the development of Buddhist tantrism in the second half of the first millennium. Indian sources for what came to be known as the Vajrayāna did not understand their texts or the ritual procedures that they describe to constitute some adjunct to prior Buddhist teaching "included" at its periphery, perhaps for some or other expedient purpose; theirs is the apex of the dharma (indeed a "secret" culmination to it), by which progress to the status of a Buddha could be made at lightening ("*vajra*") speed. As here, so also in our Buddha-nature sources: Buddhist innovators justify engagement in a form of discourse (about the self) or system of practice (esoteric ritualism) that flourished outside of the commonly acknowledged parameters of Buddhist teaching, for which there was no prior approval in extant Buddhist literature. In each instance—at least in the eyes of the authors responsible—the adoption of new ideas or activities left established Buddhist teaching intact; belief in the *tathāgatagarbha* does not lead to acceptance of erroneous or worldly notions of the self, and in the

78. See Sanderson 1994: 96–97. Elsewhere, Sanderson (2009: 128–186) attends to Buddhist adoption of explicitly Śaiva language and motifs as far back as the *Mañjuśriyamūlakalpa* (first translated into Chinese in 702 CE, though see Sanderson 2009: 129n300), in which non-Buddhist ritual elements—Śaiva and Vaiṣṇava—are presented as expedient productions by a Buddhist authority (in this context by the bodhisattva Mañjuśrī), such that "Buddhists envisaged by this text have the whole array of Śaiva Mantras at their disposal" (ibid., 130). See also Granoff 2000: 404–412; Ruegg 2008: 35–36.

79. See Hodge 2003: 52–53, which demonstrates that Buddhaguhya's commentary on the *Mahāvairocanābhisaṃbodhi* develops the theme of Vairocana's emanations further; also Sanderson 2009: 131–132, n.309; Ruegg 2008: 35–36; C. V. Jones 2016a: 159–160.

80. See Sanderson 2009: 124ff, regarding Buddhist tantrism as (at least in part) the production of rituals that could compete with the repertoire of Śaivism and other forms of tantrism. See also Ruegg 2008: 105–114; Sferra 2003.

81. Sanderson 2009: 169–172.

case of tantrism the bodhisattva's cultivation of "perfections" (*pāramitānaya*), alongside the tantric use of incantations and other ritual instruments (*mantranaya*), must still be observed.

My position, then, is that for scholarship to view Buddha-nature as some affront to teachings about absence of self—whether the *tathāgatagarbha* is presented as the Buddha's account of the self or otherwise—falls foul of privileging an essentialist perspective concerning the directions within which Buddhist authors could or could not expand the purview of teachings attributed to the Buddha.[82] In each of the literary contexts discussed above Mahāyānist authors engaged creatively with the range and popularity of ideas and practices from across the Indian religious landscape. Along the way, the account of the Buddha as a properly supermundane being—deploying myriad stratagems and devices—not only helps to accommodate non-Buddhist elements but also to contest for the authentically Buddhist origins of them. As much as Buddhist *tāntrikas* explained non-Buddhist ritual cycles to be creations or distortions of Buddhist teachings, our Buddhist *ātmavādins*—from a certainly earlier period of Buddhist history—lay claim to having the definitive account of the self, from which all limited notions of such a thing are somehow derived. In summary, use of the expression *tathāgatagarbha* to promote a Buddhist account of the self is not, from one perspective, so exceptional; it is a prime though perhaps early example of the kind of strategy that was characteristic of the Mahāyāna as it came to maturity, and in some instances pursued a catholic if not comprehensive inclusion of religious ideas and activities that Buddhist audiences may have encountered in the world.[83]

---

82. I hence disagree with accusations leveled at Buddha-nature thinking by the "Critical Buddhist" (Hihan Bukkyō) movement, which understood the alleged *dhātuvāda* orientation of the *tathāgatagarbha* tradition to constitute an "un-Buddhist" departure from core Buddhist teachings; see Hubbard and Swanson 1997: 165–335; Zimmermann 2002: 82–84; Shimoda 2020; also 5.5 above. More productively, Ruegg (1989a: 55) refers to a "common ground or substratum" to Indian thought in general, to which Buddhism, Brahmanism, and other systems were all indebted (see also Ruegg 2008: e.g., v–vi, 41–48). In this instance, a hypothetical common ground need refer to little more than a pervasive Indian occupation with the true self, or what might be essential to a sentient being across its successive lives and into liberation, rather than to any specific doctrine or practice. Regarding the diversity of the Mahāyāna tradition in India—to which our Buddha-nature sources attest—see Silk 2002, as well as the wealth of perspectives on discernibly early Mahāyānist themes and concerns collated in Harrison 2018b.

83. Though this account of the exhaustive influence of bodhisattvas is more evident in Mahāyānist sources, it should be noted that a similar claim occurs in the *Daśabhūmika* material of the Mahāsāṃghika(-Lokottaravāda) *Mahāvastu*, which declares that bodhisattvas are responsible for revealing all mantras and medicines (*agada*) that are in the world, all treatments (*bhaiṣajya*), all treatises concerned with ascertainment of truth (*śāstrāṇi tattvaniścayayuktāṇi*), as well as all means of enumeration (*saṃkhyāgaṇana*), means of writing (consisting of a list of languages and scripts), the locations of precious substances, and finally—exhaustively—all instruments (*kāraṇa*) that might be employed to benefit sentient beings; see Senart 1882: 134.17–135.10; J. J. Jones 1949: 107–108; also Granoff 2000: 422n8. This material is likely late

10.5 Closing Thoughts

The *tathāgatagarbha* was not only a Buddhist revelation of the self, but it could conveniently function as the Buddha's account of that which wider Indian religious discourse held to be of utmost importance: a kernel of human identity that gestures outside of itself toward that which is supermundane (see 10.2–3). Radich's arguments about the original doctrinal context for the Buddha-nature idea are persuasive: teaching about *tathāgatagarbha* constitutes "a positive, soteriologically-oriented substitute for the fleshly womb, which docetic Buddhology holds could not possibly be the real seed-bed for a being as perfect and exalted as a Buddha."[84] Although the nuances and possible interpretations of *tathāgatagarbha* are many, throughout Indian Buddhist literature it was understood to mark the locus (or, following Jikidō Takasaki, "matrix") from which a properly transcendent Buddha could, in time, emerge. But as far back as we are able to trace teaching about *tathāgatagarbha*—to material in the MPNMS(-tg), in which the sacred bodily essence of a Buddha (*buddhadhātu*) is relocated into the constitution of every sentient being—this was always proximate to the idea that something in all sentient beings is so precious, so unlike the rest of their person, that this qualifies to be known as the self.

Observing similarities between non-Buddhist discourse about the self and our *ātmavādin* Buddhist sources does not require us to conclude that early explanations of *tathāgatagarbha* were an infiltration into Buddhism by ideas or language of a "non-Buddhist" bent, nor that some Buddhist authors "sold out" to embrace a discourse long-eschewed by their predecessors. To argue as much submits to an essentialist understanding of Buddhist thought in India, and does a disservice to the creativity of Mahāyānist authors and their efforts to develop, defend, and expand the breadth of teachings attributed to the Buddha. While still committed to rejecting attachment to things worldly—the body, sensations, or other transient content of the mind—our earliest Buddha-nature authors recognized that the universalization of what is most essential to a Buddha, which understands each sentient being to be the site from which a fully realized Buddha can emerge, equipped them with a new perspective on how liberation could be conceptualized. Informed by a doctrinal shift begun by the SP, the *tathāgatagarbha* is that which prefigures the eventual manifestation of a new Buddha in any sentient being; but it could also compete with wider Indian discourse about something that is superlatively valuable in all beings: transcendently powerful, enduringly present, and an object of reverence hidden in each one of them.

---

in the composition of the *Mahāvastu* (Tournier 2017: 611–613), and likely does not predate the Buddha-nature literature that has concerned us here.

84. Radich 2015a: 156.

Later Mahāyānist authors attempted to salvage the expression *tathāgatagarbha* from what may have been a failed enterprise; in the eyes of some authors, Buddhist dharma could not (or should not) sustain an *ātmavādin* form. Related to this, and most visible in both the ŚDS and LAS, was the rejection of *tathāgatagarbha* as a signifier for some precious "essence" of a Buddha hidden within one's constitution, and the sense instead that this must refer to, for example, the mind as the locus at which one can find the basic nature of reality itself (e.g., "*dharmadhātugarbha*"; see 5.2, 8.6). We should not be surprised by the hermeneutic employed by the LAS, and to some extent the RGVV, to make sense of inconvenient *ātmavādin* declarations made by earlier *tathāgatagarbha* sources; where Buddha-nature is presented as an account of the self, this can only be an expediency. This revisionist interpretation is all well and good for Buddhist authors, who are compelled to interpret the diversity of ideas found in preexisting materials to fit with their own conception of the true (i.e., *sad-*)dharma. But no *sūtra* text, claiming to preserve authoritative utterances by the Buddha (*buddhavacana*), took itself to be of only provisional value, and there is little chance that the authors of the MPNMS, AMS, and MBhS understood their elaborate expositions of the Buddhist self to be less than they appear to be: teachings about the true self, which is the Buddha's great revelation, otherwise known by the expression *tathāgatagarbha*.

Was all of this effort—to present Buddha-nature in language that spoke to the wider Indian religious landscape—only an elaborate strategy to convert opponents to the dharma? This is broadly the position of both the RGVV and LAS, and at face value it seems reasonable that Buddha-nature teachings may have been developed to appeal to non-Buddhist adepts (*tīrthika*s) specifically.[85] But again this understands some teaching about *tathāgatagarbha* as a kind of expedient device—likely not what authors of the MPNMS-group intended—and one which, I believe, would have been somewhat flawed. We have seen both the MPNMS and AMS claim that wider discourse about the self is somehow derivative of Buddhist teaching, and that non-Buddhist accounts of the self have the Buddha or bodhisattvas as their originators. These would not have been terribly persuasive statements to the ears of committed advocates of non-Buddhist systems, who would have had no reason to doubt that their account of the self was original (or to believe that they or their teachings were somehow "stratagems" produced by bodhisattvas). In other words, Buddhist *ātmavāda* has little to say to teachers or adepts sworn to non-Buddhist systems, in spite of how both the RGVV and LAS couch the value of *ātmavāda tathāgatagarbha* teachings, ex post facto, as tools for something like proselytization.

Reconfiguring Buddhist dharma to have at its apex an account of the self would be a tremendous leap just for the sake of converting (or condescending to) systems of non-Buddhist renunciation, and there is no doubt that the rest of our Buddha-nature sources are very focused on what is proper

85. For example, Zimmermann 2002: 75–77.

conduct for already committed adepts or supporters of the Mahāyāna. The universalization of Buddha-nature, articulated in terms of the self, must have had other motivations, and was—I believe—a strategy proper to a far more ambitious project. The revelation of the *tathāgatagarbha* creatively expands the repertoire of Buddhist teachings to include and moreover "own" discourse about that which qualifies to be called the self. Our primary sources for this tradition follow the SP, and hold that the Buddha continues to influence the world in myriad, mysterious ways. Within the single vehicle paradigm—a radical shift in Buddhist soteriology, for which the SP is surely our earliest source—liberation is open to all persons who commit to the Mahāyāna, and if the Buddha is indeed both permanent and supremely powerful, then all manner of phenomena can be expressions of his continuing works for all of these beings, in all kinds of environments.[86] Our Buddha-nature texts do not celebrate the merits of non-Buddhist accounts of the self—no more than the SP approves of "Hīnayānist" teachings, nor Buddhist *tāntrikas* of their non-Buddhist counterparts and competitors—but rather introduce the Buddha's definitive account of to what all remotely persuasive *ātmavādin* discourse must have always referred. In so doing, our sources develop the Mahāyāna as the exhaustive treasury of all teachings and activities, at all times and in all circumstances, that aim at liberation from rebirth, in which *tathāgatagarbha* speaks directly and definitively about what is greater than, yet also "resident in," all sentient beings.

If nothing else, this study has hoped to shift scholarly attention to the sources of Buddha-nature teaching that couched *tathāgatagarbha* in terms of selfhood, in the belief that these preserve for us an older form of teaching about to what the expression *tathāgatagarbha* must refer. To better understand the world of their authors, more must be done to unpack the rich and little-studied doctrines of both the AMS and MBhS in particular, as well as their common debt to the SP: a precursor, we have seen, to Buddha-nature thinking in general. After the SP, early *tathāgatagarbha* literature attests to an expansion of the Mahāyāna to account for not simply all Buddhist teachings, but moreover all religious discourse in general, and in the process an elevation of the Buddha to a status such that he is responsible for far more than many Buddhists (let alone other Indian audiences) would have commonly accepted. I have suggested that this reflects a spirit of intersectarian competition that was alive and well in the early centuries of the Common Era, though have provided only a preliminary sketch of how and why Buddhist authors began to transform the Mahāyāna into an explanation for all manner of teachings and practices that were outside of the dharma as it had been previously understood.[87]

---

86. An eloquent statement by Ruegg (2008: 34; quoted in C. V. Jones 2016a: 161) bears repeating: if the Buddha indeed exceeds what was seen of his life, "the entire world of *saṃsāra* may then be a kind of stage on which the liberating activity of the Buddha and the Bodhisattvas is played out."

87. As this study has concerned literature proper to Indian Buddhism, I stop short of discussing the implications of my argument for our understanding of Buddhism in East

The revised trajectory of Buddha-nature teaching that we have explored is open to further interrogation. As I have focused on a single issue that courses through the *tathāgatagarbha* literature, it is perhaps with reference to other themes or motifs—such as those identified in chapter 9, or others besides—that more could be done to contextualize all of these texts in the diverse and colorful world of Indian Mahāyāna literature. It is also still the case that the varied and slippery ideas of the LAS—an influential outlier to Buddha-nature teaching that reflects on this and other earlier Mahāyānist developments besides—require more attention. Finally, and needless to say, critical editions and philologically grounded translations of all of the texts discussed in this volume, where such things do not already exist, remain desiderata if the many curiosities of the Buddha-nature tradition are to be further studied and understood.

The current volume has reevaluated a contentious development in the Indian Mahāyāna, and traced this—the history of a Buddhist account of the self—through the invention and reinvention of the expression *tathāgatagarbha,* to which it was related. We have seen that Buddha-nature teaching emerged in the context of Mahāyānist innovation and expansion, in which affirmation of the supermundane status of the Buddha played a formative and central role. In its early life, likely between the second and third centuries of the Common Era, Buddha-nature teaching came in the wake of the belief that the Buddha must endure beyond what was seen of his earthly form, and that all things that he had taught belong to the Mahāyāna. Early Buddha-nature thought, which was articulated as an account of the self, both complements and expands this paradigm of the Buddha's involvement with the world and the status of the Mahāyāna within it. Teaching about *tathāgatagarbha* provided a new account of how buddhahood can be a universal goal, and allowed for the Mahāyāna—imagined now as the single, exhaustive vehicle of Buddhist teaching—to be both the cause and culmination of all worldly discourse about liberation in general. Like the Buddha's physical relics before it, the Buddha-nature idea became enshrined in the expression *tathāgatagarbha,* and in turn this name gave life to a wealth of different perspectives on how a commonality between sentient beings and Buddhas might be understood. Even so, teaching about *tathāgatagarbha* in India carried the legacy of having been, in its earliest incarnation, a Mahāyānist account of the self—the enduring and indestructible essence of every sentient being, and the immanent yet elusive goal of all religious enterprise.

Asia, where the SP and MPNMS played important roles in systems of doctrinal classification (*panjiao* 判教), and which in some instances stretched to include—at their lower levels—teachings and practices proper to "worldly" or non-Buddhist traditions; see, for example, Gregory 1983; 1991: 255–261.

References

Abbott, Terry Rae. 1985. "Vasubandhu's Commentary to the *Saddharmapuṇḍarīka-sūtra:* A Study of Its History and Significance." Doctoral dissertation, University of California, Berkeley.

———. 2013. "The Commentary on the Lotus Sutra." In *Tiantai Lotus Texts,* 83-150. Berkeley, CA: Bukkyō Dendō Kyōkai America.

Acharya, Diwakar. 2014. "On the Śaiva Concept of Innate Impurity (*Mala*) and the Function of the Rite of Initiation." *Journal of Indian Philosophy* 42: 9–25.

Albahari, Miri. 2002. "Against No-Ātman Theories of Anattā." *Asian Philosophy* 12 (1): 5–20.

———. 2006. *Analytical Buddhism: The Two-Tiered Illusion of Self.* Basingstoke, UK: Palgrave Macmillan.

Anālayo, Bhikkhu. 2008. "The Conversion of Aṅgulimāla in the *Saṃyukta-āgama.*" *Buddhist Studies Review* 25 (2): 135–148.

———. 2009. "The Lion's Roar in Early Buddhism—A Study Based on the *Ekottarika-āgama* Parallel to the *Cūḷasīhanāda-sutta.*" *Chung-Hwa Buddhist Journal* 22: 3–23.

———. 2011. *A Comparative Study of the Majjhima-nikāya.* Vol. 1, *Introduction, Studies of Discourses 1 to 90.* Dharma Drum Publishing. Accessed December 30, 2018. https://www.buddhismuskunde.uni-hamburg.de.

———. 2017. "The Luminous Mind in Theravāda and Dharmaguptaka Discourses." *Journal of the Oxford Centre for Buddhist Studies* 13: 10–51.

Andersen, Dines, and Smith, Helmer. 1913. *Suttanipāta.* London: Pali Text Society.

Apte, Vaman Shivaram. 1957. *Revised and Enlarged Edition of Prin. V. S. Apte's "The Practical Sanskrit-English Dictionary."* Vol. 1. (A to K). Poona, India: Prasad Prakashan.

Bailey, H. W., and Johnston, E. H. 1935. "A Fragment of the '*Uttaratantra*' in Sanskrit." *Bulletin of the School of Oriental Studies, University of London* 8 (1): 77–89.

Balcerowicz, Piotr. 1997. "Jaina Concept of Religion." *Dialogue and Universalism* 11–12: 197–215.

Barber, Anthony. 2008. "Two Mahāyāna Developments along the Krishna River." In *Buddhism in the Krishna River Valley of Andhra,* edited by Sree Padma and A. W. Barber, 151–168. Albany: State University of New York Press.

Bareau, André. 1955. *Les sectes bouddhiques du Petit Véhicule.* Saigon: Ecole Française d'Extrême-Orient.

Basham, A. L. 1951. *History and Doctrines of the Ājīvikas: A Vanished Indian Religion.* London: Luzac & Co.

Bedekar, V. M. 1968. "The Doctrine of the Colours of the Souls in the *Mahābhārata:* Its Character and Implications." *Annals of the Bhandarkar Oriental Research Institute* 48–49: 329–338.

Bendall, Cecil. (1897–1902) 1970. *Çikshāsamuccaya: A Compendium of Buddhistic Teaching Compiled by Çāntideva, Chiefly from Earlier Mahāyāna-sūtras.* Bibliotheca Buddhica 1. Saint Petersburg: Imperial Academy. Reprint, Osnabrück, Germany: Biblio Verlag.

Benn, James A. 2009. "The *Lotus Sūtra* and Self-Immolation." In *Readings of the Lotus Sūtra,* edited by Jacqueline I. Stone and Stephen F. Teiser, 107–131. New York: Columbia University Press.

Bentor, Yael. 1988. "The Redactions of the *Adbhutadharmaparyāya* from Gilgit." *JIABS* 11 (2): 21–52.

Bhattacharya, Kamaleswar. 1973. *L'àtman-brahman dans le bouddhisme ancient.* Paris: l'École française d'Extrême-Orient. Vol. 90. English translation: 2015. *The Ātman-Brahman in Ancient Buddhism.* Cotopaxi, CO: Canon.

Bhattacharya, Ram Shankar. 1975. "Wrong Views about the Name and Nature of the Eighth *Siddhi* of the *Aṇimādi* Group." *Adyar Library Bulletin* 47: 48–57.

Bhattacharya, Ramkrishna. 2011. *Studies on the Cārvāka/Lokāyata.* London: Anthem.

Bielefeldt, Carl. 2009. "Expedient Devices, the One Vehicle, and the Lifespan of the Buddha." In *Readings of the Lotus Sūtra,* edited by Jacqueline I. Stone and Stephen F. Teiser, 62–82. New York: Columbia University Press.

Black, Brian. 2007. *The Character of the Self in Ancient India: Priest, Kings, and Women in the Early Upaniṣads.* Albany: State University of New York Press.

Blum, Mark. 2013. *The Nirvana Sutra (Mahāparinirvāṇa-sūtra).* Vol. 1. Berkeley, CA: Bukkyō Dendō Kyōkai America.

Brereton, Joel. 1990. "The Upanishads." In *Approaches to the Asian Classics,* edited by Wm. Theodore de Bary and Irene Bloom, 115–135. New York: Columbia University Press.

Brockington, John. 1998. *The Sanskrit Epics.* Leiden/Boston/Köln: Brill.

———. 1999. "Epic Sāṃkhya: Texts, Teachers, Terminology." *Asiatische Studien: Zeitschrift der Schweizerischen Asiengesellschaft / Études Asiatiques: Revue de la Societe Suisse-Asie* 53 (3): 473–490.

———. 2002. "The Structure of the *Mokṣa-dharma-parvan* of the *Mahā-bhārata.*" In *On the Understanding of Other Cultures: Proceedings of the International Conference on Sanskrit and Related Studies to Commemorate the Centenary of the Birth of Stanislaw Schayer (1899–1941),* edited by Piotr Balcerowicz and Marek Mejor, 99–112. Warsaw: Oriental Institute of Warsaw University.

Brodbeck, Simon. 2018. "The *Upaniṣads* and the *Bhagavadgītā.*" In Cohen 2018: 200–218.

Bronkhorst, Johannes. 2006. "Systematic Philosophy between the Empires: Some Determining Features." In *Between the Empires: Society in India 300B CE to 400 CE,* edited by Patrick Olivelle, 287–313. Oxford: Oxford University Press.

———. 2007. *Greater Magadha: Studies in the Culture of Early India.* Leiden: Brill.

———. 2011. *Buddhism in the Shadow of Brahmanism.* Leiden: Brill.

———. 2018. "Abhidharma in Early Mahāyāna." In Harrison 2018b: 119–140.

Brown, Brian Edward. 1991. *The Buddha-Nature: A Study of Tathāgatagarbha and Ālayavijñāna.* Delhi: Motilal Banarsidass.

Brunnhölzl, Karl. 2014. *When the Clouds Part: The Uttaratantra and Its Meditative Tradition as a Bridge between Sūtra and Tantra*. Boston: Snow Lion.
Bühler, Georg. 1932. *Āpastamba's Aphorisms on the Sacred Law of the Hindus*. 3rd ed. Poona, India: S. K. Belvalkar.
Burchardi, Anne. 2007. "A Look at the Diversity of the *Gzhan stong* Tradition." *Journal of the International Association of Tibetan Studies* 3. Accessed December 30, 2018. http://www.thlib.org.
Burley, Mikel. 2007. *Classical Sāṃkhya and Yoga: An Indian Metaphysics of Experience*. London: Routledge.
CBETA [Chinese Buddhist Electronic Text Association] 2015. *Taishō shinshū daizōkyō* 大正新脩大藏經, edited by Takakusu Junjirō 高楠順次郎 and Watanabe Kaigyoku 渡邊海旭. Tokyo: Taishō shinshū daizōkyō kankōkai/Daizō shuppan, 1924–1932. Accessed March 31, 2020, via the CBETA Online Reader. https://www.cbeta.org.
Chandra, Lokesh. 1959. *Tibetan-Sanskrit Dictionary*. New Delhi: International Academy of Indian Culture and Aditya Prakashan.
Chang, Garma. 1991. *A Treasury of Mahāyāna Sūtras: Selections from the Mahāratnakūṭa Sūtra*. Delhi: Motilal Banarsidass.
Chau, Thich Thien. 1984. "The Literature of the Pudgalavādins." *JIABS* 7 (1): 7–16.
Chen Jinhua. 2004. "The Indian Buddhist Missionary Dharmakṣema (385–433): A New Dating of His Arrival in Guzang and of His Translations." *T'oung-p'ao: Revue internationale de sinologie* 90 (4–5): 215–263.
Cohen, Signe. 2008. *Text and Authority in the Older Upaniṣads*. Leiden: Brill.
———, ed. 2018. *The Upaniṣads: A Complete Guide*. Abingdon, UK: Routledge.
Cole, Alan. 2005. *Text as Father: Paternal Seductions in Early Mahāyāna Buddhist Literature*. Berkeley: University of California Press.
Collins, Steven. 1982. *Selfless Persons: Imagery and Thought in Theravāda Buddhism*. Cambridge: Cambridge University Press.
———. 1998. *Nirvana and Other Buddhist Felicities*. Cambridge: Cambridge University Press.
Comans, Michael. 2000. *The Method of Early Advaita Vedānta*. Delhi: Motilal Banarsidass.
Conze, Edward. 1978. *The Prajñāpāramitā Literature*. 2nd ed., revised and enlarged. Bibliographia Philologica Buddhica, Series Maior I. Tokyo: Reiyukai.
Cousins, Lance. 1994. "Person and Self." In *Buddhism into the Year 2000: International Conference Proceedings*, 15–31. Bangkok: Dhammakāya Foundation.
Dayal, Har. 1970. *The Bodhisattva Doctrine in Buddhist Sanskrit Literature*. Delhi: Motilal Banarsidass.
de Breet, Jan A. 1992. "The Concept *Upāyakauśalya* in the *Aṣṭasāhasrikā Prajñāpāramitā*." *Wiener Zeitschrift für die Kunde Südasiens* 36: 203–216.
de Jong, Jan Willem. 1968. Review of *A Study of the Ratnagotravibhāga (Uttaratantra): Being a Treatise on the Tathāgatagarbha Theory of Mahāyāna Buddhisms* by J. Takasaki. *Indo-Iranian Journal* 2 (1): 36–54.
Deleanu, Florin. 2018. "The *Laṅkāvatārasūtra:* A Bibliographical Survey." *Bulletin of the International Institute for Buddhist Studies* 1: 15–44.
Dhammajoti, Bhikkhu K. L. 2009. *Sarvāstivāda Abhidharma*. 4th ed. Hong Kong: Centre of Buddhist Studies, University of Hong Kong.
Dhirasekera, Jotiya. 1982. *Buddhist Monastic Discipline: A Study of Its Origins and Development in Relation to the Sutta and Vinaya Pitakas*. Colombo, Sri Lanka: Ministry of Higher Education Research Publication Series.

Drewes, David. 2018. "The Forest Hypothesis." In Harrison 2018b: 73–94.

———. 2019. "Mahāyāna Sūtras and Opening of the Bodhisattva Path." Paper presented at the Eighteenth IABS Congress, Toronto, August 20–25, 2017. Updated 2019. Accessed December 30, 2019. https://www.academia.edu.

Duerlinger, James. 1993. "Reductionist and Nonreductionist Theories of Persons in Indian Buddhist Philosophy." *Journal of Indian Philosophy* 21: 79–101.

———. 2005. *Indian Buddhist Theories of Persons: Vasubandhu's "Refutation of the Theory of a Self."* London: Routledge.

———. 2012. *The Refutation of the Self in Indian Buddhism: Candrakīrti on the Selflessness of Persons.* London: Routledge.

Dundas, Paul. 2002. *The Jains.* 2nd ed. London: Routledge.

Dutt, Nalinaksha. 1934. *Pañcaviṃśatisāhasrikā Prajñāpāramitā.* London: Luzac & Co.

Eckel, Malcolm David. 2008. *Bhāviveka and His Buddhist Opponents.* Cambridge, MA: Harvard University Press.

Edgerton, Franklin. 1953. *Buddhist Hybrid Sanskrit Grammar and Dictionary.* Vol. 2, *Dictionary.* Delhi: Motilal Banarsidass.

Elizarenkova, Tatiana Yakovlevna. 2005. "The Word *Ātmán* in the *Ṛgveda.*" *Indologica Taurinesia* 31: 121–134.

Eltschinger, Vincent. 2010. "Apocalypticism, Heresy and Philosophy—Towards a Socio-historically Grounded Account of Sixth-Century Indian Philosophy." In *Investigation of Religious Pluralism and the Concept of Tolerance in India,* edited by Goshin Shaku 悟震釈 et al., 425–480. Tokyo: The Eastern Institute.

———. 2014. *Buddhist Epistemology as Apologetics.* Vienna: Verlag der Österreichischen Akademie der Wissenschaften.

Eltschinger, Vincent, and Isabelle Ratié. 2013. *Self, No-Self, and Salvation: Dharmakīrti's Critique of the Notions of Self and Person.* Vienna: Verlag der Österreichischen Akademie der Wissenschaften.

Emmerick, R. E. 1970. *The Sūtra of Golden Light—Being a Translation of the Suvarṇabhāsottamasūtra.* London: Luzac & Co.

Falk, Harry. 2005. "The Introduction of Stūpa-Worship in Bajaur." In *Afghanistan: Ancien carrefour entre l'est et l'ouest,* edited by O. Bopearachchi and M. F. Boussac, 347–358. Turnhout, Belgium: Brepols.

Falk, Nancy. 1977. "To Gaze on the Sacred Traces." *History of Religions* 16 (4): 281–293.

Feuerstein, Georg. 1979. *The Yoga-Sūtra of Patañjali: A New Translation and Commentary.* Folkestone, UK: Dawson.

Fitzgerald, James L. 2006. "Negotiating the Shape of 'Scripture': New Perspectives on the Development and Growth of the *Mahābhārata* between the Empires." In *Between the Empires: Society in India 300BCE to 400 CE,* edited by Patrick Olivelle, 257–286. Oxford: Oxford University Press.

Forte, Antonino. 2005. *Political Propaganda and Ideology in China at the End of the Seventh Century: Inquiry into the Nature, Authors, and Function of the Dunhuang Document S.6502, Followed by an Annotated Translation.* 2nd ed. Kyoto: Scuola Italiana di Studi sull'Asia Orientale.

Frauwallner, Erich. 1951. "*Amalavijñānam* und *Ālayavijñānam.*" In *Beiträge zur indischen Philologie und Altertumskunde, Walther Schubring zum 10. Geburtstag dargebracht,* edited by Gerhard Oberhammer and Ernst Steinkellner, 148–159. Hamburg: Franz Steiner Verlag.

Fujii Kyōko 藤井教孝. 1983. "*Nehangyō* ni okeru 'ga' 『涅槃経』における「我」." *Bukkyōgaku* 仏教学 16: 47–69.

———. 1993. "On the *Ātman* Theory in the *Mahāparinirvāṇasūtra*." In *Premier Colloque Étienne Lamotte (Bruxelles et Liège, 24–27 Septembre 1989)*, 27–31. Louvain-la-Neuve, Belgium: Université catholique de Louvain, Institut Orientaliste.

Fujita Kōtatsu 藤田宏達. 1975. "One Vehicle or Three." *Journal of Indian Philosophy* 3: 79–116. Translated by Leon Hurvitz.

Ganeri, Jonardon. 2007. *The Concealed Art of the Soul: Theories of Self and Practices of Truth in Indian Ethics and Epistemology*. Oxford: Oxford University Press.

Gimello, Robert M. 1976. "Apophatic and Kataphatic Discourse in Mahāyāna: A Chinese View." *Philosophy East and West* 26 (2): 117–136.

Gokhale, Pradeep P. 2015. *Lokāyata/Cārvāka: A Philosophical Inquiry*. New Delhi: Oxford University Press.

Gokhale, V. V. 1955. "A Note on *Ratnagotravibhāga* I.52 = *Bhagavadgītā* XIII.32." In *Indogaku bukkyōgaku ronsō: Yamaguchi hakushi kanreki kinen* 印度學佛教學論叢：山口博士還暦記念 [Studies in Indology and Buddhology, presented in honour of Professor S. Yamaguchi], 90–91. Kyoto: Hōzōkan.

Gombrich, Richard. 1996. *How Buddhism Began: The Conditioned Genesis of the Early Teachings*. New Delhi: Munshiram Mahoharlal.

Gonda, Jan. 1950. *Notes on Brahman*. Utrecht: J. L. Beyers.

Goudriaan, Teun. 1978. *Māyā Divine and Human: A Study of Magic and Its Religious Foundations in Sanskrit Texts, with Particular Attention to a Fragment on Viṣṇu's Māyā Preserved in Bali*. Delhi: Motilal Banarsidass.

Granoff, Phyllis. 2000. "Other People's Rituals: Ritual Eclecticism in Early Medieval Indian Religions." *Journal of Indian Philosophy* 28: 399–424.

———. 2012. "After Sinning: Some Thoughts on Remorse, Responsibility, and the Remedies for Sin in Indian Religious Tradition." In *Sins and Sinners: Perspectives from Asian Religions*, edited by Phyllis Granoff and Koichi Shinohara, 175–215. Leiden: Brill.

Gregory, Peter N. 1983. "The Teaching of Men and Gods: The Doctrinal and Social Basis of Lay Buddhist Practice in the Hua-Yen Tradition." In *Studies in Ch'an and Hua-Yen*, edited by Robert M. Gimello and Peter N. Gregor, 253–320. Honolulu: University of Hawai'i Press.

———. 1991. *Tsung-mi and the Sinification of Buddhism*. Princeton, NJ: Princeton University Press.

Griffiths, Paul. 1990. "Painting Space with Colors: Tathāgatagarbha in the *Mahāyānasūtrālaṅkāra*-Corpus IX.22–37." In *Buddha Nature: A Festschrift in Honor of Minoru Kiyota*, edited by Paul Griffiths and John Keenan, 41–63. Reno, NV: Buddhist Books International.

Grimm, George. 1958. *The Doctrine of the Buddha: The Religion of Reason and Meditation*. Berlin: Akademie-Verlag.

Grosnick, William H. 1977. "The Understanding of '*Dhātu*' in the *Anūnatvāpūrṇatvanirdeśa*." In *Transactions of the International Conference of Orientalists in Japan* 22: 30–36.

———. 1981. "Nonorigination and *Nirvāṇa* in the Early *Tathāgatagarbha* Literature." *JIABS* 4 (1): 33–43.

———. 1989. "The Categories of *T'i*, *Hsiang*, and *Yung*: Evidence that Paramārtha Composed the *Awakening of Faith*." *JIABS* 12 (1): 65–92.

———. 1990. "The Buddha-Nature as Myth." In *Buddha Nature: A Festschrift in Honor of Minoru Kiyota,* edited by Paul Griffiths and John Keenan, 66–74. Reno, NV: Buddhist Books International.

———. 1995. "The *Tathāgatagarbha Sūtra.*" In *Buddhism in Practice,* edited by Donald S. Lopez Jr., 92–106. Princeton, NJ: Princeton University Press.

Gummer, Natalie. 2015. "*Suvarṇabhāsottamasūtra.*" In *Brill's Encyclopedia of Buddhism.* vol. 1, *Literature and Languages,* edited by Jonathan Silk et al., 249–260. Brill: Leiden.

Habata Hiromi 幅田裕美. 1989. "*Daijō Nehangyō* no ichi kōsatsu: Igaku shisō ni kanren shite. 大乗『涅槃経』の一考察: 医学思想に関連して." *IBK* 37 (2): 158–160.

———. 1990. "*Daijō Nehangyō* ni okeru ātoman ron" 大乗＜涅槃経＞におけるアートマン論." *Hokkaidō indo tetsugaku bukkyō gakkai* 北海道インド哲学仏教学会 5: 173–190.

———. 1992. "*Daijō Nehangyō* to *Jū issai fukutoku zanmai kyō* 大乗〈涅槃経〉と『集一切福徳三昧経』." *Indo tetsugaku bukkyōgaku* 印度哲学仏教学 7: 153–169.

———. 1994. "Daigyō (*mahāsūtra*) toshite no daijō <*Nehangyō*> 大経 (*mahāsūtra*) としての大乗＜涅槃経＞." *IBK* 43 (1): 140–143.

———. 2007. *Die Zentralasiatischen Sanskrit-Fragmente des Mahāparinirvāṇa-Mahāsūtra.* Marburg, Germany: Indica et Tibetica Verlag.

———. 2009. "The *Mahāparinirvāṇa-mahāsūtra* Manuscripts in the Stein and Hoerle Collections (1)." In *Buddhist Manuscripts from Central Asia: The British Library Sanskrit Fragments.* Vol. 2.1, edited by Karashima Seishi and Klaus Wille, 551–588. Tokyo: International Research Institute for Advanced Buddhology, Soka University.

———. 2013. *A Critical Edition of the Tibetan Translation of the Mahāparinirvāṇa-mahāsūtra.* Wiesbaden, Germany: Dr. Ludwig Reichert Verlag.

———. 2014. "Busshō no sengen: *Nehangyō* 仏性の宣言涅槃経." In Katsura et al. 2014: 141–166.

———. 2015a. "*Daihatsunehangyō* no St. Petersburg shozō bonbun shin danpen ni tsuite 大般涅槃経の St. Petersburg 所蔵梵文新断片について." *Indo ronrigaku kenkyū* インド論理学研究 8: 235–245.

———. 2015b. "*Buddhadhātu, Tathāgatadhātu* and *Tathāgatagarbha* in the *Mahāparinirvāṇa-mahāsūtra.*" *Hōrin: Vergleichende Studien zur japanischen Kultur* 18: 176–196.

———. 2018. "Some Reflections on the Term 'Sautrāntika' in Vinaya Context: *Vinayadharaḥ Sautrāntikaḥ* in the *Mahāparinirvāṇa-mahāsūtra.*" *Journal of Indian Philosophy* 46 (2): 241–261.

———. 2019. *Aufbau und Umstrukturierung des Mahāparinirvāṇasutra: Untersuchungen zum Mahāparinirvāṇamahāsūtra unter Berücksichtigung der Sanskrit-Fragment.* Bremen, Germany: Hempen Verlag.

Halbfass, Wilhelm. 1995. *Philology and Confrontation: Paul Hacker on Traditional and Modern Vedānta.* Albany: State University of New York Press.

Hamar, Imre. 2007. "The History of the *Buddhāvataṃsaka-sūtra:* Shorter and Larger Texts." In *Reflecting Mirrors: Perspectives on Huayen Buddhism,* edited by Imre Hamar, 139–167. Wiesbaden, Germany: Harrassowitz Verlag.

Hara Minoru 原實. 1959. "A Note on the Sanskrit Word *Ni-tya.*" *Journal of the American Oriental Society* 79 (2): 90–96.

———. 1994. "*Deva-garbha* and *Tathāgata-garbha.*" In *The Buddhist Forum,* vol. 3, *Papers in Honour and Appreciation of Professor David Seyfort Ruegg's Contribution to*

Indological, Buddhist, and Tibetan Studies, edited by Tadeusz Skorupski and Ulrich Pagel, 37–56. Tring, UK: The Institute of Buddhist Studies.

Harrison, Paul. 1982. "Sanskrit Fragments of a Lokottaravādin Tradition." In *Indological and Buddhist Studies: Volume in Honour of Professor J. W. de Jong on His Sixtieth Birthday,* edited by L. A. Hercus et al., 211–234. Canberra: Faculty of Asian Studies.

———. 1987. "Who Gets to Ride in the Great Vehicle? Self-Image and Identity among the Followers of the Early Mahāyāna." *JIABS* 10 (1): 67–89.

———. 1992a. "Is the *Dharma-kāya* the Real 'Phantom Body' of the Buddha?" *JIABS* 15 (1): 44–94.

———. 1992b. "Commemoration and Identification in Buddhānusmṛti." In *In the Mirror of Memory: Reflections on Mindfulness and Remembrance in Indian and Tibetan Buddhism,* edited by Janet Gyatso, 215–238. Albany: State University of New York Press.

———. 1993. "The Earliest Chinese Translations of Mahāyāna Buddhist Sūtras: Some Notes on the Works of Lokakṣema." *Buddhist Studies Review* 10 (2): 135–178.

———. 1995a. "Searching for the Origins of the Mahāyāna: What Are We Looking For?" *Eastern Buddhist* 28 (1): 48–69.

———. 1995b. "Some Reflections on the Personality of the Buddha." *Ōtani gakuhō* 大谷學報 74 (4): 1–29.

———. 2003. "Mediums and Messages: Reflections on the Productions of *Mahāyāna Sūtras.*" *Eastern Buddhist* 35 (1): 115–151.

———. 2018a. "Early Mahāyāna: Laying out the Field." In Harrison 2018b: 7–32.

———, ed. 2018b. *Setting Out on the Great Way: Essays on Early Mahāyāna Buddhism.* Sheffield, UK: Equinox.

Harrison, Paul, Timothy Lenz, Lin Qian, and Richard Salomon. 2016. "A Gāndhārī Fragment of the *Sarvapuṇyasamuccayasamādhisūtra.*" In *Manuscripts in the Schøyen Collection,* vol. 4, edited by Jens Braarvig et al., 311–319. Oslo: Hermes Publications.

Harrison, Paul, and Watanabe Shōgo 渡辺章悟. 2006. "*Vajracchedikā Prajñāpāramitā.*" In *Manuscripts in the Schøyen Collection,* vol. 3, edited by Jens Braarvig et al., 89–132. Oslo: Hermes Publications.

Harvey, Peter. 1995. *The Selfless Mind: Personality, Consciousness, and Nirvana in Early Buddhism.* London: Curzon Press.

Hidas, Gergely. 2012. *Mahāpratisarā-Mahāvidyārājñī—The Great Amulet, Great Queen of Spells: Introduction, Critical Editions and Annotated Translations.* New Delhi: International Academy of Indian Culture and Aditya Prakashan.

Hikata Ryūshō 干潟龍祥. 1958. *Suvikrāntavikrāmi-paripṛcchā Prajñāpāramitā Sūtra.* Fukuoka, Japan: Kyushu University.

Hirakawa Akira 平川彰. 1990. *A History of Indian Buddhism: From Śākyamuni to early Mahāyāna.* Honolulu: University of Hawai'i Press.

Hodge, Stephen. 2003. *The Mahāvairocana-Abhisaṃbodhi Tantra with Buddhaguhya's Commentary.* London: Routledge-Curzon.

———. 2006. "On the Eschatology of the *Mahāparinirvāṇa Sūtra* and Related Matters." Lecture notes from the University of London, SOAS. Accessed December 30, 2018. http://www.nirvanasutra.net.

———. 2010/2012. "The *Mahāyāna Mahāparinirvāṇa Sūtra:* The Text and Its Transmission." Revised version of a paper presented at the Second International

Workshop of the *Mahāparinirvāṇa Sūtra,* Munich. Accessed August 30, 2019. https://www.buddhismuskunde.uni-hamburg.de.

Hoernle, A. F. 1916. *Manuscript Remains of Buddhist Literature found in Eastern Turkestan.* Vol. 1. Oxford: Clarendon.

Hookham, Susan K. 1991. *The Buddha Within: Tathagatagarbha Doctrine according to the Shentong Interpretation of the Ratnagotravibhaga.* Albany: State University of New York Press.

Hopkins, Jerry. 2006. *Mountain Doctrine: Tibet's Fundamental Treatise on Other-Emptiness and the Buddha-Matrix, by Döl-bo-ba shay-rap-gyel-tsen.* Translated and introduced by Jeffrey Hopkins, edited by Kevin Vose. Ithaca, NY: Snow Lion.

Horsche, Paul. 1968. "Buddhismus und Upaniṣaden." In *Pratidānam: Indian, Iranian, and Indo-European Studies Presented to Franciscus Bernardus Jacobus Kuiper on His Sixtieth Birthday,* edited by J. C. Heesterman et al., 462–477. The Hague: Mouton.

Hubbard, Jamie. 1995. "Buddhist-Buddhist Dialogue? The '*Lotus Sutra*' and the Polemic of Accommodation." *Buddhist-Christian Studies* 15: 119–136.

Hubbard, Jamie, and Paul Swanson, eds. 1997. *Pruning the Bodhi Tree: The Storm over Critical Buddhism.* Honolulu: University of Hawai'i Press.

Isayeva, Natalia. 1993. *Shankara and Indian Philosophy.* Albany: State University of New York Press.

Jacobi, Hermann. 1882. *Âyâraṃga Sutta of the Çetâmbara Jain.* Part 1, *Text.* London: Henry Frowde, for the Pali Text Society.

———. 1908. "The Metaphysics and Ethics of the Jainas." In *Transactions of the Third International Congress for the History of Religions,* vol. 2, edited by P. S. Allen and John de Monins Johnson, 59–66. Oxford: Clarendon Press.

Jain, Jagdish Chandra. 1935. "The Conception of Soul in Jainism." *Indian Historical Quarterly* 11: 137–141.

Jaini, Padmanabh S. 1977. "Bhavyatva and Abhavyatva—A Jain Doctrine of 'Predestination.'" In *Mahāvīra and His Teachings,* edited by Ā. N. Upādhye, 95–111. Bombay: Bhagavān Mahāvīra.

Jamspal, Lozang. 2010. *The Range of the Bodhisattva, A Mahāyāna Sūtra (Ārya-Bodhisattva-gocara): The Teachings of the Nirgrantha Satyaka. Introduction and Translation.* New York: American Institute of Buddhist Studies / Columbia University Center for Buddhist Studies.

Jhaveri, B. J. 1977. "Considerations of Self in Jaina Philosophy." In *Mahāvīra and His Teachings,* edited by Ā. N. Upādhye, 235–242. Bombay: Bhagavān Mahāvīra.

Jia Shanshan. 2015. "*Laṅkāvatārasūtra.*" In *Brill's Encyclopedia of Buddhism,* vol. 1, *Literature and Languages,* edited by Jonathan Silk et al., 138–143. Brill: Leiden.

Johnston, E. H. (1950) 1991. *The Ratnagotravibhāga Mahāyānottaratantraśāstra.* Reprinted in *The Uttaratantra of Maitreya: Containing Introduction, E. H. Johnston's Sanskrit Text, and E. Obermiller's English Translation,* edited by H. S. Prasad. Delhi: Sri Satguru Publications.

Jones, C. V. 2015. "The Use of, and Controversy Surrounding, the Term *Ātman* in the Indian Buddhist *Tathāgatagarbha* Literature." Doctoral dissertation, Faculty of Oriental Studies, University of Oxford.

———. 2016a. "A Self-Aggrandizing Vehicle: *Tathāgatagarbha, Tīrthika*s, and the True Self." *JIABS* 39: 115–170.

———. 2016b. "Beings, Non-Beings, and Buddhas: Contrasting Notions of *Tathāgatagarbha* in the *Anūnatvāpūrṇatvanirdeśaparivarta* and *Mahābherī Sūtra.*" *Journal of the Oxford Centre for Buddhist Studies* 10: 90–122.

———. 2020. "Reconsidering the 'Essence' of Indian Buddha-Nature Literature." *Acta Asiatica* 118: 57–78.

———. Forthcoming. "Translating the Tīrthika: An Enduring 'Heresy' in Buddhist Studies." In *Translating Buddhism: Collected Essays on Translation Theory and Practice (South Asia),* edited by Alice Collett. Albany: State University of New York Press.

Jones, J. J. 1949. *The Mahāvastu*. Vol. 1. London: Luzac & Co.

Kanō Kazuo 加納和雄. 2000. "*Ōkutsumarakyō* no kenkyū: Zentai no kōsei to naiyō gaikan 『央掘魔羅経』の研究: 全体の構成と内容概観." *Kōyasandaigaku daigakuin kiyō* 高野山大学大学院紀要 4: 57–82.

———. 2014. "*Hōshō ron* no tenkai 宝性論の展開." In Katsura et al. 2014: 204–247.

———. 2016. *Buddha-Nature and Emptiness: rNgog Blo-ldan-shes-rab and a Transmission of the Ratnagotravibhāga from India to Tibet.* Vienna: Wiener Studien zur Tibetologie und Buddhismuskunde.

———. 2017. "*Tathāgatagarbhaḥ sarvasattvānāṃ: Nehangyō ni okeru nyoraizō no fukugōgo kaishaku ni kansuru shiron / Tathāgatagarbhaḥ sarvasattvānāṃ:* 涅槃経における如来蔵の複合語解釈にかんする試論." *Critical Review for Buddhist Studies* 불교학리뷰 22: 9–61.

———. 2020. "A Syntactic Analysis of the Term *Tathāgatagarbha* in Sanskrit Fragments and Multiple Meanings of *Garbha* in the *Mahāparinirvāṇamahāsūtra.*" *Acta Asiatica* 118: 17–40.

Kapstein, Matthew. 1986. "Collins, Parfit, and the Problem of Personal Identity in Two Philosophical Traditions: A Review of 'Selfless Persons' and 'Reasons and Persons.'" *Philosophy East and West* 36 (3): 289–298.

———. 2018. "Collins and Parfit Three Decades On." *Sophia* 57 (2): 207–210.

Karashima Seishi 辛嶋静志. 2003–2006. "A Trilingual Edition of the Lotus Sūtra: New Editions of the Sanskrit, Tibetan and Chinese Versions." *Annual Report of the International Research Institute for Advanced Buddhology,* vols. 6–9.

———. 2007. "Who Were the *Icchantika*s?" *Annual Report of the International Research Institute for Advanced Buddhology at Soka University* 10: 67–80.

———. 2011. *A Critical Edition of Lokakṣema's Translation of the Aṣṭasāhasrikā Prajñāpāramitā.* Tokyo: The International Research Institute for Advanced Buddhology at Soka University.

Katsura Shōryū 桂紹隆, Saitō Akira 斎藤明, Shimoda Masahiro 下田正弘, and Sueki Fumihiko 末木文美士, eds. 2014. *Nyoraizō to busshō* 如来蔵と仏性 (*Shirīzu daijōbukkyō* シリーズ大乗仏教 Vol. 8. Tokyo: Shunjūsha.

Kazama Toshio 風間敏夫. 1962. "On the Conception of *Ātman* in the *Brāhmaṇa.*" *IBK* 10: 363–359.

Kern, Hendrik. 1884. *Saddharma-pundarika: or, the Lotus of the True Law.* Oxford: Clarendon Press.

Kern, Hendrick, and Nanjio Bunyio 南条文雄, eds. (1908–1912) 1970. *Saddharmapuṇḍarīka.* Imprimerie de l'Académie Impériale des Sciences. Reprint, Osnabrück, Germany: Biblio Verlag.

Khosla, Usha. 2015. "Study of the *Tathāgatagarbha* as True Self and the True Selves of the Brahmanic, Sāṅkhya and Jaina Traditions." Doctoral dissertation, Department of Religious Studies, University of Toronto.

Kiblinger, Kristin Beise. 2005. *Buddhist Inclusivism: Attitudes towards Religious Others.* Aldershot, UK: Ashgate.

Kieschnick, John. 2003. *The Impact of Buddhism on Chinese Material Culture.* Princeton, NJ: Princeton University Press.

Killingley, Dermot. 2018a. "The Religious and Ritual Background [of the *Upaniṣads*]." In Cohen 2018: 58–72.

———. 2018b. "The Upaniṣads and the Emergence of Theism." In Cohen 2018: 161–173.

King, Richard. 1995a. *Early Advaita Vedānta and Buddhism: The Mahāyāna Context of the Gauḍapādīya-kārikā.* Albany: State University of New York Press.

———. 1995b. "Is 'Buddha-Nature' Buddhist? Doctrinal Tensions in the *Śrīmālā Sūtra:* An Early *Tathāgatagarbha* Text." *Numen* 42 (1): 1–20.

King, Sallie. 1989. "Buddha Nature and the Concept of Person." *Philosophy East and West* 39 (2): 151–170.

———. 1991. *Buddha Nature.* Albany: State University of New York Press.

———. 1997. "The Doctrine of Buddha-Nature Is Impeccably Buddhist." In Hubbard and Swanson 1997: 174–192.

Kloppenborg, Ria. 1974. *The Paccekabuddha: A Buddhist Ascetic—A Study of the Concept of the Paccekabuddha in Pāli Canonical and Commentarial Literature.* Leiden: Brill.

Kramer, Jowita. 2016. "Some Remarks on Sthiramati and His Putative Authorship of the *Madhyāntavibhāgaṭikā,* the *Sūtrālaṃkāravṛttibhāṣya* and the *Triṃśikāvijñaptibhāṣya.*" *Buddhist Studies Review* 33 (1–2): 47–63.

Kubota Chikara 久保田力. 1999. "*Shōmangyō ni okeru ḍairikibosatsu no seiritsu* 勝鬘経』における大力菩薩の成立." *IBK* 48 (1): 269–274.

Kumāra, Śaśiprabhā. 2013. *Classical Vaiśeṣika in Indian Philosophy: On Knowing and What Is to Be Known.* London: Routledge.

Kunst, Arnold. 1977. "Some Aspects of the *Ekayāna.*" In *Prajñāpāramitā and Related Systems: Studies in Honor of Edward Conze,* edited by Lewis Lancaster, 313–323. Berkeley, CA: Berkeley Buddhist Studies Series.

———. 1980. "Some of the Polemics in the *Laṅkāvatārasūtra.*" In *Buddhist Studies in Honour of Walpola Rahula,* edited by Sōmaratna Bālasūriya et al., 103–112. London: Gordon Fraser.

Lamotte, Étienne. 1938a. *La somme du Grand Véhicule d'Asaṅga (Mahāyānasaṃgraha).* Book 1, *Versions tibétaine et chinoise (Hiuan-tsang).* Louvain, Belgium: Bureaux du Muséon.

———. 1938b. *La somme du Grand Véhicule d'Asaṅga (Mahāyānasaṃgraha).* Book 2, *Traduction et commentaire.* Louvain, Belgium: Bureaux du Muséon.

———. 1944. *Le traité de la grande vertu de sagesse.* Vol. 1. Louvain, Belgium: Publications Universitaires.

———. 1962. *L'enseignement de Vimalakīrti.* Louvain, Belgium: Publications Universitaires.

Langenberg, Amy Paris. 2017. *Birth in Buddhism: The Suffering Fetus and Female Freedom.* Oxford: Routledge.

Larson, Gerald. 1969. *Classical Sāṃkhya: An Interpretation of Its History and Meaning.* Delhi: Motilal Banarsidass.

La Vallée Poussin, Louis de. 1912. *Madhyāmakāvatāra(-Bhāṣya).* Saint Petersburg: Imprimerie de l'Académie Impériale des Sciences.

———. 1923. *L'Abhidharmakośa de Vasubandhu.* Paris: Paul Geuthner.

La Vallée Poussin, Louis de, and E. J. Thomas. 1916. *Mahāniddesa.* Vol. 1. London: Pali Text Society.

Lee, Sumi. 2014. "The Meaning of 'Mind-made Body' (S. *manomaya-kāya*, C. *yisheng shen* 意生身) in Buddhist Cosmological and Soteriological Systems." *Buddhist Studies Review* 31 (1): 65–90.
Lévi, Sylvain. 1907. *Mahāyāna-Sūtrālaṃkāra: Exposé de la doctrine du Grand Véhicule selon le système Yogācāra.* Tome 1, *Texte.* Paris: Libraire Honoré Champion.
———. 1911. *Mahāyāna-Sūtrālaṃkāra: Exposé de la doctrine du Grand Véhicule selon le système Yogācāra.* Tome 2, *Traduction, introduction, index.* Paris: Libraire Honoré Champion.
Liebenthal, Walter. 1955. "A Biography of Chu Tao-Sheng." *Monumenta Nipponica* 11 (3): 284–316.
———. 1956. "The World Conception of Chu Tao-Sheng." *Monumenta Nipponica* 12 (1–2): 65–103.
Lindtner, Christian. 1982. *Nagarjuniana: Studies in the Writings and Philosophy of Nāgārjuna.* Copenhagen: Akademisk Forlag.
———. 1992. "The *Laṅkāvatārasūtra* in Early Indian Madhyamaka Literature." *Asiatische Studien: Zeitschrift der Schweizerischen Asiengesellschaft / Études Asiatiques: Revue de la Societe Suisse-Asie* 46 (1): 244–279.
Liu Ming-Wood. 1982. "The Doctrine of the Buddha-Nature in the *Mahāyāna Mahāparinirvāṇa-Sūtra.*" *JIABS* 5 (2): 63–94.
Lopez, Donald S. Jr., and Jacqueline I. Stone. 2019. *Two Buddhas Seated Side by Side: A Guide to the Lotus Sūtra.* Princeton, NJ: Princeton University Press.
MacQueen, Graeme. 1982. "Inspired Speech in Early Mahāyāna Buddhism II." *Religion* 12: 49–65.
———. 1988. *A Study of the Śrāmaṇyaphala-Sūtra.* Wiesbaden, Germany: Harrassowitz.
Mainkar, T. G. 1964. *The Sāṃkhyakārikā of Īśvarakṛṣṇa, with the Commentary of Gauḍapāda.* Poona, India: Oriental Book Agency.
Makransky, John J. 1997. *Buddhahood Embodied: Sources of Controversy in India and Tibet.* Albany: State University of New York Press.
Malinar, Angelika. 2007. *The Bhagavadgītā: Doctrines and Contexts.* Cambridge: Cambridge University Press.
Masuda Jiryō 増田慈良. 1930. "*Saptaśatikā Prajñāpāramitā:* Text and the Hsüan-chwang Chinese Version with Notes." *Journal of the Taisho University* 6–7: 185–241.
Mathes, Klaus-Dieter. 2004. "Tāranātha's 'Twenty-One Differences with Regard to the Profound Meaning': Comparing the Views of the Two gźan stoṅ Masters Dol po pa and Śākya mchog ldan." *JIABS* 27 (2): 286–328.
———. 2008. *A Direct Path to the Buddha Within: Gö Lotsāwa's Mahāmudrā Interpretation of the Ratnagotravibhāga.* Boston: Wisdom Publications.
———. 2012. "The *Gzhan Stong* Model of Reality—Some More Material on Its Origin, Transmission, and Interpretation." *JIABS* 34 (1–2): 187–223.
———. 2015. "The Original *Ratnagotravibhāga* and Its Yogācāra Interpretation as Possible Indian Precedents of *Gzhan Stong* ("Empti[ness] of Other")." *Hōrin* 18: 119–140.
Mathes, Klaus-Dieter, and Michael Sheehy, eds. 2019. *The Other Emptiness: Rethinking the Zhentong Buddhist Discourse in Tibet.* New York: State University of New York Press.
Matsuda Kazunobu 和信松田. 2000. "*Śrīmālādevīsiṃhanādanirdeśa.*" In *Manuscripts in the Schøyen Collection,* vol. 1, edited by Jens Braarvig et al., 65–76. Oslo: Hermes Publications.

Matsumoto Shirō 松本史朗. 1997. "The Doctrine of *Tathāgata-garbha* Is Not Buddhist." In Hubbard and Swanson 1997: 165–173.

———. 2014. "Nyoraizō to Sora 如来蔵と空." In Katsura et al. 2014: 249–299.

McGovern, Nathan. 2016. "On the Origins of the 32 Marks of a Great Man." *JIABS* 39: 207–247.

———. 2019. *The Snake and the Mongoose: The Emergence of Identity in Early Indian Religion.* New York: Oxford University Press.

Mitrikeski, Drasko. 2009. "Nāgārjuna and the *Tathāgatagarbha:* A Closer Look at Some Peculiar Features in the *Niraupamyastava.*" *Journal of Religious History* 33 (2): 149–164.

Mochizuki Kaie 望月海慧. 2017. "Vasubandhu's Commentary on the *Lotus Sutra* in Tibetan Literature." *IBK* 65 (3): 225–232.

Nagao Gadjin 長尾雅人. 1964. *Madhyāntavibhāgabhāṣya: A Buddhist Philosophical Treatise Edited for the First Time from a Sanskrit Manuscript.* Tokyo: Suzuki Research Foundation.

———. 1978. "'What Remains' in Śūnyatā: A Yogācāra Interpretation of Emptiness." In *Mahāyāna Buddhist Meditation: Theory and Practice,* edited by Minoru Kiyota, assisted by Elvin W. Jones, 66–82. Honolulu: University Press of Hawai'i.

———. 1991. *Mādhyamika and Yogācāra: A Study of Mahāyāna Philosophies.* Albany: State University of New York Press.

———. 2007. *Daijōshōgonkyōron wayaku to chūkai: Nagao Gadjin kenkyū nōto 1* 『大乗荘厳経論』和訳と註解：長尾雅人研究ノート (1)』 Kyoto: Nagao Bunko.

Nakamura Hajime 中村元. 1955. "Upanisadic Tradition and the Early School of Vedānta as Noticed in Buddhist Scripture." *Harvard Journal of Asiatic Studies* 18 (1–2): 74–104.

———. (1980) 1987. *Indian Buddhism: A Survey with Bibliographical Notes.* Reprint, Delhi: Motilal Banarsidass.

———. 1980. *Bukkyōgo daijiten* 仏教語大辞典. Tokyo: Tokyo Shoseki.

Nakamura Zuiryū 中村瑞隆. 1967. *Zō Wa taiyaku Kyūkyō ichijō hōshōron kenkyū* 蔵和対訳究竟一乗宝性論研究. Tokyo: Suzuki Research Foundation.

Nanjio Bunyio 南条文雄. 1923. *The Laṅkāvatāra Sūtra.* Kyoto: Otani University Press.

Nattier, Jan. 1991. *Once Upon a Future time: Studies in a Buddhist Prophecy of Decline.* Berkeley, CA: Asian Humanities Press.

———. 1997. "The Lotus Sutra: Good News for Whom?" Paper presented at the Third International Lotus Sutra Conference ("The Lotus Sutra as Good News"). July 1997, sponsored by the Rissho Koseikai, Tokyo, Japan.

———. 2003. *A Few Good Men: The Bodhisattva Path according to the Inquiry of Ugra (Ugraparipṛcchā).* Honolulu: University of Hawai'i Press.

———. 2007. "One Vehicle (一乘) in the Chinese *Āgama*s: New Light on an Old Problem in Pāli." *Annual Report of the International Research Institute for Advanced Buddhology at Soka University* 12: 181–200.

Nilakanta Sastri, K. A. 1958. *A History of South India: From Prehistoric Times to the Fall of Vijayanagara.* Madras: Oxford University Press.

Nobel, Johannes. 1937. *Suvarṇabhāsottamasūtra: Das Goldglanz-Sūtra, ein Sanskrittext des Mahāyāna-Buddhismus, Nach den Handschriften und mit Hilfe der tibetischen und chinesischen Übertragungen.* Leipzig: Otto Harrassowitz.

Norman, K. R. 1981. "A Note on *Attā* in the *Alagaddūpama Sutta.*" In *Studies in Indian Philosophy: A Memorial Volume in Honour of Pandit Sukhlalji Sanghvi,* edited by Sukhlalji Sanghavi, 19–29. Ahmedabad, India: LD Institute of Indology.

———. 1983. "The Pratyeka-Buddha in Buddhism and Jainism." In *Buddhist Studies (Ancient and Modern)*, edited by Philip Denwood and Alexander Piatigorsky, 92–106. London: Curzon.

Oberhammer, Gerhard, ed. 1983. *Inklusivismus: Eine indische Denkform*. Vienna: Institut für Indologie der Universität Wien.

Obermiller, Eugène. (1931) 1991. *The Sublime Science of the Great Vehicle to Salvation, Being a Manual of Buddhist Monism: The Work of Ārya Maitreya with a Commentary by Āryāsaṅga, Acta Orientalia* 9: 81–306. Reprinted in *The Uttaratantra of Maitreya: Containing Introduction, E. H. Johnston's Sanskrit Text, and E. Obermiller's English Translation*, edited by H. S. Prasad. Delhi: Sri Satguru Publications.

Ogawa Ichijō 小川一乗. 1999. "*Ōkutsumara kyō* ni okeru 'Nyoraizō kanken' 『央掘魔羅経』における「如来蔵」管見." *Bukkyōgaku seminā* 仏教学セミナー 69: 1–12.

———. 2001. *Ōkutsumarakyō, Shōmangyō, Nyoraizōkyo Fuzōfugengyō* 央掘摩羅経·勝鬘経·如来蔵経·不増不減経. Shin kokuyaku daizōkyo 新国訳大蔵経. Nyoraizō Yuishiki bu 1 如来蔵・唯識部. Tokyo: Daizō Shuppan.

Olivelle, Patrick. 1986. Review of Gerhard Oberhammer, *Inklusivismus: Eine indische Denkform*, in *Journal of the American Oriental Society* 106 (4): 867–868.

———. 1998. *The Early Upaniṣads: Annotated Text and Translation*. Oxford: Oxford University Press.

———. 1999. *Dharmasūtras: The Law Codes of Āpastamba, Gautama, Baudhāyana, and Vasiṣṭha*. Oxford: Oxford University Press.

———. 2005. *Manu's Code of Law: A Critical Edition and Translation of the Mānava-Dharmaśāstra*. Oxford: Oxford University Press.

———. 2018a. "Social and Literary History of Dharmaśāstra: The Foundational Texts." In *Hindu Law: A New History of Dharmaśāstra*, edited by Patrick Olivelle and Donald R. Davis Jr., 15–29. Oxford: Oxford University Press.

———. 2018b. "Food and Dietary Rules: *Abhakṣya, Abhojya*." In *Hindu Law: A New History of Dharmaśāstra*, edited by Patrick Olivelle and Donald R. Davis Jr., 189–196. Oxford: Oxford University Press.

Parfit, Derek. 1984. *Reasons and Persons*. Oxford: Clarendon Press.

Paul, Diana. 1976a. Review of *The Lion's Roar of Queen Śrīmālā* by Alex and Hideko Wayman. *Philosophy East and West* 26 (3): 346–348.

———. 1976b. Rejoinder to Alex and Hideko Wayman's Reply, *Philosophy East and West* 26 (4): 493–494.

———. 1979. "The Concept of *Tathāgatagarbha* in the *Śrīmālādevī Sūtra* (*Sheng-Man Ching*)." *Journal of the American Oriental Society* 99 (2): 191–203.

———. 2004. *The Sutra of Queen Śrīmālā of the Lion's Roar*. Berkeley, CA: Numata Centre for Buddhist Translation and Research.

Pérez-Remón, Joaquín. 1980. *Self and Non-Self in Early Buddhism*. The Hague: Mouton Publishers.

Potter, Karl. 1963. *Presuppositions of India's Philosophies*. Englewood Cliffs, NJ: Prentice-Hall.

Pradhan, Prahlad. 1967. *The Abhidharmakośa of Vasubandhu*. Vol. 3. Patna: K. P. Jayaswal Research Institute.

Priestley, Leonard. 1999. *Pudgalavāda Buddhism: The Reality of the Indeterminate Self*. Toronto: University of Toronto.

Pye, Michael. 2003. *Skilful Means: A Concept in Mahayana Buddhism*. 2nd ed. London: Routledge.

Qvarnström, Olle. 1989. *The "Vedāntatattvaviniścaya" Chapter of Bhavya's "Madhyamakahṛdayakārikā."* Lund Studies in African and Asian Religions. Vol. 4. Lund, Sweden: Plus Ultra.

Radich, Michael. 2007. "The Somatics of Liberation: Ideas about Embodiment in Buddhism from Its Origins to the Fifth Century C.E." Doctoral dissertation, Department of East Asian Languages and Civilizations, Harvard University.

———. 2010. "Embodiments of the Buddha in Sarvāstivāda Doctrine: With Special Reference to the **Mahāvibhāṣā.*" *Annual Report of the International Research Institute for Advanced Buddhology* 13: 121–172.

———. 2011. *How Ajātaśatru Was Reformed: The Domestication of "Ajase" and Stories in Buddhist History*. Studia Philologica Buddhica. Vol. 27. Tokyo: International Institute for Buddhist Studies.

———. 2012a. "Immortal Buddhas and Their Indestructible Embodiments: The Advent of the Concept of Vajrakāya." *JIABS* 34: 227–290.

———. 2012b. "External Evidence Relating to Works Ascribed to Paramārtha, with a Focus on Traditional Chinese Catalogues." In *Shintai sanzō kenkyū ronshū* 真諦三藏研究論集, edited by Funayama Tōru 船山徹, 39–102. Kyoto: Institute for Research in Humanities, Kyoto University.

———. 2014. "On the Sources, Style and Authorship of Chapters of the Synoptic *Suvarṇaprabhāsottama-sūtra* T664 Ascribed to Paramārtha (Part 1)." *Annual Report of the International Research Institute for Advanced Buddhology* 17: 207–244.

———. 2015a. *The Mahāparinirvāṇa-mahāsūtra and the Emergence of Tathāgatagarbha Doctrine*. Hamburg Buddhist Studies Series 5. Hamburg: Hamburg University Press.

———. 2015b. "*Tathāgatagarbha Sūtras.*" In *Brill's Encyclopedia of Buddhism,* vol. 1. *Literature and Languages,* edited by Jonathan Silk et al., 261–273. Brill: Leiden.

———. 2015c. "Tibetan Evidence for the Sources of Chapters of the Synoptic *Suvarṇaprabhāsottama-sūtra* T644 Ascribed to Paramārtha." *Buddhist Studies Review* 32 (3): 245–270.

———. 2016. "Pure Mind in India: Indian Background to Paramārtha's **Amalavijñāna.*" *JIABS* 39: 249–308.

Ray, Reginald. 1994. *Buddhist Saints in India: A Study in Buddhist Values and Orientations*. Oxford: Oxford University Press.

Renou, Louis. 1952. "On the Word *Ātman.*" *Vāk* 2: 151–157.

Rocher, Ludo. 1986. *The Purāṇas*. Wiesbaden, Germany: Harrassowitz.

Rotman, Andy. 2009. *Thus Have I Seen: Visualizing Faith in Early Indian Buddhism*. Oxford: Oxford University Press.

Ruegg, David Seyfort. 1966. *The Life of Bu ston Rin po che*. Rome: Istituto Italiano per il Medio ed Estremo Oriente.

———. 1969. *La théorie du tathāgatagarbha et du gotra: Études sur la sotériologie et la gnoséologie du bouddhisme*. Paris: École Française d'Extrême-Orient.

———. 1971. "Le *Dharmadhātustava* de Nāgārjuna." In *Études tibétaines: Dédiées à la mémoire de Marcelle Lalou,* 448–471. Paris: Librairie d'Amérique et d'Orient.

———. 1973. *Le traité du tathāgatagarbha de Bu ston Rin chen grub: Traduction du De bžin gsegs pa'i sñiṅ po gsal žin 'mdzes par byed pa'i rgyan*. Paris: École française d'Extrême-Orient.

———. 1976. "The Meanings of the Term '*Gotra*' and the Textual History of the "*Ratnagotravibhāga.*" *Bulletin of the School of Oriental and African Studies* 39 (2): 341–363.

———. 1977. "The *Gotra, Ekayāna* and *Tathāgatagarbha* Theories of the Prajñāpāramitā according to Dharmamitra and Abhayākaragupta." *Prajñāpāramitā and Related Systems: Studies in Honor of Edward Conze,* edited by Lewis Lancaster, 283–312. Berkeley, CA: Berkeley Buddhist Studies Series.

———. 1981. *The Literature of the Madhyamaka School of Philosophy in India.* Wiesbaden, Germany: Otto Harrassowitz.

———. 1989a. *Buddha-nature, Mind, and the Problem of Gradualism in a Comparative Perspective: On the Transmission and Reception of Buddhism in India and Tibet.* London: University of London.

———. 1989b. "Allusiveness and Obliqueness in Buddhist Texts: *Saṃdhā, Saṃdhi, Saṃdhyā* and *Abhisaṃdhi.*" In *Dialectes dans les literatures Indo-Aryennes,* edited by Colette Caillat, 295–328. Paris: Collège de France, Institute de Civilisation Indienne.

———. 2004. "Aspects of the Study of the (Earlier) Indian Mahāyāna." *JIABS* 27 (1): 3–62.

———. 2008. *The Symbiosis of Buddhism and Brahmanism/Hinduism in South Asia and of Buddhism with "Local Cults" in Tibet and the Himalayan Region.* Vienna: Verlag der Österreichischen Akademie der Wissenschaften.

———. 2015. "Textual and Philosophical Problems in the Translation and Transmission of *Tathāgatagarbha* Texts." *Bulletin of the School of Oriental and African Studies* 78 (2): 317–332.

Rulu 如露. 2016. *The Tathāgata Store.* Bloomington, IN: AuthorHouse. Translations accessed December 30, 2018. http://www.sutrasmantras.info.

Saitō Akira 斎藤明. 2020. "Buddha-Nature or Buddha Within? Revisiting the Meaning of *Tathāgata-garbha.*" *Acta Asiatica* 118: 1–15.

Salvini, Mattia. 2016. "*Ratna:* A Buddhist World of Precious Things." In *Soulless Matter, Seats of Energy: Metals, Gems, and Minerals in South Asian Traditions,* edited by Fabrizio M. Ferrari and Thomas W. P. Dähnhardt, 219–254. Sheffield, UK: Equinox.

Sanderson, Alexis. 1988. "Śaivism and the Tantric Traditions." In *The World's Religions,* edited by Stewart Sutherland et al., 660–704. London: Routledge.

———. 1994. "Vajrayāna: Origin and Function." In *Buddhism into the Year 2000: International Conference Proceedings,* 87–102. Bangkok: Dhammakāya Foundation.

———. 2009. "The Śaiva Age: The Rise and Dominance of Śaivism during the Early Medieval Period." *Genesis and Development of Tantrism,* edited by Shingo Einō, 41–350. Tokyo: Institute of Oriental Culture, University of Tokyo.

Sargeant, Winthrop. 2009. *The Bhagavad Gītā.* Albany: State University of New York Press.

Sasaki Shizuka 佐々木閑. 1999. "Review of The *Mahāparinirvāṇa Sūtra* and the Origins of Mahāyāna Buddhism [Shimoda 1997]." *Japanese Journal of Religious Studies* 26 (1–2): 189–197.

Sasson, Venessa. 2008. "A Womb with a View: The Buddha's Final Fetal Experience." In *Imagining the Fetus: The Unborn in Myth, Ritual, Religion, and Culture,* edited by Vanessa R. Sasson and Jane Marie Law, 55–72. American Academy of Religion Cultural Criticism Series. Oxford: Oxford University Press.

Scharfe, Hartmut. 1977. *Grammatical Literature.* Wiesbaden, Germany: Otto Harrassowitz.

Schiltz, Elizabeth. 2018. "*The Kaṭha Upaniṣad.*" In Cohen 2018: 317–325.

Schmithausen, Lambert. 1971. "Philologische Bemerkungen zum *Ratnagotravibhāgaḥ.*" *Wiener Zeitschrift für die Kunde Südasiens* 15: 123–177.

———. 1973. "Zu D. Seyfort Rueggs Buch 'La théorie du *tathāgatagarbha* et du *gotra*' (Besprechungsaufsatz)." *Wiener Zeitschrift für die Kunde Südasiens* 17: 123–160.

———. 1981. "On Some Aspects of Descriptions or Theories of 'Liberating Insight' and 'Enlightenment' in Early Buddhism." In *Studien zum Jainismus und Buddhismus: Gedenkschrift für Ludwig Alsdorf,* edited by Klaus Bruhn and Albrecht Wezler, 199–250. Wiesbaden, Germany: Franz Steiner Verlag.

———. 1987. *Ālayavijñāna: On the Origin and the Early Development of a Central Concept of Yogācāra Philosophy.* Tokyo: The International Institute for Buddhist Studies.

———. 1992. "A Note on Vasubandhu and the *Laṅkāvatārasūtra*." *Asiatische Studien* 46 (1): 392–397.

———. 2002. "The Case of Vegetarianism: A Buddhist Perspective." *Journal of Indian Philosophy* (인도철학) 12 (1): 309–329.

———. 2003. "Einige besondere Aspekte der 'Bodhisattva-Ethik' in Indien und ihre Hintergründe." *Hōrin: Vergleichende Studien zur japanischen Kultur* 10: 21–46.

———. 2005. "Meat-eating and Nature: Buddhist Perspectives." In *Buddhism and Nature (Bukkyō to shizen* 仏教と自然*): Supplement to the Bulletin of the Research Institute of Bukkyō University,* 182–201.

———. 2009. *Plants in Early Buddhism and the Far Eastern Idea of the Buddha-Nature of Grasses and Trees.* Lumbini, Nepal: Lumbini International Research Institute.

———. 2014. *The Genesis of Yogācāra-Vijñānavāda: Responses and Reflections.* Tokyo: The International Institute for Buddhist Studies of the International College for Postgraduate Buddhist Studies.

———. 2017. "Some Remarks on the Genesis of Central Yogācāra-Vijñānavāda Concepts." *Journal of Indian Philosophy* 46: 263–281.

———. Forthcoming (2020). *Fleischverzehr und Vegetarismus im indischen Buddhismus. Teil 1: Studie und Übersetzungen; Teil 2: Endnoten; Teil 3: Texte (Editionen).* Hamburg Buddhist Studies 12. Bochum/Freiburg, Germany: Projektverlag.

Schopen, Gregory. 1987. "Burial *Ad Sanctos* and the Physical Presence of the Buddha in Early Indian Buddhism: A Study in the Archaeology of Religions." *Religion* 17: 193–225.

———. (1987) 2005. "The Inscription on the Kuṣān Image of Amitābha and the Character of the Early Mahāyāna in India." *JIABS* 10 (2): 99–137. Reprinted (with alterations) in *Figments and Fragments of Mahāyāna Buddhism in India: More Collected Papers,* 247–277. Honolulu: University of Hawai'i Press.

———. 1988. "On the Buddha and His Bones: The Conception of a Relic in the Inscriptions of Nāgarjunikoṇḍa." *Journal of the American Oriental Society* 108 (4): 527–537.

———. 1989. "The Manuscript of the *Vajracchedikā* Found at Gilgit: An Annotated Transcription and Translation." In *Studies in the Literature of the Great Vehicle: Three Mahāyāna Buddhist Texts,* Luis O. Gómez and Jonathan A. Silk, 89–139. Ann Arbor: Collegiate Institute for the Study of Buddhist Literature and Centre for South and Southeast Asian Studies, University of Michigan.

———. 1991. "Monks and the Relic Cult in the *Mahāparinibbānasutta:* An Old Misunderstanding in Regard to Monastic Buddhism." In *From Benares to Beijing: Essays on Buddhism and Chinese Religion in Honour of Prof. Jan Yün-hua,*

edited by Koichi Shinohara and Gregory Schopen, 187–201. Oakville, ON: Mosaic Press.
———. 1998. "Relic." In *Critical Terms for Religious Studies,* edited by Mark C. Taylor, 256–268. Chicago: University of Chicago Press.
Senart, Émile. 1882. *Le Mahāvastu: Texte sanscrit publié pour la première fois et accompagné d'introductions et d'un commentaire.* Vol. 1. Paris: Société Asiatique.
———. 1897. *Le Mahāvastu: Texte sanscrit publié pour la première fois et accompagné d'introductions et d'un commentaire.* Vol. 3. Paris: Société Asiatique.
Sferra, Francesco. 2003. "Some Considerations on the Relationship between Hindu and Buddhist Tantras." In *Buddhist Asia 1: Papers from the First Conference of Buddhist Studies Held in Naples in May 2001,* edited by Giovanni Verardi and Silvio Vita, 57–84. Kyoto: Italian School of East Asian Studies.
Sharf, Robert H. 2002. *Coming to Terms with Chinese Buddhism: A Reading of the Treasure Store Treatise.* Honolulu: University of Hawai'i Press.
Shimoda Masahiro 下田正弘. 1991. "Jō raku ga jō: bukkyō ni okeru ātoman juyō no ichi tsūro 常楽我浄: 仏教におけるアートマン受容の一通." *Bukkyōgaku* 仏教学 31: 1–23.
———. 1994. "The Relationship between the Mahāyāna *Mahāparinirvāṇasūtra* and the Mahāsāṃghika." *IBK* 42 (2): 22–27.
———. 1997. *Nehan gyō no kenkyū: Daijōkyōten no kenkyū hōhō shiron* 涅槃経の研究ー大乗経典の研究方法試論. Tokyo: Shunjūsha.
———. 2002. "Stūpa Worship as Historical Background to *Tathāgatagarbha* Theory as Suggested by Several Seemingly Irrelevant Texts." In *Buddhist and Indian Studies in Honour of Professor Sodō Mori,* 247–265. Hamamatsu, Japan: Kokusai Bukkyoto Kyokai.
———. 2014. "Nyoraizō, busshō shisō no aratana rikai ni mukete 如来蔵. 仏性思想のあらたな理解に向けて." In Katsura et al. 2014: 3–95.
———. 2015. "*Mahāparinirvāṇamahāsūtra.*" In *Brill's Encyclopedia of Buddhism,* vol. 1, *Literature and Languages,* edited by Jonathan Silk et al., 158–170. Brill: Leiden.
———. 2020. "The Structure of the Soteriology of *Tathāgatagarbha* Thought as Seen from the Perspective of Different Modes of Discourse: A Response to Critical Buddhism." *Acta Asiatica* 118: 79–97.
Siderits, Mark. 2007. *Buddhism as Philosophy: An Introduction.* Aldershot, UK: Hackett.
———. 2015. *Personal Identity and Buddhist Philosophy: Empty Persons.* 2nd ed. Farnham, UK: Ashgate.
Silk, Jonathan. 2001. "The Place of the *Lotus Sūtra* in Indian Buddhism." *Journal of Oriental Philosophy* 11: 89–107.
———. 2002. "What, If Anything, Is Mahāyāna Buddhism? Problems of Definitions and Classifications." *Numen* 49 (4): 355–405.
———. 2006. *Indic śarīra and Chinese shèlì in the Mahāparinirvāṇa-sūtra and Saddharmapuṇḍarīka.* Tokyo: International Institute for Buddhist Studies of the International College for Postgraduate Buddhist Studies.
———. 2013. "The Proof Is in the Pudding: What Is Involved in Editing and Translating a Mahāyāna *Sūtra?*" *Indo-Iranian Journal* 56 (2): 157–178.
———. 2015a. "Establishing/Interpreting/Translating: Is It Just That Easy?" *JIABS* 36/37: 205–226.
———. 2015b. *Buddhist Cosmic Unity: An Edition, Translation and Study of the Anūnatvāpūrṇatvanirdeśaparivarta.* Hamburg Buddhist Studies Series 4. Hamburg: Hamburg University Press.

———. 2016. "Peering through a Funhouse Mirror: Trying to Read Indic Texts through Tibetan and Chinese Translations." In *Cross-Cultural Transmission of Buddhist Texts,* edited by Dorji Wangchuk, 289–313. Hamburg: Department of Indian and Tibetan Studies, Universität Hamburg.

Skilling, Peter. 1997. *Mahāsūtras.* Vol. 2. Oxford: Pali Text Society.

———. 2005. "Cutting across Categories: The Ideology of Relics in Buddhism." *Annual Report of the International Research Institute for Advanced Buddhology at Soka University* 8: 269–322.

———. 2009. "Seeing the Preacher as the Teacher: A Note on *Śāstṛsaṃjñā.*" *Annual Report of the International Research Institute for Advanced Buddhology at Soka University* 12: 73–100.

———. 2018. "How the Unborn Was Born: The Riddle of Mahāyāna Origins." In Harrison 2018b: 33–71.

Stearns, Cyrus. 2010. *The Buddha from Dölpo: A Study of the Life and Thought of the Tibetan Master Dölpopa Sherab Gyaltsen.* Revised and enlarged edition. Ithaca, NY: Snow Lion.

Steinthal, Paul. 1885. *Udânaṃ.* London: Henry Frowde, for the Pali Text Society.

Strong, John. 2004. *Relics of the Buddha.* Princeton, NJ: Princeton University Press.

———. 2007. "Two Buddha Relic Traditions." *Religion Compass* 1 (3): 341–352.

Studholme, Alexander. 2002. *The Origins of Oṃ Maṇipadme Hūṃ: A Study of the Kāraṇḍavyūha Sūtra.* Albany: State University of New York Press.

Suthren Hirst, Jacqueline. 2018. "*Ātman* and *Brahman* in the Principle *Upaniṣads.*" In Cohen 2018: 107–120.

Sutton, Florin Giripescu. 1991. *Existence and Enlightenment in the Laṅkāvatāra-sūtra: A Study in the Ontology and Epistemology of the Yogācāra School of Mahāyāna Buddhism.* Albany: State University of New York Press.

Suzuki Daisetz Teitaro. 1930. *Studies in the Laṅkāvatāra Sūtra.* London: Routledge & Kegan Paul.

———. 1932. *The Laṅkāvatāra Sūtra: A Mahāyāna Text.* Delhi: Motilal Banarsidass.

Suzuki Takayasu 鈴木隆泰. 1996a. "*Daihokku kyō* no kenkyū josetsu 『大法鼓経』の研究序説." *Bukkyō bunka* 仏教文化 35: 2–22.

———. 1996b. "The *Mahāmeghasūtra* as an Origin of an Interpolated Part of the Present *Suvarṇaprabhāsa.*" *IBK* 45 (1): 28–30.

———. 1997. "Nyorai jōjū kyū toshite no *Daihokku kyō* 如来常住経としての『大法鼓経』." *Bukkyō bunka kenkyū ronshū* 仏教文化研究論集 1: 39–55.

———. 1998. "*Konkōmyō kyō Nyorai juryō hin* to *Daiun kyō* 『金光明経如来寿量品』と『大雲経』." *Tōyō bunka kenkyūjo kiyō* 東洋文化研究所紀要 135: 1–46.

———. 1999a. "*Ōkutsumara kyō* ni miru butten kaishakuhō no tekiyō 央掘魔羅経に見る仏典解釈法の適用." *IBK* 48 (1): 440–436.

———. 1999b. "Mutual Influence among the Mahāyāna Sūtras Concerning Sarvalokapriyadarśana." *IBK* 47 (2): 10–14.

———. 2000a. "*Nehangyō kyōtengun ni okeru kū to jitsuzai* 涅槃経系経典群における空と実在." *Tōyōbunka kenkyūsho kiyō* 東洋文化研究所紀要 139: 109–146.

———. 2000b. "Anisetsusha—*Ōkutsumara kyō* to *Daihokku kyō* no torēgā 安慰説者–央掘魔羅経と大法鼓経のトレーガー." *Tōyō bunka kenkyūjo kiyō* 東洋文化研究所紀要 140: 143–167.

———. 2001. "The Recompilation of the *Mahāparinirvāṇasūtra* under the Influence of the *Mahāmeghasūtra.*" *IBK* 49 (2): 34–38.

———. 2002. "The Buddhology in the *Mahābherīsūtra* Inherited from the *Saddharmapuṇḍarīka*." *IBK* 50 (2): 20–24.

———. 2003. "*Stūpa* Worship and *Dharma* Evaluation in the *Suvarṇaprabhāsa*." *IBK* 51 (2): 32–36.

———. 2004. "Rites and Buddhism: A Perspective from the *Sarasvatī-parivarta* in the *Suvarṇaprabhāsa*." *IBK* 52 (2): 12–17.

———. 2005. "The Unchanged Intention of the Compilers of the *Suvarṇaprabhāsa:* An Examination through the Verification of the Hypothesis on 'the Independence of [Mahāyāna] Buddhism.'" *IBK* 53 (2): 20–26.

———. 2006. "The Primary Introduction of the Rites for Good Fortune in the *Suvarṇaprabhāsa* Described in the *Śrī-parivarta*." *IBK* 54 (3): 42–50.

———. 2007. "An Intention of the Compilers of the *Suvarṇaprabhāsa* Expressed and Intimated in the *Dṛḍhā-parivarta*." *IBK* 55 (3): 64–72.

———. 2008. "The Characteristics of 'The Five Chapters on the Various Gods and Goddesses' in the *Suvarṇaprabhāsa*." *IBK* 56 (3): 66–73.

———. 2014. "Busshō no tenkai—*Ōkutsumara kyō, Daihokku kyō*" 仏性の展開—央掘魔羅経・大雲経." In Katsura et al. 2014: 167–204.

———. 2015. "Two Parables on 'The Wealthy Father and the Poor Son' in the *Saddharmapuṇḍarīka* and the *Mahābherīsūtra*." *IBK* 63 (6): 169–176.

Taishō University (Study Group on Buddhist Sanskrit Literature, the Institute for Comprehensive Studies of Buddhism). 2006. *Vimalakīrtinirdeśa: A Sanskrit Edition Based upon the Manuscript Newly Found at the Potala Palace.* Tokyo: Taishō University Press.

Takasaki Jikidō 高崎直道. 1958. "The '*Tathāgôtpattisaṃbhava-nirdeśa*' of the *Avataṃsaka* and the *Ratnagotravibhāga:* With Special Reference to the Term '*Tathāgata-gotra-saṃbhava*' (如來性起)." *IBK* 7 (1): 48–53.

———. 1966. *A Study of the Ratnagotravibhāga (Uttaratantra): Being a Treatise on the Tathāgatagarbha Theory of Mahāyāna Buddhism.* Rome: Istituto Italiano per il Medio ed Estremo Oriente.

———. 1971. "The *Tathāgatagarbha* Theory in the *Mahāparinirvāṇa-sūtra*." *IBK* 19 (2): 1–10.

———. 1974. *Nyoraizō shisō no keisei: Indo daijōbukkyō shisō kenkyū* 如来蔵思想の形成: インド大乗仏教思想研究. Tokyo: Shunjūsha.

———. 1980. "An Analysis of the *Laṅkāvatāra*: In Search of Its Original Form." In *Indianisme et Bouddhisme: Mélanges offerts à Mgr Étienne Lamotte,* 339–352. Louvain-la-Neuve: Université catholique de Louvain, Institut orientaliste.

———. 1981. "The Concept of Manas in the *Laṅkāvatāra*." *IBK* 29 (2): 1–8.

———. (1981) 2014. "A Revised Edition of the *Laṅkāvatāra-Sūtra, Kṣanika-Parivarta.* Tokyo: *Ippan kenkyū (C) Kenkyū seika hōkukusho* 一般研 (C) 究研究成果報告書. Reprinted in Takasaki 2014: 9–98.

———. (1982) 2014. "Sources of the *Laṅkāvatāra* and Its Position in Mahāyāna Buddhism." In *Indological and Buddhist Studies: Volume in Honour of Professor J. W. de Jong on His Sixtieth Birthday,* edited by L. A. Hercus et al., 545–568. Delhi: Sri Satguru Publications. Reprinted in Takasaki 2014: 128–155.

———. 2014. *Collected Papers on the Tathāgatagarbha Doctrine.* Delhi: Motilal Banarsidass.

Tarocco, Francesca. 2008. "Lost in Translation? The *Treatise on the Mahāyāna Awakening of Faith* (*Dasheng qixin lun*) and Its Modern Readings." *Bulletin of the School of Oriental and African Studies* 71 (2): 323–343.

Thakur, Upendra. 1963. *The History of Suicide in India: An Introduction.* Delhi: Munshi Ram Mahohar Lal.

Ṭhānissaro, Bhikkhu. 2011. *Selves and Not Self: The Buddhist Teaching on Anattā.* Accessed December 30, 2018. https://www.accesstoinsight.org.

Toganō Shōun 栂尾祥雲. (1930) 1982. *Rushukyō no kenkyū* 理趣経の研究. Wakayama, Japan: Kōyasan Daigaku. Reprint, Kyoto: Rinsen.

Tournier, Vincent. 2017. *La formation du* Mahāvastu *et la mise en place des conceptions relatives à la carrière du bodhisattva.* Paris: École français d'Extrême-Orient.

Trainor, Kevin. 2004. "Introduction: Beyond Superstition." In *Embodying the Dharma: Buddhist Relic Veneration in Asia,* edited by David Germano and Kevin Trainor, 1–26. Albany: State University of New York Press.

Tsukinowa Kenryū 月輪賢隆. 1938. "Bukkyō ni okeru 'muga no ga' no shisō 佛教に於ける「無我の我」の思想." *Bukkyōkenkyū* 佛教研究 3 (3): 120–141.

———. 1940. *Zō-Kan-Wa sanyaku gappeki Shōman gyō, Hōgatsu dōji shomon gyō* 藏・漢・和三譯合璧勝鬘經・寶月童子所問經. Kyoto: Kōkyōshoin.

Tucci, Giuseppe. 1932. "Two Hymns of the *Catuḥ-stava* of Nāgārjuna." *Journal of the Royal Asiatic Society of Great Britain and Ireland* 2: 309–325.

———. 1936. "The *Ratnavali* of Nagarjuna." *Journal of the Royal Asiatic Society of Great Britain and Ireland* 3: 237–252.

Ui Hakuju 宇井伯壽. 1959. *Hōshōron kenkyū* 宝性論研究. Tokyo: Iwanami Shoten.

Urban, Hugh B. 2001. *The Economics of Ecstasy: Tantra, Secrecy, and Power in Colonial Bengal.* Oxford: Oxford University Press.

Vaidya, P. L. 1960. *Aṣṭasāhasrikā Prajñāpāramitā, with Haribhadra's Commentary Called Āloka.* Darbhanga, India: Mithila Institute.

———. 1963. *Saddharmalaṅkāvatārasūtram.* Darbhanga, India: Mithila Institute.

———. 1967. *Daśabhūmikasūtram.* Darbhanga, India: Mithila Institute.

van Nooten, Barend, and Gary B. Holland. 1994. *Rig Veda: A Metrically Restored Text with an Introduction and Notes.* Cambridge, MA: Harvard University Press.

Verardi, Giovanni. 2011. *Hardships and Downfall of Buddhism in India.* New Delhi: Manohar Publishers and Distributors.

Vetter, Tilmann. 1978. "Die *Gauḍapādīya Kārikās*: Zur Entstehung und zur Bedeutung von (A)dvaita." *Wiener Zeitschrift für die Kunde Südasiens* 22: 95–133.

Vogel, Claus. 1970. *The Teachings of the Six Heretics according to the Pravrajyāvastu of the Tibetan Mūlasarvāstivāda Vinaya, with an Appendix Containing an English Translation of the Pertinent Sections in the Chinese Mūlasarvāstivāda Vinaya.* Wiesbaden, Germany: Kommissionsverlag F. Steiner.

von Hinüber, Oscar. 2003. *Beiträge zur Erklärung der Senavarma-Inschrift.* Mainz: Akademie der Wissenschaften und der Literatur / Stuttgart: Franz Steiner Verlag.

von Hinüber, Oscar, and, K. R. Norman. 1994. *Dhammapada: With a complete Word Index Compiled by Shoko Tabata and Tetsuya Tabata.* Oxford: Pali Text Society.

Vorobyova-Desyatovskaya, M. I. 2002. *The Kāśyapaparivarta: Romanized Text and Facsimiles.* Tokyo: International Research Institute for Advanced Buddhology.

Waldschmidt, Ernst. 1950–1951. *Der Mahāparinirvāṇasūtra: Text in Sanskrit und Tibetisch, verglichen mit dem Pāli nebst einer Übersetzung der chinesischen Entsprechung im Vinaya der Mūlasarvāstivādins auf Grund con Turfan-Handschriften.* 3 vols. Berlin: Akademie-Verlag.

Walser, Joseph. 2005. *Nāgārjuna in Context: Mahāyāna Buddhism and Early Indian Culture.* New York: Columbia University Press.

Wangchuk, Dorji. 2004. "The rÑiṅ-ma Interpretations of the *Tathāgatagarbha* Theory." *Wiener Zeitschrift für die Kunde Südasiens* 48: 171–213.

———. 2007. *The Resolve to Become a Buddha: A Study of the Bodhicitta Concept in Indo-Tibetan Buddhism.* Tokyo: International Institute for Buddhist Studies of the International College for Postgraduate Buddhist Studies.

Wangchuk, Tsering. 2017. *The Uttaratantra in the Land of Snows: Tibetan Thinkers Debate the Centrality of the Buddha-Nature Treatise.* Albany: State University of New York Press.

Watanabe Shōgo 渡辺章悟. 2009. "The Role of 'Destruction of the Dharma' and 'Predictions' in Mahāyāna *Sūtra*s: With a Focus on the *Prajñāpāramitā Sūtras*." *Acta Asiatica* 96: 77–97.

Wayman, Alex. 1976. Reply to Dina [*sic*] Paul's Review of *The Lion's Roar of Queen Śrīmālā. Philosophy East and West* 26 (4): 492–494.

———. 1978. "The Mahāsāṃghika and the *Tathāgatagarbha* (Buddhist Doctrinal History, Study 1)." *JIABS* 1 (1): 35–50.

Wayman, Alex, and Hideko Wayman. 1974. *The Lion's Roar of Queen Śrīmālā: A Buddhist Scripture on the Tathāgatagarbha Theory.* London: Columbia University Press.

Westerhoff, Jan. 2018. *The Golden Age of Indian Buddhist Philosophy.* Oxford: Oxford University Press.

Wiley, Kristi L. 2000. "Colors of the Soul: By-Products of Activity or Passions?" *Philosophy East and West* 50 (3): 348–366.

Williams, Paul. 2009. *Mahāyāna Buddhism: The Doctrinal Foundations.* 2nd ed. London: Routledge.

Wynne, Alexander. 2007. *The Origin of Buddhist Meditation.* London: Routledge.

———. 2011. "The *Ātman* and Its Negation—A Conceptual and Chronological Analysis of Early Buddhist Thought." *JIABS* 33 (1–2): 103–171.

Yamabe Nobuyoshi 山部能宜. 2017. "Once Again on "*Dhātu-vāda*." *Critical Review for Buddhist Studies* 불교학리뷰 21: 9–43.

Yamano Chieko 山野千恵子. 2008. "Nāgārjuna and Sātavāhana." *IBK* 56 (3): 121–127.

Zacchetti, Stefano. 2004. "Teaching Buddhism in Han China: A Study of the *Ahan koujie shi'er yinyuan jing* T.1508 Attributed to An Shigao." *Annual Report of the International Research Institute for Advanced Buddhology at Soka University* 15: 197–224.

———. 2005. *In Praise of the Light: A Critical Synoptic Edition with an Annotated Translation of Chapters 1–3 of Dharmarakṣa's Guang zan jing, Being the Earliest Chinese Translation of the Larger Prajñāpāramitā.* Tokyo: International Research Institute for Advanced Buddhology, Soka University.

———. 2015. "*Prajñāpāramitā Sūtra*s." In *Brill's Encyclopedia of Buddhism,* vol. 1, *Literature and Languages,* edited by Jonathan Silk et al., 171–209. Brill: Leiden.

Zapart, Jarosław. 2017. "The Buddha as I: Selfhood and Identity in *Śrīmālādevīsiṃhanāda-sūtra*." *Studia Religiologica* 50 (2): 145–161.

Zhen Liu. 2015. *The Dharmadhātustava: A Critical Edition of the Sanskrit Text with the Tibetan and Chinese Translations, a Diplomatic Transliteration of the Manuscript and Notes.* Beijing: China Tibetology Publishing House; Vienna: Austrian Academy of Sciences Press.

Zimmermann, Michael. 1999. "The *Tathāgatagarbhasūtra:* Its Basic Structure and Relation to the *Lotus Sūtra*." *Annual Report of the International Research Institute for Advanced Buddhology at Soka University* 2: 143–168.

———. 2000. "A Mahāyānist Criticism of *Arthaśāstra:* The Chapter on Royal Ethics in the *Bodhisattva-gocaropāya-viṣaya-vikurvāṇa-nirdeśa-sūtra.*" *Annual Report of the International Research Institute for Advanced Buddhology at Soka University* 3: 177–211.

———. 2002. *A Buddha Within: the Tathāgatagarbhasūtra—the earliest exposition of the Buddha-nature teaching in India.* Tokyo: The International Research Institute for Advanced Buddhology, Soka University.

———. 2014a. "The Process of Awakening in Early Texts on Buddha-Nature in India." In *A Distant Mirror: Articulating Indic Ideas in Sixth and Seventh Century Chinese Buddhism,* edited by Chen-kuo Lin and Michael Radich, 513–528. Hamburg: Hamburg University Press.

———. 2014b. "'*Nyoraizōkyō*' saikō: busshō kyū yu wo chūshin toshite『如来蔵経』再考―仏性九喩を中心として." In Katsura et al. 2014: 97–139.

———. 2020. "A Multi-associative Term: Why *Tathāgatagarbha* Is Not One and the Same." *Acta Asiatica* 118: 41–55.

Zysk, Kenneth G. 2016. *The Indian System of Human Marks.* 2 vols. Leiden: Brill.

Index

Abhayākaragupta, 198n61, 199n62
abhidharma, 10n26, 244n25
Abhidharmakośabhāṣya, 5, 34n21, 122n11, 135n53
ābhiprāyika (intentionality), 98, 109, 112, 121n10, 222
Acharya, D., 226n86
acintyapariṇāmacyuti (death through inconceivable transformation), 119n2, 135, 204, 207
ādānavijñāna (receiving consciousness). See *ālayavijñāna*
Adhyardhaśatikā-prajñāpāramitā, 195n50, 199n62
Advaita, 197n58, 227n90, 231n2, 252n60
advaya (non-duality), 60–61
Aggivacchagottasutta (MN.I.483), 172n82
aggregates. See *skandha*
agotra (without lineage). See *gotra*
aiśvarya (sovereignty), 39, 66–67, 104–107, 111, 171–173, 184n8
Aitareya-upaniṣad, 248
Ājīvikas, 4, 225
ākiṃcanya (nothing whatsoever), 220–222
akṣaras (syllables/letters), 58, 109, 184n11
Akṣayamatinirdeśasūtra, 110n47, 207n16
Alagaddūpamasutta (MN.I.130), 8n21, 237n4
ālayavijñāna (substratum consciousness), 156, 188–198, 215, 236
**amalavijñāna* (stainless consciousness), 216n50
Ambalaṭṭhikarāhulovādasutta (MN.I.414), 80n42
Amoghavajra, 144
amṛta (ambrosia; undying), 8, 229, 250n47
Anālayo, B., 5n13, 72n10, 119n1, 172n82, 214n39
anātman (not-self; absence of self), 1–10, 197–198, 211–213, 229–233, 245–246, 253, 260; in the AMS, 74–79, 81–82, 92–93; in the LAS, 183–188, 193–194; in the MBhS, 104–107, 110–114; in the MPNMS, 34–40, 46, 51, 59–62, 65–66; in the MSA(Bh), 150–153; in the RGV(V), 170–179; in the ŚDS, 128–129
Anattalakkhaṇasutta (SN.III.66), 4, 7–8, 104
Andhra, 121n8, 218, 238
Aṅgulimālīyasūtra (AMS), 13, 22, 70–96, 182n5, 185n14, 211, 217, 232, 262–263; and *ekayāna,* 204–205; and emptiness, 222–223; and the MBhS, 98–99; and the MPNMS, 54; and the ŚDS, 132–136, 137n55
Aniruddha, 81
antaryāmin (inner controller), 8
Anūnatvāpūrṇatvanirdeśaparivarta (AAN), 12, 139–142, 204, 234–236, 246; and the AMS, 87; and the MBhS, 97–98
Āpastamba-dharmasūtra, 229, 249
arhats, 2, 42, 119n2, 121, 132, 135–136, 174n85, 204–210, 239, 244
asaṃskṛta (unconditioned; uncreated), 9, 31n15, 103, 243–244
Asaṅga, 149, 155, 182n6, 238
Asaṅkhatasaṃyutta (SN.IV.359), 244n25
asceticism, 85–87, 91–94, 168, 225n79, 247
Aśoka, 18n55, 241n18
Assalāyanasutta (MN.II.147), 132–133n40
Aṣṭasāhasrikā-prajñāpāramitā, 18–19, 58n106, 81n48, 124, 165n51, 171, 214
aśūnyatā (nonemptiness), 130, 177, 218–223
*Asvabhāva/Niḥsvabhāva, 151n55
Aśvaghoṣa, 22

ātmadhātu. See *dhātu*
ātman (self), 1–10, 21–26, 115–116, 229–237, 239–247, 251–260; in the AMS, 74–87, 91–96; belonging to (*ātmanīya*), 6, 67, 101; in the LAS, 183–188, 191–195; grasping to (*ātmagrāha*), 4, 50, 170, 196; in the MBhS, 100–109; in the MPNMS, 33–62, 65–67; non-Buddhist notions of, 2–10, 37–40, 55–58, 78–79, 93–96, 164–171, 183–188, 223–228, 232–236, 247–251, 258–263; in the RGV(V), 162–165, 175–180; in the ŚDS, 127–129, 136–138. See also *ātmapāramitā*, *mahātman*
ātmapāramitā (perfection of self), 122, 129–132, 152, 167–179, 219, 233
ātmavāda (teaching/discourse about a self): across *tathāgatagarbha* literature, 13, 21–26, 213, 231–236, 245–248; in the LAS, 183–188, 191–194; in the MBhS, 114–116; in the MPNMS, 47–55, 67; of non-Buddhists, 3, 7–10, 39–40, 58, 69, 162–163, 173–174, 183–188, 223–228; in the RGV(V), 166; in the ŚDS, 127–128, 132, 137–138, 213. *See also* non-Buddhists
Atthattasutta (SN.IV.400), 5
Avalokiteśvara, 55–57
avatāra (manifestation), 256n67, 257n73
avyākṛta (unexpounded [questions]), 172
awakening. *See* buddhahood
Āyāraṅgasutta, 225n82
ayoniśomanaskāra (irrational thought), 163

bahuvrīhi, 15, 145, 160
Baoyun, 29
Barber, A., 121n8, 238n7
Basham, A. L., 4n8, 225n82
bdag gyi khams/dbyings. See *dhātu*
Bhagavadgītā, 54n88, 197n55, 225, 249, 251, 256; and the RGV(V), 162–164, 234, 237
Bhattacharya, K., 5n11
Bhāviveka, 10n28, 196–197, 227, 231n2
bhūmi (stage [of a bodhisattva's progress]), 42–43, 55, 80–81, 101, 193, 101n19, 175n90
Bimbisārapratyudgamanamahāsūtra, 38n39
Blum, M., 29, 44–45n60, 49n73, 57n102, 61n115, 212n32
Bodhibhadra, 71, 94, 98n7
bodhicitta (intention for awakening), 63n126, 127
Bodhiruci (sixth century translator), 139, 155n7, 181, 205, 206n9
Bodhiruci (eighth century translator), 120, 195n50
Bodhisattvagocaropāyaviṣayavikurvāṇanirdeśasūtra, 205–206, 231n2, 254–255
body of the Buddha, 19, 31, 40–41, 99, 115, 121n9, 129–132, 146–148, 160, 171–172, 208n21, 230–231; as diamond (*vajrakāya*), 31, 195n50. See also *dharmakāya*
brahmacārya (celibacy), 83–84, 88–89, 232, 250
Brahmajālasutta (DN.I.1), 140
brahman (Brahmanical 'power'), 7, 138n57, 248–250, 252n60
Brahmanism, 3–4, 7–8, 48–49, 56–57, 65–66, 82n51, 92–93, 132–133n40, 223–228, 234, 247–257
Bṛhadāraṇyaka-upaniṣad, 8, 9n24, 79, 193n41, 247–248
Bronkhorst, J., 3n5, 4n8, 10n26–27, 15n42, 17n50, 226n89, 227n91
Brown, B., 12, 181
Brunnhölzl, K., 12n32, 15n41, 70n3, 98n4, 154n3, 222n70
Bu ston (Rin chen grub), 37n36, 45n65–66, 50n78, 52n82, 66n141, 74n20, 100n12
Buddhāvataṃsaka, 160n29
Buddha-nature idea: definition, 13–14, 19–26; development: 229–237; in the MPNMS-group, 69, 72, 98, 132; origins: 32, 237–245; in the ŚDS, 125, 132, 137; in the TGS, 144, 147
Buddhabhadra, 29, 144
buddhadhātu (nature of a Buddha; Buddha-nature), 16–22, 230–234, 261; "above" oneself, 47n72; in the AMS, 73–76, 84–86, 95; in the body, 16n45, 41–47, 50–58, 60, 80–81, 86, 96, 146–147, 162–163, 183–184, 230–231, 242–243; in the LAS, 184; in the MBhS, 100–104; in the MPNMS, 32–33, 40–42, 49–56, 68–69; in MPNMS[D]+, 63–65; in the RGV(V), 159, 162, 165–166, 177, 179, 219; in the TGS, 146; which cannot be killed, 48–49, 52–55, 224–225. See also *dhātu*; *tathāgatagarbha*
Buddhaguhya, 259n79
buddhahood, 20, 26, 239, 245–253, 264; in the AMS, 81–83; in the LAS, 193; in the MBhS, 99–100; in the MPNMS, 33–40, 52–53, 63; in the MSA(Bh),

150; in the RGV(V), 160, 164; in the ŚDS, 129–132, 136; in the TGS, 146.
buddhajñāna (knowledge of a Buddha), 13n38, 160, 197, 213n36
buddhakṣetra (Buddha-field), 242
Buddhamati, 92–94
buddhānusmṛti (recollection of the Buddha), 241–242
buddhavacana (utterances by the Buddha), 257n73, 262

Candrakīrti, 5n10, 196, 198–199
Cārvākas, 6n14, 226. *See also* non-Buddhists.
Chāndogya-upaniṣad, 8n21, 45n62, 79, 80n42, 224, 248
China (Buddha-nature teaching in), 23–24, 30, 63n126
cittamātra (mind-only), 182n6, 188n22, 235. *See also* Yogācāra-Vijñānavāda
cittaprakṛti (nature of the mind), 119, 122–123, 136, 141–142, 159, 162–163, 166, 178, 184–185, 192, 198, 214–217, 220, 233–234; as intrinsically pure (*prakṛtipariśuddhacitta*): 119, 121n10, 122–123, 136, 141–142, 159, 178, 184n11, 214–217, 220, 233–234; as intrinsically luminous (*prakṛtiprabhāsvaracitta*): 184–185, 192, 198, 214–217
Cohen, S., 4n7, 8n21, 224n76, 225n79, 248nn32–33, nn35–37, nn39–40, 249n43
Collins, S., 2, 4n6, 6–9, 224n25
Conze, E., 61n120–121
Critical Buddhism (Hihan Bukkyō), 137–138, 260n82
cryptic utterance (*saṃdhā/sandhā-bhāṣya/vacana*), 24, 136, 210–217, 222–223, 231; in the AMS, 74–75, 81–82, 93; in the MBhS, 99; in the MPNMS, 46, 51, 60
Cūḷamāluṅkyasutta (MN.I.426), 10n26, 108n41
Cūḷasaccakasutta (MN.I.227), 104, 205n5

Da fagu jing (T.270). See *Mahābherīhārakasūtra*
Da fangdeng wuxiang jing (T.387). See *Mahāmeghasūtra*
Dabanniepan jing (T.374). See *Mahāparinirvāṇamahāsūtra*
Dabannihuan jing (T.376). See *Mahāparinirvāṇamahāsūtra*
Dafangdeng rulaizang jing (T.666). See *Tathāgatagarbhasūtra*
Dafangguang rulaizang jing (T.667). See *Tathāgatagarbhasūtra*
Daosheng, 12n34, 63n126
Daśabhūmikasūtra, 66n142, 174n85, 179n99, 260n83
Dasheng qixin lun (T.1666), 22
Dasheng rulengqie jing (T.672). See *Laṅkāvatārasūtra*
Dasheng zhuangyan jing lun (T.1604). See *Mahāyānasūtrālaṃkāra(bhāṣya)*
de bzhin gshegs pa'i snying po. See *tathāgatagarbha*
De bzhin gshegs pa'i snying po gsal zhing mdzes par byed pa'i rgyan. See Bu ston
decline (of the dharma), 32, 34n22, 71, 114, 194n48, 217–218, 238–239, 243
decrease/increase (of sentient beings), 101–104, 139–142
Devacandra, 29
devas. See gods
devotion, 17–18, 40–41, 243–244, 248–249, 255–256, 257n73
Dhammacakkappavattanasutta (SN.V.420), 133n41
Dhammapada, 59n112, 215–216
dharmadhātu (nature/realm of phenomena), 86n64, 89–90n76, 123–124, 128, 140–142, 150, 166n55, 179, 198–199, 204, 215, 234, 262
Dharmadhātustava, 140–141n6
dharmakāya ("dharma-body"), in the AAN, 140–142, 234; in the AMS, 72; in the MBhS 115; in the MPNMS, 31–32, 34, 40–41, 67, 230; in the RGV(V), 156, 160, 164, 167–180, 235–236; in the ŚDS, 121–132, 136–137, 233; and the commentary on the SP, 206n9
Dharmakṣema, 22–23, 29–31, 32n17, 62–67, 120n4, 172–173, 181, 204, 233n3, 256n68
dharmanairātmya (absence of self among *dharmas*), 11, 170–171, 186, 189, 207, 218
Dharmapada. See *Dhammapada*
dharmas ("phenomena"), 6–11, 36–37, 46–47, 123–126, 169–174, 186–187, 196–199, 218–223
Dharmatāśīla, 70
dhātu; one's own (*ātmadhātu/*svadhātu/*ma ddhātu*), 48–49, 73–77, 80–81, 83–91, 95–96, 216, 232; of sentient beings (*sattvadhātu*), 48–49, 56n96, 75, 77, 88–89, 100, 115, 140–141, 161n34, 166n55, 206n9. See also *buddhadhātu*; *dharmadhātu*

dhātuvāda, 123n13, 138n57, 260n82
docetism, 20, 88, 105–106, 208n21, 209, 240–241, 246–247, 256n67, 261–262
Dol po pa (Shes rab rgyal mtshan), 37n36, 45n63, 45n65, 50n78, 54n88, 64n134, 75n21, 76n25, 84n54, 98n8, 100n12, 114n65, 217n56
dPal brtsegs, 149
dPal gyi lhun po, 97
Drewes, D., 82n48, 240n14, 246–247
Duerlinger, J., 2n3, 5n10
Dundas, P., 3n5, 225n82, 226n83
Dunhuang, 30, 155, 182

eka(dharma)dhātu (single essence/realm [of phenomena]), 88–91, 139–142
ekarasa (single flavor), 52–53
ekaśaraṇa (single refuge), 133–135
ekayāna (single vehicle), 24, 26, 149, 164, 191, 203–210, 232–233, 238–239, 255–256, 263; in the AMS, 94–95; in Mādhyamika sources, 195, 198–199; in the MBhS, 99, 115; in the MPNMS, 63; in the ŚDS, 119, 121, 129, 132–137
Eltschinger, V., 10n28, 33n20, 57n101, 127n25, 194n48, 257n72
embryo, 14–15, 124, 140–141n6, 144, 150n47, 175, 193n43
emptiness. See *śūnyatā*

faith (*pratyaya*; *śraddhā*): in the AMS, 72, 81; in the MBhS, 111, 114; in the MPNMS, 43–45, 52, 63n127; in the RGV(V), 161, 167–170, 175, 213
Faxian, 29
Forte, A., 34n22, 72n13
Foshuo buzeng bujian jing (T.668). See *Anūnat vāpūrṇatvanirdeśaparivarta*
four truths, 6n15, 133, 137, 223
foxing. See *buddhadhātu*
Foxing lun (T.1610), 22–23n68, 167n58
Frauwallner, E., 216n50
Fujii, K., 14n39, 32n17

Gaddulabaddhasutta (SN.III.149), 9n25
Gaganagañjaparipṛcchā, 163n42, 214n42
Gauḍapāda, 227n90
Gauḍapādīyakārikā, 177n95, 227n90
Gautamīputra Śatakarṇi, 238
Ghanavyūhasūtra, 189n25
gods, 3–4, 82, 106–107, 185, 207, 248–249, 256–257
Gombrich, R., 8n21, 9n24
Gonda, J., 7n17
gotra (lineage), 146, 148–149, 157, 160, 168, 206–208; absence of (*agotra*), 148–149, 157n22, 168, 206
Granoff, P., 30n8, 259n78, 260n83
Griffiths, P., 148n41, 149, 151n55
Grosnick, W. H., 22n68, 73n16, 140n6, 144n17, 244n25
guhya (secret), 97n1, 211n29, 212n33, 213n36, 249n43, 250
Guṇabhadra, 70, 97, 119–120, 181, 182, 205, 238
guṇapāramitā (perfected qualities), 34n23, 130, 161–162, 167–176, 178–180
Guptas, 204n1, 239n8
gzhan stong (other-empty), 219–220

Habata, H., 13, 15n42, 29–32, 35n25, 41n46, 45n66, 46n70, 54n88, 64n130, 71n8–9, 166n53, 209n25, 211n28–29, 250n47
Hacker, P., 258
Haimavatas, 10n28
Hara, M., 15n41, 82n51, 124n16, 157n22
Harivarman, 225
Harrison, P., 61n118, 122n11, 242n19; on buddhahood, 31n15, 122n11, 247; on Mahāyāna studies, 11nn29–30, 17n51, 24nn74–75, 238n7, 239nn10–11, 260n82
Harvey, P., 10n28, 47n71, 78n30, 214n43
Hastikakṣyasūtra, 71n5, 182n5, 196n51
Hevajratantra, 259
Hīnayāna, 136, 209, 236. *See also* Śrāvakayāna
Hirakawa, A., 17n51
**hitopadeṣṭṛ* (teacher of what is beneficial), 71, 98
Hodge, S., 13n36, 29nn2–4, 30n8, 32–36, 50n75, 62n125, 68–69, 166n53, 212n34, 217–218, 238nn6–7, 258n77, 259n79
Hoernle, A. F., 211n28, 212n32
Hookham, S. K., 219n63
Horsche, P., 8n21
Hubbard, J., 123n13, 138n56, 209n23, 260n82
Huveṣka/Huviṣka, 204n1

*icchantika*s, 63, 84–85, 167–169, 170n72, 208n19
Ikṣvākus, 121n8
inclusivism, 254, 258–258, 260
intrinsically pure mind. See *cittaprakṛti*
Īśā-upaniṣad, 224n76, 225, 248–249

īśvara, 106–107, 255
itaretaraśūnyatā (emptiness of one thing from another), 220

Jainism, 3–4, 91–92, 168, 205, 221n67, 223–226, 252n61
Jamspal, L., 205n4
Jayānanda, 199n62
Jianyi, 155
Jinamitra, 29, 120
Jñānagarbha, 29
Jñānasārasamuccaya-nibandhana, 94, 98n7
Johnston, E. H., 154–160
Jones, C. V., 16n45, 16n47, 259n79, 263n86; on the MBhS, 97, 103n27, 110n47, 115n67, 140n5; on the MPNMS, 56n95, 91n83, 255n62; on the RGV(V), 158n24, 166n55; Jong, J. W. de, 154n5, 174n85
Jujing yisheng baoxing lun (T.1611). See *Ratnagotravibhāga(vyākhyā)*

Kaivalya-upaniṣad, 249
kaliyuga (age of decline), 194n48. *See also* decline of the dharma
Kamalaśīla, 119n2, 196–199
Kanō, K., 12, 15nn41–42, 40n45, 41n46, 47n72, 119n2, 137n55; on the AMS, 70–73, 87n66, 94n90, 211n30; on Mādhyamika commentary, 195n50, 196n51, 198, 199n62; on the RGV(V), 23n69, 154–157, 165n48, 167n58, 206n11, 214n42
Kāraṇḍavyūhasūtra, 257
Karashima, S., 25n80, 58n106, 63n126
Kāśyapa (a bodhisattva), 43–57, 68, 106–111
Kāśyapa (a Buddha), 85–86
Kāśyapaparivarta, 38n39
Kaṭha-upaniṣad, 54n88, 79, 224–227, 248–249
Kauṣītaki-upaniṣad, 248
Kena-upaniṣad, 224n76, 248n36
Kern, H., 25n80
Khādalik, 30
Khotan, 30, 155
Kiblinger, K. B., 258n75
Killingley, D., 4n6–7, 224n76, 246n42, 249n42
King, R., 120, 133n44, 227n90
King, S., 12, 22n68, 22–23n68, 131n36, 167n48, 175n88, 292n60
kleśas (afflictions), 214–216, 225, 230–233; in the AAN, 141–142; in the AMS, 73, 76, 83–87, 216, 222; in the BGVNS, 205; in the LAS, 192, 207; in the MBhS, 100–102, 108–109, 113; in the MPNMS, 44–45, 51–52, 55, 60, 63n126, 64n134, 221; in the RGV(V), 161–163, 175–177, 214–215; in the ŚDS, 122–123, 129–136, 220; in the TGS, 144–146
Kōyasan, 30
Kṛṣṇa-Vāsudeva, 249n43
kṛtayuga (ideal age), 194n48
Kṣaṇikaparivarta, 188
Kumārajīva, 25n80
Kunst, A., 183n7, 194, 204n1, 209n23
Kuśinagara, 29

La Vallée Poussin, L. de, 38n39, 135n53, 198n59
Laghuśaṃvara, 259
Lalitavistara, 20n65
Lamotte, E., 57n104, 81n45, 88n69, 104n29, 149n43
Laṅkāvatārasūtra, 13, 136, 181–199, 206–208, 235–236
Laws of Manu. See *Mānava-dharmasūtra*
Lengqie abatuoluo bao jing (T.670). See *Laṅkāvatārasūtra*
Lévi, S., 137n55, 148n41, 149, 150n47, 150nn49–52, 151nn56–57, 152n58–59, 174n85
Liebenthal, W., 12n34, 19n60, 63n126
Liu, M., 14n39, 32n17, 64n134, 67n143, 85n55
Lokakṣema, 20n63, 204n1, 239n11, 241, 242n19
lokānuvartana (conformity with the world), 20, 105–106, 209, 241
Lokānuvartanasūtra, 20, 241
Lopez, D. S. Jr., 26n82, 35–36n31
Lotus Sūtra. See *Saddharmapuṇḍarīka*

MacQueen, G., 65n137, 168n63, 258n73
Madhyamaka, 173n84, 196, 198–199, 204n1, 208n21
Madhyamakahṛdayakārikā, 197n58
Madhyamakāloka, 119n2, 198
Madhyamakāvatārabhāṣya, 5n10, 198–199
Madhyāntavibhāga(bhāṣya), 140n6, 219–220n63
mahābhāras (great burdens), 137n55
Mahābhārata, 82n51, 182n5, 225, 228n91, 253n61, 257n67
Mahābherīhārakasūtra (MBhS), 12–13, 97–116, 211, 217, 221–222, 224, 232, 245, 262–263; and the AAN, 102–104; and the AMS, 71

Mahākāśyapa, 218, 85n60
Mahāmati, 183–189
Mahāmaudgalyāna, 93
Mahāmeghasūtra, 34n22, 71n5, 72n13, 182n5, 196n51, 212n34, 217–218, 218n57, 238, 257n69
Mahānārāyana-upaniṣad, 249
Mahānidānasutta (DN.II.55), 8–9
Mahāniddesa, 38n39
Mahāparinibbānasutta (DN.II.72), 29n1, 41n48
Mahāparinirvāṇamahāsūtra (MPNMS), 12–20, 29–69, 203–214, 220–221, 224–227, 229–231, 237–240, 243–249, 253–255, 261–262; and the AMS, 71–75, 87, 91, 95–96; and the MBhS, 98–99, 103, 105, 111, 115; and the LAS, 182n5, 183–188; and the RGV(V), 156–158, 162–166, 178–179; and the ŚDS, 122–133, 136–137; and the TGS, 45, 143, 147–148
Mahāpratisarā-mahāvidyārājñī, 195n50
Mahāpuṇṇamasutta (MN.III.15), 7n16
Mahāratnakūṭa, 120
Mahāsaccakasutta (MN.I.237), 205n5
Mahāsāṃghika, 120, 238n7
mahātman/mahātmya (great self/character; majesty), 46–47, 66, 72–73, 150–153, 171–172, 235
Mahāvairocanābhisaṃbodhi, 258–259
Mahāvastu, 20n65, 120n6, 132–133n40, 260n83
Mahāyāna, 1–2, 10n26, 11, 26, 63n126, 94–95, 99, 114–115, 120–121, 134–136, 167–169, 197n58, 203–210, 238–239, 247, 253–260
Mahāyānadharmadhātunirviśeṣa, 141n10, 155
Mahāyānasaṃgraha, 149n43–44
Mahāyānasūtrālaṃkāra(bhāṣya) (MSA[Bh]), 148–153, 206, 235–236, 238; and the RGV(V), 171–173
Mahāyānasūtrālaṃkāraṭīkā, 151n55
Mahāyānottaratantraśāstra. See *Ratnagotravibhāga(vyākhyā)*
Mahāyānottaratantraṭippaṇī, 156n16
Maheśvara, 226, 255, 259
Maitreya(nātha), 149, 155, 182n6, 219n63, 238
Maitrī-upaniṣad, 248
Makransky, J. J., 31–32n15
Malinar, A., 249n43, 256n57
Mallikāsutta (SN.I.75), 9n24
Māṃsabhakṣaṇaparivarta, 182n5
Mānava-dharmaśāstra, 250–253
Māṇḍūkya-upaniṣad, 248
Mañjuśrī, 83–93, 215, 222–223
Mañjuśriyamūlakalpa, 259n78
manomayakāya (mind-made body), 135, 174n85, 204
Māra(s), 54, 217
Mathes, K., 154n3, 156, 158n24, 159n25, 161n32, 219n61, 219n63, 220n66
Mathurā, 204n1
Matsuda, K., 119n1, 120n3, 133n45
Matsumoto, S., 123n13, 131n36, 137–138, 160n29, 175n88, 252n60
Mātusutta (SN.II.189), 88n69
McGovern, N., 41–42n49, 88n67
meat eating. *See* vegetarianism
medicines, 37–39, 45–46, 52, 113, 211nn28–29, 250n47
Miaofa lianhua jing (T.262). See *Saddharmapuṇḍarīka*
Miaofa lianhua jing youbotishe (T.1519). See *Saddharmapuṇḍarīkasūtropadeśa*
Mokṣadharmaparvan, 252n61
monism, 135n54, 138n57, 141, 175n88, 252n60
Muṇḍaka-upaniṣad, 224n76, 225, 248
Munimatālaṃkāra, 198n61, 199n62

Nagao, G., 140n6, 150n47, 169n68, 219–220n63, 252n60
Nāgārjuna, 140–141n6, 204n1, 208n21, 218, 238n5, 238n7
nairātmya (absence of self). See *anātman*
nairātmyavāda, 4–11, 59–62, 67–69, 78, 114, 158, 171, 187–188, 192–194, 229, 242, 256–258
Nakamura, H., 12n33, 21n67, 44–45n60, 66n142, 172n81, 225n80–81, 239n8
Nakamura, Z., 36n33, 155n6
Nanjio, B., 25n80, 181–199
Nārāyana, 259
naṭa (dancer), 88n70, 188
Nattier, J., 23n71, 24n73, 25n79, 35–36n31, 204n1, 209n23, 218n58
neyārtha (provisional meaning), 98–99, 110, 198, 258n76
Nigantha Nātaputta, 168n63
Niraupamyastava, 208n21
Nirgrantha. See Jainism; non-Buddhists
nirmāṇa/nirmita (emanation), 57–58, 93–94, 197n58, 231, 254–255
Nirvāṇa Sūtra. See *Mahāparinirvāṇamahāsūtra*
nītārtha (definitive meaning), 98n8, 110, 133n45, 181, 198
non-Buddhists (*pāsaṇḍa, tīrthika,* etc.), 2–4, 223–228, 246–247, 253–260; in the

AMS, 91–96, 232; in the BGVNS, 205; in the LAS, 183–190, 197–198; in the MPNMS, 37–40, 55–58, 65, 230–231; in the RGV(V), 164–174, 235. *See also* Brahmanism
Norman, K. R., 8n21, 42n50, 59n112, 216n46, 216n49

Oberhammer, G., 258n75
Obermiller, E., 148n41, 155n6, 175n88, 252n60
Ogawa, I., 70
Olivelle, P., 8–9, 182n5, 224n76, 229, 247–251, 258n75; *see also* Upaniṣads

Pañcaviṃśatisahāsrikā-prajñāpāramitā, 78n30, 132–133n40
parables: of an ascetic boy, 85–86; of a magically conjured city (SP), 99, 110, 115, 210n26; of a diamond in stone (MPNMS), 54–55; of an elixir (MPNMS), 52–54; of a sick infant (MPNMS), 45–46; of two physicians (MPNMS), 37–39, 44; of a lost son (SP), 99, 110, 115; of a lost sword (MPNMS), 56–58, 69, 93–94, 184n11; of treasure beneath a house (MPNMS), 45, 64, 144n20; of a wrestler (MPNMS); 50–51, 64. *See also* similes
Paramārtha, 22, 216n50
paramātman (supreme self), 46, 130, 151, 171–174, 178–179, 235, 250
pāramitā (perfection). See *guṇapāramitā*
parinirvāṇa, 5n13, 19, 31–33, 43n55, 99, 102–103, 208n21, 211, 218
Pāśupatas, 92, 226. *See also* Śaivism
Patañjali, 66n142
Paul, D., 120
perfection of self. See *ātmapāramitā*
power (in liberation), 7–8, 31n15, 41n46, 66–69, 104–107, 135, 171–174, 207, 245–250
Prabhākaramitra, 146
prajñāpāramitā (perfection of insight), 11, 25, 124, 153, 158, 218–220; and the AMS, 77–78; and the LAS, 186; and the MPNMS, 60–62; and the RGV(V), 165, 167n58, 174, 179
prakṛti (original nature), 88n70, 160–161, 237
prakṛtipariśuddhacitta. See *cittaprakṛti*
prakṛtiprabhāsvaracitta. See *cittaprakṛti*
pramāda (negligence), 86–87, 107
Prasenajit, 97n1, 110, 120, 137n55
Praśna-upaniṣad, 224n76, 248
pratyekabuddha ('solitary' Buddha), 42–43, 75, 77–78, 81, 99, 101, 110, 121, 132–136, 137n55, 149, 168–169, 174n85, 174–177. See also *triyāna*
Pratyutpanna-sūtra, 242n19
Priestley, L., 10n28, 50n76, 193n42, 193n44
prophecy complex, 32, 34n22, 71, 114, 121, 136, 217n56, 218, 238. *See also* decline (of the dharma)
pudgala. See *pudgalavāda*; self, erroneous notions of
pudgalavāda (discourse/teaching about personhood), 10–11n28, 50n76, 168n65, 193–194
Purāṇas, 257
Pūrṇa, 74–79, 210n27, 211
puruṣa ([cosmic] person), 3n5, 88n70, 132–133n40, 197, 248–249
Puruṣasūkta, 132–133n40

Radich, M., 12–21, 22n68, 45n62, 123, 173n83, 217n51, 218, 238, 239n80, 255n64, 256n68; on Buddha-bodies, 135n53, 240–241; on the MPNMS, 30n5, 31–33, 41–42, 67–68, 203, 211nn28–29, 229–230, 261; on the pure mind, 214n39, 214n41, 216n50
Rāhula, 80–82
rang stong (self-empty), 219
Ratié, I., 10n28, 127n25, 167n58
Ratnagotravibhāga(-vyākhyā) (RGV[V]), 12–13, 15–17, 104n29, 110n47, 154–180, 206, 234–235; and the AAN, 139–141, 144; and the LAS, 182–183; and the MPNMS, 30, 35–36; and the MSA(Bh), 152, 171–173; and the ŚDS, 119, 123, 126, 134n39, 135; and the TGS, 143–144, 147, 159, 166
Ratnamati, 155, 206n9
Ratnāvalī, 208
relics, 16n45, 17–20, 25, 32–33, 40–41, 68, 72–73, 90n77, 124, 146, 230, 239–241, 243, 257n69, 264. See also *stūpa*s.
Renou, L., 3, 9
Ṛgveda, 3, 133n40
Ri chos nges don rgya mtsho zhes bya ba mthar thug thun mong ma yin pa'i man ngag. See Dol po pa
rNgog Blo ldan shes rab, 12n33, 155
Rotman, A., 241n17
Ru lengqie jing (T.671). See *Laṅkāvatārasūtra*
Rudra, 226, 255

Ruegg, D. S., 2n4, 8n21, 12–14, 32n17, 37n36, 140n6, 152, 155–157, 178n98, 196–199, 208n21, 257n72, 258nn74–76, 260n82; on emanations, 57n104, 255nn65–66, 259nn78–80, 263n80; on the pure mind, 214n39, 215n44; on *saṃdhā*, 210n27, 212n33
rulaixing. See *buddhadhātu*
rulaizang. See *tathāgatagarbha*
Rulu, 70n1, 98n4, 120n5, 144n17

Saddharmapuṇḍarīka (sūtra) (SP), 18, 24n75, 25–26, 31, 168n62, 217–218, 228, 231–233, 236, 261–263; and the AMS, 94–95; regarding the Buddha, 20; and *ekayāna*, 203–214, 239, 253–256; and the LAS, 191, 195; and the MBhS, 99, 100n17, 110, 115; and the MPNMS, 24n75, 31, 63; and the ŚDS, 121, 132–136; and the TGS, 148
**Saddharmapuṇḍarīkasūtropadeśa*, 206
Sāgaramatiparipṛcchā, 214n42
Sagāthaka, 183, 191–195, 236
Saitō, A., 15n41, 83n53, 124n16
Śaivism, 226, 259
Śākyaprabha, 70
Śākyasiṃha, 149
Samaññaphalasutta (DN.I.47), 65, 168n63
saṃdhābhāṣya/sandhāvacana. *See* cryptic utterance
Sāṃkhya, 3n5, 88n70, 168, 183, 189n23, 197, 227
Sāṃkhyakārikā, 3n5, 88n70, 189n23, 227n91
Sāṃmitīya, 10–11n28, 50n76
Sanderson, A., 226n86, 259n78–81
sangha, 17, 33, 46, 64, 81, 93–94, 133–134, 157, 159, 242–243
sangs rgyas kyi khams/dbyings. See *buddhadhātu*
Śaṅkarācārya, 227n90
Śāntideva, 34n21, 119n2, 196n51, 205
Saptaśatikā-prajñāpāramitā, 61n121
śaraṇas ([three] refuges), 133–134, 243
Sargeant, W., 58n88, 163n39, 197n55, 249n43
*Sarvalokapriyadarśana/ Sarvasattvapriyadarśana, 217–218
Sarvapuṇyasamuccayasamādhisūtra, 61
Sarvāstivāda, 10n26, 21n1, 122n11, 135n53
śāśvatavāda (eternalism), 5–6, 62, 105
Śātavāhanas, 121n8, 218, 238
satkāyadṛṣṭi (view of a worldly self), 112, 152, 175. *See also* self, erroneous notions of
sattvadhātu. See *dhātu*
Satyakaparivarta. See *Bodhisattvagocaropāyaviṣayavikurvāṇanirdeśasūtra*
**Satyasiddhiśāstra*, 225
Schmithausen, L., 10n26, 20n61, 56n95, 70, 73n16, 154n5, 240n13; on *ālavijñāna*, 182–183n6, 190; on the RGV(V), 155–160, 163, 165; on vegetarianism, 71n4, 89n74, 91n82, 182n5
Schopen, G., 17n50–51, 18n52, 165n51, 204n1, 241n18
secrecy, 64, 74–75, 97n1, 142, 210–214, 222–223, 232, 246n48, 249n43, 250–252, 259.
See also cryptic utterance; *guhya*
self, erroneous notions of, 37–40, 54, 56, 59, 77–79, 128, 192–194, 224–226; qualities associated with, 1–10, 47–50. See also *ātman; satkāyadṛṣṭi*
Senavarman, 18n52
Senglang, 206n9
Shengman furen hui (T.310, text no.48). See *Śrīmālādevīsiṃhanādasūtra*
Shengman shizihou yisheng dafangbian fangguang jing (T.353). See *Śrīmālādevīsiṃhanādasūtra*
Shimoda, M., 13–19, 30n7, 34n23, 35n28, 37n34, 44n58, 131n37, 208n21, 230, 241n17; on Critical Buddhism, 138n56; on composition of the MPNMS, 31–33, 238n7
Śikṣasamuccaya, 34n21, 119n2, 196n51, 205n3
Silk, J., 12, 25n79, 214n38; on the AAN, 98n5, 104n30, 139–141, 168n61, 213n37, 220n64; on the BGVNS, 205nn3–4; on Mahāyāna studies, 11n30, 24n73, 260n82
similes: of a bird's trail (MPNMS; AMS), 42–43, 59–60, 81–82, 231; in the BGVNS, 205–206; of a diseased eye (MPNMS; MBhS), 42–43, 101–102; of diving merchants (MPNMS), 35–36, 176; of a dizzied person (MPNMS), 34–35, 59; of gold with impurities (MBhS), 108; of a jewel in a garment (SP), 204n2; of a lamp in a jar (MPNMS; MBhS), 85, 100–101; of language learning (MBhS), 108–109; of the moon behind cloud (MBhS), 100; of Rāhula with water (AMS), 80–81; of the TGS, 144–148, 159, 162, 166, 197; of a woodworm (MPNMS), 37–39, 247, 252n61; of a wrestler with a jewel (MPNMS), 51–52; of water below

the earth (MBhS), 100. *See also* parables
Śiva, 226, 256n67, 257
skandha (heap[s]), 7, 10n28, 53–54, 87, 104, 163, 169, 174, 183–184, 188, 192–194
Skilling, P., 17n50, 38n39, 242n21, 243n22
Śrāvakayāna, 1n2, 2, 43n55, 94, 99, 121, 122, 168n65, 196, 205, 209, 216–217, 233
Śrīmālādevīsiṃhanādasūtra (ŚDS), 12–13, 104, 119–138, 204–205, 213–216; 219–220, 233–235, 238, 246; and the AAN, 139–141; and the AMS, 72, 132–136; and the LAS, 182–183, 189–191; and the MPNMS, 122–132; and the RGV(V), 156, 162–167, 177–178
Sthiramati/Sāramati, 151n55, 155
Stone, J. I., 26n82, 35–36n31
Strong, J., 18nn52–53, 18n55, 69n146, 90n77
stūpas, 15n42, 17–19, 40–41, 67–69, 72, 96, 123, 133, 146, 230, 240–243
śūnyatā (emptiness), 24, 196–199, 218–223, 226–228; in the AMS, 77–79, 222–223; in the LAS, 185–186, 190–191; in the MBhS, 109–114; in the MPNMS, 67, 220–221; in the MSA(Bh), 150–153; in the RGV(V), 166, 168–180; in the ŚDS, 121n10, 128, 130, 220
Śūraṅgamasamādhisūtra, 44n60
Surendrabodhi, 120
Suthren Hirst, J., 7n17, 248n32
Suttanipāta, 38n39
Suvarṇaprabhāsasūtra, 72–73n13, 218n57, 256, 257n69
Suvikrāntavikrāmiparipṛcchā-prajñāpāramitā, 61n120, 214
Suzuki, D. T., 181, 192, 208
Suzuki, T., 217n51, 220n66, 256n68, 257; on the AMS, 13n37, 70–71, 211n30; on the *Mahāmeghasūtra,* 34n22, 212–213n34; on the MBhS, 97–99, 104n28
Śvetāśvatara-upaniṣad, 79, 185, 224, 227, 248–249
Swanson, P., 123n13, 138n56, 260n82

Taishō shinshū daizōkyō, 23n70
Taittirīya-upaniṣad, 248
Takasaki, J., 12–14, 17, 19n58, 21–26, 139, 143, 148n41, 206n9, 214n39, 218–219, 261; on the AMS, 70; on the BGVNS, 205n3, 205n6; on the LAS, 181, 182nn5–6, 185n12, 189n24, 198n28, 213n36; on the MBhS, 97; on the MPNMS, 40n45; on the RGV(V), 154–180, 214n42; on the ŚDS, 120, 127n28, 131n37
Tanlin, 206n9
tantric Buddhism, 152n60, 195n50, 242n19, 257–260, 263. *See also* Vajrayāna
Tarānātha, 219n63
tārikas ([non-Buddhist] philosophers), 192. *See also* non-Buddhists
Tarkajvāla, 10n28, 196, 197n58, 231n2
tathāgatadhātu. See *buddhadhātu*
tathāgatagarbha (chamber/womb/embryo for a Buddha): as *ālayavijñāna,* 25n78, 156, 188–198, 215, 236; as *dharmakāya,* 122–132, 136–137, 140–142, 160–164, 175–179, 190, 206n9, 233–234; relevant literature, 11–14, 21–26, 115–116, 143, 229–237; origins, 12–21, 67–69, 237–245; translation of, 14–16, 19–20, 68, 122–124, 137, 148–150, 175, 230, 241. See also *ātman; buddhadhātu; cittaprakṛti*
Tathāgatagarbhasūtra (TGS), 13, 17, 22, 143–148, 159, 166, 204, 213, 219, 226, 234–236, 243n22; and the MPNMS, 45, 143, 147–148; and the RGV(V), 159–162, 166, 178
Tathāgataguhya (*sūtra*), 213n36
Tathāgatotpattisaṃbhavanirdeśa (sūtra), 13n38, 160n28, 197, 213n36
tathatā (reality), 141n8, 149–151, 161, 175, 179
tatpuruṣa, 115, 145
theism, 248–249, 251–252, 256n67, 257n73
Theravāda, 10n26
three jewels, 64, 94n92, 159, 242. See also *śaraṇas*
Tibet (Buddha-nature teaching in), 12, 15n41, 23–24, 30, 37n36, 154n3, 155–156. *See also* Bu ston; Dol po pa
tīrthakara. See non-Buddhists
tīrthika/tīrthya. See non-Buddhists
Tong Ācārya, 70
Tournier, V., 120n6, 261n83
Triṃśikā, 182–183n6
triyāna (three vehicles), 99, 110, 134–135, 149, 203–210, 212n33
Tsukinowa, K., 13, 14n39
twenty-five existences, 44–45, 50–53, 103, 127–128, 221

ucchedavāda (annihilationism), 5–6, 62, 65–66, 105, 113–114, 175n91, 221–222
Udāna, 244n25
Ugraparipṛcchāsūtra, 105n32

Upaniṣads, 4, 7–9, 40, 45n62, 54, 57–58, 78–79, 138n57, 185, 197, 224–227, 247–251
upāyakauśalya (skill-in-methods), 35n31, 110, 167n58, 186, 209n24, 210n27, 224
Upāyakauśalyasūtra, 20n65
uttaratantra (higher teaching), 110n47, 154, 165–166

Vacchagotta, 5
Vacchagottasutta (SN.IV.395), 5n13
Vairocanarakṣita, 156n16
Vaiśeṣika, 3n5, 168, 183
Vaiṣṇavism, 164, 197, 227, 256–257, 259n78
Vajracchedikā-prajñāpāramitā, 165n51, 227n90
Vajrayāna, 152n60, 259. *See also* tantric Buddhism
varṇa (social class), 3–4, 48–53, 225
Vasubandhu, 5, 22, 135n53, 149, 182–183n6, 206n9
Vātsīputrīya, 10–11n28, 168n65
Vedānta, 66n142, 164n47, 197n58, 227n90, 231n2, 250n49, 252n60
Vedas, 3–4, 7–9, 57n105, 248
vegetarianism, 71n4, 91, 182n5, 196n51, 226
Vidyākaraprabha, 97
vijñānavāda (teaching/discourse about consciousness), 132, 183, 188–191, 194–199. *See also* Yogācāra-Vijñānavāda
Vimalakīrtinirdeśasūtra, 31n15, 72, 124, 168n62, 210n27
Viniścayasaṅgrahaṇī, 149n44
violence, 71, 84, 89–91, 95
Vipallāsasutta (AN.II.52), 34n21
viparyāsa ([mental] distortion), 33–40, 42–44, 65, 128–131, 167–170, 175–176
Viṣṇu, 197, 256–257

waidao. See non-Buddhists
Walser, J., 218n59, 238–239n7
Wangchuk, D., 127n26, 135n49, 204n1, 207nn16–17, 219n63
Wangchuk, T., 37n36, 154n3, 219n63
Wayman, A. and H, 12, 120–121, 127n28, 238n7
Williams, P., 11n31, 12n33, 21n67, 190n29, 219n63, 239n8
womb, imagery of a, 14–21, 68, 123–124, 137, 150, 161, 175, 194, 230, 241, 261
Wynne, A., 8n21, 10n26, 49n74

xing. See *dhātu*

Yamakasutta (SN.III.109), 106n37
Ye shes sde, 120
Yogabhāṣya, 66n142
Yogācāra-Vijñānavāda, 25n78, 132, 206–210, 215, 235–238; and the LAS, 182–183, 186, 188–191, 194–199; and the MSA(Bh), 148–149; and the RGV(V), 156–157
Yogasūtra, 66n142
Yangjuemoluo jing (T.120). See *Aṅgulimālīyasūtra*

Zacchetti, S., 59n110, 61n120, 61–62n121, 78n30, 125–126n21, 172n81, 195n50
Zapart, J., 120, 123n13, 131n36
Zhonghua Dazangjing, 43n54
Zimmermann, M., 12–14, 21n67, 25–26, 83n53, 160n29, 241, 243n22, 260n82, 262n85; on the TGS, 102n23, 143–148, 204–205, 214, 234, 239n8
Zongmi, 125–126n21

About the Author

C. V. Jones is assistant professor in Buddhist studies at the Institute for South Asian, Tibetan, and Buddhist Studies, University of Vienna. His work concerns the development of Buddhist thought as represented in Sanskrit, Chinese, and Tibetan literature, with particular interest in Mahāyāna Buddhism and the interplay between Buddhist and non-Buddhist traditions of religious thought and practice in India.